D0913861

THE WILLIAM STALLINGS BOOKS ON COMPUTER

DATA AND COMPUTER COMMUNICATIONS, SEVENTH EDITION

A comprehensive survey that has become the standard in the field, covering (1) data communications, including transmission, media, signal encoding, link control, and multiplexing; (2) communication networks, including circuit- and packet-switched, frame relay, ATM, and LANs; (3) the TCP/IP protocol suite, including IPv6, TCP, MIME, and HTTP, as well as a detailed treatment of network security. **Received the 2000 Text and Academic Authors Association (TAA) award for long-term excellence in a Computer Science Textbook.** ISBN 0-13-100681-9

COMPUTER NETWORKS WITH INTERNET PROTOCOLS AND TECHNOLOGY

An up-to-date survey of developments in the area of Internet-based protocols and algorithms. Using a top-down approach, this book covers applications, transport layer, Internet QoS, Internet routing, data link layer and computer networks, security, and network management. ISBN 0-13-141098-9

COMPUTER ORGANIZATION AND ARCHITECTURE, SEVENTH EDITION

A unified view of this broad field. Covers fundamentals such as CPU, control unit, microprogramming, instruction set, I/O, and memory. Also covers advanced topics such as RISC, superscalar, and parallel organization. **Fourth and fifth editions received the TAA award for the best Computer Science and Engineering Textbook of the year.** ISBN 0-13-185644-8

WIRELESS COMMUNICATIONS AND NETWORKS, Second Edition

A comprehensive, state-of-the art survey. Covers fundamental wireless communications topics, including antennas and propagation, signal encoding techniques, spread spectrum, and error correction techniques. Examines satellite, cellular, wireless local loop networks and wireless LANs, including Bluetooth and 802.11. Covers Mobile IP and WAP. ISBN 0-13-191835-4

BUSINESS DATA COMMUNICATIONS, FIFTH EDITION

A comprehensive presentation of data communications and telecommunications from a business perspective. Covers voice, data, image, and video communications and applications technology and includes a number of case studies. ISBN 0-13-144257-0

AND DATA COMMUNICATIONS TECHNOLOGY

OPERATING SYSTEMS, FIFTH EDITION

A state-of-the art survey of operating system principles. Covers fundamental technology as well as contemporary design issues, such as threads, microkernels, SMPs, real-time systems, multiprocessor scheduling, distributed systems, clusters, security, and object-oriented design. **Fourth edition received the TAA award for the best Computer Science and Engineering Textbook of 2002.** ISBN 0-13-147954-7

NETWORK SECURITY ESSENTIALS, SECOND EDITION

A tutorial and survey on network security technology. The book covers important network security tools and applications, including S/MIME, IP Security, Kerberos, SSL/TLS, SET, and X509v3. In addition, methods for countering hackers and viruses are explored. ISBN 0-13-035128-8

LOCAL AND METROPOLITAN AREA NETWORKS, SIXTH EDITION

An in-depth presentation of the technology and architecture of local and metropolitan area networks. Covers topology, transmission media, medium access control, standards, internetworking, and network management. Provides an up-to-date coverage of LAN/MAN systems, including Fast Ethernet, Fibre Channel, and wireless LANs, plus LAN QoS. **Received the 2001 TAA award for long-term excellence in a Computer Science Textbook.** ISBN 0-13-012939-9

ISDN AND BROADBAND ISDN, WITH FRAME RELAY AND ATM: FOURTH EDITION

An in-depth presentation of the technology and architecture of integrated services digital networks (ISDN). Covers the integrated digital network (IDN), xDSL, ISDN services and architecture, signaling system no. 7 (SS7) and provides detailed coverage of the ITU-T protocol standards. Also provides detailed coverage of protocols and congestion control strategies for both frame relay and ATM. ISBN 0-13-973744-8

HIGH-SPEED NETWORKS AND INTERNETS, SECOND EDITION

A state-of-the art survey of high-speed networks. Topics covered include TCP congestion control, ATM traffic management, Internet traffic management, differentiated and integrated services, Internet routing protocols and multicast routing protocols, resource reservation and RSVP, and lossless and lossy compression. Examines important topic of self-similar data traffic. ISBN 0-13-03221-0

CRYPTOGRAPHY AND NETWORK SECURITY

PRINCIPLES AND PRACTICES

FOURTH EDITION

William Stallings

Pearson Education International

Vice President and Editorial Director, ECS: *Marcia J. Horton*
Executive Editor: *Tracy Dunkelberger*
Editorial Assistant: *Christianna Lee*
Executive Managing Editor: *Vince O'Brien*
Managing Editor: *Camille Trentacoste*
Production Editor: *Rose Kernan*
Director of Creative Services: *Paul Belfanti*
Cover Designer: *Bruce Kenselaar*
Managing Editor, AV Management and Production: *Patricia Burns*
Art Editor: *Gregory Dulles*
Manufacturing Manager: *Alexis Heydt-Long*
Manufacturing Buyer: *Lisa McDowell*
Marketing Manager: *Robin O'Brien*
Marketing Assistant: *Barrie Reinhold*

Pearson Prentice Hall
Pearson Education, Inc.
Upper Saddle River, NJ 07458

Printed in the United States of America
10 9 8 7 6 5 4 3 2 1

ISBN: 0-13-202322-9

Pearson Education LTD.
Pearson Education Australia PTY, Limited
Pearson Education Singapore, Pte. Ltd.
Pearson Education North Asia Ltd.
Pearson Education Canada, Ltd.
Pearson Educación de Mexico, S.A. de C.V.
Pearson Education—Japan
Pearson Education Malaysia, Pte. Ltd.
Pearson Education, Inc., *Upper Saddle River, New Jersey*

To Antigone
never dull
never boring
always a Sage

CONTENTS

NOTATION

Even the natives have difficulty mastering this peculiar vocabulary.

—*The Golden Bough*, Sir James George Frazer

Symbol	Expression	Meaning
D, K	D(K, Y)	Symmetric decryption of ciphertext Y using secret key K.
D, PR_a	D(PR_a, Y)	Asymmetric decryption of ciphertext Y using A's private key PR_a
D, PU_a	D(PU_a, Y)	Asymmetric decryption of ciphertext Y using A's public key PU_a
E, K	E(K, X)	Symmetric encryption of plaintext X using secret key K.
E, PR_a	E(PR_a, X)	Asymmetric encryption of plaintext X using A's private key PR_a
E, PU_a	E(PU_a, X)	Asymmetric encryption of plaintext X using A's public key PU_a
K		Secret key
PR_a		Private key of user A
PU_a		Public key of user A
C, K	C(K, X)	Message authentication code of message X using secret key K.
GF(p)		The finite field of order p, where p is prime. The field is defined as the set Z_p together with the arithmetic operations modulo p.
GF(2^n)		The finite field of order 2^n.
Z_n		Set of nonnegative integers less than n
gcd	gcd(i, j)	Greatest common divisor; the largest positive integer that divides both i and j with no remainder on division.
mod	$a \bmod m$	Remainder after division of a by m.
mod, ≡	$a \equiv b \pmod{m}$	$a \bmod m = b \bmod m$
mod, ≢	$a \not\equiv b \pmod{m}$	$a \bmod m \neq b \bmod m$
dlog	$\text{dlog}_{a,p}(b)$	Discrete logarithm of the number b for the base a (mod p)
ϕ	$\phi(n)$	The number of positive integers less than n and relatively prime to n. This is Euler's totient function.
Σ	$\sum_{i=1}^{n} a_i$	$a_1 + a_2 + \cdots + a_n$
Π	$\prod_{i=1}^{n} a_i$	$a_1 \times a_2 \times \cdots \times a_n$
|	$i \mid j$	i divides j, which means that there is no remainder when j is divided by i
|, |	$\lvert a \rvert$	Absolute value of a
‖	$x \Vert y$	x concatenated with y
≈	$x \approx y$	x is approximately equal to y
⊕	$x \oplus y$	Exclusive-OR of x and y for single-bit variables; Bitwise exclusive-OR of x and y for multiple-bit variables
⌊, ⌋	$\lfloor x \rfloor$	The largest integer less than or equal to x
∈	$x \in S$	The element x is contained in the set S.
↔	$A \leftrightarrow (a_1, a_2, \ldots, a_k)$	The integer A corresponds to the sequence of integers $(a_1, a_2, \ldots, a_k)$

PREFACE

"The tie, if I might suggest it, sir, a shade more tightly knotted. One aims at the perfect butterfly effect. If you will permit me—"

"What does it matter, Jeeves, at a time like this? Do you realize that Mr. Little's domestic happiness is hanging in the scale?"

"There is no time, sir, at which ties do not matter."

—*Very Good, Jeeves!* P. G. Wodehouse

In this age of universal electronic connectivity, of viruses and hackers, of electronic eavesdropping and electronic fraud, there is indeed no time at which security does not matter. Two trends have come together to make the topic of this book of vital interest. First, the explosive growth in computer systems and their interconnections via networks has increased the dependence of both organizations and individuals on the information stored and communicated using these systems. This, in turn, has led to a heightened awareness of the need to protect data and resources from disclosure, to guarantee the authenticity of data and messages, and to protect systems from network-based attacks. Second, the disciplines of cryptography and network security have matured, leading to the development of practical, readily available applications to enforce network security.

OBJECTIVES

It is the purpose of this book to provide a practical survey of both the principles and practice of cryptography and network security. In the first two parts of the book, the basic issues to be addressed by a network security capability are explored by providing a tutorial and survey of cryptography and network security technology. The latter part of the book deals with the practice of network security: practical applications that have been implemented and are in use to provide network security.

The subject, and therefore this book, draws on a variety of disciplines. In particular, it is impossible to appreciate the significance of some of the techniques discussed in this book without a basic understanding of number theory and some results from probability theory. Nevertheless, an attempt has been made to make the book self-contained. The book presents not only the basic mathematical results that are needed but provides the reader with an intuitive understanding of those results. Such background material is introduced as needed. This approach helps to motivate the material that is introduced, and the author considers this preferable to simply presenting all of the mathematical material in a lump at the beginning of the book.

INTENDED AUDIENCE

The book is intended for both an academic and a professional audience. As a textbook, it is intended as a one-semester undergraduate course in cryptography and network security for computer science, computer engineering, and electrical engineering majors. It covers the material in IAS2 Security Mechanisms, a core area in the Information Technology body of knowledge; NET4 Security, another core area in the Information Technology body of knowledge; and IT311, Cryptography, an advanced course; these subject areas are part of the Draft ACM/IEEE Computer Society Computing Curricula 2005.

The book also serves as a basic reference volume and is suitable for self-study.

PLAN OF THE BOOK

The book is organized in four parts:

Part One. Conventional Encryption: A detailed examination of conventional encryption algorithms and design principles, including a discussion of the use of conventional encryption for confidentiality.

Part Two. Public-Key Encryption and Hash Functions: A detailed examination of public-key encryption algorithms and design principles. This part also examines the use of message authentication codes and hash functions, as well as digital signatures and public-key certificates.

Part Three. Network Security Practice: Covers important network security tools and applications, including Kerberos, X.509v3 certificates, PGP, S/MIME, IP Security, SSL/TLS, and SET.

Part Four. System Security: Looks at system-level security issues, including the threat of and countermeasures for intruders and viruses, and the use of firewalls and trusted systems.

In addition, the book includes an extensive glossary, a list of frequently used acronyms, and a bibliography. Each chapter includes homework problems, review questions, a list of key words, suggestions for further reading, and recommended Web sites.

A more detailed, chapter-by-chapter summary of each part appears at the beginning of that part.

INTERNET SERVICES FOR INSTRUCTORS AND STUDENTS

There is a Web site for this book that provides support for students and instructors. The site includes links to other relevant sites, transparency masters of figures and tables in the book in PDF (Adobe Acrobat) format, and PowerPoint slides. The Web page is at WilliamStallings.com/Crypto/Crypto4e.html. As soon as typos or other errors are discovered, an errata list for this book will be available at WilliamStallings.com. In addition, the Computer Science Student Resource site, at WilliamStallings.com/StudentSupport.html, provides documents, information, and useful links for computer science students and professionals.

PROJECTS FOR TEACHING CRYPTOGRAPHY AND NETWORK SECURITY

For many instructors, an important component of a cryptography or security course is a project or set of projects by which the student gets hands-on experience to reinforce concepts from the text. This book provides an unparalleled degree of support for including a projects component in the course. The instructor's manual not only includes guidance on how to assign and structure the projects, but also includes a set of suggested projects that covers a broad range of topics from the text:

- **Research projects:** A series of research assignments that instruct the student to research a particular topic on the Internet and write a report
- **Programming projects:** A series of programming projects that cover a broad range of topics and that can be implemented in any suitable language on any platform
- **Lab exercises:** A series of projects that involve programming and experimenting with concepts from the book
- **Writing assignments:** A set of suggested writing assignments, by chapter
- **Reading/report assignments:** A list of papers in the literature, one for each chapter, that can be assigned for the student to read and then write a short report

See Appendix B for details.

WHAT'S NEW IN THE FOURTH EDITION

In the three years since the third edition of this book was published, the field has seen continued innovations and improvements. In this new edition, I try to capture these changes while maintaining a broad and comprehensive coverage of the entire field. To begin this process of revision, the third edition was extensively reviewed by a number of professors who teach the subject. In addition, a number of professionals working in the field reviewed individual chapters. The result is that, in many places, the narrative has been clarified and tightened, and illustrations have been improved. Also, a large number of new "field-tested" problems have been added.

Beyond these refinements to improve pedagogy and user friendliness, there have been major substantive changes throughout the book. Highlights include the following:

- **Simplified AES:** This is an educational, simplified version of AES (Advanced Encryption Standard), which enables students to grasp the essentials of AES more easily.
- **Whirlpool:** This is an important new secure hash algorithm based on the use of a symmetric block cipher.
- **CMAC:** This is a new block cipher mode of operation. CMAC (cipher-based message authentication code) provides message authentication based on the use of a symmetric block cipher.
- **Public-key infrastructure (PKI):** This important topic is treated in this new edition.
- **Distributed denial of service (DDoS) attacks:** DDoS attacks have assumed increasing significance in recent years.
- **Common Criteria for Information Technology Security Evaluation:** The Common Criteria have become the international framework for expressing security requirements and evaluating products and implementations.
- **Online appendices:** Six appendices available at this book's Web site supplement the material in the text.

In addition, much of the other material in the book has been updated and revised.

ACKNOWLEDGMENTS

This new edition has benefited from review by a number of people, who gave generously of their time and expertise. The following people reviewed all or a large part of the manuscript: Danny Krizanc (Wesleyan University), Breno de Medeiros (Florida State University), Roger H. Brown (Rensselaer at Hartford), Cristina Nita-Rotarul (Purdue University), and Jimmy McGibney (Waterford Institute of Technology).

Thanks also to the many people who provided detailed technical reviews of a single chapter: Richard Outerbridge, Jorge Nakahara, Jeroen van de Graaf, Philip Moseley, Andre Correa, Brian Bowling, James Muir, Andrew Holt, Décio Luiz Gazzoni Filho, Lucas Ferreira, Dr. Kemal Bicakci, Routo Terada, Anton Stiglic, Valery Pryamikov, and Yongge Wang.

Joan Daemen kindly reviewed the chapter on AES. Vincent Rijmen reviewed the material on Whirlpool. And Edward F. Schaefer reviewed the material on simplified AES.

The following people contributed homework problems for the new edition: Joshua Brandon Holden (Rose-Hulman Institute if Technology), Kris Gaj (George Mason University), and James Muir (University of Waterloo).

Sanjay Rao and Ruben Torres of Purdue developed the laboratory exercises that appear in the instructor's supplement. The following people contributed project assignments that appear in the instructor's supplement: Henning Schulzrinne (Columbia University); Cetin Kaya Koc (Oregon State University); and David Balenson (Trusted Information Systems and George Washington University).

Finally, I would like to thank the many people responsible for the publication of the book, all of whom did their usual excellent job. This includes the staff at Prentice Hall, particularly production manager Rose Kernan; my supplements manager Sarah Parker; and my new editor Tracy Dunkelberger. Also, Patricia M. Daly did the copy editing.

With all this assistance, little remains for which I can take full credit. However, I am proud to say that, with no help whatsoever, I selected all of the quotations.

CHAPTER 0

READER'S GUIDE

The art of war teaches us to rely not on the likelihood of the enemy's not coming, but on our own readiness to receive him; not on the chance of his not attacking, but rather on the fact that we have made our position unassailable.

—*The Art of War*, Sun Tzu

This book, with its accompanying Web site, covers a lot of material. Here we give the reader an overview.

0.1 OUTLINE OF THIS BOOK

Following an introductory chapter, Chapter 1, the book is organized into four parts:

Part One: Symmetric Ciphers: Provides a survey of symmetric encryption, including classical and modern algorithms. The emphasis is on the two most important algorithms, the Data Encryption Standard (DES) and the Advanced Encryption Standard (AES). This part also addresses message authentication and key management.

Part Two: Public-Key Encryption and Hash Functions: Provides a survey of public-key algorithms, including RSA (Rivest-Shamir-Adelman) and elliptic curve. It also covers public-key applications, including digital signatures and key exchange.

Part Three: Network Security Practice: Examines the use of cryptographic algorithms and security protocols to provide security over networks and the Internet. Topics covered include user authentication, e-mail, IP security, and Web security.

Part Four: System Security: Deals with security facilities designed to protect a computer system from security threats, including intruders, viruses, and worms. This part also looks at firewall technology.

Many of the cryptographic algorithms and network security protocols and applications described in this book have been specified as standards. The most important of these are Internet Standards, defined in Internet RFCs (Request for Comments), and Federal Information Processing Standards (FIPS), issued by the National Institute of Standards and Technology (NIST). Appendix A discusses the standards-making process and lists the standards cited in this book.

0.2 ROADMAP

Subject Matter

The material in this book is organized into three broad categories:

- **Cryptology:** This is the study of techniques for ensuring the secrecy and/or authenticity of information. The two main branches of cryptology are

cryptography, which is the study of the design of such techniques; and **cryptanalysis**, which deals with the defeating such techniques, to recover information, or forging information that will be accepted as authentic.

- **Network security:** This area covers the use of cryptographic algorithms in network protocols and network applications.
- **Computer security:** In this book, we use this term to refer to the security of computers against intruders (e.g., hackers) and malicious software (e.g., viruses). Typically, the computer to be secured is attached to a network and the bulk of the threats arise from the network.

The first two parts of the book deal with two distinct cryptographic approaches: symmetric cryptographic algorithms and public-key, or asymmetric, cryptographic algorithms. Symmetric algorithms make use of a single shared key shared by two parties. Public-key algorithms make use of two keys: a private key known only to one party, and a public key, available to other parties.

Topic Ordering

This book covers a lot of material. For the instructor or reader who wishes a shorter treatment, there are a number of opportunities.

To thoroughly cover the material in the first two parts, the chapters should be read in sequence. With the exception of the Advanced Encryption Standard (AES), none of the material in **Part One** requires any special mathematical background. To understand AES, it is necessary to have some understanding of finite fields. In turn, an understanding of finite fields requires a basic background in prime numbers and modular arithmetic. Accordingly, Chapter 4 covers all of these mathematical preliminaries just prior to their use in Chapter 5 on AES. Thus, if Chapter 5 is skipped, it is safe to skip Chapter 4 as well.

Chapter 2 introduces some concepts that are useful in later chapters of Part One. However, for the reader whose sole interest is contemporary cryptography, this chapter can be quickly skimmed. The two most important symmetric cryptographic algorithms are DES and AES, which are covered in Chapters 3 and 5, respectively. Chapter 6 covers two other interesting algorithms, both of which enjoy commercial use. This chapter can be safely skipped if these algorithms are not of interest.

For **Part Two,** the only additional mathematical background that is needed is in the area of number theory, which is covered in Chapter 8. The reader who has skipped Chapters 4 and 5 should first review the material on Sections 4.1 through 4.3.

The two most widely used general-purpose public-key algorithms are RSA and elliptic curve, with RSA enjoying much wider acceptance. The reader may wish to skip the material on elliptic curve cryptography in Chapter 10, at least on a first reading. In Chapter 12, Whirlpool and CMAC are of lesser importance.

Part Three and **Part Four** are relatively independent of each other and can be read in either order. Both parts assume a basic understanding of the material in Parts One and Two.

0.3 INTERNET AND WEB RESOURCES

There are a number of resources available on the Internet and the Web to support this book and to help one keep up with developments in this field.

Web Sites for This Book

A special Web page has been set up for this book at **WilliamStallings.com/Crypto/Crypto4e.html.** The site includes the following:

- **Useful Web sites:** There are links to other relevant Web sites, organized by chapter, including the sites listed in this section and throughout this book.
- **Errata sheet:** An errata list for this book will be maintained and updated as needed. Please e-mail any errors that you spot to me. Errata sheets for my other books are at **WilliamStallings.com.**
- **Figures:** All of the figures in this book in PDF (Adobe Acrobat) format.
- **Tables:** All of the tables in this book in PDF format.
- **Slides:** A set of PowerPoint slides, organized by chapter.
- **Cryptography and network security courses:** There are links to home pages for courses based on this book; these pages may be useful to other instructors in providing ideas about how to structure their course.

I also maintain the Computer Science Student Resource Site, at **WilliamStallings.com/StudentSupport.html.** The purpose of this site is to provide documents, information, and links for computer science students and professionals. Links and documents are organized into four categories:

- **Math:** Includes a basic math refresher, a queuing analysis primer, a number system primer, and links to numerous math sites
- **How-to:** Advice and guidance for solving homework problems, writing technical reports, and preparing technical presentations
- **Research resources:** Links to important collections of papers, technical reports, and bibliographies
- **Miscellaneous:** A variety of other useful documents and links

Other Web Sites

There are numerous Web sites that provide information related to the topics of this book. In subsequent chapters, pointers to specific Web sites can be found in the *Recommended Reading and Web Sites* section. Because the addresses for Web sites tend to change frequently, I have not included URLs in the book. For all of the Web sites listed in the book, the appropriate link can be found at this book's Web site. Other links not mentioned in this book will be added to the Web site over time.

USENET Newsgroups

A number of USENET newsgroups are devoted to some aspect of cryptography or network security. As with virtually all USENET groups, there is a high noise-to-signal ratio, but it is worth experimenting to see if any meet your needs. The most relevant are

- **sci.crypt.research:** The best group to follow. This is a moderated newsgroup that deals with research topics; postings must have some relationship to the technical aspects of cryptology.
- **sci.crypt:** A general discussion of cryptology and related topics.
- **sci.crypt.random-numbers:** A discussion of cryptographic-strength random number generators.
- **alt.security:** A general discussion of security topics.
- **comp.security.misc:** A general discussion of computer security topics.
- **comp.security.firewalls:** A discussion of firewall products and technology.
- **comp.security.announce:** News, announcements from CERT.
- **comp.risks:** A discussion of risks to the public from computers and users.
- **comp.virus:** A moderated discussion of computer viruses.

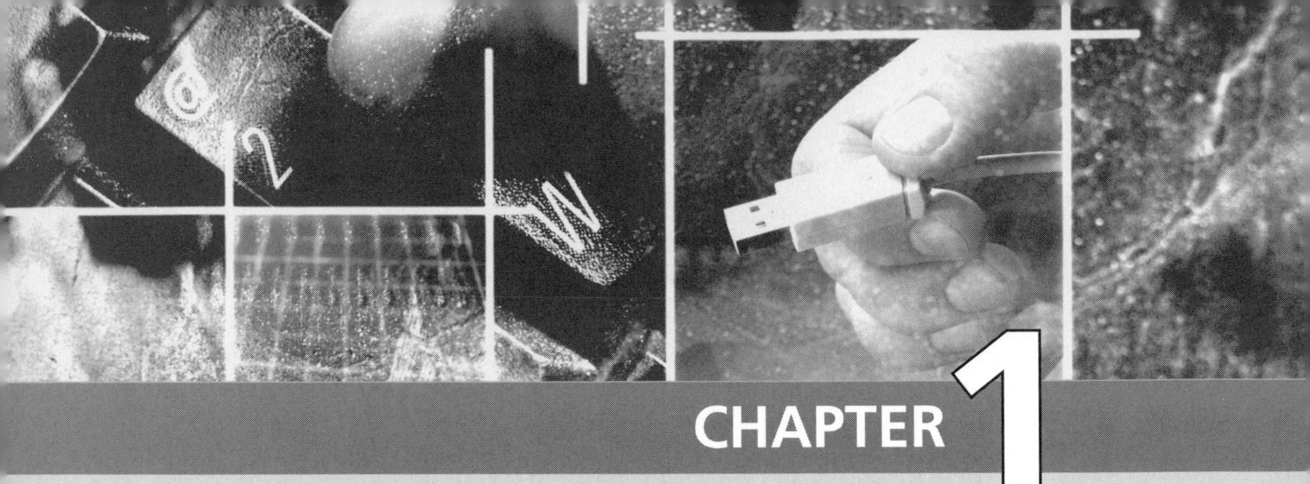

CHAPTER 1

INTRODUCTION

The combination of space, time, and strength that must be considered as the basic elements of this theory of defense makes this a fairly complicated matter. Consequently, it is not easy to find a fixed point of departure.

—*On War*, Carl Von Clausewitz

KEY POINTS

- The OSI (open systems interconnection) security architecture provides a systematic framework for defining security attacks, mechanisms, and services.
- **Security attacks** are classified as either passive attacks, which include unauthorized reading of a message of file and traffic analysis; and active attacks, such as modification of messages or files, and denial of service.
- A **security mechanism** is any process (or a device incorporating such a process) that is designed to detect, prevent, or recover from a security attack. Examples of mechanisms are encryption algorithms, digital signatures, and authentication protocols.
- **Security services** include authentication, access control, data confidentiality, data integrity, nonrepudiation, and availability.

The requirements of **information security** within an organization have undergone two major changes in the last several decades. Before the widespread use of data processing equipment, the security of information felt to be valuable to an organization was provided primarily by physical and administrative means. An example of the former is the use of rugged filing cabinets with a combination lock for storing sensitive documents. An example of the latter is personnel screening procedures used during the hiring process.

With the introduction of the computer, the need for automated tools for protecting files and other information stored on the computer became evident. This is especially the case for a shared system, such as a time-sharing system, and the need is even more acute for systems that can be accessed over a public telephone network, data network, or the Internet. The generic name for the collection of tools designed to protect data and to thwart hackers is **computer security**.

The second major change that affected security is the introduction of distributed systems and the use of networks and communications facilities for carrying data between terminal user and computer and between computer and computer. Network security measures are needed to protect data during their transmission. In fact, the term **network security** is somewhat misleading, because virtually all business, government, and academic organizations interconnect their data processing equipment with a collection of interconnected networks. Such a collection is often referred to as an internet,[1] and the term **internet security** is used.

There are no clear boundaries between these two forms of security. For example, one of the most publicized types of attack on information systems is the computer virus. A virus may be introduced into a system physically when it arrives on a diskette or optical disk and is subsequently loaded onto a computer. Viruses may also arrive over an internet. In either case, once the virus is resident on a computer system, internal computer security tools are needed to detect and recover from the virus.

This book focuses on internet security, which consists of measures to deter, prevent, detect, and correct security violations that involve the transmission of information. That is a broad statement that covers a host of possibilities. To give you a feel for the areas covered in this book, consider the following examples of security violations:

1. User A transmits a file to user B. The file contains sensitive information (e.g., payroll records) that is to be protected from disclosure. User C, who is not authorized to read the file, is able to monitor the transmission and capture a copy of the file during its transmission.
2. A network manager, D, transmits a message to a computer, E, under its management. The message instructs computer E to update an authorization file to include the identities of a number of new users who are to be given access to that computer. User F intercepts the message, alters its contents to add or delete entries, and then forwards the message to E, which accepts the message as coming from manager D and updates its authorization file accordingly.
3. Rather than intercept a message, user F constructs its own message with the desired entries and transmits that message to E as if it had come from manager D. Computer E accepts the message as coming from manager D and updates its authorization file accordingly.
4. An employee is fired without warning. The personnel manager sends a message to a server system to invalidate the employee's account. When the invalidation is accomplished, the server is to post a notice to the employee's file as confirmation of the action. The employee is able to intercept the message and delay it long enough to make a final access to the server to retrieve sensitive information. The message is then forwarded, the action taken, and the confirmation posted. The employee's action may go unnoticed for some considerable time.
5. A message is sent from a customer to a stockbroker with instructions for various transactions. Subsequently, the investments lose value and the customer denies sending the message.

Although this list by no means exhausts the possible types of security violations, it illustrates the range of concerns of network security.

---

[1]We use the term *internet*, with a lowercase "i," to refer to any interconnected collection of networks. A corporate intranet is an example of an internet. The Internet with a capital "I" may be one of the facilities used by an organization to construct its internet.

Internetwork security is both fascinating and complex. Some of the reasons follow:

1. Security involving communications and networks is not as simple as it might first appear to the novice. The requirements seem to be straightforward; indeed, most of the major requirements for security services can be given self-explanatory one-word labels: confidentiality, authentication, nonrepudiation, integrity. But the mechanisms used to meet those requirements can be quite complex, and understanding them may involve rather subtle reasoning.
2. In developing a particular security mechanism or algorithm, one must always consider potential attacks on those security features. In many cases, successful attacks are designed by looking at the problem in a completely different way, therefore exploiting an unexpected weakness in the mechanism.
3. Because of point 2, the procedures used to provide particular services are often counterintuitive: It is not obvious from the statement of a particular requirement that such elaborate measures are needed. It is only when the various countermeasures are considered that the measures used make sense.
4. Having designed various security mechanisms, it is necessary to decide where to use them. This is true both in terms of physical placement (e.g., at what points in a network are certain security mechanisms needed) and in a logical sense [e.g., at what layer or layers of an architecture such as TCP/IP (Transmission Control Protocol/Internet Protocol) should mechanisms be placed].
5. Security mechanisms usually involve more than a particular algorithm or protocol. They usually also require that participants be in possession of some secret information (e.g., an encryption key), which raises questions about the creation, distribution, and protection of that secret information. There is also a reliance on communications protocols whose behavior may complicate the task of developing the security mechanism. For example, if the proper functioning of the security mechanism requires setting time limits on the transit time of a message from sender to receiver, then any protocol or network that introduces variable, unpredictable delays may render such time limits meaningless.

Thus, there is much to consider. This chapter provides a general overview of the subject matter that structures the material in the remainder of the book. We begin with a general discussion of network security services and mechanisms and of the types of attacks they are designed for. Then we develop a general overall model within which the security services and mechanisms can be viewed.

1.1 SECURITY TRENDS

In 1994, the Internet Architecture Board (IAB) issued a report entitled "Security in the Internet Architecture" (RFC 1636). The report stated the general consensus that the Internet needs more and better security, and it identified key areas for security mechanisms. Among these were the need to secure the network infrastructure from unauthorized monitoring and control of network traffic and the need to secure end-user-to-end-user traffic using authentication and encryption mechanisms.

These concerns are fully justified. As confirmation, consider the trends reported by the Computer Emergency Response Team (CERT) Coordination Center (CERT/CC). Figure 1.1a shows the trend in Internet-related vulnerabilities reported

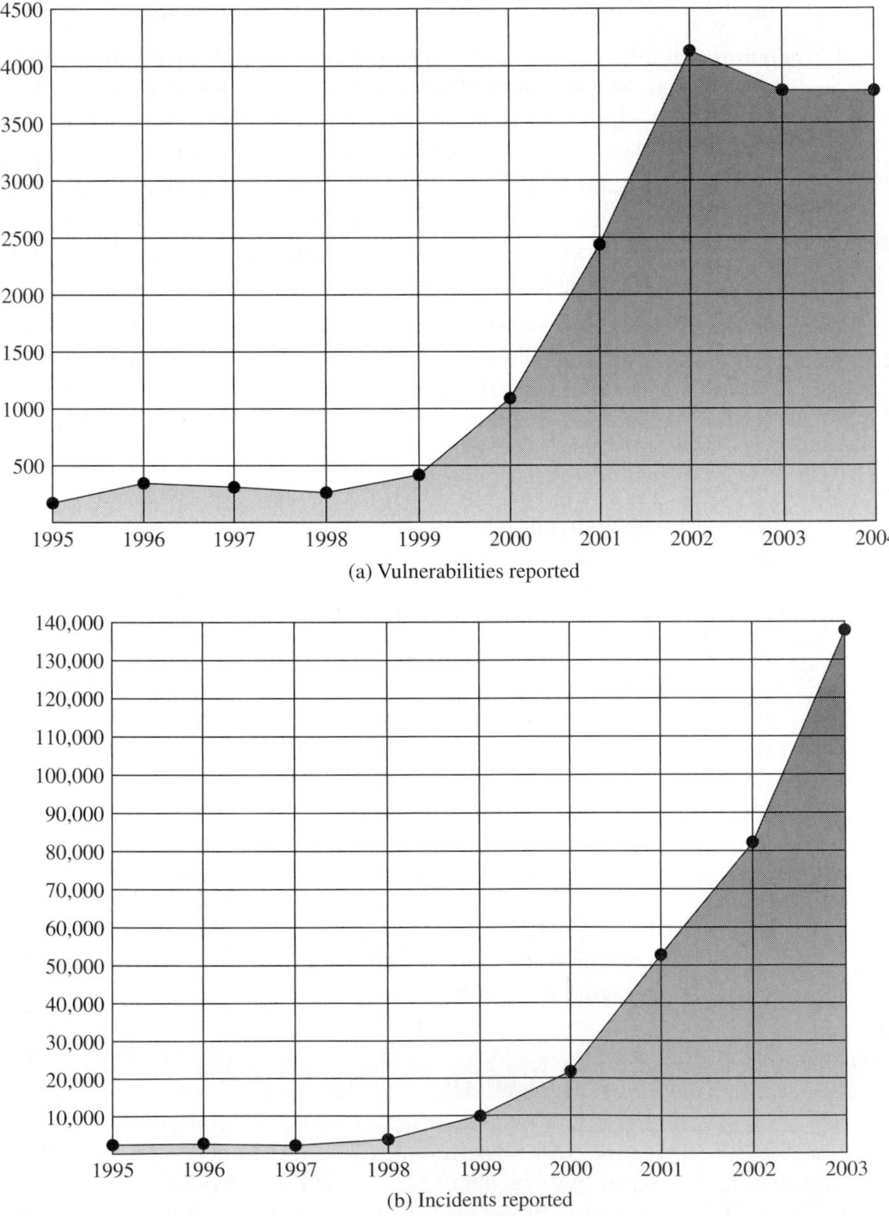

Figure 1.1 CERT Statistics

to CERT over a 10-year period. These include security weaknesses in the operating systems of attached computers (e.g., Windows, Linux) as well as vulnerabilities in Internet routers and other network devices. Figure 1.1b shows the number of security-related incidents reported to CERT. These include denial of service attacks; IP spoofing, in which intruders create packets with false IP addresses and exploit applications that use authentication based on IP; and various forms of eavesdropping and packet sniffing, in which attackers read transmitted information, including logon information and database contents.

Over time, the attacks on the Internet and Internet-attached systems have grown more sophisticated while the amount of skill and knowledge required to mount an attack has declined (Figure 1.2). Attacks have become more automated and can cause greater amounts of damage.

This increase in attacks coincides with an increased use of the Internet and with increases in the complexity of protocols, applications, and the Internet itself. Critical infrastructures increasingly rely on the Internet for operations. Individual users rely on the security of the Internet, email, the Web, and Web-based applications to a greater extent than ever. Thus, a wide range of technologies and tools are needed to counter the growing threat. At a basic level, cryptographic algorithms for confidentiality and authentication assume greater importance. As well, designers need to focus on Internet-based protocols and the vulnerabilities of attached operating systems and applications. This book surveys all of these technical areas.

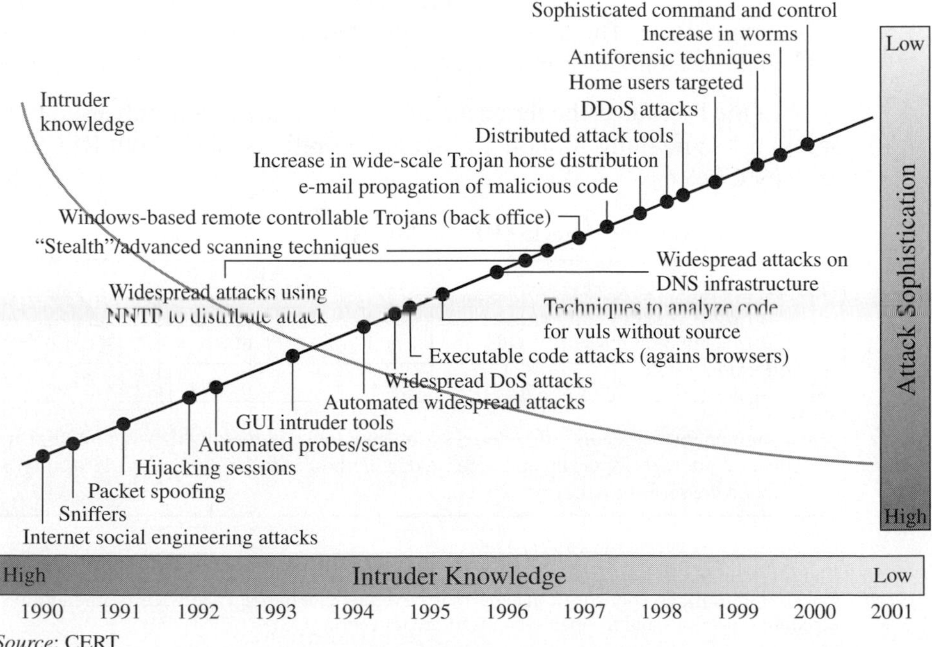

Source: CERT

Figure 1.2 Trends in Attack Sophistication and Intruder Knowledge

1.2 THE OSI SECURITY ARCHITECTURE

To assess effectively the security needs of an organization and to evaluate and choose various security products and policies, the manager responsible for security needs some systematic way of defining the requirements for security and characterizing the approaches to satisfying those requirements. This is difficult enough in a centralized data processing environment; with the use of local and wide area networks, the problems are compounded.

ITU-T[2] Recommendation X.800, *Security Architecture for OSI*, defines such a systematic approach.[3] The OSI security architecture is useful to managers as a way of organizing the task of providing security. Furthermore, because this architecture was developed as an international standard, computer and communications vendors have developed security features for their products and services that relate to this structured definition of services and mechanisms.

For our purposes, the OSI security architecture provides a useful, if abstract, overview of many of the concepts that this book deals with. The OSI security architecture focuses on security attacks, mechanisms, and services. These can be defined briefly as follows:

- **Security attack:** Any action that compromises the security of information owned by an organization.
- **Security mechanism:** A process (or a device incorporating such a process) that is designed to detect, prevent, or recover from a security attack.
- **Security service:** A processing or communication service that enhances the security of the data processing systems and the information transfers of an organization. The services are intended to counter security attacks, and they make use of one or more security mechanisms to provide the service.

In the literature, the terms *threat* and *attack* are commonly used to mean more or less the same thing. Table 1.1 provides definitions taken from RFC 2828, *Internet Security Glossary*.

Table 1.1 Threats and Attacks (RFC 2828)

Threat A potential for violation of security, which exists when there is a circumstance, capability, action, or event that could breach security and cause harm. That is, a threat is a possible danger that might exploit a vulnerability.
Attack An assault on system security that derives from an intelligent threat; that is, an intelligent act that is a deliberate attempt (especially in the sense of a method or technique) to evade security services and violate the security policy of a system.

[2]The International Telecommunication Union (ITU) Telecommunication Standardization Sector (ITU-T) is a United Nations–sponsored agency that develops standards, called Recommendations, relating to telecommunications and to open systems interconnection (OSI).

[3]The OSI security architecture was developed in the context of the OSI protocol architecture, which is described in Appendix H. However, for our purposes in this chapter, an understanding of the OSI protocol architecture is not required.

1.3 SECURITY ATTACKS

A useful means of classifying security attacks, used both in X.800 and RFC 2828, is in terms of *passive attacks* and *active attacks*. A passive attack attempts to learn or make use of information from the system but does not affect system resources. An active attack attempts to alter system resources or affect their operation.

Passive Attacks

Passive attacks are in the nature of eavesdropping on, or monitoring of, transmissions. The goal of the opponent is to obtain information that is being transmitted. Two types of passive attacks are release of message contents and traffic analysis.

The **release of message contents** is easily understood (Figure 1.3a). A telephone conversation, an electronic mail message, and a transferred file may contain sensitive or confidential information. We would like to prevent an opponent from learning the contents of these transmissions.

A second type of passive attack, **traffic analysis**, is subtler (Figure 1.3b). Suppose that we had a way of masking the contents of messages or other information traffic so that opponents, even if they captured the message, could not extract the information from the message. The common technique for masking contents is encryption. If we had encryption protection in place, an opponent might still be able to observe the pattern of these messages. The opponent could determine the location and identity of communicating hosts and could observe the frequency and length of messages being exchanged. This information might be useful in guessing the nature of the communication that was taking place.

Passive attacks are very difficult to detect because they do not involve any alteration of the data. Typically, the message traffic is sent and received in an apparently normal fashion and neither the sender nor receiver is aware that a third party has read the messages or observed the traffic pattern. However, it is feasible to prevent the success of these attacks, usually by means of encryption. Thus, the emphasis in dealing with passive attacks is on prevention rather than detection.

Active Attacks

Active attacks involve some modification of the data stream or the creation of a false stream and can be subdivided into four categories: masquerade, replay, modification of messages, and denial of service.

A **masquerade** takes place when one entity pretends to be a different entity (Figure 1.4a). A masquerade attack usually includes one of the other forms of active attack. For example, authentication sequences can be captured and replayed after a valid authentication sequence has taken place, thus enabling an authorized entity with few privileges to obtain extra privileges by impersonating an entity that has those privileges.

Replay involves the passive capture of a data unit and its subsequent retransmission to produce an unauthorized effect (Figure 1.4b).

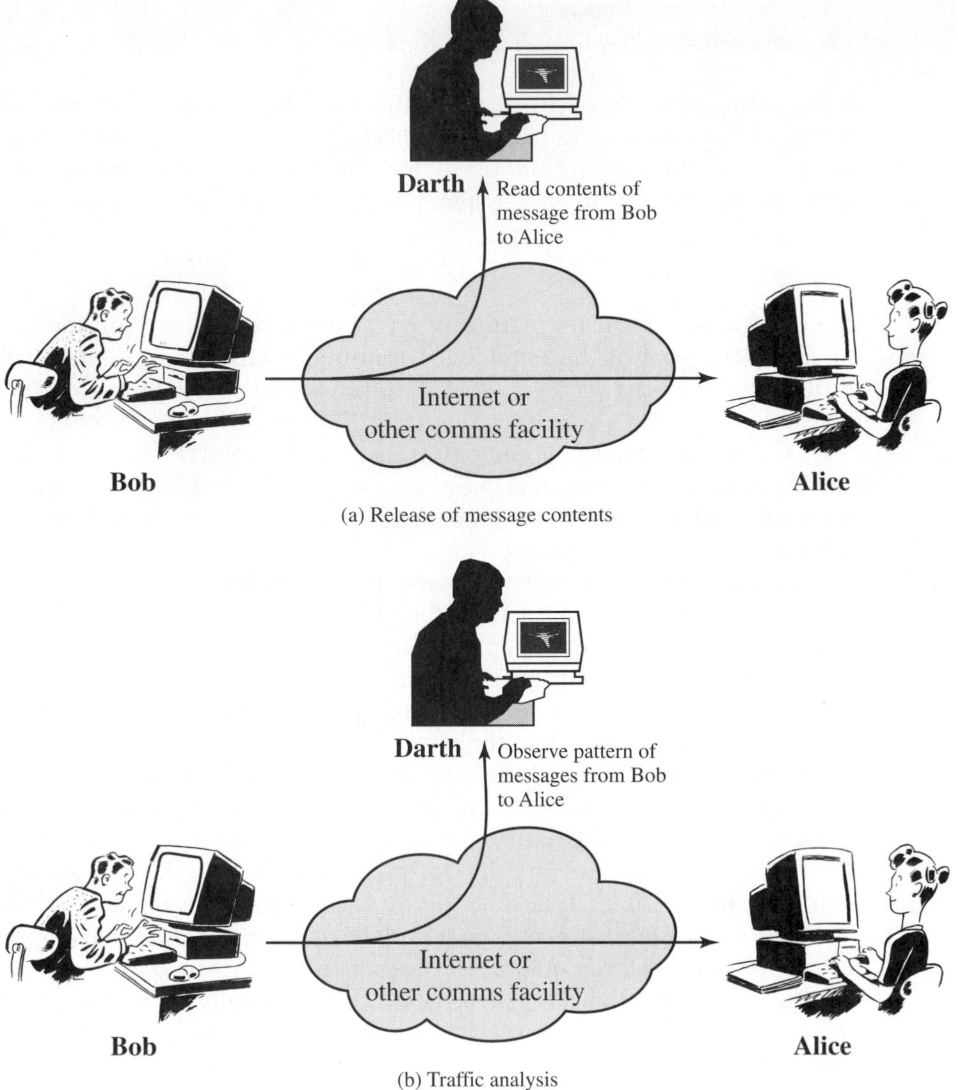

Figure 1.3 Passive Attacks

Modification of messages simply means that some portion of a legitimate message is altered, or that messages are delayed or reordered, to produce an unauthorized effect (Figure 1.4c). For example, a message meaning "Allow John Smith to read confidential file *accounts*" is modified to mean "Allow Fred Brown to read confidential file *accounts.*"

The **denial of service** prevents or inhibits the normal use or management of communications facilities (Figure 1.4d). This attack may have a specific target; for example, an entity may suppress all messages directed to a particular destination (e.g., the security audit service). Another form of service denial

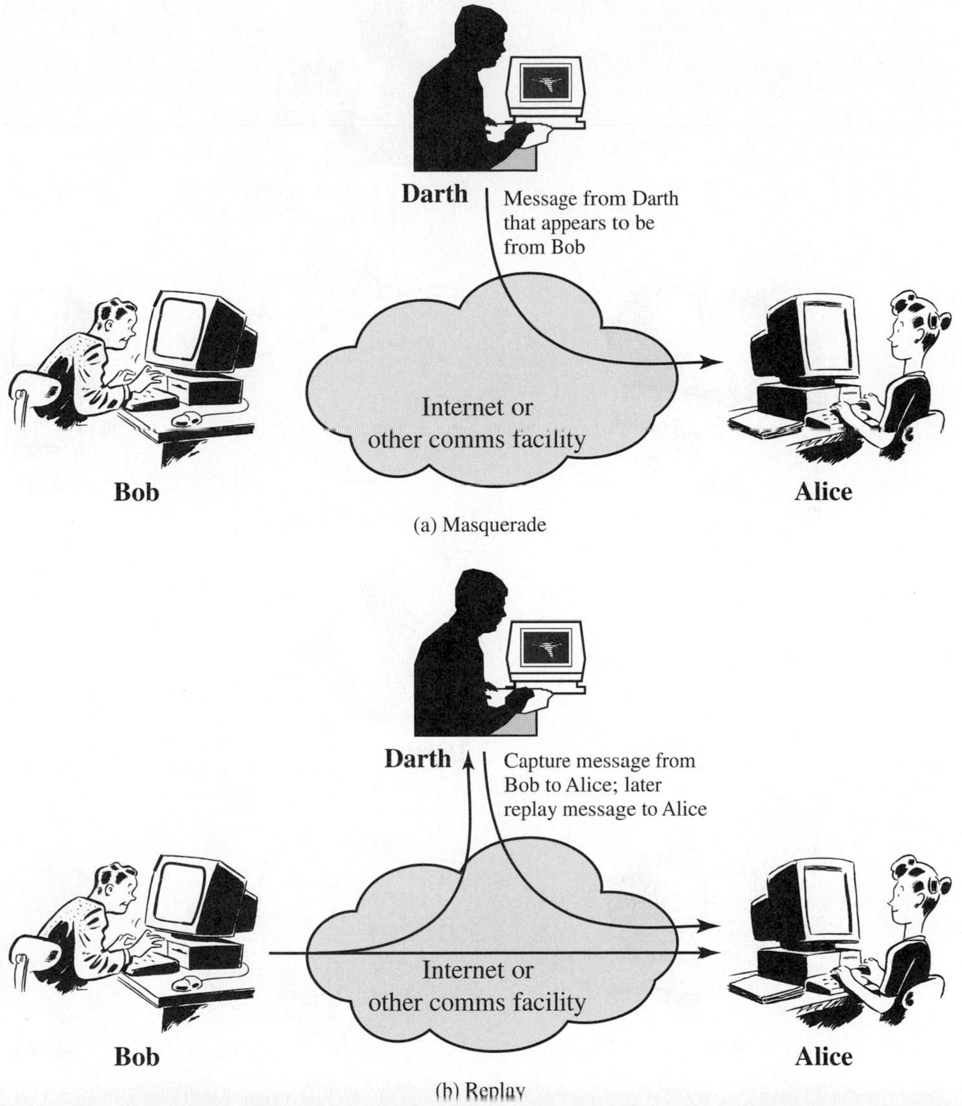

Figure 1.4 Active Attacks (page 1 of 2)

is the disruption of an entire network, either by disabling the network or by overloading it with messages so as to degrade performance.

Active attacks present the opposite characteristics of passive attacks. Whereas passive attacks are difficult to detect, measures are available to prevent their success. On the other hand, it is quite difficult to prevent active attacks absolutely, because of the wide variety of potential physical, software, and network vulnerabilities. Instead, the goal is to detect active attacks and to recover from any disruption or delays caused by them. If the detection has a deterrent effect, it may also contribute to prevention.

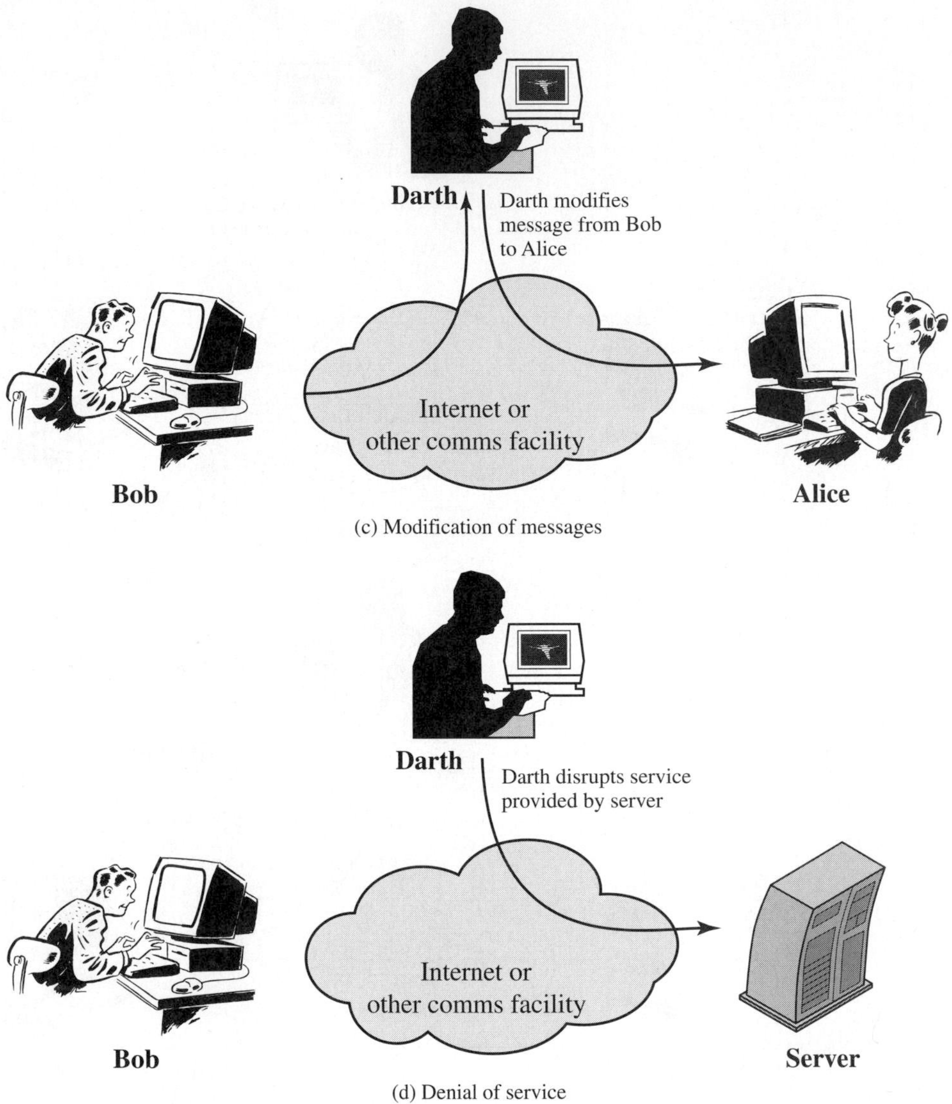

Figure 1.4 Active Attacks (page 2 of 2)

1.4 SECURITY SERVICES

X.800 defines a security service as a service provided by a protocol layer of communicating open systems, which ensures adequate security of the systems or of data transfers. Perhaps a clearer definition is found in RFC 2828, which provides the following definition: a processing or communication service that is provided by a system to give a specific kind of protection to system resources; security services implement security policies and are implemented by security mechanisms.

X.800 divides these services into five categories and fourteen specific services (Table 1.2). We look at each category in turn.[4]

Table 1.2 Security Services (X.800)

AUTHENTICATION The assurance that the communicating entity is the one that it claims to be. **Peer Entity Authentication** Used in association with a logical connection to provide confidence in the identity of the entities connected. **Data Origin Authentication** In a connectionless transfer, provides assurance that the source of received data is as claimed. **ACCESS CONTROL** The prevention of unauthorized use of a resource (i.e., this service controls who can have access to a resource, under what conditions access can occur, and what those accessing the resource are allowed to do). **DATA CONFIDENTIALITY** The protection of data from unauthorized disclosure. **Connection Confidentiality** The protection of all user data on a connection. **Connectionless Confidentiality** The protection of all user data in a single data block **Selective-Field Confidentiality** The confidentiality of selected fields within the user data on a connection or in a single data block. **Traffic Flow Confidentiality** The protection of the information that might be derived from observation of traffic flows.	**DATA INTEGRITY** The assurance that data received are exactly as sent by an authorized entity (i.e., contain no modification, insertion, deletion, or replay). **Connection Integrity with Recovery** Provides for the integrity of all user data on a connection and detects any modification, insertion, deletion, or replay of any data within an entire data sequence, with recovery attempted. **Connection Integrity without Recovery** As above, but provides only detection without recovery. **Selective-Field Connection Integrity** Provides for the integrity of selected fields within the user data of a data block transferred over a connection and takes the form of determination of whether the selected fields have been modified, inserted, deleted, or replayed. **Connectionless Integrity** Provides for the integrity of a single connectionless data block and may take the form of detection of data modification. Additionally, a limited form of replay detection may be provided. **Selective-Field Connectionless Integrity** Provides for the integrity of selected fields within a single connectionless data block; takes the form of determination of whether the selected fields have been modified. **NONREPUDIATION** Provides protection against denial by one of the entities involved in a communication of having participated in all or part of the communication. **Nonrepudiation, Origin** Proof that the message was sent by the specified party. **Nonrepudiation, Destination** Proof that the message was received by the specified party.

[4]There is no universal agreement about many of the terms used in the security literature. For example, the term *integrity* is sometimes used to refer to all aspects of information security. The term *authentication* is sometimes used to refer both to verification of identity and to the various functions listed under integrity in this chapter. Our usage here agrees with both X.800 and RFC 2828.

Authentication

The authentication service is concerned with assuring that a communication is authentic. In the case of a single message, such as a warning or alarm signal, the function of the authentication service is to assure the recipient that the message is from the source that it claims to be from. In the case of an ongoing interaction, such as the connection of a terminal to a host, two aspects are involved. First, at the time of connection initiation, the service assures that the two entities are authentic, that is, that each is the entity that it claims to be. Second, the service must assure that the connection is not interfered with in such a way that a third party can masquerade as one of the two legitimate parties for the purposes of unauthorized transmission or reception.

Two specific authentication services are defined in X.800:

- **Peer entity authentication:** Provides for the corroboration of the identity of a peer entity in an association. It is provided for use at the establishment of, or at times during the data transfer phase of, a connection. It attempts to provide confidence that an entity is not performing either a masquerade or an unauthorized replay of a previous connection.
- **Data origin authentication:** Provides for the corroboration of the source of a data unit. It does not provide protection against the duplication or modification of data units. This type of service supports applications like electronic mail where there are no prior interactions between the communicating entities.

Access Control

In the context of network security, access control is the ability to limit and control the access to host systems and applications via communications links. To achieve this, each entity trying to gain access must first be identified, or authenticated, so that access rights can be tailored to the individual.

Data Confidentiality

Confidentiality is the protection of transmitted data from passive attacks. With respect to the content of a data transmission, several levels of protection can be identified. The broadest service protects all user data transmitted between two users over a period of time. For example, when a TCP connection is set up between two systems, this broad protection prevents the release of any user data transmitted over the TCP connection. Narrower forms of this service can also be defined, including the protection of a single message or even specific fields within a message. These refinements are less useful than the broad approach and may even be more complex and expensive to implement.

The other aspect of confidentiality is the protection of traffic flow from analysis. This requires that an attacker not be able to observe the source and destination, frequency, length, or other characteristics of the traffic on a communications facility.

Data Integrity

As with confidentiality, integrity can apply to a stream of messages, a single message, or selected fields within a message. Again, the most useful and straightforward approach is total stream protection.

A connection-oriented integrity service, one that deals with a stream of messages, assures that messages are received as sent, with no duplication, insertion, modification, reordering, or replays. The destruction of data is also covered under this service. Thus, the connection-oriented integrity service addresses both message stream modification and denial of service. On the other hand, a connectionless integrity service, one that deals with individual messages without regard to any larger context, generally provides protection against message modification only.

We can make a distinction between the service with and without recovery. Because the integrity service relates to active attacks, we are concerned with detection rather than prevention. If a violation of integrity is detected, then the service may simply report this violation, and some other portion of software or human intervention is required to recover from the violation. Alternatively, there are mechanisms available to recover from the loss of integrity of data, as we will review subsequently. The incorporation of automated recovery mechanisms is, in general, the more attractive alternative.

Nonrepudiation

Nonrepudiation prevents either sender or receiver from denying a transmitted message. Thus, when a message is sent, the receiver can prove that the alleged sender in fact sent the message. Similarly, when a message is received, the sender can prove that the alleged receiver in fact received the message.

Availability Service

Both X.800 and RFC 2828 define availability to be the property of a system or a system resource being accessible and usable upon demand by an authorized system entity, according to performance specifications for the system (i.e., a system is available if it provides services according to the system design whenever users request them). A variety of attacks can result in the loss of or reduction in availability. Some of these attacks are amenable to automated countermeasures, such as authentication and encryption, whereas others require some sort of physical action to prevent or recover from loss of availability of elements of a distributed system.

X.800 treats availability as a property to be associated with various security services. However, it makes sense to call out specifically an availability service. An availability service is one that protects a system to ensure its availability. This service addresses the security concerns raised by denial-of-service attacks. It depends on proper management and control of system resources and thus depends on access control service and other security services.

1.5 SECURITY MECHANISMS

Table 1.3 lists the security mechanisms defined in X.800. As can be seen the mechanisms are divided into those that are implemented in a specific protocol layer and those that are not specific to any particular protocol layer or security service. These mechanisms will be covered in the appropriate places in the book and so we do not elaborate now, except to comment on the definition of encipherment. X.800

Table 1.3 Security Mechanisms (X.800)

SPECIFIC SECURITY MECHANISMS	PERVASIVE SECURITY MECHANISMS
May be incorporated into the appropriate protocol layer in order to provide some of the OSI security services.	Mechanisms that are not specific to any particular OSI security service or protocol layer.
Encipherment The use of mathematical algorithms to transform data into a form that is not readily intelligible. The transformation and subsequent recovery of the data depend on an algorithm and zero or more encryption keys.	**Trusted Functionality** That which is perceived to be correct with respect to some criteria (e.g., as established by a security policy).
Digital Signature Data appended to, or a cryptographic transformation of, a data unit that allows a recipient of the data unit to prove the source and integrity of the data unit and protect against forgery (e.g., by the recipient).	**Security Label** The marking bound to a resource (which may be a data unit) that names or designates the security attributes of that resource.
Access Control A variety of mechanisms that enforce access rights to resources.	**Event Detection** Detection of security-relevant events.
Data Integrity A variety of mechanisms used to assure the integrity of a data unit or stream of data units.	**Security Audit Trail** Data collected and potentially used to facilitate a security audit, which is an independent review and examination of system records and activities.
Authentication Exchange A mechanism intended to ensure the identity of an entity by means of information exchange.	**Security Recovery** Deals with requests from mechanisms, such as event handling and management functions, and takes recovery actions.
Traffic Padding The insertion of bits into gaps in a data stream to frustrate traffic analysis attempts.	
Routing Control Enables selection of particular physically secure routes for certain data and allows routing changes, especially when a breach of security is suspected.	
Notarization The use of a trusted third party to assure certain properties of a data exchange.	

distinguishes between reversible encipherment mechanisms and irreversible encipherment mechanisms. A reversible encipherment mechanism is simply an encryption algorithm that allows data to be encrypted and subsequently decrypted. Irreversible encipherment mechanisms include hash algorithms and message authentication codes, which are used in digital signature and message authentication applications.

Table 1.4, based on one in X.800, indicates the relationship between security services and security mechanisms.

Table 1.4 Relationship between Security Services and Mechanisms

	Mechanism							
Service	**Encipherment**	**Digital Signature**	**Access Control**	**Data Integrity**	**Authentication Exchange**	**Traffic Padding**	**Routing Control**	**Notarization**
Peer entity authentication	Y	Y			Y			
Data origin authentication	Y	Y						
Access control			Y					
Confidentiality	Y						Y	
Traffic flow confidentiality	Y					Y	Y	
Data integrity	Y	Y		Y				
Nonrepudiation		Y		Y				Y
Availability				Y	Y			

1.6 A MODEL FOR NETWORK SECURITY

A model for much of what we will be discussing is captured, in very general terms, in Figure 1.5. A message is to be transferred from one party to another across some sort of internet. The two parties, who are the *principals* in this transaction, must cooperate for the exchange to take place. A logical information channel is established by defining a route through the internet from source to destination and by the cooperative use of communication protocols (e.g., TCP/IP) by the two principals.

Security aspects come into play when it is necessary or desirable to protect the information transmission from an opponent who may present a threat to confidentiality, authenticity, and so on. All the techniques for providing security have two components:

- A security-related transformation on the information to be sent. Examples include the encryption of the message, which scrambles the message so that it is unreadable by the opponent, and the addition of a code based on the contents of the message, which can be used to verify the identity of the sender
- Some secret information shared by the two principals and, it is hoped, unknown to the opponent. An example is an encryption key used in conjunction with the transformation to scramble the message before transmission and unscramble it on reception.[5]

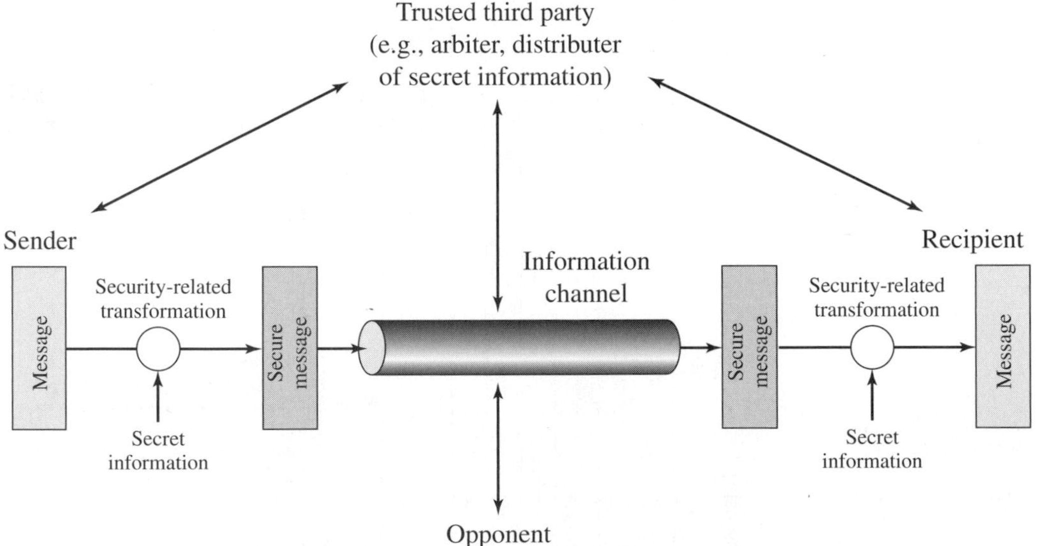

Figure 1.5 Model for Network Security

[5]Part Two discusses a form of encryption, known as public-key encryption, in which only one of the two principals needs to have the secret information.

A trusted third party may be needed to achieve secure transmission. For example, a third party may be responsible for distributing the secret information to the two principals while keeping it from any opponent. Or a third party may be needed to arbitrate disputes between the two principals concerning the authenticity of a message transmission.

This general model shows that there are four basic tasks in designing a particular security service:

1. Design an algorithm for performing the security-related transformation. The algorithm should be such that an opponent cannot defeat its purpose.
2. Generate the secret information to be used with the algorithm.
3. Develop methods for the distribution and sharing of the secret information.
4. Specify a protocol to be used by the two principals that makes use of the security algorithm and the secret information to achieve a particular security service.

Parts One through Three of this book concentrates on the types of security mechanisms and services that fit into the model shown in Figure 1.5. However, there are other security-related situations of interest that do not neatly fit this model but that are considered in this book. A general model of these other situations is illustrated by Figure 1.6, which reflects a concern for protecting an information system from unwanted access. Most readers are familiar with the concerns caused by the existence of hackers, who attempt to penetrate systems that can be accessed over a network. The hacker can be someone who, with no malign intent, simply gets satisfaction from breaking and entering a computer system. Or, the intruder can be a disgruntled employee who wishes to do damage, or a criminal who seeks to exploit computer assets for financial gain (e.g., obtaining credit card numbers or performing illegal money transfers).

Another type of unwanted access is the placement in a computer system of logic that exploits vulnerabilities in the system and that can affect application programs as well as utility programs, such as editors and compilers. Programs can present two kinds of threats:

- **Information access threats** intercept or modify data on behalf of users who should not have access to that data.
- **Service threats** exploit service flaws in computers to inhibit use by legitimate users.

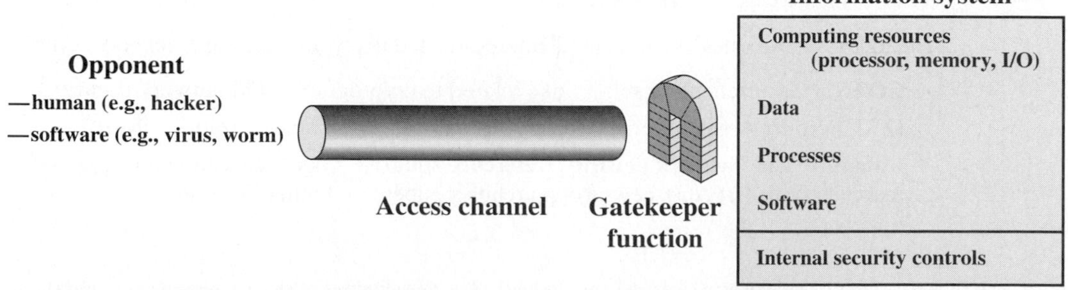

Figure 1.6 Network Access Security Model

Viruses and worms are two examples of software attacks. Such attacks can be introduced into a system by means of a disk that contains the unwanted logic concealed in otherwise useful software. They can also be inserted into a system across a network; this latter mechanism is of more concern in network security.

The security mechanisms needed to cope with unwanted access fall into two broad categories (see Figure 1.6). The first category might be termed a gatekeeper function. It includes password-based login procedures that are designed to deny access to all but authorized users and screening logic that is designed to detect and reject worms, viruses, and other similar attacks. Once either an unwanted user or unwanted software gains access, the second line of defense consists of a variety of internal controls that monitor activity and analyze stored information in an attempt to detect the presence of unwanted intruders. These issues are explored in Part Four.

1.7 RECOMMENDED READING AND WEB SITES

[PFLE02] provides a good introduction to both computer and network security. Two other excellent surveys are [PIEP03] and [BISH05]. [BISH03] covers much the same ground as [BISH05] but with more mathematical detail and rigor. [SCHN00] is valuable reading for any practitioner in the field of computer or network security: it discusses the limitations of technology, and cryptography in particular, in providing security, and the need to consider the hardware, the software implementation, the networks, and the people involved in providing and attacking security.

BISH03 Bishop, M. *Computer Security: Art and Science.* Boston: Addison-Wesley, 2003.

BISH05 Bishop, M. *Introduction to Computer Security.* Boston: Addison-Wesley, 2005.

PFLE02 Pfleeger, C. *Security in Computing.* Upper Saddle River, NJ: Prentice Hall, 2002.

PIEP03 Pieprzyk, J.; Hardjono, T.; and Seberry, J. *Fundamentals of Computer Security.* New York: Springer-Verlag, 2003.

SCHN00 Schneier, B. *Secrets and Lies: Digital Security in a Networked World.* New York: Wiley 2000.

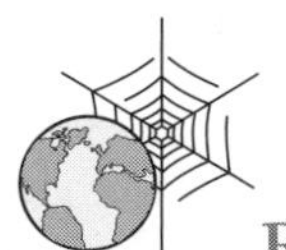

Recommended Web Sites:

The following Web sites[6] are of general interest related to cryptography and network security:

- **COAST:** Comprehensive set of links related to cryptography and network security.
- **IETF Security Area:** Material related to Internet security standardization efforts.
- **Computer and Network Security Reference Index:** A good index to vendor and commercial products, FAQs, newsgroup archives, papers, and other Web sites.

---

[6]Because URLs sometimes change, they are not included. For all of the Web sites listed in this and subsequent chapters, the appropriate link is at this book's Web site at **williamstallings.com/Crypto/Crypto4e.html**.

- **The Cryptography FAQ:** Lengthy and worthwhile FAQ covering all aspects of cryptography.
- **Tom Dunigan's Security Page:** An excellent list of pointers to cryptography and network security Web sites.
- **Helgar Lipma's Cryptology Pointers:** Another excellent list of pointers to cryptography and network security Web sites.
- **IEEE Technical Committee on Security and Privacy:** Copies of their newsletter, information on IEEE-related activities.
- **Computer Security Resource Center:** Maintained by the National Institute of Standards and Technology (NIST); contains a broad range of information on security threats, technology, and standards.
- **Security Focus:** A wide variety of security information, with an emphasis on vendor products and end-user concerns.
- **SANS Institute:** Similar to Security Focus. Extensive collection of white papers.

1.8 KEY TERMS, REVIEW QUESTIONS, AND PROBLEMS

Key Terms

access control	denial of service	passive threat
active threat	encryption	replay
authentication	integrity	security attacks
authenticity	intruder	security mechanisms
availability	masquerade	security services
data confidentiality	nonrepudiation	traffic analysis
data integrity	OSI security architecture	

Review Questions

1.1 What is the OSI security architecture?

1.2 What is the difference between passive and active security threats?

1.3 List and briefly define categories of passive and active security attacks.

1.4 List and briefly define categories of security services.

1.5 List and briefly define categories of security mechanisms.

Problems

1.1 Draw a matrix similar to Table 1.4 that shows the relationship between security services and attacks.

1.2 Draw a matrix similar to Table 1.4 that shows the relationship between security mechanisms and attacks.

PART ONE

Symmetric Ciphers

Cryptography is probably the most important aspect of communications security and is becoming increasingly important as a basic building block for computer security.

—*Computers at Risk: Safe Computing in the Information Age,* National Research Council, 1991

The increased use of computer and communications systems by industry has increased the risk of theft of proprietary information. Although these threats may require a variety of countermeasures, encryption is a primary method of protecting valuable electronic information.

—*Communications Privacy: Federal Policy and Actions,* General Accounting Office Report GAO/OSI-94-2, November 1993

By far the most important automated tool for network and communications security is encryption. Two forms of encryption are in common use: conventional, or symmetric, encryption and public-key, or asymmetric, encryption. Part One provides a survey of the basic principles of symmetric encryption, looks at widely used algorithms, and discusses applications of symmetric cryptography.

ROAD MAP FOR PART ONE

Chapter 2: Classical Encryption Techniques

Chapter 2 describes classical symmetric encryption techniques. It provides a gentle and interesting introduction to cryptography and cryptanalysis and highlights important concepts.

Chapter 3: Block Ciphers and the Data Encryption Standard

Chapter 3 introduces the principles of modern symmetric cryptography, with an emphasis on the most widely used encryption technique, the Data Encryption Standard (DES). The chapter includes a discussion of design considerations and cryptanalysis and introduces the Feistel cipher, which is the basic structure of most modern symmetric encryption schemes.

Chapter 4: Finite Fields

Finite fields have become increasingly important in cryptography. A number of cryptographic algorithms rely heavily on properties of finite fields, notably the Advanced Encryption Standard (AES) and elliptic curve cryptography. This chapter is positioned here so that concepts relevant to AES can be introduced prior to the discussion of AES. Chapter 4 provides the necessary background to the understanding of arithmetic over finite fields of the form $GF(2^n)$.

Chapter 5: Advanced Encryption Standard

The most important development in cryptography in recent years is the adoption of a new symmetric cipher standard, AES. Chapter 5 provides a thorough discussion of this cipher.

Chapter 6: More on Symmetric Ciphers

Chapter 6 explores additional topics related to symmetric ciphers. The chapter begins by examining multiple encryption and, in particular, triple DES. Next, we look at the concept of block cipher modes of operation, which deal with ways of handling plaintext longer than a single block. Finally, the chapter discusses stream ciphers and describes RC4.

Chapter 7: Confidentiality Using Symmetric Encryption

Beyond questions dealing with the actual construction of a symmetric encryption algorithm, a number of design issues relate to the use of symmetric encryption to provide confidentiality. Chapter 7 surveys the most important of these issues. The chapter includes a discussion of end-to-end versus link encryption, techniques for achieving traffic confidentiality, and key distribution techniques. An important related topic, random number generation, is also addressed.

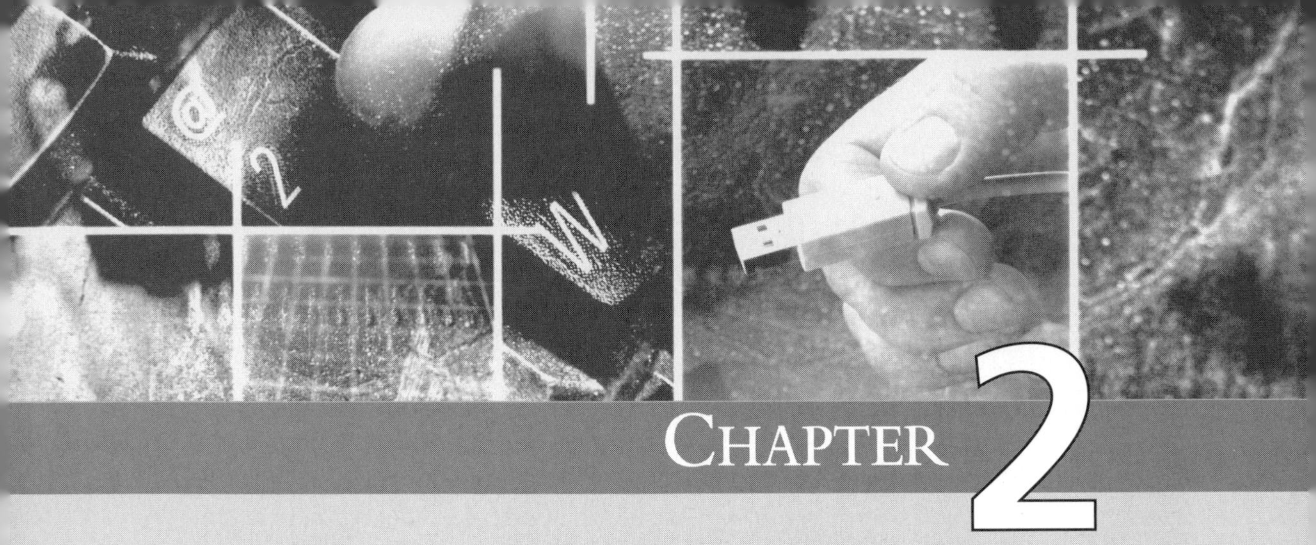

CHAPTER 2

CLASSICAL ENCRYPTION TECHNIQUES

Many savages at the present day regard their names as vital parts of themselves, and therefore take great pains to conceal their real names, lest these should give to evil-disposed persons a handle by which to injure their owners.

—*The Golden Bough,* Sir James George Frazer

KEY POINTS

- Symmetric encryption is a form of cryptosystem in which encryption and decryption are performed using the same key. It is also known as conventional encryption.
- Symmetric encryption transforms plaintext into ciphertext using a secret key and an encryption algorithm. Using the same key and a decryption algorithm, the plaintext is recovered from the ciphertext.
- The two types of attack on an encryption algorithm are cryptanalysis, based on properties of the encryption algorithm, and brute-force, which involves trying all possible keys.
- Traditional (precomputer) symmetric ciphers use substitution and/or transposition techniques. Substitution techniques map plaintext elements (characters, bits) into ciphertext elements. Transposition techniques systematically transpose the positions of plaintext elements.
- Rotor machines are sophisticated precomputer hardware devices that use substitution techniques.
- Steganography is a technique for hiding a secret message within a larger one in such a way that others cannot discern the presence or contents of the hidden message.

Symmetric encryption, also referred to as conventional encryption or single-key encryption, was the only type of encryption in use prior to the development of public-key encryption in the 1970s. It remains by far the most widely used of the two types of encryption. Part One examines a number of symmetric ciphers. In this chapter, we begin with a look at a general model for the symmetric encryption process; this will enable us to understand the context within which the algorithms are used. Next, we examine a variety of algorithms in use before the computer era. Finally, we look briefly at a different approach known as steganography. Chapter 3 examines the most widely used symmetric cipher: DES.

Before beginning, we define some terms. An original message is known as the **plaintext**, while the coded message is called the **ciphertext**. The process of converting from plaintext to ciphertext is known as **enciphering** or **encryption**; restoring the plaintext from the ciphertext is **deciphering** or **decryption**. The many schemes used for encryption constitute the area of study known as **cryptography**. Such a scheme is known as a **cryptographic system** or a **cipher**. Techniques used for deciphering a message without any knowledge of the enciphering details fall into the area of **cryptanalysis**. Cryptanalysis is what the layperson calls "breaking the code." The areas of cryptography and cryptanalysis together are called **cryptology**.

2.1 SYMMETRIC CIPHER MODEL

A symmetric encryption scheme has five ingredients (Figure 2.1):

- **Plaintext:** This is the original intelligible message or data that is fed into the algorithm as input.
- **Encryption algorithm:** The encryption algorithm performs various substitutions and transformations on the plaintext.
- **Secret key:** The secret key is also input to the encryption algorithm. The key is a value independent of the plaintext and of the algorithm. The algorithm will produce a different output depending on the specific key being used at the time. The exact substitutions and transformations performed by the algorithm depend on the key.
- **Ciphertext:** This is the scrambled message produced as output. It depends on the plaintext and the secret key. For a given message, two different keys will produce two different ciphertexts. The ciphertext is an apparently random stream of data and, as it stands, is unintelligible.
- **Decryption algorithm:** This is essentially the encryption algorithm run in reverse. It takes the ciphertext and the secret key and produces the original plaintext.

There are two requirements for secure use of conventional encryption:

1. We need a strong encryption algorithm. At a minimum, we would like the algorithm to be such that an opponent who knows the algorithm and has access to one or more ciphertexts would be unable to decipher the ciphertext or figure out the key. This requirement is usually stated in a stronger form: The opponent should be unable to decrypt ciphertext or discover the key even if he or she is

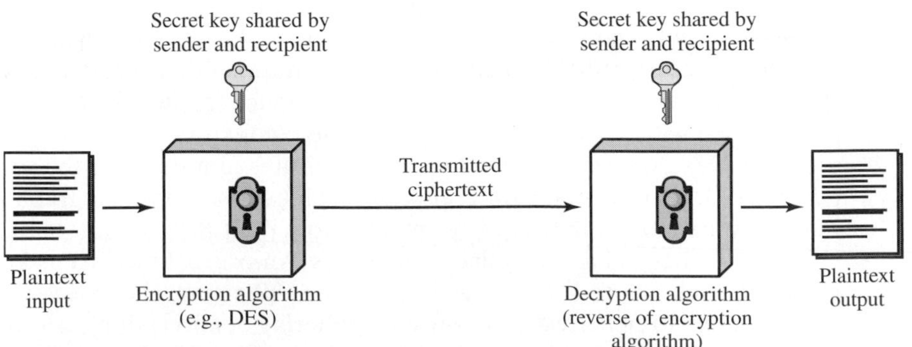

Figure 2.1 Simplified Model of Conventional Encryption

in possession of a number of ciphertexts together with the plaintext that produced each ciphertext.

2. Sender and receiver must have obtained copies of the secret key in a secure fashion and must keep the key secure. If someone can discover the key and knows the algorithm, all communication using this key is readable.

We assume that it is impractical to decrypt a message on the basis of the ciphertext *plus* knowledge of the encryption/decryption algorithm. In other words, we do not need to keep the algorithm secret; we need to keep only the key secret. This feature of symmetric encryption is what makes it feasible for widespread use. The fact that the algorithm need not be kept secret means that manufacturers can and have developed low-cost chip implementations of data encryption algorithms. These chips are widely available and incorporated into a number of products. With the use of symmetric encryption, the principal security problem is maintaining the secrecy of the key.

Let us take a closer look at the essential elements of a symmetric encryption scheme, using Figure 2.2. A source produces a message in plaintext, $X = [X_1, X_2, \ldots, X_M]$. The M elements of X are letters in some finite alphabet. Traditionally, the alphabet usually consisted of the 26 capital letters. Nowadays, the binary alphabet $\{0, 1\}$ is typically used. For encryption, a key of the form $K = [K_1, K_2, \ldots, K_J]$ is generated. If the key is generated at the message source, then it must also be provided to the destination by means of some secure channel. Alternatively, a third party could generate the key and securely deliver it to both source and destination.

With the message X and the encryption key K as input, the encryption algorithm forms the ciphertext $Y = [Y_1, Y_2, \ldots, Y_N]$. We can write this as

$$Y = E(K, X)$$

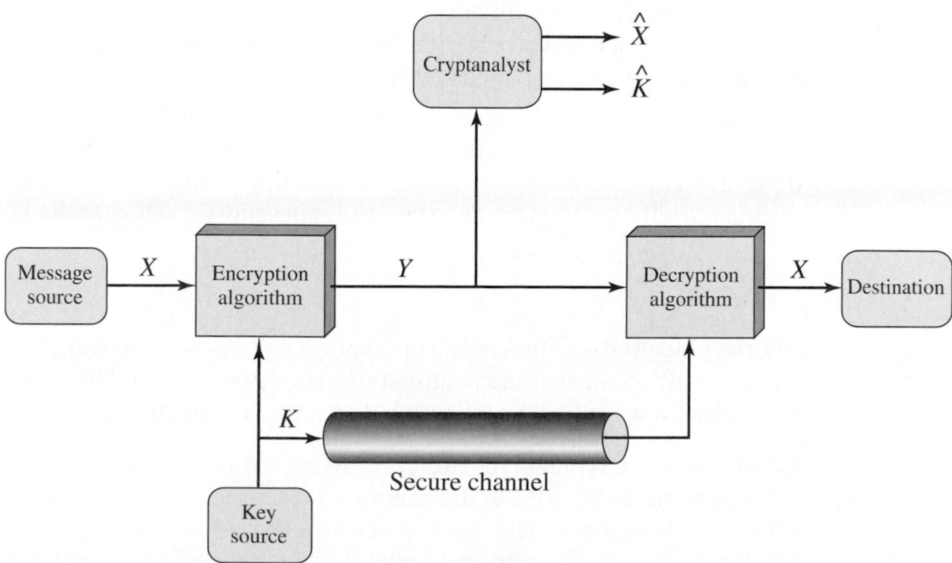

Figure 2.2 Model of Conventional Cryptosystem

This notation indicates that Y is produced by using encryption algorithm E as a function of the plaintext X, with the specific function determined by the value of the key K.

The intended receiver, in possession of the key, is able to invert the transformation:

$$X = \mathrm{D}(K, Y)$$

An opponent, observing Y but not having access to K or X, may attempt to recover X or K or both X and K. It is assumed that the opponent knows the encryption (E) and decryption (D) algorithms. If the opponent is interested in only this particular message, then the focus of the effort is to recover X by generating a plaintext estimate $\hat{X}$. Often, however, the opponent is interested in being able to read future messages as well, in which case an attempt is made to recover K by generating an estimate $\hat{K}$.

Cryptography

Cryptographic systems are characterized along three independent dimensions:

1. **The type of operations used for transforming plaintext to ciphertext.** All encryption algorithms are based on two general principles: substitution, in which each element in the plaintext (bit, letter, group of bits or letters) is mapped into another element, and transposition, in which elements in the plaintext are rearranged. The fundamental requirement is that no information be lost (that is, that all operations are reversible). Most systems, referred to as *product systems*, involve multiple stages of substitutions and transpositions.
2. **The number of keys used.** If both sender and receiver use the same key, the system is referred to as symmetric, single-key, secret-key, or conventional encryption. If the sender and receiver use different keys, the system is referred to as asymmetric, two-key, or public-key encryption.
3. **The way in which the plaintext is processed.** A *block cipher* processes the input one block of elements at a time, producing an output block for each input block. A *stream cipher* processes the input elements continuously, producing output one element at a time, as it goes along.

Cryptanalysis

Typically, the objective of attacking an encryption system is to recover the key in use rather then simply to recover the plaintext of a single ciphertext. There are two general approaches to attacking a conventional encryption scheme:

- **Cryptanalysis:** Cryptanalytic attacks rely on the nature of the algorithm plus perhaps some knowledge of the general characteristics of the plaintext or even some sample plaintext-ciphertext pairs. This type of attack exploits the characteristics of the algorithm to attempt to deduce a specific plaintext or to deduce the key being used.

- **Brute-force attack:** The attacker tries every possible key on a piece of ciphertext until an intelligible translation into plaintext is obtained. On average, half of all possible keys must be tried to achieve success.

If either type of attack succeeds in deducing the key, the effect is catastrophic: All future and past messages encrypted with that key are compromised.

We first consider cryptanalysis and then discuss brute-force attacks.

Table 2.1 summarizes the various types of **cryptanalytic attacks**, based on the amount of information known to the cryptanalyst. The most difficult problem is presented when all that is available is the *ciphertext only*. In some cases, not even the encryption algorithm is known, but in general we can assume that the opponent does know the algorithm used for encryption. One possible attack under these circumstances is the brute-force approach of trying all possible keys. If the key space is very large, this becomes impractical. Thus, the opponent must rely on an analysis of the ciphertext itself, generally applying various statistical tests to it. To use this approach, the opponent must have some general idea of the type of plaintext that is concealed, such as English or French text, an EXE file, a Java source listing, an accounting file, and so on.

The ciphertext-only attack is the easiest to defend against because the opponent has the least amount of information to work with. In many cases, however, the analyst has more information. The analyst may be able to capture one or more plaintext messages as well as their encryptions. Or the analyst may know that certain plaintext patterns will appear in a message. For example, a file that is encoded in the Postscript

Table 2.1 Types of Attacks on Encrypted Messages

Type of Attack	Known to Cryptanalyst
Ciphertext only	• Encryption algorithm • Ciphertext
Known plaintext	• Encryption algorithm • Ciphertext • One or more plaintext-ciphertext pairs formed with the secret key
Chosen plaintext	• Encryption algorithm • Ciphertext • Plaintext message chosen by cryptanalyst, together with its corresponding ciphertext generated with the secret key
Chosen ciphertext	• Encryption algorithm • Ciphertext • Purported ciphertext chosen by cryptanalyst, together with its corresponding decrypted plaintext generated with the secret key
Chosen text	• Encryption algorithm • Ciphertext • Plaintext message chosen by cryptanalyst, together with its corresponding ciphertext generated with the secret key • Purported ciphertext chosen by cryptanalyst, together with its corresponding decrypted plaintext generated with the secret key

format always begins with the same pattern, or there may be a standardized header or banner to an electronic funds transfer message, and so on. All these are examples of *known plaintext.* With this knowledge, the analyst may be able to deduce the key on the basis of the way in which the known plaintext is transformed.

Closely related to the known-plaintext attack is what might be referred to as a probable-word attack. If the opponent is working with the encryption of some general prose message, he or she may have little knowledge of what is in the message. However, if the opponent is after some very specific information, then parts of the message may be known. For example, if an entire accounting file is being transmitted, the opponent may know the placement of certain key words in the header of the file. As another example, the source code for a program developed by Corporation X might include a copyright statement in some standardized position.

If the analyst is able somehow to get the source system to insert into the system a message chosen by the analyst, then a *chosen-plaintext* attack is possible. An example of this strategy is differential cryptanalysis, explored in Chapter 3. In general, if the analyst is able to choose the messages to encrypt, the analyst may deliberately pick patterns that can be expected to reveal the structure of the key.

Table 2.1 lists two other types of attack: chosen ciphertext and chosen text. These are less commonly employed as cryptanalytic techniques but are nevertheless possible avenues of attack.

Only relatively weak algorithms fail to withstand a ciphertext-only attack. Generally, an encryption algorithm is designed to withstand a known-plaintext attack.

Two more definitions are worthy of note. An encryption scheme is **unconditionally secure** if the ciphertext generated by the scheme does not contain enough information to determine uniquely the corresponding plaintext, no matter how much ciphertext is available. That is, no matter how much time an opponent has, it is impossible for him or her to decrypt the ciphertext, simply because the required information is not there. With the exception of a scheme known as the one-time pad (described later in this chapter), there is no encryption algorithm that is unconditionally secure. Therefore, all that the users of an encryption algorithm can strive for is an algorithm that meets one or both of the following criteria:

- The cost of breaking the cipher exceeds the value of the encrypted information.
- The time required to break the cipher exceeds the useful lifetime of the information.

An encryption scheme is said to be **computationally secure** if either of the foregoing two criteria are met. The rub is that it is very difficult to estimate the amount of effort required to cryptanalyze ciphertext successfully.

All forms of cryptanalysis for symmetric encryption schemes are designed to exploit the fact that traces of structure or pattern in the plaintext may survive encryption and be discernible in the ciphertext. This will become clear as we examine various symmetric encryption schemes in this chapter. We will see in Part Two that cryptanalysis for public-key schemes proceeds from a fundamentally different premise, namely, that the mathematical properties of the pair of keys may make it possible for one of the two keys to be deduced from the other.

Table 2.2 Average Time Required for Exhaustive Key Search

Key size (bits)	Number of alternative keys	Time required at 1 decryption/μs	Time required at 10^6 decryptions/μs
32	$2^{32} = 4.3 \times 10^9$	2^{31} μs = 35.8 minutes	2.15 milliseconds
56	$2^{56} = 7.2 \times 10^{16}$	2^{55} μs = 1142 years	10.01 hours
128	$2^{128} = 3.4 \times 10^{38}$	2^{127} μs = 5.4×10^{24} years	5.4×10^{18} years
168	$2^{168} = 3.7 \times 10^{50}$	2^{167} μs = 5.9×10^{36} years	5.9×10^{30} years
26 characters (permutation)	$26! = 4 \times 10^{26}$	2×10^{26} μs = 6.4×10^{12} years	6.4×10^6 years

A **brute-force attack** involves trying every possible key until an intelligible translation of the ciphertext into plaintext is obtained. On average, half of all possible keys must be tried to achieve success. Table 2.2 shows how much time is involved for various key spaces. Results are shown for four binary key sizes. The 56-bit key size is used with the DES (Data Encryption Standard) algorithm, and the 168-bit key size is used for triple DES. The minimum key size specified for AES (Advanced Encryption Standard) is 128 bits. Results are also shown for what are called substitution codes that use a 26-character key (discussed later), in which all possible permutations of the 26 characters serve as keys. For each key size, the results are shown assuming that it takes 1 μs to perform a single decryption, which is a reasonable order of magnitude for today's machines. With the use of massively parallel organizations of microprocessors, it may be possible to achieve processing rates many orders of magnitude greater. The final column of Table 2.2 considers the results for a system that can process 1 million keys per microsecond. As you can see, at this performance level, DES can no longer be considered computationally secure.

2.2 SUBSTITUTION TECHNIQUES

In this section and the next, we examine a sampling of what might be called classical encryption techniques. A study of these techniques enables us to illustrate the basic approaches to symmetric encryption used today and the types of cryptanalytic attacks that must be anticipated.

The two basic building blocks of all encryption techniques are substitution and transposition. We examine these in the next two sections. Finally, we discuss a system that combines both substitution and transposition.

A substitution technique is one in which the letters of plaintext are replaced by other letters or by numbers or symbols.[1] If the plaintext is viewed as a sequence of bits, then substitution involves replacing plaintext bit patterns with ciphertext bit patterns.

[1]When letters are involved, the following conventions are used in this book. Plaintext is always in lowercase; ciphertext is in uppercase; key values are in italicized lowercase.

Caesar Cipher

The earliest known use of a substitution cipher, and the simplest, was by Julius Caesar. The Caesar cipher involves replacing each letter of the alphabet with the letter standing three places further down the alphabet. For example,

```
plain:  meet me after the toga party
cipher: PHHW PH DIWHU WKH WRJD SDUWB
```

Note that the alphabet is wrapped around, so that the letter following Z is A. We can define the transformation by listing all possibilities, as follows:

```
plain:   a b c d e f g h i j k l m n o p q r s t u v w x y z
cipher:  D E F G H I J K L M N O P Q R S T U V W X Y Z A B C
```

Let us assign a numerical equivalent to each letter:

a	b	c	d	e	f	g	h	i	j	k	l	m
0	1	2	3	4	5	6	7	8	9	10	11	12

n	o	p	q	r	s	t	u	v	w	x	y	z
13	14	15	16	17	18	19	20	21	22	23	24	25

Then the algorithm can be expressed as follows. For each plaintext letter p, substitute the ciphertext letter C:[2]

$$C = \mathrm{E}(3, p) = (p + 3) \bmod 26$$

A shift may be of any amount, so that the general Caesar algorithm is

$$C = \mathrm{E}(k, p) = (p + k) \bmod 26$$

where k takes on a value in the range 1 to 25. The decryption algorithm is simply

$$p = \mathrm{D}(k, C) = (C - k) \bmod 26$$

If it is known that a given ciphertext is a Caesar cipher, then a brute-force cryptanalysis is easily performed: Simply try all the 25 possible keys. Figure 2.3 shows the results of applying this strategy to the example ciphertext. In this case, the plaintext leaps out as occupying the third line.

Three important characteristics of this problem enabled us to use a brute-force cryptanalysis:

1. The encryption and decryption algorithms are known.
2. There are only 25 keys to try.
3. The language of the plaintext is known and easily recognizable.

---

[2]We define $a \bmod n$ to be the remainder when a is divided by n. For example, $11 \bmod 7 = 4$. See Chapter 4 for a further discussion of modular arithmetic.

KEY	PHHW PH DIWHU WKH WRJD SDUWB
1	oggv og chvgt vjg vqic rctva
2	nffu nf bgufs uif uphb qbsuz
3	meet me after the toga party
4	ldds ld zesdq sgd snfz ozqsx
5	kccr kc ydrcp rfc rmey nyprw
6	jbbq jb xcqbo qeb qldx mxoqv
7	iaap ia wbpan pda pkcw lwnpu
8	hzzo hz vaozm ocz ojbv kvmot
9	gyyn gy uznyl nby niau julns
10	fxxm fx tymxk max mhzt itkmr
11	ewwl ew sxlwj lzw lgys hsjlq
12	dvvk dv rwkvi kyv kfxr grikp
13	cuuj cu qvjuh jxu jewq fqhjo
14	btti bt puitg iwt idvp epgin
15	assh as othsf hvs hcuo dofhm
16	zrrg zr nsgre gur gbtn cnegl
17	yqqf yq mrfqd ftq fasm bmdfk
18	xppe xp lqepc esp ezrl alcej
19	wood wo kpdob dro dyqk zkbdi
20	vnnc vn jocna cqn cxpj yjach
21	ummb um inbmz bpm bwoi xizbg
22	tlla tl hmaly aol avnh whyaf
23	skkz sk glzkx znk zumg vgxze
24	rjjy rj fkyjw ymj ytlf ufwyd
25	qiix qi ejxiv xli xske tevxc

Figure 2.3 Brute-Force Cryptanalysis of Caesar Cipher

In most networking situations, we can assume that the algorithms are known. What generally makes brute-force cryptanalysis impractical is the use of an algorithm that employs a large number of keys. For example, the triple DES algorithm, examined in Chapter 6, makes use of a 168-bit key, giving a key space of 2^{168} or greater than 3.7×10^{50} possible keys.

The third characteristic is also significant. If the language of the plaintext is unknown, then plaintext output may not be recognizable. Furthermore, the input may be abbreviated or compressed in some fashion, again making recognition difficult. For example, Figure 2.4 shows a portion of a text file compressed using an algorithm called ZIP. If this file is then encrypted with a simple substitution cipher (expanded to include more than just 26 alphabetic characters), then the plaintext may not be recognized when it is uncovered in the brute-force cryptanalysis.

```
~+Wµ"- Ω-O)≤4{∞‡¸ ë~Ω%ràu·¯Í ◊¯Z-
Ú≠2Ò#Åæ∂ œ«q7¸Ωn·®3N◊Ú ŒzʼY-ƒ∞Í[±Û_ èΩ,<NO¬±«˘xã  Åä£èü3Å
x}ö§kºÂ
_yÍ ^ΔÉ] ˛¤ J/˚iTê&ı 'c<uΩ-
 ÄD(G WÄC~y_ïõÄW PÔı«ÎÜ†ç],¤¡˘Ì^üÑπ˘≈˘L˘9Ogfl0˘&Œ≤ ¬≤ ØÔ§˝:
 ˘Œ!SGqèvo^ ú\¸S>h<-*6ø‡%x´˝|ﬁÓ#≈~my‰˘≥ñP‹,ƒi Áj Å◊¿˝Zù-
Ω¨Õ¯6Œÿ{% „ΩÊó ¸ï π÷ÁÎ˚úO2çSÿ´O-
2ÄflßiAi /@^˝∏Kºª PŒπ¸úé^´3∑˘ö˘ÔZÌ"Y¬ŸΩœY› Ω+eô/˙‹K£¿*÷˜"≤û˜
B ZøK˜Qßÿüƒ˛!ÒflÎzsS/]›ÈQ ü
```

Figure 2.4 Sample of Compressed Text

Monoalphabetic Ciphers

With only 25 possible keys, the Caesar cipher is far from secure. A dramatic increase in the key space can be achieved by allowing an arbitrary substitution. Recall the assignment for the Caesar cipher:

```
plain:  a b c d e f g h i j k l m n o p q r s t u v w x y z
cipher: D E F G H I J K L M N O P Q R S T U V W X Y Z A B C
```

If, instead, the "cipher" line can be any permutation of the 26 alphabetic characters, then there are 26! or greater than 4×10^{26} possible keys. This is 10 orders of magnitude greater than the key space for DES and would seem to eliminate brute-force techniques for cryptanalysis. Such an approach is referred to as a **monoalphabetic substitution cipher**, because a single cipher alphabet (mapping from plain alphabet to cipher alphabet) is used per message.

There is, however, another line of attack. If the cryptanalyst knows the nature of the plaintext (e.g., noncompressed English text), then the analyst can exploit the regularities of the language. To see how such a cryptanalysis might proceed, we give a partial example here that is adapted from one in [SINK66]. The ciphertext to be solved is

```
UZQSOVUOHXMOPVGPOZPEVSGZWSZOPFPESXUDBMETSXAIZ
VUEPHZHMDZSHZOWSFPAPPDTSVPQUZWYMXUZUHSX
EPYEPOPDZSZUFPOMBZWPFUPZHMDJUDTMOHMQ
```

As a first step, the relative frequency of the letters can be determined and compared to a standard frequency distribution for English, such as is shown in Figure 2.5 (based on [LEWA00]). If the message were long enough, this technique alone might be sufficient, but because this is a relatively short message, we cannot expect an exact match. In any case, the relative frequencies of the letters in the ciphertext (in percentages) are as follows:

P 13.33	H 5.83	F 3.33	B 1.67	C 0.00
Z 11.67	D 5.00	W 3.33	G 1.67	K 0.00
S 8.33	E 5.00	Q 2.50	Y 1.67	L 0.00
U 8.33	V 4.17	T 2.50	I 0.83	N 0.00
O 7.50	X 4.17	A 1.67	J 0.83	R 0.00
M 6.67				

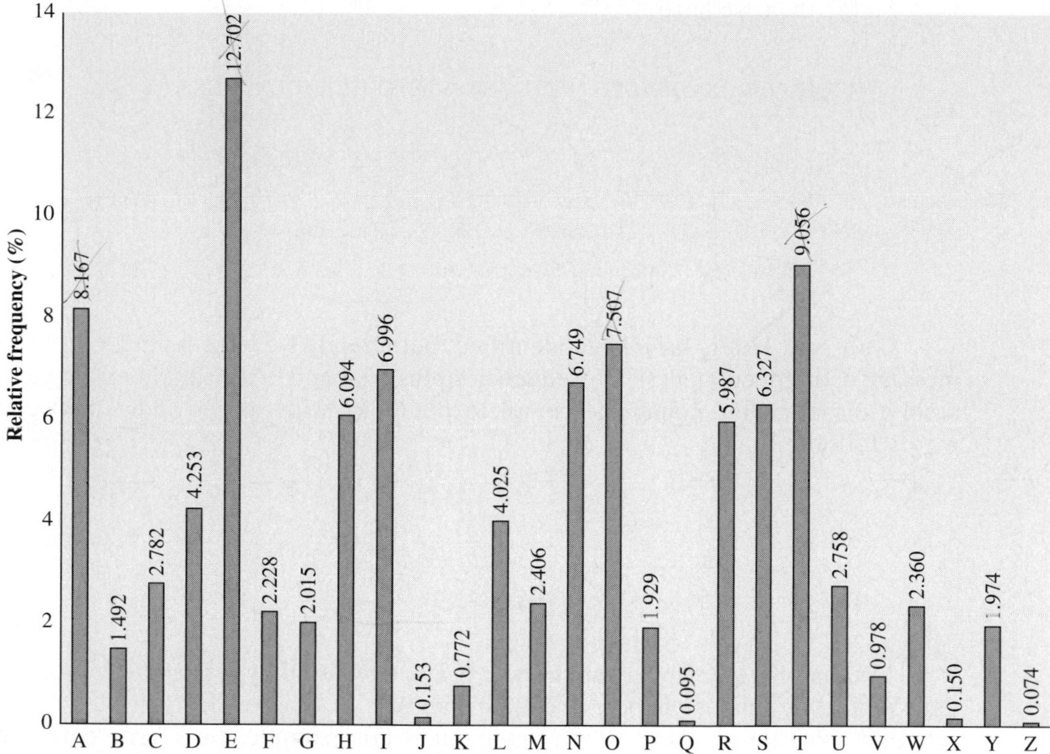

Figure 2.5 Relative Frequency of Letters in English Text

Comparing this breakdown with Figure 2.5, it seems likely that cipher letters P and Z are the equivalents of plain letters e and t, but it is not certain which is which. The letters S, U, O, M, and H are all of relatively high frequency and probably correspond to plain letters from the set {a, h, i, n, o, r, s}. The letters with the lowest frequencies (namely, A, B, G, Y, I, J) are likely included in the set {b, j, k, q, v, x, z}.

There are a number of ways to proceed at this point. We could make some tentative assignments and start to fill in the plaintext to see if it looks like a reasonable "skeleton" of a message. A more systematic approach is to look for other regularities. For example, certain words may be known to be in the text. Or we could look for repeating sequences of cipher letters and try to deduce their plaintext equivalents.

A powerful tool is to look at the frequency of two-letter combinations, known as digrams. A table similar to Figure 2.5 could be drawn up showing the relative frequency of digrams. The most common such digram is th. In our ciphertext, the most common digram is ZW, which appears three times. So we make the correspondence of Z with t and W with h. Then, by our earlier hypothesis, we can equate P with e. Now notice that the sequence ZWP appears in the ciphertext, and we can translate that sequence as "the." This is the most frequent trigram (three-letter combination) in English, which seems to indicate that we are on the right track.

Next, notice the sequence ZWSZ in the first line. We do not know that these four letters form a complete word, but if they do, it is of the form th_t. If so, S equates with a.

So far, then, we have

```
UZQSOVUOHXMOPVGPOZPEVSGZWSZOPFPESXUDBMETSXAIZ
 t a        e  e te  a that e e a         a
VUEPHZHMDZSHZOWSFPAPPDTSVPQUZWYMXUZUHSX
   e t    ta t ha e ee   a e  th    t  a
EPYEPOPDZSZUFPOMBZWPFUPZHMDJUDTMOHMQ
 e  e e tat  e    the   t
```

Only four letters have been identified, but already we have quite a bit of the message. Continued analysis of frequencies plus trial and error should easily yield a solution from this point. The complete plaintext, with spaces added between words, follows:

```
it was disclosed yesterday that several informal but
direct contacts have been made with political
representatives of the viet cong in moscow
```

Monoalphabetic ciphers are easy to break because they reflect the frequency data of the original alphabet. A countermeasure is to provide multiple substitutes, known as homophones, for a single letter. For example, the letter e could be assigned a number of different cipher symbols, such as 16, 74, 35, and 21, with each homophone used in rotation, or randomly. If the number of symbols assigned to each letter is proportional to the relative frequency of that letter, then single-letter frequency information is completely obliterated. The great mathematician Carl Friedrich Gauss believed that he had devised an unbreakable cipher using homophones. However, even with homophones, each element of plaintext affects only one element of ciphertext, and multiple-letter patterns (e.g., digram frequencies) still survive in the ciphertext, making cryptanalysis relatively straightforward.

Two principal methods are used in substitution ciphers to lessen the extent to which the structure of the plaintext survives in the ciphertext: One approach is to encrypt multiple letters of plaintext, and the other is to use multiple cipher alphabets. We briefly examine each.

Playfair Cipher

The best-known multiple-letter encryption cipher is the Playfair, which treats digrams in the plaintext as single units and translates these units into ciphertext digrams.[3]

---

[3]This cipher was actually invented by British scientist Sir Charles Wheatstone in 1854, but it bears the name of his friend Baron Playfair of St. Andrews, who championed the cipher at the British foreign office.

The Playfair algorithm is based on the use of a 5×5 matrix of letters constructed using a keyword. Here is an example, solved by Lord Peter Wimsey in Dorothy Sayers's *Have His Carcase*:[4]

M	O	N	A	R
C	H	Y	B	D
E	F	G	I/J	K
L	P	Q	S	T
U	V	W	X	Z

In this case, the keyword is *monarchy*. The matrix is constructed by filling in the letters of the keyword (minus duplicates) from left to right and from top to bottom, and then filling in the remainder of the matrix with the remaining letters in alphabetic order. The letters I and J count as one letter. Plaintext is encrypted two letters at a time, according to the following rules:

1. Repeating plaintext letters that are in the same pair are separated with a filler letter, such as x, so that balloon would be treated as ba lx lo on.
2. Two plaintext letters that fall in the same row of the matrix are each replaced by the letter to the right, with the first element of the row circularly following the last. For example, ar is encrypted as RM.
3. Two plaintext letters that fall in the same column are each replaced by the letter beneath, with the top element of the column circularly following the last. For example, mu is encrypted as CM.
4. Otherwise, each plaintext letter in a pair is replaced by the letter that lies in its own row and the column occupied by the other plaintext letter. Thus, hs becomes BP and ea becomes IM (or JM, as the encipherer wishes).

The Playfair cipher is a great advance over simple monoalphabetic ciphers. For one thing, whereas there are only 26 letters, there are $26 \times 26 = 676$ digrams, so that identification of individual digrams is more difficult. Furthermore, the relative frequencies of individual letters exhibit a much greater range than that of digrams, making frequency analysis much more difficult. For these reasons, the Playfair cipher was for a long time considered unbreakable. It was used as the standard field system by the British Army in World War I and still enjoyed considerable use by the U.S. Army and other Allied forces during World War II.

Despite this level of confidence in its security, the Playfair cipher is relatively easy to break because it still leaves much of the structure of the plaintext language intact. A few hundred letters of ciphertext are generally sufficient.

One way of revealing the effectiveness of the Playfair and other ciphers is shown in Figure 2.6, based on [SIMM93]. The line labeled *plaintext* plots the frequency distribution of the more than 70,000 alphabetic characters in the *Encyclopaedia Brittanica* article on cryptology.[5] This is also the frequency distribution of any

[4]The book provides an absorbing account of a probable-word attack.

[5]I am indebted to Gustavus Simmons for providing the plots and explaining their method of construction.

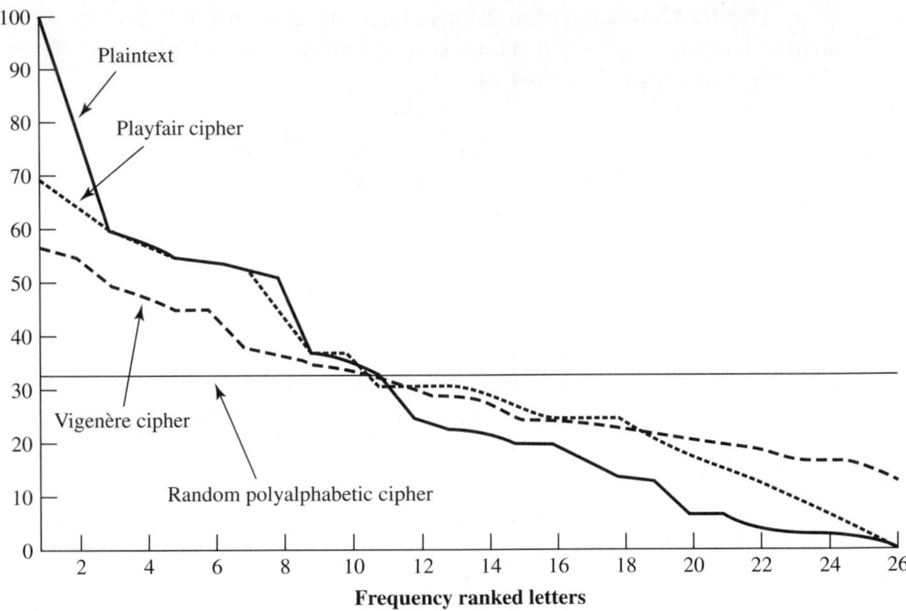

Figure 2.6 Relative Frequency of Occurrence of Letters

monoalphabetic substitution cipher. The plot was developed in the following way: The number of occurrences of each letter in the text was counted and divided by the number of occurrences of the letter e (the most frequently used letter). As a result, e has a relative frequency of 1, t of about 0.76, and so on. The points on the horizontal axis correspond to the letters in order of decreasing frequency.

Figure 2.6 also shows the frequency distribution that results when the text is encrypted using the Playfair cipher. To normalize the plot, the number of occurrences of each letter in the ciphertext was again divided by the number of occurrences of e in the plaintext. The resulting plot therefore shows the extent to which the frequency distribution of letters, which makes it trivial to solve substitution ciphers, is masked by encryption. If the frequency distribution information were totally concealed in the encryption process, the ciphertext plot of frequencies would be flat, and cryptanalysis using ciphertext only would be effectively impossible. As the figure shows, the Playfair cipher has a flatter distribution than does plaintext, but nevertheless it reveals plenty of structure for a cryptanalyst to work with.

Hill Cipher[6]

Another interesting multiletter cipher is the Hill cipher, developed by the mathematician Lester Hill in 1929. The encryption algorithm takes m successive plaintext letters and substitutes for them m ciphertext letters. The substitution is determined

[6]This cipher is somewhat more difficult to understand than the others in this chapter, but it illustrates an important point about cryptanalysis that will be useful later on. This subsection can be skipped on a first reading.

by m linear equations in which each character is assigned a numerical value (a = 0, b = 1, ... z = 25). For $m = 3$, the system can be described as follows:

$$c_1 = (k_{11}p_1 + k_{12}p_2 + k_{13}p_3) \bmod 26$$
$$c_2 = (k_{21}p_1 + k_{22}p_2 + k_{23}p_3) \bmod 26$$
$$c_3 = (k_{31}p_1 + k_{32}p_2 + k_{33}p_3) \bmod 26$$

This can be expressed in term of column vectors and matrices:

$$\begin{pmatrix} c_1 \\ c_2 \\ c_3 \end{pmatrix} = \begin{pmatrix} k_{11} & k_{12} & k_{13} \\ k_{21} & k_{22} & k_{23} \\ k_{31} & k_{32} & k_{33} \end{pmatrix} \begin{pmatrix} p_1 \\ p_2 \\ p_3 \end{pmatrix} \bmod 26$$

or

$$\mathbf{C} = \mathbf{KP} \bmod 26$$

where **C** and **P** are column vectors of length 3, representing the plaintext and ciphertext, and **K** is a 3×3 matrix, representing the encryption key. Operations are performed mod 26.

For example, consider the plaintext "paymoremoney" and use the encryption key

$$\mathbf{K} = \begin{pmatrix} 17 & 17 & 5 \\ 21 & 18 & 21 \\ 2 & 2 & 19 \end{pmatrix}$$

The first three letters of the plaintext are represented by the vector $\begin{pmatrix} 15 \\ 0 \\ 24 \end{pmatrix}$. Then $\mathbf{K}\begin{pmatrix} 15 \\ 0 \\ 24 \end{pmatrix} = \begin{pmatrix} 375 \\ 819 \\ 486 \end{pmatrix} \bmod 26 = \begin{pmatrix} 11 \\ 13 \\ 18 \end{pmatrix}$ = LNS. Continuing in this fashion, the ciphertext for the entire plaintext is LNSHDLEWMTRW.

Decryption requires using the inverse of the matrix **K**. The inverse $\mathbf{K}^{-1}$ of a matrix **K** is defined by the equation $\mathbf{KK}^{-1} = \mathbf{K}^{-1}\mathbf{K} = \mathbf{I}$, where **I** is the matrix that is all zeros except for ones along the main diagonal from upper left to lower right. The inverse of a matrix does not always exist, but when it does, it satisfies the preceding equation. In this case, the inverse is:

$$\mathbf{K}^{-1} = \begin{pmatrix} 4 & 9 & 15 \\ 15 & 17 & 6 \\ 24 & 0 & 17 \end{pmatrix}$$

This is demonstrated as follows:

$$\begin{pmatrix} 17 & 17 & 5 \\ 21 & 18 & 21 \\ 2 & 2 & 19 \end{pmatrix} \begin{pmatrix} 4 & 9 & 15 \\ 15 & 17 & 6 \\ 24 & 0 & 17 \end{pmatrix} = \begin{pmatrix} 443 & 442 & 442 \\ 858 & 495 & 780 \\ 494 & 52 & 365 \end{pmatrix} \bmod 26 = \begin{pmatrix} 1 & 0 & 0 \\ 0 & 1 & 0 \\ 0 & 0 & 1 \end{pmatrix}$$

It is easily seen that if the matrix $\mathbf{K}^{-1}$ is applied to the ciphertext, then the plaintext is recovered. To explain how the inverse of a matrix is determined, we make an exceedingly brief excursion into linear algebra.[7] For any square matrix $(m \times m)$, the **determinant** equals the sum of all the products that can be formed by taking exactly one element from each row and exactly one element from each column, with certain of the product terms preceded by a minus sign. For a 2×2 matrix

$$\begin{pmatrix} k_{11} & k_{12} \\ k_{21} & k_{22} \end{pmatrix}$$

the determinant is $k_{11}k_{22} - k_{12}k_{21}$. For a 3×3 matrix, the value of the determinant is $k_{11}k_{22}k_{33} + k_{21}k_{32}k_{13} + k_{31}k_{12}k_{23} - k_{31}k_{22}k_{13} - k_{21}k_{12}k_{33} - k_{11}k_{32}k_{23}$. If a square matrix **A** has a nonzero determinant, then the inverse of the matrix is computed as $[\mathbf{A}^{-1}]_{ij} = (-1)^{i+j}(\mathrm{D}_{ji})/\det(\mathbf{A})$, where (D_{ij}) is the subdeterminant formed by deleting the ith row and the jth column of **A** and det(**A**) is the determinant of **A**. For our purposes, all arithmetic is done mod 26.

In general terms, the Hill system can be expressed as follows:

$$\mathbf{C} = \mathrm{E}(\mathbf{K}, \mathbf{P}) = \mathbf{KP} \bmod 26$$
$$\mathbf{P} = \mathrm{D}(\mathbf{K}, \mathbf{P}) = \mathbf{K}^{-1}\mathbf{C} \bmod 26 = \mathbf{K}^{-1}\mathbf{KP} = \mathbf{P}$$

As with Playfair, the strength of the Hill cipher is that it completely hides single-letter frequencies. Indeed, with Hill, the use of a larger matrix hides more frequency information. Thus a 3×3 Hill cipher hides not only single-letter but also two-letter frequency information.

Although the Hill cipher is strong against a ciphertext-only attack, it is easily broken with a known plaintext attack. For an $m \times m$ Hill cipher, suppose we have m plaintext-ciphertext pairs, each of length m. We label the pairs $\mathbf{P}_j = \begin{pmatrix} p_{1j} \\ p_{2j} \\ \vdots \\ p_{mj} \end{pmatrix}$ and $\mathbf{C}_j = \begin{pmatrix} c_{1j} \\ c_{2j} \\ \vdots \\ c_{mj} \end{pmatrix}$ such that $\mathbf{C}_j = \mathbf{KP}_j$ for $1 \le j \le m$ and for some unknown key matrix **K**. Now define two $m \times m$ matrices $\mathbf{X} = (p_{ij})$ and $\mathbf{Y} = (c_{ij})$. Then we can form the matrix equation $\mathbf{Y} = \mathbf{KX}$. If **X** has an inverse, then we can determine $\mathbf{K} = \mathbf{YX}^{-1}$. If **X** is not invertible, then a new version of **X** can be formed with additional plaintext-ciphertext pairs until an invertible **X** is obtained.

We use an example based on one in [STIN02]. Suppose that the plaintext "friday" is encrypted using a 2×2 Hill cipher to yield the ciphertext PQCFKU. Thus, we know that $\mathbf{K}\begin{pmatrix} 5 \\ 17 \end{pmatrix} \bmod 26 = \begin{pmatrix} 15 \\ 16 \end{pmatrix}$; $\mathbf{K}\begin{pmatrix} 8 \\ 3 \end{pmatrix} \bmod 26 = \begin{pmatrix} 2 \\ 5 \end{pmatrix}$; and $\mathbf{K}\begin{pmatrix} 0 \\ 24 \end{pmatrix} \bmod 26 = \begin{pmatrix} 10 \\ 20 \end{pmatrix}$. Using the first two plaintext-ciphertext pairs, we have

$$\begin{pmatrix} 15 & 2 \\ 16 & 5 \end{pmatrix} = \mathbf{K}\begin{pmatrix} 5 & 8 \\ 17 & 3 \end{pmatrix} \bmod 26$$

---

[7]The basic concepts of linear algebra are summarized in the Math Refresher document at the Computer Science Student Resource site at WilliamStallings.com/StudentSupport.hmtl. The interested reader may consult any text on linear algebra for greater detail.

The inverse of **X** can be computed:

$$\begin{pmatrix} 5 & 8 \\ 17 & 3 \end{pmatrix}^{-1} = \begin{pmatrix} 9 & 2 \\ 1 & 15 \end{pmatrix}$$

so

$$\mathbf{K} = \begin{pmatrix} 15 & 2 \\ 16 & 5 \end{pmatrix}\begin{pmatrix} 9 & 2 \\ 1 & 15 \end{pmatrix} = \begin{pmatrix} 137 & 60 \\ 149 & 107 \end{pmatrix} \bmod 26 = \begin{pmatrix} 7 & 8 \\ 19 & 3 \end{pmatrix}$$

This result is verified by testing the remaining plaintext-ciphertext pair.

Polyalphabetic Ciphers

Another way to improve on the simple monoalphabetic technique is to use different monoalphabetic substitutions as one proceeds through the plaintext message. The general name for this approach is **polyalphabetic substitution cipher**. All these techniques have the following features in common:

1. A set of related monoalphabetic substitution rules is used.
2. A key determines which particular rule is chosen for a given transformation.

The best known, and one of the simplest, such algorithm is referred to as the Vigenère cipher. In this scheme, the set of related monoalphabetic substitution rules consists of the 26 Caesar ciphers, with shifts of 0 through 25. Each cipher is denoted by a key letter, which is the ciphertext letter that substitutes for the plaintext letter a. Thus, a Caesar cipher with a shift of 3 is denoted by the key value *d*.

To aid in understanding the scheme and to aid in its use, a matrix known as the Vigenère tableau is constructed (Table 2.3). Each of the 26 ciphers is laid out horizontally, with the key letter for each cipher to its left. A normal alphabet for the plaintext runs across the top. The process of encryption is simple: Given a key letter *x* and a plaintext letter y, the ciphertext letter is at the intersection of the row labeled *x* and the column labeled y; in this case the ciphertext is V.

To encrypt a message, a key is needed that is as long as the message. Usually, the key is a repeating keyword. For example, if the keyword is *deceptive*, the message "we are discovered save yourself" is encrypted as follows:

```
key:           deceptivedeceptivedeceptive
plaintext:     wearediscoveredsaveyourself
ciphertext:    ZICVTWQNGRZGVTWAVZHCQYGLMGJ
```

Decryption is equally simple. The key letter again identifies the row. The position of the ciphertext letter in that row determines the column, and the plaintext letter is at the top of that column.

The strength of this cipher is that there are multiple ciphertext letters for each plaintext letter, one for each unique letter of the keyword. Thus, the letter frequency information is obscured. However, not all knowledge of the plaintext structure is lost. For example, Figure 2.6 shows the frequency distribution for a Vigenère cipher with a keyword of length 9. An improvement is achieved over the Playfair cipher, but considerable frequency information remains.

Table 2.3 The Modern Vigenère Tableau

Key	Plaintext																									
	a	**b**	**c**	**d**	**e**	**f**	**g**	**h**	**i**	**j**	**k**	**l**	**m**	**n**	**o**	**p**	**q**	**r**	**s**	**t**	**u**	**v**	**w**	**x**	**y**	**z**
a	A	B	C	D	E	F	G	H	I	J	K	L	M	N	O	P	Q	R	S	T	U	V	W	X	Y	Z
b	B	C	D	E	F	G	H	I	J	K	L	M	N	O	P	Q	R	S	T	U	V	W	X	Y	Z	A
c	C	D	E	F	G	H	I	J	K	L	M	N	O	P	Q	R	S	T	U	V	W	X	Y	Z	A	B
d	D	E	F	G	H	I	J	K	L	M	N	O	P	Q	R	S	T	U	V	W	X	Y	Z	A	B	C
e	E	F	G	H	I	J	K	L	M	N	O	P	Q	R	S	T	U	V	W	X	Y	Z	A	B	C	D
f	F	G	H	I	J	K	L	M	N	O	P	Q	R	S	T	U	V	W	X	Y	Z	A	B	C	D	E
g	G	H	I	J	K	L	M	N	O	P	Q	R	S	T	U	V	W	X	Y	Z	A	B	C	D	E	F
h	H	I	J	K	L	M	N	O	P	Q	R	S	T	U	V	W	X	Y	Z	A	B	C	D	E	F	G
i	I	J	K	L	M	N	O	P	Q	R	S	T	U	V	W	X	Y	Z	A	B	C	D	E	F	G	H
j	J	K	L	M	N	O	P	Q	R	S	T	U	V	W	X	Y	Z	A	B	C	D	E	F	G	H	I
k	K	L	M	N	O	P	Q	R	S	T	U	V	W	X	Y	Z	A	B	C	D	E	F	G	H	I	J
l	L	M	N	O	P	Q	R	S	T	U	V	W	X	Y	Z	A	B	C	D	E	F	G	H	I	J	K
m	M	N	O	P	Q	R	S	T	U	V	W	X	Y	Z	A	B	C	D	E	F	G	H	I	J	K	L
n	N	O	P	Q	R	S	T	U	V	W	X	Y	Z	A	B	C	D	E	F	G	H	I	J	K	L	M
o	O	P	Q	R	S	T	U	V	W	X	Y	Z	A	B	C	D	E	F	G	H	I	J	K	L	M	N
p	P	Q	R	S	T	U	V	W	X	Y	Z	A	B	C	D	E	F	G	H	I	J	K	L	M	N	O
q	Q	R	S	T	U	V	W	X	Y	Z	A	B	C	D	E	F	G	H	I	J	K	L	M	N	O	P
r	R	S	T	U	V	W	X	Y	Z	A	B	C	D	E	F	G	H	I	J	K	L	M	N	O	P	Q
s	S	T	U	V	W	X	Y	Z	A	B	C	D	E	F	G	H	I	J	K	L	M	N	O	P	Q	R
t	T	U	V	W	X	Y	Z	A	B	C	D	E	F	G	H	I	J	K	L	M	N	O	P	Q	R	S
u	U	V	W	X	Y	Z	A	B	C	D	E	F	G	H	I	J	K	L	M	N	O	P	Q	R	S	T
v	V	W	X	Y	Z	A	B	C	D	E	F	G	H	I	J	K	L	M	N	O	P	Q	R	S	T	U
w	W	X	Y	Z	A	B	C	D	E	F	G	H	I	J	K	L	M	N	O	P	Q	R	S	T	U	V
x	X	Y	Z	A	B	C	D	E	F	G	H	I	J	K	L	M	N	O	P	Q	R	S	T	U	V	W
y	Y	Z	A	B	C	D	E	F	G	H	I	J	K	L	M	N	O	P	Q	R	S	T	U	V	W	X
z	Z	A	B	C	D	E	F	G	H	I	J	K	L	M	N	O	P	Q	R	S	T	U	V	W	X	Y

It is instructive to sketch a method of breaking this cipher, because the method reveals some of the mathematical principles that apply in cryptanalysis.

First, suppose that the opponent believes that the ciphertext was encrypted using either monoalphabetic substitution or a Vigenère cipher. A simple test can be made to make a determination. If a monoalphabetic substitution is used, then the statistical properties of the ciphertext should be the same as that of the language of the plaintext. Thus, referring to Figure 2.5, there should be one cipher letter with a relative frequency of occurrence of about 12.7%, one with about 9.06%, and so on. If only a single message is available for analysis, we would not expect an exact match of this small sample with the statistical profile of the plaintext language. Nevertheless, if the correspondence is close, we can assume a monoalphabetic substitution.

If, on the other hand, a Vigenère cipher is suspected, then progress depends on determining the length of the keyword, as will be seen in a moment. For now, let us concentrate on how the keyword length can be determined. The important insight that leads to a solution is the following: If two identical sequences of plaintext letters occur at a distance that is an integer multiple of the keyword length, they will generate identical ciphertext sequences. In the foregoing example, two instances of the sequence "red" are separated by nine character positions. Consequently, in both cases, r is encrypted using key letter *e*, e is encrypted using key letter *p*, and d is encrypted using key letter *t*. Thus, in both cases the ciphertext sequence is VTW.

An analyst looking at only the ciphertext would detect the repeated sequences VTW at a displacement of 9 and make the assumption that the keyword is either three or nine letters in length. The appearance of VTW twice could be by chance and not reflect identical plaintext letters encrypted with identical key letters. However, if the message is long enough, there will be a number of such repeated ciphertext sequences. By looking for common factors in the displacements of the various sequences, the analyst should be able to make a good guess of the keyword length.

Solution of the cipher now depends on an important insight. If the keyword length is N, then the cipher, in effect, consists of N monoalphabetic substitution ciphers. For example, with the keyword DECEPTIVE, the letters in positions 1, 10, 19, and so on are all encrypted with the same monoalphabetic cipher. Thus, we can use the known frequency characteristics of the plaintext language to attack each of the monoalphabetic ciphers separately.

The periodic nature of the keyword can be eliminated by using a nonrepeating keyword that is as long as the message itself. Vigenère proposed what is referred to as an **autokey system**, in which a keyword is concatenated with the plaintext itself to provide a running key. For our example,

```
key:          deceptivewearediscoveredsav
plaintext:    wearediscoveredsaveyourself
ciphertext:   ZICVTWQNGKZEIIGASXSTSLVVWLA
```

Even this scheme is vulnerable to cryptanalysis. Because the key and the plaintext share the same frequency distribution of letters, a statistical technique can be applied. For example, e enciphered by *e*, by Figure 2.5, can be expected to occur with a frequency of $(0.127)^2 \approx 0.016$, whereas t enciphered by t would occur only about half as often. These regularities can be exploited to achieve successful cryptanalysis.[8]

The ultimate defense against such a cryptanalysis is to choose a keyword that is as long as the plaintext and has no statistical relationship to it. Such a system was introduced by an AT&T engineer named Gilbert Vernam in 1918. His system works on binary data rather than letters. The system can be expressed succinctly as follows:

$$c_i = p_i \oplus k_i$$

where

$$\begin{aligned} p_i &= i\text{th binary digit of plaintext} \\ k_i &= i\text{th binary digit of key} \\ c_i &= i\text{th binary digit of ciphertext} \\ \oplus &= \text{exclusive-or (XOR) operation} \end{aligned}$$

Thus, the ciphertext is generated by performing the bitwise XOR of the plaintext and the key. Because of the properties of the XOR, decryption simply involves the same bitwise operation:

$$p_i = c_i \oplus k_i$$

The essence of this technique is the means of construction of the key. Vernam proposed the use of a running loop of tape that eventually repeated the key, so that in fact the system worked with a very long but repeating keyword. Although such a scheme, with a long key, presents formidable cryptanalytic difficulties, it can be broken with sufficient ciphertext, the use of known or probable plaintext sequences, or both.

One-Time Pad

An Army Signal Corp officer, Joseph Mauborgne, proposed an improvement to the Vernam cipher that yields the ultimate in security. Mauborgne suggested using a random key that is as long as the message, so that the key need not be repeated. In addition, the key is to be used to encrypt and decrypt a single message, and then is discarded. Each new message requires a new key of the same length as the new message. Such a scheme, known as a **one-time pad**, is unbreakable. It produces random output that bears no statistical relationship to the plaintext. Because the ciphertext contains no information whatsoever about the plaintext, there is simply no way to break the code.

An example should illustrate our point. Suppose that we are using a Vigenère scheme with 27 characters in which the twenty-seventh character is the space character, but with a one-time key that is as long as the message. Thus, the tableau of Table 2.3 must be expanded to 27×27. Consider the ciphertext

ANKYODKYUREPFJBYOJDSPLREYIUNOFDOIUERFPLUYTS

[8]Although the techniques for breaking a Vigenère cipher are by no means complex, a 1917 issue of *Scientific American* characterized this system as "impossible of translation." This is a point worth remembering when similar claims are made for modern algorithms.

We now show two different decryptions using two different keys:

```
ciphertext: ANKYODKYUREPFJBYOJDSPLREYIUNOFDOIUERFPLUYTS
key:        pxlmvmsydofuyrvzwc tnlebnecvgdupahfzzlmnyih
plaintext:  mr mustard with the candlestick in the hall

ciphertext: ANKYODKYUREPFJBYOJDSPLREYIUNOFDOIUERFPLUYTS
key:        mfugpmiydgaxgoufhklllmhsqdqogtewbqfgyovuhwt
plaintext:  miss scarlet with the knife in the library
```

Suppose that a cryptanalyst had managed to find these two keys. Two plausible plaintexts are produced. How is the cryptanalyst to decide which is the correct decryption (i.e., which is the correct key)? If the actual key were produced in a truly random fashion, then the cryptanalyst cannot say that one of these two keys is more likely than the other. Thus, there is no way to decide which key is correct and therefore which plaintext is correct.

In fact, given any plaintext of equal length to the ciphertext, there is a key that produces that plaintext. Therefore, if you did an exhaustive search of all possible keys, you would end up with many legible plaintexts, with no way of knowing which was the intended plaintext. Therefore, the code is unbreakable.

The security of the one-time pad is entirely due to the randomness of the key. If the stream of characters that constitute the key is truly random, then the stream of characters that constitute the ciphertext will be truly random. Thus, there are no patterns or regularities that a cryptanalyst can use to attack the ciphertext.

In theory, we need look no further for a cipher. The one-time pad offers complete security but, in practice, has two fundamental difficulties:

1. There is the practical problem of making large quantities of random keys. Any heavily used system might require millions of random characters on a regular basis. Supplying truly random characters in this volume is a significant task.
2. Even more daunting is the problem of key distribution and protection. For every message to be sent, a key of equal length is needed by both sender and receiver. Thus, a mammoth key distribution problem exists.

Because of these difficulties, the one-time pad is of limited utility, and is useful primarily for low-bandwidth channels requiring very high security.

2.3 TRANSPOSITION TECHNIQUES

All the techniques examined so far involve the substitution of a ciphertext symbol for a plaintext symbol. A very different kind of mapping is achieved by performing some sort of permutation on the plaintext letters. This technique is referred to as a transposition cipher.

The simplest such cipher is the rail fence technique, in which the plaintext is written down as a sequence of diagonals and then read off as a sequence of rows. For example, to encipher the message "meet me after the toga party" with a rail fence of depth 2, we write the following:

```
m e m a t r h t g p r y
 e t e f e t e o a a t
```

The encrypted message is

MEMATRHTGPRYETEFETEOAAT

This sort of thing would be trivial to cryptanalyze. A more complex scheme is to write the message in a rectangle, row by row, and read the message off, column by column, but permute the order of the columns. The order of the columns then becomes the key to the algorithm. For example,

```
Key:          4 3 1 2 5 6 7
Plaintext:    a t t a c k p
              o s t p o n e
              d u n t i l t
              w o a m x y z
Ciphertext:   TTNAAPTMTSUOAODWCOIXKNLYPETZ
```

A pure transposition cipher is easily recognized because it has the same letter frequencies as the original plaintext. For the type of columnar transposition just shown, cryptanalysis is fairly straightforward and involves laying out the ciphertext in a matrix and playing around with column positions. Digram and trigram frequency tables can be useful.

The transposition cipher can be made significantly more secure by performing more than one stage of transposition. The result is a more complex permutation that is not easily reconstructed. Thus, if the foregoing message is reencrypted using the same algorithm,

```
Key:          4 3 1 2 5 6 7
Input:        t t n a a p t
              m t s u o a o
              d w c o i x k
              n l y p e t z
Output:       NSCYAUOPTTWLTMDNAOIEPAXTTOKZ
```

To visualize the result of this double transposition, designate the letters in the original plaintext message by the numbers designating their position. Thus, with 28 letters in the message, the original sequence of letters is

```
01 02 03 04 05 06 07 08 09 10 11 12 13 14
15 16 17 18 19 20 21 22 23 24 25 26 27 28
```

After the first transposition we have

```
03 10 17 24 04 11 18 25 02 09 16 23 01 08
15 22 05 12 19 26 06 13 20 27 07 14 21 28
```

which has a somewhat regular structure. But after the second transposition, we have

```
17 09 05 27 24 16 12 07 10 02 22 20 03 25
15 13 04 23 19 14 11 01 26 21 18 08 06 28
```

This is a much less structured permutation and is much more difficult to cryptanalyze.

2.4 ROTOR MACHINES

The example just given suggests that multiple stages of encryption can produce an algorithm that is significantly more difficult to cryptanalyze. This is as true of substitution ciphers as it is of transposition ciphers. Before the introduction of DES, the most important application of the principle of multiple stages of encryption was a class of systems known as rotor machines.[9]

The basic principle of the rotor machine is illustrated in Figure 2.7. The machine consists of a set of independently rotating cylinders through which electrical pulses can flow. Each cylinder has 26 input pins and 26 output pins, with internal wiring that connects each input pin to a unique output pin. For simplicity, only three of the internal connections in each cylinder are shown.

If we associate each input and output pin with a letter of the alphabet, then a single cylinder defines a monoalphabetic substitution. For example, in Figure 2.7, if an operator depresses the key for the letter A, an electric signal is applied to the first pin of the first cylinder and flows through the internal connection to the twenty-fifth output pin.

Consider a machine with a single cylinder. After each input key is depressed, the cylinder rotates one position, so that the internal connections are shifted accordingly. Thus, a different monoalphabetic substitution cipher is defined. After 26 letters of plaintext, the cylinder would be back to the initial position. Thus, we have a polyalphabetic substitution algorithm with a period of 26.

A single-cylinder system is trivial and does not present a formidable cryptanalytic task. The power of the rotor machine is in the use of multiple cylinders, in which the output pins of one cylinder are connected to the input pins of the next. Figure 2.7 shows a three-cylinder system. The left half of the figure shows a position in which the input from the operator to the first pin (plaintext letter a) is routed through the three cylinders to appear at the output of the second pin (ciphertext letter B).

With multiple cylinders, the one closest to the operator input rotates one pin position with each keystroke. The right half of Figure 2.7 shows the system's configuration after a single keystroke. For every complete rotation of the inner

[9]Machines based on the rotor principle were used by both Germany (Enigma) and Japan (Purple) in World War II. The breaking of both codes by the Allies was a significant factor in the war's outcome.

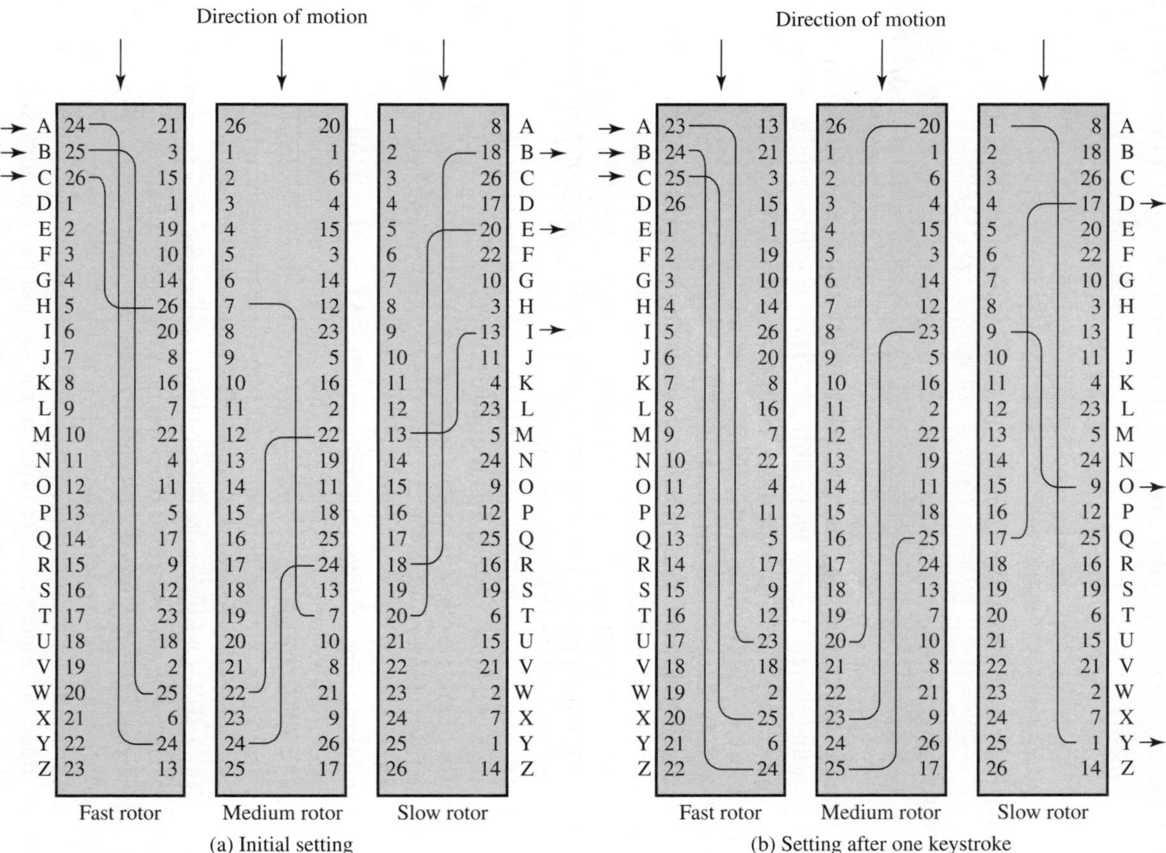

Figure 2.7 Three-Rotor Machine with Wiring Represented by Numbered Contacts

cylinder, the middle cylinder rotates one pin position. Finally, for every complete rotation of the middle cylinder, the outer cylinder rotates one pin position. This is the same type of operation seen with an odometer. The result is that there are $26 \times 26 \times 26 = 17{,}576$ different substitution alphabets used before the system repeats. The addition of fourth and fifth rotors results in periods of 456,976 and 11,881,376 letters, respectively. As David Kahn eloquently put it, referring to a five-rotor machine [KAHN96, page 413]:

> A period of that length thwarts any practical possibility of a straightforward solution on the basis of letter frequency. This general solution would need about 50 letters per cipher alphabet, meaning that all five rotors would have to go through their combined cycle 50 times. The ciphertext would have to be as long as all the speeches made on the floor of the Senate and the House of Representatives in three successive sessions of Congress. No cryptanalyst is likely to bag that kind of trophy in his lifetime; even diplomats, who can be as verbose as politicians, rarely scale those heights of loquacity.

The significance of the rotor machine today is that it points the way to the most widely used cipher ever: the Data Encryption Standard (DES). This we examine in Chapter 3.

2.5 STEGANOGRAPHY

We conclude with a discussion of a technique that is, strictly speaking, not encryption, namely, steganography.

A plaintext message may be hidden in one of two ways. The methods of steganography conceal the existence of the message, whereas the methods of cryptography render the message unintelligible to outsiders by various transformations of the text.[10]

A simple form of steganography, but one that is time-consuming to construct, is one in which an arrangement of words or letters within an apparently innocuous text spells out the real message. For example, the sequence of first letters of each word of the overall message spells out the hidden message. Figure 2.8 shows an example in which a subset of the words of the overall message is used to convey the hidden message.

Various other techniques have been used historically; some examples are the following [MYER91]:

- **Character marking:** Selected letters of printed or typewritten text are overwritten in pencil. The marks are ordinarily not visible unless the paper is held at an angle to bright light.
- **Invisible ink:** A number of substances can be used for writing but leave no visible trace until heat or some chemical is applied to the paper.

[10] *Steganography* was an obsolete word that was revived by David Kahn and given the meaning it has today [KAHN96].

3rd March

Dear George,

Greetings to all at Oxford. Many thanks for your
letter and for the Summer examination package.
All Entry Forms and Fees Forms should be ready
for final despatch to the Syndicate by Friday
20th or at the very latest, I'm told. by the 21st.
Admin has improved here, though there's room
for improvement still; just give us all two or three
more years and we'll really show you! Please
don't let these wretched 16+ proposals destroy
your basis O and A pattern. Certainly this
sort of change, if implemented immediately,
would bring chaos.

Sincerely yours.

Figure 2.8 A Puzzle for Inspector Morse
(From The Silent World of Nicholas Quinn, *by Colin Dexter)*

- **Pin punctures:** Small pin punctures on selected letters are ordinarily not visible unless the paper is held up in front of a light.
- **Typewriter correction ribbon:** Used between lines typed with a black ribbon, the results of typing with the correction tape are visible only under a strong light.

Although these techniques may seem archaic, they have contemporary equivalents. [WAYN93] proposes hiding a message by using the least significant bits of frames on a CD. For example, the Kodak Photo CD format's maximum resolution is 2048 by 3072 pixels, with each pixel containing 24 bits of RGB color information. The least significant bit of each 24-bit pixel can be changed without greatly affecting the quality of the image. The result is that you can hide a 2.3-megabyte message in a single digital snapshot. There are now a number of software packages available that take this type of approach to steganography.

Steganography has a number of drawbacks when compared to encryption. It requires a lot of overhead to hide a relatively few bits of information, although using some scheme like that proposed in the preceding paragraph may make it more effective. Also, once the system is discovered, it becomes virtually worthless. This problem, too, can be overcome if the insertion method depends on some sort of key (e.g., see Problem 2.11). Alternatively, a message can be first encrypted and then hidden using steganography.

The advantage of steganography is that it can be employed by parties who have something to lose should the fact of their secret communication (not necessarily the content) be discovered. Encryption flags traffic as important or secret or may identify the sender or receiver as someone with something to hide.

2.6 RECOMMENDED READING AND WEB SITES

For anyone interested in the history of code making and code breaking, the book to read [KAHN96]. Although it is concerned more with the impact of cryptology than its technical development, it is an excellent introduction and makes for exciting reading. Another excellent historical account is [SING99].

A short treatment covering the techniques of this chapter, and more, is [GARD72]. There are many books that cover classical cryptography in a more technical vein; one of the best is [SINK66]. [KORN96] is a delightful book to read and contains a lengthy section on classical techniques. Two cryptography books that contain a fair amount of technical material on classical techniques are [GARR01] and [NICH99]. For the truly interested reader, the two-volume [NICH96] covers numerous classical ciphers in detail and provides many ciphertexts to be cryptanalyzed, together with the solutions.

An excellent treatment of rotor machines, including a discussion of their cryptanalysis is found in [KUMA97].

[KATZ00] provides a thorough treatment of steganography. Another good source is [WAYN96].

GARD72 Gardner, M. *Codes, Ciphers, and Secret Writing.* New York: Dover, 1972.

GARR01 Garrett, P. *Making, Breaking Codes: An Introduction to Cryptology.* Upper Saddle River, NJ: Prentice Hall, 2001.

KAHN96 Kahn, D. *The Codebreakers: The Story of Secret Writing.* New York: Scribner, 1996.

KATZ00 Katzenbeisser, S., ed. *Information Hiding Techniques for Steganography and Digital Watermarking.* Boston: Artech House, 2000.

KORN96 Korner, T. *The Pleasures of Counting.* Cambridge, England: Cambridge University Press, 1996.

KUMA97 Kumar, I. *Cryptology.* Laguna Hills, CA: Aegean Park Press, 1997.

NICH96 Nichols, R. *Classical Cryptography Course.* Laguna Hills, CA: Aegean Park Press, 1996.

NICH99 Nichols, R. ed. *ICSA Guide to Cryptography.* New York: McGraw-Hill, 1999.

SING99 Singh, S. *:The Code Book: The Science of Secrecy from Ancient Egypt to Quantum Cryptography.* New York: Anchor Books, 1999.

SINK66 Sinkov, A. *Elementary Cryptanalysis: A Mathematical Approach.* Washington, DC: The Mathematical Association of America, 1966.

WAYN96 Wayner, P. *Disappearing Cryptography.* Boston: AP Professional Books, 1996.

Recommended Web Sites:

- **American Cryptogram Association:** An association of amateur cryptographers. The Web site includes information and links to sites concerned with classical cryptography.

- **Crypto Corner:** Simon Singh's Web site. Lots of good information, plus interactive tools for learning about cryptography.
- **Steganography:** Good collection of links and documents.

2.7 KEY TERMS, REVIEW QUESTIONS, AND PROBLEMS

Key Terms

block cipher	cryptology	polyalphabetic cipher
brute-force attack	deciphering	rail fence cipher
Caesar cipher	decryption	single-key encryption
cipher	enciphering	steganography
ciphertext	encryption	stream cipher
computationally secure	Hill cipher	symmetric encryption
conventional encryption	monoalphabetic cipher	transposition cipher
cryptanalysis	one-time pad	unconditionally secure
cryptographic system	plaintext	Vigenère cipher
cryptography	Playfair cipher	

Review Questions

2.1 What are the essential ingredients of a symmetric cipher?

2.2 What are the two basic functions used in encryption algorithms?

2.3 How many keys are required for two people to communicate via a cipher?

2.4 What is the difference between a block cipher and a stream cipher?

2.5 What are the two general approaches to attacking a cipher?

2.6 List and briefly define types of cryptanalytic attacks based on what is known to the attacker.

2.7 What is the difference between an unconditionally secure cipher and a computationally secure cipher?

2.8 Briefly define the Caesar cipher.

2.9 Briefly define the monoalphabetic cipher.

2.10 Briefly define the Playfair cipher.

2.11 What is the difference between a monoalphabetic cipher and a polyalphabetic cipher?

2.12 What are two problems with the one-time pad?

2.13 What is a transposition cipher?

2.14 What is steganography?

Problems

2.1 A generalization of the Caesar cipher, knows as the affine Caesar cipher, has the following form: For each plaintext letter p, substitute the ciphertext letter C:

$$C = \mathrm{E}([a, b], p) = (ap + b) \bmod 26$$

A basic requirement of any encryption algorithm is that it be one-to-one. That is, if $p \neq q$, then $E(k, p) \neq E(k, q)$. Otherwise, decryption is impossible, because more than one plaintext character maps into the same ciphertext character. The affine Caesar cipher is not one-to-one for all values of a. For example, for $a = 2$ and $b = 3$, then $E([a, b], 0) = E([a, b], 13) = 3$.

a. Are there any limitations on the value of b? Explain why or why not.
b. Determine which values of a are not allowed.
c. Provide a general statement of which values of a are and are not allowed. Justify your statement.

2.2 How many one-to-one affine Caesar ciphers are there?

2.3 A ciphertext has been generated with an affine cipher. The most frequent letter of the ciphertext is 'B', and the second most frequent letter of the ciphertext is 'U'. Break this code.

2.4 The following ciphertext was generated using a simple substitution algorithm:

53‡‡†305))6*;4826)4‡.)4‡);806*;48†8¶60))85;;]8*;:‡*8†83
(88)5*†;46(;88*96*?;8)*‡(;485);5*†2:*‡(;4956*2(5*-4)88*
;4069285);)6†8)4‡[ddagger];1(‡9;48081;8:8‡1;48†85;4)485†528806*81
(‡9;48;(88;4(‡?34;48)4‡;161;:188;‡?;

Decrypt this message. *Hints:*

1. As you know, the most frequently occurring letter in English is e. Therefore, the first or second (or perhaps third?) most common character in the message is likely to stand for e. Also, e is often seen in pairs (e.g., meet, fleet, speed, seen, been, agree, etc.). Try to find a character in the ciphertext that decodes to e.
2. The most common word in English is "the." Use this fact to guess the characters that stand for t and h.
3. Decipher the rest of the message by deducing additional words.

Warning: The resulting message is in English but may not make much sense on a first reading.

2.5 One way to solve the key distribution problem is to use a line from a book that both the sender and the receiver possess. Typically, at least in spy novels, the first sentence of a book serves as the key. The particular scheme discussed in this problem is from one of the best suspense novels involving secret codes, *Talking to Strange Men*, by Ruth Rendell. Work this problem without consulting that book!

Consider the following message:

SIDKHKDM AF HCRKIABIE SHIMC KD LFEAILA

This ciphertext was produced using the first sentence of *The Other Side of Silence* (a book about the spy Kim Philby):

> The snow lay thick on the steps and the snowflakes driven by the wind looked black in the headlights of the cars.

A simple substitution cipher was used.

a. What is the encryption algorithm?
b. How secure is it?
c. To make the key distribution problem simple, both parties can agree to use the first or last sentence of a book as the key. To change the key, they simply need to agree on a new book. The use of the first sentence would be preferable to the use of the last. Why?

2.6 In one of his cases, Sherlock Holmes was confronted with the following message.

534 C2 13 127 36 31 4 17 21 41
DOUGLAS 109 293 5 37 BIRLSTONE
26 BIRLSTONE 9 127 171

Although Watson was puzzled, Holmes was able immediately to deduce the type of cipher. Can you?

2.7 This problem uses a real-world example, from an old U.S. Special Forces manual (public domain). A copy is available at **ftp://shell.shore.net/members/w/s/ws/Support/Crypto/FM-31-4.pdf**

a. Using the two keys (memory words) *cryptographic* and *network security*, encrypt the following message:

Be at the third pillar from the left outside the lyceum theatre tonight at seven.
If you are distrustful bring two friends.

Make reasonable assumptions about how to treat redundant letters and excess letters in the memory words and how to treat spaces and punctuation. Indicate what your assumptions are. *Note:* The message is from the Sherlock Holmes novel, *The Sign of Four*.

b. Decrypt the ciphertext. Show your work.

c. Comment on when it would be appropriate to use this technique and what its advantages are.

2.8 A disadvantage of the general monoalphabetic cipher is that both sender and receiver must commit the permuted cipher sequence to memory. A common technique for avoiding this is to use a keyword from which the cipher sequence can be generated. For example, using the keyword *CIPHER*, write out the keyword followed by unused letters in normal order and match this against the plaintext letters:

```
plain:    a b c d e f g h i j k l m n o p q r s t u v w x y z
cipher:   C I P H E R A B D F G J K L M N O Q S T U V W X Y Z
```

If it is felt that this process does not produce sufficient mixing, write the remaining letters on successive lines and then generate the sequence by reading down the columns:

```
C I P H E R
A B D F G J
K L M N O Q
S T U V W X
Y Z
```

This yields the sequence

```
C A K S Y I B L T Z P D M U H F N V E G O W R J Q X
```

Such a system is used in the example in Section 2.2 (the one that begins "it was disclosed yesterday"). Determine the keyword.

2.9 When the PT-109 American patrol boat, under the command of Lieutenant John F. Kennedy, was sunk by a Japanese destroyer, a message was received at an Australian wireless station in Playfair code:

```
KXJEY UREBE ZWEHE WRYTU HEYFS
KREHE GOYFI WTTTU OLKSY CAJPO
BOTEI ZONTX BYBNT GONEY CUZWR
GDSON SXBOU YWRHE BAAHY USEDQ
```

The key used was *royal new zealand navy*. Decrypt the message. Translate TT into tt.

2.10 a. Construct a Playfair matrix with the key *largest*.

b. Construct a Playfair matrix with the key *occurrence*. Make a reasonable assumption about how to treat redundant letters in the key.

2.11 a. Using this Playfair matrix

M	F	H	I/J	K
U	N	O	P	Q
Z	V	W	X	Y
E	L	A	R	G
D	S	T	B	C

encrypt this message:

Must see you over Cadogan West. Coming at once.

Note: The message is from the Sherlock Holmes story, *The Adventure of the Bruce-Partington Plans*.

b. Repeat part (a) using the Playfair matrix from Problem 2.10a.

c. How do you account for the results of this problem? Can you generalize your conclusion?

2.12 a. How many possible keys does the Playfair cipher have? Ignore the fact that some keys might produce identical encryption results. Express your answer as an approximate power of 2.

b. Now take into account the fact that some Playfair keys produce the same encryption results. How many effectively unique keys does the Playfair cipher have?

2.13 What substitution system results when we use a 25×1 Playfair matrix?

2.14 a. Decipher the message YITJP GWJOW FAQTQ XCSMA ETSQU SQAPU SQGKC PQTYJ using the Hill cipher with the inverse key $\begin{pmatrix} 5 & 1 \\ 2 & 7 \end{pmatrix}$. Show your calculations and the result.

b. Decipher the message MWALO LIAIW WTGBH JNTAK QZJKA ADAWS SKQKU AYARN CSODN IIAES OQKJY B using the Hill cipher with the inverse key $\begin{pmatrix} 2 & 23 \\ 21 & 7 \end{pmatrix}$. Show your calculations and the result.

2.15 a. Encrypt the message "meet me at the usual place at ten rather than eight oclock" using the Hill cipher with the key $\begin{pmatrix} 9 & 4 \\ 5 & 7 \end{pmatrix}$. Show your calculations and the result.

b. Show the calculations for the corresponding decryption of the ciphertext to recover the original plaintext.

2.16 We have shown that the Hill cipher succumbs to a known plaintext attack if sufficient plaintext-ciphertext pairs are provided. It is even easier to solve the Hill cipher if a chosen plaintext attack can be mounted. Describe such an attack.

2.17 It can be shown that the Hill cipher with the matrix $\begin{pmatrix} a & b \\ c & d \end{pmatrix}$ requires that $(ad - bc)$ is relatively prime to 26; that is the only common positive factor of $(ad - bc)$ and 26 is 1. Thus, if $(ad - bc) = 13$ or is even, the matrix is not allowed. Determine the number of different (good) keys there are for a 2×2 Hill cipher without counting them one by one, using the following steps:

a. Find the number of matrices whose determinant is even because one or both rows are even. (A row is "even" if both entries in the row are even.)

b. Find the number of matrices whose determinant is even because one or both columns are even. (A column is "even" if both entries in the column are even.)

c. Find the number of matrices whose determinant is even because all of the entries are odd.

d. Taking into account overlaps, find the total number of matrices whose determinant is even.

e. Find the number of matrices whose determinant is a multiple of 13 because the first column is a multiple of 13.

f. Find the number of matrices whose determinant is a multiple of 13 where the first column is not a multiple of 13 but the second column is a multiple of the first modulo 13.

g. Find the total number of matrices whose determinant is a multiple of 13.

h. Find the number of matrices whose determinant is a multiple of 26 because they fit case (a) and (e). (b) and (e). (c) and (e). (a) and (f). And so on ...

i. Find the total number of matrices whose determinant is neither a multiple of 2 nor a multiple of 13.

2.18 Using the Vigenère cipher, encrypt the word "explanation" using the key *leg*.

2.19 This problem explores the use of a one-time pad version of the Vigenère cipher. In this scheme, the key is a stream of random numbers between 0 and 26. For example, if the key is 3 19 5 . . . , then the first letter of plaintext is encrypted with a shift of 3 letters, the second with a shift of 19 letters, the third with a shift of 5 letters, and so on.

a. Encrypt the plaintext sendmoremoney with the key stream 9 0 1 7 23 15 21 14 11 11 2 8 9.

b. Using the ciphertext produced in part a, find a key so that the cipher text decrypts to the plaintext cashnotneeded.

2.20 What is the message embedded in Figure 2.8?

2.21 In one of Dorothy Sayers's mysteries, Lord Peter is confronted with the message shown in Figure 2.9. He also discovers the key to the message, which is a sequence of integers:

787656543432112343456567878878765654
3432112343456567878878765654433211234

a. Decrypt the message. *Hint:* What is the largest integer value?

b. If the algorithm is known but not the key, how secure is the scheme?

c. If the key is known but not the algorithm, how secure is the scheme?

Programming Problems

2.22 Write a program that can encrypt and decrypt using the general Caesar cipher, also known as an additive cipher.

2.23 Write a program that can encrypt and decrypt using the affine cipher described in Problem 2.1.

2.24 Write a program that can perform a letter frequency attack on an additive cipher without human intervention. Your software should produce possible plaintexts in rough

I thought to see the fairies in the
fields, but I saw only the evil elephants
with their black backs. Woe! how that
sight awed me! The elves danced all
around and about while I heard voices
calling clearly. Ah! how I tried to
see-throw off the ugly cloud-but no blind
eye of a mortal was permitted to spy
them. So then came minstrels, having gold
trumpets, harps and drums. These played
very loudly beside me, breaking that spell.
So the dream vanished, whereat I thanked
Heaven. I shed many tears before the thin
moon rose up, frail and faint as a sickle of
straw. Now though the Enchanter gnash
his teeth vainly, yet shall he return as the
Spring returns. Oh, wretched man! Hell
gapes, Erebus now lies open. The mouths
of Death wait on thy end.

Figure 2.9 A Puzzle for Lord Peter

order of likelihood. It would be good if your user interface allowed the user to specify "give me the top 10 possible plaintexts".

2.25 Write a program that can perform a letter frequency attack on any monoalphabetic substitution cipher without human intervention. Your software should produce possible plaintexts in rough order of likelihood. It would be good if your user interface allowed the user to specify "give me the top 10 possible plaintexts".

2.26 Create software that can encrypt and decrypt using a 2×2 Hill cipher.

2.27 Create software that can perform a fast known plaintext attack on a Hill cipher, given the dimension m. How fast are your algorithms, as a function of m?

CHAPTER 3

Block Ciphers and the Data Encryption Standard

All the afternoon Mungo had been working on Stern's code, principally with the aid of the latest messages which he had copied down at the Nevin Square drop. Stern was very confident. He must be well aware London Central knew about that drop. It was obvious that they didn't care how often Mungo read their messages, so confident were they in the impenetrability of the code.

—*Talking to Strange Men,* Ruth Rendell

KEY POINTS

- A **block cipher** is an encryption/decryption scheme in which a block of plaintext is treated as a whole and used to produce a ciphertext block of equal length.
- Many block ciphers have a Feistel structure. Such a structure consists of a number of identical rounds of processing. In each round, a substitution is performed on one half of the data being processed, followed by a permutation that interchanges the two halves. The original key is expanded so that a different key is used for each round.
- The Data Encryption Standard (DES) has been the most widely used encryption algorithm until recently. It exhibits the classic Feistel structure. DES uses a 64-bit block and a 56-bit key.
- Two important methods of cryptanalysis are differential cryptanalysis and linear cryptanalysis. DES has been shown to be highly resistant to these two types of attack.

The objective of this chapter is to illustrate the principles of modern symmetric ciphers. For this purpose, we focus on the most widely used symmetric cipher: the Data Encryption Standard (DES). Although numerous symmetric ciphers have been developed since the introduction of DES, and although it is destined to be replaced by the Advanced Encryption Standard (AES), DES remains the most important such algorithm. Further, a detailed study of DES provides an understanding of the principles used in other symmetric ciphers. We examine other important symmetric ciphers, including AES, in Chapters 5 and 6.

This chapter begins with a discussion of the general principles of symmetric block ciphers, which are the type of symmetric ciphers studied in this book (with the exception of the stream cipher RC4 in Chapter 6). Next, we cover full DES. Following this look at a specific algorithm, we return to a more general discussion of block cipher design.

Compared to public-key ciphers such as RSA, the structure of DES, and most symmetric ciphers, is very complex and cannot be explained as easily as RSA and similar algorithms. Accordingly, the reader may with to begin with a simplified version of DES, which is described in Appendix C. This version allows the reader to perform encryption and decryption by hand and gain a good understanding of the working of the algorithm details. Classroom experience indicates that a study of this simplified version enhances understanding of DES.[1]

3.1 BLOCK CIPHER PRINCIPLES

Most symmetric block encryption algorithms in current use are based on a structure referred to as a Feistel block cipher [FEIS73]. For that reason, it is important to examine the design principles of the Feistel cipher. We begin with a comparison of stream ciphers and block ciphers. Then we discuss the motivation for the Feistel block cipher structure. Finally, we discuss some of its implications.

Stream Ciphers and Block Ciphers

A **stream cipher** is one that encrypts a digital data stream one bit or one byte at a time. Examples of classical stream ciphers are the autokeyed Vigenère cipher and the Vernam cipher. A **block cipher** is one in which a block of plaintext is treated as a whole and used to produce a ciphertext block of equal length. Typically, a block size of 64 or 128 bits is used. Using some of the modes of operation explained in Chapter 6, a block cipher can be used to achieve the same effect as a stream cipher.

Far more effort has gone into analyzing block ciphers. In general, they seem applicable to a broader range of applications than stream ciphers. The vast majority of network-based symmetric cryptographic applications make use of block ciphers. Accordingly, the concern in this chapter, and in our discussions throughout the book of symmetric encryption, will focus on block ciphers.

Motivation for the Feistel Cipher Structure

A block cipher operates on a plaintext block of n bits to produce a ciphertext block of n bits. There are 2^n possible different plaintext blocks and, for the encryption to be reversible (i.e., for decryption to be possible), each must produce a unique ciphertext block. Such a transformation is called reversible, or nonsingular. The following examples illustrate nonsingular and singular transformation for $n = 2$.

Reversible Mapping

Plaintext	Ciphertext
00	11
01	10
10	00
11	01

Irreversible Mapping

Plaintext	Ciphertext
00	11
01	10
10	01
11	01

In the latter case, a ciphertext of 01 could have been produced by one of two plaintext blocks. So if we limit ourselves to reversible mappings, the number of different transformations is $2^n!$.

[1]However, you may safely skip Appendix C, at least on a first reading. If you get lost or bogged down in the details of DES, then you can go back and start with simplified DES.

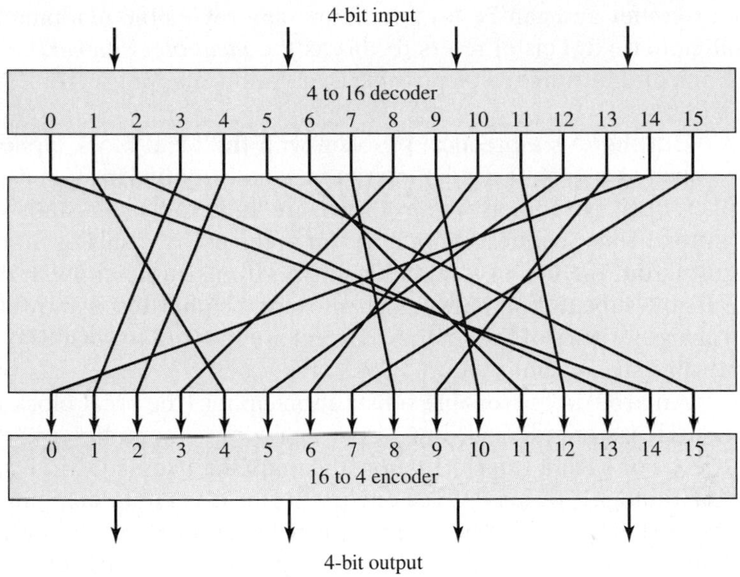

Figure 3.1 General n-bit-n-bit Block Substitution (shown with $n = 4$)

Figure 3.1 illustrates the logic of a general substitution cipher for $n = 4$. A 4-bit input produces one of 16 possible input states, which is mapped by the substitution cipher into a unique one of 16 possible output states, each of which is represented by 4 ciphertext bits. The encryption and decryption mappings can be defined by a tabulation, as shown in Table 3.1. This is the most general form of

Table 3.1 Encryption and Decryption Tables for Substitution Cipher of Figure 3.4

Plaintext	Ciphertext
0000	1110
0001	0100
0010	1101
0011	0001
0100	0010
0101	1111
0110	1011
0111	1000
1000	0011
1001	1010
1010	0110
1011	1100
1100	0101
1101	1001
1110	0000
1111	0111

Ciphertext	Plaintext
0000	1110
0001	0011
0010	0100
0011	1000
0100	0001
0101	1100
0110	1010
0111	1111
1000	0111
1001	1101
1010	1001
1011	0110
1100	1011
1101	0010
1110	0000
1111	0101

block cipher and can be used to define any reversible mapping between plaintext and ciphertext. Feistel refers to this as the *ideal block cipher*, because it allows for the maximum number of possible encryption mappings from the plaintext block [FEIS75].

But there is a practical problem with the ideal block cipher. If a small block size, such as $n = 4$, is used, then the system is equivalent to a classical substitution cipher. Such systems, as we have seen, are vulnerable to a statistical analysis of the plaintext. This weakness is not inherent in the use of a substitution cipher but rather results from the use of a small block size. If n is sufficiently large and an arbitrary reversible substitution between plaintext and ciphertext is allowed, then the statistical characteristics of the source plaintext are masked to such an extent that this type of cryptanalysis is infeasible.

An arbitrary reversible substitution cipher (the ideal block cipher) for a large block size is not practical, however, from an implementation and performance point of view. For such a transformation, the mapping itself constitutes the key. Consider again Table 3.1, which defines one particular reversible mapping from plaintext to ciphertext for $n = 4$. The mapping can be defined by the entries in the second column, which show the value of the ciphertext for each plaintext block. This, in essence, is the key that determines the specific mapping from among all possible mappings. In this case, using this straightforward method of defining the key, the required key length is (4 bits) $\times$ (16 rows) $=$ 64 bits. In general, for an n-bit ideal block cipher, the length of the key defined in this fashion is $n \times 2^n$ bits. For a 64-bit block, which is a desirable length to thwart statistical attacks, the required key length is $64 \times 2^{64} = 2^{70} \approx 10^{21}$ bits.

In considering these difficulties, Feistel points out that what is needed is an approximation to the ideal block cipher system for large n, built up out of components that are easily realizable [FEIS75]. But before turning to Feistel's approach, let us make one other observation. We could use the general block substitution cipher but, to make its implementation tractable, confine ourselves to a subset of the $2^n!$ possible reversible mappings. For example, suppose we define the mapping in terms of a set of linear equations. In the case of $n = 4$, we have

$$
\begin{aligned}
y_1 &= k_{11}x_1 + k_{12}x_2 + k_{13}x_3 + k_{14}x_4 \\
y_2 &= k_{21}x_1 + k_{22}x_2 + k_{23}x_3 + k_{24}x_4 \\
y_3 &= k_{31}x_1 + k_{32}x_2 + k_{33}x_3 + k_{34}x_4 \\
y_4 &= k_{41}x_1 + k_{42}x_2 + k_{43}x_3 + k_{44}x_4
\end{aligned}
$$

where the x_i are the four binary digits of the plaintext block, the y_i are the four binary digits of the ciphertext block, the k_{ij} are the binary coefficients, and arithmetic is mod 2. The key size is just n^2, in this case 16 bits. The danger with this kind of formulation is that it may be vulnerable to cryptanalysis by an attacker that is aware of the structure of the algorithm. In this example, what we have is essentially the Hill cipher discussed in Chapter 2, applied to binary data rather than characters. As we saw in Chapter 2, a simple linear system such as this is quite vulnerable.

The Feistel Cipher

Feistel proposed [FEIS73] that we can approximate the ideal block cipher by utilizing the concept of a product cipher, which is the execution of two or more simple ciphers in sequence in such a way that the final result or product is cryptographically stronger than any of the component ciphers. The essence of the approach is to develop a block cipher with a key length of k bits and a block length of n bits, allowing a total of 2^k possible transformations, rather than the $2^n!$ transformations available with the ideal block cipher.

In particular, Feistel proposed the use of a cipher that alternates substitutions and permutations. In fact, this is a practical application of a proposal by Claude Shannon to develop a product cipher that alternates *confusion* and *diffusion* functions [SHAN49]. We look next at these concepts of diffusion and confusion and then present the Feistel cipher. But first, it is worth commenting on this remarkable fact: The Feistel cipher structure, which dates back over a quarter century and which, in turn, is based on Shannon's proposal of 1945, is the structure used by many significant symmetric block ciphers currently in use.

Diffusion and Confusion The terms *diffusion* and *confusion* were introduced by Claude Shannon to capture the two basic building blocks for any cryptographic system [SHAN49].[2] Shannon's concern was to thwart cryptanalysis based on statistical analysis. The reasoning is as follows. Assume the attacker has some knowledge of the statistical characteristics of the plaintext. For example, in a human-readable message in some language, the frequency distribution of the various letters may be known. Or there may be words or phrases likely to appear in the message (probable words). If these statistics are in any way reflected in the ciphertext, the cryptanalyst may be able to deduce the encryption key, or part of the key, or at least a set of keys likely to contain the exact key. In what Shannon refers to as a strongly ideal cipher, all statistics of the ciphertext are independent of the particular key used. The arbitrary substitution cipher that we discussed previously (Figure 3.1) is such a cipher, but as we have seen, is impractical.

Other than recourse to ideal systems, Shannon suggests two methods for frustrating statistical cryptanalysis: diffusion and confusion. In **diffusion**, the statistical structure of the plaintext is dissipated into long-range statistics of the ciphertext. This is achieved by having each plaintext digit affect the value of many ciphertext digits; generally this is equivalent to having each ciphertext digit be affected by many plaintext digits. An example of diffusion is to encrypt a message $M = m_1, m_2, m_3, \ldots$ of characters with an averaging operation:

$$y_n = \left(\sum_{i=1}^{k} m_{n+i} \right) \bmod 26$$

adding k successive letters to get a ciphertext letter y_n. One can show that the statistical structure of the plaintext has been dissipated. Thus, the letter frequencies in

[2]Shannon's 1949 paper appeared originally as a classified report in 1945. Shannon enjoys an amazing and unique position in the history of computer and information science. He not only developed the seminal ideas of modern cryptography but is also responsible for inventing the discipline of information theory. In addition, he founded another discipline, the application of Boolean algebra to the study of digital circuits; this last he managed to toss off as a master's thesis.

the ciphertext will be more nearly equal than in the plaintext; the digram frequencies will also be more nearly equal, and so on. In a binary block cipher, diffusion can be achieved by repeatedly performing some permutation on the data followed by applying a function to that permutation; the effect is that bits from different positions in the original plaintext contribute to a single bit of ciphertext.[3]

Every block cipher involves a transformation of a block of plaintext into a block of ciphertext, where the transformation depends on the key. The mechanism of diffusion seeks to make the statistical relationship between the plaintext and ciphertext as complex as possible in order to thwart attempts to deduce the key. On the other hand, **confusion** seeks to make the relationship between the statistics of the ciphertext and the value of the encryption key as complex as possible, again to thwart attempts to discover the key. Thus, even if the attacker can get some handle on the statistics of the ciphertext, the way in which the key was used to produce that ciphertext is so complex as to make it difficult to deduce the key. This is achieved by the use of a complex substitution algorithm. In contrast, a simple linear substitution function would add little confusion.

As [ROBS95b] points out, so successful are diffusion and confusion in capturing the essence of the desired attributes of a block cipher that they have become the cornerstone of modern block cipher design.

Feistel Cipher Structure Figure 3.2 depicts the structure proposed by Feistel. The inputs to the encryption algorithm are a plaintext block of length $2w$ bits and a key K. The plaintext block is divided into two halves, L_0 and R_0. The two halves of the data pass through n rounds of processing and then combine to produce the ciphertext block. Each round i has as inputs L_{i-1} and R_{i-1}, derived from the previous round, as well as a subkey K_i, derived from the overall K. In general, the subkeys K_i are different from K and from each other.

All rounds have the same structure. A **substitution** is performed on the left half of the data. This is done by applying a *round function* F to the right half of the data and then taking the exclusive-OR of the output of that function and the left half of the data. The round function has the same general structure for each round but is parameterized by the round subkey K_i. Following this substitution, a **permutation** is performed that consists of the interchange of the two halves of the data.[4] This structure is a particular form of the substitution-permutation network (SPN) proposed by Shannon.

The exact realization of a Feistel network depends on the choice of the following parameters and design features:

- **Block size:** Larger block sizes mean greater security (all other things being equal) but reduced encryption/decryption speed for a given algorithm. The greater security is achieved by greater diffusion Traditionally, a block size of 64 bits has

---

[3]Some books on cryptography equate permutation with diffusion. This is incorrect. Permutation, *by itself*, does not change the statistics of the plaintext at the level of individual letters or permuted blocks. For example, in DES, the permutation swaps two 32-bit blocks, so statistics of strings of 32 bits or less are preserved.

[4]The final round is followed by an interchange that undoes the interchange that is part of the final round. One could simply leave both interchanges out of the diagram, at the sacrifice of some consistency of presentation. In any case, the effective lack of a swap in the final round is done to simplify the implementation of the decryption process, as we shall see.

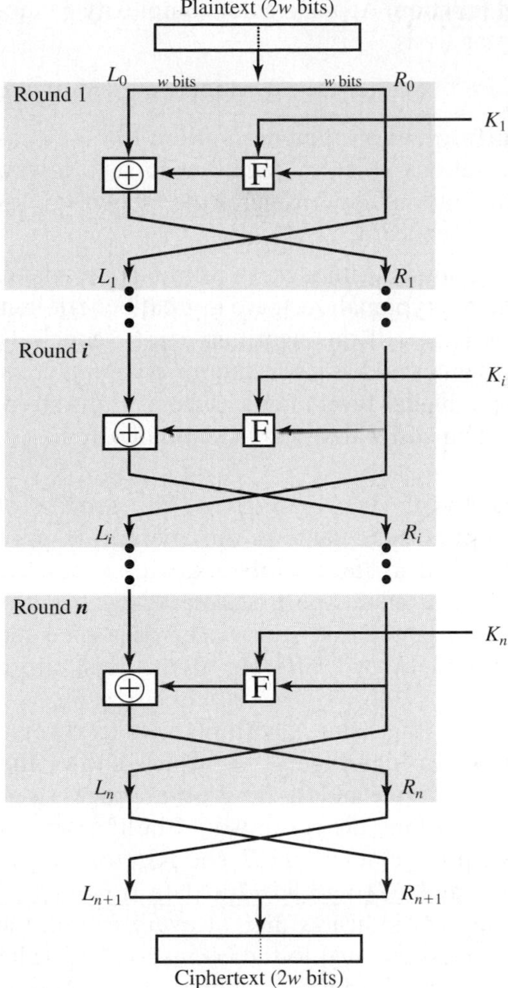

Figure 3.2 Classical Feistel Network

been considered a reasonable tradeoff and was nearly universal in block cipher design. However, the new AES uses a 128-bit block size.

- **Key size:** Larger key size means greater security but may decrease encryption/decryption speed. The greater security is achieved by greater resistance to brute-force attacks and greater confusion. Key sizes of 64 bits or less are now widely considered to be inadequate, and 128 bits has become a common size.
- **Number of rounds:** The essence of the Feistel cipher is that a single round offers inadequate security but that multiple rounds offer increasing security. A typical size is 16 rounds.
- **Subkey generation algorithm:** Greater complexity in this algorithm should lead to greater difficulty of cryptanalysis.

- **Round function:** Again, greater complexity generally means greater resistance to cryptanalysis.

There are two other considerations in the design of a Feistel cipher:

- **Fast software encryption/decryption:** In many cases, encryption is embedded in applications or utility functions in such a way as to preclude a hardware implementation. Accordingly, the speed of execution of the algorithm becomes a concern.
- **Ease of analysis:** Although we would like to make our algorithm as difficult as possible to cryptanalyze, there is great benefit in making the algorithm easy to analyze. That is, if the algorithm can be concisely and clearly explained, it is easier to analyze that algorithm for cryptanalytic vulnerabilities and therefore develop a higher level of assurance as to its strength. DES, for example, does not have an easily analyzed functionality.

Feistel Decryption Algorithm The process of decryption with a Feistel cipher is essentially the same as the encryption process. The rule is as follows: Use the ciphertext as input to the algorithm, but use the subkeys K_i in reverse order. That is, use K_n in the first round, K_{n-1} in the second round, and so on until K_1 is used in the last round. This is a nice feature because it means we need not implement two different algorithms, one for encryption and one for decryption.

To see that the same algorithm with a reversed key order produces the correct result, consider Figure 3.3, which shows the encryption process going down the left-hand side and the decryption process going up the right-hand side for a 16-round algorithm (the result would be the same for any number of rounds). For clarity, we use the notation LE_i and RE_i for data traveling through the encryption algorithm and LD_i and RD_i for data traveling through the decryption algorithm. The diagram indicates that, at every round, the intermediate value of the decryption process is equal to the corresponding value of the encryption process with the two halves of the value swapped. To put this another way, let the output of the ith encryption round be $\mathrm{LE}_i \| \mathrm{RE}_i$ (L_i concatenated with R_i). Then the corresponding input to the $(16 - i)$th decryption round is $\mathrm{RE}_i \| \mathrm{LE}_i$ or, equivalently, $\mathrm{RD}_{16-i} \| LD_{16-i}$.

Let us walk through Figure 3.3 to demonstrate the validity of the preceding assertions.[5] After the last iteration of the encryption process, the two halves of the output are swapped, so that the ciphertext is $\mathrm{RE}_{16} \| \mathrm{LE}_{16}$. The output of that round is the ciphertext. Now take that ciphertext and use it as input to the same algorithm. The input to the first round is $\mathrm{RE}_{16} \| \mathrm{LE}_{16}$, which is equal to the 32-bit swap of the output of the sixteenth round of the encryption process.

[5] To simplify the diagram, it is untwisted, not showing the swap that occurs at the end of each iteration. But please note that the intermediate result at the end of the ith stage of the encryption process is the $2w$-bit quantity formed by concatenating LE_i and RE_i, and that the intermediate result at the end of the ith stage of the decryption process is the $2w$-bit quantity formed by concatenating LD_i and RD_i.

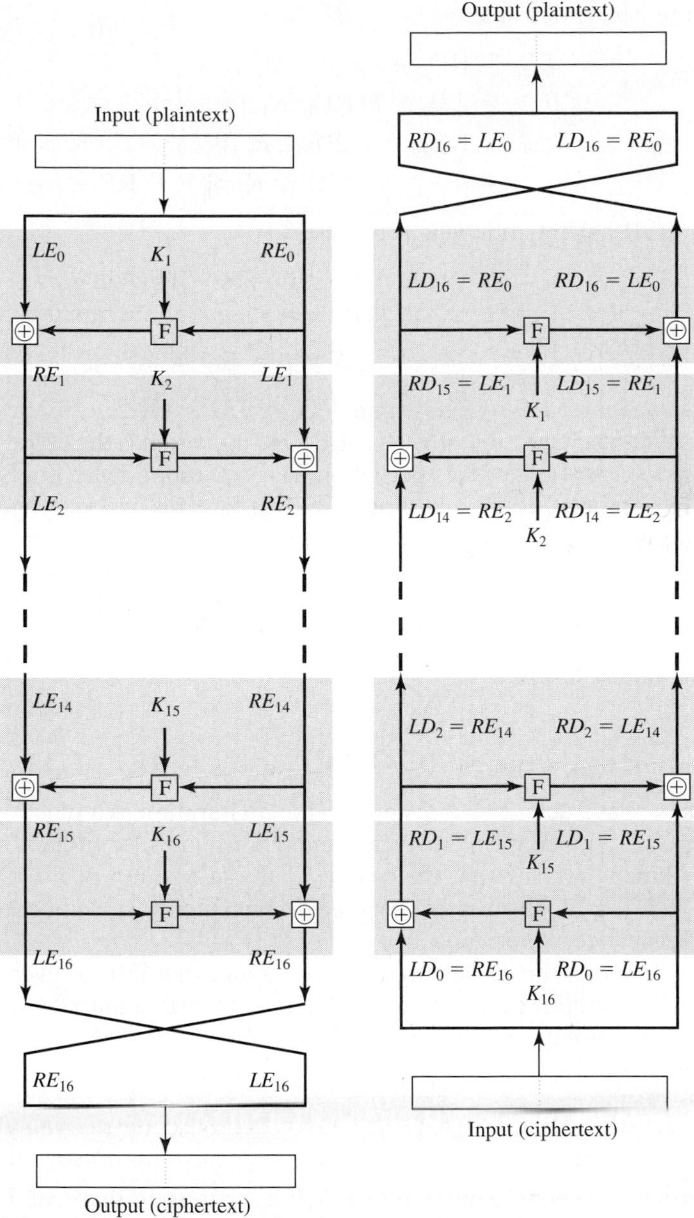

Figure 3.3 Feistel Encryption and Decryption

Now we would like to show that the output of the first round of the decryption process is equal to a 32-bit swap of the input to the sixteenth round of the encryption process. First, consider the encryption process. We see that

$$\begin{aligned} \mathrm{LE}_{16} &= \mathrm{RE}_{15} \\ \mathrm{RE}_{16} &= \mathrm{LE}_{15} \times \mathrm{F}(\mathrm{RE}_{15}, K_{16}) \end{aligned}$$

On the decryption side,

$$\begin{aligned} LD_1 &= \mathrm{RD}_0 = \mathrm{LE}_{16} = \mathrm{RE}_{15} \\ \mathrm{RD}_1 &= LD_0 \times \mathrm{F}(\mathrm{RD}_0, K_{16}) \\ &= \mathrm{RE}_{16} \times \mathrm{F}(\mathrm{RE}_{15}, K_{16}) \\ &= [\mathrm{LE}_{15} \times \mathrm{F}(\mathrm{RE}_{15}, K_{16})] \times \mathrm{F}(\mathrm{RE}_{15}, K_{16}) \end{aligned}$$

The XOR has the following properties:

$$\begin{aligned} [A \times B] \times C &= A \times [B \times C] \\ D \times D &= 0 \\ E \times 0 &= \mathrm{E} \end{aligned}$$

Thus, we have $LD_1 = \mathrm{RE}_{15}$ and $\mathrm{RD}_1 = \mathrm{LE}_{15}$. Therefore, the output of the first round of the decryption process is $\mathrm{LE}_{15} \| \mathrm{RE}_{15}$, which is the 32-bit swap of the input to the sixteenth round of the encryption. This correspondence holds all the way through the 16 iterations, as is easily shown. We can cast this process in general terms. For the ith iteration of the encryption algorithm,

$$\begin{aligned} \mathrm{LE}_i &= \mathrm{RE}_{i-1} \\ \mathrm{RE}_i &= \mathrm{LE}_{i-1} \times \mathrm{F}(\mathrm{RE}_{i-1}, \mathrm{K}_i) \end{aligned}$$

Rearranging terms,

$$\begin{aligned} \mathrm{RE}_{i-1} &= \mathrm{LE}_i \\ \mathrm{LE}_{i-1} &= \mathrm{RE}_i \times \mathrm{F}(\mathrm{RE}_{i-1}, \mathrm{K}_i) = \mathrm{RE}_i \times \mathrm{F}(\mathrm{LE}_i, \mathrm{K}_i) \end{aligned}$$

Thus, we have described the inputs to the ith iteration as a function of the outputs, and these equations confirm the assignments shown in the right-hand side of Figure 3.3.

Finally, we see that the output of the last round of the decryption process is $\mathrm{RE}_0 \| \mathrm{LE}_0$. A 32-bit swap recovers the original plaintext, demonstrating the validity of the Feistel decryption process.

Note that the derivation does not require that F be a reversible function. To see this, take a limiting case in which F produces a constant output (e.g., all ones) regardless of the values of its two arguments. The equations still hold.

3.2 THE DATA ENCRYPTION STANDARD

The most widely used encryption scheme is based on the Data Encryption Standard (DES) adopted in 1977 by the National Bureau of Standards, now the National Institute of Standards and Technology (NIST), as Federal Information Processing Standard 46 (FIPS PUB 46). The algorithm itself is referred to as the Data Encryption Algorithm (DEA).[6] For DES, data are encrypted in 64-bit blocks using a 56-bit key.

[6]The terminology is a bit confusing. Until recently, the terms *DES* and *DEA* could be used interchangeably. However, the most recent edition of the DES document includes a specification of the DEA described here plus the triple DEA (TDEA) described in Chapter 6. Both DEA and TDEA are part of the Data Encryption Standard. Further, until the recent adoption of the official term *TDEA*, the triple DEA algorithm was typically referred to as *triple DES* and written as 3DES. For the sake of convenience, we use the term 3DES.

The algorithm transforms 64-bit input in a series of steps into a 64-bit output. The same steps, with the same key, are used to reverse the encryption.

The DES enjoys widespread use. It has also been the subject of much controversy concerning how secure the DES is. To appreciate the nature of the controversy, let us quickly review the history of the DES.

In the late 1960s, IBM set up a research project in computer cryptography led by Horst Feistel. The project concluded in 1971 with the development of an algorithm with the designation LUCIFER [FEIS73], which was sold to Lloyd's of London for use in a cash-dispensing system, also developed by IBM. LUCIFER is a Feistel block cipher that operates on blocks of 64 bits, using a key size of 128 bits. Because of the promising results produced by the LUCIFER project, IBM embarked on an effort to develop a marketable commercial encryption product that ideally could be implemented on a single chip. The effort was headed by Walter Tuchman and Carl Meyer, and it involved not only IBM researchers but also outside consultants and technical advice from NSA. The outcome of this effort was a refined version of LUCIFER that was more resistant to cryptanalysis but that had a reduced key size of 56 bits, to fit on a single chip.

In 1973, the National Bureau of Standards (NBS) issued a request for proposals for a national cipher standard. IBM submitted the results of its Tuchman-Meyer project. This was by far the best algorithm proposed and was adopted in 1977 as the Data Encryption Standard.

Before its adoption as a standard, the proposed DES was subjected to intense criticism, which has not subsided to this day. Two areas drew the critics' fire. First, the key length in IBM's original LUCIFER algorithm was 128 bits, but that of the proposed system was only 56 bits, an enormous reduction in key size of 72 bits. Critics feared that this key length was too short to withstand brute-force attacks. The second area of concern was that the design criteria for the internal structure of DES, the S-boxes, were classified. Thus, users could not be sure that the internal structure of DES was free of any hidden weak points that would enable NSA to decipher messages without benefit of the key. Subsequent events, particularly the recent work on differential cryptanalysis, seem to indicate that DES has a very strong internal structure. Furthermore, according to IBM participants, the only changes that were made to the proposal were changes to the S-boxes, suggested by NSA, that removed vulnerabilities identified in the course of the evaluation process.

Whatever the merits of the case, DES has flourished and is widely used, especially in financial applications. In 1994, NIST reaffirmed DES for federal use for another five years; NIST recommended the use of DES for applications other than the protection of classified information. In 1999, NIST issued a new version of its standard (FIPS PUB 46-3) that indicated that DES should only be used for legacy systems and that triple DES (which in essence involves repeating the DES algorithm three times on the plaintext using two or three different keys to produce the ciphertext) be used. We study triple DES in Chapter 6. Because the underlying encryption and decryption algorithms are the same for DES and triple DES, it remains important to understand the DES cipher.

DES Encryption

The overall scheme for DES encryption is illustrated in Figure 3.4. As with any encryption scheme, there are two inputs to the encryption function: the plaintext to

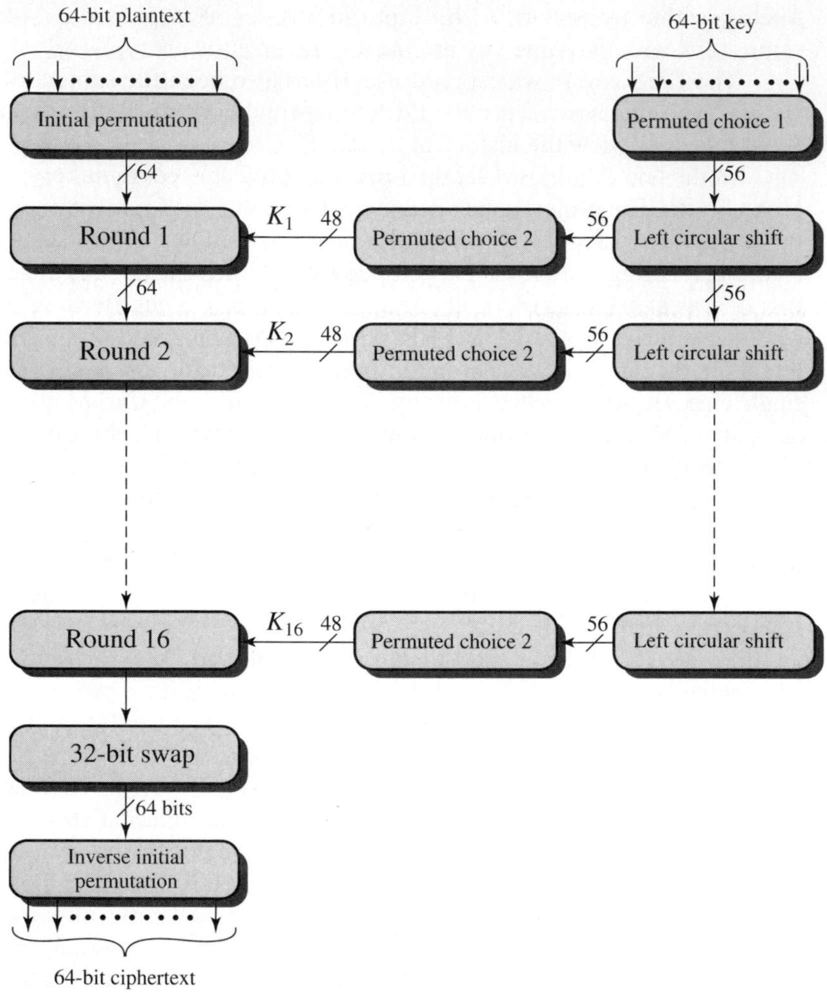

Figure 3.4 General Depiction of DES Encryption Algorithm

be encrypted and the key. In this case, the plaintext must be 64 bits in length and the key is 56 bits in length.[7]

Looking at the left-hand side of the figure, we can see that the processing of the plaintext proceeds in three phases. First, the 64-bit plaintext passes through an initial permutation (IP) that rearranges the bits to produce the *permuted input*. This is followed by a phase consisting of 16 rounds of the same function, which involves both permutation and substitution functions. The output of the last (sixteenth) round consists of 64 bits that are a function of the input plaintext and the key. The left and right halves of the output are swapped to produce the **preoutput**. Finally, the preoutput is passed through a permutation (IP^{-1}) that is the inverse of the initial permutation function, to

[7]Actually, the function expects a 64-bit key as input. However, only 56 of these bits are ever used; the other 8 bits can be used as parity bits or simply set arbitrarily.

produce the 64-bit ciphertext. With the exception of the initial and final permutations, DES has the exact structure of a Feistel cipher, as shown in Figure 3.2.

The right-hand portion of Figure 3.4 shows the way in which the 56-bit key is used. Initially, the key is passed through a permutation function. Then, for each of the 16 rounds, a *subkey* (K_i) is produced by the combination of a left circular shift and a permutation. The permutation function is the same for each round, but a different subkey is produced because of the repeated shifts of the key bits.

Initial Permutation The initial permutation and its inverse are defined by tables, as shown in Tables 3.2a and 3.2b, respectively. The tables are to be interpreted as follows. The input to a table consists of 64 bits numbered from 1 to 64. The 64 entries in the permutation table contain a permutation of the numbers from 1 to 64. Each entry in the permutation table indicates the position of a numbered input bit in the output, which also consists of 64 bits.

To see that these two permutation functions are indeed the inverse of each other, consider the following 64-bit input M:

M_1	M_2	M_3	M_4	M_5	M_6	M_7	M_8
M_9	M_{10}	M_{11}	M_{12}	M_{13}	M_{14}	M_{15}	M_{16}
M_{17}	M_{18}	M_{19}	M_{20}	M_{21}	M_{22}	M_{23}	M_{24}
M_{25}	M_{26}	M_{27}	M_{28}	M_{29}	M_{30}	M_{31}	M_{32}
M_{33}	M_{34}	M_{35}	M_{36}	M_{37}	M_{38}	M_{39}	M_{40}
M_{41}	M_{42}	M_{43}	M_{44}	M_{45}	M_{46}	M_{47}	M_{48}
M_{49}	M_{50}	M_{51}	M_{52}	M_{53}	M_{54}	M_{55}	M_{56}
M_{57}	M_{58}	M_{59}	M_{60}	M_{61}	M_{62}	M_{63}	M_{64}

where M_i is a binary digit. Then the permutation $X = \mathrm{IP}(M)$ is as follows:

M_{58}	M_{50}	M_{42}	M_{34}	M_{26}	M_{18}	M_{10}	M_2
M_{60}	M_{52}	M_{44}	M_{36}	M_{28}	M_{20}	M_{12}	M_4
M_{62}	M_{54}	M_{46}	M_{38}	M_{30}	M_{22}	M_{14}	M_6
M_{64}	M_{56}	M_{48}	M_{40}	M_{32}	M_{24}	M_{16}	M_8
M_{57}	M_{49}	M_{41}	M_{33}	M_{25}	M_{17}	M_9	M_1
M_{59}	M_{51}	M_{43}	M_{35}	M_{27}	M_{19}	M_{11}	M_3
M_{61}	M_{53}	M_{45}	M_{37}	M_{29}	M_{21}	M_{13}	M_5
M_{63}	M_{55}	M_{47}	M_{39}	M_{31}	M_{23}	M_{15}	M_7

If we then take the inverse permutation $Y = \mathrm{IP}^{-1}(X) = \mathrm{IP}^{-1}(\mathrm{IP}(M))$, it can be seen that the original ordering of the bits is restored.

Details of Single Round Figure 3.5 shows the internal structure of a single round. Again, begin by focusing on the left-hand side of the diagram. The left and right halves of each 64-bit intermediate value are treated as separate 32-bit quantities,

Table 3.2 Permutation Tables for DES

(a) Initial Permutation (IP)

58	50	42	34	26	18	10	2
60	52	44	36	28	20	12	4
62	54	46	38	30	22	14	6
64	56	48	40	32	24	16	8
57	49	41	33	25	17	9	1
59	51	43	35	27	19	11	3
61	53	45	37	29	21	13	5
63	55	47	39	31	23	15	7

(b) Inverse Initial Permutation (IP^{-1})

40	8	48	16	56	24	64	32
39	7	47	15	55	23	63	31
38	6	46	14	54	22	62	30
37	5	45	13	53	21	61	29
36	4	44	12	52	20	60	28
35	3	43	11	51	19	59	27
34	2	42	10	50	18	58	26
33	1	41	9	49	17	57	25

(c) Expansion Permutation (E)

32	1	2	3	4	5
4	5	6	7	8	9
8	9	10	11	12	13
12	13	14	15	16	17
16	17	18	19	20	21
20	21	22	23	24	25
24	25	26	27	28	29
28	29	30	31	32	1

(d) Permutation Function (P)

16	7	20	21	29	12	28	17
1	15	23	26	5	18	31	10
2	8	24	14	32	27	3	9
19	13	30	6	22	11	4	25

labeled L (left) and R (right). As in any classic Feistel cipher, the overall processing at each round can be summarized in the following formulas:

$$L_i = R_{i-1}$$
$$R_i = L_{i-1} \times \mathrm{F}(R_{i-1}, K_i)$$

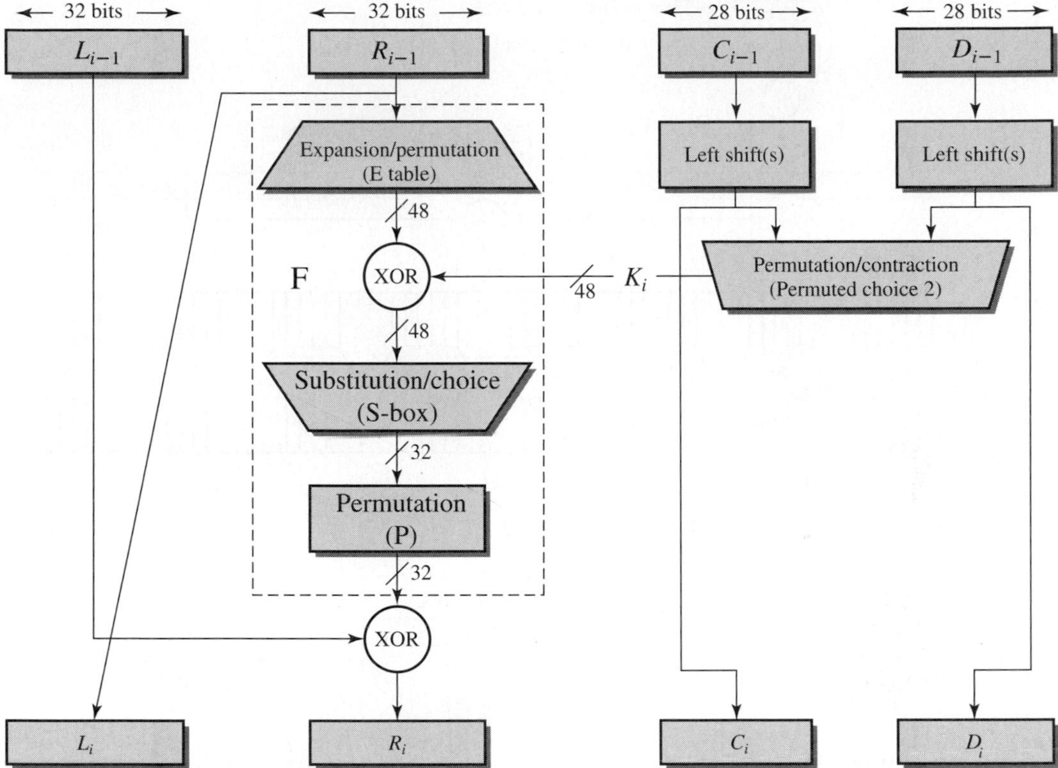

Figure 3.5 Single Round of DES Algorithm

The round key K_i is 48 bits. The R input is 32 bits. This R input is first expanded to 48 bits by using a table that defines a permutation plus an expansion that involves duplication of 16 of the R bits (Table 3.2c). The resulting 48 bits are XORed with K_i. This 48-bit result passes through a substitution function that produces a 32-bit output, which is permuted as defined by Table 3.2d.

The role of the S-boxes in the function F is illustrated in Figure 3.6. The substitution consists of a set of eight S-boxes, each of which accepts 6 bits as input and produces 4 bits as output. These transformations are defined in Table 3.3, which is interpreted as follows: The first and last bits of the input to box S_i form a 2-bit binary number to select one of four substitutions defined by the four rows in the table for S_i. The middle four bits select one of the sixteen columns. The decimal value in the cell selected by the row and column is then converted to its 4-bit representation to produce the output. For example, in S_1, for input 011001, the row is 01 (row 1) and the column is 1100 (column 12). The value in row 1, column 12 is 9, so the output is 1001.

Each row of an S-box defines a general reversible substitution. Figure 3.1 may be useful in understanding the mapping. The figure shows the substitution for row 0 of box S_1.

The operation of the S-boxes is worth further comment. Ignore for the moment the contribution of the key (K_i). If you examine the expansion table, you

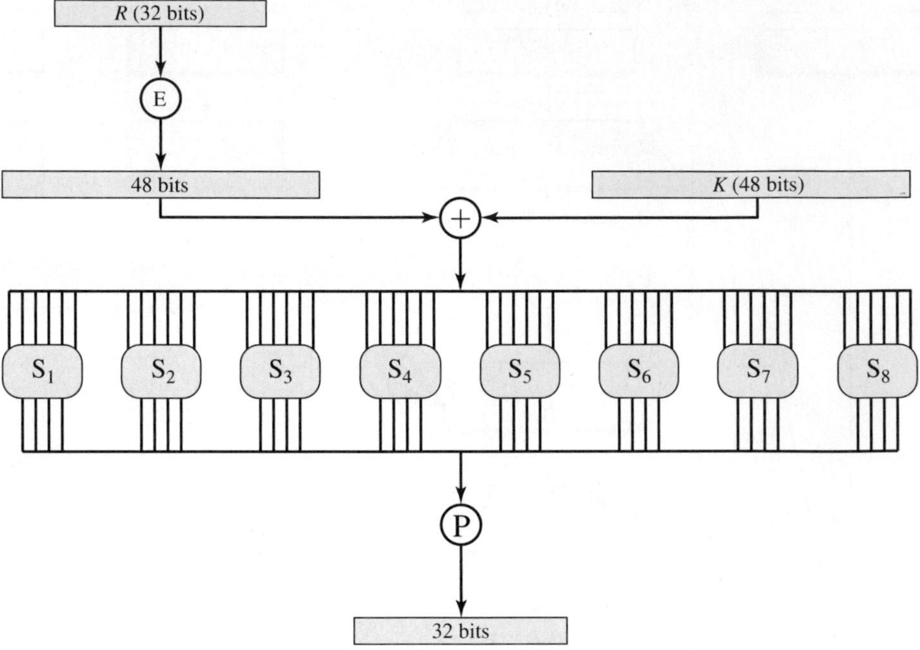

Figure 3.6 Calculation of F(R, K)

see that the 32 bits of input are split into groups of 4 bits, and then become groups of 6 bits by taking the outer bits from the two adjacent groups. For example, if part of the input word is

... efgh ijkl mnop ...

this becomes

... defghi hijklm lmnopq ...

The outer two bits of each group select one of four possible substitutions (one row of an S-box). Then a 4-bit output value is substituted for the particular 4-bit input (the middle four input bits). The 32-bit output from the eight S-boxes is then permuted, so that on the next round the output from each S-box immediately affects as many others as possible.

Key Generation Returning to Figures 3.4 and 3.5, we see that a 64-bit key is used as input to the algorithm. The bits of the key are numbered from 1 through 64; every eighth bit is ignored, as indicated by the lack of shading in Table 3.4a. The key is first subjected to a permutation governed by a table labeled Permuted Choice One (Table 3.4b). The resulting 56-bit key is then treated as two 28-bit quantities, labeled C_0 and D_0. At each round, C_{i-1} and D_{i-1} are separately subjected to a circular left shift, or rotation, of 1 or 2 bits, as governed by Table 3.4d. These shifted values serve as input to the next round. They also serve as input to Permuted Choice Two (Table 3.4c), which produces a 48-bit output that serves as input to the function $F(R_{i-1}, K_i)$.

Table 3.3 Definition of DES S-Boxes

S_1	14	4	13	1	2	15	11	8	3	10	6	12	5	9	0	7
	0	15	7	4	14	2	13	1	10	6	12	11	9	5	3	8
	4	1	14	8	13	6	2	11	15	12	9	7	3	10	5	0
	15	12	8	2	4	9	1	7	5	11	3	14	10	0	6	13
S_2	15	1	8	14	6	11	3	4	9	7	2	13	12	0	5	10
	3	13	4	7	15	2	8	14	12	0	1	10	6	9	11	5
	0	14	7	11	10	4	13	1	5	8	12	6	9	3	2	15
	13	8	10	1	3	15	4	2	11	6	7	12	0	5	14	9
S_3	10	0	9	14	6	3	15	5	1	13	12	7	11	4	2	8
	13	7	0	9	3	4	6	10	2	8	5	14	12	11	15	1
	13	6	4	9	8	15	3	0	11	1	2	12	5	10	14	7
	1	10	13	0	6	9	8	7	4	15	14	3	11	5	2	12
S_4	7	13	14	3	0	6	9	10	1	2	8	5	11	12	4	15
	13	8	11	5	6	15	0	3	4	7	2	12	1	10	14	9
	10	6	9	0	12	11	7	13	15	1	3	14	5	2	8	4
	3	15	0	6	10	1	13	8	9	4	5	11	12	7	2	14
S_5	2	12	4	1	7	10	11	6	8	5	3	15	13	0	14	9
	14	11	2	12	4	7	13	1	5	0	15	10	3	9	8	6
	4	2	1	11	10	13	7	8	15	9	12	5	6	3	0	14
	11	8	12	7	1	14	2	13	6	15	0	9	10	4	5	3
S_6	12	1	10	15	9	2	6	8	0	13	3	4	14	7	5	11
	10	15	4	2	7	12	9	5	6	1	13	14	0	11	3	8
	9	14	15	5	2	8	12	3	7	0	4	10	1	13	11	6
	4	3	2	12	9	5	15	10	11	14	1	7	6	0	8	13
S_7	4	11	2	14	15	0	8	13	3	12	9	7	5	10	6	1
	13	0	11	7	4	9	1	10	14	3	5	12	2	15	8	6
	1	4	11	13	12	3	7	14	10	15	6	8	0	5	9	2
	6	11	13	8	1	4	10	7	9	5	0	15	14	2	3	12
S_8	13	2	8	4	6	15	11	1	10	9	3	14	5	0	12	7
	1	15	13	8	10	3	7	4	12	5	6	11	0	14	9	2
	7	11	4	1	9	12	14	2	0	6	10	13	15	3	5	8
	2	1	14	7	4	10	8	13	15	12	9	0	3	5	6	11

Table 3.4 DES Key Schedule Calculation

(a) Input Key

1	2	3	4	5	6	7	8
9	10	11	12	13	14	15	16
17	18	19	20	21	22	23	24
25	26	27	28	29	30	31	32
33	34	35	36	37	38	39	40
41	42	43	44	45	46	47	48
49	50	51	52	53	54	55	56
57	58	59	60	61	62	63	64

(b) Permuted Choice One (PC-1)

57	49	41	33	25	17	9
1	58	50	42	34	26	18
10	2	59	51	43	35	27
19	11	3	60	52	44	36
63	55	47	39	31	23	15
7	62	54	46	38	30	22
14	6	61	53	45	37	29
21	13	5	28	20	12	4

(c) Permuted Choice Two (PC-2)

14	17	11	24	1	5	3	28
15	6	21	10	23	19	12	4
26	8	16	7	27	20	13	2
41	52	31	37	47	55	30	40
51	45	33	48	44	49	39	56
34	53	46	42	50	36	29	32

(d) Schedule of Left Shifts

Round number	1	2	3	4	5	6	7	8	9	10	11	12	13	14	15	16
Bits rotated	1	1	2	2	2	2	2	2	1	2	2	2	2	2	2	1

DES Decryption

As with any Feistel cipher, decryption uses the same algorithm as encryption, except that the application of the subkeys is reversed.

The Avalanche Effect

A desirable property of any encryption algorithm is that a small change in either the plaintext or the key should produce a significant change in the ciphertext. In particular, a change in one bit of the plaintext or one bit of the key should produce a change in many bits of the ciphertext. If the change were small, this might provide a way to reduce the size of the plaintext or key space to be searched.

DES exhibits a strong avalanche effect. Table 3.5 shows some results taken from [KONH81]. In Table 3.5a, two plaintexts that differ by one bit were used:

00000000 00000000 00000000 00000000 00000000 00000000 00000000 00000000

10000000 00000000 00000000 00000000 00000000 00000000 00000000 00000000

with the key

0000001 1001011 0100100 1100010 0011100 0011000 0011100 0110010

The Table 3.5a shows that after just three rounds, 21 bits differ between the two blocks. On completion, the two ciphertexts differ in 34 bit positions.

Table 3.5b shows a similar test in which a single plaintext is input:

01101000 10000101 00101111 01111010 00010011 01110110 11101011 10100100

with two keys that differ in only one bit position:

1110010 1111011 1101111 0011000 0011101 0000100 0110001 11011100

0110010 1111011 1101111 0011000 0011101 0000100 0110001 11011100

Again, the results show that about half of the bits in the ciphertext differ and that the avalanche effect is pronounced after just a few rounds.

Table 3.5 Avalanche Effect in DES

(a) Change in Plaintext		(b) Change in Key	
Round	**Number of bits that differ**	**Round**	**Number of bits that differ**
0	1	0	0
1	6	1	2
2	21	2	14
3	35	3	28
4	39	4	32
5	34	5	30
6	32	6	32
7	31	7	35
8	29	8	34
9	42	9	40
10	44	10	38
11	32	11	31
12	30	12	33
13	30	13	28
14	26	14	26
15	29	15	34
16	34	16	35

3.3 THE STRENGTH OF DES

Since its adoption as a federal standard, there have been lingering concerns about the level of security provided by DES. These concerns, by and large, fall into two areas: key size and the nature of the algorithm.

The Use of 56-Bit Keys

With a key length of 56 bits, there are 2^{56} possible keys, which is approximately 7.2×10^{16} keys. Thus, on the face of it, a brute-force attack appears impractical. Assuming that, on average, half the key space has to be searched, a single machine performing one DES encryption per microsecond would take more than a thousand years (see Table 2.2) to break the cipher.

However, the assumption of one encryption per microsecond is overly conservative. As far back as 1977, Diffie and Hellman postulated that the technology existed to build a parallel machine with 1 million encryption devices, each of which could perform one encryption per microsecond [DIFF77]. This would bring the average search time down to about 10 hours. The authors estimated that the cost would be about $20 million in 1977 dollars.

DES finally and definitively proved insecure in July 1998, when the Electronic Frontier Foundation (EFF) announced that it had broken a DES encryption using a special-purpose "DES cracker" machine that was built for less than $250,000. The attack took less than three days. The EFF has published a detailed description of the machine, enabling others to build their own cracker [EFF98]. And, of course, hardware prices will continue to drop as speeds increase, making DES virtually worthless.

It is important to note that there is more to a key-search attack than simply running through all possible keys. Unless known plaintext is provided, the analyst must be able to recognize plaintext as plaintext. If the message is just plain text in English, then the result pops out easily, although the task of recognizing English would have to be automated. If the text message has been compressed before encryption, then recognition is more difficult. And if the message is some more general type of data, such as a numerical file, and this has been compressed, the problem becomes even more difficult to automate. Thus, to supplement the brute-force approach, some degree of knowledge about the expected plaintext is needed, and some means of automatically distinguishing plaintext from garble is also needed. The EFF approach addresses this issue as well and introduces some automated techniques that would be effective in many contexts.

Fortunately, there are a number of alternatives to DES, the most important of which are AES and triple DES, discussed in Chapters 5 and 6, respectively.

The Nature of the DES Algorithm

Another concern is the possibility that cryptanalysis is possible by exploiting the characteristics of the DES algorithm. The focus of concern has been on the eight substitution tables, or S-boxes, that are used in each iteration. Because the design criteria for these boxes, and indeed for the entire algorithm, were not made public, there is a suspicion that the boxes were constructed in such a way that cryptanalysis is possible for an opponent who knows the weaknesses in the S-boxes. This assertion is tantalizing, and over the years a number of regularities and unexpected behaviors of the S-boxes have been discovered. Despite this, no one has so far succeeded in discovering the supposed fatal weaknesses in the S-boxes.[8]

Timing Attacks

We discuss timing attacks in more detail in Part Two, as they relate to public-key algorithms. However, the issue may also be relevant for symmetric ciphers. In essence, a timing attack is one in which information about the key or the plaintext is obtained by observing how long it takes a given implementation to perform decryptions on various ciphertexts. A timing attack exploits the fact that an encryption or decryption algorithm often takes slightly different amounts of time on different inputs. [HEVI99] reports on an approach that yields the Hamming weight (number of bits equal to one) of the secret key. This is a long way from knowing the actual key, but it is an intriguing first step. The authors conclude that DES appears to be fairly resistant to a successful timing attack but suggest some avenues to explore. Although this is an interesting line of attack, it so far appears unlikely that this technique will ever be successful against DES or more powerful symmetric ciphers such as triple DES and AES.

3.4 DIFFERENTIAL AND LINEAR CRYPTANALYSIS

For most of its life, the prime concern with DES has been its vulnerability to brute-force attack because of its relatively short (56 bits) key length. However, there has also been interest in finding cryptanalytic attacks on DES. With the increasing popularity of block ciphers with longer key lengths, including triple DES, brute-force attacks have become increasingly impractical. Thus, there has been increased emphasis on cryptanalytic attacks on DES and other symmetric block ciphers. In this section, we provide a brief overview of the two most powerful and promising approaches: differential cryptanalysis and linear cryptanalysis.

Differential Cryptanalysis

One of the most significant advances in cryptanalysis in recent years is differential cryptanalysis. In this section, we discuss the technique and its applicability to DES.

History Differential cryptanalysis was not reported in the open literature until 1990. The first published effort appears to have been the cryptanalysis of a block cipher called FEAL by Murphy [MURP90]. This was followed by a number of papers by Biham and Shamir, who demonstrated this form of attack on a variety of encryption algorithms and hash functions; their results are summarized in [BIHA93].

The most publicized results for this approach have been those that have application to DES. Differential cryptanalysis is the first published attack that is capable of breaking DES in less than 2^{55} complexity. The scheme, as reported in [BIHA93], can successfully cryptanalyze DES with an effort on the order of 2^{47} encryptions, requiring 2^{47} chosen plaintexts. Although 2^{47} is certainly significantly less than 2^{55}, the need for the adversary to find 2^{47} chosen plaintexts makes this attack of only theoretical interest.

[8]At least, no one has publicly acknowledged such a discovery.

Although differential cryptanalysis is a powerful tool, it does not do very well against DES. The reason, according to a member of the IBM team that designed DES [COPP94], is that differential cryptanalysis was known to the team as early as 1974. The need to strengthen DES against attacks using differential cryptanalysis played a large part in the design of the S-boxes and the permutation P. As evidence of the impact of these changes, consider these comparable results reported in [BIHA93]. Differential cryptanalysis of an eight-round LUCIFER algorithm requires only 256 chosen plaintexts, whereas an attack on an eight-round version of DES requires 2^{14} chosen plaintexts.

Differential Cryptanalysis Attack The differential cryptanalysis attack is complex; [BIHA93] provides a complete description. The rationale behind differential cryptanalysis is to observe the behavior of pairs of text blocks evolving along each round of the cipher, instead of observing the evolution of a single text block. Here, we provide a brief overview so that you can get the flavor of the attack.

We begin with a change in notation for DES. Consider the original plaintext block m to consist of two halves m_0, m_1. Each round of DES maps the right-hand input into the left-hand output and sets the right-hand output to be a function of the left-hand input and the subkey for this round. So, at each round, only one new 32-bit block is created. If we label each new block m_i $(2 \leq i \leq 17)$, then the intermediate message halves are related as follows:

$$m_{i+1} = m_{i-1} \oplus \mathrm{f}(m_i, K_i), \qquad i = 1, 2, \ldots, 16$$

In differential cryptanalysis, we start with two messages, m and m', with a known XOR difference $\Delta m = m \oplus m'$, and consider the difference between the intermediate message halves: $\Delta m_i = m_i \oplus m_i'$. Then we have:

$$\begin{aligned}
\Delta m_{i+1} &= m_{i+1} \oplus m_{i+1}' \\
&= [m_{i-1} \oplus \mathrm{f}(m_i, K_i)] \oplus [m_{i-1}' \oplus \mathrm{f}(m_i', K_i)] \\
&= \Delta m_{i-1} \oplus [\mathrm{f}(m_i, K_i) \oplus \mathrm{f}(m_i', K_i)]
\end{aligned}$$

Now, suppose that many pairs of inputs to f with the same difference yield the same output difference if the same subkey is used. To put this more precisely, let us say that *X may cause Y with probability p*, if for a fraction *p* of the pairs in which the input XOR is *X*, the output XOR equals *Y*. We want to suppose that there are a number of values of *X* that have high probability of causing a particular output difference. Therefore, if we know Δm_{i-1} and Δm_i with high probability, then we know Δm_{i+1} with high probability. Furthermore, if a number of such differences are determined, it is feasible to determine the subkey used in the function f.

The overall strategy of differential cryptanalysis is based on these considerations for a single round. The procedure is to begin with two plaintext messages m and m' with a given difference and trace through a probable pattern of differences after each round to yield a probable difference for the ciphertext. Actually, there are two probable patterns of differences for the two 32-bit halves: $(\Delta m_{17} \| \Delta m_{16})$. Next, we submit m and m' for encryption to determine the actual difference under the unknown key and compare the result to the probable difference. If there is a match,

$$\mathrm{E}(K, m) \oplus \mathrm{E}(K, m') = (\Delta m_{17} \| \Delta m_{16})$$

then we suspect that all the probable patterns at all the intermediate rounds are correct. With that assumption, we can make some deductions about the key bits. This procedure must be repeated many times to determine all the key bits.

Figure 3.7, based on a figure in [BIHA93], illustrates the propagation of differences through three rounds of DES. The probabilities shown on the right refer to the probability that a given set of intermediate differences will appear as a function of the input differences. Overall, after three rounds the probability that the output difference is as shown is equal to $0.25 \times 1 \times 0.25 = 0.0625$.

Linear Cryptanalysis

A more recent development is linear cryptanalysis, described in [MATS93]. This attack is based on finding linear approximations to describe the transformations performed in DES. This method can find a DES key given 2^{43} known plaintexts, as compared to 2^{47} chosen plaintexts for differential cryptanalysis. Although this is a minor improvement,

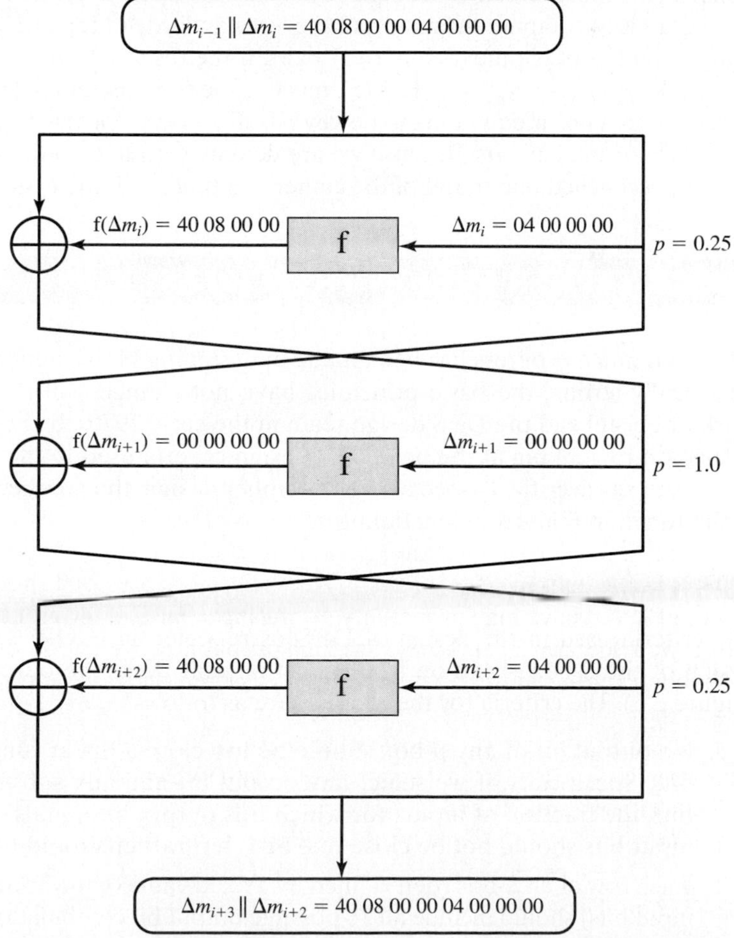

Figure 3.7 Differential Propagation through Three Round of DES (numbers in hexadecimal)

because it may be easier to acquire known plaintext rather than chosen plaintext, it still leaves linear cryptanalysis infeasible as an attack on DES. So far, little work has been done by other groups to validate the linear cryptanalytic approach.

We now give a brief summary of the principle on which linear cryptanalysis is based. For a cipher with n-bit plaintext and ciphertext blocks and an m-bit key, let the plaintext block be labeled P[1], ... P[n], the cipher text block C[1], ... C[n], and the key K[1], ..., K[m]. Then define

$$A[i, j, \ldots, k] = A[i] \oplus A[j] \oplus \ldots \oplus A[k]$$

The objective of linear cryptanalysis is to find an effective *linear* equation of the form:

$$\mathrm{P}[\alpha_1, \alpha_2, \ldots, \alpha_a] \oplus \mathrm{C}[\beta_1, \beta_2, \ldots, \beta_b] = \mathrm{K}[\gamma_1, \gamma_2, \ldots, \gamma_c]$$

(where $x = 0$ or $1; 1 \leq a, b \leq n, 1 \leq c \leq m$, and where the α, β, and γ terms represent fixed, unique bit locations) that holds with probability $p \neq 0.5$. The further p is from 0.5, the more effective the equation. Once a proposed relation is determined, the procedure is to compute the results of the left-hand side of the preceding equation for a large number of plaintext-ciphertext pairs. If the result is 0 more than half the time, assume $\mathrm{K}[\gamma_1, \gamma_2, \ldots, \gamma_c] = 0$. If it is 1 most of the time, assume $\mathrm{K}[\gamma_1, \gamma_2, \ldots, \gamma_c] = 1$. This gives us a linear equation on the key bits. Try to get more such relations so that we can solve for the key bits. Because we are dealing with linear equations, the problem can be approached one round of the cipher at a time, with the results combined.

3.5 BLOCK CIPHER DESIGN PRINCIPLES

Although much progress has been made in designing block ciphers that are cryptographically strong, the basic principles have not changed all that much since the work of Feistel and the DES design team in the early 1970s. It is useful to begin this discussion by looking at the published design criteria used in the DES effort. Then we look at three critical aspects of block cipher design: the number of rounds, design of the function F, and key scheduling.

DES Design Criteria

The criteria used in the design of DES, as reported in [COPP94], focused on the design of the S-boxes and on the P function that takes the output of the S boxes (Figure 3.6). The criteria for the S-boxes are as follows:

1. No output bit of any S-box should be too close a linear function of the input bits. Specifically, if we select any output bit and any subset of the six input bits, the fraction of inputs for which this output bit equals the XOR of these input bits should not be close to 0 or 1, but rather should be near 1/2.
2. Each row of an S-box (determined by a fixed value of the leftmost and rightmost input bits) should include all 16 possible output bit combinations.
3. If two inputs to an S-box differ in exactly one bit, the outputs must differ in at least two bits.

4. If two inputs to an S-box differ in the two middle bits exactly, the outputs must differ in at least two bits.
5. If two inputs to an S-box differ in their first two bits and are identical in their last two bits, the two outputs must not be the same.
6. For any nonzero 6-bit difference between inputs, no more than 8 of the 32 pairs of inputs exhibiting that difference may result in the same output difference.
7. This is a criterion similar to the previous one, but for the case of three S-boxes.

Coppersmith pointed out that the first criterion in the preceding list was needed because the S-boxes are the only nonlinear part of DES. If the S-boxes were linear (i.e., each output bit is a linear combination of the input bits), the entire algorithm would be linear and easily broken. We have seen this phenomenon with the Hill cipher, which is linear. The remaining criteria were primarily aimed at thwarting differential cryptanalysis and at providing good confusion properties.

The criteria for the permutation P are as follows:

1. The four output bits from each S-box at round i are distributed so that two of them affect (provide input for) "middle bits" of round $(i + 1)$ and the other two affect end bits. The two middle bits of input to an S-box are not shared with adjacent S-boxes. The end bits are the two left-hand bits and the two right-hand bits, which are shared with adjacent S-boxes.
2. The four output bits from each S-box affect six different S-boxes on the next round, and no two affect the same S-box.
3. For two S-boxes j, k, if an output bit from S_j affects a middle bit of S_k on the next round, then an output bit from S_k cannot affect a middle bit of S_j. This implies that for $j = k$, an output bit from S_j must not affect a middle bit of S_j.

These criteria are intended to increase the diffusion of the algorithm.

Number of Rounds

The cryptographic strength of a Feistel cipher derives from three aspects of the design: the number of rounds, the function F, and the key schedule algorithm. Let us look first at the choice of the number of rounds.

The greater the number of rounds, the more difficult it is to perform cryptanalysis, even for a relatively weak F. In general, the criterion should be that the number of rounds is chosen so that known cryptanalytic efforts require greater effort than a simple brute-force key search attack. This criterion was certainly used in the design of DES. Schneier [SCHN96] observes that for 16-round DES, a differential cryptanalysis attack is slightly less efficient than brute force: the differential cryptanalysis attack requires $2^{55.1}$ operations,[9] whereas brute force requires 2^{55}. If DES had 15 or fewer rounds, differential cryptanalysis would require less effort than brute-force key search.

This criterion is attractive because it makes it easy to judge the strength of an algorithm and to compare different algorithms. In the absence of a cryptanalytic

[9]Recall that differential cryptanalysis of DES requires 2^{47} *chosen* plaintext. If all you have to work with is known plaintext, then you must sort through a large quantity of known plaintext-ciphertext pairs looking for the useful ones. This brings the level of effort up to $2^{55.1}$.

breakthrough, the strength of any algorithm that satisfies the criterion can be judged solely on key length.

Design of Function F

The heart of a Feistel block cipher is the function F. As we have seen, in DES, this function relies on the use of S-boxes. This is also the case for most other symmetric block ciphers, as we shall see in Chapter 4. However, we can make some general comments about the criteria for designing F. After that, we look specifically at S-box design.

Design Criteria for F The function F provides the element of confusion in a Feistel cipher. Thus, it must be difficult to "unscramble" the substitution performed by F. One obvious criterion is that F be nonlinear, as we discussed previously. The more nonlinear F, the more difficult any type of cryptanalysis will be. There are several measures of nonlinearity, which are beyond the scope of this book. In rough terms, the more difficult it is to approximate F by a set of linear equations, the more nonlinear F is.

Several other criteria should be considered in designing F. We would like the algorithm to have good avalanche properties. Recall that, in general, this means that a change in one bit of the input should produce a change in many bits of the output. A more stringent version of this is the **strict avalanche criterion (SAC)** [WEBS86], which states that any output bit j of an S-box should change with probability 1/2 when any single input bit i is inverted for all i, j. Although SAC is expressed in terms of S-boxes, a similar criterion could be applied to F as a whole. This is important when considering designs that do not include S-boxes.

Another criterion proposed in [WEBS86] is the **bit independence criterion (BIC)**, which states that output bits j and k should change independently when any single input bit i is inverted, for all i, j, and k. The SAC and BIC criteria appear to strengthen the effectiveness of the confusion function.

S-Box Design One of the most intense areas of research in the field of symmetric block ciphers is that of S-box design. The papers are almost too numerous to count.[10] Here we mention some general principles. In essence, we would like any change to the input vector to an S-box to result in random-looking changes to the output. The relationship should be nonlinear and difficult to approximate with linear functions.

One obvious characteristic of the S-box is its size. An $n \times m$ S-box has n input bits and m output bits. DES has 6×4 S-boxes. Blowfish, described in Chapter 6, has 8×32 S-boxes. Larger S-boxes, by and large, are more resistant to differential and linear cryptanalysis [SCHN96]. On the other hand, the larger the dimension n, the (exponentially) larger the lookup table. Thus, for practical reasons, a limit of n equal to about 8 to 10 is usually imposed. Another practical consideration is that the larger the S-box, the more difficult it is to design it properly.

S-boxes are typically organized in a different manner than used in DES. An $n \times m$ S-box typically consists of 2^n rows of m bits each. The n bits of input select one of the rows of the S-box, and the m bits in that row are the output. For example, in an 8×32 S-box, if the input is 00001001, the output consists of the 32 bits in row 9 (the first row is labeled row 0).

---

[10] A good summary of S-box design studies through early 1996 can be found in [SCHN96].

Mister and Adams [MIST96] propose a number of criteria for S-box design. Among these are that the S-box should satisfy both SAC and BIC. They also suggest that all linear combinations of S-box columns should be *bent*. Bent functions are a special class of Boolean functions that are highly nonlinear according to certain mathematical criteria [ADAM90]. There has been increasing interest in designing and analyzing S-boxes using bent functions.

A related criterion for S-boxes is proposed and analyzed in [HEYS95]. The authors define the **guaranteed avalanche (GA)** criterion as follows: An S-box satisfies GA of order π if, for a 1-bit input change, at least π output bits change. The authors conclude that a GA in the range of order 2 to order 5 provides strong diffusion characteristics for the overall encryption algorithm.

For larger S-boxes, such as 8×32, the question arises as to the best method of selecting the S-box entries in order to meet the type of criteria we have been discussing. Nyberg, who has written a lot about the theory and practice of S-box design, suggests the following approaches (quoted in [ROBS95b]):

- **Random:** Use some pseudorandom number generation or some table of random digits to generate the entries in the S-boxes. This may lead to boxes with undesirable characteristics for small sizes (e.g., 6×4) but should be acceptable for large S-boxes (e.g., 8×32).
- **Random with testing:** Choose S-box entries randomly, then test the results against various criteria, and throw away those that do not pass.
- **Human-made:** This is a more or less manual approach with only simple mathematics to support it. It is apparently the technique used in the DES design. This approach is difficult to carry through for large S-boxes.
- **Math-made:** Generate S-boxes according to mathematical principles. By using mathematical construction, S-boxes can be constructed that offer proven security against linear and differential cryptanalysis, together with good diffusion.

A variation on the first technique is to use S-boxes that are both random and key dependent. An example of this approach is Blowfish, described in Chapter 6, which starts with S-boxes filled with pseudorandom digits and then alters the contents using the key. A tremendous advantage of key-dependent S-boxes is that, because they are not fixed, it is impossible to analyze the S-boxes ahead of time to look for weaknesses.

Key Schedule Algorithm

A final area of block cipher design, and one that has received less attention than S-box design, is the key schedule algorithm. With any Feistel block cipher, the key is used to generate one subkey for each round. In general, we would like to select subkeys to maximize the difficulty of deducing individual subkeys and the difficulty of working back to the main key. No general principles for this have yet been promulgated.

Hall suggests [ADAM94] that, at minimum, the key schedule should guarantee key/ciphertext Strict Avalanche Criterion and Bit Independence Criterion.

3.6 RECOMMENDED READING

There is a wealth of information on symmetric encryption. Some of the more worthwhile references are listed here. An essential reference work is [SCHN96]. This remarkable work contains descriptions of virtually every cryptographic algorithm and protocol published up to the time of the writing of the book. The author pulls together results from journals, conference proceedings, government publications, and standards documents and organizes these into a comprehensive and comprehensible survey. Another worthwhile and detailed survey is [MENE97]. A rigorous mathematical treatment is [STIN02].

The foregoing references provide coverage of public-key as well as symmetric encryption.

Perhaps the most detailed description of DES is [SIMO95]; the book also contains an extensive discussion of differential and linear cryptanalysis of DES. [BARK91] provides a readable and interesting analysis of the structure of DES and of potential cryptanalytic approaches to DES. [EFF98] details the most effective brute-force attack on DES. [COPP94] looks at the inherent strength of DES and its ability to stand up to cryptanalysis.

BARK91 Barker, W. *Introduction to the Analysis of the Data Encryption Standard (DES).* Laguna Hills, CA: Aegean Park Press, 1991.

COPP94 Coppersmith, D. "The Data Encryption Standard (DES) and Its Strength Against Attacks." *IBM Journal of Research and Development*, May 1994.

EFF98 Electronic Frontier Foundation. *Cracking DES: Secrets of Encryption Research, Wiretap Politics, and Chip Design.* Sebastopol, CA: O'Reilly, 1998

MENE97 Menezes, A.; van Oorschot, P.; and Vanstone, S. *Handbook of Applied Cryptography.* Boca Raton, FL: CRC Press, 1997.

SCHN96 Schneier, B. *Applied Cryptography.* New York: Wiley, 1996.

SIMO95 Simovits, M. *The DES: An Extensive Documentation and Evaluation.* Laguna Hills, CA: Aegean Park Press, 1995.

STIN02 Stinson, D. *Cryptography: Theory and Practice.* Boca Raton, FL: CRC Press, 2002.

3.7 KEY TERMS, REVIEW QUESTIONS, AND PROBLEMS

Key Terms

avalanche effect	diffusion	product cipher
block cipher	Feistel cipher	reversible mapping
confusion	irreversible mapping	round
Data Encryption Standard (DES)	key	round function
	linear cryptanalysis	subkey
differential cryptanalysis	permutation	substitution

Review Questions

3.1 Why is it important to study the Feistel cipher?

3.2 What is the difference between a block cipher and a stream cipher?

3.3 Why is it not practical to use an arbitrary reversible substitution cipher of the kind shown in Table 3.1?

3.4 What is a product cipher?

3.5 What is the difference between diffusion and confusion?

3.6 Which parameters and design choices determine the actual algorithm of a Feistel cipher?

3.7 What is the purpose of the S-boxes in DES?

3.8 Explain the avalanche effect.

3.9 What is the difference between differential and linear cryptanalysis?

Problems

3.1 **a.** In Section 3.1, under the subsection on the motivation for the Feistel cipher structure, it was stated that, for a block of n bits, the number of different reversible mappings for the ideal block cipher is $2^n!$. Justify.

b. In that same discussion, it was stated that for the ideal block cipher, which allows all possible reversible mappings, the size of the key is $n \times 2^n$ bits. But, if there are $2^n!$ possible mappings, it should take $\log_2 2^n!$ bits to discriminate among the different mappings, and so the key length should be $\log_2 2^n!$. However, $\log_2 2^n! < n \times 2^n$. Explain the discrepancy.

3.2 Consider a Feistel cipher composed of 16 rounds with block length 128 bits and key length 128 bits. Suppose that, for a given k, the key scheduling algorithm determines values for the first 8 round keys, $k_1, k_2, \ldots k_8$, and then sets

$$k_9 = k_8, k_{10} = k_7, k_{11} = k_6, \ldots, k_{16} = k_1$$

Suppose you have a ciphertext c. Explain how, with access to an encryption oracle, you can decrypt c and determine m using just a single oracle query. This shows that such a cipher is vulnerable to a chosen plaintext attack. (An encryption oracle can be thought of as a device that, when given a plaintext, returns the corresponding ciphertext. The internal details of the device are not known to you and you cannot break open the device. You can only gain information from the oracle by making queries to it and observing its responses.)

3.3 Consider a block encryption algorithm that encrypts blocks of length n, and let $N = 2^n$. Say we have t plaintext-ciphertext pairs $P_i, C_i = \mathrm{E}(K, P_1)$, where we assume that the key K selects one of the $N!$ possible mappings. Imagine that we wish to find K by exhaustive search. We could generate key K' and test whether $C_i = \mathrm{E}(K', P_i)$ for $1 \neq i \neq t$. If K' encrypts each P_i to its proper C_i, then we have evidence that $K = K'$. However, it may be the case that the mappings $\mathrm{E}(K, \cdot)$ and $\mathrm{E}(K', \cdot)$ exactly agree on the t plaintext-ciphertext pairs P_i, C_i and agree on no other pairs.

a. What is the probability that $\mathrm{E}(K, \cdot)$ and $\mathrm{E}(K', \cdot)$ are in fact distinct mappings?

b. What is the probability that $\mathrm{E}(K, \cdot)$ and $\mathrm{E}(K', \cdot)$ agree on another t' plaintext-ciphertext pairs where $0 \neq t' \neq N - t$?

3.4 Let π be a permutation of the integers $0, 1, 2, \ldots (2^n - 1)$, such that $\pi(m)$ gives the permuted value of m, $0 \neq m < 2^n$. Put another way, π maps the set of n-bit integers into itself and no two integers map into the same integer. DES is such a permutation for 64-bit integers. We say that π has a fixed point at m if $\pi(m) = m$. That is, if π is an encryption mapping, then a fixed point corresponds to a message that encrypts to itself. We are interested in the probability that π has no fixed points. Show the somewhat unexpected result that over 60% of mappings will have at least one fixed point.

3.5 Consider the substitution defined by row 1 of S-box S_1 in Table 3.3. Show a block diagram similar to Figure 3.1 that corresponds to this substitution.

3.6 Compute the bits number 1, 16, 33, and 48 at the output of the first round of the DES decryption, assuming that the ciphertext block is composed of all ones and the external key is composed of all ones.

3.7 Suppose the DES F function mapped every 32-bit input R, regardless of the value of the input K, to

a. 32-bit string of ones,
b. bitwise complement of R.

Hint: Use the following properties of the XOR operation:

1. What function would DES then compute?
2. What would the decryption look like?

$$(A \otimes B) \otimes C = A \otimes (B \otimes C)$$
$$A \otimes A = \mathbf{0}$$
$$A \otimes 0 = A$$
$$A \otimes \mathbf{1} = \text{bitwise complement of } A$$

where

A, B, C are n-bit strings of bits
0 is an n-bit string of zeros
1 is an n-bit string of one

3.8 This problem provides a numerical example of encryption using a one-round version of DES. We start with the same bit pattern for the key K and the plaintext, namely:

in hexadecimal notation:	0 1 2 3 4 5 6 7 8 9 A B C D E F
in binary notation:	0000 0001 0010 0011 0100 0101 0110 0111
	1000 1001 1010 1011 0100 1101 1110 1111

a. Derive K_1, the first-round subkey.
b. Derive L_0, R_0.
c. Expand R_0 to get E[R_0], where E[·] is the expansion function of Figure 3.8.
d. Calculate $A = \text{E}[R_0] \otimes K_1$.
e. Group the 48-bit result of (d) into sets of 6 bits and evaluate the corresponding S-box substitutions.
f. Concatenate the results of (e) to get a 32-bit result, B.
g. Apply the permutation to get P(B).
h. Calculate $R_1 = \text{P}(B) \otimes L_0$.
i. Write down the ciphertext.

3.9 Show that DES decryption is, in fact, the inverse of DES encryption.

3.10 The 32-bit swap after the sixteenth iteration of the DES algorithm is needed to make the encryption process invertible by simply running the ciphertext back through the algorithm with the key order reversed. This was demonstrated in Problem 3.7. However, it still may not be entirely clear why the 32-bit swap is needed. To demonstrate why, solve the following exercises. First, some notation:

$A \| B$ = the concatenation of the bit strings A and B

$\text{T}_i(R \| L)$ = the transformation defined by the ith iteration of the encryption algorithm, for $1 \neq I \neq 16$

$\text{TD}_i(R \| L)$ = the transformation defined by the ith iteration of the decryption algorithm, for $1 \neq i \neq 16$

$T_{17}(R \| L)$ = $L \| R$. This transformation occurs after the sixteenth iteration of the encryption algorithm.

a. Show that the composition $\mathrm{TD}_1(\mathrm{IP}(\mathrm{IP}^{-1}(\mathrm{T}_{17}(\mathrm{T}_{16}(L_{15}\|R_{15})))))$ is equivalent to the transformation that interchanges the 32-bit halves, L_{15} and R_{15}. That is, show that

$$\mathrm{TD}_1(\mathrm{IP}(\mathrm{IP}^{-1}(\mathrm{T}_{17}(\mathrm{T}_{16}(L_{15}\|R_{15}))))) = R_{15}\|L_{15}$$

b. Now suppose that we did away with the final 32-bit swap in the encryption algorithm. Then we would want the following equality to hold:

$$\mathrm{TD}_1(\mathrm{IP}(\mathrm{IP}^{-1}(\mathrm{T}_{16}(L_{15}\|R_{15})))) = L_{15}\|R_{15}$$

Does it?

3.11 Compare the initial permutation table (Table 3.2a) with the permuted choice one table (Table 3.4b). Are the structures similar? If so, describe the similarities. What conclusions can you draw from this analysis?

3.12 When using the DES algorithm for decryption, the 16 keys ($K_1, K_2, \ldots, K_{16}$) are used in reverse order. Therefore, the right-hand side of Figure 3.5 is no longer valid. Design a key-generation scheme with the appropriate shift schedule (analogous to Table 3.4d) for the decryption process.

3.13 a. Let X' be the bitwise complement of X. Prove that if the complement of the plaintext block is taken and the complement of an encryption key is taken, then the result of DES encryption with these values is the complement of the original ciphertext. That is,

$$\text{If } \quad Y = \mathrm{E}(K, X)$$
$$\text{Then } Y' = \mathrm{E}(K', X')$$

Hint: Begin by showing that for any two bit strings of equal length, A and B, $(A \otimes B)' = A \otimes \; \times B$.

b. It has been said that a brute-force attack on DES requires searching a key space of 2^{56} keys. Does the result of part (a) change that?

3.14 Show that in DES the first 24 bits of each subkey come from the same subset of 28 bits of the initial key and that the second 24 bits of each subkey come from a disjoint subset of 28 bits of the initial key.

3.15 For any block cipher, the fact that it is a nonlinear function is crucial to its security. To see this, suppose that we have a linear block cipher EL that encrypts 128-bit blocks of plaintext into 128-bit blocks of ciphertext. Let EL(k, m) denote the encryption of a 128-bit message m under a key k (the actual bit length of k is irrelevant). Thus

$$\mathrm{EL}(k, [m_1 \otimes m_2]) = \mathrm{EL}(k, m_1) \otimes \mathrm{EL}(k, m_1) \text{ for all 128-bit patterns } m_1, m_2$$

Describe how, with 128 chosen ciphertexts, an adversary can decrypt any ciphertext without knowledge of the secret key k. (A "chosen ciphertext" means that an adversary has the ability to choose a ciphertext and then obtain its decryption. Here, you have 128 plaintext/ciphertext pairs to work with and you have the ability to chose the value of the ciphertexts.)

Note: The following problems refer to simplified DES, described in Appendix C.

3.16 Refer to Figure C.2, which depicts key generation for S-DES.

a. How important is the initial P10 permutation function?

b. How important are the two LS-1 shift functions?

3.17 The equations for the variables q and r for S-DES are defined in the section on S-DES analysis. Provide the equations for s and t.

3.18 Using S-DES, decrypt the string (10100010) using the key (0111111101) by hand. Show intermediate results after each function (IP, F_K, SW, F_K, IP^{-1}). Then decode the first 4 bits of the plaintext string to a letter and the second 4 bits to another letter where we encode A through P in base 2 (i.e., A = 0000, B = 0001, . . . , P = 1111). *Hint:* As a midway check, after the application of SW, the string should be (00010011).

Programming Problems

3.19 Create software that can encrypt and decrypt using a general substitution block cipher.

3.20 Create software that can encrypt and decrypt using S-DES. Test data: Use plaintext, ciphertext, and key of Problem 3.15.

CHAPTER 4

FINITE FIELDS

The next morning at daybreak, Star flew indoors, seemingly keen for a lesson. I said, "Tap eight." She did a brilliant exhibition, first tapping it in 4, 4, then giving me a hasty glance and doing it in 2, 2, 2, 2, before coming for her nut.

It is astonishing that Star learned to count up to 8 with no difficulty, and of her own accord discovered that each number could be given with various different divisions, this leaving no doubt that she was consciously thinking each number. In fact, she did mental arithmetic, although unable, like humans, to name the numbers. But she learned to recognize their spoken names almost immediately and was able to remember the sounds of the names. Star is unique as a wild bird, who of her own free will pursued the science of numbers with keen interest and astonishing intelligence.

—*Living with Birds*, Len Howard

KEY POINTS

- A field is a set of elements on which two arithmetic operations (addition and multiplication) have been defined and which has the properties of ordinary arithmetic, such as closure, associativity, commutativity, distributivity, and having both additive and multiplicative inverses.
- Modular arithmetic is a kind of integer arithmetic that reduces all numbers to one of a fixed set $[0 \ldots n - 1]$ for some number n. Any integer outside this range is reduced to one in this range by taking the remainder after division by n.
- The greatest common divisor of two integers is the largest positive integer that exactly divides both integers.
- Finite fields are important in several areas of cryptography. A finite field is simply a field with a finite number of elements. It can be shown that the order of a finite field (number of elements in the field) must be a power of a prime p^n, where n is a positive integer.
- Finite fields of order p can be defined using arithmetic mod p.
- Finite fields of order p^n, for $n > 1$ can be defined using arithmetic over polynomials.

Finite fields have become increasingly important in cryptography. A number of cryptographic algorithms rely heavily on properties of finite fields, notably the Advanced Encryption Standard (AES) and elliptic curve cryptography.

The chapter begins with a brief overview of the concepts of group, ring, and field. This section is somewhat abstract; the reader may prefer to quickly skim this section on a first reading. Next, we need some elementary background in modular arithmetic and the Euclidean algorithm. We are then ready to discuss finite fields of the form GF(p), where p is a prime number. Next, we need some additional background, this time in polynomial arithmetic. The chapter concludes with a discussion of finite fields of the form GF(2^n), where n is a positive integer.

The concepts and techniques of number theory are quite abstract, and it is often difficult to grasp them intuitively without examples [RUBI97]. Accordingly, this chapter and Chapter 8 include a number of examples, each of which is highlighted in a shaded box.

4.1 GROUPS, RINGS, AND FIELDS

Groups, rings, and fields are the fundamental elements of a branch of mathematics known as abstract algebra, or modern algebra. In abstract algebra, we are concerned with sets on whose elements we can operate algebraically; that is, we can combine two elements of the set, perhaps in several ways, to obtain a third element of the set. These operations are subject to specific rules, which define the nature of the set. By convention, the notation for the two principal classes of operations on set elements is usually the same as the notation for addition and multiplication on ordinary numbers. However, it is important to note that, in abstract algebra, we are not limited to ordinary arithmetical operations. All this should become clear as we proceed.

Groups

A **group** G, sometimes denoted by $\{G, \cdot\}$, is a set of elements with a binary operation, denoted by $\cdot$, that associates to each ordered pair (a, b) of elements in G an element $(a \cdot b)$ in G, such that the following axioms are obeyed:[1]

(A1) Closure:	If a and b belong to G, then $a \cdot b$ is also in G.
(A2) Associative:	$a \cdot (b \cdot c) = (a \cdot b) \cdot c$ for all a, b, c in G.
(A3) Identity element:	There is an element e in G such that $a \cdot \mathrm{e} = \mathrm{e} \cdot a = a$ for all a in G.
(A4) Inverse element:	For each a in G there is an element a' in G such that $a \cdot a' = a' \cdot a = \mathrm{e}$.

Let N_n denote a set of n distinct symbols that, for convenience, we represent as $\{1, 2, \ldots, n\}$. A permutation of n distinct symbols is a one-to-one mapping from N_n to N_n. Define S_n to be the set of all permutations of n distinct symbols. Each element of S_n is represented by a permutation of the integers in $\{1, 2, \ldots, n\}$. It is easy to demonstrate that S_n is a group:

A1: If $\pi, \rho \in S_n$, then the composite mapping $\pi \cdot \rho$ is formed by permuting the elements of ρ according to the permutation π. For example, $\{3, 2, 1\} \cdot \{1, 3, 2\} = \{2, 3, 1\}$. Clearly, $\pi \cdot \rho \in S_n$.

[1]The operator $\cdot$ is generic and can refer to addition, multiplication, or some other mathematical operation.

A2: The composition of mappings is also easily seen to be associative.
A3: The identity mapping is the permutation that does not alter the order of the n elements. For S_n, the identity element is $\{1, 2, \ldots, n\}$.
A4: For any $\pi \in S_n$, the mapping that undoes the permutation defined by π is the inverse element for π. There will always be such an inverse. For example $\{2, 3, 1\} \cdot \{3, 1, 2\} = \{1, 2, 3\}$

If a group has a finite number of elements, it is referred to as a **finite group**, and the **order** of the group is equal to the number of elements in the group. Otherwise, the group is an **infinite group**.

A group is said to be **abelian** if it satisfies the following additional condition:

(A5) Commutative: $a \cdot b = b \cdot a$ for all a, b in G.

The set of integers (positive, negative, and 0) under addition is an abelian group. The set of nonzero real numbers under multiplication is an abelian group. The set S_n from the preceding example is a group but not an abelian group for $n > 2$.

When the group operation is addition, the identity element is 0; the inverse element of a is $-a$; and subtraction is defined with the following rule: $a - b = a + (-b)$.

Cyclic Group We define exponentiation within a group as repeated application of the group operator, so that $a^3 = a \cdot a \cdot a$. Further, we define $a^0 = \mathrm{e}$, the identity element; and $a^{-n} = (a')^n$. A group G is **cyclic** if every element of G is a power a^k (k is an integer) of a fixed element $a \in G$. The element a is said to **generate** the group G, or to be a **generator** of G. A cyclic group is always abelian, and may be finite or infinite.

The additive group of integers is an infinite cyclic group generated by the element 1. In this case, powers are interpreted additively, so that n is the nth power of 1.

Rings

A **ring** R, sometimes denoted by $\{R, +, \times\}$, is a set of elements with two binary operations, called *addition* and *multiplication*,[2] such that for all a, b, c in R the following axioms are obeyed:

(A1-A5) R is an abelian group with respect to addition; that is, R satisfies axioms A1 through A5. For the case of an additive group, we denote the identity element as 0 and the inverse of a as $-a$.

(M1) Closure under multiplication: If a and b belong to R, then ab is also in R.

(M2) Associativity of multiplication: $a(bc) = (ab)c$ for all a, b, c in R.

(M3) Distributive laws: $a(b + c) = ab + ac$ for all a, b, c in R.
$(a + b)c = ac + bc$ for all a, b, c in R.

[2]Generally, we do not use the multiplication symbol, $\times$, but denote multiplication by the concatenation of two elements.

In essence, a ring is a set in which we can do addition, subtraction $[a - b = a + (-b)]$, and multiplication without leaving the set.

With respect to addition and multiplication, the set of all n-square matrices over the real numbers is a ring.

A ring is said to be **commutative** if it satisfies the following additional condition:

(M4) Commutativity of multiplication: $ab = ba$ for all a, b in R.

Let S be the set of even integers (positive, negative, and 0) under the usual operations of addition and multiplication. S is a commutative ring. The set of all n-square matrices defined in the preceding example is not a commutative ring.

Next, we define an **integral domain**, which is a commutative ring that obeys the following axioms:

(M5) Multiplicative identity: There is an element 1 in R such that $a1 = 1a = a$ for all a in R.

(M6) No zero divisors: If a, b in R and $ab = 0$, then either $a = 0$ or $b = 0$.

Let S be the set of integers, positive, negative, and 0, under the usual operations of addition and multiplication. S is an integral domain.

Fields

A **field** F, sometimes denoted by $\{F, +, \times\}$, is a set of elements with two binary operations, called *addition* and *multiplication*, such that for all a, b, c in F the following axioms are obeyed:

(A1–M6) F is an integral domain; that is, F satisfies axioms A1 through A5 and M1 through M6.

(M7) Multiplicative inverse: For each a in F, except 0, there is an element a^{-1} in F such that $aa^{-1} = (a^{-1})a = 1$.

In essence, a field is a set in which we can do addition, subtraction, multiplication, and division without leaving the set. Division is defined with the following rule: $a/b = a(b^{-1})$.

Familiar examples of fields are the rational numbers, the real numbers, and the complex numbers. Note that the set of all integers is not a field, because not every element of the set has a multiplicative inverse; in fact, only the elements 1 and -1 have multiplicative inverses in the integers.

Figure 4.1 summarizes the axioms that define groups, rings, and fields.

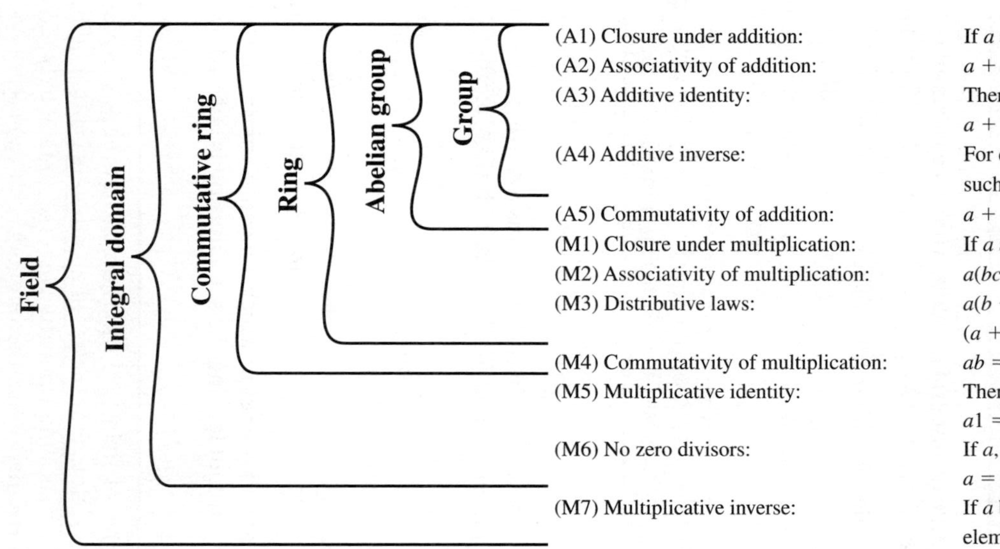

(A1) Closure under addition:	If a and b belong to S, then $a + b$ is also in S
(A2) Associativity of addition:	$a + (b + c) = (a + b) + c$ for all a, b, c in S
(A3) Additive identity:	There is an element 0 in R such that $a + 0 = 0 + a = a$ for all a in S
(A4) Additive inverse:	For each a in S there is an element $-a$ in S such that $a + (-a) = (-a) + a = 0$
(A5) Commutativity of addition:	$a + b = b + a$ for all a, b in S
(M1) Closure under multiplication:	If a and b belong to S, then ab is also in S
(M2) Associativity of multiplication:	$a(bc) = (ab)c$ for all a, b, c in S
(M3) Distributive laws:	$a(b + c) = ab + ac$ for all a, b, c in S $(a + b)c = ac + bc$ for all a, b, c in S
(M4) Commutativity of multiplication:	$ab = ba$ for all a, b in S
(M5) Multiplicative identity:	There is an element 1 in S such that $a1 = 1a = a$ for all a in S
(M6) No zero divisors:	If a, b in S and $ab = 0$, then either $a = 0$ or $b = 0$
(M7) Multiplicative inverse:	If a belongs to S and $a \neq 0$, there is an element a^{-1} in S such that $aa^{-1} = a^{-1}a = 1$

Figure 4.1 Group, Ring, and Field

4.2 MODULAR ARITHMETIC

Given any positive integer n and any nonnegative integer a, if we divide a by n, we get an integer quotient q and an integer remainder r that obey the following relationship:

$$a = qn + r \qquad 0 \le r < n; q = \lfloor a/n \rfloor \tag{4.1}$$

where $\lfloor x \rfloor$ is the largest integer less than or equal to x.

Figure 4.2 demonstrates that, given a and positive n, it is always possible to find q and r that satisfy the preceding relationship. Represent the integers on the number line; a will fall somewhere on that line (positive a is shown, a similar demonstration can be made for negative a). Starting at 0, proceed to n, $2n$, up to qn such that $qn \le a$ and $(q + 1)n > a$. The distance from qn to a is r, and we have found the unique values of q and r. The remainder r is often referred to as a **residue**.

$a = 11;$	$n = 7;$	$11 = 1 \times 7 + 4;$	$r = 4$	$q = 1$
$a = -11;$	$n = 7;$	$-11 = (-2) \times 7 + 3;$	$r = 3$	$q = -2$

If a is an integer and n is a positive integer, we define $a \bmod n$ to be the remainder when a is divided by n. The integer n is called the **modulus**. Thus, for any integer a, we can always write:

$$a = \lfloor a/n \rfloor \times n + (a \bmod n)$$

$11 \bmod 7 = 4; \qquad -11 \bmod 7 = 3$

Two integers a and b are said to be **congruent modulo** n, if $(a \bmod n) = (b \bmod n)$. This is written as $a \equiv b \pmod{n}$.[3]

$73 \equiv 4 \pmod{23}; \qquad 21 \equiv -9 \pmod{10}$

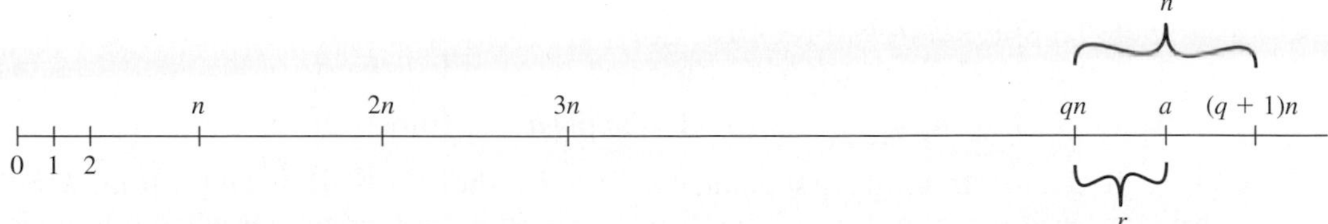

Figure 4.2 The Relationship $a = qn + r, 0 \le r < n$

[3]We have just used the operator mod in two different ways: first as a binary operator that produces a remainder, as in the expression $a \bmod b$; second as a congruence relation that shows the equivalence of two integers, as in the expression $a \equiv b \pmod{n}$. To distinguish the two uses, the mod term is enclosed in parentheses for a congruence relation; this is common but not universal in the literature. See Appendix D for a further discussion.

Divisors

We say that a nonzero b divides a if $a = mb$ for some m, where a, b, and m are integers. That is, b divides a if there is no remainder on division. The notation $b|a$ is commonly used to mean b divides a. Also, if $b|a$, we say that b is a **divisor** of a.

The positive divisors of 24 are 1, 2, 3, 4, 6, 8, 12, and 24.

The following relations hold:

- If $a|1$, then $a = \pm 1$.
- If $a|b$ and $b|a$, then $a = \pm b$.
- Any $b \neq 0$ divides 0.
- If $b|g$ and $b|h$, then $b|(mg + nh)$ for arbitrary integers m and n.

To see this last point, note that

If $b|g$, then g is of the form $g = b \times g_1$ for some integer g_1.
If $b|h$, then h is of the form $h = b \times h_1$ for some integer h_1.

So

$$mg + nh = mbg_1 + nbh_1 = b \times (mg_1 + nh_1)$$

and therefore b divides $mg + nh$.

$b = 7; g = 14; h = 63; m = 3; n = 2.$ $7|14$ and $7|63$. To show: $7|(3 \times 14 + 2 \times 63)$ We have $(3 \times 14 + 2 \times 63) = 7(3 \times 2 + 2 \times 9)$ And it is obvious that $7|(7(3 \times 2 + 2 \times 9))$

Note that if $a \equiv 0 \pmod{n}$, then $n|a$.

Properties of Congruences

Congruences have the following properties:

1. $a \equiv b \pmod{n}$ if $n|(a - b)$.
2. $a \equiv b \pmod{n}$ implies $b \equiv a \pmod{n}$..
3. $a \equiv b \pmod{n}$ and $b \equiv c \pmod{n}$ imply $a \equiv c \pmod{n}$.

To demonstrate the first point, if $n|(a - b)$, then $(a - b) = kn$ for some k. So we can write $a = b + kn$. Therefore, $(a \bmod n)$ = (remainder when $b + kn$ is divided by n) = (remainder when b is divided by n) = $(b \bmod n)$

$23 \equiv 8 \pmod{5}$	because	$23 - 8 = 15 = 5 \times 3$
$-11 \equiv 5 \pmod{8}$	because	$-11 - 5 = -16 = 8 \times (-2)$
$81 \equiv 0 \pmod{27}$	because	$81 - 0 = 81 = 27 \times 3$

The remaining points are as easily proved.

Modular Arithmetic Operations

Note that, by definition (Figure 4.2), the (mod n) operator maps all integers into the set of integers $\{0, 1, \ldots (n - 1)\}$. This suggests the question: Can we perform arithmetic operations within the confines of this set? It turns out that we can; this technique is known as **modular arithmetic**.

Modular arithmetic exhibits the following properties:

1. $[(a \bmod n) + (b \bmod n)] \bmod n = (a + b) \bmod n$
2. $[(a \bmod n) - (b \bmod n)] \bmod n = (a - b) \bmod n$
3. $[(a \bmod n) \times (b \bmod n)] \bmod n = (a \times b) \bmod n$

We demonstrate the first property. Define $(a \bmod n) = r_a$ and $(b \bmod n) = r_b$. Then we can write $a = r_a + jn$ for some integer j and $b = r_b + kn$ for some integer k. Then

$$\begin{aligned}(a + b) \bmod n &= (r_a + jn + r_b + kn) \bmod n \\ &= (r_a + r_b + (k + j)n) \bmod n \\ &= (r_a + r_b) \bmod n \\ &= [(a \bmod n) + (b \bmod n)] \bmod n\end{aligned}$$

The remaining properties are as easily proved. Here are examples of the three properties:

$11 \bmod 8 = 3; \quad 15 \bmod 8 = 7$
$[(11 \bmod 8) + (15 \bmod 8)] \bmod 8 = 10 \bmod 8 = 2$
$(11 + 15) \bmod 8 = 26 \bmod 8 = 2$

$[(11 \ mod\ 8) - (15 \ mod\ 8)] \ mod\ 8 = -4 \ mod\ 8 = 4$
$(11 - 15) \ mod\ 8 = -4 \ mod\ 8 = 4$

$[(11 \bmod 8) \times (15 \bmod 8)] \bmod 8 = 21 \bmod 8 = 5$
$(11 \times 15) \bmod 8 = 165 \bmod 8 = 5$

Exponentiation is performed by repeated multiplication, as in ordinary arithmetic. (We have more to say about exponentiation in Chapter 8.)

To find $11^7 \bmod 13$, we can proceed as follows:

$11^2 = 121 \equiv 4 \pmod{13}$
$11^4 = (11^2)^2 \equiv 4^2 \equiv 3 \pmod{13}$
$11^7 \equiv 11 \times 4 \times 3 \equiv 132 \equiv 2 \pmod{13}$

Thus, the rules for ordinary arithmetic involving addition, subtraction, and multiplication carry over into modular arithmetic.

Table 4.1 provides an illustration of modular addition and multiplication modulo 8. Looking at addition, the results are straightforward and there is a regular pattern to the matrix. Both matrices are symmetric about the main diagonal, in conformance to the commutative property of addition and multiplication. As in ordinary addition, there is an additive inverse, or negative, to each integer in modular arithmetic. In this case, the negative of an integer x is the integer y such that $(x + y) \bmod 8 = 0$. To find the additive inverse of an integer in the left-hand column, scan across the corresponding row of the matrix to find the value 0; the integer at the top of that column is the additive inverse; thus $(2 + 6) \bmod 8 = 0$. Similarly, the entries in the multiplication table are straightforward. In ordinary arithmetic, there is a multiplicative inverse, or reciprocal, to each integer. In modular arithmetic mod 8, the multiplicative inverse of x is the integer y such that $(x \times y) \bmod 8 = 1 \bmod 8$. Now, to find the multiplicative inverse of an integer from the multiplication table, scan across the matrix in the row for that integer to find the value 1; the integer at the top of that column is the multiplicative inverse; thus $(3 \times 3) \bmod 8 = 1$. Note that not all integers mod 8 have a multiplicative inverse; more about that later.

Table 4.1 Arithmetic Modulo 8

+	0	1	2	3	4	5	6	7
0	0	1	2	3	4	5	6	7
1	1	2	3	4	5	6	7	0
2	2	3	4	5	6	7	0	1
3	3	4	5	6	7	0	1	2
4	4	5	6	7	0	1	2	3
5	5	6	7	0	1	2	3	4
6	6	7	0	1	2	3	4	5
7	7	0	1	2	3	4	5	6

(a) Addition modulo 8

×	0	1	2	3	4	5	6	7
0	0	0	0	0	0	0	0	0
1	0	1	2	3	4	5	6	7
2	0	2	4	6	0	2	4	6
3	0	3	6	1	4	7	2	5
4	0	4	0	4	0	4	0	4
5	0	5	2	7	4	1	6	3
6	0	6	4	2	0	6	4	2
7	0	7	6	5	4	3	2	1

(b) Multiplication modulo 8

w	$-w$	w^{-1}
0	0	—
1	7	1
2	6	—
3	5	3
4	4	—
5	3	5
6	2	—
7	1	7

(c) Additive and multiplicative inverses modulo 8

Properties of Modular Arithmetic

Define the set Z_n as the set of nonnegative integers less than n:

$$Z_n = \{0, 1, \ldots, (n - 1)\}$$

This is referred to as the **set of residues**, or **residue classes** modulo n. To be more precise, each integer in Z_n represents a residue class. We can label the residue classes modulo n as $[0], [1], [2], \ldots, [n - 1]$, where

$$[r] = \{a: a \text{ is an integer}, a \equiv r \pmod{n}\}$$

The residue classes modulo 4 are

$$[0] = \{\ldots, -16, -12, -8, -4, 0, 4, 8, 12, 16, \ldots\}$$
$$[1] = \{\ldots, -15, -11, -7, -3, 1, 5, 9, 13, 17, \ldots\}$$
$$[2] = \{\ldots, -14, -10, -6, -2, 2, 6, 10, 14, 18, \ldots\}$$
$$[3] = \{\ldots, -13, -9, -5, -1, 3, 7, 11, 15, 19, \ldots\}$$

Of all the integers in a residue class, the smallest nonnegative integer is the one usually used to represent the residue class. Finding the smallest nonnegative integer to which k is congruent modulo n is called **reducing *k* modulo *n***.

If we perform modular arithmetic within Z_n, the properties shown in Table 4.2 hold for integers in Z_n. Thus, Z_n is a commutative ring with a multiplicative identity element (Figure 4.1).

There is one peculiarity of modular arithmetic that sets it apart from ordinary arithmetic. First, observe that, as in ordinary arithmetic, we can write the following:

$$\textbf{if } (a + b) \equiv (a + c) \pmod{n} \quad \textbf{then} \quad b \equiv c \pmod{n} \qquad \textbf{(4.2)}$$

$$(5 + 23) \equiv (5 + 7) \pmod{8}; \quad 23 \equiv 7 \pmod{8}$$

Table 4.2 Properties of Modular Arithmetic for Integers in $\mathbf{Z}_n$

Property	Expression
Commutative laws	$(w + x) \bmod n = (x + w) \bmod n$ $(w \times x) \bmod n = (x \times w) \bmod n$
Associative laws	$[(w + x) + y] \bmod n = [w + (x + y)] \bmod n$ $[(w \times x) \times y] \bmod n = [w \times (x \times y)] \bmod n$
Distributive laws	$[w \times (x + y)] \bmod n = [(w \times x) + (w \times y)] \bmod n$ $[w + (x \times y)] \bmod n = [(w + x) \times (w + y)] \bmod n$
Identities	$(0 + w) \bmod n = w \bmod n$ $(1 \times w) \bmod n = w \bmod n$
Additive inverse $(-w)$	For each $w \in Z_n$, there exists a z such that $w + z \equiv 0 \bmod n$

Equation (4.2) is consistent with the existence of an additive inverse. Adding the additive inverse of a to both sides of Equation (4.2), we have:

$$((-a) + a + b) \equiv ((-a) + a + c)(\text{mod } n)$$
$$b \equiv c \ (\text{mod } n)$$

However, the following statement is true only with the attached condition:

$$\textbf{if}(a \times b) \equiv (a \times c)(\text{mod } n) \textbf{ then } b \equiv c \ (\text{mod } n) \quad \textbf{if } a \text{ is relatively prime to } n \quad \textbf{(4.3)}$$

where the term *relatively prime* is defined as follows: two integers are **relatively prime** if their only common positive integer factor is 1. Similar to the case of Equation (4.2), we can say that Equation (4.3) is consistent with the existence of a multiplicative inverse. Applying the multiplicative inverse of a to both sides of Equation (4.2), we have:

$$((a^{-1})ab) \equiv ((a^{-1})ac)(\text{mod } n)$$
$$b \equiv c \ (\text{mod } n)$$

To see this, consider an example in which the condition of Equation (4.3) does not hold. The integers 6 and 8 are not relatively prime, since they have the common factor 2. We have the following:

$$6 \times 3 = 18 \equiv 2 \ (\text{mod } 8)$$
$$6 \times 7 = 42 \equiv 2 \ (\text{mod } 8)$$

Yet $3 \not\equiv 7 \ (\text{mod } 8)$.

The reason for this strange result is that for any general modulus n, a multiplier a that is applied in turn to the integers 0 through $(n - 1)$ will fail to produce a complete set of residues if a and n have any factors in common.

With $a = 6$ and $n = 8$,

Z_8	0	1	2	3	4	5	6	7
Multiply by 6	0	6	12	18	24	30	36	42
Residues	0	6	4	2	0	6	4	2

Because we do not have a complete set of residues when multiplying by 6, more than one integer in Z_8 maps into the same residue. Specifically, $6 \times 0 \text{ mod } 8 = 6 \times 4 \text{ mod } 8$; $6 \times 1 \text{ mod } 8 = 6 \times 5 \text{ mod } 8$; and so on. Because this is a many-to-one mapping, there is not a unique inverse to the multiply operation.

However, if we take $a = 5$ and $n = 8$, whose only common factor is 1,

Z_8	0	1	2	3	4	5	6	7
Multiply by 5	0	5	10	15	20	25	30	35
Residues	0	5	2	7	4	1	6	3

The line of residues contains all the integers in Z_8, in a different order.

In general, an integer has a multiplicative inverse in Z_n if that integer is relatively prime to n. Table 4.1c shows that the integers 1, 3, 5, and 7 have a multiplicative inverse in Z_8, but 2, 4, and 6 do not.

4.3 THE EUCLIDEAN ALGORITHM

One of the basic techniques of number theory is the Euclidean algorithm, which is a simple procedure for determining the greatest common divisor of two positive integers.

Greatest Common Divisor

Recall that nonzero b is defined to be a divisor of a if $a = mb$ for some m, where a, b, and m are integers. We will use the notation $\gcd(a, b)$ to mean the **greatest common divisor** of a and b. The positive integer c is said to be the greatest common divisor of a and b if

1. c is a divisor of a and of b;
2. any divisor of a and b is a divisor of c.

An equivalent definition is the following:

$$\gcd(a, b) = \max[k, \text{ such that } k|a \text{ and } k|b]$$

Because we require that the greatest common divisor be positive, $\gcd(a, b) = \gcd(a, -b) = \gcd(-a, b) = \gcd(-a, -b)$. In general, $\gcd(a, b) = \gcd(|a|, |b|)$.

$$\gcd(60, 24) = \gcd(60, -24) = 12$$

Also, because all nonzero integers divide 0, we have $\gcd(a, 0) = |a|$.

We stated that two integers a and b are relatively prime if their only common positive integer factor is 1. This is equivalent to saying that a and b are relatively prime if $\gcd(a, b) = 1$.

> 8 and 15 are relatively prime because the positive divisors of 8 are 1, 2, 4, and 8, and the positive divisors of 15 are 1, 3, 5, and 15, so 1 is the only integer on both lists.

Finding the Greatest Common Divisor

The Euclidean algorithm is based on the following theorem: For any nonnegative integer a and any positive integer b,

$$\gcd(a, b) = \gcd(b, a \bmod b) \tag{4.4}$$

$$\gcd(55, 22) = \gcd(22, 55 \bmod 22) = \gcd(22, 11) = 11$$

To see that Equation (4.4) works, let $d = \gcd(a, b)$. Then, by the definition of gcd, $d|a$ and $d|b$. For any positive integer b, a can be expressed in the form

$$a = kb + r \equiv r \pmod{b}$$
$$a \bmod b = r$$

with k, r integers. Therefore, $(a \bmod b) = a - kb$ for some integer k. But because $d|b$, it also divides kb. We also have $d|a$. Therefore, $d|(a \bmod b)$. This shows that d is a common divisor of b and $(a \bmod b)$. Conversely, if d is a common divisor of b and $(a \bmod b)$, then $d|kb$ and thus $d|[kb + (a \bmod b)]$, which is equivalent to $d|a$. Thus, the set of common divisors of a and b is equal to the set of common divisors of b and $(a \bmod b)$. Therefore, the gcd of one pair is the same as the gcd of the other pair, proving the theorem.

Equation (4.4) can be used repetitively to determine the greatest common divisor.

$$\gcd(18, 12) = \gcd(12, 6) = \gcd(6, 0) = 6$$
$$\gcd(11, 10) = \gcd(10, 1) = \gcd(1, 0) = 1$$

The Euclidean algorithm makes repeated use of Equation (4.4) to determine the greatest common divisor, as follows. The algorithm assumes $a > b > 0$. It is acceptable to restrict the algorithm to positive integers because $\gcd(a, b) = \gcd(|a|, |b|)$.

```
EUCLID(a, b)
1.   A ← a; B ← b
2.   if B = 0  return  A = gcd(a, b)
3.   R = A mod B
4.   A ← B
5.   B ← R
6.   goto 2
```

The algorithm has the following progression:

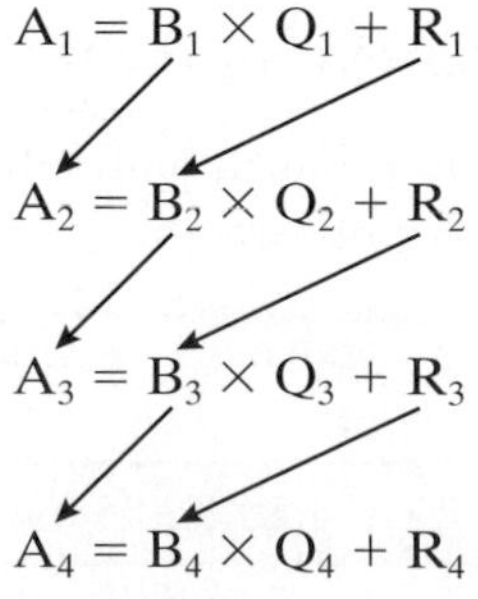

$$A_1 = B_1 \times Q_1 + R_1$$
$$A_2 = B_2 \times Q_2 + R_2$$
$$A_3 = B_3 \times Q_3 + R_3$$
$$A_4 = B_4 \times Q_4 + R_4$$

To find gcd(1970, 1066)

$1970 = 1 \times 1066 + 904$	gcd(1066, 904)
$1066 = 1 \times 904 + 162$	gcd(904, 162)
$904 = 5 \times 162 + 94$	gcd(162, 94)
$162 = 1 \times 94 + 68$	gcd(94, 68)
$94 = 1 \times 68 + 26$	gcd(68, 26)
$68 = 2 \times 26 + 16$	gcd(26, 16)
$26 = 1 \times 16 + 10$	gcd(16, 10)
$16 = 1 \times 10 + 6$	gcd(10, 6)
$10 = 1 \times 6 + 4$	gcd(6, 4)
$6 = 1 \times 4 + 2$	gcd(4, 2)
$4 = 2 \times 2 + 0$	gcd(2, 0)

Therefore, gcd(1970, 1066) = 2

The alert reader may ask how we can be sure that this process terminates. That is, how can we be sure that at some point B divides A? If not, we would get an endless sequence of positive integers, each one strictly smaller than the one before, and this is clearly impossible.

4.4 FINITE FIELDS OF THE FORM GF(p)

In Section 4.1, we defined a field as a set that obeys all of the axioms of Figure 4.1 and gave some examples of infinite fields. Infinite fields are not of particular interest in the context of cryptography. However, finite fields play a crucial role in many cryptographic algorithms. It can be shown that the order of a finite field (number of elements in the field) must be a power of a prime p^n, where n is a positive integer. We discuss prime numbers in detail in Chapter 8. Here, we need only say that a prime number is an integer whose only positive integer factors are itself and 1. That is, the only positive integers that are divisors of p are p and 1.

The finite field of order p^n is generally written GF(p^n); GF stands for Galois field, in honor of the mathematician who first studied finite fields. Two special cases are of interest for our purposes. For $n = 1$, we have the finite field GF(p); this finite field has a different structure than that for finite fields with $n > 1$ and is studied in this section. In Section 4.6, we look at finite fields of the form GF(2^n).

Finite Fields of Order p

For a given prime, p, the finite field of order p, GF(p) is defined as the set Z_p of integers $\{0, 1, \ldots, p - 1\}$, together with the arithmetic operations modulo p.

Recall that we showed in Section 4.2 that the set Z_n of integers $\{0, 1, \ldots, n - 1\}$, together with the arithmetic operations modulo n, is a commutative ring (Table 4.2). We further observed that any integer in Z_n has a multiplicative inverse if and only if that integer is relatively prime to n [see discussion of Equation (4.3)].[4] If n is prime,

[4]As stated in the discussion of Equation (4.3), two integers are **relatively prime** if their only common positive integer factor is 1.

then all of the nonzero integers in Z_n are relatively prime to n, and therefore there exists a multiplicative inverse for all of the nonzero integers in Z_n. Thus, we can add the following properties to those listed in Table 4.2 for Z_p:

Multiplicative inverse (w^{-1})	For each $w \in Z_p$, $w \neq 0$, there exists a $z \in Z_p$ such that $w \times z \equiv 1 \pmod{p}$

Because w is relatively prime to p, if we multiply all the elements of Z_p by w, the resulting residues are all of the elements of Z_p permuted. Thus, exactly one of the residues has the value 1. Therefore, there is some integer in Z_p that, when multiplied by w, yields the residue 1. That integer is the multiplicative inverse of w, designated w^{-1}. Therefore, Z_p is in fact a finite field. Further, Equation (4.3) is consistent with the existence of a multiplicative inverse and can be rewritten without the condition:

$$\textbf{if } (a \times b) \equiv (a \times c) \pmod{p} \textbf{ then } b \equiv c \pmod{p} \qquad \textbf{(4.5)}$$

Multiplying both sides of Equation (4.5) by the multiplicative inverse of a, we have:

$$((a^{-1}) \times a \times b) \equiv ((a^{-1}) \times a \times c) \pmod{p}$$
$$b \equiv c \pmod{p}$$

The simplest finite field is GF(2). Its arithmetic operations are easily summarized:

+	0	1
0	0	1
1	1	0

Addition

×	0	1
0	0	0
1	0	1

Multiplication

w	$-w$	w^{-1}
0	0	—
1	1	1

Inverses

In this case, addition is equivalent to the exclusive-OR (XOR) operation, and multiplication is equivalent to the logical AND operation.

Table 4.3 shows GF(7). This is a field of order 7 using modular arithmetic modulo 7. As can be seen, it satisfies all of the properties required of a field (Figure 4.1). Compare this table with Table 4.1. In the latter case, we see that the set Z_8, using modular arithmetic modulo 8, is not a field. Later in this chapter, we show how to define addition and multiplication operations on Z_8 in such a way as to form a finite field.

Finding the Multiplicative Inverse in GF(p)

It is easy to find the multiplicative inverse of an element in GF(p) for small values of p. You simply construct a multiplication table, such as shown in Table 4.3b, and the desired result can be read directly. However, for large values of p, this approach is not practical.

If $\gcd(m, b) = 1$, then b has a multiplicative inverse modulo m. That is, for positive integer $b < m$, there exists a $b^{-1} < m$ such that $bb^{-1} = 1 \bmod m$. The Euclidean algorithm can be extended so that, in addition to finding $\gcd(m, b)$, if the gcd is 1, the algorithm returns the multiplicative inverse of b.

Table 4.3 Arithmetic in GF(7)

+	0	1	2	3	4	5	6
0	0	1	2	3	4	5	6
1	1	2	3	4	5	6	0
2	2	3	4	5	6	0	1
3	3	4	5	6	0	1	2
4	4	5	6	0	1	2	3
5	5	6	0	1	2	3	4
6	6	0	1	2	3	4	5

(a) Addition modulo 7

×	0	1	2	3	4	5	6
0	0	0	0	0	0	0	0
1	0	1	2	3	4	5	6
2	0	2	4	6	1	3	5
3	0	3	6	2	5	1	4
4	0	4	1	5	2	6	3
5	0	5	3	1	6	4	2
6	0	6	5	4	3	2	1

(b) Multiplication modulo 7

w	$-w$	w^{-1}
0	0	—
1	6	1
2	5	4
3	4	5
4	3	2
5	2	3
6	1	6

(c) Additive and multiplicative inverses modulo 7

```
EXTENDED EUCLID(m, b)
1. (A1, A2, A3) ← (1, 0, m); (B1, B2, B3) ← (0, 1, b)
2. if B3 = 0 return A3 = gcd(m, b); no inverse
3. if B3 = 1 return B3 = gcd(m, b); B2 = b^-1 mod m
4. Q = ⌊A3 / B3⌋
5. (T1, T2, T3) ← (A1 - QB1, A2 - QB2, A3 - QB3)
6. (A1, A2, A3) ← (B1, B2, B3)
7. (B1, B2, B3) ← (T1, T2, T3)
8. goto 2
```

Throughout the computation, the following relationships hold:

$$m\mathrm{T1} + b\mathrm{T2} = \mathrm{T3} \qquad m\mathrm{A1} + b\mathrm{A2} = \mathrm{A3} \qquad m\mathrm{B1} + b\mathrm{B2} = \mathrm{B3}$$

To see that this algorithm correctly returns gcd(m, b), note that if we equate A and B in the Euclidean algorithm with A3 and B3 in the extended Euclidean algorithm, then the treatment of the two variables is identical. At each iteration of the Euclidean algorithm, A is set equal to the previous value of B and B is set equal to the previous value of A mod B. Similarly, at each step of the extended

Euclidean algorithm, A3 is set equal to the previous value of B3, and B3 is set equal to the previous value of A3 minus the integer quotient of A3 multiplied by B3. This latter value is simply the remainder of A3 divided by B3, which is A3 mod B3.

Note also that if $\gcd(m, b) = 1$, then on the final step we would have B3 = 0 and A3 = 1. Therefore, on the preceding step, B3 = 1. But if B3 = 1, then we can say the following:

$$\begin{aligned} m\text{B1} + b\text{B2} &= \text{B3} \\ m\text{B1} + b\text{B2} &= 1 \\ b\text{B2} &= 1 - m\text{B1} \\ b\text{B2} &\equiv 1 \pmod{m} \end{aligned}$$

And B2 is the multiplicative inverse of b, modulo m.

Table 4.4 is an example of the execution of the algorithm. It shows that $\gcd(1759, 550) = 1$ and that the multiplicative inverse of 550 is 355; that is, $550 \times 355 \equiv 1 \pmod{1759}$.

For a more detailed proof of this algorithm, see [KNUT97].

Summary

In this section, we have shown how to construct a finite field of order p, where p is prime. Specifically, we defined GF(p) with the following properties:

1. GF(p) consists of p elements.
2. The binary operations + and × are defined over the set. The operations of addition, subtraction, multiplication, and division can be performed without leaving the set. Each element of the set other than 0 has a multiplicative inverse.

We have shown that the elements of GF(p) are the integers $\{0, 1, \ldots, p\}$ and that the arithmetic operations are addition and multiplication mod p.

Table 4.4 Finding the Multiplicative Inverse of 550 in GF(1759)

Q	A1	A2	A3	B1	B2	B3
—	1	0	1759	0	1	550
3	0	1	550	1	−3	109
5	1	−3	109	−5	16	5
21	−5	16	5	106	−339	4
1	106	−339	4	−111	355	1

4.5 POLYNOMIAL ARITHMETIC

Before pursuing our discussion of finite fields, we need to introduce the interesting subject of polynomial arithmetic. We are concerned with polynomials in a single variable x, and we can distinguish three classes of polynomial arithmetic:

- Ordinary polynomial arithmetic, using the basic rules of algebra
- Polynomial arithmetic in which the arithmetic on the coefficients is performed modulo p; that is, the coefficients are in GF(p)
- Polynomial arithmetic in which the coefficients are in GF(p), and the polynomials are defined modulo a polynomial $m(x)$ whose highest power is some integer n

This section examines the first two classes, and the next section covers the last class.

Ordinary Polynomial Arithmetic

A **polynomial** of degree n (integer $n \geq 0$) is an expression of the form

$$f(x) = a_n x^n + a_{n-1}x^{n-1} + \cdots + a_1 x + a_0 = \sum_{i=0}^{n} a_i x^i$$

where the a_i are elements of some designated set of numbers S, called the **coefficient set**, and $a_n \neq 0$. We say that such polynomials are defined over the coefficient set S.

A zeroth-degree polynomial is called a **constant polynomial** and is simply an element of the set of coefficients. An nth-degree polynomial is said to be a **monic polynomial** if $a_n = 1$.

In the context of abstract algebra, we are usually not interested in evaluating a polynomial for a particular value of x [e.g., $f(7)$]. To emphasize this point, the variable x is sometimes referred to as the **indeterminate**.

Polynomial arithmetic includes the operations of addition, subtraction, and multiplication. These operations are defined in a natural way as though the variable x was an element of S. Division is similarly defined, but requires that S be a field. Examples of fields include the real numbers, rational numbers, and Z_p for p prime. Note that the set of all integers is not a field and does not support polynomial division.

Addition and subtraction are performed by adding or subtracting corresponding coefficients. Thus, if

$$f(x) = \sum_{i=0}^{n} a_i x^i; \quad g(x) = \sum_{i=0}^{m} b_i x^i; \quad n \geq m$$

then addition is defined as

$$f(x) + g(x) = \sum_{i=0}^{m} (a_i + b_i)x^i + \sum_{i=m+1}^{n} a_i x^i$$

and multiplication is defined as

$$f(x) \times g(x) = \sum_{i=0}^{n+m} c_i x^i$$

where

$$c_k = a_0 b_k + a_1 b_{k-1} + \cdots + a_{k-1} b_1 + a_k b_0$$

In the last formula, we treat a_i as zero for $i > n$ and b_i as zero for $i > m$. Note that the degree of the product is equal to the sum of the degrees of the two polynomials.

> As an example, let $f(x) = x^3 + x^2 + 2$ and $g(x) = x^2 - x + 1$, where S is the set of integers. Then
>
> $$f(x) + g(x) = x^3 + 2x^2 - x + 3$$
> $$f(x) - g(x) = x^3 + x + 1$$
> $$f(x) \times g(x) = x^5 + 3x^2 - 2x + 2$$
>
> Figures 4.3a through 4.3c show the manual calculations. We comment on division subsequently.

Polynomial Arithmetic with Coefficients in Zp

Let us now consider polynomials in which the coefficients are elements of some field F. We refer to this as a polynomial over the field F. In that case, it is easy to show that the set of such polynomials is a ring, referred to as a **polynomial ring**. That is, if we consider each distinct polynomial to be an element of the set, then that set is a ring.[5]

$$\begin{array}{r} x^3 + x^2 \qquad + 2 \\ + \;(x^2 - x + 1) \\ \hline x^3 + 2x^2 - x + 3 \end{array}$$

(a) Addition

$$\begin{array}{r} x^3 + x^2 \qquad + 2 \\ - \;(x^2 - x + 1) \\ \hline x^3 \qquad + x + 1 \end{array}$$

(b) Subtraction

$$\begin{array}{r} x^3 + x^2 \qquad + 2 \\ \times \;(x^2 - x + 1) \\ \hline x^3 + x^2 \qquad + 2 \\ -x^4 - x^3 \qquad - 2x \quad \\ x^5 + x^4 \qquad + 2x^2 \qquad\quad \\ \hline x^5 \qquad + 3x^2 - 2x + 2 \end{array}$$

(c) Multiplication

$$\begin{array}{r} x + 2 \\ x^2 - x + 1 \;\big)\; x^3 + x^2 \qquad + 2 \\ x^3 - x^2 + x \quad \\ \hline 2x^2 - x + 2 \\ 2x^2 - 2x + 2 \\ \hline x \end{array}$$

(d) Division

Figure 4.3 Examples of Polynomial Arithmetic

---

[5]In fact, the set of polynomials whose coefficients are elements of a commutative ring forms a polynomial ring, but that is of no interest in the present context.

When polynomial arithmetic is performed on polynomials over a field, then division is possible. Note that this does not mean that *exact division* is possible. Let us clarify this distinction. Within a field, given two elements a and b, the quotient a/b is also an element of the field. However, given a ring R that is not a field, in general division will result in both a quotient and a remainder; this is not exact division.

> Consider the division 5/3 within a set S. If S is the set of rational numbers, which is a field, then the result is simply expressed as 5/3 and is an element of S. Now suppose that S is the field Z_7. In this case, we calculate (using Table 4.3c):
>
> $$5/3 = (5 \times 3^{-1}) \bmod 7 = (5 \times 5) \bmod 7 = 4$$
>
> which is an exact solution. Finally, suppose that S is the set of integers, which is a ring but not a field. Then 5/3 produces a quotient of 1 and a remainder of 2:
>
> $$5/3 = 1 + 2/3$$
> $$5 = 1 \times 3 + 2$$
>
> Thus, division is not exact over the set of integers.

Now, if we attempt to perform polynomial division over a coefficient set that is not a field, we find that division is not always defined.

> If the coefficient set is the integers, then $(5x^2)/(3x)$ does not have a solution, because it would require a coefficient with a value of 5/3, which is not in the coefficient set. Suppose that we perform the same polynomial division over Z_7. Then we have $(5x^2)/(3x) = 4x$, which is a valid polynomial over Z_7.

However, as we demonstrate presently, even if the coefficient set is a field, polynomial division is not necessarily exact. In general, division will produce a quotient and a remainder:

$$\frac{f(x)}{g(x)} = q(x) + \frac{r(x)}{g(x)}$$
$$f(x) = q(x)g(x) + r(x) \quad \textbf{(4.6)}$$

If the degree of $f(x)$ is n and the degree of $g(x)$ is m, $(m \geq n)$, then the degree of the quotient $q(x)$ is $m - n$ and the degree of the remainder is at most $m - 1$. With the understanding that remainders are allowed, we can say that polynomial division is possible if the coefficient set is a field.

In an analogy to integer arithmetic, we can write $f(x) \bmod g(x)$ for the remainder $r(x)$ in Equation (4.6). That is, $r(x) = f(x) \bmod g(x)$. If there is no remainder [i.e., $r(x) = 0$], then we can say $g(x)$ **divides** $f(x)$, written as $g(x)|f(x)$; equivalently, we can say that $g(x)$ is a **factor** of $f(x)$ or $g(x)$ is a **divisor** of $f(x)$.

For the preceding example [$f(x) = x^3 + x^2 + 2$ and $g(x) = x^2 - x + 1$], $f(x)/g(x)$ produces a quotient of $q(x) = x + 2$ and a remainder $r(x) = x$, as shown in Figure 4.3d. This is easily verified by noting that

$$q(x)g(x) + r(x) = (x + 2)(x^2 - x + 1) + x = (x^3 + x^2 - x + 2) + x$$
$$= x^3 + x^2 + 2 = f(x)$$

For our purposes, polynomials over GF(2) are of most interest. Recall from Section 4.4 that in GF(2), addition is equivalent to the XOR operation, and multiplication is equivalent to the logical AND operation. Further, addition and subtraction are equivalent mod 2: $1 + 1 = 1 - 1 = 0$; $1 + 0 = 1 - 0 = 1$; $0 + 1 = 0 - 1 = 1$.

Figure 4.4 shows an example of polynomial arithmetic over GF(2). For $f(x) = (x^7 + x^5 + x^4 + x^3 + x + 1)$ and $g(x) = (x^3 + x + 1)$, the figure shows $f(x) + g(x)$; $f(x) - g(x)$; $f(x) \times g(x)$; and $f(x)/g(x)$. Note that $g(x)|f(x)$

$$\begin{array}{r} x^7 + x^5 + x^4 + x^3 + x + 1 \\ +\,(x^3 + x + 1) \\ \hline x^7 + x^5 + x^4 \end{array}$$

(a) Addition

$$\begin{array}{r} x^7 + x^5 + x^4 + x^3 + x + 1 \\ -\,(x^3 + x + 1) \\ \hline x^7 + x^5 + x^4 \end{array}$$

(b) Subtraction

$$\begin{array}{r} x^7 + x^5 + x^4 + x^3 + x + 1 \\ \times\,(x^3 + x + 1) \\ \hline x^7 + x^5 + x^4 + x^3 + x + 1 \\ x^8 + x^6 + x^5 + x^4 + x^2 + x \\ x^{10} + x^8 + x^7 + x^6 + x^4 + x^3 \\ \hline x^{10} + x^4 + x^2 + 1 \end{array}$$

(c) Multiplication

$$\begin{array}{r|l} & x^4 + 1 \\ \hline x^3 + x + 1 & x^7 + x^5 + x^4 + x^3 + x + 1 \\ & x^7 + x^5 + x^4 \\ \hline & x^3 + x + 1 \\ & x^3 + x + 1 \\ \hline \end{array}$$

(d) Division

Figure 4.4 Examples of Polynomial Arithmetic over GF(2)

A polynomial $f(x)$ over a field F is called **irreducible** if and only if $f(x)$ cannot be expressed as a product of two polynomials, both over F, and both of degree lower than that of $f(x)$. By analogy to integers, an irreducible polynomial is also called a **prime polynomial**.

The polynomial[6] $f(x) = x^4 + 1$ over GF(2) is reducible, because $x^4 + 1 = (x + 1)(x^3 + x^2 + x + 1)$

Consider the polynomial $f(x) = x^3 + x + 1$. It is clear by inspection that x is not a factor of $f(x)$. We easily show that $x + 1$ is not a factor of $f(x)$:

$$\begin{array}{r@{}l} & x^2 + x \\ x + 1 & \overline{/x^3 \qquad + x + 1} \\ & \underline{x^3 + x^2} \\ & \qquad x^2 + x \\ & \qquad \underline{x^2 + x} \\ & \qquad\qquad\quad 1 \end{array}$$

Thus $f(x)$ has no factors of degree 1. But it is clear by inspection that if $f(x)$ is reducible, it must have one factor of degree 2 and one factor of degree 1. Therefore, $f(x)$ is irreducible.

Finding the Greatest Common Divisor

We can extend the analogy between polynomial arithmetic over a field and integer arithmetic by defining the greatest common divisor as follows. The polynomial $c(x)$ is said to be the greatest common divisor of $a(x)$ and $b(x)$ if

1. $c(x)$ divides both $a(x)$ and $b(x)$;
2. any divisor of $a(x)$ and $b(x)$ is a divisor of $c(x)$.

An equivalent definition is the following: $\gcd[a(x), b(x)]$ is the polynomial of maximum degree that divides both $a(x)$ and $b(x)$.

We can adapt the Euclidean algorithm to compute the greatest common divisor of two polynomials. The equality in Equation (4.4) can be rewritten as the following theorem:

$$\gcd[a(x), b(x)] = \gcd[b(x), a(x) \bmod b(x)] \qquad \textbf{(4.7)}$$

[6]In the remainder of this chapter, unless otherwise noted, all examples are of polynomials over GF(2).

The Euclidean algorithm for polynomials can be stated as follows. The algorithm assumes that the degree of $a(x)$ is greater than the degree of $b(x)$. Then, to find gcd[$a(x), b(x)$],

```
EUCLID[a(x), b(x)]
1.  A(x) ← a(x); B(x) ← b(x)
2.  if B(x) = 0     return A(x) = gcd[a(x), b(x)]
3.  R(x) = A(x) mod B(x)
4.  A(x) ← B(x)
5.  B(x) ← R(x)
6.  goto 2
```

Find gcd[$a(x), b(x)$] for $a(x) = x^6 + x^5 + x^4 + x^3 + x^2 + x + 1$ and $b(x) = x^4 + x^2 + x + 1$.
$A(x) = a(x); B(x) = b(x)$

$$
\begin{array}{r|l}
 & x^2 + x \\
\hline
x^4 + x^2 + x + 1 & x^6 + x^5 + x^4 + x^3 + x^2 + x + 1 \\
 & x^6 \qquad + x^4 + x^3 + x^2 \\
\cline{2-2}
 & \quad x^5 \qquad\qquad\qquad + x + 1 \\
 & \quad x^5 \qquad + x^3 + x^2 + x \\
\cline{2-2}
 & \qquad\qquad x^3 + x^2 \qquad + 1
\end{array}
$$

$R(x) = A(x) \bmod B(x) = x^3 + x^2 + 1$
$A(x) = x^4 + x^2 + x + 1; B(x) = x^3 + x^2 + 1$

$$
\begin{array}{r|l}
 & x + 1 \\
\hline
x^3 + x^2 + 1 & x^4 \qquad + x^2 + x + 1 \\
 & x^4 + x^3 \qquad + x \\
\cline{2-2}
 & \quad x^3 + x^2 \qquad + 1 \\
 & \quad x^3 + x^2 \qquad + 1 \\
\cline{2-2}
\end{array}
$$

$R(x) = A(x) \bmod B(x) = 0$
$\gcd[a(x), b(x)] = A(x) = x^3 + x^2 + 1$

Summary

We began this section with a discussion of arithmetic with ordinary polynomials. In ordinary polynomial arithmetic, the variable is not evaluated; that is, we do not plug a value in for the variable of the polynomials. Instead, arithmetic operations are performed on polynomials (addition, subtraction, multiplication, division) using the ordinary rules of algebra. Polynomial division is not allowed unless the coefficients are elements of a field.

Next, we discussed polynomial arithmetic in which the coefficients are elements of GF(p). In this case, polynomial addition, subtraction, multiplication, and division are allowed. However, division is not exact; that is, in general division results in a quotient and a remainder.

Finally, we showed that the Euclidean algorithm can be extended to find the greatest common divisor of two polynomials whose coefficients are elements of a field.

All of the material in this section provides a foundation for the following section, in which polynomials are used to define finite fields of order p^n.

4.6 FINITE FIELDS OF THE FORM GF(2^n)

Earlier in this chapter, we mentioned that the order of a finite field must be of the form p^n, where p is a prime and n is a positive integer. In Section 4.4, we looked at the special case of finite fields with order p. We found that, using modular arithmetic in Z_p, all of the axioms for a field (Figure 4.1) are satisfied. For polynomials over p^n, with $n > 1$, operations modulo p^n do not produce a field. In this section, we show what structure satisfies the axioms for a field in a set with p^n elements, and concentrate on GF(2^n).

Motivation

Virtually all encryption algorithms, both symmetric and public key, involve arithmetic operations on integers. If one of the operations that is used in the algorithm is division, then we need to work in arithmetic defined over a field. For convenience and for implementation efficiency, we would also like to work with integers that fit exactly into a given number of bits, with no wasted bit patterns. That is, we wish to work with integers in the range 0 through $2^n - 1$, which fit into an n-bit word.

> Suppose we wish to define a conventional encryption algorithm that operates on data 8 bits at a time and we wish to perform division. With 8 bits, we can represent integers in the range 0 through 255. However, 256 is not a prime number, so that if arithmetic is performed in Z_{256} (arithmetic modulo 256), this set of integers will not be a field. The closest prime number less than 256 is 251. Thus, the set Z_{251}, using arithmetic modulo 251, is a field. However, in this case the 8-bit patterns representing the integers 251 through 255 would not be used, resulting in inefficient use of storage.

As the preceding example points out, if all arithmetic operations are to be used, and we wish to represent a full range of integers in n bits, then arithmetic modulo 2^n will not work; equivalently, the set of integers modulo 2^n, for $n > 1$, is not a field. Furthermore, even if the encryption algorithm uses only addition and multiplication, but not division, the use of the set Z_{2^n} is questionable, as the following example illustrates.

Suppose we wish to use 3-bit blocks in our encryption algorithm, and use only the operations of addition and multiplication. Then arithmetic modulo 8 is well defined, as shown in Table 4.1. However, note that in the multiplication table, the nonzero integers do not appear an equal number of times. For example, there are only four occurrences of 3, but twelve occurrences of 4. On the other hand, as was mentioned, there are finite fields of the form GF(2^n), so there is in particular a finite field of order $2^3 = 8$. Arithmetic for this field is shown in Table 4.5. In this case, the number of occurrences of the nonzero integers is uniform for multiplication. To summarize,

Integer	1	2	3	4	5	6	7
Occurrences in Z_8	4	8	4	12	4	8	4
Occurrences in GF(2^3)	7	7	7	7	7	7	7

For the moment, let us set aside the question of how the matrices of Table 4.5 were constructed and instead make some observations.

1. The addition and multiplication tables are symmetric about the main diagonal, in conformance to the commutative property of addition and multiplication. This property is also exhibited in Table 4.1, which uses mod 8 arithmetic.
2. All the nonzero elements defined by Table 4.5 have a multiplicative inverse, unlike the case with Table 4.1.
3. The scheme defined by Table 4.5 satisfies all the requirements for a finite field. Thus, we can refer to this scheme as GF(2^3).
4. For convenience, we show the 3-bit assignment used for each of the elements of GF(2^3).

Intuitively, it would seem that an algorithm that maps the integers unevenly onto themselves might be cryptographically weaker than one that provides a uniform mapping. Thus, the finite fields of the form GF(2^n) are attractive for cryptographic algorithms.

To summarize, we are looking for a set consisting of 2^n elements, together with a definition of addition and multiplication over the set that define a field. We can assign a unique integer in the range 0 through $2^n - 1$ to each element of the set. Keep in mind that we will not use modular arithmetic, as we have seen that this does not result in a field. Instead, we will show how polynomial arithmetic provides a means for constructing the desired field.

Modular Polynomial Arithmetic

Consider the set S of all polynomials of degree $n - 1$ or less over the field Z_p. Thus, each polynomial has the form

$$f(x) = a_{n-1}x^{n-1} + a_{n-2}x^{n-2} + \cdots + a_1x + a_0 = \sum_{i=0}^{n-1} a_ix^i$$

where each a_i takes on a value in the set $\{0, 1, \ldots, p - 1\}$. There are a total of p^n different polynomials in S.

Table 4.5 Arithmetic in GF(2^3)

		000	001	010	011	100	101	110	111
	+	0	1	2	3	4	5	6	7
000	0	0	1	2	3	4	5	6	7
001	1	1	0	3	2	5	4	7	6
010	2	2	3	0	1	6	7	4	5
011	3	3	2	1	0	7	6	5	4
100	4	4	5	6	7	0	1	2	3
101	5	5	4	7	6	1	0	3	2
110	6	6	7	4	5	2	3	0	1
111	7	7	6	5	4	3	2	1	0

(a) Addition

		000	001	010	011	100	101	110	111
	×	0	1	2	3	4	5	6	7
000	0	0	0	0	0	0	0	0	0
001	1	0	1	2	3	4	5	6	7
010	2	0	2	4	6	3	1	7	5
011	3	0	3	6	5	7	4	1	2
100	4	0	4	3	7	6	2	5	1
101	5	0	5	1	4	2	7	3	6
110	6	0	6	7	1	5	3	2	4
111	7	0	7	5	2	1	6	4	3

(b) Multiplication

w	$-w$	w^{-1}
0	0	—
1	1	1
2	2	5
3	3	6
4	4	7
5	5	2
6	6	3
7	7	4

(c) Additive and multiplicative inverses

For $p = 3$ and $n = 2$, the $3^2 = 9$ polynomials in the set are

0	x	$2x$
1	$x + 1$	$2x + 1$
2	$x + 2$	$2x + 2$

For $p = 2$ and $n = 3$, the $2^3 = 8$ polynomials in the set are

0	$x + 1$	$x^2 + x$
1	x^2	$x^2 + x + 1$
x	$x^2 + 1$	

With the appropriate definition of arithmetic operations, each such set S is a finite field. The definition consists of the following elements:

1. Arithmetic follows the ordinary rules of polynomial arithmetic using the basic rules of algebra, with the following two refinements.
2. Arithmetic on the coefficients is performed modulo p. That is, we use the rules of arithmetic for the finite field Z_p.

3. If multiplication results in a polynomial of degree greater than $n - 1$, then the polynomial is reduced modulo some irreducible polynomial $m(x)$ of degree n. That is, we divide by $m(x)$ and keep the remainder. For a polynomial $f(x)$, the remainder is expressed as $r(x) = f(x) \bmod m(x)$.

The Advanced Encryption Standard (AES) uses arithmetic in the finite field GF(2^8), with the irreducible polynomial $m(x) = x^8 + x^4 + x^3 + x + 1$. Consider the two polynomials $f(x) = x^6 + x^4 + x^2 + x + 1$ and $g(x) = x^7 + x + 1$. Then

$$\begin{aligned} f(x) + g(x) &= x^6 + x^4 + x^2 + x + 1 + x^7 + x + 1 \\ &= x^7 + x^6 + x^4 + x^2 \end{aligned}$$

$$\begin{aligned} f(x) \times g(x) &= x^{13} + x^{11} + x^9 + x^8 + x^7 + \\ &\quad x^7 + x^5 + x^3 + x^2 + x + \\ &\quad x^6 + x^4 + x^2 + x + 1 \\ &= x^{13} + x^{11} + x^9 + x^8 + x^6 + x^5 + x^4 + x^3 + 1 \end{aligned}$$

$$\begin{array}{r|l} & x^5 + x^3 \\ \hline x^8 + x^4 + x^3 + x + 1 & x^{13} + x^{11} + x^9 + x^8 + x^7 + x^6 + x^5 + x^4 + x^3 + \quad + 1 \\ & \underline{x^{13} \quad + x^9 + x^8 \quad + x^6 + x^5} \\ & x^{11} \quad + x^4 + x^3 \\ & \underline{x^{11} \quad + x^7 + x^6 \quad + x^4 + x^3} \\ & x^7 + x^6 \quad + 1 \end{array}$$

Therefore, $f(x) \times g(x) \bmod m(x) = x^7 + x^6 + 1$.

As with ordinary modular arithmetic, we have the notion of a set of residues in modular polynomial arithmetic. The set of residues modulo $m(x)$, an nth-degree polynomial, consists of p^n elements. Each of these elements is represented by one of the p^n polynomials of degree $m < n$.

The residue class $[x + 1]$, modulo $m(x)$, consists of all polynomials $a(x)$ such that $a(x) \in (x + 1) \pmod{m(x)}$. Equivalently, the residue class $[x + 1]$ consists of all polynomials $a(x)$ that satisfy the equality $a(x) \bmod m(x) = x + 1$.

It can be shown that the set of all polynomials modulo an irreducible nth-degree polynomial $m(x)$ satisfies the axioms in Figure 4.1, and thus forms a finite field. Furthermore, all finite fields of a given order are isomorphic; that is, any two finite-field structures of a given order have the same structure, but the representation, or labels, of the elements may be different.

To construct the finite field GF(2^3), we need to choose an irreducible polynomial of degree 3. There are only two such polynomials: $(x^3 + x^2 + 1)$ and $(x^3 + x + 1)$. Using the latter, Table 4.6 shows the addition and multiplication tables for GF(2^3). Note that this set of tables has the identical structure to those of Table 4.5. Thus, we have succeeded in finding a way to define a field of order 2^3.

Finding the Multiplicative Inverse

Just as the Euclidean algorithm can be adapted to find the greatest common divisor of two polynomials, the extended Euclidean algorithm can be adapted to find the multiplicative inverse of a polynomial. Specifically, the algorithm will find the multiplicative inverse of $b(x)$ modulo $m(x)$ if the degree of $b(x)$ is less than the degree of $m(x)$ and $\gcd[m(x), b(x)] = 1$. If $m(x)$ is an irreducible polynomial, then it has no factor other than itself or 1, so that $\gcd[m(x), b(x)] = 1$. The algorithm is as follows:

```
EXTENDED EUCLID[m(x), b(x)]
1.  [A1(x), A2(x), A3(x)] ← [1, 0, m(x)]; [B1(x), B2(x),
    B3(x)] ← [0, 1, b(x)]
2.  if B3(x) = 0     return  A3(x) = gcd[m(x), b(x)];  no
    inverse
3.  if B3(x) = 1     return  B3(x) = gcd[m(x), b(x)];
    B2(x) = b(x)^-1 mod m(x)
4.  Q(x) = quotient of A3(x)/B3(x)
5.  [T1(x), T2(x), T3(x)] ← [A1(x) - Q(x)B1(x), A2(x) -
    Q(x)B2(x), A3(x) - QB3(x)]
6.  [A1(x), A2(x), A3(x)] ← [B1(x), B2(x), B3(x)]
7.  [B1(x), B2(x), B3(x)] ← [T1(x), T2(x), T3(x)]
8.  goto 2
```

Table 4.7 shows the calculation of the multiplicative inverse of $(x^7 + x + 1)$ mod $(x^8 + x^4 + x^3 + x + 1)$. The result is that $(x^7 + x + 1)^{-1} = (x^7)$ That is, $(x^7 + x + 1)(x^7) \equiv 1 \pmod{(x^8 + x^4 + x^3 + x + 1)}$.

Computational Considerations

A polynomial $f(x)$ in GF(2^n)

$$f(x) = a_{n-1}x^{n-1} + a_{n-2}x^{n-2} + \cdots + a_1x + a_0 = \sum_{i=0}^{n-1} a_ix^i$$

can be uniquely represented by its n binary coefficients $(a_{n-1}a_{n-2} \ldots a_0)$. Thus, every polynomial in GF(2^n) can be represented by an n-bit number.

Table 4.6 Polynomial Arithmetic Modulo $(x^3 + x + 1)$

		000	001	010	011	100	101	110	111
	+	0	1	x	$x + 1$	x^2	$x^2 + 1$	$x^2 + x$	$x^2 + x + 1$
000	0	0	1	x	$x + 1$	x^2	$x^2 + 1$	$x^2 + x$	$x^2 + x + 1$
001	1	1	0	$x + 1$	x	$x^2 + 1$	x^2	$x^2 + x + 1$	$x^2 + x$
010	x	x	$x + 1$	0	1	$x^2 + x$	$x^2 + x + 1$	x^2	$x^2 + 1$
011	$x + 1$	$x + 1$	x	1	0	$x^2 + x + 1$	$x^2 + x$	$x^2 + 1$	x^2
100	x^2	x^2	$x^2 + 1$	$x^2 + x$	$x^2 + x + 1$	0	1	x	$x + 1$
101	$x^2 + 1$	$x^2 + 1$	x^2	$x^2 + x + 1$	$x^2 + x$	1	0	$x + 1$	x
110	$x^2 + x$	$x^2 + x$	$x^2 + x + 1$	x^2	$x^2 + 1$	x	$x + 1$	0	1
111	$x^2 + x + 1$	$x^2 + x + 1$	$x^2 + x$	$x^2 + 1$	x^2	$x + 1$	x	1	0

(a) Addition

		000	001	010	011	100	101	110	111
	×	0	1	x	$x + 1$	x^2	$x^2 + 1$	$x^2 + x$	$x^2 + x + 1$
000	0	0	0	0	0	0	0	0	0
001	1	0	1	x	$x + 1$	x^2	$x^2 + 1$	$x^2 + x$	$x^2 + x + 1$
010	x	0	x	x^2	$x^2 + x$	$x + 1$	1	$x^2 + x + 1$	$x^2 + 1$
011	$x + 1$	0	$x + 1$	$x^2 + x$	$x^2 + 1$	$x^2 + x + 1$	x^2	1	x
100	x^2	0	x^2	$x + 1$	$x^2 + x + 1$	$x^2 + x$	x	$x^2 + 1$	1
101	$x^2 + 1$	0	$x^2 + 1$	1	x^2	x	$x^2 + x + 1$	$x + 1$	$x^2 + x$
110	$x^2 + x$	0	$x^2 + x$	$x^2 + x + 1$	1	$x^2 + 1$	$x + 1$	x	x^2
111	$x^2 + x + 1$	0	$x^2 + x + 1$	$x^2 + 1$	x	1	$x^2 + x$	x^2	$x + 1$

(b) Multiplication

Table 4.7 Extended Euclid [$(x^8 + x^4 + x^3 + x + 1), (x^7 + x + 1)$]

Initialization	A1(x) = 1; A2(x) = 0; A3(x) = $x^8 + x^4 + x^3 + x + 1$ B1(x) = 0; B2(x) = 1; B3(x) = $x^7 + x + 1$
Iteration 1	Q(x) = x A1(x) = 0; A2(x) = 1; A3(x) = $x^7 + x + 1$ B1(x) = 1; B2(x) = x; B3(x) = $x^4 + x^3 + x^2 + 1$
Iteration 2	Q(x) = $x^3 + x^2 + 1$ A1(x) = 1; A2(x) = x; A3(x) = $x^4 + x^3 + x^2 + 1$ B1(x) = $x^3 + x^2 + 1$; B2(x) = $x^4 + x^3 + x + 1$; B3(x) = x
Iteration 3	Q(x) = $x^3 + x^2 + x$ A1(x) = $x^3 + x^2 + 1$; A2(x) = $x^4 + x^3 + x + 1$; A3(x) = x B1(x) = $x^6 + x^2 + x + 1$; B2(x) = x^7; B3(x) = 1
Iteration 4	B3(x) = gcd[$(x^7 + x + 1), (x^8 + x^4 + x^3 + x + 1)$] = 1 B2($x$) = $(x^7 + x + 1)^{-1} \bmod (x^8 + x^4 + x^3 + x + 1) = x^7$

Tables 4.5 and 4.6 show the addition and multiplication tables for GF(2^3) modulo $m(x) = (x^3 + x + 1)$. Table 4.5 uses the binary representation, and Table 4.6 uses the polynomial representation.

Addition We have seen that addition of polynomials is performed by adding corresponding coefficients, and, in the case of polynomials over Z_2, addition is just the XOR operation. So, addition of two polynomials in GF(2^n) corresponds to a bitwise XOR operation.

Consider the two polynomials in GF(2^8) from our earlier example: $f(x) = x^6 + x^4 + x^2 + x + 1$ and $g(x) = x^7 + x + 1$.

$(x^6 + x^4 + x^2 + x + 1) + (x^7 + x + 1)$	$= x^7 + x^6 + x^4 + x^2$	(polynomial notation)
(01010111) ⊕ (10000011)	= (11010100)	(binary notation)
{57} ⊕ {83}	= {D4}	(hexadecimal notation)[7]

Multiplication There is no simple XOR operation that will accomplish multiplication in GF(2^n). However, a reasonably straightforward, easily implemented technique is available. We will discuss the technique with reference to GF(2^8) using $m(x) = x^8 + x^4 + x^3 + x + 1$, which is the finite field used in AES. The technique readily generalizes to GF(2^n).

The technique is based on the observation that

$$x^8 \bmod m(x) = [m(x) - x^8] = (x^4 + x^3 + x + 1) \quad \textbf{(4.8)}$$

[7]A basic refresher on number systems (decimal, binary, hexadecimal) can be found at the Computer Science Student Resource Site at WilliamStallings.com/StudentSupport.html. Here each of two groups of 4 bits in a byte is denoted by a single hexadecimal character, the two characters enclosed in brackets.

A moment's thought should convince you that Equation (4.8) is true; if not, divide it out. In general, in GF(2^n) with an nth-degree polynomial $p(x)$, we have $x^n \bmod p(x) = [p(x) - x^n]$.

Now, consider a polynomial in GF(2^8), which has the form $f(x) = b_7x^7 + b_6x^6 + b_5x^5 + b_4x^4 + b_3x^3 + b_2x^2 + b_1x + b_0$. If we multiply by x, we have

$$x \times f(x) = (b_7x^8 + b_6x^7 + b_5x^6 + b_4x^5 + b_3x^4 + b_2x^3 + b_1x^2 + b_0x) \bmod m(x) \quad \textbf{(4.9)}$$

If $b_7 = 0$, then the result is a polynomial of degree less than 8, which is already in reduced form, and no further computation is necessary. If $b_7 = 1$, then reduction modulo $m(x)$ is achieved using Equation (4.8):

$$x \times f(x) = (b_6x^7 + b_5x^6 + b_4x^5 + b_3x^4 + b_2x^3 + b_1x^2 + b_0x) + (x^4 + x^3 + x + 1)$$

It follows that multiplication by x (i.e., 00000010) can be implemented as a 1-bit left shift followed by a conditional bitwise XOR with (00011011), which represents $(x^4 + x^3 + x + 1)$. To summarize,

$$x \times f(x) = \begin{cases} (b_6b_5b_4b_3b_2b_1b_00) & \text{if } b_7 = 0 \\ (b_6b_5b_4b_3b_2b_1b_00) \oplus (00011011) & \text{if } b_7 = 1 \end{cases} \quad \textbf{(4.10)}$$

Multiplication by a higher power of x can be achieved by repeated application of Equation (4.10). By adding intermediate results, multiplication by any constant in GF(2^8) can be achieved.

In an earlier example, we showed that for $f(x) = x^6 + x^4 + x^2 + x + 1$, $g(x) = x^7 + x + 1$, and $m(x) = x^8 + x^4 + x^3 + x + 1$, $f(x) \times g(x) \bmod m(x) = x^7 + x^6 + 1$. Redoing this in binary arithmetic, we need to compute $(01010111) \times (10000011)$. First, we determine the results of multiplication by powers of x:

$$\begin{aligned}
(01010111) \times (00000010) &= (10101110) \\
(01010111) \times (00000100) &= (01011100) \oplus (00011011) = (01000111) \\
(01010111) \times (00001000) &= (10001110) \\
(01010111) \times (00010000) &= (00011100) \oplus (00011011) = (00000111) \\
(01010111) \times (00100000) &= (00001110) \\
(01010111) \times (01000000) &= (00011100) \\
(01010111) \times (10000000) &= (00111000)
\end{aligned}$$

So,

$$\begin{aligned}
(01010111) \times (10000011) &= (01010111) \times [(00000001) \times (00000010) \times (10000000)] \\
&= (01010111) \oplus (10101110) \oplus (00111000) = (11000001)
\end{aligned}$$

which is equivalent to $x^7 + x^6 + 1$.

Using a Generator

An equivalent technique for defining a finite field of the form GF(2^n) using the same irreducible polynomial, is sometimes more convenient. To begin, we need two definitions: A **generator** g of a finite field F of order q (contains q elements) is an element whose first $q - 1$ powers generate all the nonzero elements of F. That is, the elements of F consist of $0, g^0, g^1, \ldots, g^{q-2}$. Consider a field F defined by a polynomial $f(x)$. An element b contained in F is called a **root** of the polynomial if $f(b) = 0$. Finally, it can be shown that a root g of an irreducible polynomial is a generator of the finite field defined on that polynomial.

Let us consider the finite field GF(2^3), defined over the irreducible polynomial $x^3 + x + 1$, discussed previously. Thus, the generator g must satisfy $f(g) = g^3 + g + 1 = 0$. Keep in mind, as discussed previously, that we need not find a numerical solution to this equality. Rather, we deal with polynomial arithmetic in which arithmetic on the coefficients is performed modulo 2. Therefore, the solution to the preceding equality is $g^3 = -g - 1 = g + 1$. We now show that g in fact generates all of the polynomials of degree less than 3. We have the following:

$$g^4 = g(g^3) = g(g + 1) = g^2 + g$$
$$g^5 = g(g^4) = g(g^2 + g) = g^3 + g^2 = g^2 + g + 1$$
$$g^6 = g(g^5) = g(g^2 + g + 1) = g^3 + g^2 + g = g^2 + g + g + 1 = g^2 + 1$$
$$g^7 = g(g^6) = g(g^2 + 1) = g^3 + g = g + g + 1 = 1 = g^0$$

We see that the powers of g generate all the nonzero polynomials in GF(2^3). Also, it should be clear that $g^k = g^{k \bmod 7}$ for any integer k. Table 4.8 shows the power representation, as well as the polynomial and binary representations.

This power representation makes multiplication easy. To multiply in the power notation, add exponents modulo 7. For example, $g^4 \times g^6 = g^{(10 \bmod 7)} = g^3 = g + 1$. The same result is achieved using polynomial arithmetic, as follows: we

(Continued)

Table 4.8 Generator for GF(2^3) using $x^3 + x + 1$

Power Representation	Polynomial Representation	Binary Representation	Decimal (Hex) Representation
0	0	000	0
g^0 (= g^7)	1	001	1
g^1	g	010	2
g^2	g^2	100	4
g^3	$g + 1$	011	3
g^4	$g^2 + g$	110	6
g^5	$g^2 + g + 1$	111	7
g^6	$g^2 + 1$	101	5

Table 4.9 GF(2^3) Arithmetic Using Generator for the Polynomial ($x^3 + x + 1$)

		000	001	010	100	011	110	111	101
	+	0	1	g	g^2	g^3	g^4	g^5	g^6
000	0	0	1	g	g^2	$g + 1$	$g^2 + g$	$g^2 + g + 1$	$g^2 + 1$
001	1	1	0	$g + 1$	$g^2 + 1$	g	$g^2 + g + 1$	$g^2 + g$	g^2
010	g	g	$g + 1$	0	$g^2 + g$	1	g^2	$g^2 + 1$	$g^2 + g + 1$
100	g^2	g^2	$g^2 + 1$	$g^2 + g$	0	$g^2 + g + 1$	g	$g + 1$	1
011	g^3	$g + 1$	g	1	$g^2 + g + 1$	0	$g^2 + 1$	g^2	$g^2 + g$
110	g^4	$g^2 + g$	$g^2 + g + 1$	g^2	g	$g^2 + 1$	0	1	$g + 1$
111	g^5	$g^2 + g + 1$	$g^2 + g$	$g^2 + 1$	$g + 1$	g^2	1	0	g
101	g^6	$g^2 + 1$	g^2	$g^2 + g + 1$	1	$g^2 + g$	$g + 1$	g	0

(a) Addition

		000	001	010	100	011	110	111	101
	×	0	1	g	g^2	g^3	g^4	g^5	g^6
000	0	0	0	0	0	0	0	0	0
001	1	0	1	g	g^2	$g + 1$	$g^2 + g$	$g^2 + g + 1$	$g^2 + 1$
010	g	0	g	g^2	$g + 1$	$g^2 + g$	$g^2 + g + 1$	$g^2 + 1$	1
100	g^2	0	g^2	$g + 1$	$g^2 + g$	$g^2 + g + 1$	$g^2 + 1$	1	g
011	g^3	0	$g + 1$	$g^2 + g$	$g^2 + g + 1$	$g^2 + 1$	1	G	g^2
110	g^4	0	$g^2 + g$	$g^2 + g + 1$	$g^2 + 1$	1	g	g^2	$g + 1$
111	g^5	0	$g^2 + g + 1$	$g^2 + 1$	1	g	g^2	$g + 1$	$g^2 + g$
101	g^6	0	$g^2 + 1$	1	g	g^2	$g + 1$	$g^2 + g$	$g^2 + g + 1$

(b) Multiplication

(Continued)

have $g^4 = g^2 + g$ and $g^6 = g^2 + 1$. Then, $(g^2 + g) \times (g^2 + 1) = g^4 + g^3 + g^2 + 1$. Next, we need to determine $(g^4 + g^3 + g^2 + 1) \bmod (g^3 + g + 1)$ by division:

$$
\begin{array}{r}
g \quad + 1 \\
g^3 + g^2 + 1 \overline{)\, g^4 + g^3 + g^2 + g} \\
\underline{g^4 + \qquad g^2 + g} \\
g^3 \qquad\qquad \\
\underline{g^3 + \qquad g + 1} \\
g + 1
\end{array}
$$

We get a result of $g + 1$, which agrees with the result obtained using the power representation.

Table 4.9 shows the addition and multiplication tables for $GF(2^3)$ using the power represenation. Note that this yields the identical results to the polynomial representation (Table 4.6) with some of the rows and columns interchanged.

In general, for $GF(2^n)$ with irreducible polynomial $f(x)$, determine $g^n = f(g) - g^n$. Then calculate all of the powers of g from g^{n+1} through g^{2^n-2}. The elements of the field correspond to the powers of g from g^0 through g^{2^n-2}, plus the value 0. For multiplication of two elements in the field, use the equality $g^k = g^{k \bmod (2^n-1)}$ for any integer k.

Summary

In this section, we have shown how to construct a finite field of order 2^n. Specifically, we defined $GF(2^n)$ with the following properties:

1. $GF(2^n)$ consists of 2^n elements.
2. The binary operations + and $\times$ are defined over the set. The operations of addition, subtraction, multiplication, and division can be performed without leaving the set. Each element of the set other than 0 has a multiplicative inverse.

We have shown that the elements of $GF(2^n)$ can be defined as the set of all polynomials of degree $n - 1$ or less with binary coefficients. Each such polynomial can be represented by a unique n-bit value. Arithmetic is defined as polynomial arithmetic modulo some irreducible polynomial of degree n. We have also seen that an equivalent definition of a finite field $GF(2^n)$ makes use of a generator and that arithmetic is defined using powers of the generator.

4.7 RECOMMENDED READING AND WEB SITES

[HERS75], still in print, is the classic treatment of abstract algebra; it is readable and rigorous; [DESK92] is another good resource. [KNUT98] provides good coverage of polynomial arithmetic.

One of the best treatments of the topics of this chapter is [BERL84], still in print. [GARR01] also has extensive coverage. A thorough and rigorous treatment of finite fields is [LIDL94]. [HORO71] is a good overview of the topics of this chapter.

BERL84 Berlekamp, E. *Algebraic Coding Theory.* Laguna Hills, CA: Aegean Park Press, 1984.

DESK92 Deskins, W. *Abstract Algebra.* New York: Dover, 1992.

GARR01 Garrett, P. *Making, Breaking Codes: An Introduction to Cryptology.* Upper Saddle River, NJ: Prentice Hall, 2001.

HERS75 Herstein, I. *Topics in Algebra.* New York: Wiley, 1975.

HORO71 Horowitz, E. "Modular Arithmetic and Finite Field Theory: A Tutorial." *Proceedings of the Second ACM Symposium and Symbolic and Algebraic Manipulation*, March 1971.

KNUT98 Knuth, D. *The Art of Computer Programming, Volume 2: Seminumerical Algorithms.* Reading, MA: Addison-Wesley, 1998.

LIDL94 Lidl, R., and Niederreiter, H. *Introduction to Finite Fields and Their Applications.* Cambridge: Cambridge University Press, 1994.

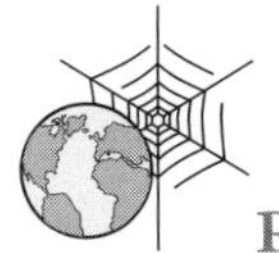

Recommended Web Sites:

- **PascGalois Project:** Contains a clever set of examples and projects to aid in giving students a visual understanding of key concepts in abstract algebra

4.8 KEY TERMS, REVIEW QUESTIONS, AND PROBLEMS

Key Terms

abelian group	generator	modulo operator
associative	greatest common divisor	modulus
coefficient set	group	monic polynomial
commutative	identity element	order
commutative ring	infinite group	polynomial
cyclic group	infinite ring	polynomial arithmetic
divisor	infinite field	polynomial ring
Euclidean algorithm	integral domain	prime number
field	inverse element	prime polynomial
finite group	irreducible polynomial	relatively prime
finite ring	modular arithmetic	residue
finite field	modular polynomial arithmetic	ring

Review Questions

4.1. Briefly define a group.
4.2. Briefly define a ring.
4.3. Briefly define a field.
4.4. What does it mean to say that b is a divisor of a?
4.5. What is the difference between modular arithmetic and ordinary arithmetic?
4.6. List three classes of polynomial arithmetic.

Problems

4.1 For the group S_n of all permutations of n distinct symbols,
 a. What is the number of elements in S_n?
 b. Show that S_n is not abelian for $n > 2$.

4.2 Does the set of residue classes modulo 3 form a group
 a. with respect to addition?
 b. with respect to multiplication?

4.3 Consider the set $S = \{a, b\}$ with addition and multiplication defined by the tables:

+	a	b
a	a	b
b	b	a

×	a	b
a	a	a
b	a	b

Is S a ring? Justify your answer.

4.4 Reformulate Equation (4.1), removing the restriction that a is a nonnegative integer. That is, let a be any integer.

4.5 Draw a figure similar to Figure 4.2 for $a < 0$.

4.6 Find integers x such that
 a. $5x \equiv 4 \pmod 3$
 b. $7x \equiv 6 \pmod 5$
 c. $9x \equiv 8 \pmod 7$

4.7 In this text we assume that the modulus is a positive integer. But the definition of the expression $a \bmod n$ also makes perfect sense if n is negative. Determine the following:
 a. $5 \bmod 3$
 b. $5 \bmod -3$
 c. $-5 \bmod 3$
 d. $-5 \bmod -3$

4.8 A modulus of 0 does not fit the definition, but is defined by convention as follows: $a \bmod 0 = a$. With this definition in mind, what does the following expression mean: $a \equiv b \pmod 0$?

4.9 In Section 4.2, we define the congruence relationship as follows: Two integers a and b are said to be congruent modulo n, if $(a \bmod n) = (b \bmod n)$. We then proved that $a \equiv b \pmod n$ if $n|(a - b)$. Some texts on number theory use this latter relationship as the definition of congruence: Two integers a and b are said to be congruent modulo n, if $n|(a - b)$. Using this latter definition as the starting point, prove that if $(a \bmod n) = (b \bmod n)$, then n divides $(a - b)$.

4.10 What is the smallest positive integer that has exactly k divisors, for $1 \le k \le 6$?

4.11 Prove the following:
 a. $a \equiv b \pmod n$ implies $b \equiv a \pmod n$
 b. $a \equiv b \pmod n$ and $b \equiv c \pmod n$ imply $a \equiv c \pmod n$

4.12 Prove the following:
 a. $[(a \bmod n) - (b \bmod n)] \bmod n = (a - b) \bmod n$
 b. $[(a \bmod n) \times (b \bmod n)] \bmod n = (a \times b) \bmod n$

4.13 Find the multiplicative inverse of each nonzero element in Z_5.

4.14 Show that an integer N is congruent modulo 9 to the sum of its decimal digits. For example, $475 \equiv 4 + 7 + 5 \equiv 16 \equiv 1 + 6 \equiv 7 \pmod 9$. This is the basis for the familiar procedure of "casting out 9's" when checking computations in arithmetic.

4.15 **a.** Determine gcd(24140, 16762).
b. Determine gcd(4655, 12075).

4.16 The purpose of this problem is to set an upper bound on the number of iterations of the Euclidean algorithm.
a. Suppose that $m = qn + r$ with $q > 0$ and $0 \leq r < n$. Show that $m/2 > r$.
b. Let A_i be the value of A in the Euclidean algorithm after the ith iteration. Show that

$$A_{i+2} < \frac{A_i}{2}$$

c. Show that if m, n, and N are integers with $1 \leq m, n, \leq 2^N$, then the Euclidean algorithm takes at most $2N$ steps to find gcd(m, n).

4.17 The Euclidean algorithm has been known for over 2000 years and has always been a favorite among number theorists. After these many years, there is now a potential competitor, invented by J. Stein in 1961. Stein's algorithms is as follows. Determine $\gcd(A, B)$ with $A, B \geq 1$.

STEP 1 Set $A_1 = A, B_1 = B, C_1 = 1$
STEP n (1) If $A_n = B_n$ stop. $\gcd(A, B) = A_nC_n$
(2) If A_n and B_n are both even, set $A_{n+1} = A_n/2, B_{n+1} = B_n/2, C_{n+1} = 2C_n$
(3) If A_n is even and B_n is odd, set $A_{n+1} = A_n/2, B_{n+1} = B_n, C_{n+1} = C_n$
(4) If A_n is odd and B_n is even, set $A_{n+1} = A_n, B_{n+1} = B_n/2, C_{n+1} = C_n$
(5) If A_n and B_n are both odd, set $A_{n+1} = |A_n - B_n|, B_{n+1} = \min(B_n, A_n)$, $C_{n+1} = C_n$

Continue to step $n + 1$.

a. To get a feel for the two algorithms, compute gcd(2152, 764) using both the Euclidean and Stein's algorithm.
b. What is the apparent advantage of Stein's algorithm over the Euclidean algorithm?

4.18 **a.** Show that if Stein's algorithm does not stop before the nth step, then

$$C_{n+1} \times \gcd(A_{n+1}, B_{n+1}) = C_n \times \gcd(A_n, B_n)$$

b. Show that if the algorithm does not stop before step $(n - 1)$, then

$$A_{n+2}B_{n+2} \leq \frac{A_nB_n}{2}$$

c. Show that if $1 \leq A, B \leq 2^N$, then Stein's algorithm takes at most $4N$ steps to find gcd(m, n). Thus, Stein's algorithm works in roughly the same number of steps as the Euclidean algorithm.
d. Demonstrate that Stein's algorithm does indeed return gcd(A, B).

4.19 Using the extended Euclidean algorithm, find the multiplicative inverse of
a. 1234 mod 4321
b. 24140 mod 40902
c. 550 mod 1769

4.20 Develop a set of tables similar to Table 4.3 for GF(5).

4.21 Demonstrate that the set of polynomials whose coefficients form a field is a ring.

4.22 Demonstrate whether each of these statements is true or false for polynomials over a field:
a. The product of monic polynomials is monic.
b. The product of polynomials of degrees m and n has degree $m + n$.
c. The sum of polynomials of degrees m and n has degree max[m, n].

4.23 For polynomial arithmetic with coefficients in Z_{10}, perform the following calculations:
   a. $(7x + 2) - (x^2 + 5)$
   b. $(6x^2 + x + 3) \times (5x^2 + 2)$

4.24 Determine which of the following are reducible over GF(2):
   a. $x^3 + 1$
   b. $x^3 + x^2 + 1$
   c. $x^4 + 1$ (be careful)

4.25 Determine the gcd of the following pairs of polynomials:
   a. $x^3 + x + 1$ and $x^2 + x + 1$ over GF(2)
   b. $x^3 - x + 1$ and $x^2 + 1$ over GF(3)
   c. $x^5 + x^4 + x^3 - x^2 - x + 1$ and $x^3 + x^2 + x + 1$ over GF(3)
   d. $x^5 + 88x^4 + 73x^3 + 83x^2 + 51x + 67$ and $x^3 + 97x^2 + 40x + 38$ over GF(101)

4.26 Develop a set of tables similar to Table 4.6 for GF(4) with $m(x) = x^2 + x + 1$.

4.27 Determine the multiplicative inverse of $x^3 + x + 1$ in GF(2^4), with $m(x) = x^4 + x + 1$.

4.28 Develop a table similar to Table 4.8 for GF(2^4) with $m(x) = x^4 + x + 1$.

Programming Problems

4.29 Write a simple four-function calculator in GF(2^4). You may use table lookups for the multiplicative inverses.

4.30 Write a simple four-function calculator in GF(2^8). You should compute the multiplicative inverses on the fly.

CHAPTER 5

ADVANCED ENCRYPTION STANDARD

"It seems very simple."
"It is very simple. But if you don't know what the key is it's virtually indecipherable."

—*Talking to Strange Men,* Ruth Rendell

KEY POINTS

- AES is a block cipher intended to replace DES for commercial applications. It uses a 128-bit block size and a key size of 128, 192, or 256 bits.
- AES does not use a Feistel structure. Instead, each full round consists of four separate functions: byte substitution, permutation, arithmetic operations over a finite field, and XOR with a key.

The Advanced Encryption Standard (AES) was published by NIST (National Institute of Standards and Technology) in 2001. AES is a symmetric block cipher that is intended to replace DES as the approved standard for a wide range of applications. In this chapter, we first look at the evaluation criteria used by NIST to select a candidate for AES and then examine the cipher itself.

Compared to public-key ciphers such as RSA, the structure of AES, and most symmetric ciphers, is very complex and cannot be explained as easily as RSA and similar algorithms. Accordingly, the reader may with to begin with a simplified version of AES, which is described in Appendix 5B. This version allows the reader to perform encryption and decryption by hand and gain a good understanding of the working of the algorithm details. Classroom experience indicates that a study of this simplified version enhances understanding of AES.[1]

5.1 EVALUATION CRITERIA FOR AES

The Origins of AES

We mentioned in Chapter 3 that in 1999, NIST issued a new version of its DES standard (FIPS PUB 46-3) that indicated that DES should only be used for legacy systems and that triple DES (3DES) be used. We describe 3DES in Chapter 6. 3DES has two attractions that assure its widespread use over the next few years. First, with its 168-bit key length, it overcomes the vulnerability to brute-force attack of DES. Second, the underlying encryption algorithm in 3DES is the same as in DES. This algorithm has been subjected to more scrutiny than any other encryption algorithm over a longer period of time, and no effective cryptanalytic attack based on the algorithm rather

[1]However, you may safely skip Appendix 5B, at least on a first reading. If you get lost or bogged down in the details of AES, then you can go back and start with simplified AES.

than brute force has been found. Accordingly, there is a high level of confidence that 3DES is very resistant to cryptanalysis. If security were the only consideration, then 3DES would be an appropriate choice for a standardized encryption algorithm for decades to come.

The principal drawback of 3DES is that the algorithm is relatively sluggish in software. The original DES was designed for mid-1970s hardware implementation and does not produce efficient software code. 3DES, which has three times as many rounds as DES, is correspondingly slower. A secondary drawback is that both DES and 3DES use a 64-bit block size. For reasons of both efficiency and security, a larger block size is desirable.

Because of these drawbacks, 3DES is not a reasonable candidate for long-term use. As a replacement, NIST in 1997 issued a call for proposals for a new Advanced Encryption Standard (AES), which should have a security strength equal to or better than 3DES and significantly improved efficiency. In addition to these general requirements, NIST specified that AES must be a symmetric block cipher with a block length of 128 bits and support for key lengths of 128, 192, and 256 bits.

In a first round of evaluation, 15 proposed algorithms were accepted. A second round narrowed the field to 5 algorithms. NIST completed its evaluation process and published a final standard (FIPS PUB 197) in November of 2001. NIST selected Rijndael as the proposed AES algorithm. The two researchers who developed and submitted Rijndael for the AES are both cryptographers from Belgium: Dr. Joan Daemen and Dr. Vincent Rijmen.

Ultimately, AES is intended to replace 3DES, but this process will take a number of years. NIST anticipates that 3DES will remain an approved algorithm (for U.S. government use) for the foreseeable future.

AES Evaluation

It is worth examining the criteria used by NIST to evaluate potential candidates. These criteria span the range of concerns for the practical application of modern symmetric block ciphers. In fact, two set of criteria evolved. When NIST issued its original request for candidate algorithm nominations in 1997 [NIST97], the request stated that candidate algorithms would be compared based on the factors shown in Table 5.1 (ranked in descending order of relative importance). The three categories of criteria were as follows:

- **Security:** This refers to the effort required to cryptanalyze an algorithm. The emphasis in the evaluation was on the practicality of the attack. Because the minimum key size for AES is 128 bits, brute-force attacks with current and projected technology were considered impractical. Therefore, the emphasis, with respect to this point, is cryptanalysis other than a brute-force attack.
- **Cost:** NIST intends AES to be practical in a wide range of applications. Accordingly, AES must have high computational efficiency, so as to be usable in high-speed applications, such as broadband links.

Table 5.1 NIST Evaluation Criteria for AES (September 12, 1997)

SECURITY

- **Actual security:** compared to other submitted algorithms (at the same key and block size).
- **Randomness:** the extent to which the algorithm output is indistinguishable from a random permutation on the input block.
- **Soundness:** of the mathematical basis for the algorithm's security.
- **Other security factors:** raised by the public during the evaluation process, including any attacks which demonstrate that the actual security of the algorithm is less than the strength claimed by the submitter.

COST

- **Licensing requirements:** NIST intends that when the AES is issued, the algorithm(s) specified in the AES shall be available on a worldwide, non-exclusive, royalty-free basis.
- **Computational efficiency:** The evaluation of computational efficiency will be applicable to both hardware and software implementations. Round 1 analysis by NIST will focus primarily on software implementations and specifically on one key-block size combination (128-128); more attention will be paid to hardware implementations and other supported key-block size combinations during Round 2 analysis. Computational efficiency essentially refers to the speed of the algorithm. Public comments on each algorithm's efficiency (particularly for various platforms and applications) will also be taken into consideration by NIST.
- **Memory requirements:** The memory required to implement a candidate algorithm—for both hardware and software implementations of the algorithm—will also be considered during the evaluation process. Round 1 analysis by NIST will focus primarily on software implementations; more attention will be paid to hardware implementations during Round 2. Memory requirements will include such factors as gate counts for hardware implementations, and code size and RAM requirements for software implementations.

ALGORITHM AND IMPLEMENTATION CHARACTERISTICS

- **Flexibility:** Candidate algorithms with greater flexibility will meet the needs of more users than less flexible ones, and therefore, inter alia, are preferable. However, some extremes of functionality are of little practical application (e.g., extremely short key lengths); for those cases, preference will not be given. Some examples of flexibility may include (but are not limited to) the following:
  a. The algorithm can accommodate additional key- and block-sizes (e.g., 64-bit block sizes, key sizes other than those specified in the Minimum Acceptability Requirements section, [e.g., keys between 128 and 256 that are multiples of 32 bits, etc.])
  b. The algorithm can be implemented securely and efficiently in a wide variety of platforms and applications (e.g., 8-bit processors, ATM networks, voice & satellite communications, HDTV, B-ISDN, etc.).
  c. The algorithm can be implemented as a stream cipher, message authentication code (MAC) generator, pseudorandom number generator, hashing algorithm, etc.
- **Hardware and software suitability:** A candidate algorithm shall not be restrictive in the sense that it can only be implemented in hardware. If one can also implement the algorithm efficiently in firmware, then this will be an advantage in the area of flexibility.
- **Simplicity:** A candidate algorithm shall be judged according to relative simplicity of design.

- **Algorithm and implementation characteristics:** This category includes a variety of considerations, including flexibility; suitability for a variety of hardware and software implementations; and simplicity, which will make an analysis of security more straightforward.

Using these criteria, the initial field of 21 candidate algorithms was reduced first to 15 candidates and then to 5 candidates. By the time that a final evaluation had been done the evaluation criteria, as described in [NECH00], had evolved. The following criteria were used in the final evaluation:

- **General security:** To assess general security, NIST relied on the public security analysis conducted by the cryptographic community. During the course of the three-year evaluation process, a number of cryptographers published their analyses of the strengths and weaknesses of the various candidates. There was particular emphasis on analyzing the candidates with respect to known attacks, such as differential and linear cryptanalysis. However, compared to the analysis of DES, the amount of time and the number of cryptographers devoted to analyzing Rijndael are quite limited. Now that a single AES cipher has been chosen, we can expect to see a more extensive security analysis by the cryptographic community.
- **Software implementations:** The principal concerns in this category are execution speed, performance across a variety of platforms, and variation of speed with key size.
- **Restricted-space environments:** In some applications, such as smart cards, relatively small amounts of random-access memory (RAM) and/or read-only memory (ROM) are available for such purposes as code storage (generally in ROM); representation of data objects such as S-boxes (which could be stored in ROM or RAM, depending on whether pre-computation or Boolean representation is used); and subkey storage (in RAM).
- **Hardware implementations:** Like software, hardware implementations can be optimized for speed or for size. However, in the case of hardware, size translates much more directly into cost than is usually the case for software implementations. Doubling the size of an encryption program may make little difference on a general-purpose computer with a large memory, but doubling the area used in a hardware device typically more than doubles the cost of the device.
- **Attacks on implementations:** The criterion of general security, discussed in the first bullet, is concerned with cryptanalytic attacks that exploit mathematical properties of the algorithms. There is another class of attacks that use physical measurements conducted during algorithm execution to gather information about quantities such as keys. Such attacks exploit a combination of intrinsic algorithm characteristics and implementation-dependent features. Examples of such attacks are timing attacks and power analysis. Timing attacks are described in Chapter 3. The basic idea behind power analysis [KOCH98, BIHA00] is the observation that the power consumed by a smart card at any particular time during the cryptographic operation is related to the instruction being executed and to the data being processed. For example, multiplication consumes more power than addition, and writing 1s consumes more power than writing 0s.
- **Encryption versus decryption:** This criterion deals with several issues related to considerations of both encryption and decryption. If the encryption and decryption algorithms differ, then extra space is needed for the decryption.

Also, whether the two algorithms are the same or not, there may be timing differences between encryption and decryption.

- **Key agility:** Key agility refers to the ability to change keys quickly and with a minimum of resources. This includes both subkey computation and the ability to switch between different ongoing security associations when subkeys may already be available.
- **Other versatility and flexibility:** [NECH00] indicates two areas that fall into this category. Parameter flexibility includes ease of support for other key and block sizes and ease of increasing the number of rounds in order to cope with newly discovered attacks. Implementation flexibility refers to the possibility of optimizing cipher elements for particular environments.
- **Potential for instruction-level parallelism:** This criterion refers to the ability to exploit ILP features in current and future processors.

Table 5.2 shows the assessment that NIST provided for Rijndael based on these criteria.

Table 5.2 Final NIST Evaluation of Rijndael (October 2, 2000)

General Security Rijndael has no known security attacks. Rijndael uses S-boxes as nonlinear components. Rijndael appears to have an adequate security margin, but has received some criticism suggesting that its mathematical structure may lead to attacks. On the other hand, the simple structure may have facilitated its security analysis during the timeframe of the AES development process.
Software Implementations Rijndael performs encryption and decryption very well across a variety of platforms, including 8-bit and 64-bit platforms, and DSPs. However, there is a decrease in performance with the higher key sizes because of the increased number of rounds that are performed. Rijndael's high inherent parallelism facilitates the efficient use of processor resources, resulting in very good software performance even when implemented in a mode not capable of interleaving. Rijndael's key setup time is fast.
Restricted-Space Environments In general, Rijndael is very well suited for restricted-space environments where either encryption or decryption is implemented (but not both). It has very low RAM and ROM requirements. A drawback is that ROM requirements will increase if both encryption and decryption are implemented simultaneously, although it appears to remain suitable for these environments. The key schedule for decryption is separate from encryption.
Hardware Implementations Rijndael has the highest throughput of any of the finalists for feedback modes and second highest for non-feedback modes. For the 192 and 256-bit key sizes, throughput falls in standard and unrolled implementations because of the additional number of rounds. For fully pipelined implementations, the area requirement increases, but the throughput is unaffected.
Attacks on Implementations The operations used by Rijndael are among the easiest to defend against power and timing attacks. The use of masking techniques to provide Rijndael with some defense against these attacks does not cause significant performance degradation relative to the other finalists, and its RAM requirement remains reasonable. Rijndael appears to gain a major speed advantage over its competitors when such protections are considered.

(*Continued*)

Table 5.2 Continued

Encryption vs. Decryption The encryption and decryption functions in Rijndael differ. One FPGA study reports that the implementation of both encryption and decryption takes about 60% more space than the implementation of encryption alone. Rijndael's speed does not vary significantly between encryption and decryption, although the key setup performance is slower for decryption than for encryption.
Key Agility Rijndael supports on-the-fly subkey computation for encryption. Rijndael requires a one-time execution of the key schedule to generate all subkeys prior to the first decryption with a specific key. This places a slight resource burden on the key agility of Rijndael.
Other Versatility and Flexibility Rijndael fully supports block sizes and key sizes of 128 bits, 192 bits and 256 bits, in any combination. In principle, the Rijndael structure can accommodate any block sizes and key sizes that are multiples of 32, as well as changes in the number of rounds that are specified.
Potential for Instruction-Level Parallelism Rijndael has an excellent potential for parallelism for a single block encryption.

5.2 THE AES CIPHER[2]

The Rijndael proposal for AES defined a cipher in which the block length and the key length can be independently specified to be 128, 192, or 256 bits. The AES specification uses the same three key size alternatives but limits the block length to 128 bits. A number of AES parameters depend on the key length (Table 5.3). In the description of this section, we assume a key length of 128 bits, which is likely to be the one most commonly implemented.

Rijndael was designed to have the following characteristics:

- Resistance against all known attacks
- Speed and code compactness on a wide range of platforms
- Design simplicity

Figure 5.1 shows the overall structure of AES. The input to the encryption and decryption algorithms is a single 128-bit block. In FIPS PUB 197, this block is depicted as a square matrix of bytes. This block is copied into the **State** array, which is

Table 5.3 AES Parameters

Key size (words/bytes/bits)	4/16/128	6/24/192	8/32/256
Plaintext block size (words/bytes/bits)	4/16/128	4/16/128	4/16/128
Number of rounds	10	12	14
Round key size (words/bytes/bits)	4/16/128	4/16/128	4/16/128
Expanded key size (words/bytes)	44/176	52/208	60/240

[2]Much of the material in this section originally appeared in [STAL02].

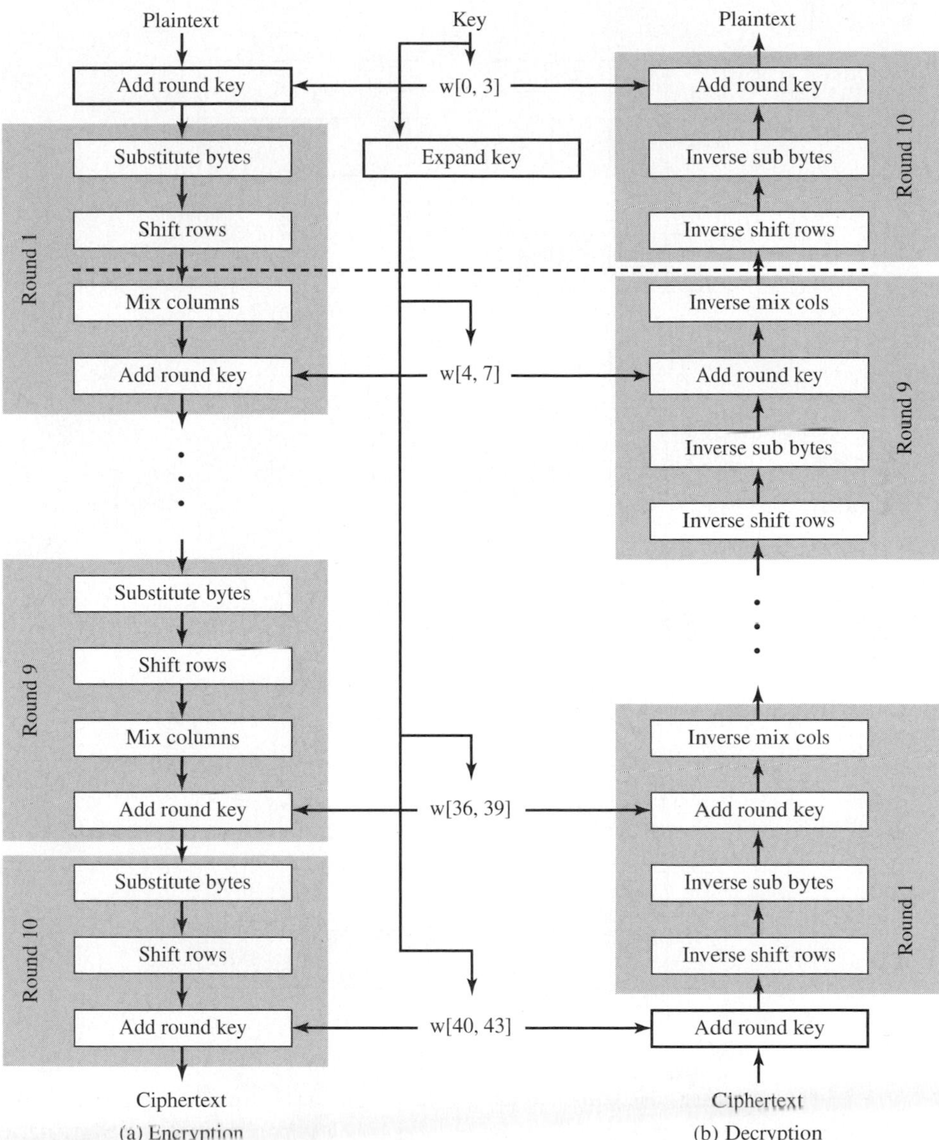

Figure 5.1 AES Encryption and Decryption

modified at each stage of encryption or decryption. After the final stage, **State** is copied to an output matrix. These operations are depicted in Figure 5.2a. Similarly, the 128-bit key is depicted as a square matrix of bytes. This key is then expanded into an array of key schedule words; each word is four bytes and the total key schedule is 44 words for the 128-bit key (Figure 5.2b). Note that the ordering of bytes within a matrix is by column. So, for example, the first four bytes of a 128-bit plaintext input to the encryption cipher occupy the first column of the **in** matrix, the second four bytes occupy the second column, and so on. Similarly, the first four bytes of the expanded key, which form a word, occupy the first column of the **w** matrix.

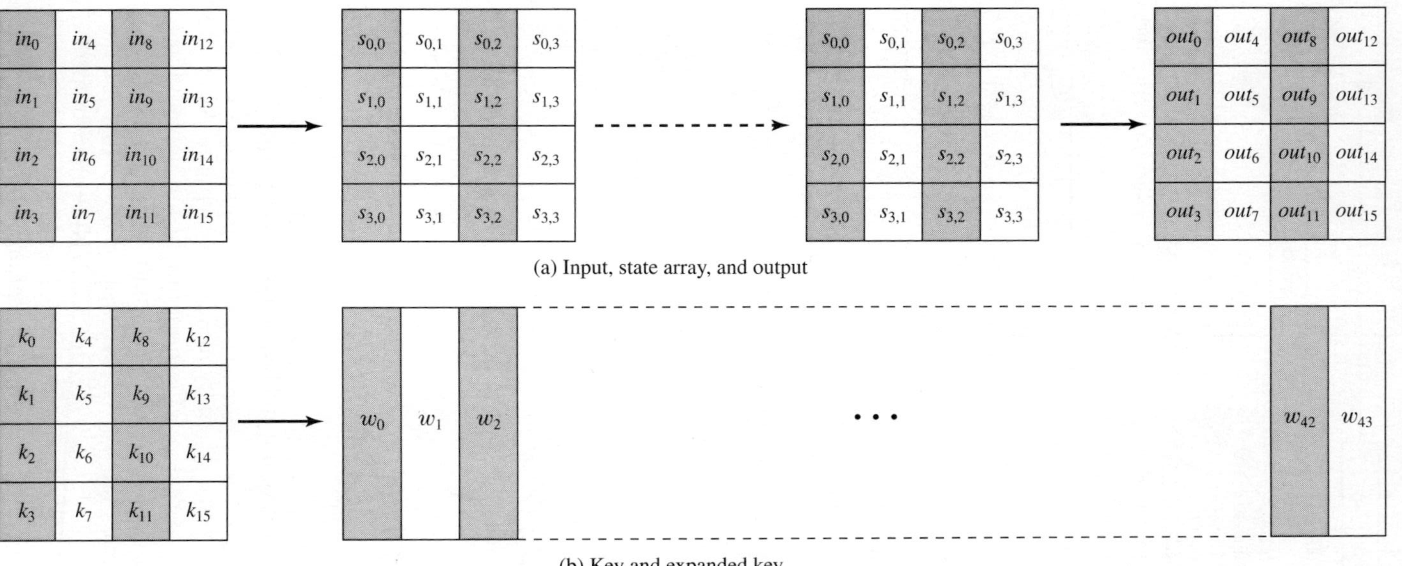

Figure 5.2 AES Data Structures

Before delving into details, we can make several comments about the overall AES structure:

1. One noteworthy feature of this structure is that it is not a Feistel structure. Recall that in the classic Feistel structure, half of the data block is used to modify the other half of the data block, and then the halves are swapped. Two of the AES finalists, including Rijndael, do not use a Feistel structure but process the entire data block in parallel during each round using substitutions and permutation.
2. The key that is provided as input is expanded into an array of forty-four 32-bit words, **w**[*i*]. Four distinct words (128 bits) serve as a round key for each round; these are indicated in Figure 5.1.
3. Four different stages are used, one of permutation and three of substitution:
   - **Substitute bytes:** Uses an S-box to perform a byte-by-byte substitution of the block
   - **ShiftRows:** A simple permutation
   - **MixColumns:** A substitution that makes use of arithmetic over GF(2^8)
   - **AddRoundKey:** A simple bitwise XOR of the current block with a portion of the expanded key
4. The structure is quite simple. For both encryption and decryption, the cipher begins with an AddRoundKey stage, followed by nine rounds that each includes all four stages, followed by a tenth round of three stages. Figure 5.3 depicts the structure of a full encryption round.
5. Only the AddRoundKey stage makes use of the key. For this reason, the cipher begins and ends with an AddRoundKey stage. Any other stage, applied at the beginning or end, is reversible without knowledge of the key and so would add no security.
6. The AddRoundKey stage is, in effect, a form of Vernam cipher and by itself would not be formidable. The other three stages together provide confusion, diffusion, and nonlinearity, but by themselves would provide no security because they do not use the key. We can view the cipher as alternating operations of XOR encryption (AddRoundKey) of a block, followed by scrambling of the block (the other three stages), followed by XOR encryption, and so on. This scheme is both efficient and highly secure.
7. Each stage is easily reversible. For the Substitute Byte, ShiftRows, and MixColumns stages, an inverse function is used in the decryption algorithm. For the AddRoundKey stage, the inverse is achieved by XORing the same round key to the block, using the result that $A \oplus A \oplus B = B$.
8. As with most block ciphers, the decryption algorithm makes use of the expanded key in reverse order. However, the decryption algorithm is not identical to the encryption algorithm. This is a consequence of the particular structure of AES.
9. Once it is established that all four stages are reversible, it is easy to verify that decryption does recover the plaintext. Figure 5.1 lays out encryption and decryption going in opposite vertical directions. At each horizontal

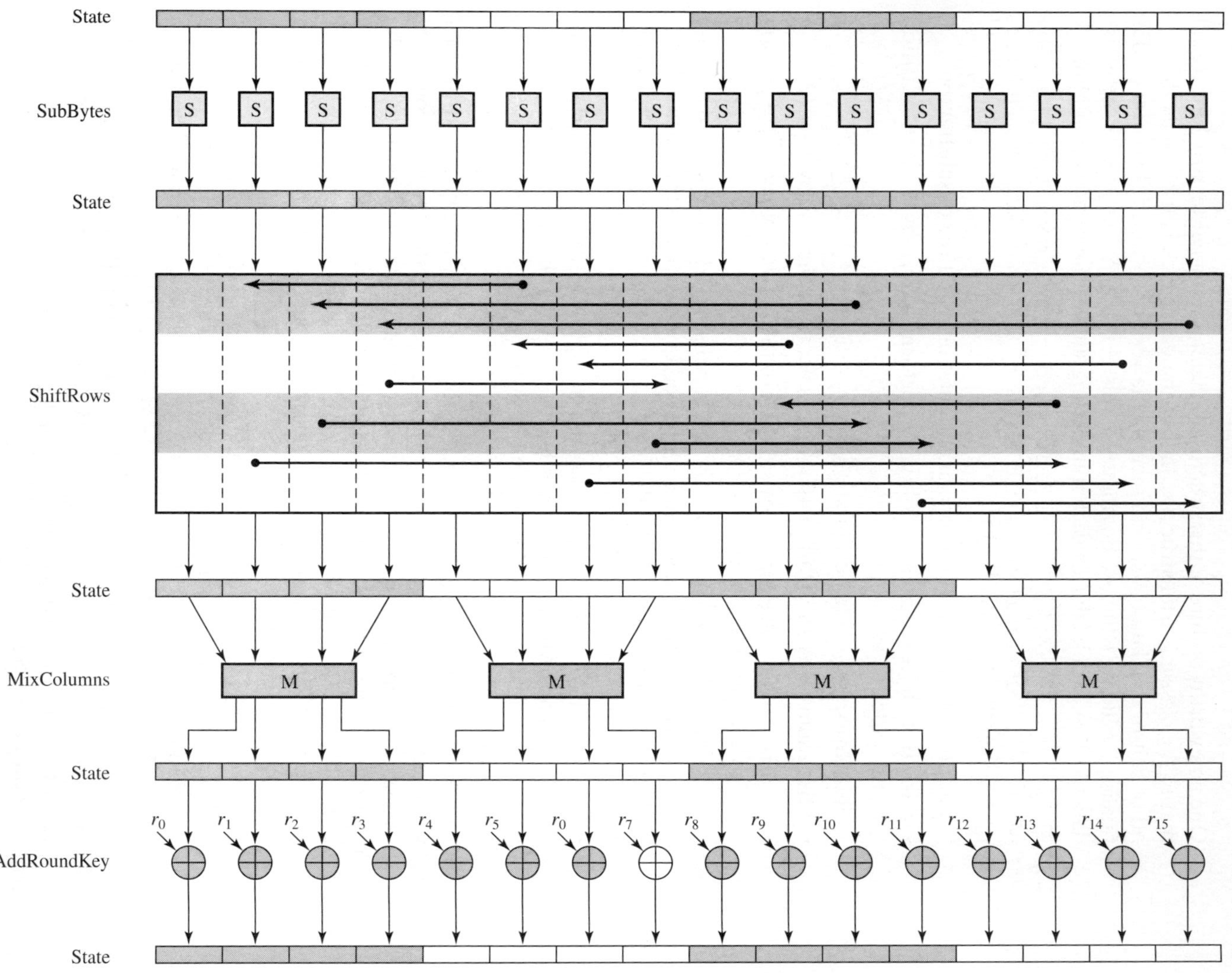

Figure 5.3 AES Encryption Round

point (e.g., the dashed line in the figure), **State** is the same for both encryption and decryption.

10. The final round of both encryption and decryption consists of only three stages. Again, this is a consequence of the particular structure of AES and is required to make the cipher reversible.

We now turn to a discussion of each of the four stages used in AES. For each stage, we describe the forward (encryption) algorithm, the inverse (decryption) algorithm, and the rationale for the stage. This is followed by a discussion of key expansion.

As was mentioned in Chapter 4, AES uses arithmetic in the finite field GF(2^8), with the irreducible polynomial[3] $m(x) = x^8 + x^4 + x^3 + x + 1$. The developers of Rijndael give as their motivation for selecting this one of the 30 possible irreducible polynomials of degree 8 that it is the first one on the list given in [LIDL94].

Substitute Bytes Transformation

Forward and Inverse Transformations The **forward substitute byte transformation**, called SubBytes, is a simple table lookup (Figure 5.4a). AES defines a 16 × 16 matrix of byte values, called an S-box (Table 5.4a), that contains a permutation of all

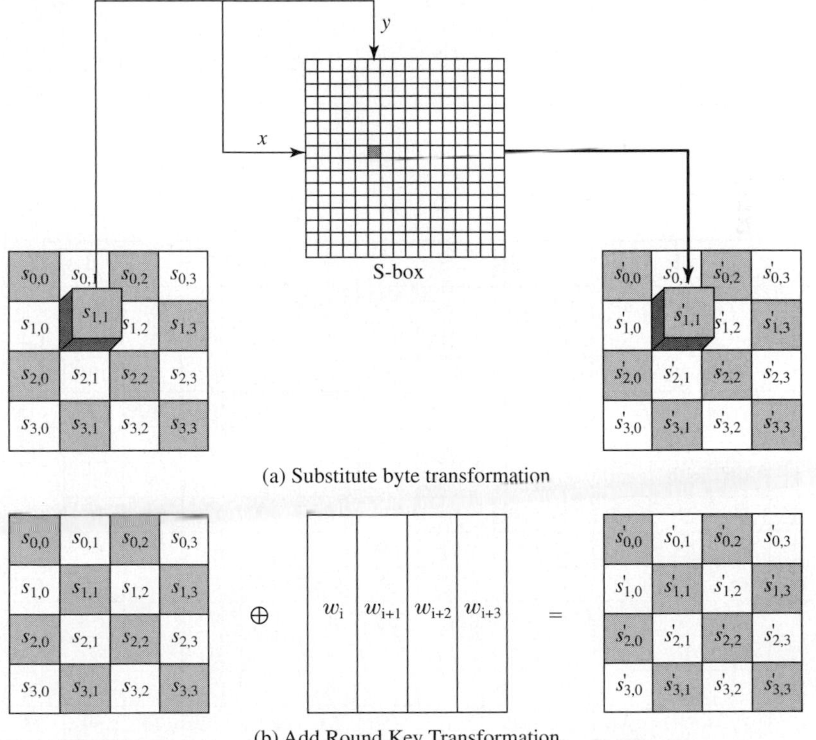

Figure 5.4 AES Byte-Level Operations

[3]In the remainder of this discussion, references to GF(2^8) refer to the finite field defined with this polynomial.

Table 5.4 AES S-Boxes

(a) S-box

		y															
		0	**1**	**2**	**3**	**4**	**5**	**6**	**7**	**8**	**9**	**A**	**B**	**C**	**D**	**E**	**F**
	0	63	7C	77	7B	F2	6B	6F	C5	30	01	67	2B	FE	D7	AB	76
	1	CA	82	C9	7D	FA	59	47	F0	AD	D4	A2	AF	9C	A4	72	C0
	2	B7	FD	93	26	36	3F	F7	CC	34	A5	E5	F1	71	D8	31	15
	3	04	C7	23	C3	18	96	05	9A	07	12	80	E2	EB	27	B2	75
	4	09	83	2C	1A	1B	6E	5A	A0	52	3B	D6	B3	29	E3	2F	84
	5	53	D1	00	ED	20	FC	B1	5B	6A	CB	BE	39	4A	4C	58	CF
	6	D0	EF	AA	FB	43	4D	33	85	45	F9	02	7F	50	3C	9F	A8
x	**7**	51	A3	40	8F	92	9D	38	F5	BC	B6	DA	21	10	FF	F3	D2
	8	CD	0C	13	EC	5F	97	44	17	C4	A7	7E	3D	64	5D	19	73
	9	60	81	4F	DC	22	2A	90	88	46	EE	B8	14	DE	5E	0B	DB
	A	E0	32	3A	0A	49	06	24	5C	C2	D3	AC	62	91	95	E4	79
	B	E7	C8	37	6D	8D	D5	4E	A9	6C	56	F4	EA	65	7A	AE	08
	C	BA	78	25	2E	1C	A6	B4	C6	E8	DD	74	1F	4B	BD	8B	8A
	D	70	3E	B5	66	48	03	F6	0E	61	35	57	B9	86	C1	1D	9E
	E	E1	F8	98	11	69	D9	8E	94	9B	1E	87	E9	CE	55	28	DF
	F	8C	A1	89	0D	BF	E6	42	68	41	99	2D	0F	B0	54	BB	16

(b) Inverse S-box

		y															
		0	**1**	**2**	**3**	**4**	**5**	**6**	**7**	**8**	**9**	**A**	**B**	**C**	**D**	**E**	**F**
	0	52	09	6A	D5	30	36	A5	38	BF	40	A3	9E	81	F3	D7	FB
	1	7C	E3	39	82	9B	2F	FF	87	34	8E	43	44	C4	DE	E9	CB
	2	54	7B	94	32	A6	C2	23	3D	EE	4C	95	0B	42	FA	C3	4E
	3	08	2E	A1	66	28	D9	24	B2	76	5B	A2	49	6D	8B	D1	25
	4	72	F8	F6	64	86	68	98	16	D4	A4	5C	CC	5D	65	B6	92
	5	6C	70	48	50	FD	ED	B9	DA	5E	15	46	57	A7	8D	9D	84
	6	90	D8	AB	00	8C	BC	D3	0A	F7	E4	58	05	B8	B3	45	06
x	**7**	D0	2C	1E	8F	CA	3F	0F	02	C1	AF	BD	03	01	13	8A	6B
	8	3A	91	11	41	4F	67	DC	EA	97	F2	CF	CE	F0	B4	E6	73
	9	96	AC	74	22	E7	AD	35	85	E2	F9	37	E8	1C	75	DF	6E
	A	47	F1	1A	71	1D	29	C5	89	6F	B7	62	0E	AA	18	BE	1B
	B	FC	56	3E	4B	C6	D2	79	20	9A	DB	C0	FE	78	CD	5A	F4
	C	1F	DD	A8	33	88	07	C7	31	B1	12	10	59	27	80	EC	5F
	D	60	51	7F	A9	19	B5	4A	0D	2D	E5	7A	9F	93	C9	9C	EF
	E	A0	E0	3B	4D	AE	2A	F5	B0	C8	EB	BB	3C	83	53	99	61
	F	17	2B	04	7E	BA	77	D6	26	E1	69	14	63	55	21	0C	7D

possible 256 8-bit values. Each individual byte of **State** is mapped into a new byte in the following way: The leftmost 4 bits of the byte are used as a row value and the rightmost 4 bits are used as a column value. These row and column values serve as indexes into the S-box to select a unique 8-bit output value. For example, the hexadecimal value[4] {95} references row 9, column 5 of the S-box, which contains the value {2A}. Accordingly, the value {95} is mapped into the value {2A}.

Here is an example of the SubBytes transformation:

EA	04	65	85
83	45	5D	96
5C	33	98	B0
F0	2D	AD	C5

→

87	F2	4D	97
EC	6E	4C	90
4A	C3	46	E7
8C	D8	95	A6

The S-box is constructed in the following fashion:

1. Initialize the S-box with the byte values in ascending sequence row by row. The first row contains {00}, {01}, {02},.... {0F}; the second row contains {10}, {11}, etc.; and so on. Thus, the value of the byte at row x, column y is $\{xy\}$.
2. Map each byte in the S-box to its multiplicative inverse in the finite field GF(2^8); the value {00} is mapped to itself.
3. Consider that each byte in the S-box consists of 8 bits labeled $(b_7, b_6, b_5, b_4, b_3, b_2, b_1, b_0)$. Apply the following transformation to each bit of each byte in the S-box:

$$b_i' = b_i \oplus b_{(i+4) \bmod 8} \oplus b_{(i+5) \bmod 8} \oplus b_{(i+6) \bmod 8} \oplus b_{(i+7) \bmod 8} \oplus c_i \qquad \textbf{(5.1)}$$

where c_i is the ith bit of byte c with the value {63}; that is, $(c_7c_6c_5c_4c_3c_2c_1c_0) = (01100011)$. The prime (′) indicates that the variable is to be updated by the value on the right. The AES standard depicts this transformation in matrix form as follows:

$$\begin{bmatrix} b_0' \\ b_1' \\ b_2' \\ b_3' \\ b_4' \\ b_5' \\ b_6' \\ b_7' \end{bmatrix} = \begin{bmatrix} 1 & 0 & 0 & 0 & 1 & 1 & 1 & 1 \\ 1 & 1 & 0 & 0 & 0 & 1 & 1 & 1 \\ 1 & 1 & 1 & 0 & 0 & 0 & 1 & 1 \\ 1 & 1 & 1 & 1 & 0 & 0 & 0 & 1 \\ 1 & 1 & 1 & 1 & 1 & 0 & 0 & 0 \\ 0 & 1 & 1 & 1 & 1 & 1 & 0 & 0 \\ 0 & 0 & 1 & 1 & 1 & 1 & 1 & 0 \\ 0 & 0 & 0 & 1 & 1 & 1 & 1 & 1 \end{bmatrix} \begin{bmatrix} b_0 \\ b_1 \\ b_2 \\ b_3 \\ b_4 \\ b_5 \\ b_6 \\ b_7 \end{bmatrix} + \begin{bmatrix} 1 \\ 1 \\ 0 \\ 0 \\ 0 \\ 1 \\ 1 \\ 0 \end{bmatrix} \qquad \textbf{(5.2)}$$

[4]In FIPS PUB 197, a hexadecimal number is indicated by enclosing it in curly brackets. We use that convention in this chapter.

Equation (5.2) has to be interpreted carefully. In ordinary matrix multiplication,[5] each element in the product matrix is the sum of products of the elements or one row and one column. In this case, each element in the product matrix is the bitwise XOR of products of elements of one row and one column. Further, the final addition shown in Equation (5.2) is a bitwise XOR.

As an example, consider the input value {95}. The multiplicative inverse in GF(2^8) is $\{95\}^{-1} = \{8A\}$, which is 10001010 in binary. Using Equation (5.2),

$$\begin{bmatrix} 1&0&0&0&1&1&1&1\\ 1&1&0&0&0&1&1&1\\ 1&1&1&0&0&0&1&1\\ 1&1&1&1&0&0&0&1\\ 1&1&1&1&1&0&0&0\\ 0&1&1&1&1&1&0&0\\ 0&0&1&1&1&1&1&0\\ 0&0&0&1&1&1&1&1 \end{bmatrix} \begin{bmatrix}0\\1\\0\\1\\0\\0\\0\\1\end{bmatrix} \oplus \begin{bmatrix}1\\1\\0\\0\\0\\1\\1\\0\end{bmatrix} = \begin{bmatrix}1\\0\\0\\1\\0\\0\\1\\0\end{bmatrix} \oplus \begin{bmatrix}1\\1\\0\\0\\0\\1\\1\\0\end{bmatrix} = \begin{bmatrix}0\\1\\0\\1\\0\\1\\0\\0\end{bmatrix}$$

The result is {2A}, which should appear in row {09} column {05} of the S-box. This is verified by checking Table 5.4a.

The **inverse substitute byte transformation**, called InvSubBytes, makes use of the inverse S-box shown in Table 5.4b. Note, for example, that the input {2A} produces the output {95}, and the input {95} to the S-box produces {2A}. The inverse S-box is constructed by applying the inverse of the transformation in Equation (5.1) followed by taking the multiplicative inverse in GF(2^8). The inverse transformation is:

$$b_i' = b_{(i+2) \bmod 8} \oplus b_{(i+5) \bmod 8} \oplus b_{(i+7) \bmod 8} \oplus d_i$$

where byte $d = \{05\}$, or 00000101. We can depict this transformation as follows:

$$\begin{bmatrix} b_0'\\ b_1'\\ b_2'\\ b_3'\\ b_4'\\ b_5'\\ b_6'\\ b_7' \end{bmatrix} = \begin{bmatrix} 0&0&1&0&0&1&0&1\\ 1&0&0&1&0&0&1&0\\ 0&1&0&0&1&0&0&1\\ 1&0&1&0&0&1&0&0\\ 0&1&0&1&0&0&1&0\\ 0&0&1&0&1&0&0&1\\ 1&0&0&1&0&1&0&0\\ 0&1&0&0&1&0&1&0 \end{bmatrix} \begin{bmatrix} b_0\\ b_1\\ b_2\\ b_3\\ b_4\\ b_5\\ b_6\\ b_7 \end{bmatrix} + \begin{bmatrix}1\\0\\1\\0\\0\\0\\0\\0\end{bmatrix}$$

To see that InvSubBytes is the inverse of SubBytes, label the matrices in SubBytes and InvSubBytes as **X** and **Y**, respectively, and the vector versions of constants c

[5]For a brief review of the rules of matrix and vector multiplication, see the Math Refresher document and the Computer Science Student Resource site at **williamstallings.com/StudentSupport.html**.

and d as **C** and **D**, respectively. For some 8-bit vector **B**, Equation (5.2) becomes $\mathbf{B}' = \mathbf{XB} \oplus \mathbf{C}$. We need to show that $\mathbf{Y}(\mathbf{XB} \oplus \mathbf{C}) \oplus \mathbf{D} = \mathbf{B}$. Multiply out, we must show $\mathbf{YXB} \oplus \mathbf{YC} \oplus \mathbf{D} = \mathbf{B}$. This becomes

$$\begin{bmatrix} 0 & 0 & 1 & 0 & 0 & 1 & 0 & 1 \\ 1 & 0 & 0 & 1 & 0 & 0 & 1 & 0 \\ 0 & 1 & 0 & 0 & 1 & 0 & 0 & 1 \\ 1 & 0 & 1 & 0 & 0 & 1 & 0 & 0 \\ 0 & 1 & 0 & 1 & 0 & 0 & 1 & 0 \\ 0 & 0 & 1 & 0 & 1 & 0 & 0 & 1 \\ 1 & 0 & 0 & 1 & 0 & 1 & 0 & 0 \\ 0 & 1 & 0 & 0 & 1 & 0 & 1 & 0 \end{bmatrix} \begin{bmatrix} 1 & 0 & 0 & 0 & 1 & 1 & 1 & 1 \\ 1 & 1 & 0 & 0 & 0 & 1 & 1 & 1 \\ 1 & 1 & 1 & 0 & 0 & 0 & 1 & 1 \\ 1 & 1 & 1 & 1 & 0 & 0 & 0 & 1 \\ 1 & 1 & 1 & 1 & 1 & 0 & 0 & 0 \\ 0 & 1 & 1 & 1 & 1 & 1 & 0 & 0 \\ 0 & 0 & 1 & 1 & 1 & 1 & 1 & 0 \\ 0 & 0 & 0 & 1 & 1 & 1 & 1 & 1 \end{bmatrix} \begin{bmatrix} b_0 \\ b_1 \\ b_2 \\ b_3 \\ b_4 \\ b_5 \\ b_6 \\ b_7 \end{bmatrix} \oplus$$

$$\begin{bmatrix} 0 & 0 & 1 & 0 & 0 & 1 & 0 & 1 \\ 1 & 0 & 0 & 1 & 0 & 0 & 1 & 0 \\ 0 & 1 & 0 & 0 & 1 & 0 & 0 & 1 \\ 1 & 0 & 1 & 0 & 0 & 1 & 0 & 0 \\ 0 & 1 & 0 & 1 & 0 & 0 & 1 & 0 \\ 0 & 0 & 1 & 0 & 1 & 0 & 0 & 1 \\ 1 & 0 & 0 & 1 & 0 & 1 & 0 & 0 \\ 0 & 1 & 0 & 0 & 1 & 0 & 1 & 0 \end{bmatrix} \begin{bmatrix} 1 \\ 0 \\ 1 \\ 0 \\ 0 \\ 1 \\ 1 \\ 0 \end{bmatrix} \oplus \begin{bmatrix} 1 \\ 0 \\ 1 \\ 0 \\ 0 \\ 0 \\ 0 \\ 0 \end{bmatrix} =$$

$$\begin{bmatrix} 1 & 0 & 0 & 0 & 0 & 0 & 0 & 0 \\ 0 & 1 & 0 & 0 & 0 & 0 & 0 & 0 \\ 0 & 0 & 1 & 0 & 0 & 0 & 0 & 0 \\ 0 & 0 & 0 & 1 & 0 & 0 & 0 & 0 \\ 0 & 0 & 0 & 0 & 1 & 0 & 0 & 0 \\ 0 & 0 & 0 & 0 & 0 & 1 & 0 & 0 \\ 0 & 0 & 0 & 0 & 0 & 0 & 1 & 0 \\ 0 & 0 & 0 & 0 & 0 & 0 & 0 & 1 \end{bmatrix} \begin{bmatrix} b_0 \\ b_1 \\ b_2 \\ b_3 \\ b_4 \\ b_5 \\ b_6 \\ b_7 \end{bmatrix} \oplus \begin{bmatrix} 1 \\ 0 \\ 1 \\ 0 \\ 0 \\ 0 \\ 0 \\ 0 \end{bmatrix} \oplus \begin{bmatrix} 1 \\ 0 \\ 1 \\ 0 \\ 0 \\ 0 \\ 0 \\ 0 \end{bmatrix} = \begin{bmatrix} b_0 \\ b_1 \\ b_2 \\ b_3 \\ b_4 \\ b_5 \\ b_6 \\ b_7 \end{bmatrix}$$

We have demonstrated that **YX** equals the identity matrix, and the **YC** = **D**, so that $\mathbf{YC} \oplus \mathbf{D}$ equals the null vector.

Rationale The S-box is designed to be resistant to known cryptanalytic attacks. Specifically, the Rijndael developers sought a design that has a low correlation between input bits and output bits, and the property that the output cannot be described as a simple mathematical function of the input [DAEM01]. In addition, the constant in Equation (5.1) was chosen so that the S-box has no fixed points [S-box(a) = a] and no "opposite fixed points" [S-box(a) = $\bar{a}$], where $\bar{a}$ is the bitwise complement of a.

Of course, the S-box must be invertible, that is, IS-box[S-box(a)] = a. However, the S-box is not self-inverse in the sense that it is not true that S-box(a) = IS-box(a). For example, S-box({95}) = {2A}, but IS-box({95}) = {AD}.

ShiftRows Transformation

Forward and Inverse Transformations The **forward shift row transformation**, called ShiftRows, is depicted in Figure 5.5a. The first row of **State** is not altered. For the second row, a 1-byte circular left shift is performed. For the third row, a 2-byte circular left shift is performed. For the fourth row, a 3-byte circular left shift is performed. The following is an example of ShiftRows:

87	F2	4D	97		87	F2	4D	97
EC	6E	4C	90	→	6E	4C	90	EC
4A	C3	46	E7		46	E7	4A	C3
8C	D8	95	A6		A6	8C	D8	95

The **inverse shift row transformation**, called InvShiftRows, performs the circular shifts in the opposite direction for each of the last three rows, with a one-byte circular right shift for the second row, and so on.

Rationale The shift row transformation is more substantial than it may first appear. This is because the **State**, as well as the cipher input and output, is treated as an array of four 4-byte columns. Thus, on encryption, the first 4 bytes of the plaintext are copied to the first column of **State**, and so on. Further, as will be seen, the round key is applied to **State** column by column. Thus, a row shift moves an individual byte from one column to another, which is a linear distance of a multiple of 4 bytes. Also note that the transformation ensures that the 4 bytes of one column are spread out to four different columns. Figure 5.3 illustrates the effect.

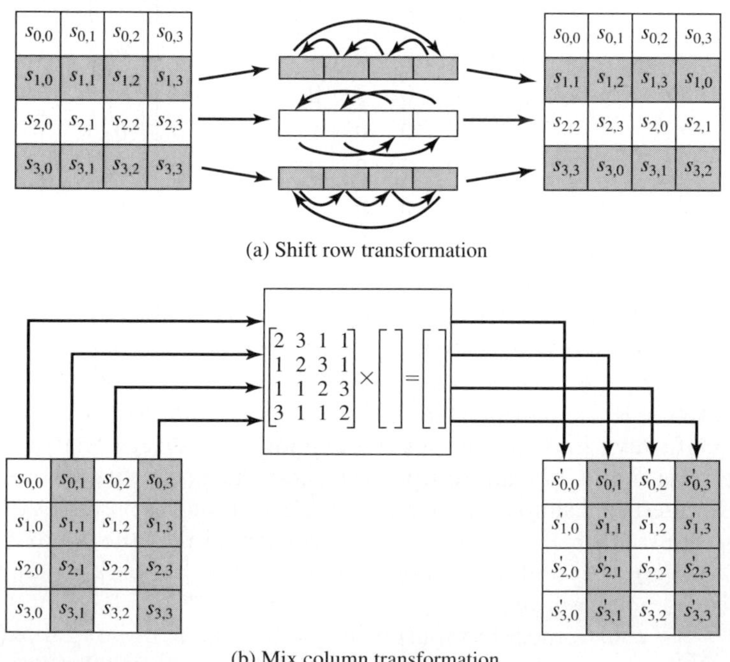

(a) Shift row transformation

(b) Mix column transformation

Figure 5.5 AES Row and Column Operations

MixColumns Transformation

Forward and Inverse Transformations The **forward mix column transformation**, called MixColumns, operates on each column individually. Each byte of a column is mapped into a new value that is a function of all four bytes in that column. The transformation can be defined by the following matrix multiplication on **State** (Figure 5.5b):

$$\begin{bmatrix} 02 & 03 & 01 & 01 \\ 01 & 02 & 03 & 01 \\ 01 & 01 & 02 & 03 \\ 03 & 01 & 01 & 02 \end{bmatrix} \begin{bmatrix} s_{0,0} & s_{0,1} & s_{0,2} & s_{0,3} \\ s_{1,0} & s_{1,1} & s_{1,2} & s_{1,3} \\ s_{2,0} & s_{2,1} & s_{2,2} & s_{2,3} \\ s_{3,0} & s_{3,1} & s_{3,2} & s_{3,3} \end{bmatrix} = \begin{bmatrix} s'_{0,0} & s'_{0,1} & s'_{0,2} & s'_{0,3} \\ s'_{1,0} & s'_{1,1} & s'_{1,2} & s'_{1,3} \\ s'_{2,0} & s'_{2,1} & s'_{2,2} & s'_{2,3} \\ s'_{3,0} & s'_{3,1} & s'_{3,2} & s'_{3,3} \end{bmatrix} \quad (5.3)$$

Each element in the product matrix is the sum of products of elements of one row and one column. In this case, the individual additions and multiplications[6] are performed in GF(2^8). The MixColumns transformation on a single column $j (0 \le j \le 3)$ of **State** can be expressed as

$$\begin{aligned} s'_{0,j} &= (2 \bullet s_{0,j}) \oplus (3 \bullet s_{1,j}) \oplus s_{2,j} \oplus s_{3,j} \\ s'_{1,j} &= s_{0,j} \oplus (2 \bullet s_{1,j}) \oplus (3 \bullet s_{2,j}) \oplus s_{3,j} \\ s'_{2,j} &= s_{0,j} \oplus s_{1,j} \oplus (2 \bullet s_{2,j}) \oplus (3 \bullet s_{3,j}) \\ s'_{3,j} &= (3 \bullet s_{0,j}) \oplus s_{1,j} \oplus s_{2,j} \oplus (2 \bullet s_{3,j}) \end{aligned} \quad (5.4)$$

The following is an example of MixColumns:

87	F2	4D	97
6E	4C	90	EC
46	E7	4A	C3
A6	8C	D8	95

→

47	40	A3	4C
37	D4	70	9F
94	E4	3A	42
ED	A5	A6	BC

Let us verify the first column of this example. Recall from Section 4.6 that, in GF(2^8), addition is the bitwise XOR operation and that multiplication can be performed according to the rule established in Equation (4.10). In particular, multiplication of a value by x (i.e., by $\{02\}$) can be implemented as a 1-bit left shift followed by a conditional bitwise XOR with (0001 1011) if the leftmost bit of the original value (prior to the shift) is 1. Thus, to verify the MixColumns transformation on the first column, we need to show that

$$\begin{aligned} &(\{02\} \bullet \{87\}) \oplus (\{03\} \bullet \{6E\}) \oplus \{46\} \oplus \{A6\} = \{47\} \\ &\{87\} \oplus (\{02\} \bullet \{6E\}) \oplus (\{03\} \bullet \{46\}) \oplus \{A6\} = \{37\} \\ &\{87\} \oplus \{6E\} \oplus (\{02\} \bullet \{46\}) \oplus (\{03\} \bullet \{A6\}) = \{94\} \\ &(\{03\} \bullet \{87\}) \oplus \{6E\} \oplus \{46\} \oplus (\{02\} \bullet \{A6\}) = \{ED\} \end{aligned}$$

[6]We follow the convention of FIPS PUB 197 and use the symbol • to indicate multiplication over the finite field GF(2^8) and $\oplus$ to indicate bitwise XOR, which corresponds to addition in GF(2^8).

For the first equation, we have $\{02\} \cdot \{87\} = (0000\,1110) \oplus (0001\,1011) = (0001\,0101)$; and $\{03\} \cdot \{6E\} = \{6E\} \oplus (\{02\} \cdot \{6E\}) = (0110\,1110) \oplus (1101\,1100) = (1011\,0010)$. Then

$$\begin{array}{lll} \{02\} \cdot \{87\} & = & 0001\,0101 \\ \{03\} \cdot \{6E\} & = & 1011\,0010 \\ \{46\} & = & 0100\,0110 \\ \{A6\} & = & \underline{1010\,0110} \\ & & 0100\,0111 = \{47\} \end{array}$$

The other equations can be similarly verified.

The **inverse mix column transformation**, called InvMixColumns, is defined by the following matrix multiplication:

$$\begin{bmatrix} 0E & 0B & 0D & 09 \\ 09 & 0E & 0B & 0D \\ 0D & 09 & 0E & 0B \\ 0B & 0D & 09 & 0E \end{bmatrix} \begin{bmatrix} s_{0,0} & s_{0,1} & s_{0,2} & s_{0,3} \\ s_{1,0} & s_{1,1} & s_{1,2} & s_{1,3} \\ s_{2,0} & s_{2,1} & s_{2,2} & s_{2,3} \\ s_{3,0} & s_{3,1} & s_{3,2} & s_{3,3} \end{bmatrix} = \begin{bmatrix} s'_{0,0} & s'_{0,1} & s'_{0,2} & s'_{0,3} \\ s'_{1,0} & s'_{1,1} & s'_{1,2} & s'_{1,3} \\ s'_{2,0} & s'_{2,1} & s'_{2,2} & s'_{2,3} \\ s'_{3,0} & s'_{3,1} & s'_{3,2} & s'_{3,3} \end{bmatrix} \quad \textbf{(5.5)}$$

It is not immediately clear that Equation (5.5) is the **inverse** of Equation (5.3). We need to show that:

$$\begin{bmatrix} 0E & 0B & 0D & 09 \\ 09 & 0E & 0B & 0D \\ 0D & 09 & 0E & 0B \\ 0B & 0D & 09 & 0E \end{bmatrix} \begin{bmatrix} 02 & 03 & 01 & 01 \\ 01 & 02 & 03 & 01 \\ 01 & 01 & 02 & 03 \\ 03 & 01 & 01 & 02 \end{bmatrix} \begin{bmatrix} s_{0,0} & s_{0,1} & s_{0,2} & s_{0,3} \\ s_{1,0} & s_{1,1} & s_{1,2} & s_{1,3} \\ s_{2,0} & s_{2,1} & s_{2,2} & s_{2,3} \\ s_{3,0} & s_{3,1} & s_{3,2} & s_{3,3} \end{bmatrix} = \begin{bmatrix} s_{0,0} & s_{0,1} & s_{0,2} & s_{0,3} \\ s_{1,0} & s_{1,1} & s_{1,2} & s_{1,3} \\ s_{2,0} & s_{2,1} & s_{2,2} & s_{2,3} \\ s_{3,0} & s_{3,1} & s_{3,2} & s_{3,3} \end{bmatrix}$$

which is equivalent to showing that:

$$\begin{bmatrix} 0E & 0B & 0D & 09 \\ 09 & 0E & 0B & 0D \\ 0D & 09 & 0E & 0B \\ 0B & 0D & 09 & 0E \end{bmatrix} \begin{bmatrix} 02 & 03 & 01 & 01 \\ 01 & 02 & 03 & 01 \\ 01 & 01 & 02 & 03 \\ 03 & 01 & 01 & 02 \end{bmatrix} = \begin{bmatrix} 1 & 0 & 0 & 0 \\ 0 & 1 & 0 & 0 \\ 0 & 0 & 1 & 0 \\ 0 & 0 & 0 & 1 \end{bmatrix} \quad \textbf{(5.6)}$$

That is, the inverse transformation matrix times the forward transformation matrix equals the identity matrix. To verify the first column of Equation (5.6), we need to show that:

$$\begin{aligned} (\{0E\} \cdot \{02\}) \oplus \{0B\} \oplus \{0D\} \oplus (\{09\} \cdot \{03\}) &= \{01\} \\ (\{09\} \cdot \{02\}) \oplus \{0E\} \oplus \{0B\} \oplus (\{0D\} \cdot \{03\}) &= \{00\} \\ (\{0D\} \cdot \{02\}) \oplus \{09\} \oplus \{0E\} \oplus (\{0B\} \cdot \{03\}) &= \{00\} \\ (\{0B\} \cdot \{02\}) \oplus \{0D\} \oplus \{09\} \oplus (\{0E\} \cdot \{03\}) &= \{00\} \end{aligned}$$

For the first equation, we have $\{0E\} \cdot \{02\} = 00011100$; and $\{09\} \cdot \{03\} = \{09\} \oplus (\{09\} \cdot \{02\}) = 00001001 \oplus 00010010 = 00011011$. Then

$$\begin{array}{ll} \{0E\} \cdot \{02\} & = 00011100 \\ \{0B\} & = 00001011 \\ \{0D\} & = 00001101 \\ \{09\} \cdot \{03\} & = \underline{00011011} \\ & \ 00000001 \end{array}$$

The other equations can be similarly verified.

The AES document describes another way of characterizing the MixColumns transformation, which is in terms of polynomial arithmetic. In the standard, MixColumns is defined by considering each column of **State** to be a four-term polynomial with coefficients in GF(2^8). Each column is multiplied modulo $(x^4 + 1)$ by the fixed polynomial $a(x)$, given by

$$a(x) = \{03\}x^3 + \{01\}x^2 + \{01\}x + \{02\} \quad \textbf{(5.7)}$$

Appendix 5A demonstrates that multiplication of each column of **State** by $a(x)$ can be written as the matrix multiplication of Equation (5.3). Similarly, it can be seen that the transformation in Equation (5.5) corresponds to treating each column as a four-term polynomial and multiplying each column by $b(x)$, given by

$$b(x) = \{0B\}x^3 + \{0D\}x^2 + \{09\}x + \{0E\} \quad \textbf{(5.8)}$$

It can readily be shown that $b(x) = a^{-1}(x) \bmod (x^4 + 1)$.

Rationale The coefficients of the matrix in Equation (5.3) are based on a linear code with maximal distance between code words, which ensures a good mixing among the bytes of each column. The mix column transformation combined with the shift row transformation ensures that after a few rounds, all output bits depend on all input bits. See [DAEM99] for a discussion.

In addition, the choice of coefficients in MixColumns, which are all {01}, {02}, or {03}, was influenced by implementation considerations. As was discussed, multiplication by these coefficients involves at most a shift and an XOR. The coefficients in InvMixColumns are more formidable to implement. However, encryption was deemed more important than decryption for two reasons:

1. For the CFB and OFB cipher modes (Figures 6.5 and 6.6; described in Chapter 6), only encryption is used.
2. As with any block cipher, AES can be used to construct a message authentication code (Part Two), and for this only encryption is used.

AddRoundKey Transformation

Forward and Inverse Transformations In the **forward add round key transformation**, called AddRoundKey, the 128 bits of **State** are bitwise XORed with the 128 bits of the round key. As shown in Figure 5.4b, the operation is viewed as a columnwise operation between the 4 bytes of a **State** column and one word of the round key; it can also be viewed as a byte-level operation. The following is an example of AddRoundKey:

47	40	A3	4C
37	D4	70	9F
94	E4	3A	42
ED	A5	A6	BC

⊕

AC	19	28	57
77	FA	D1	5C
66	DC	29	00
F3	21	41	6A

=

EB	59	8B	1B
40	2E	A1	C3
F2	38	13	42
1E	84	E7	D2

The first matrix is **State**, and the second matrix is the round key.

The **inverse add round key transformation** is identical to the forward add round key transformation, because the XOR operation is its own inverse.

Rationale The add round key transformation is as simple as possible and affects every bit of **State**. The complexity of the round key expansion, plus the complexity of the other stages of AES, ensure security.

AES Key Expansion

Key Expansion Algorithm The AES key expansion algorithm takes as input a 4-word (16-byte) key and produces a linear array of 44 words (176 bytes). This is sufficient to provide a 4-word round key for the initial AddRoundKey stage and each of the 10 rounds of the cipher. The following pseudocode describes the expansion:

```
KeyExpansion (byte key[16], word w[44])
{
    word temp
    for (i = 0; i < 4; i++)    w[i] = (key[4*i], key[4*i+1],
                                       key[4*i+2],
                                       key[4*i+3]);

    for (i = 4; i < 44; i++)
    {
     temp = w[i - 1];
     if (i mod 4 = 0)     temp = SubWord(RotWord(temp))
                                 ⊕ Rcon[i/4];
     w[i] = w[i-4] ≈ temp
    }
}
```

The key is copied into the first four words of the expanded key. The remainder of the expanded key is filled in four words at a time. Each added word **w**[i] depends on the immediately preceding word, **w**[i − 1], and the word four positions back, **w**[i − 4]. In three out of four cases, a simple XOR is used. For a word whose position in the **w** array is a multiple of 4, a more complex function is used. Figure 5.6 illustrates the generation of the first eight words of the expanded key, using the symbol g to represent that complex function. The function g consists of the following subfunctions:

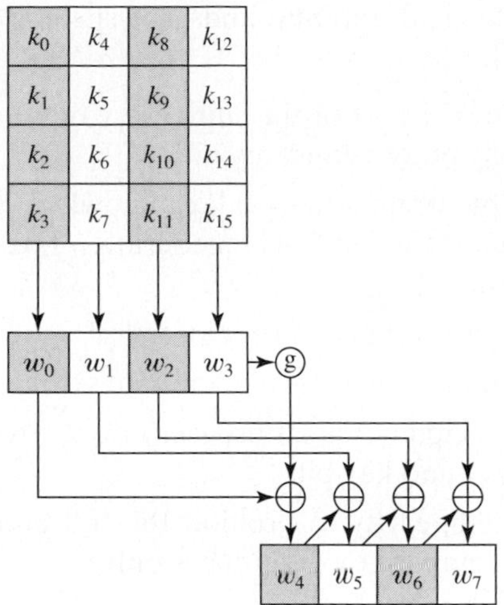

Figure 5.6 AES Key Expansion

1. RotWord performs a one-byte circular left shift on a word. This means that an input word [b0, b1, b2, b3] is transformed into [b1, b2, b3, b0].
2. SubWord performs a byte substitution on each byte of its input word, using the S-box (Table 5.4a).
3. The result of steps 1 and 2 is XORed with a round constant, Rcon[j].

The round constant is a word in which the three rightmost bytes are always 0. Thus the effect of an XOR of a word with Rcon is to only perform an XOR on the left-most byte of the word. The round constant is different for each round and is defined as Rcon[j] = (RC[j], 0, 0, 0), with RC[1] = 1, RC[j] = 2 · RC[j − 1] and with multiplication defined over the field GF(2^8). The values of RC[j] in hexadecimal are

j	1	2	3	4	5	6	7	8	9	10
RC[j]	01	02	04	08	10	20	40	80	1B	36

For example, suppose that the round key for round 8 is

EA D2 73 21 B5 8D BA D2 31 2B F5 60 7F 8D 29 2F

Then the first 4 bytes (first column) of the round key for round 9 are calculated as follows:

i (decimal)	temp	After RotWord	After SubWord	Rcon (9)	After XOR with Rcon	w[i − 4]	w[i] = temp ⊕ w[i − 4]
36	7F8D292F	8D292F7F	5DA515D2	1B000000	46A515D2	EAD27321	AC7766F3

Rationale The Rijndael developers designed the expansion key algorithm to be resistant to known cryptanalytic attacks. The inclusion of a round-dependent round constant eliminates the symmetry, or similarity, between the ways in which round keys are generated in different rounds. The specific criteria that were used are as follows [DAEM99]:

- Knowledge of a part of the cipher key or round key does not enable calculation of many other round key bits
- An invertible transformation [i.e., knowledge of any *Nk* consecutive words of the Expanded Key enables regeneration the entire expanded key (*Nk* = key size in words)]
- Speed on a wide range of processors
- Usage of round constants to eliminate symmetries
- Diffusion of cipher key differences into the round keys; that is, each key bit affects many round key bits
- Enough nonlinearity to prohibit the full determination of round key differences from cipher key differences only
- Simplicity of description

The authors do not quantify the first point on the preceding list, but the idea is that if you know less than *Nk* consecutive words of either the cipher key or one of the round keys, then it is difficult to reconstruct the remaining unknown bits. The fewer bits one knows, the more difficult it is to do the reconstruction or to determine other bits in the key expansion.

Equivalent Inverse Cipher

As was mentioned, the AES decryption cipher is not identical to the encryption cipher (Figure 5.1). That is, the sequence of transformations for decryption differs from that for encryption, although the form of the key schedules for encryption and decryption is the same. This has the disadvantage that two separate software or firmware modules are needed for applications that require both encryption and decryption. There is, however, an equivalent version of the decryption algorithm that has the same structure as the encryption algorithm. The equivalent version has the same sequence of transformations as the encryption algorithm (with transformations replaced by their inverses). To achieve this equivalence, a change in key schedule is needed.

Two separate changes are needed to bring the decryption structure in line with the encryption structure. An encryption round has the structure SubBytes, ShiftRows, MixColumns, AddRoundKey. The standard decryption round has the structure InvShiftRows, InvSubBytes, AddRoundKey, InvMixColumns. Thus, the first two stages of the decryption round need to be interchanged, and the second two stages of the decryption round need to be interchanged.

Interchanging InvShiftRows and InvSubBytes InvShiftRows affects the sequence of bytes in **State** but does not alter byte contents and does not depend on byte contents to perform its transformation. InvSubBytes affects the contents of bytes in **State** but does not alter byte sequence and does not depend on byte sequence to perform its transformation. Thus, these two operations commute and can be interchanged. For a given **State** S_i,

$$\text{InvShiftRows}\,[\text{InvSubBytes}\,(S_i)] = \text{InvSubBytes}\,[\text{InvShiftRows}\,(S_i)]$$

Interchanging AddRoundKey and InvMixColumns The transformations AddRoundKey and InvMixColumns do not alter the sequence of bytes in **State**. If we view the key as a sequence of words, then both AddRoundKey and InvMix-Columns operate on **State** one column at a time. These two operations are linear with respect to the column input. That is, for a given **State** S_i and a given round key w_j:

$$\text{InvMixColumns}\ (S_i \oplus w_j) = [\text{InvMixColumns}\ (S_i)] \oplus [\text{InvMixColumns}\ (w_j)]$$

To see this, suppose that the first column of **State** S_i is the sequence (y_0, y_1, y_2, y_3) and the first column of the round key w_j is (k_0, k_1, k_2, k_3). Then we need to show that

$$\begin{bmatrix} 0E & 0B & 0D & 09 \\ 09 & 0E & 0B & 0D \\ 0D & 09 & 0E & 0B \\ 0B & 0D & 09 & 0E \end{bmatrix} \begin{bmatrix} y_0 \oplus k_0 \\ y_1 \oplus k_1 \\ y_2 \oplus k_2 \\ y_3 \oplus k_3 \end{bmatrix} = \begin{bmatrix} 0E & 0B & 0D & 09 \\ 09 & 0E & 0B & 0D \\ 0D & 09 & 0E & 0B \\ 0B & 0D & 09 & 0E \end{bmatrix} \begin{bmatrix} y_0 \\ y_1 \\ y_2 \\ y_3 \end{bmatrix} \oplus \begin{bmatrix} 0E & 0B & 0D & 09 \\ 09 & 0E & 0B & 0D \\ 0D & 09 & 0E & 0B \\ 0B & 0D & 09 & 0E \end{bmatrix} \begin{bmatrix} k_0 \\ k_1 \\ k_2 \\ k_3 \end{bmatrix}$$

Let us demonstrate that for the first column entry. We need to show that:

$$\begin{aligned} &[\{0E\} \cdot (y_0 \oplus k_0)] \oplus [\{0B\} \cdot (y_1 \oplus k_1)] \oplus [\{0D\} \cdot (y_2 \oplus k_2)] \oplus [\{09\} \cdot (y_3 \oplus k_3)] \\ &\quad = [\{0E\} \cdot y_0] \oplus [\{0B\} \cdot y_1] \oplus [\{0D\} \cdot y_2] \oplus [\{09\} \cdot y_3] \\ &\quad \oplus [\{0E\} \cdot k_0] \oplus [\{0B\} \cdot k_1] \oplus [\{0D\} \cdot k_2] \oplus [\{09\} \cdot k_3] \end{aligned}$$

This equation is valid by inspection. Thus, we can interchange AddRoundKey and InvMixColumns, provided that we first apply InvMixColumns to the round key. Note that we do not need to apply InvMixColumns to the round key for the input to the first AddRoundKey transformation (preceding the first round) nor to the last AddRoundKey transformation (in round 10). This is because these two AddRoundKey transformations are not interchanged with InvMixColumns to produce the equivalent decryption algorithm.

Figure 5.7 illustrates the equivalent decryption algorithm.

Implementation Aspects

The Rijndael proposal [DAEM99] provides some suggestions for efficient implementation on 8-bit processors, typical for current smart cards, and on 32-bit processors, typical for PCs.

8-Bit Processor AES can be implemented very efficiently on an 8-bit processor. AddRoundKey is a bytewise XOR operation. ShiftRows is a simple byte shifting operation. SubBytes operates at the byte level and only requires a table of 256 bytes.

The transformation MixColumns requires matrix multiplication in the field $GF(2^8)$, which means that all operations are carried out on bytes. MixColumns only requires multiplication by {02} and {03}, which, as we have seen, involved simple shifts, conditional XORs, and XORs. This can be implemented in a more efficient way

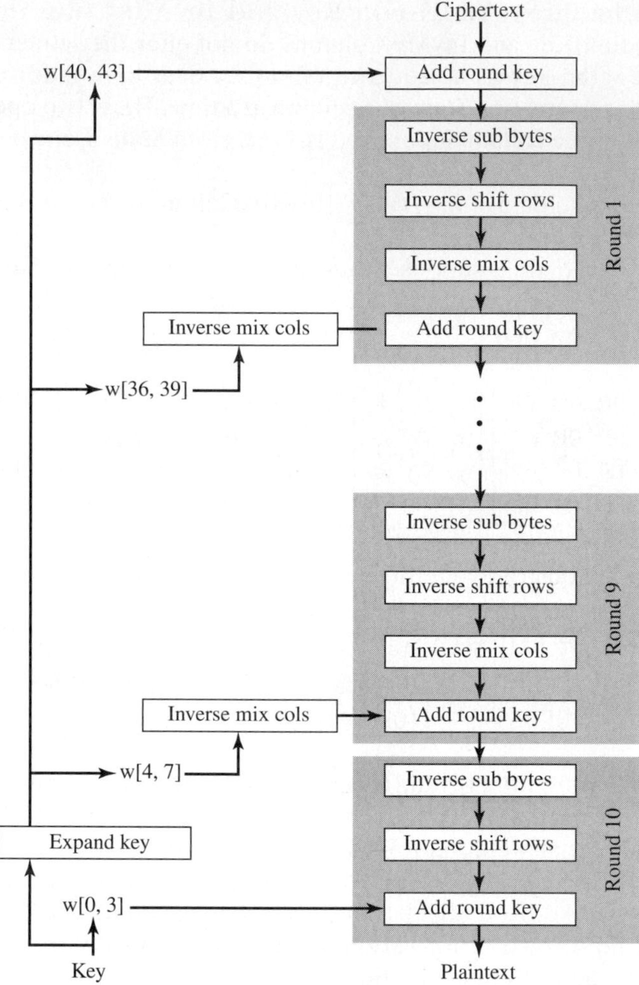

Figure 5.7 Equivalent Inverse Cipher

that eliminates the shifts and conditional XORs. Equation Set (5.4) shows the equations for the MixColumns transformation on a single column. Using the identity $\{03\} \cdot x = (\{02\} \cdot x) \oplus x$, we can rewrite Equation Set (5.4) as follows:

$$\begin{aligned} Tmp &= s_{0,j} \oplus s_{1,j} \oplus s_{2,j} \oplus s_{3,j} \\ s'_{0,j} &= s_{0,j} \oplus Tmp \oplus [2 \cdot (s_{0,j} \oplus s_{1,j})] \\ s'_{1,j} &= s_{1,j} \oplus Tmp \oplus [2 \cdot (s_{1,j} \oplus s_{2,j})] \\ s'_{2,j} &= s_{2,j} \oplus Tmp \oplus [2 \cdot (s_{2,j} \oplus s_{3,j})] \\ s'_{3,j} &= s_{3,j} \oplus Tmp \oplus [2 \cdot (s_{3,j} \oplus s_{0,j})] \end{aligned} \tag{5.9}$$

Equation Set (5.9) is verified by expanding and eliminating terms.

The multiplication by {02} involves a shift and a conditional XOR. Such an implementation may be vulnerable to a timing attack of the sort described in Section 3.4. To counter this attack and to increase processing efficiency at the cost of some storage, the multiplication can be replaced by a table lookup. Define the 256-byte table X2, such that X2[i] = {02} • i. Then Equation Set (5.9) can be rewritten as

$$\begin{aligned}
Tmp &= s_{0,j} \oplus s_{1,j} \oplus s_{2,j} \oplus s_{3,j} \\
s'_{0,j} &= s_{0,j} \oplus Tmp \oplus X2[s_{0,j} \oplus s_{1,j}] \\
s'_{1,c} &= s_{1,j} \oplus Tmp \oplus X2[s_{1,j} \oplus s_{2,j}] \\
s'_{2,c} &= s_{2,j} \oplus Tmp \oplus X2[s_{2,j} \oplus s_{3,j}] \\
s'_{3,j} &= s_{3,j} \oplus Tmp \oplus X2[s_{3,j} \oplus s_{0,j}]
\end{aligned}$$

32-Bit Processor The implementation described in the preceding subsection uses only 8-bit operations. For a 32-bit processor, a more efficient implementation can be achieved if operations are defined on 32-bit words. To show this, we first define the four transformations of a round in algebraic form. Suppose we begin with a **State** matrix consisting of elements $a_{i,j}$ and a round key matrix consisting of elements $k_{i,j}$. Then the transformations can be expressed as follows:

SubBytes	$b_{i,j} = S[a_{i,j}]$
ShiftRows	$\begin{bmatrix} c_{0,j} \\ c_{1,j} \\ c_{2,j} \\ c_{3,j} \end{bmatrix} = \begin{bmatrix} b_{0,j} \\ b_{1,j-1} \\ b_{2,j-2} \\ b_{3,j-3} \end{bmatrix}$
MixColumns	$\begin{bmatrix} d_{0,j} \\ d_{1,j} \\ d_{2,j} \\ d_{3,j} \end{bmatrix} = \begin{bmatrix} 02 & 03 & 01 & 01 \\ 01 & 02 & 03 & 01 \\ 01 & 01 & 02 & 03 \\ 03 & 01 & 01 & 02 \end{bmatrix} \begin{bmatrix} c_{0,j} \\ c_{1,j} \\ c_{2,j} \\ c_{3,j} \end{bmatrix}$
AddRoundKey	$\begin{bmatrix} e_{0,j} \\ e_{1,j} \\ e_{2,j} \\ e_{3,j} \end{bmatrix} = \begin{bmatrix} d_{0,j} \\ d_{1,j} \\ d_{2,j} \\ d_{3,j} \end{bmatrix} \oplus \begin{bmatrix} k_{0,j} \\ k_{1,j} \\ k_{2,j} \\ k_{3,j} \end{bmatrix}$

In the ShiftRows equation, the column indices are taken mod 4. We can combine all of these expressions into a single equation:

$$\begin{bmatrix} e_{0,j} \\ e_{1,j} \\ e_{2,j} \\ e_{3,j} \end{bmatrix} = \begin{bmatrix} 02 & 03 & 01 & 01 \\ 01 & 02 & 03 & 01 \\ 01 & 01 & 02 & 03 \\ 03 & 01 & 01 & 02 \end{bmatrix} \begin{bmatrix} S[a_{0,j}] \\ S[a_{1,j-1}] \\ S[a_{2,j-2}] \\ S[a_{3,j-3}] \end{bmatrix} \oplus \begin{bmatrix} k_{0,j} \\ k_{1,j} \\ k_{2,j} \\ k_{3,j} \end{bmatrix}$$

$$= \left(\begin{bmatrix} 02 \\ 01 \\ 01 \\ 03 \end{bmatrix} \bullet \mathrm{S}[a_{0,j}] \right) \oplus \left(\begin{bmatrix} 03 \\ 02 \\ 01 \\ 01 \end{bmatrix} \bullet \mathrm{S}[a_{1,j-1}] \right) \oplus \left(\begin{bmatrix} 01 \\ 03 \\ 02 \\ 01 \end{bmatrix} \bullet \mathrm{S}[a_{2,j-2}] \right)$$

$$\oplus \left(\begin{bmatrix} 01 \\ 01 \\ 03 \\ 02 \end{bmatrix} \bullet \mathrm{S}[a_{3,j-3}] \right) \oplus \begin{bmatrix} k_{0,j} \\ k_{1,j} \\ k_{2,j} \\ k_{3,j} \end{bmatrix}$$

In the second equation, we are expressing the matrix multiplication as a linear combination of vectors. We define four 256-word (1024-byte) tables as follows:

$T_0[x] = \left(\begin{bmatrix} 02 \\ 01 \\ 01 \\ 03 \end{bmatrix} \bullet \mathrm{S}[x] \right)$	$T_1[x] = \left(\begin{bmatrix} 03 \\ 02 \\ 01 \\ 01 \end{bmatrix} \bullet \mathrm{S}[x] \right)$	$T_2[x] = \left(\begin{bmatrix} 01 \\ 03 \\ 02 \\ 01 \end{bmatrix} \bullet \mathrm{S}[x] \right)$	$T_3[x] = \left(\begin{bmatrix} 01 \\ 01 \\ 03 \\ 02 \end{bmatrix} \bullet \mathrm{S}[x] \right)$

Thus, each table takes as input a byte value and produces a column vector (a 32-bit word) that is a function of the S-box entry for that byte value. These tables can be calculated in advance.

We can define a round function operating on a column in the following fashion:

$$\begin{bmatrix} s'_{0,j} \\ s'_{1,j} \\ s'_{2,j} \\ s'_{3,j} \end{bmatrix} = T_0[s_{0,j}] \oplus T_1[s_{1,j-1}] \oplus T_2[s_{2,j-2}] \oplus T_3[s_{3,j-3}] \oplus \begin{bmatrix} k_{0,j} \\ k_{1,j} \\ k_{2,j} \\ k_{3,j} \end{bmatrix}$$

As a result, an implementation based on the preceding equation requires only four table lookups and four XORs per column per round, plus 4 Kbytes to store the table. The developers of Rijndael believe that this compact, efficient implementation was probably one of the most important factors in the selection of Rijndael for AES.

5.3 RECOMMENDED READING AND WEB SITES

The most thorough description of AES so far available is the book by the developers of AES, [DAEM02]. The authors also provide a brief description and design rationale in [DAEM01]. [LAND04] is a rigorous mathematical treatment of AES and its cryptanalysis.

DAEM01 Daemen, J., and Rijmen, V. "Rijndael: The Advanced Encryption Standard." *Dr. Dobb's Journal*, March 2001.

DAEM02 Daemen, J., and Rijmen, V. *The Design of Rijndael: The Wide Trail Strategy Explained.* New York, Springer-Verlag, 2002.

LAND04 Landau, S. "Polynomials in the Nation's Service: Using Algebra to Design the Advanced Encryption Standard." *American Mathematical Monthly*, February 2004.

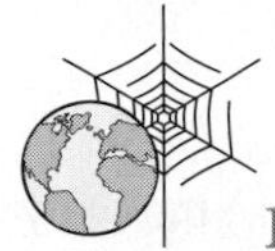

Recommended Web Sites:

- **AES home page:** NIST's page on AES. Contains the standard plus a number of other relevant documents.
- **The AES Lounge:** Contains a comprehensive bibliography of documents and papers on AES, with access to electronic copies.

5.4 KEY TERMS, REVIEW QUESTIONS, AND PROBLEMS

Key Terms

Advanced Encryption Standard (AES) National Institute of Standards and Technology (NIST)	power analysis Rijndael	S-box

Review Questions

5.1 What was the original set of criteria used by NIST to evaluate candidate AES ciphers?
5.2 What was the final set of criteria used by NIST to evaluate candidate AES ciphers?
5.3 What is power analysis?
5.4 What is the difference between Rijndael and AES?
5.5 What is the purpose of the **State** array?
5.6 How is the S-box constructed?
5.7 Briefly describe SubBytes.
5.8 Briefly describe ShiftRows.
5.9 How many bytes in **State** are affected by ShiftRows?
5.10 Briefly describe MixColumns.
5.11 Briefly describe AddRoundKey.
5.12 Briefly describe the key expansion algorithm.
5.13 What is the difference between SubBytes and SubWord?
5.14 What is the difference between ShiftRows and RotWord?
5.15 What is the difference between the AES decryption algorithm and the equivalent inverse cipher?

Problems

5.1 In the discussion of MixColumns and Inverse MixColumns, it was stated that

$$b(x) = a^{-1}(x) \bmod (x^4 + 1)$$

where $a(x) = \{03\}x^3 + \{01\}x^2 + \{01\}x + \{02\}$ and $b(x) = \{0B\}x^3 + \{0D\}x^2 + \{09\}x + \{0E\}$. Show that this is true.

5.2 a. What is $\{01\}^{-1}$ in GF(2^8)?
b. Verify the entry for {01} in the S-box.

5.3 Show the first eight words of the key expansion for a 128-bit key of all zeros.

5.4 Given the plaintext {000102030405060708090A0B0C0D0E0F} and the key {01010101010101010101010101010101},
a. Show the original contents of **State**, displayed as a 4 × 4 matrix.
b. Show the value of **State** after initial AddRoundKey.
c. Show the value of **State** after SubBytes.
d. Show the value of **State** after ShiftRows.
e. Show the value of **State** after MixColumns.

5.5 Verify Equation (5.11). That is show that $x^i \bmod (x^4 + 1) = x^{i \bmod 4}$.

5.6 Compare AES to DES. For each of the following elements of DES, indicate the comparable element in AES or explain why it is not needed in AES.
a. XOR of subkey material with the input to the f function
b. XOR of the f function output with the left half of the block
c. The f function
d. Permutation P
e. Swapping of halves of the block

5.7 In the subsection on implementation aspects, it is mentioned that the use of tables helps thwart timing attacks. Suggest an alternative technique.

5.8 In the subsection on implementation aspects, a single algebraic equation is developed that describes the four stages of a typical round of the encryption algorithm. Provide the equivalent equation for the tenth round.

5.9 Compute the output of the MixColumns transformation for the following sequence of input bytes "67 89 AB CD". Apply the InvMixColumns transformation to the obtained result to verify your calculations. Change the first byte of the input from '67' to '77', perform the MixColumns transformation again for the new input, and determine how many bits have changed in the output. *Note:* You can perform all calculations by hand or write a program supporting these computations. If you choose to write a program, it should be written entirely by you; no use of libraries or public domain source code is allowed in this assignment.

5.10 Use the key 1010 0111 0011 1011 to encrypt the plaintext "ok" as expressed in ASCII, that is 0110 1111 0110 1011. The designers of S-AES got the ciphertext 0000 0111 0011 1000. Do you?

5.11 Show that the matrix given below, with entries in GF(2^4), is the inverse of the matrix used in the MixColumns step of S-AES.

$$\begin{pmatrix} x^3 + 1 & x \\ x & x^3 + 1 \end{pmatrix}$$

5.12 Carefully write up a complete decryption of the ciphertext 0000 0111 0011 1000, using the key 1010 0111 0011 1011 and the S-AES algorithm. You should get the plaintext we started with in Problem 5.10. Note that the inverse of the S-boxes can be done with a reverse table lookup. The inverse of the MixColumns step is given by the matrix in the previous problem.

Programming Problems

5.13 Create software that can encrypt and decrypt using S-AES. Test data: a binary plaintext of 0110 1111 0110 1011 encrypted with a binary key of 1010 0111 0011 1011 should give a binary ciphertext of 0000 0111 0011 1000 less ecb $$$). Decryption should work correspondingly

5.14 Implement a differential cryptanalysis attack on 1-round S-AES.

APPENDIX 5A POLYNOMIALS WITH COEFFICIENTS IN GF(2^8)

In Section 4.5, we discussed polynomial arithmetic in which the coefficients are in Z_p, and the polynomials are defined modulo a polynomial $M(x)$ whose highest power is some integer n. In this case, addition and multiplication of coefficients occurred within the field Z_p; that is, addition and multiplication were performed modulo p.

The AES document defines polynomial arithmetic for polynomials of degree 3 or less with coefficients in GF(2^8). The following rules apply:

1. Addition is performed by adding corresponding coefficients in GF(2^8). As was pointed out Section 4.5, if we treat the elements of GF(2^8) as 8-bit strings, then addition is equivalent to the XOR operation. So, if we have

$$a(x) = a_3x^3 + a_2x^2 + a_1x + a_0 \tag{5.8}$$

$$b(x) = b_3x^3 + b_2x^2 + b_1x + b_0 \tag{5.9}$$

then

$$a(x) + b(x) = (a_3 \oplus b_3)x^3 + (a_2 \oplus b_2)x^2 + (a_1 \oplus b_1)x + (a_0 \oplus b_0)$$

2. Multiplication is performed as in ordinary polynomial multiplication, with two refinements:
   a. Coefficients are multiplied in GF(2^8).
   b. The resulting polynomial is reduced mod $(x^4 + 1)$.

We need to keep straight which polynomial we are talking about. Recall from Section 4.6 that each element of GF(2^8) is a polynomial of degree 7 or less with binary coefficients, and multiplication is carried out modulo a polynomial of degree 8. Equivalently, each element of GF(2^8) can be viewed as an 8-bit byte whose bit values correspond to the binary coefficients of the corresponding polynomial. For the sets defined in this section, we are defining a polynomial ring in which each element of this ring is a polynomial of degree 3 or less with coefficients in GF(2^8), and multiplication is carried out modulo a polynomial of degree 4. Equivalently, each element of this ring can be viewed as a 4-byte word whose byte values are elements of GF(2^8) that correspond to the 8-bit coefficients of the corresponding polynomial.

We denote the modular product of $a(x)$ and $b(x)$ by $a(x) \otimes b(x)$. To compute $d(x) = a(x) \otimes b(x)$, the first step is to perform a multiplication without the modulo operation and to collect coefficients of like powers. Let us express this as $c(x) = a(x) \times b(x)$. Then

$$c(x) = c_6x^6 + c_5x^5 + c_4x^4 + c_3x^3 + c_2x^2 + c_1x + c_0 \tag{5.10}$$

where

$$c_0 = a_0 \bullet b_0 \qquad\qquad c_4 = (a_3 \bullet b_1) \oplus (a_2 \bullet b_2) \oplus (a_1 \bullet b_3)$$
$$c_1 = (a_1 \bullet b_0) \oplus (a_0 \bullet b_1) \qquad\qquad c_5 = (a_3 \bullet b_2) \oplus (a_2 \bullet b_3)$$
$$c_2 = (a_2 \bullet b_0) \oplus (a_1 \bullet b_1) \oplus (a_0 \bullet b_2) \qquad\qquad c_6 = a_3 \bullet b_3$$
$$c_3 = (a_3 \bullet b_0) \oplus (a_2 \bullet b_1) \oplus (a_1 \bullet b_2) \oplus (a_0 \bullet b_3)$$

The final step is to perform the modulo operation:

$$d(x) = c(x) \bmod (x^4 + 1)$$

That is, $d(x)$ must satisfy the equation

$$c(x) = [(x^4 + 1) \times q(x)] \oplus d(x)$$

such that the degree of $d(x)$ is 3 or less.

A practical technique for performing multiplication over this polynomial ring is based on the observation that

$$x^i \bmod (x^4 + 1) = x^{i \bmod 4} \tag{5.11}$$

If we now combine Equations (5.10) and (5.11), we end up with

$$\begin{aligned} d(x) = c(x) \bmod (x^4 + 1) &= [c_6x^6 + c_5x^5 + c_4x^4 + c_3x^3 + c_2x^2 + c_1x + c_0] \bmod (x^4 + 1) \\ &= c_3x^3 + (c_2 \oplus c_6)x^2 + (c_1 \oplus c_5)x + (c_0 \oplus c_4) \end{aligned}$$

Expanding the c_i coefficients, we have the following equations for the coefficients of $d(x)$:

$$\begin{aligned} d_0 &= (a_0 \bullet b_0) \oplus (a_3 \bullet b_1) \oplus (a_2 \bullet b_2) \oplus (a_1 \bullet b_3) \\ d_1 &= (a_1 \bullet b_0) \oplus (a_0 \bullet b_1) \oplus (a_3 \bullet b_2) \oplus (a_2 \bullet b_3) \\ d_2 &= (a_2 \bullet b_0) \oplus (a_1 \bullet b_1) \oplus (a_0 \bullet b_2) \oplus (a_3 \bullet b_3) \\ d_3 &= (a_3 \bullet b_0) \oplus (a_2 \bullet b_1) \oplus (a_1 \bullet b_2) \oplus (a_0 \bullet b_3) \end{aligned}$$

This can be written in matrix form:

$$\begin{bmatrix} d_0 \\ d_1 \\ d_2 \\ d_3 \end{bmatrix} = \begin{bmatrix} a_0 & a_3 & a_2 & a_1 \\ a_1 & a_0 & a_3 & a_2 \\ a_2 & a_1 & a_0 & a_3 \\ a_3 & a_2 & a_1 & a_0 \end{bmatrix} \begin{bmatrix} b_0 \\ b_1 \\ b_2 \\ b_3 \end{bmatrix} \tag{5.12}$$

MixColumns Transformation

In the discussion of MixColumns, it was stated that there were two equivalent ways of defining the transformation. The first is the matrix multiplication shown in Equation (5.3), repeated here:

$$\begin{bmatrix} 02 & 03 & 01 & 01 \\ 01 & 02 & 03 & 01 \\ 01 & 01 & 02 & 03 \\ 03 & 01 & 01 & 02 \end{bmatrix} \begin{bmatrix} s_{0,0} & s_{0,1} & s_{0,2} & s_{0,3} \\ s_{1,0} & s_{1,1} & s_{1,2} & s_{1,3} \\ s_{2,0} & s_{2,1} & s_{2,2} & s_{2,3} \\ s_{3,0} & s_{3,1} & s_{3,2} & s_{3,3} \end{bmatrix} = \begin{bmatrix} s'_{0,0} & s'_{0,1} & s'_{0,2} & s'_{0,3} \\ s'_{1,0} & s'_{1,1} & s'_{1,2} & s'_{1,3} \\ s'_{2,0} & s'_{2,1} & s'_{2,2} & s'_{2,3} \\ s'_{3,0} & s'_{3,1} & s'_{3,2} & s'_{3,3} \end{bmatrix}$$

The second method is to treat each column of **State** as a four-term polynomial with coefficients in GF(2^8). Each column is multiplied modulo $(x^4 + 1)$ by the fixed polynomial $a(x)$, given by

$$a(x) = \{03\}x^3 + \{01\}x^2 + \{01\}x + \{02\}$$

From Equation (5.8), we have $a_3 = \{03\}$; $a_2 = \{01\}$; $a_1 = \{01\}$; $a_0 = \{02\}$. For the jth column of **State**, we have the polynomial $\text{col}_j(x) = s_{3,j}x^3 + s_{2,j}x^2 + s_{1,j}x + s_{0,j}$. Substituting into Equation (5.12), we can express $d(x) = a(x) \times \text{col}_j(x)$ as

$$\begin{bmatrix} d_0 \\ d_1 \\ d_2 \\ d_3 \end{bmatrix} = \begin{bmatrix} a_0 & a_3 & a_2 & a_1 \\ a_1 & a_0 & a_3 & a_2 \\ a_2 & a_1 & a_0 & a_3 \\ a_3 & a_2 & a_1 & a_0 \end{bmatrix} \begin{bmatrix} s_{0,j} \\ s_{1,j} \\ s_{2,j} \\ s_{3,j} \end{bmatrix} = \begin{bmatrix} 02 & 03 & 01 & 01 \\ 01 & 02 & 03 & 01 \\ 01 & 01 & 02 & 03 \\ 03 & 01 & 01 & 02 \end{bmatrix} \begin{bmatrix} s_{0,j} \\ s_{1,j} \\ s_{2,j} \\ s_{3,j} \end{bmatrix}$$

which is equivalent to Equation (5.3).

Multiplication by x

Consider the multiplication of a polynomial in the ring by x: $c(x) = x \otimes b(x)$. We have

$$c(x) = x \otimes b(x) = [x \times (b_3x^3 + b_2x^2 + b_1x + b_0)] \bmod (x^4 + 1)$$

$$= (b_3x^4 + b_2x^3 + b_1x^2 + b_0x) \bmod (x^4 + 1)$$
$$= b_2x^3 + b_1x^2 + b_0x + b_3$$

Thus, multiplication by x corresponds to a 1-byte circular left shift of the 4 bytes in the word representing the polynomial. If we represent the polynomial as a 4-byte column vector, then we have

$$\begin{bmatrix} c_0 \\ c_1 \\ c_2 \\ c_3 \end{bmatrix} = \begin{bmatrix} 00 & 00 & 00 & 01 \\ 01 & 00 & 00 & 00 \\ 00 & 01 & 00 & 00 \\ 00 & 00 & 01 & 00 \end{bmatrix} \begin{bmatrix} b_0 \\ b_1 \\ b_2 \\ b_3 \end{bmatrix}$$

APPENDIX 5B SIMPLIFIED AES

Simplified AES (S-AES) was developed by Professor Edward Schaefer of Santa Clara University and several of his students [MUSA03]. It is an educational rather than a secure encryption algorithm. It has similar properties and structure to AES with much smaller parameters. The reader might find it useful to work through an example by hand while following the discussion in this appendix. A good grasp of S-AES will make it easier for the student to appreciate the structure and workings of AES.

Overview

Figure 5.8 illustrates the overall structure of S-AES. The encryption algorithm takes a 16-bit block of plaintext as input and a 16-bit key and produces a 16-bit block of ciphertext as output. The

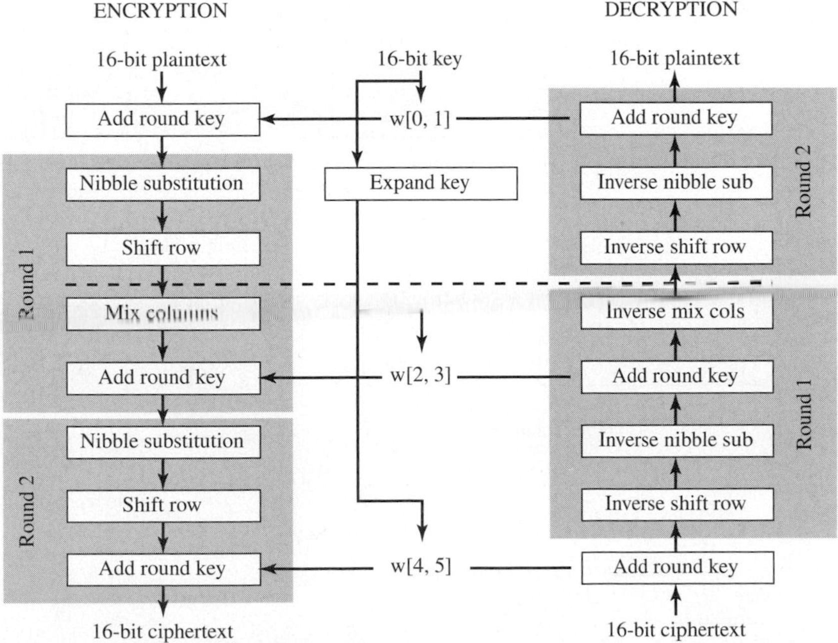

Figure 5.8 S-AES Encryption and Decryption

S-AES decryption algorithm takes an 16-bit block of ciphertext and the same 16-bit key used to produce that ciphertext as input and produces the original 16-bit block of plaintext as output.

The encryption algorithm involves the use of four different functions, or transformations: add key (A_K), nibble substitution (NS), shift row (SR), and mix column (MC), whose operation is explained subsequently.

We can concisely express the encryption algorithm as a composition[7] of functions:

$$A_{K_2} \circ SR \circ NS \circ A_{K_1} \circ MC \circ SR \circ NS \circ A_{K_0}$$

so that A_{K_0} is applied first.

The encryption algorithm is organized into three rounds. Round 0 is simply an add key round; round 1 is a full round of four functions; and round 2 contains only 3 functions. Each round includes the add key function, which makes use of 16 bits of key. The initial 16-bit key is expanded to 48 bits, so that each round uses a distinct 16-bit round key.

Each function operates on a 16-bit state, treated as a 2 × 2 matrix of nibbles, where one nibble equals 4 bits. The initial value of the state matrix is the 16-bit plaintext; the state matrix is modified by each subsequent function in the encryption process, producing after the last function the 16-bit ciphertext. As Figure 5.9a shows, the ordering of nibbles within the matrix is by column. So, for example, the first eight bits of a 16-bit plaintext input to the encryption cipher occupy the first column of the matrix, and the second eight bits occupy the second column. The 16-bit key is similarly organized, but it is somewhat more convenient to view the key as two bytes rather than four nibbles (Figure 5.9b). The expanded key of 48 bits is treated as three round keys, whose bits are labeled as follows: $K_0 = k_0 \ldots k_{15}$; $K_1 = k_{16} \ldots k_{31}$; $K_2 = k_{32} \ldots k_{47}$.

Figure 5.10 shows the essential elements of a full round of S-AES.

Decryption is also shown in Figure 5.8 and is essentially the reverse of encryption:

$$A_{K_0} \circ INS \circ ISR \circ IMC \circ A_{K_1} \circ INS \circ ISR \circ A_{K_2}$$

$b_0b_1b_2b_3$	$b_8b_9b_{10}b_{11}$
$b_4b_5b_6b_7$	$b_{12}b_{13}b_{14}b_{15}$

Bit representation

$S_{0,0}$	$S_{0,1}$
$S_{1,0}$	$S_{1,1}$

Nibble representation

(a) State matrix

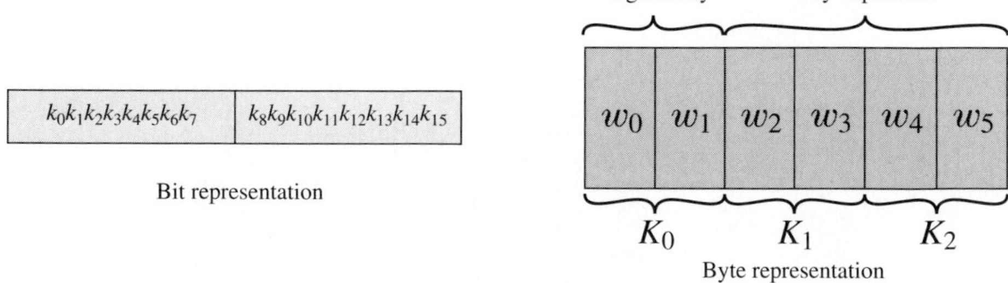

(b) Key

Figure 5.9 S-AES Data Structures

[7]**Definition:** If f and g are two functions, then the function F with the equation y = F(x) = g[f(x)] is called the **composition** of f and g and is denoted as F = g ∘ f.

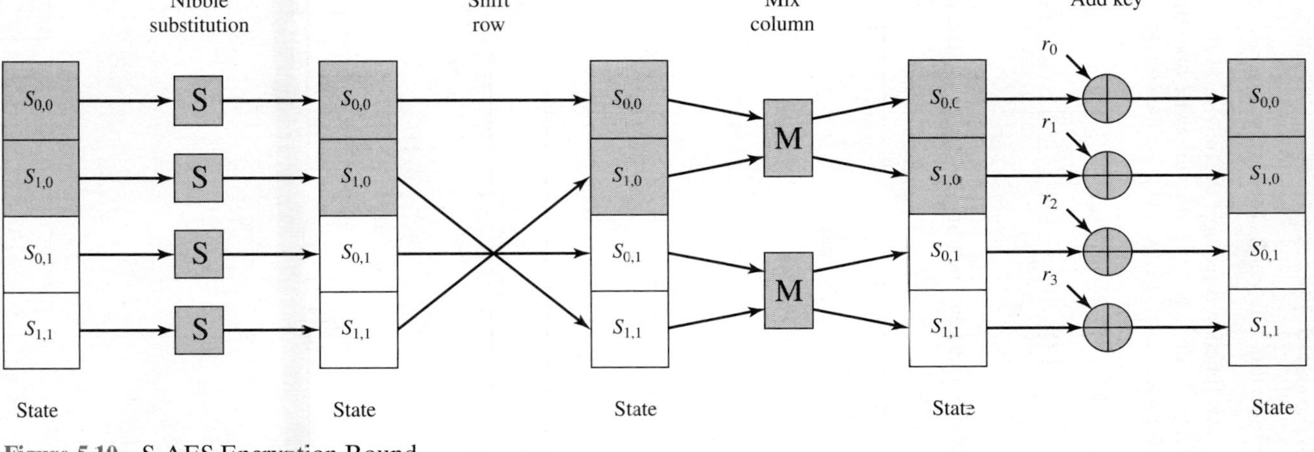

Figure 5.10 S-AES Encryption Round

in which three of the functions have a corresponding inverse function: inverse nibble substitution (INS), inverse shift row (ISR), and inverse mix column (IMC).

S-AES Encryption and Decryption

We now look at the individual functions that are part of the encryption algorithm.

Add Key The add key function consists of the bitwise XOR of the 16-bit state matrix and the 16-bit round key. Figure 5.11 depicts this as a columnwise operation, but it can also be viewed as a nibble-wise or bitwise operation. The following is an example:

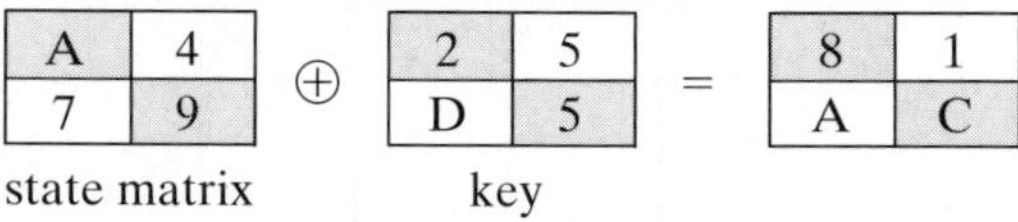

The inverse of the add key function is identical to the add key function, because the XOR operation is its own inverse.

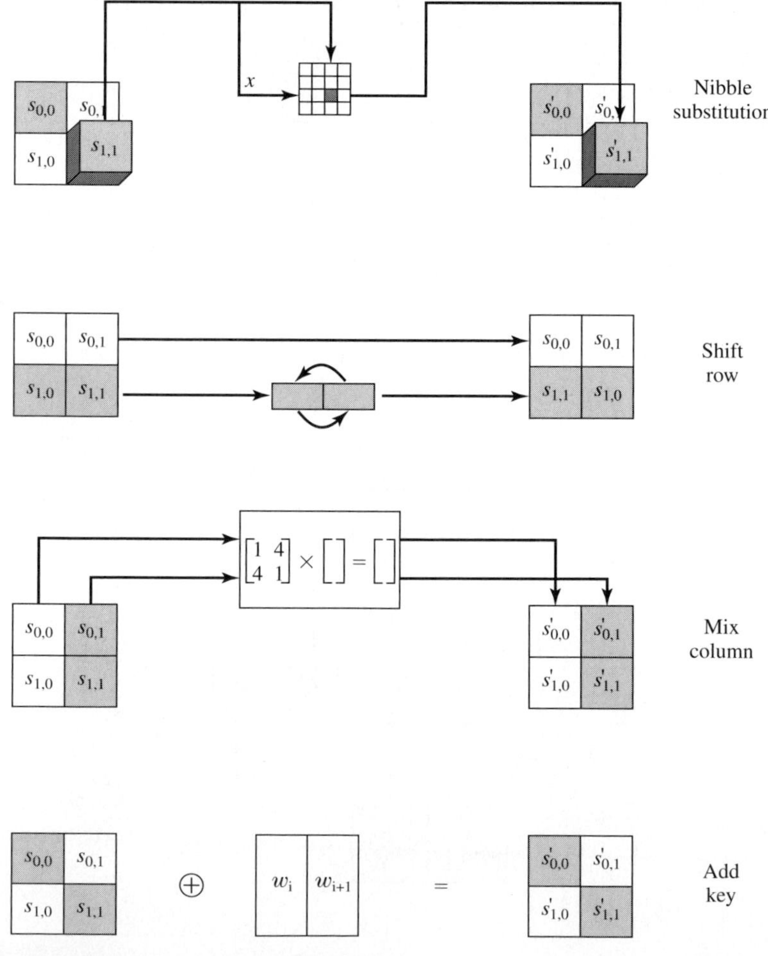

Figure 5.11 S-AES Transformations

Table 5.5 S-AES S-Boxes

(a) S-Box

		j			
		00	**01**	**10**	**11**
i	00	9	4	A	B
	01	D	1	8	5
	10	6	2	0	3
	11	C	E	F	7

(b) Inverse S-Box

		j			
		00	**01**	**10**	**11**
i	00	A	5	9	B
	01	1	7	8	F
	10	6	0	2	3
	11	C	4	D	E

Note: Hexadecimal numbers in shaded boxes; binary numbers in unshaded boxes.

Nibble Substitution The nibble substitution function is a simple table lookup (Figure 5.11). AES defines a 4×4 matrix of nibble values, called an S-box (Table 5.5a), that contains a permutation of all possible 4-bit values. Each individual nibble of the state matrix is mapped into a new nibble in the following way: The leftmost 2 bits of the nibble are used as a row value and the rightmost 2 bits are used as a column value. These row and column values serve as indexes into the S-box to select a unique 4-bit output value. For example, the hexadecimal value A references row 2, column 2 of the S-box, which contains the value 0. Accordingly, the value A is mapped into the value 0.

Here is an example of the nibble substitution transformation:

8	1	→	6	4
A	C		0	C

The inverse nibble substitution function makes use of the inverse S-box shown in Table 5.5b. Note, for example, that the input 0 produces the output A, and the input A to the S-box produces 0.

Shift Row The shift row function performs a one-nibble circular shift of the second row of the state matrix; the first row is not altered (Figure 5.11). The following is an example:

6	4	→	6	4
0	C		C	0

The inverse shift row function is identical to the shift row function, because it shifts the second row back to its original position.

Mix Column The mix column function operates on each column individually. Each nibble of a column is mapped into a new value that is a function of both nibbles in that column. The transformation can be defined by the following matrix multiplication on the state matrix (Figure 5.11):

$$\begin{bmatrix} 1 & 4 \\ 4 & 1 \end{bmatrix} \begin{bmatrix} S_{0,0} & S_{0,1} \\ S_{1,0} & S_{1,1} \end{bmatrix} = \begin{bmatrix} S'_{0,0} & S'_{0,1} \\ S'_{1,0} & S'_{1,1} \end{bmatrix}$$

Performing the matrix multiplication, we get:

$$\begin{aligned} S'_{0,0} &= S_{0,0} \oplus (4 \cdot S_{1,0}) \\ S'_{1,0} &= (4 \cdot S_{0,0}) \oplus S_{1,0} \\ S'_{0,1} &= S_{0,1} \oplus (4 \cdot S_{1,1}) \\ S'_{1,1} &= (4 \cdot S_{0,1}) \oplus S_{1,1} \end{aligned}$$

Where arithmetic is performed in GF(2^4), and the symbol $\cdot$ refers to multiplication in GF(2^4). Appendix E provides the addition and multiplication tables. The following is an example:

$$\begin{bmatrix} 1 & 4 \\ 4 & 1 \end{bmatrix} \begin{bmatrix} 6 & 4 \\ C & 0 \end{bmatrix} = \begin{bmatrix} 3 & 4 \\ 7 & 3 \end{bmatrix}$$

The inverse mix column function is defined as follows:

$$\begin{bmatrix} 9 & 2 \\ 2 & 9 \end{bmatrix} \begin{bmatrix} S_{0,0} & S_{0,1} \\ S_{1,0} & S_{1,1} \end{bmatrix} = \begin{bmatrix} S'_{0,0} & S'_{0,1} \\ S'_{1,0} & S'_{1,1} \end{bmatrix}$$

We demonstrate that we have indeed defined the inverse in the following fashion:

$$\begin{bmatrix} 9 & 2 \\ 2 & 9 \end{bmatrix} \begin{bmatrix} 1 & 4 \\ 4 & 1 \end{bmatrix} \begin{bmatrix} S_{0,0} & S_{0,1} \\ S_{1,0} & S_{1,1} \end{bmatrix} = \begin{bmatrix} 1 & 0 \\ 0 & 1 \end{bmatrix} \begin{bmatrix} S_{0,0} & S_{0,1} \\ S_{1,0} & S_{1,1} \end{bmatrix} = \begin{bmatrix} S_{0,0} & S_{0,1} \\ S_{1,0} & S_{1,1} \end{bmatrix}$$

The preceding matrix multiplication makes use of the following results in GF(2^4): $9 + (2 \cdot 4) = 9 + 8 = 1$; $(9 \cdot 4) + 2 = 2 + 2 = 0$. These operations can be verified using the arithmetic tables in Appendix E or by polynomial arithmetic.

The mix column function is the most difficult to visualize. Accordingly, we provide an additional perspective on it in Appendix E.

Key Expansion

For key expansion, the 16 bits of the initial key are grouped into a row of two 8-bit words. Figure 5.12 shows the expansion into 6 words, by the calculation of 4 new words from the initial 2 words. The algorithm is as follows:

$$\begin{aligned} w_2 &= w_0 \oplus g(w_1) = w_0 \oplus \text{RCON}(1) \oplus \text{SubNib}(\text{RotNib}(w_1)) \\ w_3 &= w_2 \oplus w_1 \\ w_4 &= w_2 \oplus g(w_3) = w_2 \oplus \text{RCON}(2) \oplus \text{SubNib}(\text{RotNib}(w_3)) \\ w_5 &= w_4 \oplus w_3 \end{aligned}$$

RCON is a round constant, defined as follows: $\text{RC}[i] = x^{i+2}$, so that $\text{RC}[1] = x^3 = 1000$ and $\text{RC}[2] = x^4 \bmod (x^4 + x + 1) = x + 1 = 0011$. RC[$i$] forms the leftmost nibble of a byte, with the rightmost nibble being all zeros. Thus, RCON(1) = 10000000 and RCON(2) = 00110000.

For example, suppose the key is 2D55 = 0010 1101 0101 0101 = $w_0 w_1$. Then

$$\begin{aligned} w_2 &= 00101101 \oplus 10000000 \oplus \text{SubNib}(01010101) \\ &= 00101101 \oplus 10000000 \oplus 00010001 = 10111100 \\ w_3 &= 10111100 \oplus 01010101 = 11101001 \\ w_4 &= 10111100 \oplus 00110000 \oplus \text{SubNib}(10011110) \\ &= 10111100 \oplus 00110000 \oplus 00101111 = 10100011 \\ w_5 &= 10100011 \oplus 11101001 = 01001010 \end{aligned}$$

The S-Box

The S-box is constructed as follows:

1. Initialize the S-box with the nibble values in ascending sequence row by row. The first row contains the hexadecimal values 0, 1, 2, 3; the second row contains 4, 5, 6, 7; and so on. Thus, the value of the nibble at row i, column j is $4i + j$.

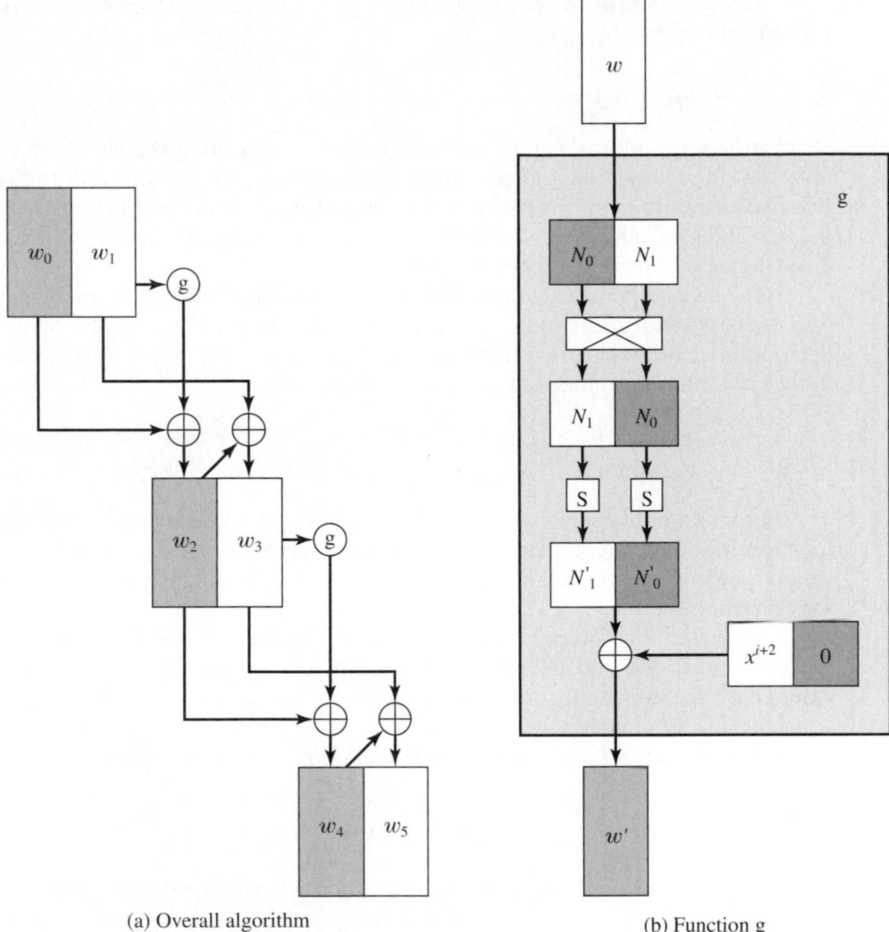

(a) Overall algorithm

(b) Function g

Figure 5.12 S-AES Key Expansion

2. Treat each nibble as an element of the finite field $GF(2^4)$ modulo $x^4 + x + 1$. Each nibble $a_0a_1a_2a_3$ represents a polynomial of degree 3.
3. Map each byte in the S-box to its multiplicative inverse in the finite field $GF(2^4)$ modulo $x^4 + x + 1$; the value 0 is mapped to itself.
4. Consider that each byte in the S-box consists of 4 bits labeled (b_0, b_1, b_2, b_3). Apply the following transformation to each bit of each byte in the S-box: The AES standard depicts this transformation in matrix form as follows:

$$\begin{bmatrix} b'_0 \\ b'_1 \\ b'_2 \\ b'_3 \end{bmatrix} = \begin{bmatrix} 1 & 0 & 1 & 1 \\ 1 & 1 & 0 & 1 \\ 1 & 1 & 1 & 0 \\ 0 & 1 & 1 & 1 \end{bmatrix} \begin{bmatrix} b_0 \\ b_1 \\ b_2 \\ b_3 \end{bmatrix} \oplus \begin{bmatrix} 1 \\ 0 \\ 0 \\ 1 \end{bmatrix}$$

The prime (′) indicates that the variable is to be updated by the value on the right. Remember that addition and multiplication are being calculated modulo 2.

Table 5.5a shows the resulting S-box. This is a nonlinear, invertible matrix. The inverse S-box is shown in Table 5.5b.

S-AES Structure

We can now examine several aspects of interest concerning the structure of AES. First, note that the encryption and decryption algorithms begin and end with the add key function. Any other function, at the beginning or end, is easily reversible without knowledge of the key and so would add no security but just a processing overhead. Thus, there is a round 0 consisting of only the add key function.

The second point to note is that round 2 does not include the mix column function. The explanation for this in fact relates to a third observation, which is that although the decryption algorithm is the reverse of the encryption algorithm, as clearly seen in Figure 5.8, it does not follow the same sequence of functions. Thus

$$\begin{array}{ll} \text{Encryption:} & \text{A}_{K_2} \circ \text{SR} \circ \text{NS} \circ \text{A}_{K_1} \circ \text{MC} \circ \text{SR} \circ \text{NS} \circ \text{A}_{K_0} \\ \text{Decryption:} & \text{A}_{K_0} \circ \text{INS} \circ \text{ISR} \circ \text{IMC} \circ \text{A}_{K_1} \circ \text{INS} \circ \text{ISR} \circ \text{A}_{K_2} \end{array}$$

From an implementation point of view, it would be desirable to have the decryption function follow the same function sequence as encryption. This allows the decryption algorithm to be implemented in the same way as the encryption algorithm, creating opportunities for efficiency.

Note that if we were able to interchange the second and third functions, the fourth and fifth functions, and the sixth and seventh functions in the decryption sequence, we would have the same structure as the encryption algorithm. Let's see if this is possible. First, consider the interchange of INS and ISR. Given a state N consisting of the nibbles (N_0, N_1, N_2, N_3), the transformation INS(ISR(N)) proceeds as follows:

$$\begin{pmatrix} N_0 & N_2 \\ N_1 & N_3 \end{pmatrix} \rightarrow \begin{pmatrix} N_0 & N_2 \\ N_3 & N_1 \end{pmatrix} \rightarrow \begin{pmatrix} \text{IS}[N_0] & \text{IS}[N_2] \\ \text{IS}[N_3] & \text{IS}[N_1] \end{pmatrix}$$

Where IS refers to the inverse S-Box. Reversing the operations, the transformation ISR(INS(N) proceeds as follows:

$$\begin{pmatrix} N_0 & N_2 \\ N_1 & N_3 \end{pmatrix} \rightarrow \begin{pmatrix} \text{IS}[N_0] & \text{IS}[N_2] \\ \text{IS}[N_1] & \text{IS}[N_3] \end{pmatrix} \rightarrow \begin{pmatrix} \text{IS}[N_0] & \text{IS}[N_2] \\ \text{IS}[N_3] & \text{IS}[N_1] \end{pmatrix}$$

which is the same result. Thus, INS(ISR(N)) = ISR(INS(N)).

Now consider the operation of inverse mix column followed by add key: IMC(A_{K_1}(N)) where the round key K_1 consists of the nibbles $(k_{0,0}, k_{1,0}, k_{0,1}, k_{1,1})$. Then:

$$\begin{aligned} \begin{pmatrix} 9 & 2 \\ 2 & 9 \end{pmatrix}\left(\begin{pmatrix} k_{0,0} & k_{0,1} \\ k_{1,0} & k_{1,1} \end{pmatrix} \oplus \begin{pmatrix} N_0 & N_2 \\ N_1 & N_3 \end{pmatrix}\right) &= \begin{pmatrix} 9 & 2 \\ 2 & 9 \end{pmatrix}\begin{pmatrix} k_{0,0} \oplus N_0 & k_{0,1} \oplus N_2 \\ k_{1,0} \oplus N_1 & k_{1,1} \oplus N_3 \end{pmatrix} \\ &= \begin{pmatrix} 9(k_{0,0} \oplus N_0) \oplus 2(K_{1,0} \oplus N_1) & 9(k_{0,1} \oplus N_2) \oplus 2(K_{1,1} \oplus N_3) \\ 2(k_{0,0} \oplus N_0) \oplus 9(K_{1,0} \oplus N_1) & 2(k_{0,1} \oplus N_2) \oplus 9(K_{1,1} \oplus N_3) \end{pmatrix} \\ &= \begin{pmatrix} (9k_{0,0} \oplus 2k_{1,0}) \oplus (9N_0 \oplus 2N_1) & (9k_{0,1} \oplus 2k_{1,1}) \oplus (9N_2 \oplus 2N_3) \\ (2k_{0,0} \oplus 9k_{1,0}) \oplus (2N_0 \oplus 9N_1) & (2k_{0,1} \oplus 9k_{1,1}) \oplus (2N_2 \oplus 9N_3) \end{pmatrix} \\ &= \begin{pmatrix} (9k_{0,0} \oplus 2k_{1,0}) & (9k_{0,1} \oplus 2k_{1,1}) \\ (2k_{0,0} \oplus 9k_{1,0}) & (2k_{0,1} \oplus 9k_{1,1}) \end{pmatrix} \oplus \begin{pmatrix} (9N_0 \oplus 2N_1) & (9N_2 \oplus 2N_3) \\ (2N_0 \oplus 9N_1) & (2N_2 \oplus 9N_3) \end{pmatrix} \\ &= \begin{pmatrix} 9 & 2 \\ 2 & 9 \end{pmatrix}\begin{pmatrix} k_{0,0} & k_{0,1} \\ k_{1,0} & k_{1,1} \end{pmatrix} \oplus \begin{pmatrix} 9 & 2 \\ 2 & 9 \end{pmatrix}\begin{pmatrix} N_0 & N_2 \\ N_1 & N_3 \end{pmatrix} \end{aligned}$$

All of the above steps make use of the properties of finite field arithmetic. The result is that $\text{IMC}(\text{A}_{K_1}(N)) = \text{IMC}(K_1) \oplus \text{IMC}(N)$. Now let us define the inverse round key for round 1 to be $\text{IMC}(K_1)$ and the inverse add key operation IA_{K_1} to be the bitwise XOR of the inverse round key with the state vector. Then we have $\text{IMC}(\text{A}_{K_1}(N)) = \text{IA}_{K_1}(\text{IMC}(N))$. As a result, we can write the following:

$$\begin{array}{ll} \text{Encryption:} & \text{A}_{K_2} \circ \text{SR} \circ \text{NS} \circ \text{A}_{K_1} \circ \text{MC} \circ \text{SR} \circ \text{NS} \circ \text{A}_{K_0} \\ \text{Decryption:} & \text{A}_{K_0} \circ \text{INS} \circ \text{ISR} \circ \text{IMC} \circ \text{A}_{K_1} \circ \text{INS} \circ \text{ISR} \circ \text{A}_{K_2} \\ \text{Decryption:} & \text{A}_{K_0} \circ \text{ISR} \circ \text{INS} \circ \text{A}_{\text{IMC}(K_1)} \circ \text{IMC} \circ \text{ISR} \circ \text{INS} \circ \text{A}_{K_2} \end{array}$$

Both encryption and decryption now follow the same sequence. Note that this derivation would not work as effectively if round 2 of the encryption algorithm included the MC function. In that case, we would have

$$\begin{array}{ll} \text{Encryption:} & \text{A}_{K_2} \circ \text{MC} \circ \text{SR} \circ \text{NS} \circ \text{A}_{K_1} \circ \text{MC} \circ \text{SR} \circ \text{NS} \circ \text{A}_{K_0} \\ \text{Decryption:} & \text{A}_{K_0} \circ \text{INS} \circ \text{ISR} \circ \text{IMC} \circ \text{A}_{K_1} \circ \text{INS} \circ \text{ISR} \circ \text{IMC} \circ \text{A}_{K_2} \end{array}$$

There is now no way to interchange pairs of operations in the decryption algorithm so as to achieve the same structure as the encryption algorithm.

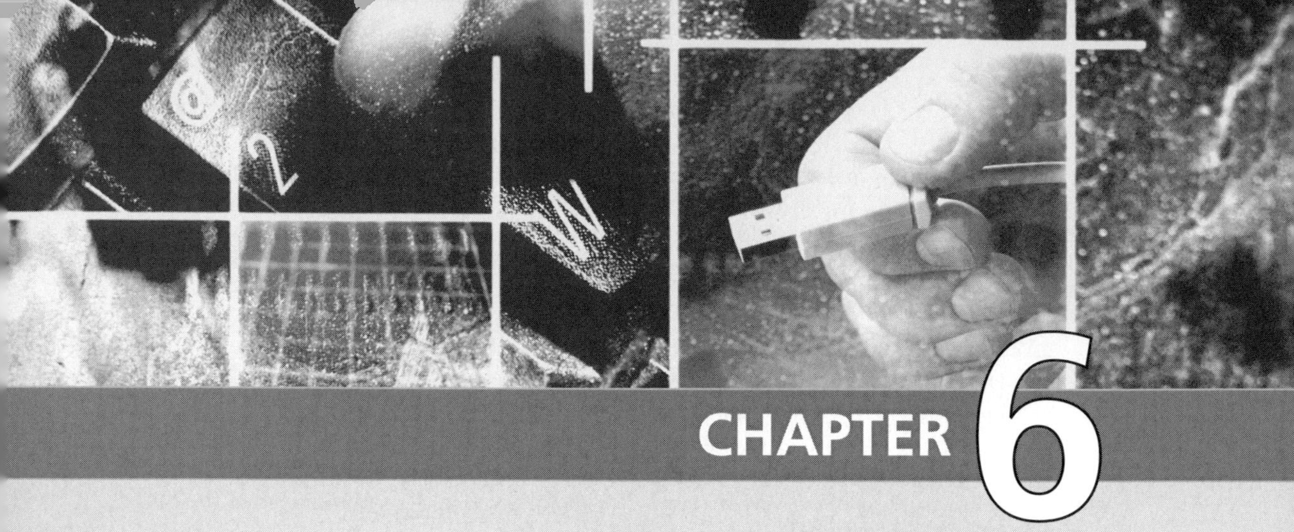

CHAPTER 6

MORE ON SYMMETRIC CIPHERS

"I am fairly familiar with all the forms of secret writings, and am myself the author of a trifling monograph upon the subject, in which I analyze one hundred and sixty separate ciphers," said Holmes.

—*The Adventure of the Dancing Men,* Sir Arthur Conan Doyle

KEY POINTS

- Multiple encryption is a technique in which an encryption algorithm is used multiple times. In the first instance, plaintext is converted to ciphertext using the encryption algorithm. This ciphertext is then used as input and the algorithm is applied again. This process may be repeated through any number of stages.
- Triple DES makes use of three stages of the DES algorithm, using a total of two or three distinct keys.
- A mode of operation is a technique for enhancing the effect of a cryptographic algorithm or adapting the algorithm for an application, such as applying a block cipher to a sequence of data blocks or a data stream.
- Five modes of operation have been standardized for use with symmetric block ciphers such as DES and AES: electronic codebook mode, cipher block chaining mode, cipher feedback mode, output feedback mode, and counter mode.
- A stream cipher is a symmetric encryption algorithm in which ciphertext output is produced bit-by-bit or byte-by-byte from a stream of plaintext input. The most widely used such cipher is RC4.

This chapter continues our discussion of symmetric ciphers. We begin with the topic of multiple encryption, looking in particular at the most widely used multiple-encryption scheme: triple DES.

The chapter next turns to the subject of block cipher modes of operation. We find that there are a number of different ways to apply a block cipher to plaintext, each with its own advantages and particular applications.

Finally, this chapter addresses the subject of symmetric stream ciphers, which differ in significant ways from symmetric block ciphers. We also look at the most important such cipher, RC4.

6.1 MULTIPLE ENCRYPTION AND TRIPLE DES

Given the potential vulnerability of DES to a brute-force attack, there has been considerable interest in finding an alternative. One approach is to design a completely new algorithm, of which AES is a prime example. Another alternative, which would preserve the existing investment in software and equipment, is to use multiple encryption with DES and multiple keys. We begin by examining the simplest example of this second alternative. We then look at the widely accepted triple DES (3DES) approach.

Double DES

The simplest form of multiple encryption has two encryption stages and two keys (Figure 6.1a). Given a plaintext P and two encryption keys K_1 and K_2, ciphertext C is generated as

$$C = \mathrm{E}(K_2, \mathrm{E}(K_1, P))$$

Decryption requires that the keys be applied in reverse order:

$$P = \mathrm{D}(K_1, \mathrm{D}(K_2, C))$$

For DES, this scheme apparently involves a key length of $56 \times 2 = 112$ bits, resulting in a dramatic increase in cryptographic strength. But we need to examine the algorithm more closely.

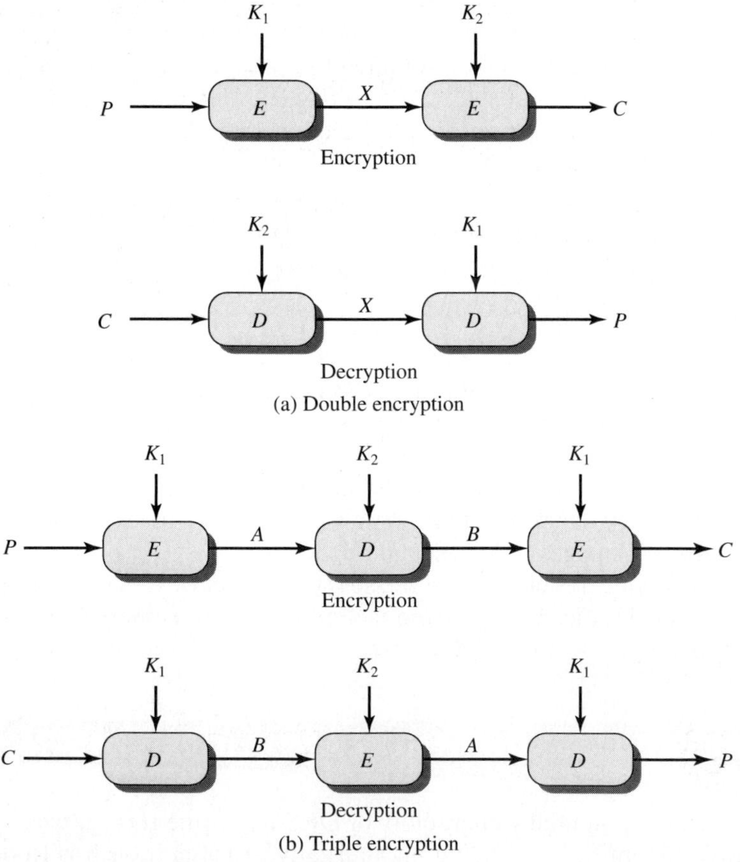

Figure 6.1 Multiple Encryption

Reduction to a Single Stage Suppose it were true for DES, for all 56-bit key values, that given any two keys K_1 and K_2, it would be possible to find a key K_3 such that

$$\mathrm{E}(K_2, \mathrm{E}(K_1, P)) = \mathrm{E}(K_3, P) \tag{6.1}$$

If this were the case, then double encryption, and indeed any number of stages of multiple encryption with DES, would be useless because the result would be equivalent to a single encryption with a single 56-bit key.

On the face of it, it does not appear that Equation (6.1) is likely to hold. Consider that encryption with DES is a mapping of 64-bit blocks to 64-bit blocks. In fact, the mapping can be viewed as a permutation. That is, if we consider all 2^{64} possible input blocks, DES encryption with a specific key will map each block into a unique 64-bit block. Otherwise, if, say, two given input blocks mapped to the same output block, then decryption to recover the original plaintext would be impossible. With 2^{64} possible inputs, how many different mappings are there that generate a permutation of the input blocks? The value is easily seen to be

$$\left(2^{64}\right)! = 10^{347380000000000000000} > \left(10^{10^{20}}\right)$$

On the other hand, DES defines one mapping for each different key, for a total number of mappings:

$$2^{56} < 10^{17}$$

Therefore, it is reasonable to assume that if DES is used twice with different keys, it will produce one of the many mappings that are not defined by a single application of DES. Although there was much supporting evidence for this assumption, it was not until 1992 that the assumption was proved [CAMP92].

Meet-in-the-Middle Attack Thus, the use of double DES results in a mapping that is not equivalent to a single DES encryption. But there is a way to attack this scheme, one that does not depend on any particular property of DES but that will work against any block encryption cipher.

The algorithm, known as a meet-in-the-middle attack, was first described in [DIFF77]. It is based on the observation that, if we have

$$C = \mathrm{E}(K_2, \mathrm{E}(K_1, P))$$

then (see Figure 6.1a)

$$X = \mathrm{E}(K_1, P) = \mathrm{D}(K_2, P)$$

Given a known pair, (P, C), the attack proceeds as follows. First, encrypt P for all 2^{56} possible values of K_1. Store these results in a table and then sort the table by the values of X. Next, decrypt C using all 2^{56} possible values of K_2. As each decryption is produced, check the result against the table for a match. If a match occurs, then test the two resulting keys against a new known plaintext-ciphertext pair. If the two keys produce the correct ciphertext, accept them as the correct keys.

For any given plaintext P, there are 2^{64} possible ciphertext values that could be produced by double DES. Double DES uses, in effect, a 112-bit key, so that there are 2^{112} possible keys. Therefore, on average, for a given plaintext P, the number of different 112-bit keys that will produce a given ciphertext C is $2^{112}/2^{64} = 2^{48}$. Thus, the foregoing procedure will produce about 2^{48} false alarms on the first (P, C) pair. A similar argument indicates that with an additional 64 bits of known plaintext and ciphertext, the false alarm rate is reduced to $2^{48-64} = 2^{-16}$. Put another way, if the meet-in-the-middle attack is performed on two blocks of known plaintext-ciphertext, the probability that the correct keys are determined is $1 - 2^{-16}$. The result is that a known plaintext attack will succeed against double DES, which has a key size of 112 bits, with an effort on the order of 2^{56}, not much more than the 2^{55} required for single DES.

Triple DES with Two Keys

An obvious counter to the meet-in-the-middle attack is to use three stages of encryption with three different keys. This raises the cost of the known-plaintext attack to 2^{112}, which is beyond what is practical now and far into the future. However, it has the drawback of requiring a key length of $56 \times 3 = 168$ bits, which may be somewhat unwieldy.

As an alternative, Tuchman proposed a triple encryption method that uses only two keys [TUCH79]. The function follows an encrypt-decrypt-encrypt (EDE) sequence (Figure 6.1b):

$$C = \mathrm{E}(K_1, \mathrm{D}(K_2, \mathrm{E}(K_1, P)))$$

There is no cryptographic significance to the use of decryption for the second stage. Its only advantage is that it allows users of 3DES to decrypt data encrypted by users of the older single DES:

$$C = \mathrm{E}(K_1, \mathrm{D}(K_1, \mathrm{E}(K_1, P))) = \mathrm{E}(K_1, P)$$

3DES with two keys is a relatively popular alternative to DES and has been adopted for use in the key management standards ANS X9.17 and ISO 8732.[1]

Currently, there are no practical cryptanalytic attacks on 3DES. Coppersmith [COPP94] notes that the cost of a brute-force key search on 3DES is on the order of $2^{112} \approx (5 \times 10^{33})$ and estimates that the cost of differential cryptanalysis suffers an exponential growth, compared to single DES, exceeding 10^{52}.

It is worth looking at several proposed attacks on 3DES that, although not practical, give a flavor for the types of attacks that have been considered and that could form the basis for more successful future attacks.

[1](ANS) American National Standard: Financial Institution Key Management (Wholesale). From its title, X9.17 appears to be a somewhat obscure standard. Yet a number of techniques specified in this standard have been adopted for use in other standards and applications, as we shall see throughout this book.

The first serious proposal came from Merkle and Hellman [MERK81]. Their plan involves finding plaintext values that produce a first intermediate value of $A = 0$ (Figure 6.1b) and then using the meet-in-the-middle attack to determine the two keys. The level of effort is 2^{56}, but the technique requires 2^{56} chosen plaintext-ciphertext pairs, a number unlikely to be provided by the holder of the keys.

A known-plaintext attack is outlined in [VANO90]. This method is an improvement over the chosen-plaintext approach but requires more effort. The attack is based on the observation that if we know A and C (Figure 6.1b), then the problem reduces to that of an attack on double DES. Of course, the attacker does not know A, even if P and C are known, as long as the two keys are unknown. However, the attacker can choose a potential value of A and then try to find a known (P, C) pair that produces A. The attack proceeds as follows:

1. Obtain n (P, C) pairs. This is the known plaintext. Place these in a table (Table 1) sorted on the values of P (Figure 6.2b).
2. Pick an arbitrary value a for A, and create a second table (Figure 6.2c) with entries defined in the following fashion. For each of the 2^{56} possible keys $K_1 = i$, calculate the plaintext value P_i that produces a:

$$P_i = D(i, a)$$

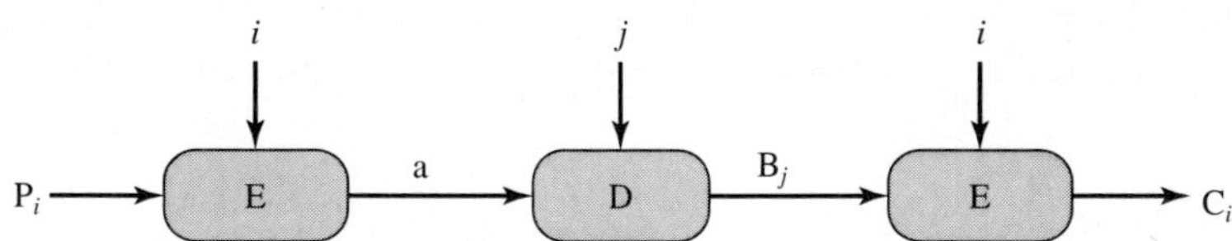

(a) Two-key triple encryption with candidate pair of keys

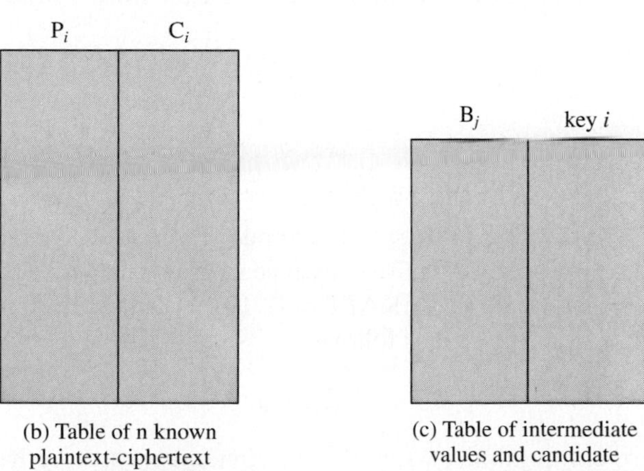

(b) Table of n known plaintext-ciphertext pairs, sorted on P

(c) Table of intermediate values and candidate keys

Figure 6.2 Known-Plaintext Attack on Triple DES

For each P_i that matches an entry in Table 1, create an entry in Table 2 consisting of the K_1 value and the value of B that is produced for the (P, C) pair from Table 1, assuming that value of K_1:

$$B = \mathrm{D}(i, C)$$

At the end of this step, sort Table 2 on the values of B.

3. We now have a number of candidate values of K_1 in Table 2 and are in a position to search for a value of K_2. For each of the 2^{56} possible keys $K_2 = j$, calculate the second intermediate value for our chosen value of a:

$$B_j = \mathrm{D}(j, a)$$

At each step, look up B_j in Table 2. If there is a match, then the corresponding key i from Table 2 plus this value of j are candidate values for the unknown keys (K_1, K_2). Why? Because we have found a pair of keys (i, j) that produce a known (P, C) pair (Figure 6.2a).

4. Test each candidate pair of keys (i, j) on a few other plaintext-ciphertext pairs. If a pair of keys produces the desired ciphertext, the task is complete. If no pair succeeds, repeat from step 1 with a new value of a.

For a given known (P, C), the probability of selecting the unique value of a that leads to success is $1/2^{64}$. Thus, given n (P, C) pairs, the probability of success for a single selected value of a is $n/2^{64}$. A basic result from probability theory is that the expected number of draws required to draw one red ball out of a bin containing n red balls and $N - n$ green balls is $(N + 1)/(n + 1)$ if the balls are not replaced. So the expected number of values of a that must be tried is, for large n,

$$\frac{2^{64} + 1}{n + 1} \approx \frac{2^{64}}{n}$$

Thus, the expected running time of the attack is on the order of

$$\left(2^{56}\right)\frac{2^{64}}{n} = 2^{120 - \log_2 n}$$

Triple DES with Three Keys

Although the attacks just described appear impractical, anyone using two-key 3DES may feel some concern. Thus, many researchers now feel that three-key 3DES is the preferred alternative (e.g., [KALI96a]). Three-key 3DES has an effective key length of 168 bits and is defined as follows:

$$C = \mathrm{E}(K_3, \mathrm{D}(K_2, \mathrm{E}(K_1, P)))$$

Backward compatibility with DES is provided by putting $K_3 = K_2$ or $K_1 = K_2$.

A number of Internet-based applications have adopted three-key 3DES, including PGP and S/MIME, both discussed in Chapter 15.

6.2 BLOCK CIPHER MODES OF OPERATION

A block cipher algorithm is a basic building block for providing data security. To apply a block cipher in a variety of applications, four "modes of operation" have been defined by NIST (FIPS 81). In essence, a mode of operation is a technique for enhancing the effect of a cryptographic algorithm or adapting the algorithm for an application, such as applying a block cipher to a sequence of data blocks or a data stream. The four modes are intended to cover virtually all the possible applications of encryption for which a block cipher could be used. As new applications and requirements have appeared, NIST has expanded the list of recommended modes to five in Special Publication 800-38A. These modes are intended for use with any symmetric block cipher, including triple DES and AES. The modes are summarized in Table 6.1 and described briefly in the remainder of this section.

Electronic Codebook Mode

The simplest mode is the electronic codebook (ECB) mode, in which plaintext is handled one block at a time and each block of plaintext is encrypted using the same key (Figure 6.3). The term *codebook* is used because, for a given key, there is a unique

Table 6.1 Block Cipher Modes of Operation

Mode	Description	Typical Application
Electronic Codebook (ECB)	Each block of 64 plaintext bits is encoded independently using the same key.	• Secure transmission of single values (e.g., an encryption key)
Cipher Block Chaining (CBC)	The input to the encryption algorithm is the XOR of the next 64 bits of plaintext and the preceding 64 bits of ciphertext.	• General-purpose block-oriented transmission • Authentication
Cipher Feedback (CFB)	Input is processed *j* bits at a time. Preceding ciphertext is used as input to the encryption algorithm to produce pseudorandom output, which is XORed with plaintext to produce next unit of ciphertext.	• General-purpose stream-oriented transmission • Authentication
Output Feedback (OFB)	Similar to CFB, except that the input to the encryption algorithm is the preceding DES output.	• Stream-oriented transmission over noisy channel (e.g., satellite communication)
Counter (CTR)	Each block of plaintext is XORed with an encrypted counter. The counter is incremented for each subsequent block.	• General-purpose block-oriented transmission • Useful for high-speed requirements

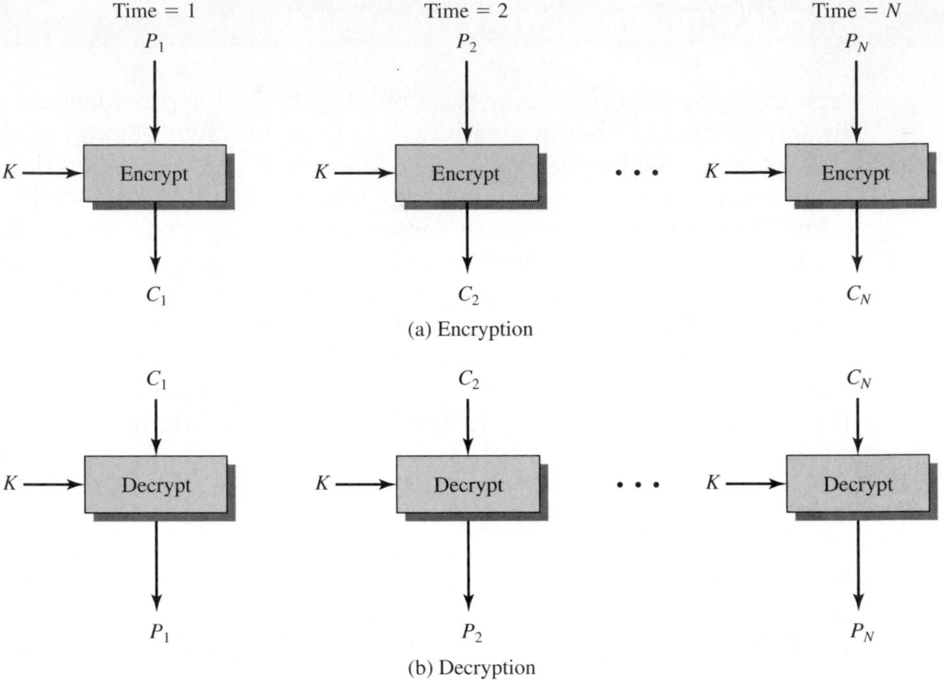

Figure 6.3 Electronic Codebook (ECB) Mode

ciphertext for every b-bit block of plaintext. Therefore, we can imagine a gigantic codebook in which there is an entry for every possible b-bit plaintext pattern showing its corresponding ciphertext.

For a message longer than b bits, the procedure is simply to break the message into b-bit blocks, padding the last block if necessary. Decryption is performed one block at a time, always using the same key. In Figure 6.3, the plaintext (padded as necessary) consists of a sequence of b-bit blocks, $P_1, P_2, \ldots, P_N$; the corresponding sequence of ciphertext blocks is $C_1, C_2, \ldots, C_N$.

The ECB method is ideal for a short amount of data, such as an encryption key. Thus, if you want to transmit a DES key securely, ECB is the appropriate mode to use.

The most significant characteristic of ECB is that the same b-bit block of plaintext, if it appears more than once in the message, always produces the same ciphertext.

For lengthy messages, the ECB mode may not be secure. If the message is highly structured, it may be possible for a cryptanalyst to exploit these regularities. For example, if it is known that the message always starts out with certain predefined fields, then the cryptanalyst may have a number of known plaintext-ciphertext pairs to work with. If the message has repetitive elements, with a period of repetition a multiple of b bits, then these elements can be identified by the analyst. This may help in the analysis or may provide an opportunity for substituting or rearranging blocks.

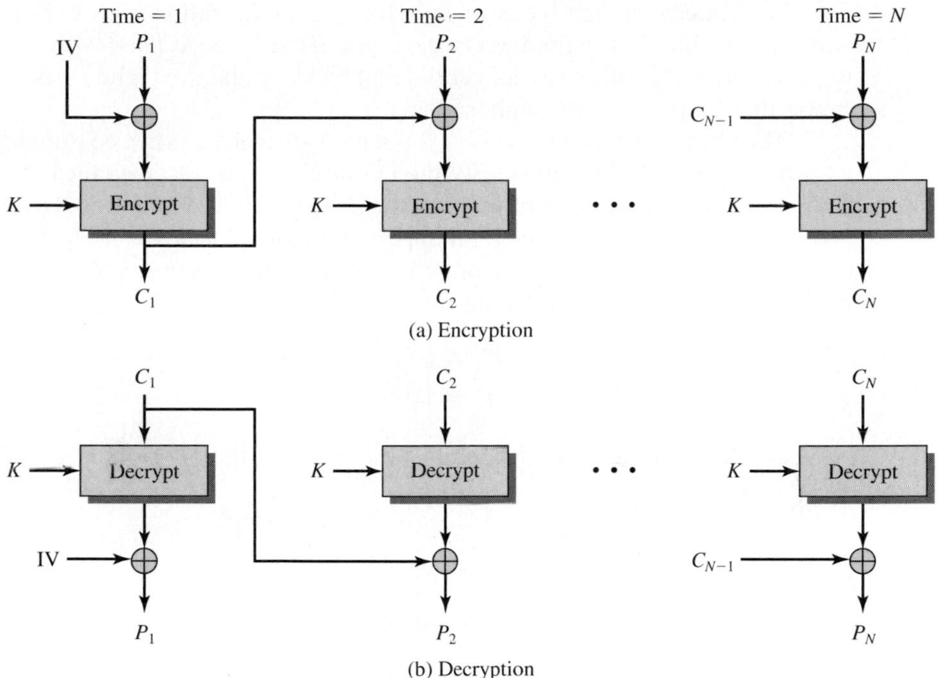

Figure 6.4 Cipher Block Chaining (CBC) Mode

Cipher Block Chaining Mode

To overcome the security deficiencies of ECB, we would like a technique in which the same plaintext block, if repeated, produces different ciphertext blocks. A simple way to satisfy this requirement is the cipher block chaining (CBC) mode (Figure 6.4). In this scheme, the input to the encryption algorithm is the XOR of the current plaintext block and the preceding ciphertext block; the same key is used for each block. In effect, we have chained together the processing of the sequence of plaintext blocks. The input to the encryption function for each plaintext block bears no fixed relationship to the plaintext block. Therefore, repeating patterns of b bits are not exposed.

For decryption, each cipher block is passed through the decryption algorithm. The result is XORed with the preceding ciphertext block to produce the plaintext block. To see that this works, we can write

$$C_j = \mathrm{E}(K, [C_{j-1} \oplus P_j])$$

Then

$$\begin{aligned} \mathrm{D}(K, C_j) &= \mathrm{D}(K, \mathrm{E}(K, [C_{j-1} \oplus P_j])) \\ \mathrm{D}(K, C_j) &= C_{j-1} \oplus P_j \\ C_{j-1} \oplus \mathrm{D}(K, C_j) &= C_{j-1} \oplus C_{j-1} \oplus P_j = P_j \end{aligned}$$

To produce the first block of ciphertext, an initialization vector (IV) is XORed with the first block of plaintext. On decryption, the IV is XORed with the output of the decryption algorithm to recover the first block of plaintext. The IV is a data block that is that same size as the cipher block.

The IV must be known to both the sender and receiver but be unpredictable by a third party. For maximum security, the IV should be protected against unauthorized changes. This could be done by sending the IV using ECB encryption. One reason for protecting the IV is as follows: If an opponent is able to fool the receiver into using a different value for IV, then the opponent is able to invert selected bits in the first block of plaintext. To see this, consider the following:

$$C_1 = \mathrm{E}(K, [\mathrm{IV} \oplus P_1])$$
$$P_1 = \mathrm{IV} \oplus \mathrm{D}(K, C_1)$$

Now use the notation that X[i] denotes the ith bit of the b-bit quantity X. Then

$$P_1[i] = \mathrm{IV}[i] \oplus \mathrm{D}(K, C_1)[i]$$

Then, using the properties of XOR, we can state

$$P_1[i]' = \mathrm{IV}[i]' \oplus \mathrm{D}(K, C_1)[i]$$

where the prime notation denotes bit complementation. This means that if an opponent can predictably change bits in IV, the corresponding bits of the received value of P_1 can be changed.

For other possible attacks based on knowledge of IV, see [VOYD83].

In conclusion, because of the chaining mechanism of CBC, it is an appropriate mode for encrypting messages of length greater than b bits.

In addition to its use to achieve confidentiality, the CBC mode can be used for authentication. This use is described in Part Two.

Cipher Feedback Mode

The DES scheme is essentially a block cipher technique that uses b-bit blocks. However, it is possible to convert DES into a stream cipher, using either the cipher feedback (CFB) or the output feedback mode. A stream cipher eliminates the need to pad a message to be an integral number of blocks. It also can operate in real time. Thus, if a character stream is being transmitted, each character can be encrypted and transmitted immediately using a character-oriented stream cipher.

One desirable property of a stream cipher is that the ciphertext be of the same length as the plaintext. Thus, if 8-bit characters are being transmitted, each character should be encrypted to produce a cipher text output of 8 bits. If more than 8 bits are produced, transmission capacity is wasted.

Figure 6.5 depicts the CFB scheme. In the figure, it is assumed that the unit of transmission is s bits; a common value is $s = 8$. As with CBC, the units of plaintext are chained together, so that the ciphertext of any plaintext unit is a function of all the preceding plaintext. In this case, rather than units of b bits, the plaintext is divided into *segments* of s bits.

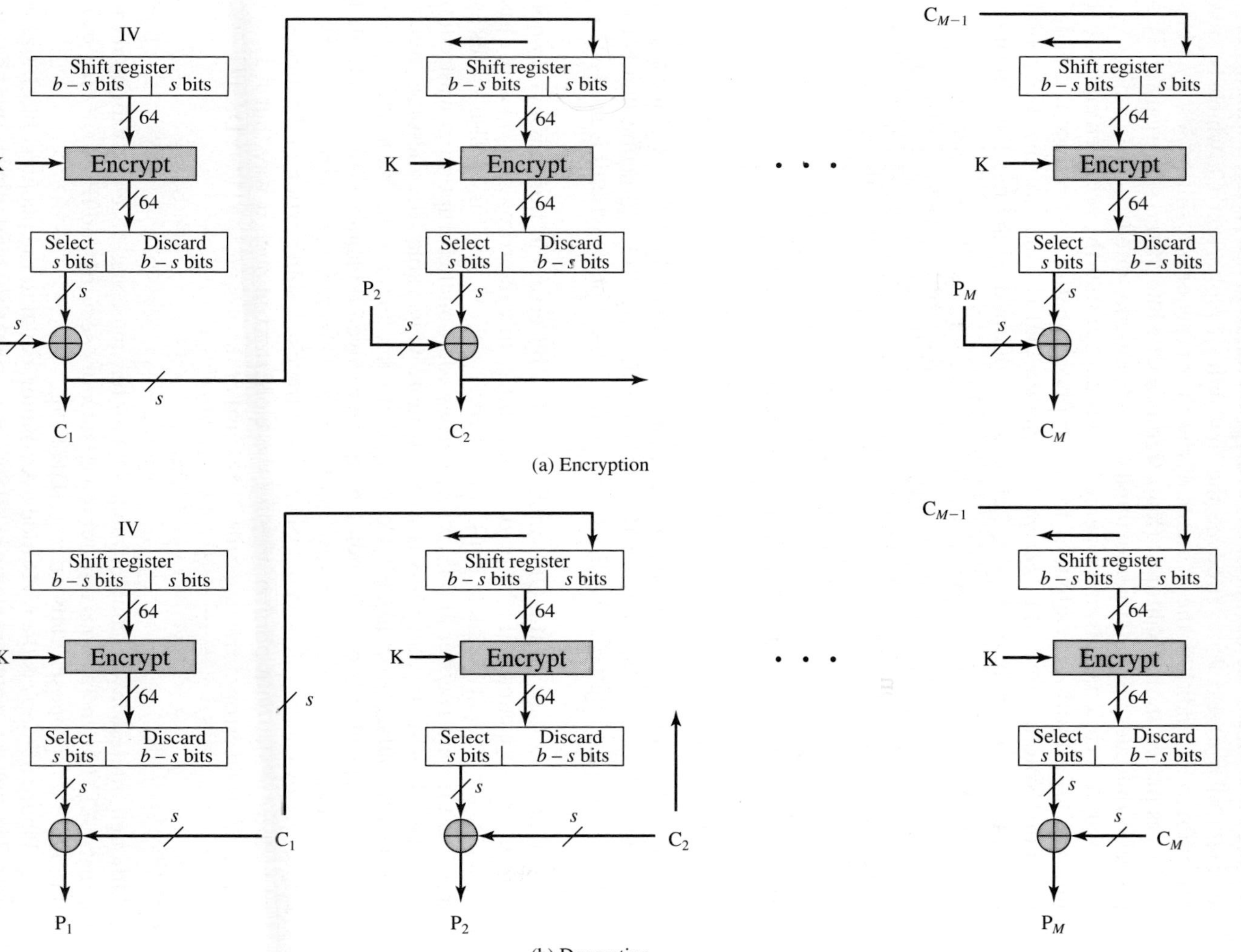

Figure 6.5 *s*-bit Cipher Feedback (CFB) Mode

First, consider encryption. The input to the encryption function is a b-bit shift register that is initially set to some initialization vector (IV). The leftmost (most significant) s bits of the output of the encryption function are XORed with the first segment of plaintext P_1 to produce the first unit of ciphertext C_1, which is then transmitted. In addition, the contents of the shift register are shifted left by s bits and C_1 is placed in the rightmost (least significant) s bits of the shift register. This process continues until all plaintext units have been encrypted.

For decryption, the same scheme is used, except that the received ciphertext unit is XORed with the output of the encryption function to produce the plaintext unit. Note that it is the *encryption* function that is used, not the decryption function. This is easily explained. Let $S_s(X)$ be defined as the most significant s bits of X. Then

$$C_1 = P_1 \oplus S_s[\mathrm{E}(K, \mathrm{IV})]$$

Therefore,

$$P_1 = C_1 \oplus S_s[\mathrm{E}(K, \mathrm{IV})]$$

The same reasoning holds for subsequent steps in the process.

Output Feedback Mode

The output feedback (OFB) mode is similar in structure to that of CFB, as illustrated in Figure 6.6. As can be seen, it is the output of the encryption function that is fed back to the shift register in OFB, whereas in CFB the ciphertext unit is fed back to the shift register.

One advantage of the OFB method is that bit errors in transmission do not propagate. For example, if a bit error occurs in C_1, only the recovered value of P_1 is affected; subsequent plaintext units are not corrupted. With CFB, C_1 also serves as input to the shift register and therefore causes additional corruption downstream.

The disadvantage of OFB is that it is more vulnerable to a message stream modification attack than is CFB. Consider that complementing a bit in the ciphertext complements the corresponding bit in the recovered plaintext. Thus, controlled changes to the recovered plaintext can be made. This may make it possible for an opponent, by making the necessary changes to the checksum portion of the message as well as to the data portion, to alter the ciphertext in such a way that it is not detected by an error-correcting code. For a further discussion, see [VOYD83].

Counter Mode

Although interest in the counter mode (CTR) has increased recently, with applications to ATM (asynchronous transfer mode) network security and IPSec (IP security), this mode was proposed early on (e.g., [DIFF79]).

Figure 6.7 depicts the CTR mode. A counter, equal to the plaintext block size is used. The only requirement stated in SP 800-38A is that the counter value must be different for each plaintext block that is encrypted. Typically, the counter is initialized to some value and then incremented by 1 for each subsequent block (modulo 2^b, where b is the block size). For encryption, the counter is encrypted and then XORed with the

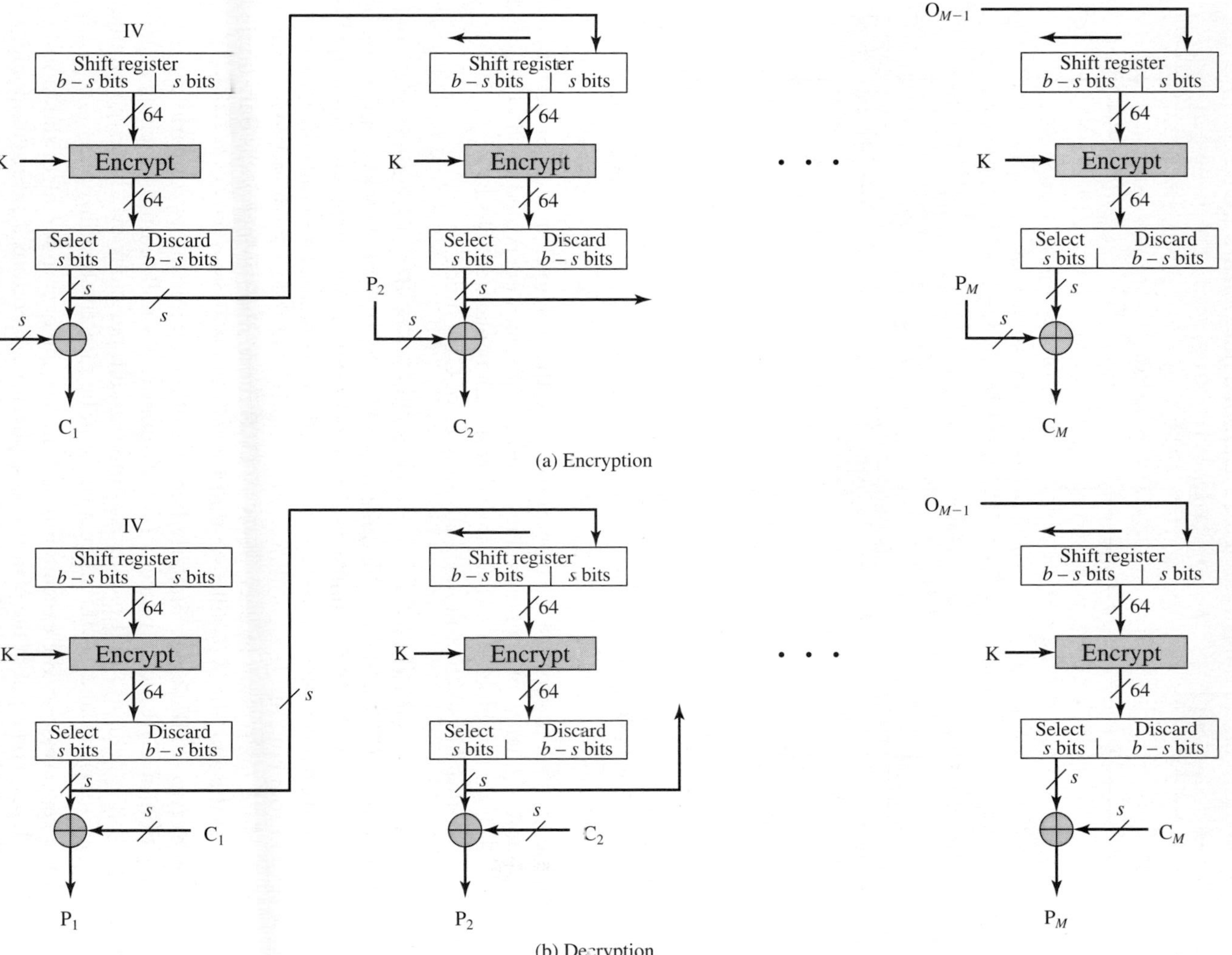

Figure 6.6 *s*-bit Output Feedback (OFB) Mode

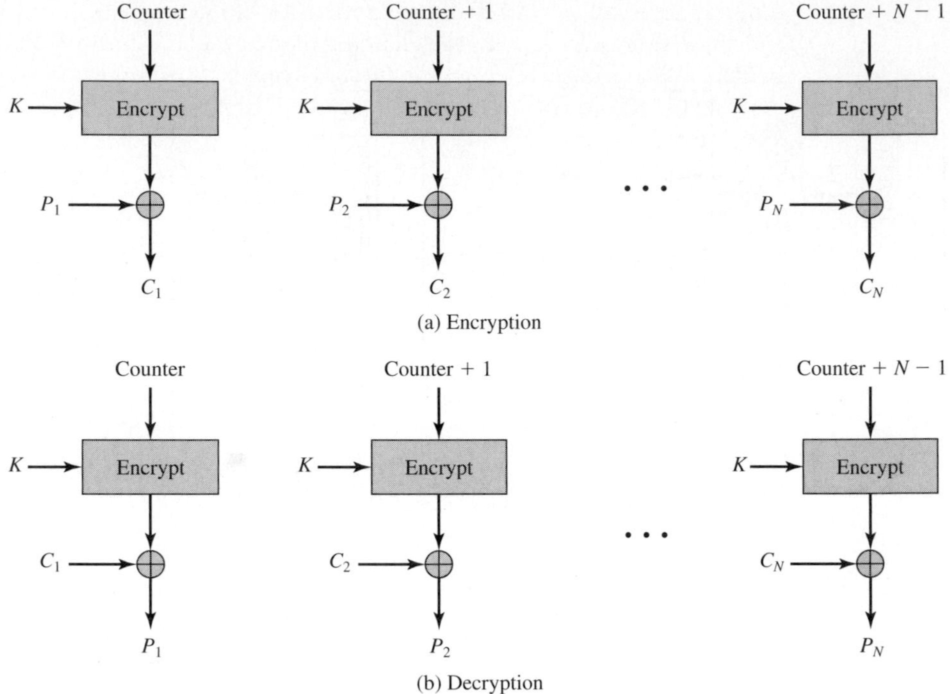

Figure 6.7 Counter (CTR) Mode

plaintext block to produce the ciphertext block; there is no chaining. For decryption, the same sequence of counter values is used, with each encrypted counter XORed with a ciphertext block to recover the corresponding plaintext block.

[LIPM00] lists the following advantages of CTR mode:

- **Hardware efficiency:** Unlike the three chaining modes, encryption (or decryption) in CTR mode can be done in parallel on multiple blocks of plaintext or ciphertext. For the chaining modes, the algorithm must complete the computation on one block before beginning on the next block. This limits the maximum throughput of the algorithm to the reciprocal of the time for one execution of block encryption or decryption. In CTR mode, the throughput is only limited by the amount of parallelism that is achieved.
- **Software efficiency:** Similarly, because of the opportunities for parallel execution in CTR mode, processors that support parallel features, such as aggressive pipelining, multiple instruction dispatch per clock cycle, a large number of registers, and SIMD instructions, can be effectively utilized.
- **Preprocessing:** The execution of the underlying encryption algorithm does not depend on input of the plaintext or ciphertext. Therefore, if sufficient memory is available and security is maintained, preprocessing can be used to prepare the output of the encryption boxes that feed into the XOR functions in Figure 6.7. When the plaintext or ciphertext input is presented, then the only computation is a series of XORs. Such a strategy greatly enhances throughput.

- **Random access:** The *i*th block of plaintext or ciphertext can be processed in random-access fashion. With the chaining modes, block C_i cannot be computed until the $i - 1$ prior block are computed. There may be applications in which a ciphertext is stored and it is desired to decrypt just one block; for such applications, the random access feature is attractive.
- **Provable security:** It can be shown that CTR is at least as secure as the other modes discussed in this section.
- **Simplicity:** Unlike ECB and CBC modes, CTR mode requires only the implementation of the encryption algorithm and not the decryption algorithm. This matters most when the decryption algorithm differs substantially from the encryption algorithm, as it does for AES. In addition, the decryption key scheduling need not be implemented.

6.3 STREAM CIPHERS AND RC4

In this section we look at perhaps the most popular symmetric stream cipher, RC4. We begin with an overview of stream cipher structure, and then examine RC4.

Stream Cipher Structure

A typical stream cipher encrypts plaintext one byte at a time, although a stream cipher may be designed to operate on one bit at a time or on units larger than a byte at a time. Figure 6.8 is a representative diagram of stream cipher structure. In this structure a key is input to a pseudorandom bit generator that produces a stream of 8-bit numbers that are apparently random. We discuss pseudorandom number generators in Chapter 7. For now, we simply say that a pseudorandom

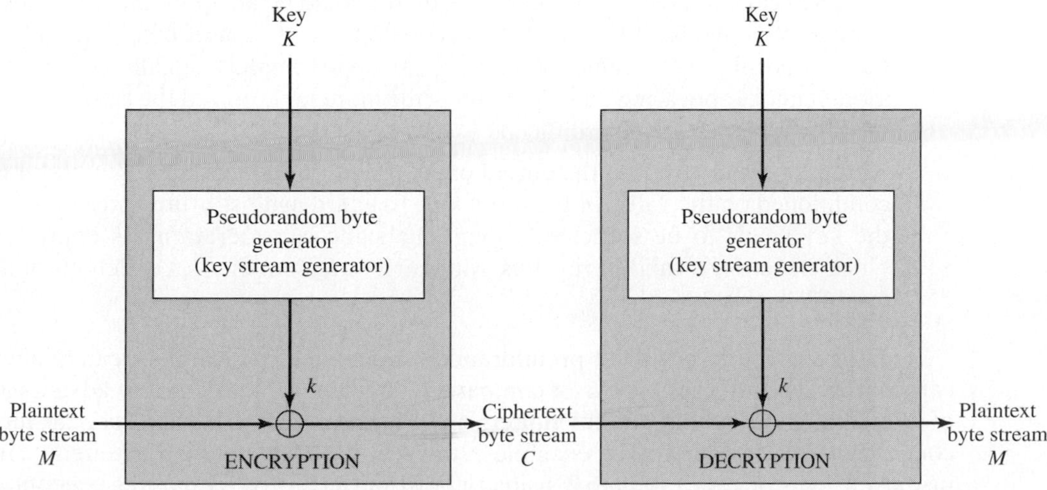

Figure 6.8 Stream Cipher Diagram

stream is one that is unpredictable without knowledge of the input key. The output of the generator, called a **keystream**, is combined one byte at a time with the plaintext stream using the bitwise exclusive-OR (XOR) operation. For example, if the next byte generated by the generator is 01101100 and the next plaintext byte is 11001100, then the resulting ciphertext byte is

```
  11001100   plaintext
⊕ 01101100   key stream
  10100000   ciphertext
```

Decryption requires the use of the same pseudorandom sequence:

```
  10100000   ciphertext
⊕ 01101100   key stream
  11001100   plaintext
```

The stream cipher is similar to the one-time pad discussed in Chapter 2. The difference is that a one-time pad uses a genuine random number stream, whereas a stream cipher uses a pseudorandom number stream.

[KUMA97] lists the following important design considerations for a stream cipher:

1. The encryption sequence should have a large period. A pseudorandom number generator uses a function that produces a deterministic stream of bits that eventually repeats. The longer the period of repeat the more difficult it will be to do cryptanalysis. This is essentially the same consideration that was discussed with reference to the Vigenère cipher, namely that the longer the keyword the more difficult the cryptanalysis.
2. The keystream should approximate the properties of a true random number stream as close as possible. For example, there should be an approximately equal number of 1s and 0s. If the keystream is treated as a stream of bytes, then all of the 256 possible byte values should appear approximately equally often. The more random-appearing the keystream is, the more randomized the ciphertext is, making cryptanalysis more difficult.
3. Note from Figure 6.8 that the output of the pseudorandom number generator is conditioned on the value of the input key. To guard against brute-force attacks, the key needs to be sufficiently long. The same considerations as apply for block ciphers are valid here. Thus, with current technology, a key length of at least 128 bits is desirable.

With a properly designed pseudorandom number generator, a stream cipher can be as secure as block cipher of comparable key length. The primary advantage of a stream cipher is that stream ciphers are almost always faster and use far less code than do block ciphers. The example in this section, RC4, can be implemented in just a few lines of code. Table 6.2, using data from [RESC01], compares execution times of RC4 with three well-known symmetric block ciphers. The advantage of a

Table 6.2 Speed Comparisons of Symmetric Ciphers on a Pentium II

Cipher	Key Length	Speed (Mbps)
DES	56	9
3DES	168	3
RC2	variable	0.9
RC4	variable	45

block cipher is that you can reuse keys. However, if two plaintexts are encrypted with the same key using a stream cipher, then cryptanalysis is often quite simple [DAWS96]. If the two ciphertext streams are XORed together, the result is the XOR of the original plaintexts. If the plaintexts are text strings, credit card numbers, or other byte streams with known properties, then cryptanalysis may be successful.

For applications that require encryption/decryption of a stream of data, such as over a data communications channel or a browser/Web link, a stream cipher might be the better alternative. For applications that deal with blocks of data, such as file transfer, e-mail, and database, block ciphers may be more appropriate. However, either type of cipher can be used in virtually any application.

The RC4 Algorithm

RC4 is a stream cipher designed in 1987 by Ron Rivest for RSA Security. It is a variable key-size stream cipher with byte-oriented operations. The algorithm is based on the use of a random permutation. Analysis shows that the period of the cipher is overwhelmingly likely to be greater than 10^{100} [ROBS95a]. Eight to sixteen machine operations are required per output byte, and the cipher can be expected to run very quickly in software. RC4 is used in the SSL/TLS (Secure Sockets Layer/Transport Layer Security) standards that have been defined for communication between Web browsers and servers. It is also used in the WEP (Wired Equivalent Privacy) protocol and the newer WiFi Protected Access (WPA) protocol that are part of the IEEE 802.11 wireless LAN standard. RC4 was kept as a trade secret by RSA Security. In September 1994, the RC4 algorithm was anonymously posted on the Internet on the Cypherpunks anonymous remailers list.

The RC4 algorithm is remarkably simply and quite easy to explain. A variable-length key of from 1 to 256 bytes (8 to 2048 bits) is used to initialize a 256-byte state vector S, with elements S[0], S[1], ..., S[255]. At all times, S contains a permutation of all 8-bit numbers from 0 through 255. For encryption and decryption, a byte k (see Figure 6.8) is generated from S by selecting one of the 255 entries in a systematic fashion. As each value of k is generated, the entries in S are once again permuted.

Initialization of S To begin, the entries of S are set equal to the values from 0 through 255 in ascending order; that is; S[0] = 0, S[1] = 1, ..., S[255] = 255. A temporary vector, T, is also created. If the length of the key K is 256 bytes, then K is transferred to T. Otherwise, for a key of length *keylen* bytes, the first *keylen* elements of T are copied from K and then K is repeated as many times as necessary to fill out T. These preliminary operations can be summarized as follows:

```
/* Initialization */
for  i = 0 to 255 do
S[i] = i;
T[i] = K[i mod keylen];
```

Next we use T to produce the initial permutation of S. This involves starting with S[0] and going through to S[255], and, for each S[i], swapping S[i] with another byte in S according to a scheme dictated by T[i]:

```
/* Initial Permutation of S */
j = 0;
for  i = 0 to 255 do
  j = (j + S[i] + T[i]) mod 256;
  Swap (S[i], S[j]);
```

Because the only operation on S is a swap, the only effect is a permutation. S still contains all the numbers from 0 through 255.

Stream Generation Once the S vector is initialized, the input key is no longer used. Stream generation involves cycling through all the elements of S[i], and, for each S[i], swapping S[i] with another byte in S according to a scheme dictated by the current configuration of S. After S[255] is reached, the process continues, starting over again at S[0]:

```
/* Stream Generation */
i, j = 0;
while (true)
  i = (i + 1) mod 256;
  j = (j + S[i]) mod 256;
  Swap (S[i], S[j]);
  t = (S[i] + S[j]) mod 256;
  k = S[t];
```

To encrypt, XOR the value *k* with the next byte of plaintext. To decrypt, XOR the value *k* with the next byte of ciphertext.

Figure 6.9 illustrates the RC4 logic.

Strength of RC4 A number of papers have been published analyzing methods of attacking RC4 [e.g., [KNUD98], [MIST98], [FLUH00], [MANT01]). None of these approaches is practical against RC4 with a reasonable key length, such as 128 bits. A more serious problem is reported in [FLUH01]. The authors demonstrate that the WEP protocol, intended to provide confidentiality on 802.11 wireless LAN networks, is vulnerable to a particular attack approach. In essence, the problem is not with RC4 itself but the way in which keys are generated for use as input to RC4.

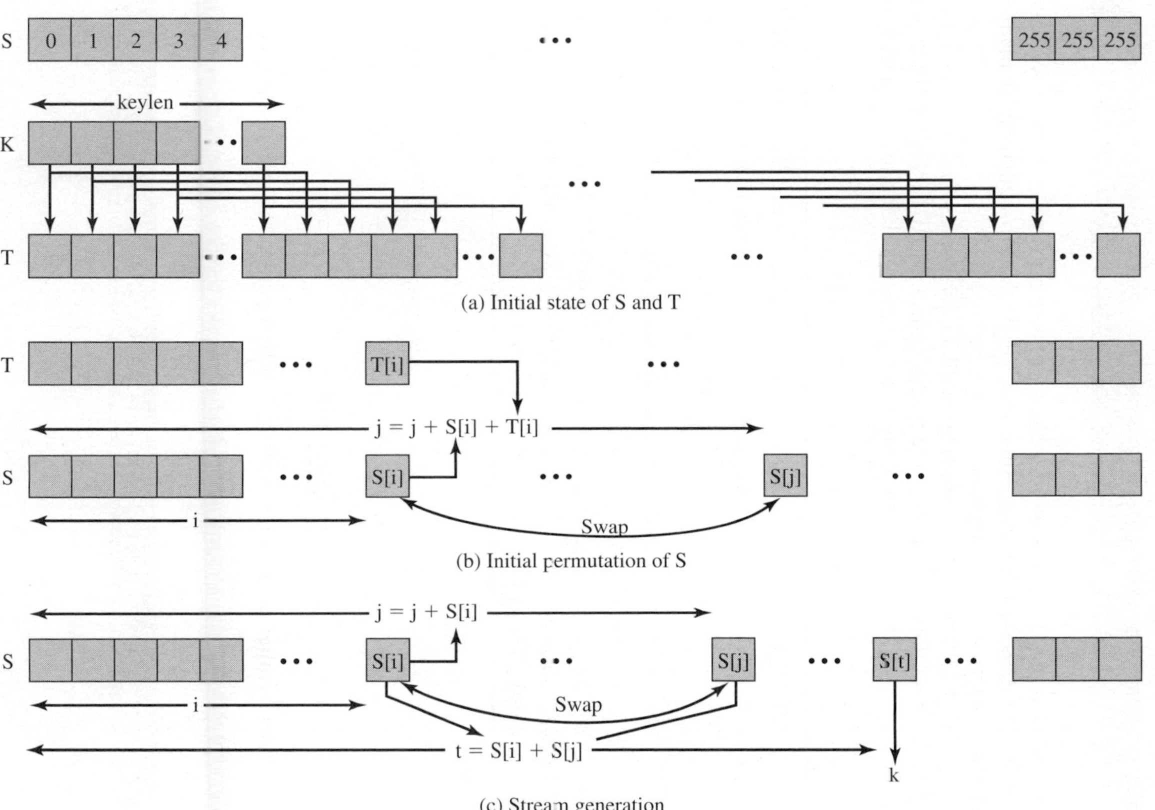

(a) Initial state of S and T

(b) Initial permutation of S

(c) Stream generation

Figure 6.9 RC4

This particular problem does not appear to be relevant to other applications using RC4 and can be remedied in WEP by changing the way in which keys are generated. This problem points out the difficulty in designing a secure system that involves both cryptographic functions and protocols that make use of them.

6.4 RECOMMENDED READING AND WEB SITE

[SCHN96] provides details on numerous symmetric block ciphers as well as some stream ciphers. [ROBS95b] is an interesting and worthwhile examination of many design issues related to symmetric block ciphers.

[KUMA97] contains an excellent and lengthy discussion of stream cipher design principles. Another good treatment, quite mathematical, is [RUEP92]. [ROBS95a] is an interesting and worthwhile examination of many design issues related to stream ciphers.

KUMA97 Kumar, I. *Cryptology.* Laguna Hills, CA: Aegean Park Press, 1997.

ROBS95a Robshaw, M. *Stream Ciphers.* RSA Laboratories Technical Report TR-701, July 1995. **http://www.rsasecurity.com/rsalabs**

ROBS95b Robshaw, M. *Block Ciphers.* RSA Laboratories Technical Report TR-601, August 1995. **http://www.rsasecurity.com/rsalabs**

RUEP92 Rueppel, T. "Stream Ciphers." In [SIMM92].

SCHN96 Schneier, B. *Applied Cryptography.* New York: Wiley, 1996.

SIMM92 Simmons, G., ed. *Contemporary Cryptology: The Science of Information Integrity.* Piscataway, NJ: IEEE Press, 1992.

Recommended Web Site:

- **Block cipher modes of operation:** NIST page with full information on NIST-approved modes of operation

6.5 KEY TERMS, REVIEW QUESTIONS, AND PROBLEMS

Key Terms

Block cipher modes of operation	meet-in-the-middle attack	RC4
cipher block chaining mode (CBC)	counter mode (CTR)	stream cipher
cipher feedback mode (CFB)	electronic codebook mode (ECB)	Triple DES (3DES)
	output feedback mode (OFB)	

Review Questions

6.1 What is triple encryption?
6.2 What is a meet-in-the-middle attack?
6.3 How many keys are used in triple encryption?
6.4 Why is the middle portion of 3DES a decryption rather than an encryption?
6.5 List important design considerations for a stream cipher.
6.6 Why is it not desirable to reuse a stream cipher key?
6.7 What primitive operations are used in RC4?
6.8 Why do some block cipher modes of operation only use encryption while others use both encryption and decryption?

Problems

6.1 You want to build a hardware device to do block encryption in the cipher block chaining (CBC) mode using an algorithm stronger than DES. 3DES is a good candidate. Figure 6.10 shows two possibilities, both of which follow from the definition of CBC. Which of the two would you choose:

a. For security?
b. For performance?

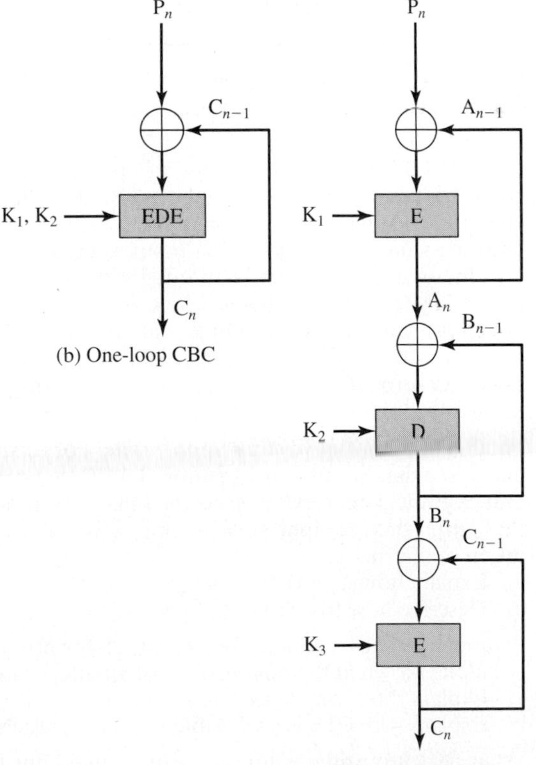

Figure 6.10 Use of Triple DES in CBC Mode

6.2 Can you suggest a security improvement to either option in Figure 6.10, using only three DES chips and some number of XOR functions? Assume you are still limited to two keys.

6.3 The Merkle-Hellman attack on 3DES begins by assuming a value of A = 0 (Figure 6.1b). Then, for each of the 2^{56} possible values of K_1, the plaintext P that produces A = 0 is determined. Describe the rest of the algorithm.

6.4 With the ECB mode of DES, if there is an error in a block of the transmitted ciphertext, only the corresponding plaintext block is affected. However, in the CBC mode, this error propagates. For example, an error in the transmitted C_1 (Figure 6.4) obviously corrupts P_1 and P_2.

a. Are any blocks beyond P_2 affected?

b. Suppose that there is a bit error in the source version of P_1. Through how many ciphertext blocks is this error propagated? What is the effect at the receiver?

6.5 If a bit error occurs in the transmission of a ciphertext character in 8-bit CFB mode, how far does the error propagate?

6.6 Fill in the remainder of this table:

Mode	**Encrypt**	**Decrypt**
ECB	$C_j = E(K, P_j) \quad j = 1, \ldots, N$	$P_j = D(K, C_j) \quad j = 1, \ldots, N$
CBC	$C_1 = E(K, [P_1 \oplus IV])$ $C_j = E(K, [P_j \oplus C_{j-1}]) \quad j = 2, \ldots, N$	$P_1 = D(K, C_1) \oplus IV$ $P_j = D(K, C_j) \oplus C_{j-1} \quad j = 2, \ldots, N$
CFB		
OFB		
CTR		

6.7 CBC-Pad is a block cipher mode of operation used in the RC5 block cipher, but it could be used in any block cipher. CBC-Pad handles plaintext of any length. The ciphertext is longer then the plaintext by at most the size of a single block. Padding is used to assure that the plaintext input is a multiple of the block length. It is assumed that the original plaintext is an integer number of bytes. This plaintext is padded at the end by from 1 to *bb* bytes, where *bb* equals the block size in bytes. The pad bytes are all the same and set to a byte that represents the number of bytes of padding. For example, if there are 8 bytes of padding, each byte has the bit pattern 00001000. Why not allow zero bytes of padding? That is, if the original plaintext is an integer multiple of the block size, why not refrain from padding?

6.8 Padding may not always be appropriate. For example, one might wish to store the encrypted data in the same memory buffer that originally contained the plaintext. In that case, the ciphertext must be the same length as the original plaintext. A mode for that purpose is the ciphertext stealing (CTS) mode. Figure 6.11a shows an implementation of this mode.

a. Explain how it works.

b. Describe how to decrypt C_{n-1} and C_n.

6.9 Figure 6.11b shows an alternative to CTS for producing ciphertext of equal length to the plaintext when the plaintext is not an integer multiple of the block size.

a. Explain the algorithm.

b. Explain why CTS is preferable to this approach illustrated in Figure 6.11b.

6.10 What RC4 key value will leave S unchanged during initialization? That is, after the initial permutation of S, the entries of S will be equal to the values from 0 through 255 in ascending order.

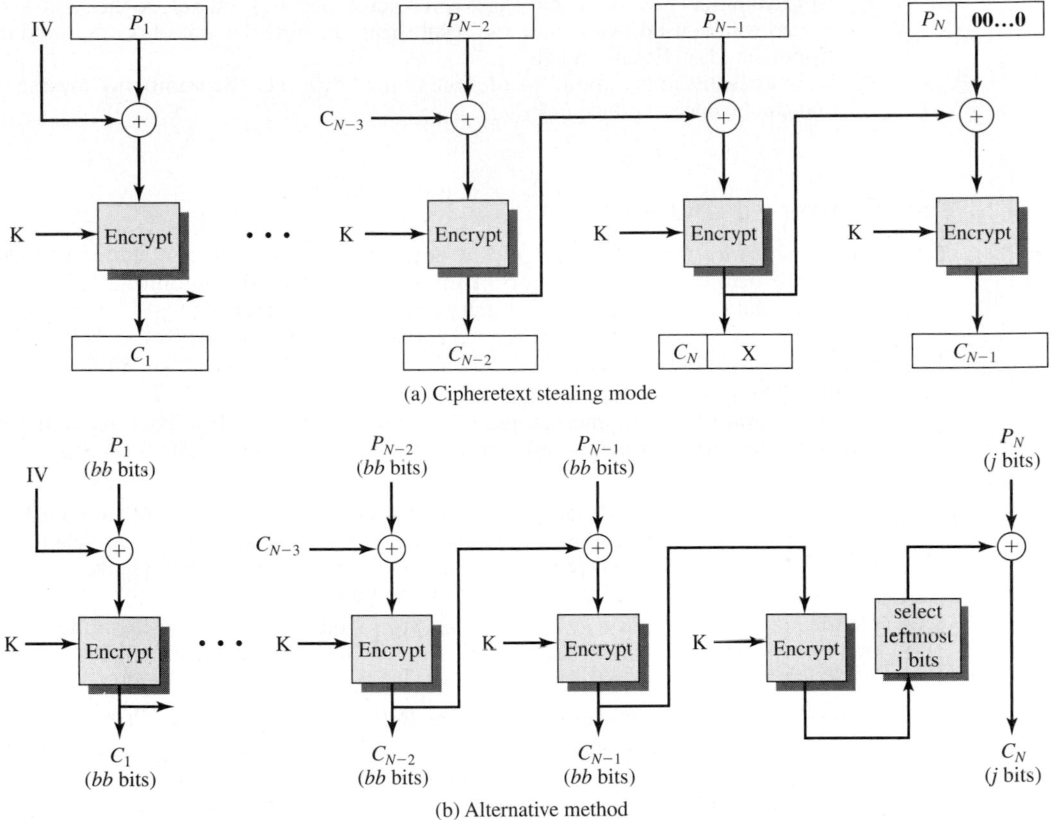

Figure 6.11 Block Cipher Modes for Plaintext not a Multiple of Block Size

6.11 RC4 has a secret internal state which is a permutation of all the possible values of the vector **S** and the two indices *i* and *j*.

a. Using a straightforward scheme to store the internal state, how many bits are used?

b. Suppose we think of it from the point of view of how much information is represented by the state. In that case, we need to determine how may different states there are, than take the log to the base 2 to find out how many bits of information this represents. Using this approach, how many bits would be needed to represent the state?

6.12 Alice and Bob agree to communicate privately via email using a scheme based on RC4, but want to avoid using a new secret key for each transmission. Alice and Bob privately agree on a 128-bit key *k*. To encrypt a message *m*, consisting of a string of bits, the following procedure is used:

1. Choose a random 80-bit value *v*
2. Generate the ciphertext $c = \text{RC4}(v \| k) \oplus m$
3. Send the bit string $(v \| c)$

a. Suppose Alice uses this procedure to send a message *m* to Bob. Describe how Bob can recover the message *m* from $(v \| c)$ using *k*.

b. If an adversary observes several values $(v_1 \| c_1)$, $(v_2 \| c_2)$, ... transmitted between Alice and Bob, how can he/she determine when the same key stream has been used to encrypt two messages?

c. Approximately how many messages can Alice expect to send before the same key stream will be used twice? Use the result from the birthday paradox described in Appendix 11A [Equation (11.7)].

d. What does this imply about the lifetime of the key k (i.e., the number of messages that can be encrypted using k)?

Programming Problems

6.13 Create software that can encrypt and decrypt in Cipher Block Chaining mode using one of the following ciphers: affine modulo 256, Hill modulo 256, S-DES, DES. Test data for S-DES: using a binary initialization vector of 1010 1010, a binary plaintext of 0000 0001 0010 0011 encrypted with a binary key of 01111 11101 should give a binary plaintext of 1111 0100 0000 1011. Decryption should work correspondingly.

6.14 Create software that can encrypt and decrypt in 4-bit Cipher Feedback mode using one of the following ciphers: additive modulo 256, affine modulo 256, S-DES;

or

8-bit Cipher Feedback mode using one of the following ciphers: 2 × 2 Hill modulo 256. Test data for S-DES: using a binary initialization vector of 1010 1011, a binary plaintext of 0001 0010 0011 0100 encrypted with a binary key of 01111 11101 should give a binary plaintext of 1110 1100 1111 1010. Decryption should work correspondingly.

6.15 Create software that can encrypt and decrypt in 4-bit Output Feedback mode using one of the following ciphers: additive modulo 256, affine modulo 256, S-DES;

or

8-bit Output Feedback mode using one of the following ciphers: 2 × 2 Hill modulo 256,

6.16 Create software that can encrypt and decrypt in Counter mode using one of the following ciphers: affine modulo 256, Hill modulo 256, S-DES.

Test data for S-DES: using a counter starting at 0000 0000, a binary plaintext of 0000 0001 0000 0010 0000 0100 encrypted with a binary key of 01111 11101 should give a binary plaintext of 0011 1000 0100 1111 0011 0010. Decryption should work correspondingly.

6.17 Implement a differential cryptanalysis attack on 3-round S-DES.

CHAPTER 7

Confidentiality Using Symmetric Encryption

Amongst the tribes of Central Australia every man, woman, and child has a secret or sacred name which is bestowed by the older men upon him or her soon after birth, and which is known to none but the fully initiated members of the group. This secret name is never mentioned except upon the most solemn occasions; to utter it in the hearing of men of another group would be a most serious breach of tribal custom. When mentioned at all, the name is spoken only in a whisper, and not until the most elaborate precautions have been taken that it shall be heard by no one but members of the group. The native thinks that a stranger knowing his secret name would have special power to work him ill by means of magic.

—*The Golden Bough*, Sir James George Frazer

John wrote the letters of the alphabet under the letters in its first lines and tried it against the message. Immediately he knew that once more he had broken the code. It was extraordinary the feeling of triumph he had. He felt on top of the world. For not only had he done it, had he broken the July code, but he now had the key to every future coded message, since instructions as to the source of the next one must of necessity appear in the current one at the end of each month.

—*Talking to Strange Men,* Ruth Rendell

KEY POINTS

- In a distributed environment, encryption devices can be placed to support either link encryption or end-to-end encryption. With link encryption, each vulnerable communications link is equipped on both ends with an encryption device. With end-to-end encryption, the encryption process is carried out at the two end systems.
- Even if all traffic between users is encrypted, a traffic analysis may yield information of value to an opponent. An effective countermeasure is traffic padding, which involves sending random bits during periods when no encrypted data are available for transmission.
- Key distribution is the function that delivers a key to two parties who wish to exchange secure encrypted data. Some sort of mechanism or protocol is needed to provide for the secure distribution of keys.
- Key distribution often involves the use of master keys, which are infrequently used and are long lasting, and session keys, which are generated and distributed for temporary use between two parties.
- A capability with application to a number of cryptographic functions is random or pseudorandom number generation. The principle requirement for this capability is that the generated number stream be unpredictable.

Historically, the focus of cryptology has been on the use of symmetric encryption to provide confidentiality. It is only in the last several decades that other considerations, such as authentication, integrity, digital signatures, and the use of public-key encryption, have been included in the theory and practice of cryptology.

Before examining some of these more recent topics, we concentrate in this chapter on the use of symmetric encryption to provide confidentiality. This topic remains important in itself. In addition, an understanding of the issues involved here helps to motivate the development of public-key encryption and clarifies the issues involved in other applications of encryption, such as authentication.

We begin with a discussion of the location of encryption logic; the main choice here is between what are known as link encryption and end-to-end encryption. Next, we look at the use of encryption to counter traffic analysis attacks. Then we discuss the difficult problem of key distribution. Finally, we discuss the principles underlying an important tool in providing a confidentiality facility: random number generation.

7.1 PLACEMENT OF ENCRYPTION FUNCTION

If encryption is to be used to counter attacks on confidentiality, we need to decide what to encrypt and where the encryption function should be located. To begin, this section examines the potential locations of security attacks and then looks at the two major approaches to encryption placement: link and end to end.

Potential Locations for Confidentiality Attacks

As an example, consider a user workstation in a typical business organization. Figure 7.1 suggests the types of communications facilities that might be employed by such a workstation and therefore gives an indication of the points of vulnerability.

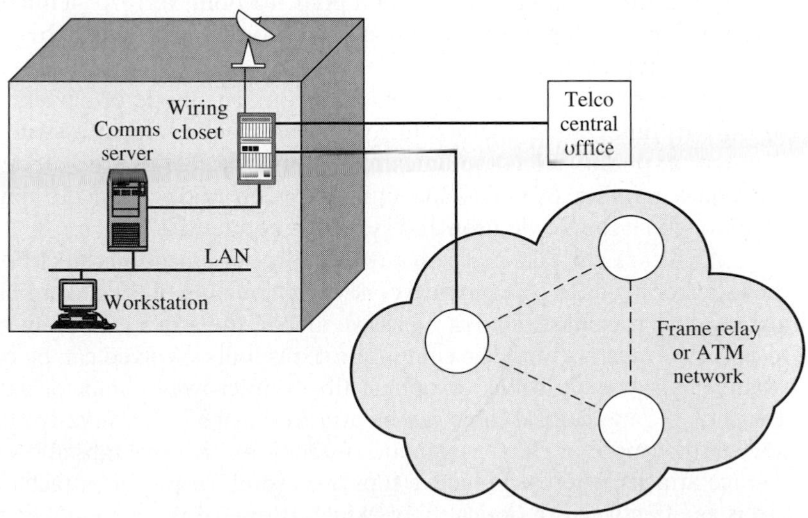

Figure 7.1 Points of Vulnerability

In most organizations, workstations are attached to local area networks (LANs). Typically, the user can reach other workstations, hosts, and servers directly on the LAN or on other LANs in the same building that are interconnected with bridges and routers. Here, then, is the first point of vulnerability. In this case, the main concern is eavesdropping by another employee. Typically, a LAN is a broadcast network: Transmission from any station to any other station is visible on the LAN medium to all stations. Data are transmitted in the form of frames, with each frame containing the source and destination address. An eavesdropper can monitor the traffic on the LAN and capture any traffic desired on the basis of source and destination addresses. If part or all of the LAN is wireless, then the potential for eavesdropping is greater.

Furthermore, the eavesdropper need not necessarily be an employee in the building. If the LAN, through a communications server or one of the hosts on the LAN, offers a dial-in capability, then it is possible for an intruder to gain access to the LAN and monitor traffic.

Access to the outside world from the LAN is almost always available in the form of a router that connects to the Internet, a bank of dial-out modems, or some other type of communications server. From the communications server, there is a line leading to a wiring closet. The wiring closet serves as a patch panel for interconnecting internal data and phone lines and for providing a staging point for external communications.

The wiring closet itself is vulnerable. If an intruder can penetrate to the closet, he or she can tap into each wire to determine which are used for data transmission. After isolating one or more lines, the intruder can attach a low-power radio transmitter. The resulting signals can be picked up from a nearby location (e.g., a parked van or a nearby building).

Several routes out of the wiring closet are possible. A standard configuration provides access to the nearest central office of the local telephone company. Wires in the closet are gathered into a cable, which is usually consolidated with other cables in the basement of the building. From there, a larger cable runs underground to the central office.

In addition, the wiring closet may provide a link to a microwave antenna, either an earth station for a satellite link or a point-to-point terrestrial microwave link. The antenna link can be part of a private network, or it can be a local bypass to hook in to a long-distance carrier.

The wiring closet may also provide a link to a node of a packet-switching network. This link can be a leased line, a direct private line, or a switched connection through a public telecommunications network. Inside the network, data pass through a number of nodes and links between nodes until the data arrive at the node to which the destination end system is connected.

An attack can take place on any of the communications links. For active attacks, the attacker needs to gain physical control of a portion of the link and be able to insert and capture transmissions. For a passive attack, the attacker merely needs to be able to observe transmissions. The communications links involved can be cable (telephone twisted pair, coaxial cable, or optical fiber), microwave links, or satellite channels. Twisted pair and coaxial cable can be attacked using either invasive taps or inductive devices that monitor electromagnetic emanations. Invasive taps allow both active and passive attacks, whereas inductive taps are useful for passive attacks. Neither type of tap is as effective with optical fiber, which is one of the advantages of this medium.

The fiber does not generate electromagnetic emanations and hence is not vulnerable to inductive taps. Physically breaking the cable seriously degrades signal quality and is therefore detectable. Microwave and satellite transmissions can be intercepted with little risk to the attacker. This is especially true of satellite transmissions, which cover a broad geographic area. Active attacks on microwave and satellite are also possible, although they are more difficult technically and can be quite expensive.

In addition to the potential vulnerability of the various communications links, the various processors along the path are themselves subject to attack. An attack can take the form of attempts to modify the hardware or software, to gain access to the memory of the processor, or to monitor the electromagnetic emanations. These attacks are less likely than those involving communications links but are nevertheless a source of risk.

Thus, there are a large number of locations at which an attack can occur. Furthermore, for wide area communications, many of these locations are not under the physical control of the end user. Even in the case of local area networks, in which physical security measures are possible, there is always the threat of the disgruntled employee.

Link versus End-to-End Encryption

The most powerful and most common approach to securing the points of vulnerability highlighted in the preceding section is encryption. If encryption is to be used to counter these attacks, then we need to decide what to encrypt and where the encryption gear should be located. As Figure 7.2 indicates, there are two fundamental alternatives: link encryption and end-to-end encryption.

Basic Approaches With link encryption, each vulnerable communications link is equipped on both ends with an encryption device. Thus, all traffic over all communications links is secured. Although this recourse requires a lot of encryption devices in a large network, its value is clear. One of its disadvantages is that the message must be decrypted each time it enters a switch (such as a frame relay switch) because the switch must read the address (logical connection number) in the packet header in order to route the frame. Thus, the message is vulnerable at each switch. If working with a public network, the user has no control over the security of the nodes.

Several implications of link encryption should be noted. For this strategy to be effective, all the potential links in a path from source to destination must use link encryption. Each pair of nodes that share a link should share a unique key, with a different key used on each link. Thus, many keys must be provided.

With end-to-end encryption, the encryption process is carried out at the two end systems. The source host or terminal encrypts the data. The data in encrypted form are then transmitted unaltered across the network to the destination terminal or host. The destination shares a key with the source and so is able to decrypt the data. This plan seems to secure the transmission against attacks on the network links or switches. Thus, end-to-end encryption relieves the end user of concerns about the degree of security of networks and links that support the communication. There is, however, still a weak spot.

Consider the following situation. A host connects to a frame relay or ATM network, sets up a logical connection to another host, and is prepared to transfer data to that other host by using end-to-end encryption. Data are transmitted over such a network in the form of packets that consist of a header and some user data. What part of each packet will the host encrypt? Suppose that the host encrypts the entire packet,

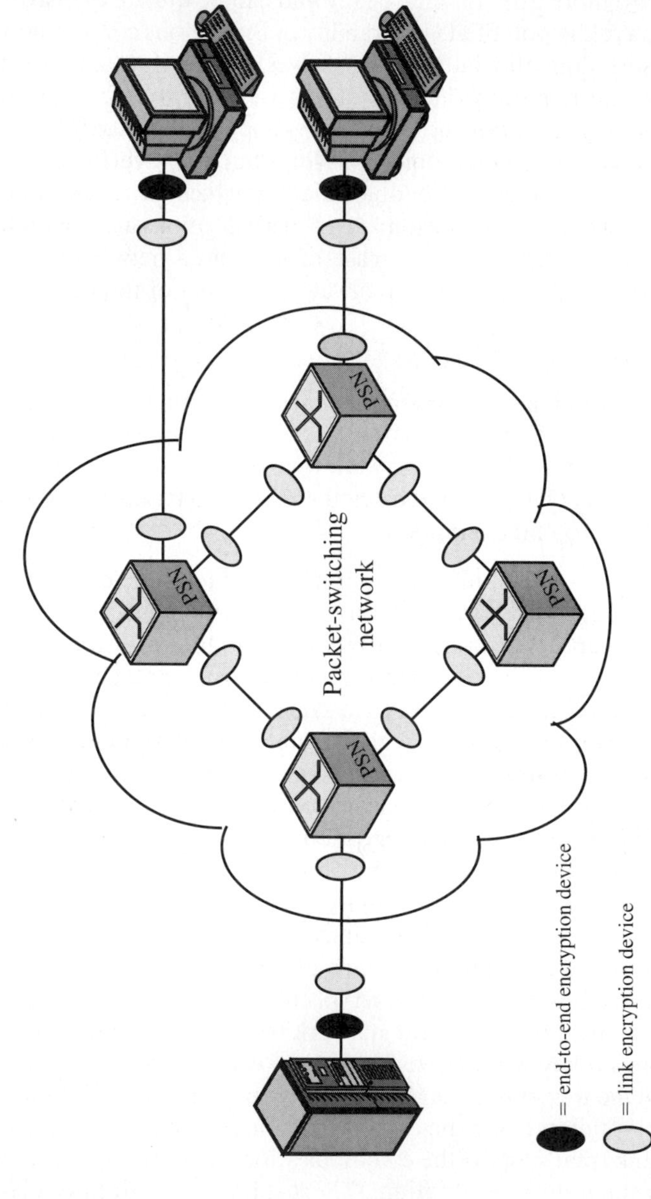

Figure 7.2 Encryption Across a Packet-Switching Network

including the header. This will not work because, remember, only the other host can perform the decryption. The frame relay or ATM switch will receive an encrypted packet and be unable to read the header. Therefore, it will not be able to route the packet. It follows that the host may encrypt only the user data portion of the packet and must leave the header in the clear.

Thus, with end-to-end encryption, the user data are secure. However, the traffic pattern is not, because packet headers are transmitted in the clear. On the other hand, end-to-end encryption does provide a degree of authentication. If two end systems share an encryption key, then a recipient is assured that any message that it receives comes from the alleged sender, because only that sender shares the relevant key. Such authentication is not inherent in a link encryption scheme.

To achieve greater security, both link and end-to-end encryption are needed, as is shown in Figure 7.2. When both forms of encryption are employed, the host encrypts the user data portion of a packet using an end-to-end encryption key. The entire packet is then encrypted using a link encryption key. As the packet traverses the network, each switch decrypts the packet, using a link encryption key to read the header, and then encrypts the entire packet again for sending it out on the next link. Now the entire packet is secure except for the time that the packet is actually in the memory of a packet switch, at which time the packet header is in the clear.

Table 7.1 summarizes the key characteristics of the two encryption strategies.

Logical Placement of End-to-End Encryption Function With link encryption, the encryption function is performed at a low level of the communications hierarchy. In terms of the Open Systems Interconnection (OSI) model, link encryption occurs at either the physical or link layers.

Table 7.1 Characteristics of Link and End-to-End Encryption [PFLE02]

Link Encryption	End-to-End Encryption
Security within End Systems and Intermediate Systems	
Message exposed in sending host	Message encrypted in sending host
Message exposed in intermediate nodes	Message encrypted in intermediate nodes
Role of User	
Applied by sending host	Applied by sending process
Transparent to user	User applies encryption
Host maintains encryption facility	User must determine algorithm
One facility for all users	Users selects encryption scheme
Can be done in hardware	Software implementation
All or no messages encrypted	User chooses to encrypt, or not, for each message
Implementation Concerns	
Requires one key per (host-intermediate node) pair and (intermediate node-intermediate node) pair	Requires one key per user pair
Provides host authentication	Provides user authentication

For end-to-end encryption, several choices are possible for the logical placement of the encryption function. At the lowest practical level, the encryption function could be performed at the network layer. Thus, for example, encryption could be associated with the frame relay or ATM protocol, so that the user data portion of all frames or ATM cells is encrypted.

With network-layer encryption, the number of identifiable and separately protected entities corresponds to the number of end systems in the network. Each end system can engage in an encrypted exchange with another end system if the two share a secret key. All the user processes and applications within each end system would employ the same encryption scheme with the same key to reach a particular target end system. With this arrangement, it might be desirable to off-load the encryption function to some sort of front-end processor (typically a communications board in the end system).

Figure 7.3 shows the encryption function of the front-end processor (FEP). On the host side, the FEP accepts packets. The user data portion of the packet is encrypted, while the packet header bypasses the encryption process.[1] The resulting packet is delivered to the network. In the opposite direction, for packets arriving from the network, the user data portion is decrypted and the entire packet is delivered to the host. If the transport layer functionality (e.g., TCP) is implemented in the front end, then the transport-layer header would also be left in the clear and the user data portion of the transport protocol data unit is encrypted.

Deployment of encryption services on end-to-end protocols, such as a network-layer frame relay or TCP, provides end-to-end security for traffic within a fully integrated internetwork. However, such a scheme cannot deliver the necessary service for traffic that crosses internetwork boundaries, such as electronic mail, electronic data interchange (EDI), and file transfers.

Figure 7.4 illustrates the issues involved. In this example, an electronic mail gateway is used to interconnect an internetwork that uses an OSI-based architecture

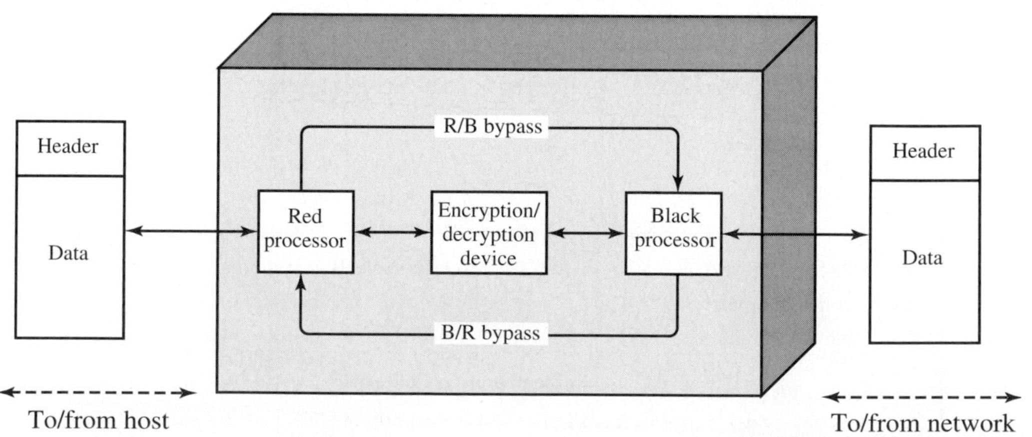

Figure 7.3 Front-End Processor Function

[1]The terms *red* and *black* are frequently used. Red data are sensitive or classified data in the clear. Black data are encrypted data.

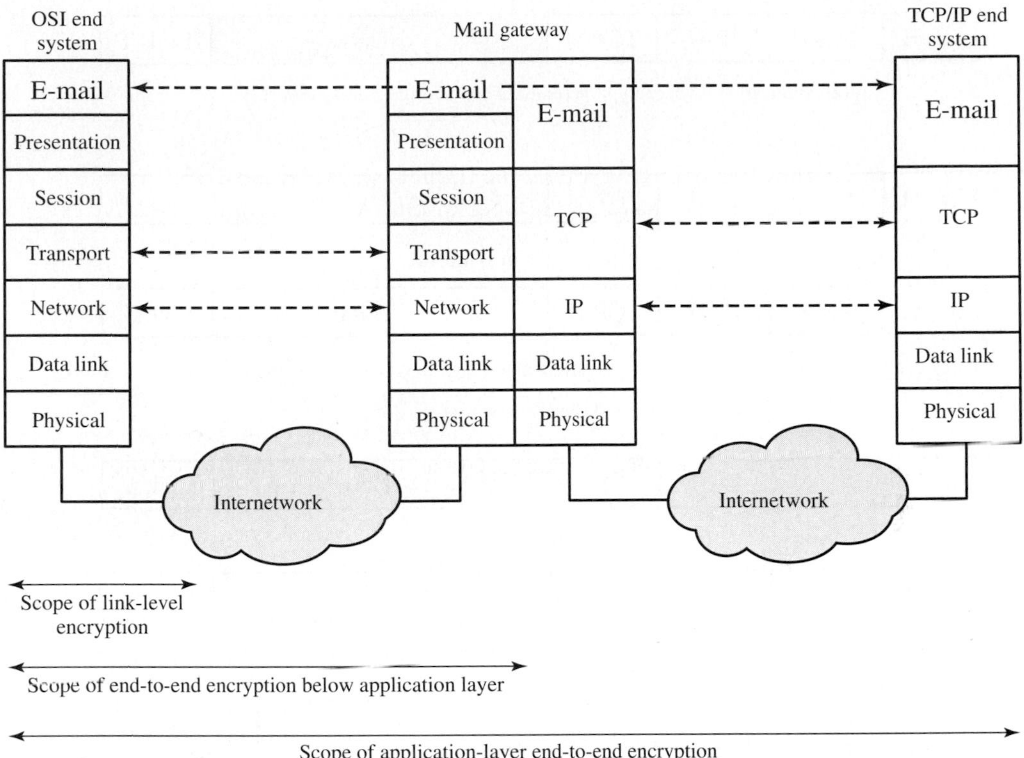

Figure 7.4 Encryption Coverage Implications of Store-and-Forward Communications

with one that uses a TCP/IP-based architecture.[2] In such a configuration, there is no end-to-end protocol below the application layer. The transport and network connections from each end system terminate at the mail gateway, which sets up new transport and network connections to link to the other end system. Furthermore, such a scenario is not limited to the case of a gateway between two different architectures. Even if both end systems use TCP/IP or OSI, there are plenty of instances in actual configurations in which mail gateways sit between otherwise isolated internetworks. Thus, for applications like electronic mail that have a store-and-forward capability, the only place to achieve end-to end encryption is at the application layer.

A drawback of application-layer encryption is that the number of entities to consider increases dramatically. A network that supports hundreds of hosts may support thousands of users and processes. Thus, many more secret keys need to be generated and distributed.

An interesting way of viewing the alternatives is to note that as we move up the communications hierarchy, less information is encrypted but it is more secure. Figure 7.5 highlights this point, using the TCP/IP architecture as an example. In the figure, an application-level gateway refers to a store-and-forward device that operates at the application level.[3]

---

[2]Appendix H provides a brief overview of the OSI and TCP/IP protocol architectures.

[3]Unfortunately, most TCP/IP documents use the term *gateway* to refer to what is more commonly referred to as a *router*.

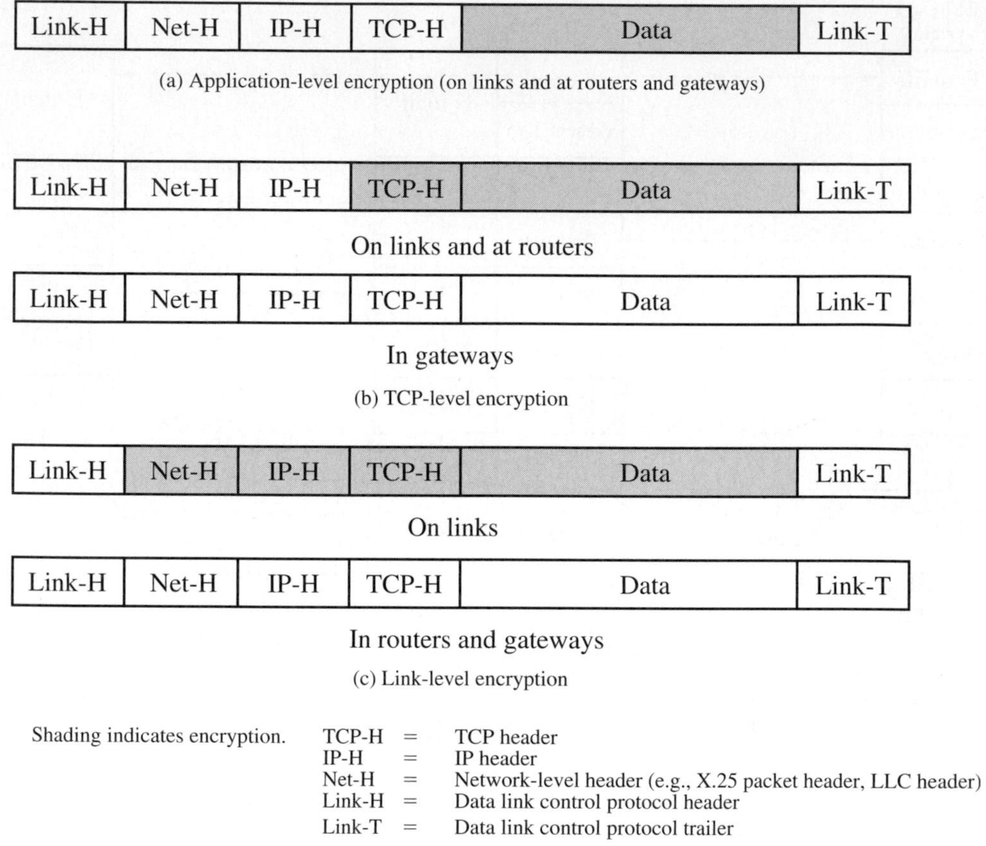

Figure 7.5 Relationship between Encryption and Protocol Levels

With application-level encryption (Figure 7.5a), only the user data portion of a TCP segment is encrypted. The TCP, IP, network-level, and link-level headers and link-level trailer are in the clear. By contrast, if encryption is performed at the TCP level (Figure 7.5b), then, on a single end-to-end connection, the user data and the TCP header are encrypted. The IP header remains in the clear because it is needed by routers to route the IP datagram from source to destination. Note, however, that if a message passes through a gateway, the TCP connection is terminated and a new transport connection is opened for the next hop. Furthermore, the gateway is treated as a destination by the underlying IP. Thus, the encrypted portions of the data unit are decrypted at the gateway. If the next hop is over a TCP/IP network, then the user data and TCP header are encrypted again before transmission. However, in the gateway itself the data unit is buffered entirely in the clear. Finally, for link-level encryption (Figure 7.5c), the entire data unit except for the link header and trailer is encrypted on each link, but the entire data unit is in the clear at each router and gateway.[4]

[4]The figure actually shows but one alternative. It is also possible to encrypt part or even all of the link header and trailer except for the starting and ending frame flags.

7.2 TRAFFIC CONFIDENTIALITY

We mentioned in Chapter 1 that, in some cases, users are concerned about security from traffic analysis. Knowledge about the number and length of messages between nodes may enable an opponent to determine who is talking to whom. This can have obvious implications in a military conflict. Even in commercial applications, traffic analysis may yield information that the traffic generators would like to conceal. [MUFT89] lists the following types of information that can be derived from a traffic analysis attack:

- Identities of partners
- How frequently the partners are communicating
- Message pattern, message length, or quantity of messages that suggest important information is being exchanged
- The events that correlate with special conversations between particular partners

Another concern related to traffic is the use of traffic patterns to create a **covert channel**. A covert channel is a means of communication in a fashion unintended by the designers of the communications facility. Typically, the channel is used to transfer information in a way that violates a security policy. For example, an employee may wish to communicate information to an outsider in a way that is not detected by management and that requires simple eavesdropping on the part of the outsider. The two participants could set up a code in which an apparently legitimate message of a less than a certain length represents binary zero, whereas a longer message represents a binary one. Other such schemes are possible.

Link Encryption Approach

With the use of link encryption, network-layer headers (e.g., frame or cell header) are encrypted, reducing the opportunity for traffic analysis. However, it is still possible in those circumstances for an attacker to assess the amount of traffic on a network and to observe the amount of traffic entering and leaving each end system. An effective countermeasure to this attack is traffic padding, illustrated in Figure 7.6.

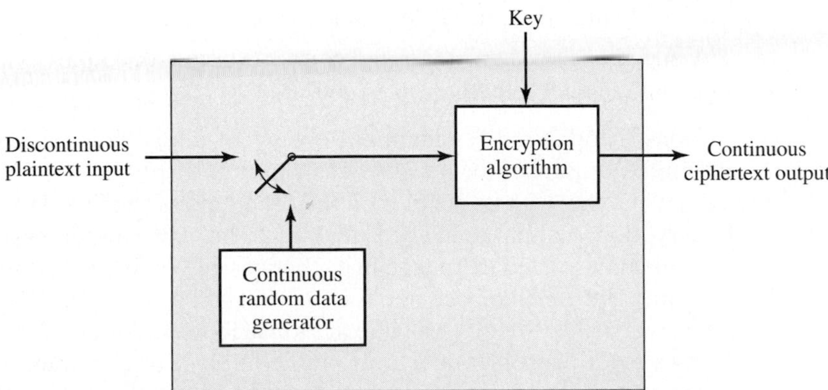

Figure 7.6 Traffic-Padding Encryption Device

Traffic padding produces ciphertext output continuously, even in the absence of plaintext. A continuous random data stream is generated. When plaintext is available, it is encrypted and transmitted. When input plaintext is not present, random data are encrypted and transmitted. This makes it impossible for an attacker to distinguish between true data flow and padding and therefore impossible to deduce the amount of traffic.

End-to-End Encryption Approach

Traffic padding is essentially a link encryption function. If only end-to-end encryption is employed, then the measures available to the defender are more limited. For example, if encryption is implemented at the application layer, then an opponent can determine which transport entities are engaged in dialogue. If encryption techniques are housed at the transport layer, then network-layer addresses and traffic patterns remain accessible.

One technique that might prove useful is to pad out data units to a uniform length at either the transport or application level. In addition, null messages can be inserted randomly into the stream. These tactics deny an opponent knowledge about the amount of data exchanged between end users and obscure the underlying traffic pattern.

7.3 KEY DISTRIBUTION

For symmetric encryption to work, the two parties to an exchange must share the same key, and that key must be protected from access by others. Furthermore, frequent key changes are usually desirable to limit the amount of data compromised if an attacker learns the key. Therefore, the strength of any cryptographic system rests with the *key distribution technique*, a term that refers to the means of delivering a key to two parties who wish to exchange data, without allowing others to see the key. For two parties A and B, key distribution can be achieved in a number of ways, as follows:

1. A can select a key and physically deliver it to B.
2. A third party can select the key and physically deliver it to A and B.
3. If A and B have previously and recently used a key, one party can transmit the new key to the other, encrypted using the old key.
4. If A and B each has an encrypted connection to a third party C, C can deliver a key on the encrypted links to A and B.

Options 1 and 2 call for manual delivery of a key. For link encryption, this is a reasonable requirement, because each link encryption device is going to be exchanging data only with its partner on the other end of the link. However, for end-to-end encryption, manual delivery is awkward. In a distributed system, any given host or terminal may need to engage in exchanges with many other hosts and terminals over time. Thus, each device needs a number of keys supplied dynamically. The problem is especially difficult in a wide area distributed system.

The scale of the problem depends on the number of communicating pairs that must be supported. If end-to-end encryption is done at a network or IP level, then a key is needed for each pair of hosts on the network that wish to communicate. Thus, if

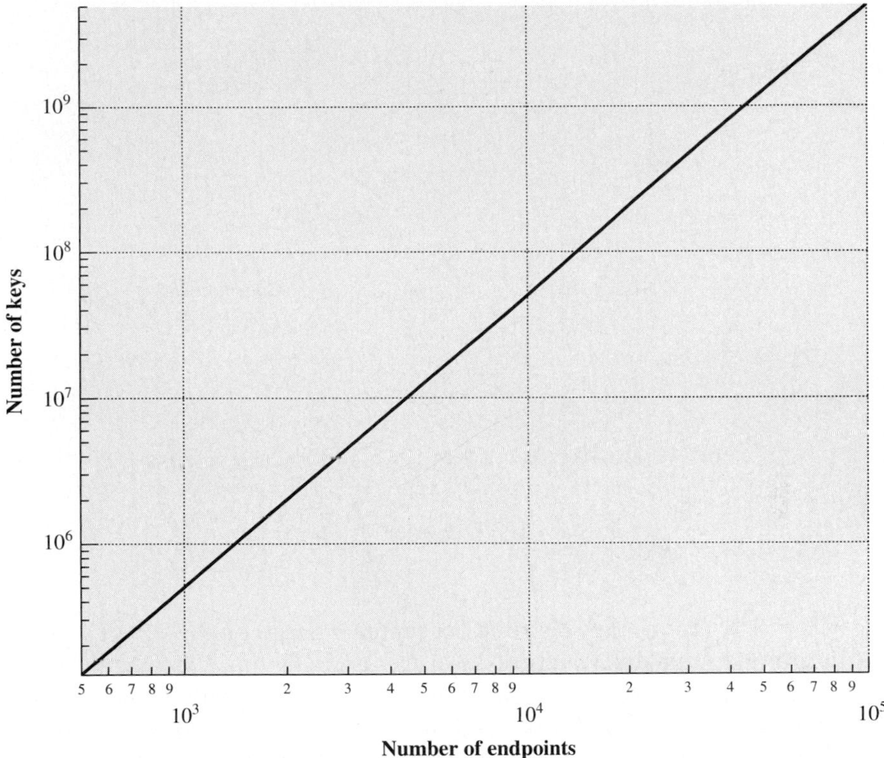

Figure 7.7 Number of Keys Required to Support Arbitrary Connections between Endpoints

there are N hosts, the number of required keys is $[N(N - 1)]/2$. If encryption is done at the application level, then a key is needed for every pair of users or processes that require communication. Thus, a network may have hundreds of hosts but thousands of users and processes. Figure 7.7 illustrates the magnitude of the key distribution task for end-to-end encryption.[5] A network using node-level encryption with 1000 nodes would conceivably need to distribute as many as half a million keys. If that same network supported 10,000 applications, then as many as 50 million keys may be required for application-level encryption.

Returning to our list, option 3 is a possibility for either link encryption or end-to-end encryption, but if an attacker ever succeeds in gaining access to one key, then all subsequent keys will be revealed. Furthermore, the initial distribution of potentially millions of keys must still be made.

For end-to-end encryption, some variation on option 4 has been widely adopted. In this scheme, a key distribution center is responsible for distributing keys to pairs of users (hosts, processes, applications) as needed. Each user must share a unique key with the key distribution center for purposes of key distribution.

[5]Note that this figure uses a log-log scale, so that a linear graph indicates exponential growth. A basic review of log scales is in the math refresher document at the Computer Science Student Resource Site at **WilliamStallings.com/StudentSupport.html.**

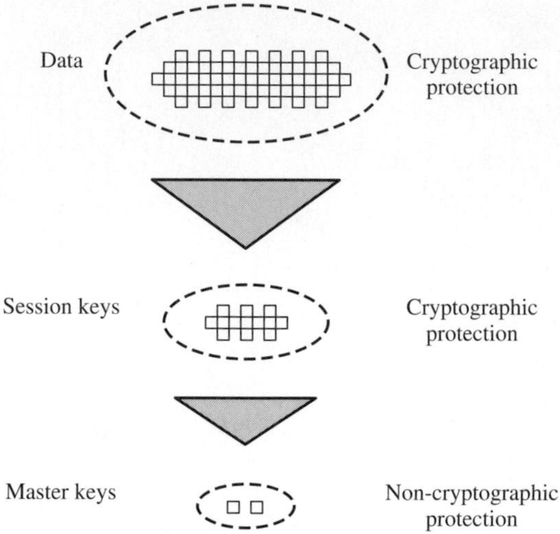

Figure 7.8 The Use of a Key Hierarchy

The use of a key distribution center is based on the use of a hierarchy of keys. At a minimum, two levels of keys are used (Figure 7.8). Communication between end systems is encrypted using a temporary key, often referred to as a **session key**. Typically, the session key is used for the duration of a logical connection, such as a frame relay connection or transport connection, and then discarded. Each session key is obtained from the key distribution center over the same networking facilities used for end-user communication. Accordingly, session keys are transmitted in encrypted form, using a **master key** that is shared by the key distribution center and an end system or user.

For each end system or user, there is a unique master key that it shares with the key distribution center. Of course, these master keys must be distributed in some fashion. However, the scale of the problem is vastly reduced. If there are N entities that wish to communicate in pairs, then, as was mentioned, as many as $[N(N-1)]/2$ session keys are needed at any one time. However, only N master keys are required, one for each entity. Thus, master keys can be distributed in some noncryptographic way, such as physical delivery.

A Key Distribution Scenario

The key distribution concept can be deployed in a number of ways. A typical scenario is illustrated in Figure 7.9, which is based on a figure in [POPE79]. The scenario assumes that each user shares a unique master key with the key distribution center (KDC).

Let us assume that user A wishes to establish a logical connection with B and requires a one-time session key to protect the data transmitted over the connection. A has a master key, K_a, known only to itself and the KDC; similarly, B shares the master key K_b with the KDC. The following steps occur:

1. A issues a request to the KDC for a session key to protect a logical connection to B. The message includes the identity of A and B and a unique identifier, N_1, for

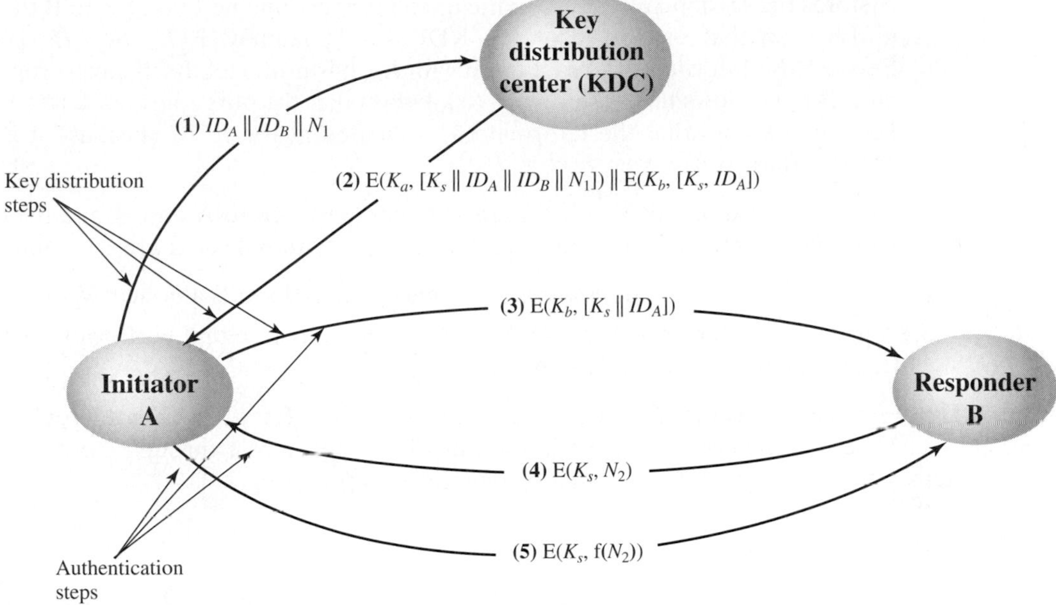

Figure 7.9 Key Distribution Scenario

this transaction, which we refer to as a **nonce**.[6] The nonce may be a timestamp, a counter, or a random number; the minimum requirement is that it differs with each request. Also, to prevent masquerade, it should be difficult for an opponent to guess the nonce. Thus, a random number is a good choice for a nonce.

2. The KDC responds with a message encrypted using K_a. Thus, A is the only one who can successfully read the message, and A knows that it originated at the KDC. The message includes two items intended for A:
   - The one-time session key, K_s, to be used for the session
   - The original request message, including the nonce, to enable A to match this response with the appropriate request

   Thus, A can verify that its original request was not altered before reception by the KDC and, because of the nonce, that this is not a replay of some previous request.

   In addition, the message includes two items intended for B:
   - The one-time session key, K_s, to be used for the session
   - An identifier of A (e.g., its network address), ID_A

   These last two items are encrypted with K_b (the master key that the KDC shares with B). They are to be sent to B to establish the connection and prove A's identity.

[6]The following definitions are useful in understanding the purpose of the nonce component. **Nonce:** The present or particular occasion. **Nonce word:** A word occurring, invented, or used just for a particular occasion. From the *American Heritage Dictionary of the English Language*, 3rd ed.

3. A stores the session key for use in the upcoming session and forwards to B the information that originated at the KDC for B, namely, $E(K_b, [K_s \| ID_A])$. Because this information is encrypted with K_b, it is protected from eavesdropping. B now knows the session key (K_s), knows that the other party is A (from ID_A), and knows that the information originated at the KDC (because it is encrypted using K_b).

At this point, a session key has been securely delivered to A and B, and they may begin their protected exchange. However, two additional steps are desirable:

4. Using the newly minted session key for encryption, B sends a nonce, N_2, to A.
5. Also using K_s, A responds with $f(N_2)$, where f is a function that performs some transformation on N_2 (e.g., adding one).

These steps assure B that the original message it received (step 3) was not a replay.

Note that the actual key distribution involves only steps 1 through 3 but that steps 4 and 5, as well as 3, perform an authentication function.

Hierarchical Key Control

It is not necessary to limit the key distribution function to a single KDC. Indeed, for very large networks, it may not be practical to do so. As an alternative, a hierarchy of KDCs can be established. For example, there can be local KDCs, each responsible for a small domain of the overall internetwork, such as a single LAN or a single building. For communication among entities within the same local domain, the local KDC is responsible for key distribution. If two entities in different domains desire a shared key, then the corresponding local KDCs can communicate through a global KDC. In this case, any one of the three KDCs involved can actually select the key. The hierarchical concept can be extended to three or even more layers, depending on the size of the user population and the geographic scope of the internetwork.

A hierarchical scheme minimizes the effort involved in master key distribution, because most master keys are those shared by a local KDC with its local entities. Furthermore, such a scheme limits the damage of a faulty or subverted KDC to its local area only.

Session Key Lifetime

The more frequently session keys are exchanged, the more secure they are, because the opponent has less ciphertext to work with for any given session key. On the other hand, the distribution of session keys delays the start of any exchange and places a burden on network capacity. A security manager must try to balance these competing considerations in determining the lifetime of a particular session key.

For connection-oriented protocols, one obvious choice is to use the same session key for the length of time that the connection is open, using a new session key for each new session. If a logical connection has a very long lifetime, then it would be prudent to change the session key periodically, perhaps every time the PDU (protocol data unit) sequence number cycles.

For a connectionless protocol, such as a transaction-oriented protocol, there is no explicit connection initiation or termination. Thus, it is not obvious how often one needs to change the session key. The most secure approach is to use a new session key for each exchange. However, this negates one of the principal benefits of connectionless protocols, which is minimum overhead and delay for each transaction. A better strategy is to use a given session key for a certain fixed period only or for a certain number of transactions.

A Transparent Key Control Scheme

The approach suggested in Figure 7.9 has many variations, one of which is described in this subsection. The scheme (Figure 7.10) is useful for providing end-to-end encryption at a network or transport level in a way that is transparent to the end users. The approach assumes that communication makes use of a connection-oriented end-to-end protocol, such as TCP. The noteworthy element of this approach is a session security module (SSM), which may consists of functionality at one protocol layer, that performs end-to-end encryption and obtains session keys on behalf of its host or terminal.

The steps involved in establishing a connection are shown in the figure. When one host wishes to set up a connection to another host, it transmits a connection-request packet (step 1). The SSM saves that packet and applies to the KDC for permission to establish the connection (step 2). The communication between the SSM and the KDC is encrypted using a master key shared only by this SSM and the KDC. If the KDC approves the connection request, it generates the session key and delivers it to the two appropriate SSMs, using a unique permanent key for each SSM (step 3). The requesting SSM can now release the connection request packet, and a connection is set up between the two end systems (step 4). All user data exchanged between the two end systems are encrypted by their respective SSMs using the one-time session key.

The automated key distribution approach provides the flexibility and dynamic characteristics needed to allow a number of terminal users to access a number of hosts and for the hosts to exchange data with each other.

Decentralized Key Control

The use of a key distribution center imposes the requirement that the KDC be trusted and be protected from subversion. This requirement can be avoided if key distribution is fully decentralized. Although full decentralization is not practical for larger networks using symmetric encryption only, it may be useful within a local context.

A decentralized approach requires that each end system be able to communicate in a secure manner with all potential partner end systems for purposes of session key distribution. Thus, there may need to be as many as $[n(n - 1)]/2$ master keys for a configuration with n end systems.

A session key may be established with the following sequence of steps (Figure 7.11):

1. A issues a request to B for a session key and includes a nonce, N_1.
2. B responds with a message that is encrypted using the shared master key. The response includes the session key selected by B, an identifier of B, the value $f(N_1)$, and another nonce, N_2.
3. Using the new session key, A returns $f(N_2)$ to B.

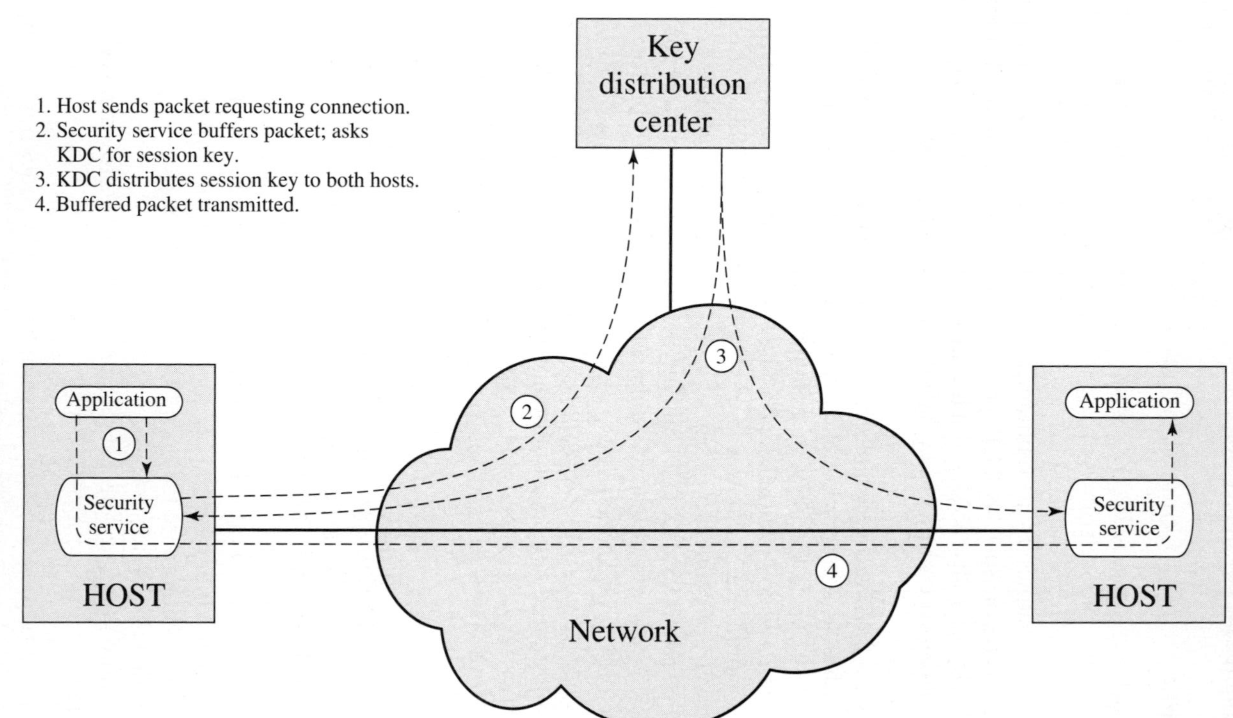
1. Host sends packet requesting connection.
2. Security service buffers packet; asks KDC for session key.
3. KDC distributes session key to both hosts.
4. Buffered packet transmitted.
Key distribution center
Application
Security service
HOST
Application
Security service
HOST
Network
1
2
3
4

Figure 7.10 Automatic Key Distribution for Connection-Oriented Protocol

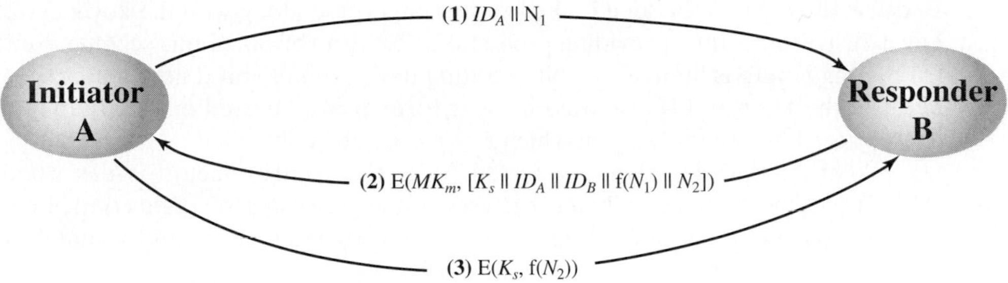

Figure 7.11 Decentralized Key Distribution

Thus, although each node must maintain at most $(n - 1)$ master keys, as many session keys as required may be generated and used. Because the messages transferred using the master key are short, cryptanalysis is difficult. As before, session keys are used for only a limited time to protect them.

Controlling Key Usage

The concept of a key hierarchy and the use of automated key distribution techniques greatly reduce the number of keys that must be manually managed and distributed. It may also be desirable to impose some control on the way in which automatically distributed keys are used. For example, in addition to separating master keys from session keys, we may wish to define different types of session keys on the basis of use, such as

- Data-encrypting key, for general communication across a network
- PIN-encrypting key, for personal identification numbers (PINs) used in electronic funds transfer and point-of-sale applications
- File-encrypting key, for encrypting files stored in publicly accessible locations

To illustrate the value of separating keys by type, consider the risk that a master key is imported as a data-encrypting key into a device. Normally, the master key is physically secured within the cryptographic hardware of the key distribution center and of the end systems. Session keys encrypted with this master key are available to application programs, as are the data encrypted with such session keys. However, if a master key is treated as a session key, it may be possible for an unauthorized application to obtain plaintext of session keys encrypted with that master key.

Thus, it may be desirable to institute controls in systems that limit the ways in which keys are used, based on characteristics associated with those keys. One simple plan is to associate a tag with each key ([JONE82]; see also [DAVI89]). The proposed technique is for use with DES and makes use of the extra 8 bits in each 64-bit DES key. That is, the 8 nonkey bits ordinarily reserved for parity checking form the key tag. The bits have the following interpretation:

- One bit indicates whether the key is a session key or a master key.
- One bit indicates whether the key can be used for encryption.
- One bit indicates whether the key can be used for decryption.
- The remaining bits are spares for future use.

Because the tag is embedded in the key, it is encrypted along with the key when that key is distributed, thus providing protection. The drawbacks of this scheme are that (1) the tag length is limited to 8 bits, limiting its flexibility and functionality; and (2) because the tag is not transmitted in clear form, it can be used only at the point of decryption, limiting the ways in which key use can be controlled.

A more flexible scheme, referred to as the control vector, is described in [MATY91a and b]. In this scheme, each session key has an associated control vector consisting of a number of fields that specify the uses and restrictions for that session key. The length of the control vector may vary.

The control vector is cryptographically coupled with the key at the time of key generation at the KDC. The coupling and decoupling processes are illustrated in Figure 7.12. As a first step, the control vector is passed through a hash function that produces a value whose length is equal to the encryption key length. Hash functions are discussed in detail in Chapter 11. In essence, a hash function maps values from a larger range into a smaller range, with a reasonably uniform spread. Thus, for example, if numbers in the range 1 to 100 are hashed into numbers in the range 1 to 10, approximately 10% of the source values should map into each of the target values.

The hash value is then XORed with the master key to produce an output that is used as the key input for encrypting the session key. Thus,

$$\begin{aligned} \text{Hash value} &= H = \text{h(CV)} \\ \text{Key input} &= K_m \oplus H \\ \text{Ciphertext} &= \text{E}([K_m \oplus H], K_s) \end{aligned}$$

where K_m is the master key and K_s is the session key. The session key is recovered in plaintext by the reverse operation:

$$\text{D}([K_m \oplus H], \text{E}([K_m \oplus H], K_s))$$

When a session key is delivered to a user from the KDC, it is accompanied by the control vector in clear form. The session key can be recovered only by using both the master key that the user shares with the KDC and the control vector. Thus, the linkage between the session key and its control vector is maintained.

Use of the control vector has two advantages over use of an 8-bit tag. First, there is no restriction on length of the control vector, which enables arbitrarily complex controls to be imposed on key use. Second, the control vector is available in clear form at all stages of operation. Thus, control of key use can be exercised in multiple locations.

7.4 RANDOM NUMBER GENERATION

Random numbers play an important role in the use of encryption for various network security applications. In this section, we provide a brief overview of the use of random numbers in network security and then look at some approaches to generating random numbers.

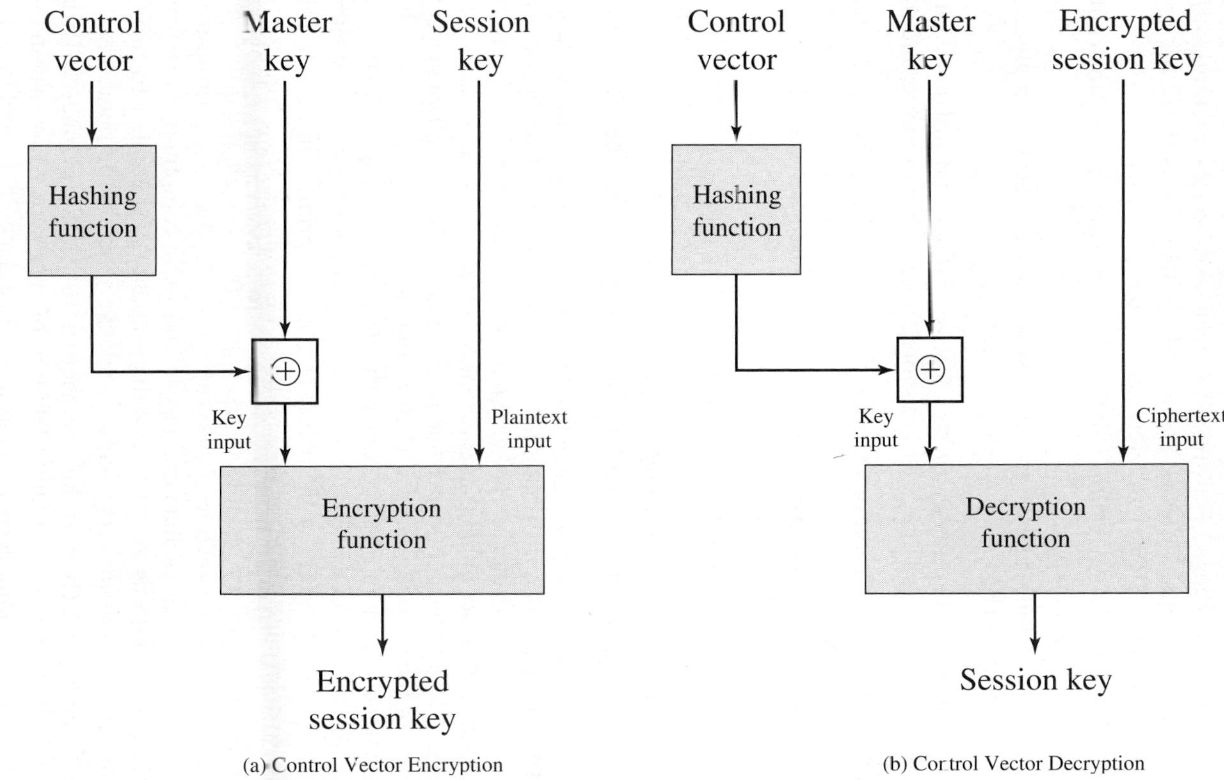

Figure 7.12 Control Vector Encryption and Decryption

The Use of Random Numbers

A number of network security algorithms based on cryptography make use of random numbers. For example,

- Reciprocal authentication schemes, such as illustrated in Figures 7.9 and 7.11. In both of these key distribution scenarios, nonces are used for handshaking to prevent replay attacks. The use of random numbers for the nonces frustrates opponents' efforts to determine or guess the nonce.
- Session key generation, whether done by a key distribution center or by one of the principals.
- Generation of keys for the RSA public-key encryption algorithm (described in Chapter 9).

These applications give rise to two distinct and not necessarily compatible requirements for a sequence of random numbers: randomness and unpredictability.

Randomness Traditionally, the concern in the generation of a sequence of allegedly random numbers has been that the sequence of numbers be random in some well-defined statistical sense. The following two criteria are used to validate that a sequence of numbers is random:

- **Uniform distribution:** The distribution of numbers in the sequence should be uniform; that is, the frequency of occurrence of each of the numbers should be approximately the same.
- **Independence:** No one value in the sequence can be inferred from the others.

Although there are well-defined tests for determining that a sequence of numbers matches a particular distribution, such as the uniform distribution, there is no such test to "prove" independence. Rather, a number of tests can be applied to demonstrate if a sequence does not exhibit independence. The general strategy is to apply a number of such tests until the confidence that independence exists is sufficiently strong.

In the context of our discussion, the use of a sequence of numbers that appear statistically random often occurs in the design of algorithms related to cryptography. For example, a fundamental requirement of the RSA public-key encryption scheme discussed in Chapter 9 is the ability to generate prime numbers. In general, it is difficult to determine if a given large number N is prime. A brute-force approach would be to divide N by every odd integer less than $\sqrt{N}$. If N is on the order, say, of 10^{150}, a not uncommon occurrence in public-key cryptography, such a brute-force approach is beyond the reach of human analysts and their computers. However, a number of effective algorithms exist that test the primality of a number by using a sequence of randomly chosen integers as input to relatively simple computations. If the sequence is sufficiently long (but far, far less than $\sqrt{10^{150}}$), the primality of a number can be determined with near certainty. This type of approach, known as randomization, crops up frequently in the design of algorithms. In essence, if a problem is too hard or time-consuming to solve exactly, a simpler, shorter approach based on randomization is used to provide an answer with any desired level of confidence.

Unpredictability In applications such as reciprocal authentication and session key generation, the requirement is not so much that the sequence of numbers be statistically random but that the successive members of the sequence are unpredictable. With "true" random sequences, each number is statistically independent of other numbers in the sequence and therefore unpredictable. However, as is discussed shortly, true random numbers are seldom used; rather, sequences of numbers that appear to be random are generated by some algorithm. In this latter case, care must be taken that an opponent not be able to predict future elements of the sequence on the basis of earlier elements.

Pseudorandom Number Generators (PRNGs)

Cryptographic applications typically make use of algorithmic techniques for random number generation. These algorithms are deterministic and therefore produce sequences of numbers that are not statistically random. However, if the algorithm is good, the resulting sequences will pass many reasonable tests of randomness. Such numbers are referred to as **pseudorandom numbers**.

You may be somewhat uneasy about the concept of using numbers generated by a deterministic algorithm as if they were random numbers. Despite what might be called philosophical objections to such a practice, it generally works. As one expert on probability theory puts it [HAMM91]:

> For practical purposes we are forced to accept the awkward concept of "relatively random" meaning that with regard to the proposed use we can see no reason why they will not perform as if they were random (as the theory usually requires). This is highly subjective and is not very palatable to purists, but it is what statisticians regularly appeal to when they take "a random sample"—they hope that any results they use will have approximately the same properties as a complete counting of the whole sample space that occurs in their theory.

Linear Congruential Generators

By far, the most widely used technique for pseudorandom number generation is an algorithm first proposed by Lehmer [LEHM51], which is known as the linear congruential method. The algorithm is parameterized with four numbers, as follows:

m	the modulus	$m > 0$
a	the multiplier	$0 < a < m$
c	the increment	$0 \le c < m$
X_0	the starting value, or seed	$0 \le X_0 < m$

The sequence of random numbers $\{X_n\}$ is obtained via the following iterative equation:

$$X_{n+1} = (aX_n + c) \bmod m$$

If m, a, c, and X_0 are integers, then this technique will produce a sequence of integers with each integer in the range $0 \le X_n < m$.

The selection of values for a, c, and m is critical in developing a good random number generator. For example, consider $a = c = 1$. The sequence produced is obviously not satisfactory. Now consider the values $a = 7, c = 0, m = 32$, and $X_0 = 1$. This generates the sequence $\{7, 17, 23, 1, 7, \text{etc.}\}$, which is also clearly unsatisfactory. Of the 32 possible values, only 4 are used; thus, the sequence is said to have a period of 4. If, instead, we change the value of a to 5, then the sequence is $\{5, 25, 29, 17, 21, 9, 13, 1, 5, \text{etc.}\}$, which increases the period to 8.

We would like m to be very large, so that there is the potential for producing a long series of distinct random numbers. A common criterion is that m be nearly equal to the maximum representable nonnegative integer for a given computer. Thus, a value of m near to or equal to 2^{31} is typically chosen.

[PARK88] proposes three tests to be used in evaluating a random number generator:

T_1: The function should be a full-period generating function. That is, the function should generate all the numbers between 0 and m before repeating.

T_2: The generated sequence should appear random. Because it is generated deterministically, the sequence is not random. There is a variety of statistical tests that can be used to assess the degree to which a sequence exhibits randomness.

T_3: The function should implement efficiently with 32-bit arithmetic.

With appropriate values of a, c, and m, these three tests can be passed. With respect to T_1, it can be shown that if m is prime and $c = 0$, then for certain values of a, the period of the generating function is $m - 1$, with only the value 0 missing. For 32-bit arithmetic, a convenient prime value of m is $2^{31} - 1$. Thus, the generating function becomes

$$X_{n+1} = (aX_n) \bmod (2^{31} - 1)$$

Of the more than 2 billion possible choices for a, only a handful of multipliers pass all three tests. One such value is $a = 7^5 = 16807$, which was originally designed for use in the IBM 360 family of computers [LEWI69]. This generator is widely used and has been subjected to a more thorough testing than any other PRNG. It is frequently recommended for statistical and simulation work (e.g., [JAIN91], [SAUE81]).

The strength of the linear congruential algorithm is that if the multiplier and modulus are properly chosen, the resulting sequence of numbers will be statistically indistinguishable from a sequence drawn at random (but without replacement) from the set $1, 2, \ldots, m - 1$. But there is nothing random at all about the algorithm, apart from the choice of the initial value X_0. Once that value is chosen, the remaining numbers in the sequence follow deterministically. This has implications for cryptanalysis.

If an opponent knows that the linear congruential algorithm is being used and if the parameters are known (e.g., $a = 7^5$, $c = 0$, $m = 2^{31} - 1$), then once a single number is discovered, all subsequent numbers are known. Even if the opponent knows only that a linear congruential algorithm is being used, knowledge of a small part of the sequence is sufficient to determine the parameters of the algorithm. Suppose that the opponent is able to determine values for X_0, X_1, X_2, and X_3. Then

$$\begin{aligned} X_1 &= (aX_0 + c) \bmod m \\ X_2 &= (aX_1 + c) \bmod m \\ X_3 &= (aX_2 + c) \bmod m \end{aligned}$$

These equations can be solved for a, c, and m.

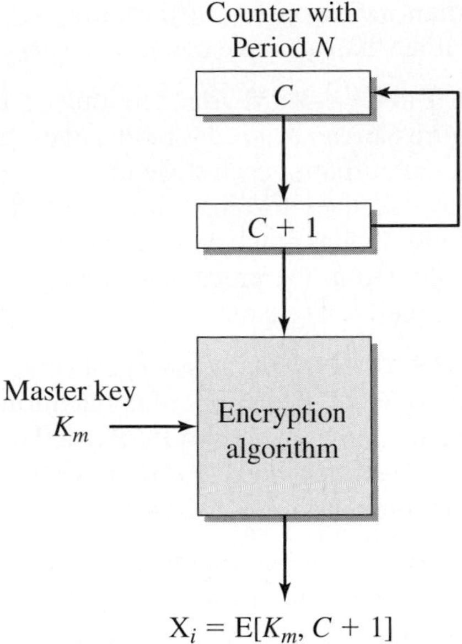

Figure 7.13 Pseudorandom Number Generation from a Counter

Thus, although it is nice to be able to use a good PRNG, it is desirable to make the actual sequence used nonreproducible, so that knowledge of part of the sequence on the part of an opponent is insufficient to determine future elements of the sequence. This goal can be achieved in a number of ways. For example, [BRIG79] suggests using an internal system clock to modify the random number stream. One way to use the clock would be to restart the sequence after every N numbers using the current clock value (mod m) as the new seed. Another way would be simply to add the current clock value to each random number (mod m).

Cryptographically Generated Random Numbers

For cryptographic applications, it makes some sense to take advantage of the encryption logic available to produce random numbers. A number of means have been used, and in this subsection we look at three representative examples.

Cyclic Encryption Figure 7.13 illustrates an approach suggested in [MEYE82]. In this case, the procedure is used to generate session keys from a master key. A counter with period N provides input to the encryption logic. For example, if 56-bit DES keys are to be produced, then a counter with period 2^{56} can be used. After each key is produced, the counter is incremented by one. Thus, the pseudorandom numbers produced by this scheme cycle through a full period: Each of the outputs $X_0, X_1, \ldots X_{N-1}$ is based on a different counter value and therefore $X_0 \neq X_1 \neq \ldots \neq X_{N-1}$. Because the master key is protected, it is not computationally feasible to deduce any of the session keys (random numbers) through knowledge of one or more earlier session keys.

To strengthen the algorithm further, the input could be the output of a full-period PRNG rather than a simple counter.

DES Output Feedback Mode The output feedback (OFB) mode of DES, illustrated in Figure 6.6, can be used for key generation as well as for stream encryption. Notice that the output of each stage of operation is a 64-bit value, of which the s leftmost bits are fed back for encryption. Successive 64-bit outputs constitute a sequence of pseudorandom numbers with good statistical properties. Again, as with the approach suggested in the preceding subsection, the use of a protected master key protects the generated session keys.

ANSI X9.17 PRNG One of the strongest (cryptographically speaking) PRNGs is specified in ANSI X9.17. A number of applications employ this technique, including financial security applications and PGP (the latter described in Chapter 15).

Figure 7.14 illustrates the algorithm, which makes use of triple DES for encryption. The ingredients are as follows:

- **Input:** Two pseudorandom inputs drive the generator. One is a 64-bit representation of the current date and time, which is updated on each number generation. The other is a 64-bit seed value; this is initialized to some arbitrary value and is updated during the generation process.
- **Keys:** The generator makes use of three triple DES encryption modules. All three make use of the same pair of 56-bit keys, which must be kept secret and are used only for pseudorandom number generation.
- **Output:** The output consists of a 64-bit pseudorandom number and a 64-bit seed value.

Define the following quantities:

DT_i	Date/time value at the beginning of ith generation stage
V_i	Seed value at the beginning of ith generation stage
R_i	Pseudorandom number produced by the ith generation stage
K_1, K_2	DES keys used for each stage

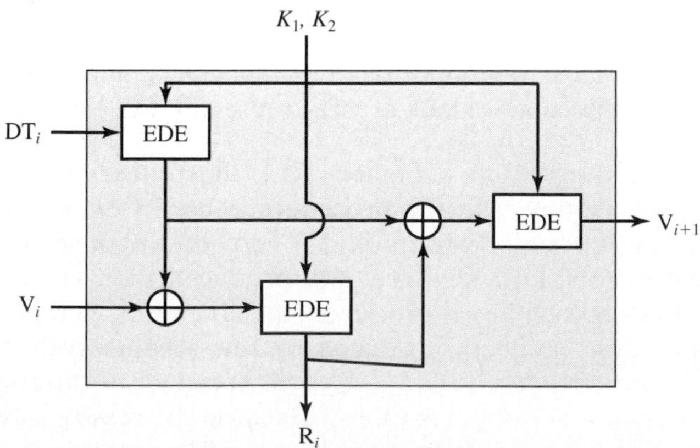

Figure 7.14 ANSI X9.17 Pseudorandom Number Generator

Then

$$R_i = \text{EDE}([K_1, K_2], [V_i \oplus \text{EDE}([K_1, K_2], \text{DT}_i)])$$
$$V_{i+1} = \text{EDE}([K_1, K_2], [R_i \oplus \text{EDE}([K_1, K_2], \text{DT}_i)])$$

where EDE($[K_1, K_2]$, X) refers to the sequence encrypt-decrypt-encrypt using two-key triple DES to encrypt X.

Several factors contribute to the cryptographic strength of this method. The technique involves a 112-bit key and three EDE encryptions for a total of nine DES encryptions. The scheme is driven by two pseudorandom inputs, the date and time value, and a seed produced by the generator that is distinct from the pseudorandom number produced by the generator. Thus, the amount of material that must be compromised by an opponent is overwhelming. Even if a pseudorandom number R_i were compromised, it would be impossible to deduce the V_{i+1} from the R_i because an additional EDE operation is used to produce the V_{i+1}.

Blum Blum Shub Generator

A popular approach to generating secure pseudorandom number is known as the Blum, Blum, Shub (BBS) generator, named for its developers [BLUM86]. It has perhaps the strongest public proof of its cryptographic strength. The procedure is as follows. First, choose two large prime numbers, p and q, that both have a remainder of 3 when divided by 4. That is,

$$p \equiv q \equiv 3 \pmod 4$$

This notation, explained more fully in Chapter 4, simply means that $(p \bmod 4) = (q \bmod 4) = 3$. For example, the prime numbers 7 and 11 satisfy $7 \equiv 11 \equiv 3 \pmod 4$. Let $n = p \times q$. Next, choose a random number s, such that s is relatively prime to n; this is equivalent to saying that neither p nor q is a factor of s. Then the BBS generator produces a sequence of bits B_i according to the following algorithm:

```
X0 = s^2 mod n
for i = 1 to ∞
    Xi = (Xi-1)^2 mod n
    Bi = Xi mod 2
```

Thus, the least significant bit is taken at each iteration. Table 7.2, shows an example of BBS operation. Here, $n = 192649 = 383 \times 503$ and the seed $s = 101355$.

The BBS is referred to as a **cryptographically secure pseudorandom bit generator** (CSPRBG). A CSPRBG is defined as one that passes the *next-bit test*, which, in turn, is defined as follows [MENE97]: A pseudorandom bit generator is said to pass the next-bit test if there is not a polynomial-time algorithm[7] that, on input of the first k bits of an output sequence, can predict the $(k + 1)^{\text{st}}$ bit with probability significantly greater than 1/2. In other words, given the first k bits of the sequence, there is not a practical algorithm that can even allow you to state that the next bit will be 1 (or 0) with probability greater than 1/2. For all practical purposes, the

[7]A polynomial-time algorithm of order k is one whose running time is bounded by a polynomial of order k.

Table 7.2 Example Operation of BBS Generator

i	X_i	B_i
0	20749	
1	143135	1
2	177671	1
3	97048	0
4	89992	0
5	174051	1
6	80649	1
7	45663	1
8	69442	0
9	186894	0
10	177046	0

i	X_i	B_i
11	137922	0
12	123175	1
13	8630	0
14	114386	0
15	14863	1
16	133015	1
17	106065	1
18	45870	0
19	137171	1
20	48060	0

sequence is unpredictable. The security of BBS is based on the difficulty of factoring n. That is, given n, we need to determine its two prime factors p and q.

True Random Number Generators

A true random number generator (TRNG) uses a nondeterministic source to produce randomness. Most operate by measuring unpredictable natural processes, such as pulse detectors of ionizing radiation events, gas discharge tubes, and leaky capacitors. Intel has developed a commercially available chip that samples thermal noise by amplifying the voltage measured across undriven resistors [JUN99]. A group at Bell Labs has developed a technique that uses the variations in the response time of raw read requests for one disk sector of a hard disk [JAKO98]. LavaRnd is an open source project for creating truly random numbers using inexpensive cameras, open source code, and inexpensive hardware. The system uses a saturated CCD in a light-tight can as a chaotic source to produce the seed. Software processes the result into truly random numbers in a variety of formats.

There are problems both with the randomness and the precision of such numbers [BRIG79], to say nothing of the clumsy requirement of attaching one of these devices to every system in an internetwork. Another alternative is to dip into a published collection of good-quality random numbers (e.g., [RAND55], [TIPP27]). However, these collections provide a very limited source of numbers compared to the potential requirements of a sizable network security application. Furthermore, although the numbers in these books do indeed exhibit statistical randomness, they are predictable, because an opponent who knows that the book is in use can obtain a copy.

Skew

A true random number generator may produce an output that is biased in some way, such as having more ones than zeros or vice versa. Various methods of modifying a bit stream to reduce or eliminate the bias have been developed. These are referred to as *deskewing algorithms*. One approach to deskew is to pass the bit stream through a hash function such as MD5 or SHA-1 (described in Part Two). The hash function produces an n-bit output from an input of arbitrary length. For deskewing, blocks of m input bits, with $m \geq n$, can be passed through the hash function.

7.5 RECOMMENDED READING AND WEB SITES

[FUMY93] is a good survey of key management principles.

Perhaps the best treatment of PRNGs is found in [KNUT98]. An alternative to the standard linear congruential algorithm, known as the linear recurrence algorithm, is explained in some detail in [BRIG79]. [ZENG91] assesses various PRNG algorithms for use in generating variable-length keys for Vernam types of ciphers.

An excellent survey of PRNGs, with an extensive bibliography, is [RITT91]. [MENE97] also provides a good discussions of secure PRNGs. Another good treatment, with an emphasis on practical implementation issues, is RFC 1750. This RFC also describes a number of deskewing techniques. [KELS98] is a good survey of secure PRNG techniques and cryptanalytic attacks on them.

BRIG79 Bright, H., and Enison, R. "Quasi-Random Number Sequences from Long-Period TLP Generator with Remarks on Application to Cryptography." *Computing Surveys*, December 1979.

FUMY93 Fumy, S., and Landrock, P. "Principles of Key Management." *IEEE Journal on Selected Areas in Communications*, June 1993.

KELS98 Kelsey, J.; Schneier, B.; and Hall, C. "Cryptanalytic Attacks on Pseudorandom Number Generators." *Proceedings, Fast Software Encryption*, 1998. **http://www.schneier. com/paper-prngs.html**

KNUT98 Knuth, D. *The Art of Computer Programming, Volume 2: Seminumerical Algorithms.* Reading, MA: Addison-Wesley, 1998.

MENE97 Menezes, A.; Oorshcot, P.; and Vanstone, S. *Handbook of Applied Cryptography.* Boca Raton, FL: CRC Press, 1997.

RITT91 Ritter, T. "The Efficient Generation of Cryptographic Confusion Sequences." *Cryptologia*, vol. 15 no. 2, 1991. **http://www.ciphersbyritter.com/ARTS/CRNG2ART.HTM**

ZENG91 Zeng. K.; Yang, C.; Wei, D.; and Rao, T. "Pseudorandom Bit Generators in Stream-Cipher Cryptography." *Computer*, February 1991.

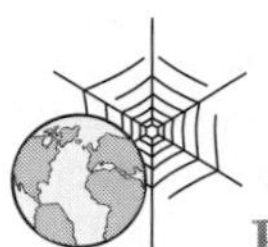

Recommended Web Sites:

- **NIST Random Number Generation Technical Working Group:** Contains documents and tests developed by NIST that related to PRNGs for cryptographic applications. Also has useful set of links.

- **LavaRnd:** LavaRnd is an open source project that uses a chaotic source to generate truly random numbers. The site also has background information on random numbers in general.
- **A Million Random Digits:** Compiled by the RAND Corporation.

7.6 KEY TERMS, REVIEW QUESTIONS, AND PROBLEMS

Key Terms

Blum, Blum, Shub generator	linear congruential	session key
covert channel	link encryption	skew
deskewing	master key	traffic padding
end-to-end encryption	nonce	true random number generator
key distribution	pseudorandom number generator (PRNG)	wiring closet
key distribution center (KDC)		

Review Questions

7.1 For a user workstation in a typical business environment, list potential locations for confidentiality attacks.

7.2 What is the difference between link and end-to-end encryption?

7.3 What types of information might be derived from a traffic analysis attack?

7.4 What is traffic padding and what is its purpose?

7.5 List ways in which secret keys can be distributed to two communicating parties.

7.6 What is the difference between a session key and a master key?

7.7 What is a nonce?

7.8 What is a key distribution center?

7.9 What is the difference between statistical randomness and unpredictability?

Problems

7.1 Electronic mail systems differ in the manner in which multiple recipients are handled. In some systems, the originating mail-handler makes all the necessary copies, and these are sent out independently. An alternative approach is to determine the route for each destination first. Then a single message is sent out on a common portion of the route, and copies are made only when the routes diverge; this process is referred to as *mail bagging*.
  a. Leaving aside considerations of security, discuss the relative advantages and disadvantages of the two methods.
  b. Discuss the security requirements and implications of the two methods.

7.2 Section 7.2 describes the use of message length as a means of constructing a covert channel. Describe three additional schemes for using traffic patterns to construct a covert channel.

7.3 One local area network vendor provides a key distribution facility, as illustrated in Figure 7.15.
  a. Describe the scheme.
  b. Compare this scheme to that of Figure 7.9. What are the pros and cons?

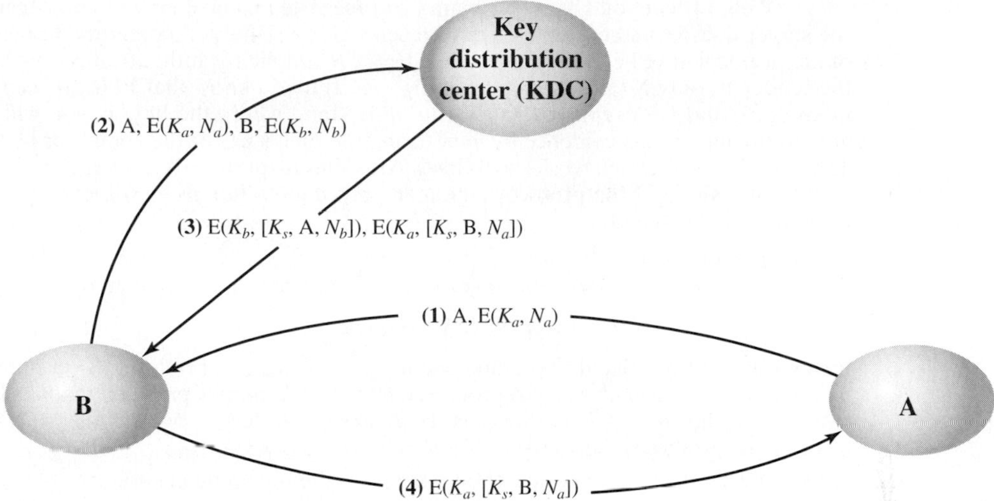

Figure 7.15 Figure for Problem 7.3

7.4 "We are under great pressure, Holmes." Detective Lestrade looked nervous. "We have learned that copies of sensitive government documents are stored in computers of one foreign embassy here in London. Normally these documents exist in electronic form only on a selected few government computers that satisfy the most stringent security requirements. However, sometimes they must be sent through the network connecting all government computers. But all messages in this network are encrypted using a top secret encryption algorithm certified by our best crypto experts. Even the NSA and the KGB are unable to break it. And now these documents have appeared in hands of diplomats of a small, otherwise insignificant, country. And we have no idea how it could happen."

"But you do have some suspicion who did it, do you?" asked Holmes.

"Yes, we did some routine investigation. There is a man who has legal access to one of the government computers and has frequent contacts with diplomats from the embassy. But the computer he has access to is not one of the trusted ones where these documents are normally stored. He is the suspect, but we have no idea how he could obtain copies of the documents. Even if he could obtain a copy of an encrypted document, he couldn't decrypt it."

"Hmm, please describe the communication protocol used on the network." Holmes opened his eyes, thus proving that he had followed Lestrade's talk with an attention that contrasted with his sleepy look.

"Well, the protocol is as follows. Each node N of the network has been assigned a unique secret key K_n. This key is used to secure communication between the node and a trusted server. That is, all the keys are stored also on the server. User A, wishing to send a secret message M to user B, initiates the following protocol:

1. A generates a random number R and sends to the server his name A, destination B, and $E(K_a, R)$.
2. Server responds by sending $E(K_b, R)$ to A.
3. A sends $E(R, M)$ together with $E(K_b, R)$ to B.
4. B knows K_b, thus decrypts $E(K_b, R)$ to get R and will subsequently use R to decrypt $E(R, M)$ to get M.

You see that a random key is generated every time a message has to be sent. I admit the man could intercept messages sent between the top secret trusted nodes, but I see no way he could decrypt them."

"Well, I think you have your man, Lestrade. The protocol isn't secure because the server doesn't authenticate users who send him a request. Apparently designers of the protocol have believed that sending $E(K_x, R)$ implicitly authenticates user X as the sender, as only X (and the server) knows K_x. But you know that $E(K_x, R)$ can be intercepted and later replayed. Once you understand where the hole is, you will be able to obtain enough evidence by monitoring the man's use of the computer he has access to. Most likely he works as follows. After intercepting $E(K_a, R)$ and $E(R, M)$ (see steps 1 and 3 of the protocol), the man, let's denote him as Z, will continue by pretending to be A and . . .

Finish the sentence for Holmes.

7.5 If we take the linear congruential algorithm with an additive component of 0:

$$X_{n+1} = (aX_n) \bmod m$$

then it can be shown that if m is prime, and if a given value of a produces the maximum period of $m - 1$, then a^k will also produce the maximum period, provided that k is less than m and that $m - 1$ is not divisible by k. Demonstrate this by using $X_0 = 1$ and $m = 31$ and producing the sequences for $a = 3, 3^2, 3^3$, and 3^4.

7.6 a. What is the maximum period obtainable from the following generator?

$$X_{n+1} = (aX_n) \bmod 2^4$$

b. What should be the value of a?

c. What restrictions are required on the seed?

7.7 You may wonder why the modulus $m = 2^{31} - 1$ was chosen for the linear congruential method instead of simply 2^{31}, because this latter number can be represented with no additional bits and the mod operation should be easier to perform. In general, the modulus $2^k - 1$ is preferable to 2^k. Why is this so?

7.8 With the linear congruential algorithm, a choice of parameters that provides a full period does not necessarily provide a good randomization. For example, consider the following two generators:

$$X_{n+1} = (6X_n) \bmod 13$$
$$X_{n+1} = (7X_n) \bmod 13$$

Write out the two sequences to show that both are full period. Which one appears more random to you?

7.9 In any use of pseudorandom numbers, whether for encryption, simulation, or statistical design, it is dangerous to trust blindly the random number generator that happens to be available in your computer's system library. [PARK88] found that many contemporary textbooks and programming packages make use of flawed algorithms for pseudorandom number generation. This exercise will enable you to test your system.

The test is based on a theorem attributed to Ernesto Cesaro (see [KNUT98] for a proof), which states the following: Given two randomly chosen integers, x and y, the probability that $\gcd(x, y) = 1$ is $6/\pi^2$. Use this theorem in a program to determine statistically the value of π. The main program should call three subprograms: the random number generator from the system library to generate the random integers; a subprogram to calculate the greatest common divisor of two integers using Euclid's Algorithm; and a subprogram that calculates square roots. If these latter two programs are not available, you will have to write them as well. The main program should loop through a large number of random numbers to give an estimate of the aforementioned probability. From this, it is a simple matter to solve for your estimate of π.

If the result is close to 3.14, congratulations! If not, then the result is probably low, usually a value of around 2.7. Why would such an inferior result be obtained?

7.10 Suppose you have a true random bit generator where each bit in the generated stream has the same probability of being a 0 or 1 as any other bit in the stream and that the bits are not correlated; that is the bits are generated from identical independent distribution. However, the bit stream is biased. The probability of a 1 is $0.5 + \partial$ and the probability of a 0 is $0.5 - \partial$, where $0 < \partial < 0.5$. A simple deskewing algorithm is as follows: Examine the bit stream as a sequence of non-overlapping pairs. Discard all 00 and 11 pairs. Replace each 01 pair with 0 and each 10 pair with 1.

a. What is the probability of occurrence of each pair in the original sequence?
b. What is the probability of occurrence of 0 and 1 in the modified sequence?
c. What is the expected number of input bits to produce x output bits?
d. Suppose that the algorithm uses overlapping successive bit pairs instead of nonoverlapping successive bit pairs. That is, the first output bit is based on input bits 1 and 2, the second output bit is based on input bits 2 and 3, and so on. What can you say about the output bit stream?

7.11 Another approach to deskewing is to consider the bit stream as a sequence of non-overlapping groups of n bits each and the output the parity of each group. That is, if a group contains an odd number of ones, the output is 1; otherwise the output is 0.

a. Express this operation in terms of a basic Boolean function.
b. Assume, as in the preceding problem, that the probability of a 1 is $0.5 + \partial$. If each group consists of 2 bits, what is the probability of an output of 1?
c. If each group consists of 4 bits, what is the probability of an output of 1?
d. Generalize the result to find the probability of an output of 1 for input groups of n bits.

7.12 Suppose that someone suggests the following way to confirm that the two of you are both in possession of the same secret key. You create a random bit string the length of the key, XOR it with the key, and send the result over the channel. Your partner XORs the incoming block with the key (which should be the same as your key) and sends it back. You check, and if what you receive is your original random string, you have verified that your partner has the same secret key, yet neither of you has ever transmitted the key. Is there a flaw in this scheme?

PART TWO

Public-Key Encryption and Hash Functions

For practical reasons, it is desirable to use different encryption and decryption keys in a crypto-system. Such asymmetric systems allow the encryption key to be made available to anyone while preserving confidence that only people who hold the decryption key can decipher the information.

—*Computers at Risk: Safe Computing in the Information Age*, National Research Council, 1991

After symmetric encryption, the other major form of encryption is public-key encryption, which has revolutionized communications security. A related cryptographic area is that of cryptographic hash functions. Hash functions are used in conjunction with symmetric ciphers for digital signatures. In addition, hash functions are used for message authentication. Symmetric ciphers are also used for key management. All of these areas are discussed in Part Two.

ROAD MAP FOR PART TWO

Chapter 8: Introduction to Number Theory

Most public-key schemes are based on number theory. While the reader can take the number theoretic results on faith, it is useful to have a basic grasp of the concepts of number theory. Chapter 8 provides an overview and numerous examples to clarify the concepts.

Chapter 9: Public-Key Cryptography and RSA

Chapter 9 introduces public-key cryptography and concentrates on its use to provide confidentiality. This chapter also examines the most widely used public-key cipher, the Rivest-Shamir-Adleman (RSA) algorithm.

Chapter 10: Key Management; Other Public-Key Cryptosystems

Chapter 10 revisits the issue of key management in light of the capabilities of symmetric ciphers. The chapter also covers the widely used Diffie-Hellman key exchange technique and looks at a more recent public-key approach based on elliptic curves.

Chapter 11: Message Authentication and Hash Functions

Of equal importance to confidentiality as a security measure is authentication. At a minimum, message authentication assures that a message comes from the alleged source. In addition, authentication can include protection against modification, delay, replay, and reordering. Chapter 11 begins with an analysis of the requirements for authentication and then provides a systematic presentation of approaches to authentication. A key element of authentication schemes is the use of an authenticator, usually either a message authentication code (MAC) or a hash function. Design considerations for both of these types of algorithms are examined, and several specific examples are analyzed.

Chapter 12: Hash and MAC Algorithms

Chapter 12 extends the discussion of the preceding chapter to discuss two of the most important cryptographic hash functions (SHA and Whirlpool) and two of the most important MACs (HMAC) and CMAC.

Chapter 13: Digital Signatures and Authentication Protocols

An important type of authentication is the digital signature. Chapter 13 examines the techniques used to construct digital signatures and looks at an important standard, the Digital Signature Standard (DSS).

The various authentication techniques based on digital signatures are building blocks in putting together authentication algorithms. The design of such algorithms involves the analysis of subtle attacks that can defeat many apparently secure protocols. This issue is also addressed in Chapter 14.

Introduction to Number Theory

The Devil said to Daniel Webster: "Set me a task I can't carry out, and I'll give you anything in the world you ask for."

Daniel Webster: "Fair enough. Prove that for n greater than 2, the equation $a^n + b^n = c^n$ has no non-trivial solution in the integers."

They agreed on a three-day period for the labor, and the Devil disappeared.

At the end of three days, the Devil presented himself, haggard, jumpy, biting his lip. Daniel Webster said to him, "Well, how did you do at my task? Did you prove the theorem?"

"Eh? No . . . no, I haven't proved it."

"Then I can have whatever I ask for? Money? The Presidency?"

"What? Oh, that of course. But listen! If we could just prove the following two lemmas—"

—*The Mathematical Magpie,* Clifton Fadiman

KEY POINTS

- A prime number is an integer that can only be divided without remainder by positive and negative values of itself and 1. Prime numbers play a critical role both in number theory and in cryptography.
- Two theorems that play important roles in public-key cryptography are Fermat's theorem and Euler's theorem.
- An important requirement in a number of cryptographic algorithms is the ability to choose a large prime number. An area of ongoing research is the development of efficient algorithms for determining if a randomly chosen large integer is a prime number.
- Discrete logarithms are fundamental to a number of public-key algorithms. Discrete logarithms are analogous to ordinary logarithms, but operate over modular arithmetic.

A number of concepts from number theory are essential in the design of public-key cryptographic algorithms. This chapter provides an overview of the concepts referred to in other chapters. The reader familiar with these topics can safely skip this chapter.

As with Chapter 4, this chapter includes a number of examples, each of which is highlighted in a shaded box.

8.1 PRIME NUMBERS[1]

A central concern of number theory is the study of prime numbers. Indeed, whole books have been written on the subject (e.g., [CRAN01], [RIBE96]). In this section we provide an overview relevant to the concerns of this book.

An integer $p > 1$ is a prime number if and only if its only divisors[2] are ± 1 and $\pm p$. Prime numbers play a critical role in number theory and in the techniques discussed in this chapter. Table 8.1 shows the primes less than 2000. Note the way the primes are distributed. In particular, note the number of primes in each range of 100 numbers.

Any integer $a > 1$ can be factored in a unique way as

$$a = p_1^{a_1} p_2^{a_2} \ldots p_t^{a_t} \quad \textbf{(8.1)}$$

where $p_1 < p_2 < \cdots < p_t$ are prime numbers and where each a_i is a positive integer. This is known as the fundamental theorem of arithmetic; a proof can be found in any text on number theory.

$$91 = 7 \times 13$$
$$3600 = 2^4 \times 3^2 \times 5^2$$
$$11011 = 7 \times 11^2 \times 13$$

It is useful for what follows to express this another way. If P is the set of all prime numbers, then any positive integer a can be written uniquely in the following form:

$$a = \prod_{p \in \mathrm{P}} p^{a_p} \quad \text{where each } a_p \geq 0$$

The right-hand side is the product over all possible prime numbers p; for any particular value of a, most of the exponents a_p will be 0.

The value of any given positive integer can be specified by simply listing all the nonzero exponents in the foregoing formulation.

The integer 12 is represented by $\{a_2 = 2, a_3 = 1\}$.
The integer 18 is represented by $\{a_2 = 1, a_3 = 2\}$.
The integer 91 is represented by $\{a_7 = 1, a_{13} = 1\}$.

Multiplication of two numbers is equivalent to adding the corresponding exponents. Given $a = \prod_{p \in \mathrm{P}} p^{a_p}$, $b = \prod_{p \in \mathrm{P}} p^{b_p}$. Define $k = ab$. We know that the integer

[1] In this section, unless otherwise noted, we deal only with the nonnegative integers. The use of negative integers would introduce no essential differences.

[2] Recall from Chapter 4 that integer a is said to be a divisor of integer b if there is no remainder on division. Equivalently, we say that a divides b.

Table 8.1 Primes under 2000

2	101	211	307	401	503	601	701	809	0	1009	1103	1201	1301	1409	1511	1601	1709	1801	1901
3	103	223	311	409	509	607	709	811	911	1013	1109	1213	1303	1423	1523	1607	1721	1811	1907
5	107	227	313	419	521	613	719	821	919	1019	1117	1217	1307	1427	1531	1609	1723	1823	1913
7	109	229	317	421	523	617	727	823	929	1021	1123	1223	1319	1429	1543	1613	1733	1831	1931
11	113	233	331	431	541	619	733	827	937	1031	1129	1229	1321	1433	1549	1619	1741	1847	1933
13	127	239	337	433	547	631	739	829	941	1033	1151	1231	1327	1439	1553	1621	1747	1861	1949
17	131	241	347	439	557	641	743	839	947	1039	1153	1237	1361	1447	1559	1627	1753	1867	1951
19	137	251	349	443	563	643	751	853	953	1049	1163	1249	1367	1451	1567	1637	1759	1871	1973
23	139	257	353	449	569	647	757	857	967	1051	1171	1259	1373	1453	1571	1657	1777	1873	1979
29	149	263	359	457	571	653	761	859	971	1061	1181	1277	1381	1459	1579	1663	1783	1877	1987
31	151	269	367	461	577	659	769	863	977	1063	1187	1279	1399	1471	1583	1667	1787	1879	1999
37	157	271	373	463	587	661	773	877	983	1069	1193	1283		1481	1597	1669	1789	1889	1997
41	163	277	379	467	593	673	787	881	991	1087		1289		1483		1693			1999
43	167	281	383	479	599	677	797	883	997	1091		1291		1487		1697			
47	173	283	389	487		683		887		1093		1297		1489		1699			
53	179	293	397	491		691				1097				1493					
59	181			499										1499					
61	191																		
67	193																		
71	197																		
73	199																		
79																			
83																			
89																			
97																			

k can be expressed as the product of powers of primes: $k = \prod_{p \in P} p^{k_p}$. It follows that $k_p = a_p + b_p$ for all $p \in P$.

$k = 12 \times 18 = (2^2 \times 3) \times (2 \times 3^2) = 216$
$k_2 = 2 + 1 = 3; k_3 = 1 + 2 = 3$
$216 = 2^3 \times 3^3 = 8 \times 27$

What does it mean, in terms of the prime factors of a and b, to say that a divides b? Any integer of the form p^n can be divided only by an integer that is of a lesser or equal power of the same prime number, p^j with $j \leq n$. Thus, we can say the following:

$$\text{Given } a = \prod_{p \in P} p^{a_p}, b = \prod_{p \in P} p^{b_p}. \text{ If } a|b, \text{ then } a_p \leq b_p \text{ for all } p.$$

$a = 12; b = 36; 12|36$
$12 = 2^2 \times 3; 36 = 2^2 \times 3^2$
$a_2 = 2 = b_2$
$a_3 = 1 \leq 2 = b_3$
Thus, the inequality $a_p \leq b_p$ is satisfied for all prime numbers.

It is easy to determine the greatest common divisor[3] of two positive integers if we express each integer as the product of primes.

$$300 = 2^2 \times 3^1 \times 5^2$$
$$18 = 2^1 \times 3^2$$
$$\gcd(18, 300) = 2^1 \times 3^1 \times 5^0 = 6$$

The following relationship always holds:

$$\text{If } \quad k = \gcd(a, b) \qquad \text{then} \quad k_p = \min(a_p, b_p) \quad \text{for all } p$$

Determining the prime factors of a large number is no easy task, so the preceding relationship does not directly lead to a practical method of calculating the greatest common divisor.

8.2 FERMAT'S AND EULER'S THEOREMS

Two theorems that play important roles in public-key cryptography are Fermat's theorem and Euler's theorem.

[3]Recall from Chapter 4 that the greatest common divisor of integers a and b, expressed $\gcd(a, b)$, is an integer c that divides both a and b without remainder and that any divisor of a and b is a divisor of c.

Fermat's Theorem[4]

Fermat's theorem states the following: If p is prime and a is a positive integer not divisible by p, then

$$a^{p-1} \equiv 1(\bmod p) \quad \textbf{(8.2)}$$

Proof: Consider the set of positive integers less than p: $\{1, 2, \ldots, p - 1\}$ and multiply each element by a, modulo p, to get the set $X = \{a \bmod p, 2a \bmod p, \ldots (p - 1)a \bmod p\}$. None of the elements of X is equal to zero because p does not divide a. Furthermore no two of the integers in X are equal. To see this, assume that $ja \equiv ka(\bmod p)$ where $1 \leq j < k \leq p - 1$. Because a is relatively prime[5] to p, we can eliminate a from both sides of the equation [see Equation (4.3)] resulting in: $j \equiv k(\bmod p)$. This last equality is impossible because j and k are both positive integers less than p. Therefore, we know that the $(p - 1)$ elements of X are all positive integers, with no two elements equal. We can conclude the X consists of the set of integers $\{1, 2, \ldots, p - 1\}$ in some order. Multiplying the numbers in both sets and taking the result mod p yields

$$a \times 2a \times \ldots \times (p - 1) \equiv [(1 \times 2 \times \ldots \times (p - 1)](\bmod p)$$
$$a^{p-1}(p - 1)! \equiv (p - 1)!(\bmod p)$$

We can cancel the $(p - 1)!$ term because it is relatively prime to p [see Equation (4.3)]. This yields Equation (8.2).

$a = 7, p = 19$
$7^2 = 49 \equiv 11(\bmod 19)$
$7^4 \equiv 121 \equiv 7(\bmod 19)$
$7^8 \equiv 49 \equiv 11(\bmod 19)$
$7^{16} \equiv 121 \equiv 7(\bmod 19)$
$a^{p-1} = 7^{18} = 7^{16} \times 7^2 \equiv 7 \times 11 \equiv 1(\bmod 19)$

An alternative form of Fermat's theorem is also useful: If p is prime and a is a positive integer, then

$$a^p = a(\bmod p) \quad \textbf{(8.3)}$$

Note that the first form of the theorem [Equation (8.2)] requires that a be relatively prime to p, but this form does not.

$p = 5, a = 3$	$a^p = 3^5 = 243 \equiv 3(\bmod 5) = a(\bmod p)$
$p = 5, a = 10$	$a^p = 10^5 = 100000 \equiv 10(\bmod 5) = 0(\bmod 5) = a(\bmod p)$

[4]This is sometimes referred to as Fermat's little theorem.

[5]Recall from Chapter 4 that two numbers are relatively prime if they have no prime factors in common; that is, their only common divisor is 1. This is equivalent to saying that two numbers are relatively prime if their greatest common divisor is 1.

Euler's Totient Function

Before presenting Euler's theorem, we need to introduce an important quantity in number theory, referred to as Euler's totient function and written $\phi(n)$, defined as the number of positive integers less than n and relatively prime to n. By convention, $\phi(1) = 1$.

> Determine $\phi(37)$ and $\phi(35)$.
> Because 37 is prime, all of the positive integers from 1 through 36 are relatively prime to 37. Thus $\phi(37) = 36$.
> To determine $\phi(35)$, we list all of the positive integers less than 35 that are relatively prime to it:
>
> $$1, 2, 3, 4, 6, 8, 9, 11, 12, 13, 16, 17, 18,$$
> $$19, 22, 23, 24, 26, 27, 29, 31, 32, 33, 34.$$
>
> There are 24 numbers on the list, so $\phi(35) = 24$.

Table 8.2 lists the first 30 values of $\phi(n)$. The value $\phi(1)$ is without meaning but is defined to have the value 1.

It should be clear that for a prime number p,

$$\phi(p) = p - 1$$

Now suppose that we have two prime numbers p and q, with $p \neq q$. Then we can show that for $n = pq$,

$$\phi(n) = \phi(pq) = \phi(p) \times \phi(q) = (p - 1) \times (q - 1)$$

To see that $\phi(n) = \phi(p) \times \phi(q)$, consider that the set of positive integers less that n is the set $\{1, \ldots, (pq - 1)\}$. The integers in this set that are not relatively

Table 8.2 Some Values of Euler's Totient Function $\phi(n)$

n	$\phi(n)$
1	1
2	1
3	2
4	2
5	4
6	2
7	6
8	4
9	6
10	4

n	$\phi(n)$
11	10
12	4
13	12
14	6
15	8
16	8
17	16
18	6
19	18
20	8

n	$\phi(n)$
21	12
22	10
23	22
24	8
25	20
26	12
27	18
28	12
29	28
30	8

prime to n are the set $\{p, 2p, \ldots, (q - 1)p\}$ and the set $\{q, 2q, \ldots, (p - 1)q\}$. Accordingly,

$$\begin{aligned}\phi(n) &= (pq - 1) - [(q - 1) + (p - 1)] \\ &= pq - (p + q) + 1 \\ &= (p - 1) \times (q - 1) \\ &= \phi(p) \times \phi(q)\end{aligned}$$

> $\phi(21) = \phi(3) \times \phi(7) = (3 - 1) \times (7 - 1) = 2 \times 6 = 12$
> where the 12 integers are $\{1, 2, 4, 5, 8, 10, 11, 13, 16, 17, 19, 20\}$

Euler's Theorem

Euler's theorem states that for every a and n that are relatively prime:

$$a^{\phi(n)} \equiv 1(\text{mod } n) \qquad \textbf{(8.4)}$$

$a = 3; n = 10; \phi(10) = 4$	$a^{\phi(n)} = 3^4 = 81 \equiv 1(\text{mod } 10) = 1(\text{mod } n)$
$a = 2; n = 11; \phi(11) = 10$	$a^{\phi(n)} = 2^{10} = 1024 \equiv 1(\text{mod } 11) = 1(\text{mod } n)$

Proof: Equation (8.4) is true if n is prime, because in that case $\phi(n) = (n - 1)$ and Fermat's theorem holds. However, it also holds for any integer n. Recall that $\phi(n)$ is the number of positive integers less than n that are relatively prime to n. Consider the set of such integers, labeled as follows:

$$R = \{x_1, x_2, \ldots, x_{\phi(n)}\}$$

That is, each element x_i of R is a unique positive integer less than n with $\gcd(x_i, n) = 1$. Now multiply each element by a, modulo n:

$$S = \{(ax_1 \text{ mod } n), (ax_2 \text{ mod } n), \ldots, (ax_{\phi(n)} \text{ mod } n)\}$$

The set S is a permutation of R, by the following line of reasoning:

1. Because a is relatively prime to n and x_i is relatively prime to n, ax_i must also be relatively prime to n. Thus, all the members of S are integers that are less than n and that are relatively prime to n.
2. There are no duplicates in S. Refer to Equation (4.3). If $ax_i \text{ mod } n = ax_j \text{ mod } n$, then $x_i = x_j$.

Therefore,

$$\prod_{i=1}^{\phi(n)} (ax_i \text{ mod } n) = \prod_{i=1}^{\phi(n)} x_i$$

$$\prod_{i=1}^{\phi(n)} ax_i \equiv \prod_{i=1}^{\phi(n)} x_i \quad (\text{mod } n)$$

$$a^{\phi(n)} \times \left[\prod_{i=1}^{\phi(n)} x_i\right] \equiv \prod_{i=1}^{\phi(n)} x_i \pmod n$$

$$a^{\phi(n)} \equiv 1 \pmod n$$

This is the same line of reasoning applied to the proof of Fermat's theorem. As is the case for Fermat's theorem, an alternative form of the theorem is also useful:

$$a^{\phi(n)+1} \equiv a(\text{mod } n) \qquad \textbf{(8.5)}$$

Again, similar to the case with Fermat's theorem, the first form of Euler's theorem [Equation (8.4)] requires that a be relatively prime to n, but this form does not.

8.3 TESTING FOR PRIMALITY

For many cryptographic algorithms, it is necessary to select one or more very large prime numbers at random. Thus we are faced with the task of determining whether a given large number is prime. There is no simple yet efficient means of accomplishing this task.

In this section, we present one attractive and popular algorithm. You may be surprised to learn that this algorithm yields a number that is not necessarily a prime. However, the algorithm can yield a number that is almost certainly a prime. This will be explained presently. We also make reference to a deterministic algorithm for finding primes. The section closes with a discussion concerning the distribution of primes.

Miller-Rabin Algorithm[6]

The algorithm due to Miller and Rabin [MILL75, RABI80] is typically used to test a large number for primality. Before explaining the algorithm, we need some background. First, any positive odd integer $n \geq 3$ can be expressed as follows:

$$n - 1 = 2^k q \qquad \text{with } k > 0, q \text{ odd}$$

To see this, note that $(n - 1)$ is an even integer. Then, divide $(n - 1)$ by 2 until the result is an odd number q, for a total of k divisions. If n is expressed as a binary number, then the result is achieved by shifting the number to the right until the rightmost digit is a 1, for a total of k shifts. We now develop two properties of prime numbers that we will need.

Two Properties of Prime Numbers The **first property** is stated as follows: If p is prime and a is a positive integer less than p, then $a^2 \bmod p = 1$ if and only if either $a \bmod p = 1$ or $a \bmod p = -1 \bmod p = p - 1$. By the rules of modular arithmetic $(a \bmod p)(a \bmod p) = a^2 \bmod p$. Thus if either $a \bmod p = 1$ or $a \bmod p = -1$, then $a^2 \bmod p = 1$. Conversely, if $a^2 \bmod p = 1$, then $(a \bmod p)^2 = 1$, which is true only for $a \bmod p = 1$ or $a \bmod p = -1$.

[6]Also referred to in the literature as the Rabin-Miller algorithm, or the Rabin-Miller test, or the Miller-Rabin test.

The **second property** is stated as follows: Let p be a prime number greater than 2. We can then write $p - 1 = 2^k q$, with $k > 0$, q odd. Let a be any integer in the range $1 < a < p - 1$. Then one of the two following conditions is true:

1. a^q is congruent to 1 modulo p. That is, $a^q \bmod p = 1$, or equivalently, $a^q \equiv 1 (\bmod p)$.
2. One of the numbers $a^q, a^{2q}, a^{4q}, \ldots, a^{2^{k-1}q}$ is congruent to -1 modulo p. That is, there is some number j in the range $(1 \le j \le k)$ such that $a^{2^{j-1}q} \bmod p = -1 \bmod p = p - 1$, or equivalently, $a^{2^{j-1}q} \equiv -1 (\bmod p)$.

Proof: Fermat's theorem [Equation (8.2)] states that $a^{n-1} \equiv 1 (\bmod n)$ if n is prime. We have $p - 1 = 2^k q$. Thus, we know that $a^{p-1} \bmod p = a^{2^k q} \bmod p = 1$. Thus, if we look at the sequence of numbers

$$a^q \bmod p, a^{2q} \bmod p, a^{4q} \bmod p, \ldots, a^{2^{k-1}q} \bmod p, a^{2^k q} \bmod p \quad \textbf{(8.6)}$$

we know that the last number in the list has value 1. Further, each number in the list is the square of the previous number. Therefore, one of the following possibilities must be true:

1. The first number on the list, and therefore all subsequent numbers on the list, equals 1.
2. Some number on the list does not equal 1, but its square mod p does equal 1. By virtue of the first property of prime numbers defined above, we know that the only number that satisfies this condition is $p - 1$. So, in this case, the list contains an element equal to $p - 1$.

This completes the proof.

Details of the Algorithm These considerations lead to the conclusion that if n is prime, then either the first element in the list of residues, or remainders, $(a^q, a^{2q}, \ldots, a^{2^{k-1}q}, a^{2^k q})$ modulo n equals 1, or some element in the list equals $(n - 1)$; otherwise n is composite (i.e., not a prime). On the other hand, if the condition is met, that does not necessarily mean that n is prime. For example, if $n = 2047 = 23 \times 89$, then $n - 1 = 2 \times 1023$. Computing, $2^{1023} \bmod 2047 = 1$, so that 2047 meets the condition but is not prime.

We can use the preceding property to devise a test for primality. The procedure TEST takes a candidate integer n as input and returns the result `composite` if n is definitely not a prime, and the result `inconclusive` if n may or may not be a prime.

```
TEST (n)
Find integers k, q, with k > 0, q odd, so that (n - 1
= 2^k q);
Select a random integer a, 1 < a < n - 1;
if a^q mod n = 1 then return("inconclusive");
for j = 0 to k - 1 do
   if a^(2^j q) mod n ≡ n - 1 then return("inconclusive");
return("composite");
```

Let us apply the test to the prime number $n = 29$. We have $(n - 1) = 28 = 2^2(7) = 2^k q$. First, let us try $a = 10$. We compute $10^7 \bmod 29 = 17$, which is neither 1 nor 28, so we continue the test. The next calculation finds that $(10^7)^2 \bmod 29 = 28$, and the test returns **inconclusive** (i.e., 29 may be prime). Let's try again with $a = 2$. We have the following calculations: $2^7 \bmod 29 = 12$; $2^{14} \bmod 29 = 28$; and the test again returns **inconclusive**. If we perform the test for all integers a in the range 1 through 28, we get the same inconclusive result, which is compatible with n being a prime number.

Now let us apply the test to the composite number $n = 13 \times 17 = 221$. Then $(n - 1) = 220 = 2^2(55) = 2^k q$. Let us try $a = 5$. Then we have $5^{55} \bmod 221 = 112$, which is neither 1 nor 220; $(5^{55})^2 \bmod 221 = 168$. Because we have used all values of j (i.e., $j = 0$ and $j = 1$) in line 4 of the TEST algorithm, the test returns **composite**, indicating that 221 is definitely a composite number. But suppose we had selected $a = 21$. Then we have $21^{55} \bmod 221 = 200$; $(21^{55})^2 \bmod 221 = 220$; and the test returns **inconclusive**, indicating that 221 may be prime. In fact, of the 218 integers from 2 through 219, four of these will return an inconclusive result, namely 21, 47, 174, and 200.

Repeated Use of the Miller-Rabin Algorithm How can we use the Miller-Rabin algorithm to determine with a high degree of confidence whether or not an integer is prime? It can be shown [KNUT98] that given an odd number n that is not prime and a randomly chosen integer, a with $1 < a < n - 1$, the probability that TEST will return **inconclusive** (i.e., fail to detect that n is not prime) is less than 1/4. Thus, if t different values of a are chosen, the probability that all of them will pass TEST (return inconclusive) for n is less than $(1/4)^t$. For example, for $t = 10$, the probability that a nonprime number will pass all ten tests is less than 10^{-6}. Thus, for a sufficiently large value of t, we can be confident that n is prime if Miller's test always returns **inconclusive**.

This gives us a basis for determining whether an odd integer n is prime with a reasonable degree of confidence. The procedure is as follows: Repeatedly invoke TEST (n) using randomly chosen values for a. If, at any point, TEST returns **composite**, then n is determined to be nonprime. If TEST continues to return **inconclusive** for t tests, for a sufficiently large value of t, assume that n is prime.

A Deterministic Primality Algorithm

Prior to 2002, there was no known method of efficiently proving the primality of very large numbers. All of the algorithms in use, including the most popular (Miller-Rabin), produced a probabilistic result. In 2002, Agrawal, Kayal, and Saxena [AGRA02] developed a relatively simple deterministic algorithm that efficiently determines whether a given large number is a prime. The algorithm, known as the AKS algorithm, does not appear to be as efficient as the Miller-Rabin algorithm. Thus far, it has not supplanted this older, probabilistic technique [BORN03].

Distribution of Primes

It is worth noting how many numbers are likely to be rejected before a prime number is found using the Miller-Rabin test, or any other test for primality. A result from number theory, known as the prime number theorem, states that the primes near n are spaced on the average one every $(\ln n)$ integers. Thus, on average, one would have to test on the order of $\ln(n)$ integers before a prime is found. Because all even integers can be immediately rejected, the correct figure is $0.5 \ln(n)$. For example, if a prime on the order of magnitude of 2^{200} were sought, then about $0.5 \ln(2^{200}) = 69$ trials would be needed to find a prime. However, this figure is just an average. In some places along the number line, primes are closely packed, and in other places there are large gaps.

> The two consecutive odd integers 1,000,000,000,061 and 1,000,000,000,063 are both prime. On the other hand, $1001! + 2, 1001! + 3, \ldots, 1001! + 1000, 1001! + 1001$ is a sequence of 1000 consecutive composite integers.

8.4 THE CHINESE REMAINDER THEOREM

One of the most useful results of number theory is the Chinese remainder theorem (CRT).[7] In essence, the CRT says it is possible to reconstruct integers in a certain range from their residues modulo a set of pairwise relatively prime moduli.

> The 10 integers in Z_{10}, that is the integers 0 through 9, can be reconstructed from their two residues modulo 2 and 5 (the relatively prime factors of 10). Say the known residues of a decimal digit x are $r_2 = 0$ and $r_5 = 3$; that is, $x \bmod 2 = 0$ and $x \bmod 5 = 3$. Therefore, x is an even integer in Z_{10} whose remainder, on division by 5, is 3. The unique solution is $x = 8$.

The CRT can be stated in several ways. We present here a formulation that is most useful from the point of view of this text. An alternative formulation is explored in Problem 8.17. Let

$$M = \prod_{i=1}^{k} m_i$$

where the m_i are pairwise relatively prime; that is, $\gcd(m_i, m_j) = 1$ for $1 \leq i, j \leq k$, and $i \neq j$. We can represent any integer A in Z_M by a k-tuple whose elements are in Z_{m_i} using the following correspondence:

$$A \leftrightarrow (a_1, a_2, \ldots, a_k) \qquad \textbf{(8.7)}$$

where $A \in Z_M$, $a_i \in Z_{m_i}$, and $a_i = A \bmod m_i$ for $1 \leq i \leq k$. The CRT makes two assertions.

---

[7]The CRT is so called because it is believed to have been discovered by the Chinese mathematician Sun-Tsu in around 100 A.D.

1. The mapping of Equation (8.7) is a one-to-one correspondence (called a **bijection**) between Z_M and the Cartesian product $Z_{m_1} \times Z_{m_2} \times \ldots \times Z_{m_k}$. That is, for every integer A such that $0 \leq A < M$ there is a unique k-tuple $(a_1, a_2, \ldots, a_k)$ with $0 \leq a_i < m_i$ that represents it, and for every such k-tuple $(a_1, a_2, \ldots, a_k)$ there is a unique integer A in Z_M.
2. Operations performed on the elements of Z_M can be equivalently performed on the corresponding k-tuples by performing the operation independently in each coordinate position in the appropriate system.

Let us demonstrate the **first assertion**. The transformation from A to $(a_1, a_2, \ldots, a_k)$ is obviously unique; that is, each a_i is uniquely calculated as $a_i = A \bmod m_i$. Computing A from $(a_1, a_2, \ldots, a_k)$ can be done as follows. Let $M_i = M/m_i$ for $1 \leq i \leq k$. Note that $M_i = m_1 \times m_2 \times \ldots \times m_{i-1} \times m_{i+1} \times \ldots \times m_k$, so that $M_i \equiv 0 (\text{mod } m_j)$ for all $j \neq i$. Then let

$$c_i = M_i \times (M_i^{-1} \bmod m_i) \quad \text{for } 1 \leq i \leq k \qquad \textbf{(8.8)}$$

By the definition of M_i, it is relatively prime to m_i and therefore has a unique multiplicative inverse mod m_i. So Equation (8.8) is well defined and produces a unique value c_i. We can now compute:

$$A \equiv \left(\sum_{i=1}^{k} a_i c_i \right) (\text{mod } M) \qquad \textbf{(8.9)}$$

To show that the value of A produced by Equation (8.9) is correct, we must show that $a_i = A \bmod m_i$, for $1 \leq i \leq k$. Note that $c_j \equiv M_j \equiv 0 (\text{mod } m_i)$ if $j \neq i$ and that $c_i \equiv 1 (\text{mod } m_i)$. It follows that $a_i = A \bmod m_i$.

The **second assertion** of the CRT, concerning arithmetic operations, follows from the rules for modular arithmetic. That is, the second assertion can be stated as follows: If

$$A \longleftrightarrow (a_1, a_2, \ldots, a_k)$$
$$B \longleftrightarrow (b_1, b_2, \ldots, b_k)$$

then

$$(A + B) \bmod M \longleftrightarrow ((a_1 + b_1) \bmod m_1, \ldots, (a_k + b_k) \bmod m_k)$$
$$(A - B) \bmod M \longleftrightarrow ((a_1 - b_1) \bmod m_1, \ldots, (a_k - b_k) \bmod m_k)$$
$$(A \times B) \bmod M \longleftrightarrow ((a_1 \times b_1) \bmod m_1, \ldots, (a_k \times b_k) \bmod m_k)$$

One of the useful features of the Chinese remainder theorem is that it provides a way to manipulate (potentially very large) numbers mod M in terms of tuples of smaller numbers. This can be useful when M is 150 digits or more. However, note that it is necessary to know beforehand the factorization of M.

To represent 973 mod 1813 as a pair of numbers mod 37 and 49, define[8]

$$\begin{aligned} m_1 &= 37 \\ m_2 &= 49 \\ M &= 1813 \\ A &= 973 \end{aligned}$$

We also have $M_1 = 49$ and $M_2 = 37$. Using the extended Euclidean algorithm, we compute $M_1^{-1} = 34 \bmod m_1$ and $M_2^{-1} = 4 \bmod m_2$. (Note that we only need to compute each M_i and each M_i^{-1} once.) Taking residues modulo 37 and 49, our representation of 973 is (11, 42), because 973 mod 37 = 11 and 973 mod 49 = 42.

Now suppose we want to add 678 to 973. What do we do to (11, 42)? First we compute $(678) \leftrightarrow (678 \bmod 37, 678 \bmod 49) = (12, 41)$. Then we add the tuples element-wise and reduce $(11 + 12 \bmod 37, 42 + 41 \bmod 49) = (23, 34)$. To verify that this has the correct effect, we compute

$$\begin{aligned} (23, 34) \longleftrightarrow\ & a_1 M_1 M_1^{-1} + a_2 M_2 M_2^{-1} \bmod M \\ &= [(23)(49)(34) + (34)(37)(4)] \bmod 1813 \\ &= 43350 \bmod 1813 \\ &= 1651 \end{aligned}$$

and check that it is equal to $(973 + 678) \bmod 1813 = 1651$. Remember that in the above derivation, M_1^{-1} is the multiplicative inverse of M_1 modulo m_1, and M_2^{-1} is the multiplicative inverse of M_2 modulo m_2.

Suppose we want to multiply 1651 (mod 1813) by 73. We multiply (23, 34) by 73 and reduce to get $(23 \times 73 \bmod 37, 34 \times 73 \bmod 49) = (14, 32)$. It is easily verified that

$$\begin{aligned} (14, 32) \longleftrightarrow\ & [(14)(49)(34) + (32)(37)(4)] \bmod 1813 \\ &= 865 \\ &= 1651 \times 73 \bmod 1813 \end{aligned}$$

8.5 DISCRETE LOGARITHMS

Discrete logarithms are fundamental to a number of public-key algorithms, including Diffie-Hellman key exchange and the digital signature algorithm (DSA). This section provides a brief overview of discrete logarithms. For the interested reader, more detailed developments of this topic can be found in [ORE67] and [LEVE90].

[8]This example was provided by Professor Ken Calvert of Georgia Tech.

The Powers of an Integer, Modulo *n*

Recall from Euler's theorem [Equation (8.4)] that, for every a and n that are relatively prime:

$$a^{\phi(n)} \equiv 1(\text{mod } n)$$

where $\phi(n)$, Euler's totient function, is the number of positive integers less than n and relatively prime to n. Now consider the more general expression:

$$a^m \equiv 1(\text{mod } n) \qquad \textbf{(8.10)}$$

If a and n are relatively prime, then there is at least one integer m that satisfies Equation (8.10), namely, $m = \phi(n)$. The least positive exponent m for which Equation (8.10) holds is referred to in several ways:

- the order of a (mod n)
- the exponent to which a belongs (mod n)
- the length of the period generated by a

To see this last point, consider the powers of 7, modulo 19:

$$\begin{aligned}
7^1 &\equiv && 7(\text{mod } 19)\\
7^2 &= 49 = 2 \times 19 + 11 \equiv && 11(\text{mod } 19)\\
7^3 &= 343 = 18 \times 19 + 1 \equiv && 1(\text{mod } 19)\\
7^4 &= 2401 = 126 \times 19 + 7 \equiv && 7(\text{mod } 19)\\
7^5 &= 16807 = 884 \times 19 + 11 \equiv && 11(\text{mod } 19)
\end{aligned}$$

There is no point in continuing because the sequence is repeating. This can be proven by noting that $7^3 \equiv 1(\text{mod } 19)$ and therefore $7^{3+j} \equiv 7^3 7^j \equiv 7^j(\text{mod } 19)$, and hence any two powers of 7 whose exponents differ by 3 (or a multiple of 3) are congruent to each other (mod 19). In other words, the sequence is periodic, and the length of the period is the smallest positive exponent m such that $7^m \equiv 1(\text{mod } 19)$.

Table 8.3 shows all the powers of a, modulo 19 for all positive $a < 19$. The length of the sequence for each base value is indicated by shading. Note the following:

1. All sequences end in 1. This is consistent with the reasoning of the preceding few paragraphs.
2. The length of a sequence divides $\phi(19) = 18$. That is, an integral number of sequences occur in each row of the table.
3. Some of the sequences are of length 18. In this case, it is said that the base integer a generates (via powers) the set of nonzero integers modulo 19. Each such integer is called a primitive root of the modulus 19.

Table 8.3 Powers of Integers, Modulo 19

a	a^2	a^3	a^4	a^5	a^6	a^7	a^8	a^9	a^{10}	a^{11}	a^{12}	a^{13}	a^{14}	a^{15}	a^{16}	a^{17}	a^{18}
1	1	1	1	1	1	1	1	1	1	1	1	1	1	1	1	1	1
2	4	8	16	13	7	14	9	18	17	15	11	3	6	12	5	10	1
3	9	8	5	15	7	2	6	18	16	10	11	14	4	12	17	13	1
4	16	7	9	17	11	6	5	1	4	16	7	9	17	11	6	5	1
5	6	11	17	9	7	16	4	1	5	6	11	17	9	7	16	4	1
6	17	7	4	5	11	9	16	1	6	17	7	4	5	11	9	16	1
7	11	1	7	11	1	7	11	1	7	11	1	7	11	1	7	11	1
8	7	18	11	12	1	8	7	18	11	12	1	8	7	18	11	12	1
9	5	7	6	16	11	4	17	1	9	5	7	6	16	11	4	17	1
10	5	12	6	3	11	15	17	18	9	14	7	13	16	8	4	2	1
11	7	1	11	7	1	11	7	1	11	7	1	11	7	1	11	7	1
12	11	18	7	8	1	12	11	18	7	8	1	12	11	18	7	8	1
13	17	12	4	14	11	10	16	18	6	2	7	15	5	8	9	3	1
14	6	8	17	10	7	3	4	18	5	13	11	2	9	12	16	15	1
15	16	12	9	2	11	13	5	18	4	3	7	10	17	8	6	14	1
16	9	11	5	4	7	17	6	1	16	9	11	5	4	7	17	6	1
17	4	11	16	6	7	5	9	1	17	4	11	16	6	7	5	9	1
18	1	18	1	18	1	18	1	18	1	18	1	18	1	18	1	18	1

More generally, we can say that the highest possible exponent to which a number can belong (mod n) is $\phi(n)$. If a number is of this order, it is referred to as a **primitive root** of n. The importance of this notion is that if a is a primitive root of n, then its powers

$$a, a^2, \ldots, a^{\phi(n)}$$

are distinct (mod n) and are all relatively prime to n. In particular, for a prime number p, if a is a primitive root of p, then

$$a, a^2, \ldots, a^{p-1}$$

are distinct (mod p). For the prime number 19, its primitive roots are 2, 3, 10, 13, 14, and 15.

Not all integers have primitive roots. In fact, the only integers with primitive roots are those of the form 2, 4, p^α, and $2p^\alpha$, where p is any odd prime and α is a positive integer. The proof is not simple but can be found in many number theory books, including [ORE76].

Logarithms for Modular Arithmetic

With ordinary positive real numbers, the logarithm function is the inverse of exponentiation. An analogous function exists for modular arithmetic.

Let us briefly review the properties of ordinary logarithms. The logarithm of a number is defined to be the power to which some positive base (except 1) must be raised in order to equal the number. That is, for base x and for a value y:

$$y = x^{\log_x(y)}$$

The properties of logarithms include the following:

$$\log_x(1) = 0$$

$$\log_x(x) = 1$$

$$\log_x(yz) = \log_x(y) + \log_x(z) \quad \textbf{(8.11)}$$

$$\log_x(y^r) = r \times \log_x(y) \quad \textbf{(8.12)}$$

Consider a primitive root a for some prime number p (the argument can be developed for nonprimes as well). Then we know that the powers of a from 1 through $(p - 1)$ produce each integer from 1 through $(p - 1)$ exactly once. We also know that any integer b satisfies

$$b \equiv r (\text{mod } p) \text{ for some } r, \text{ where } 0 \leq r \leq (p - 1)$$

by the definition of modular arithmetic. It follows that for any integer b and a primitive root a of prime number p, we can find a unique exponent i such that

$$b \equiv a^i (\text{mod } p) \text{ where } 0 \leq i \leq (p - 1)$$

This exponent i is referred to as the **discrete logarithm** of the number b for the base a (mod p). We denote this value as $\text{dlog}_{a,p}(b)$.[9]

Note the following:

$$\text{dlog}_{a,p}(1) = 0, \text{ because } a^0 \bmod p = 1 \bmod p = 1 \quad \textbf{(8.13)}$$
$$\text{dlog}_{a,p}(a) = 1, \text{ because } a^1 \bmod p = a \quad \textbf{(8.14)}$$

Here is an example using a nonprime modulus, $n = 9$. Here $\phi(n) = 6$ and $a = 2$ is a primitive root. We compute the various powers of a and find

$$\begin{array}{ll} 2^0 = 1 & 2^4 \equiv 7 (\text{mod } 9) \\ 2^1 = 2 & 2^5 \equiv 5 (\text{mod } 9) \\ 2^2 = 4 & 2^6 \equiv 1 (\text{mod } 9) \\ 2^3 = 8 & \end{array}$$

This gives us the following table of the numbers with given discrete logarithms (mod 9) for the root $a = 2$:

Logarithm	0	1	2	3	4	5
Number	1	2	4	8	7	5

To make it easy to obtain the discrete logarithms of a given number, we rearrange the table:

Number	1	2	4	5	7	8
Logarithm	0	1	2	5	4	3

Now consider

$$x = a^{\text{dlog}_{a,p}(x)} \bmod p \qquad y = a^{\text{dlog}_{a,p}(y)} \bmod p$$
$$xy = a^{\text{dlog}_{a,p}(xy)} \bmod p$$

Using the rules of modular multiplication,

$$xy \bmod p = [(x \bmod p)(y \bmod p)] \bmod p$$
$$a^{\text{dlog}_{a,p}(xy)} \bmod p = \left[\left(a^{\text{dlog}_{a,p}(x)} \bmod p\right)\left(a^{\text{dlog}_{a,p}(y)} \bmod p\right)\right] \bmod p$$
$$= \left(a^{\text{dlog}_{a,p}(x) + d\text{log}_{a,p}(y)}\right) \bmod p$$

But now consider Euler's theorem, which states that, for every a and n that are relatively prime:

$$a^{\phi(n)} \equiv 1 (\text{mod } n)$$

---

[9] Many texts refer to the discrete logarithm as the *index*. There is no generally agreed notation for this concept, much less an agreed name.

Table 8.4 Tables of Discrete Logarithms, Modulo 19

(a) Discrete logarithms to the base 2, modulo 19

a	1	2	3	4	5	6	7	8	9	10	11	12	13	14	15	16	17	18
$\log_{2,19}(a)$	18	1	13	2	16	14	6	3	8	17	12	15	5	7	11	4	10	9

(b) Discrete logarithms to the base 3, modulo 19

a	1	2	3	4	5	6	7	8	9	10	11	12	13	14	15	16	17	18
$\log_{3,19}(a)$	18	7	1	14	4	8	6	3	2	11	12	15	17	13	5	10	16	9

(c) Discrete logarithms to the base 10, modulo 19

a	1	2	3	4	5	6	7	8	9	10	11	12	13	14	15	16	17	18
$\log_{10,19}(a)$	18	17	5	16	2	4	12	15	10	1	6	3	13	11	7	14	8	9

(d) Discrete logarithms to the base 13, modulo 19

a	1	2	3	4	5	6	7	8	9	10	11	12	13	14	15	16	17	18
$\log_{13,19}(a)$	18	11	17	4	14	10	12	15	16	7	6	3	1	5	13	8	2	9

(e) Discrete logarithms to the base 14, modulo 19

a	1	2	3	4	5	6	7	8	9	10	11	12	13	14	15	16	17	18
$\log_{14,19}(a)$	18	13	7	8	10	2	6	3	14	5	12	15	11	1	17	16	4	9

(f) Discrete logarithms to the base 15, modulo 19

a	1	2	3	4	5	6	7	8	9	10	11	12	13	14	15	16	17	18
$\log_{15,19}(a)$	18	5	11	10	8	16	12	15	4	13	6	3	7	17	1	2	14	9

Any positive integer z can be expressed in the form $z = q + k\phi(n)$, with $0 \leq q < \phi(n)$. Therefore, by Euler's theorem,

$$a^z \equiv a^q (\text{mod } n) \qquad \text{if } z \equiv q \text{ mod } \phi(n)$$

Applying this to the foregoing equality, we have

$$\text{dlog}_{a,p}(xy) \equiv [\text{dlog}_{a,p}(x) + \text{dlog}_{a,p}(y)]\ (\text{mod } \phi(p))$$

and generalizing,

$$\text{dlog}_{a,p}(y^r) \equiv [r \times \text{dlog}_{a,p}(y)]\ (\text{mod } \phi(p))$$

This demonstrates the analogy between true logarithms and discrete logarithms.

Keep in mind that unique discrete logarithms mod m to some base a exist only if a is a primitive root of m.

Table 8.4, which is directly derived from Table 8.3, shows the sets of discrete logarithms that can be defined for modulus 19.

Calculation of Discrete Logarithms

Consider the equation

$$y = g^x \text{ mod } p$$

Given g, x, and p, it is a straightforward matter to calculate y. At the worst, we must perform x repeated multiplications, and algorithms exist for achieving greater efficiency (see Chapter 9).

However, given y, g, and p, it is, in general, very difficult to calculate x (take the discrete logarithm). The difficulty seems to be on the same order of magnitude as that of factoring primes required for RSA. At the time of this writing, the asymptotically fastest known algorithm for taking discrete logarithms modulo a prime number is on the order of [BETH91]:

$$e^{((\ln p)^{1/3}(\ln(\ln p))^{2/3})}$$

which is not feasible for large primes.

8.6 RECOMMENDED READING AND WEB SITES

There are many basic texts on the subject of number theory that provide far more detail than most readers of this book will desire. An elementary but nevertheless useful short introduction is [ORE67]. For the reader interested in a more in-depth treatment, two excellent textbooks on the subject are [KUMA98] and [ROSE05]. [LEVE90] is a readable and detailed account as well. All of these books include problems with solutions, enhancing their value for self-study.

For readers willing to commit the time, perhaps the best way to get a solid grasp of the fundamentals of number theory is to work their way through [BURN97], which consists solely of a series of exercises with solutions that lead the student step by step through the concepts of number theory; working through all of the exercises is equivalent to completing an undergraduate course in number theory.

BURN97 Burn, R. *A Pathway to Number Theory*. Cambridge, England: Cambridge University Press, 1997.

KUMA98 Kumanduri, R., and Romero, C. *Number Theory with Computer Applications*. Upper Saddle River, NJ: Prentice Hall, 1998.

LEVE90 Leveque, W. *Elementary Theory of Numbers*. New York: Dover, 1990.

ORE67 Ore, O. *Invitation to Number Theory*. Washington, DC: The Mathematical Association of America, 1967,

ROSE05 Rosen, K. *Elementary Number Theory and its Applications*. Reading, MA: Addison-Wesley, 2000.

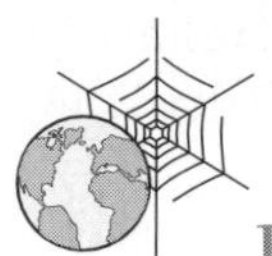

Recommended Web Site:

- **The Prime Pages:** Prime number research, records, and resources

8.7 KEY TERMS, REVIEW QUESTIONS, AND PROBLEMS

Key Terms

bijection	Euler's theorem	order
composite number	Euler's totient function	prime number
Chinese remainder theorem	Fermat's theorem	primitive root
discrete logarithm	index	

Review Questions

8.1 What is a prime number?

8.2 What is the meaning of the expression *a divides b*?

8.3 What is Euler's totient function?

8.4 The Miller-Rabin test can determine if a number is not prime but cannot determine if a number is prime. How can such an algorithm be used to test for primality?

8.5 What is a primitive root of a number?

8.6 What is the difference between an index and a discrete logarithm?

Problems

8.1 The purpose of this problem is to determine how many prime numbers there are. Suppose there are a total of n prime numbers, and we list these in order: $p_1 = 2 < p_2 = 3 < p_3 = 5 < \cdots < p_n$.

a. Define $X = 1 + p_1p_2 \ldots p_n$. That is, X is equal to one plus the product of all the primes. Can we find a prime number p_m that divides X?

b. What can you say about m?

c. Deduce that the total number of primes cannot be finite.

d. Show that $p_{n+1} \leq 1 + p_1p_2 \ldots p_n$.

8.2 The purpose of this problem is to demonstrate that the probability that two random numbers are relatively prime is about 0.6.

a. Let $P = \Pr[\gcd(a, b) = 1]$. Show that $\Pr[\gcd(a, b) = d] = P/d^2$. *Hint:* Consider the quantity $\gcd\left(\frac{a}{d}, \frac{b}{d}\right)$.

b. The sum of the result of part (a) over all possible values of d is 1. That is: $\sum_{d \geq 1} \Pr[\gcd(a, b) = d] = 1$. Use this equality to determine the value of P. *Hint:* Use the identity $\sum_{i=1}^{\infty} \frac{1}{i^2} = \frac{\pi^2}{6}$.

8.3 Why is $\gcd(n, n + 1) = 1$ for two consecutive integers n and $n + 1$?

8.4 Using Fermat's theorem, find 3^{201} mod 11.

8.5 Use Fermat's Theorem to find a number a between 0 and 72 with a congruent to 9794 modulo 73.

8.6 Use Fermat's Theorem to find a number x between 0 and 28 with x^{85} congruent to 6 modulo 29. (You should not need to use any brute force searching.)

8.7 Use Euler's Theorem to find a number a between 0 and 9 such that a is congruent to 7^{1000} modulo 10. (Note that this is the same as the last digit of the decimal expansion of 7^{1000}.)

8.8 Use Euler's Theorem to find a number x between 0 and 28 with x^{85} congruent to 6 modulo 35. (You should not need to use any brute force searching.)

8.9 Notice in Table 8.2 that $\phi(n)$ is even for $n > 2$. This is true for all $n > 2$. Give a concise argument why this is so.

8.10 Prove the following: If p is prime, then $\phi(p^i) = p^i - p^{i-1}$. *Hint:* What numbers have a factor in common with p^i?

8.11 It can be shown (see any book on number theory) that if $\gcd(m, n) = 1$ then $\phi(mn) = \phi(m)\phi(n)$. Using this property and the property developed in the preceding problem and the property that $\phi(p) = p - 1$ for p prime, it is straightforward to determine the value of $\phi(n)$ for any n. Determine the following:

a. $\phi(41)$
b. $\phi(27)$
c. $\phi(231)$
d. $\phi(440)$

8.12 It can also be shown that for arbitrary positive integer a, $\phi(a)$ is given by:

$$\phi(a) = \prod_{i=1}^{t} \left[p_i^{a_i - 1}(p_i - 1)\right]$$

where a is given by Equation (8.1), namely: $a = p_1^{a_1} p_2^{a_2} \ldots p_t^{a_t}$. Demonstrate this result.

8.13 Consider the function: $f(n)$ = number of elements in the set $\{a: 0 \leq a < n \text{ and } \gcd(a, n) = 1\}$. What is this function?

8.14 Although ancient Chinese mathematicians did good work coming up with their remainder theorem, they did not always get it right. They had a test for primality. The test said that n is prime if and only if n divides $(2^n - 2)$.

a. Give an example that satisfies the condition using an odd prime.

b. The condition is obviously true for $n = 2$. Prove that the condition is true if n is an odd prime (proving the **if** condition)

c. Give an example of an odd n that is not prime and that does not satisfy the condition. You can do this with nonprime numbers up to a very large value. This misled the Chinese mathematicians into thinking that if the condition is true then n is prime.

d. Unfortunately, the ancient Chinese never tried $n = 341$, which is nonprime $(341 = 11 \times 31)$ and yet 341 divides $2^{341} - 2$ with out remainder. Demonstrate that $2^{341} \equiv 2 \pmod{341}$ (disproving the **only if** condition). *Hint:* It is not necessary to calculate 2^{341}; play around with the congruences instead.

8.15 Show that if n is an odd composite integer, then the Miller-Rabin test will return `inconclusive` for $a = 1$ and $a = (n - 1)$.

8.16 If n is composite and passes the Miller-Rabin test for the base a, then n is called a *strong pseudoprime to the base a*. Show that 2047 is a strong pseudoprime to the base 2.

8.17 A common formulation of the Chinese remainder theorem (CRT) is as follows: Let $m_1, \ldots, m_k$ be integers that are pairwise relatively prime for $1 \leq i, j \leq k$, and $i \neq j$. Define M to be the product of all the m_i's. Let $a_1, \ldots, a_k$ be integers. Then the set of congruences:

$$
\begin{aligned}
x &\equiv a_1 (\text{mod } m_1) \\
x &\equiv a_2 (\text{mod } m_2) \\
&\vdots \\
x &\equiv a_k (\text{mod } m_k)
\end{aligned}
$$

has a unique solution modulo M. Show that the theorem stated in this form is true.

8.18 The example used by Sun-Tsu to illustrate the CRT was

$$x \equiv 2(\text{mod } 3); \quad x \equiv 3(\text{mod } 5); \quad x \equiv 2(\text{mod } 7)$$

Solve for x.

8.19 Six professors begin courses on Monday, Tuesday, Wednesday, Thursday, Friday, and Saturday, respectively, and announce their intentions of lecturing at intervals of 2, 3, 4, 1, 6, and 5 days, respectively. The regulations of the university forbid Sunday lectures (so that a Sunday lecture must be omitted). When first will all six professors find themselves compelled to omit a lecture? *Hint:* Use the CRT.

8.20 Find all primitive roots of 25.

8.21 Given 2 as a primitive root of 29, construct a table of discrete logarithms, and use it to solve the following congruences:

a. $17x^2 \equiv 10(\text{mod } 29)$
b. $x^2 - 4x - 16 \equiv 0(\text{mod } 29)$
c. $x^7 \equiv 17(\text{mod } 29)$

Programming Problems

8.22 Write a computer program that implements fast exponentiation (successive squaring) modulo n.

8.23 Write a computer program that implements the Miller-Rabin algorithm for a user-specified n. The program should allow the user two choices: (1) specify a possible witness a to test using the Witness procedure, or (2) specify a number s of random witnesses for the Miller-Rabin test to check.

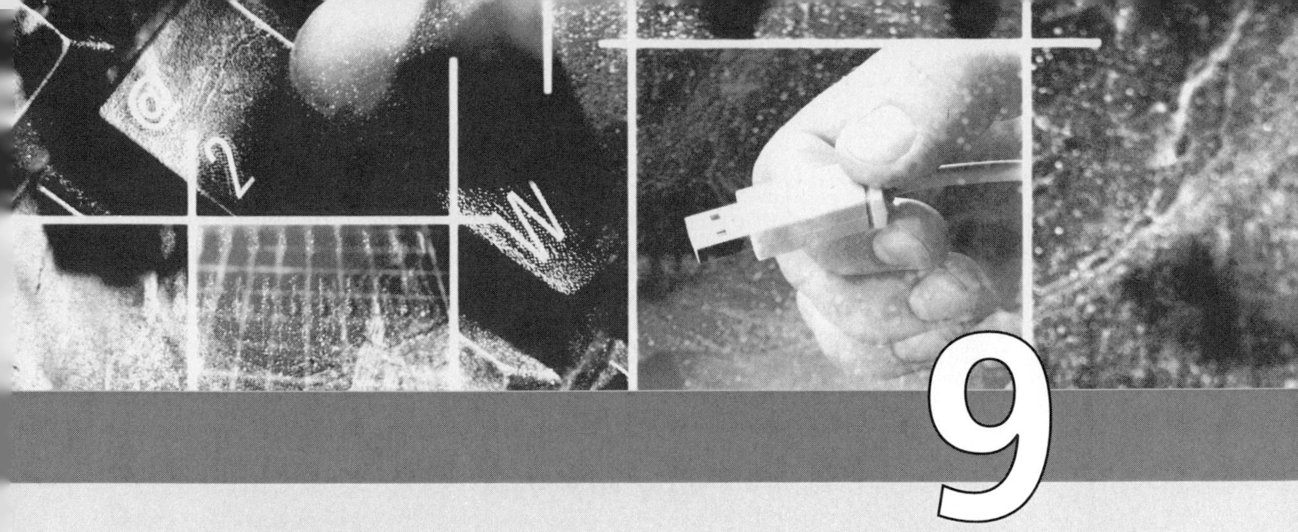

Chapter 9

Public-Key Cryptography and RSA

Every Egyptian received two names, which were known respectively as the true name and the good name, or the great name and the little name; and while the good or little name was made public, the true or great name appears to have been carefully concealed.

—*The Golden Bough,* Sir James George Frazer

KEY POINTS

- Asymmetric encryption is a form of cryptosystem in which encryption and decryption are performed using the different keys—one a public key and one a private key. It is also known as public-key encryption.
- Asymmetric encryption transforms plaintext into ciphertext using a one of two keys and an encryption algorithm. Using the paired key and a decryption algorithm, the plaintext is recovered from the ciphertext.
- Asymmetric encryption can be used for confidentiality, authentication, or both.
- The most widely used public-key cryptosystem is RSA. The difficulty of attacking RSA is based on the difficulty of finding the prime factors of a composite number.

The development of public-key cryptography is the greatest and perhaps the only true revolution in the entire history of cryptography. From its earliest beginnings to modern times, virtually all cryptographic systems have been based on the elementary tools of substitution and permutation. After millennia of working with algorithms that could essentially be calculated by hand, a major advance in symmetric cryptography occurred with the development of the rotor encryption/decryption machine. The electromechanical rotor enabled the development of fiendishly complex cipher systems. With the availability of computers, even more complex systems were devised, the most prominent of which was the Lucifer effort at IBM that culminated in the Data Encryption Standard (DES). But both rotor machines and DES, although representing significant advances, still relied on the bread-and-butter tools of substitution and permutation.

Public-key cryptography provides a radical departure from all that has gone before. For one thing, public-key algorithms are based on mathematical functions rather than on substitution and permutation. More important, public-key cryptography is asymmetric, involving the use of two separate keys, in contrast to symmetric encryption, which uses only one key. The use of two keys has profound consequences in the areas of confidentiality, key distribution, and authentication, as we shall see.

Before proceeding, we should mention several common misconceptions concerning public-key encryption. One such misconception is that public-key encryption is more secure from cryptanalysis than is symmetric encryption. In fact, the security of any encryption scheme depends on the length of the key and the computational work involved in breaking a cipher. There is nothing in principle about either symmetric or public-key encryption that makes one superior to another from the point of view of resisting cryptanalysis.

A second misconception is that public-key encryption is a general-purpose technique that has made symmetric encryption obsolete. On the contrary, because of the computational overhead of current public-key encryption schemes, there seems no foreseeable likelihood that symmetric encryption will be abandoned. As one of the inventors of public-key encryption has put it [DIFF88], "the restriction of public-key cryptography to key management and signature applications is almost universally accepted."

Finally, there is a feeling that key distribution is trivial when using public-key encryption, compared to the rather cumbersome handshaking involved with key distribution centers for symmetric encryption. In fact, some form of protocol is needed, generally involving a central agent, and the procedures involved are not simpler nor any more efficient than those required for symmetric encryption (e.g., see analysis in [NEED78]).

This chapter and the next provide an overview of public-key cryptography. First, we look at its conceptual framework. Interestingly, the concept for this technique was developed and published before it was shown to be practical to adopt it. Next, we examine the RSA algorithm, which is the most important encryption/decryption algorithm that has been shown to be feasible for public-key encryption. Further topics are explored in Chapter 10 and Appendix F.

Much of the theory of public-key cryptosystems is based on number theory. If one is prepared to accept the results given in this chapter, an understanding of number theory is not strictly necessary. However, to gain a full appreciation of public-key algorithms, some understanding of number theory is required. Chapter 8 provides the necessary background in number theory.

9.1 PRINCIPLES OF PUBLIC-KEY CRYPTOSYSTEMS

The concept of public-key cryptography evolved from an attempt to attack two of the most difficult problems associated with symmetric encryption. The first problem is that of key distribution, which was examined in some detail in Chapter 7.

As we have seen, key distribution under symmetric encryption requires either (1) that two communicants already share a key, which somehow has been distributed to them; or (2) the use of a key distribution center. Whitfield Diffie, one of the discoverers of public-key encryption (along with Martin Hellman, both at Stanford University at the time), reasoned that this second requirement negated the very essence of cryptography: the ability to maintain total secrecy over your own communication. As Diffie put it [DIFF88], "what good would it do after all to develop impenetrable cryptosystems, if their users were forced to share their keys with a KDC that could be compromised by either burglary or subpoena?"

The second problem that Diffie pondered, and one that was apparently unrelated to the first was that of "digital signatures." If the use of cryptography was to become widespread, not just in military situations but for commercial and private purposes, then electronic messages and documents would need the equivalent of signatures used in paper documents. That is, could a method be devised that would stipulate, to the satisfaction of all parties, that a digital message had been sent by a particular person? This is a somewhat broader requirement than that of authentication, and its characteristics and ramifications are explored in Chapter 13.

Diffie and Hellman achieved an astounding breakthrough in 1976 [DIFF76a, b] by coming up with a method that addressed both problems and that was radically different from all previous approaches to cryptography, going back over four millennia.[1]

In the next subsection, we look at the overall framework for public-key cryptography. Then we examine the requirements for the encryption/decryption algorithm that is at the heart of the scheme.

Public-Key Cryptosystems

Asymmetric algorithms rely on one key for encryption and a different but related key for decryption. These algorithms have the following important characteristic:

- It is computationally infeasible to determine the decryption key given only knowledge of the cryptographic algorithm and the encryption key.

In addition, some algorithms, such as RSA, also exhibit the following characteristic:

- Either of the two related keys can be used for encryption, with the other used for decryption.

A public-key encryption scheme has six ingredients (Figure 9.1a; compare with Figure 2.1):

- **Plaintext:** This is the readable message or data that is fed into the algorithm as input.
- **Encryption algorithm:** The encryption algorithm performs various transformations on the plaintext.
- **Public and private keys:** This is a pair of keys that have been selected so that if one is used for encryption, the other is used for decryption. The exact transformations performed by the algorithm depend on the public or private key that is provided as input.
- **Ciphertext:** This is the scrambled message produced as output. It depends on the plaintext and the key. For a given message, two different keys will produce two different ciphertexts.
- **Decryption algorithm:** This algorithm accepts the ciphertext and the matching key and produces the original plaintext.

[1]Diffie and Hellman first *publicly* introduced the concepts of public-key cryptography in 1976. However, this is not the true beginning. Admiral Bobby Inman, while director of the National Security Agency (NSA), claimed that public-key cryptography had been discovered at NSA in the mid-1960s [SIMM93]. The first *documented* introduction of these concepts came in 1970, from the Communications-Electronics Security Group, Britain's counterpart to NSA, in a classified report by James Ellis [ELLI70]. Ellis referred to the technique as nonsecret encryption and describes the discovery in [ELLI99].

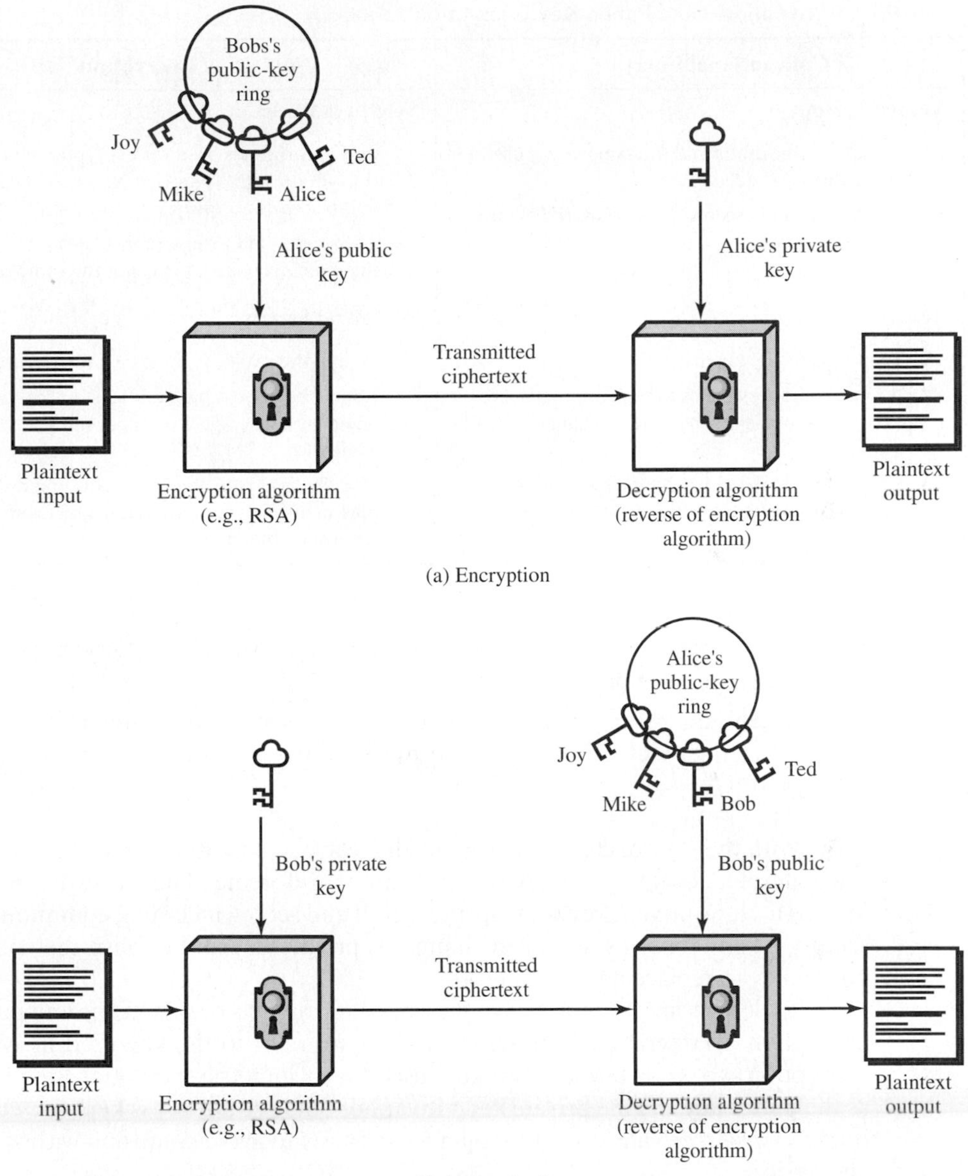

Figure 9.1 Public-Key Cryptography

The essential steps are the following:

1. Each user generates a pair of keys to be used for the encryption and decryption of messages.
2. Each user places one of the two keys in a public register or other accessible file. This is the public key. The companion key is kept private. As Figure 9.1a suggests, each user maintains a collection of public keys obtained from others.

Table 9.1 Conventional and Public-Key Encryption

Conventional Encryption	Public-Key Encryption
Needed to Work:	**Needed to Work:**
1. The same algorithm with the same key is used for encryption and decryption.	1. One algorithm is used for encryption and decryption with a pair of keys, one for encryption and one for decryption.
2. The sender and receiver must share the algorithm and the key.	2. The sender and receiver must each have one of the matched pair of keys (not the same one).
Needed for Security:	**Needed for Security:**
1. The key must be kept secret.	1. One of the two keys must be kept secret.
2. It must be impossible or at least impractical to decipher a message if no other information is available.	2. It must be impossible or at least impractical to decipher a message if no other information is available.
3. Knowledge of the algorithm plus samples of ciphertext must be insufficient to determine the key.	3. Knowledge of the algorithm plus one of the keys plus samples of ciphertext must be insufficient to determine the other key.

3. If Bob wishes to send a confidential message to Alice, Bob encrypts the message using Alice's public key.
4. When Alice receives the message, she decrypts it using her private key. No other recipient can decrypt the message because only Alice knows Alice's private key.

With this approach, all participants have access to public keys, and private keys are generated locally by each participant and therefore need never be distributed. As long as a user's private key remains protected and secret, incoming communication is secure. At any time, a system can change its private key and publish the companion public key to replace its old public key.

Table 9.1 summarizes some of the important aspects of symmetric and public-key encryption. To discriminate between the two, we refer to the key used in symmetric encryption as a **secret key**. The two keys used for asymmetric encryption are referred to as the **public key** and the **private key**.[2] Invariably, the private key is kept secret, but it is referred to as a private key rather than a secret key to avoid confusion with symmetric encryption.

Let us take a closer look at the essential elements of a public-key encryption scheme, using Figure 9.2 (compare with Figure 2.2). There is some source A that produces a message in plaintext, $X = [X_1, X_2, \ldots, X_M]$. The M elements of X are letters in

[2]The following notation is used consistently throughout. A secret key is represented by K_m, where m is some modifier; for example, K_a is a secret key owned by user A. A public key is represented by PU_a, for user A, and the corresponding private key is PR_a. Encryption of plaintext X can be performed with a secret key, a public key, or a private key, denoted by $E(K_a, X)$, $E(PU_a, X)$, and $E(PR_a, X)$, respectively. Similarly, decryption of ciphertext C can be performed with a secret key, a public key, or a private key, denoted by $D(K_a, X)$, $D(PU_a, X)$, and $D(PR_a, X)$, respectively.

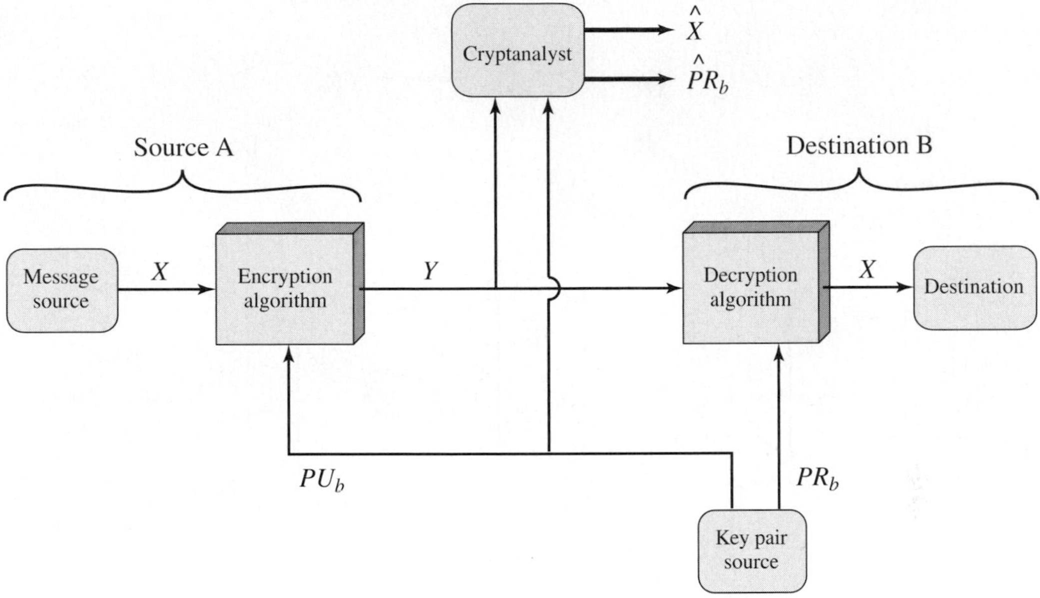

Figure 9.2 Public-Key Cryptosystem: Secrecy

some finite alphabet. The message is intended for destination B. B generates a related pair of keys: a public key, PU_b, and a private key, PR_b. PR_b is known only to B, whereas PU_b is publicly available and therefore accessible by A.

With the message X and the encryption key PU_b as input, A forms the ciphertext $Y = [Y_1, Y_2, \ldots, Y_N]$:

$$Y = \mathrm{E}(PU_b, X)$$

The intended receiver, in possession of the matching private key, is able to invert the transformation:

$$X = \mathrm{D}(PR_b, Y)$$

An adversary, observing Y and having access to PU_b, but not having access to PR_b or X, must attempt to recover X and/or PR_b. It is assumed that the adversary does have knowledge of the encryption (E) and decryption (D) algorithms. If the adversary is interested only in this particular message, then the focus of effort is to recover X, by generating a plaintext estimate $\hat{X}$. Often, however, the adversary is interested in being able to read future messages as well, in which case an attempt is made to recover PR_b by generating an estimate $\hat{PR}_b$.

We mentioned earlier that either of the two related keys can be used for encryption, with the other being used for decryption. This enables a rather different cryptographic scheme to be implemented. Whereas the scheme illustrated in Figure 9.2

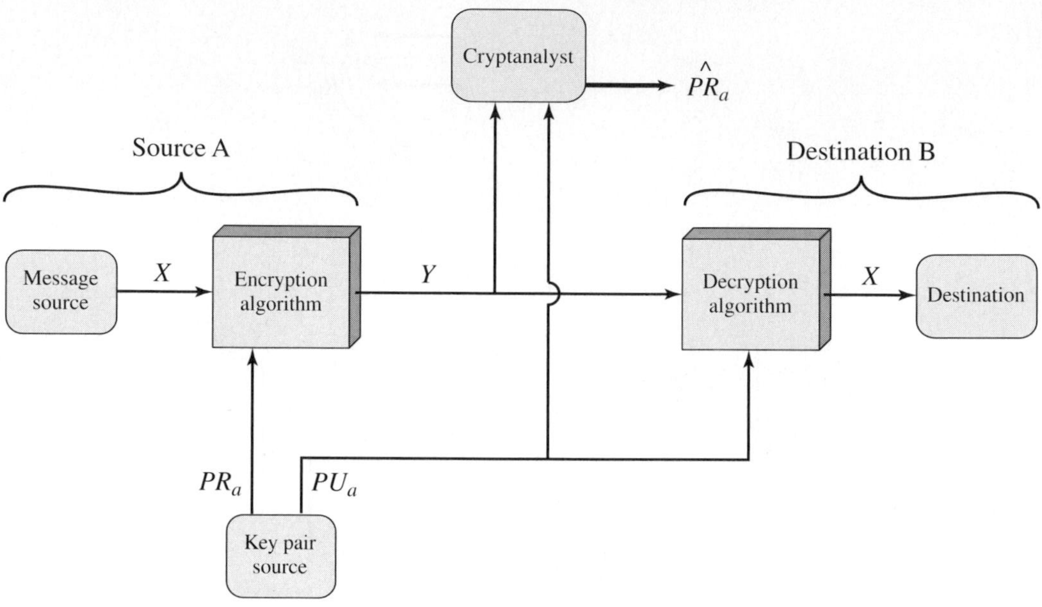

Figure 9.3 Public-Key Cryptosystem: Authentication

provides confidentiality, Figures 9.1b and 9.3 show the use of public-key encryption to provide authentication:

$$Y = E(PR_a, X)$$
$$X = D(PU_a, Y)$$

In this case, A prepares a message to B and encrypts it using A's private key before transmitting it. B can decrypt the message using A's public key. Because the message was encrypted using A's private key, only A could have prepared the message. Therefore, the entire encrypted message serves as a *digital signature*. In addition, it is impossible to alter the message without access to A's private key, so the message is authenticated both in terms of source and in terms of data integrity.

In the preceding scheme, the entire message is encrypted, which, although validating both author and contents, requires a great deal of storage. Each document must be kept in plaintext to be used for practical purposes. A copy also must be stored in ciphertext so that the origin and contents can be verified in case of a dispute. A more efficient way of achieving the same results is to encrypt a small block of bits that is a function of the document. Such a block, called an authenticator, must have the property that it is infeasible to change the document without changing the authenticator. If the authenticator is encrypted with the sender's private key, it serves as a signature that verifies origin, content, and sequencing. Chapter 13 examines this technique in detail.

It is important to emphasize that the encryption process depicted in Figures 9.1b and 9.3 does not provide confidentiality. That is, the message being sent is safe from alteration but not from eavesdropping. This is obvious in the case of a signature based on a portion of the message, because the rest of the message is transmitted in the clear. Even in the case of complete encryption, as shown in Figure 9.3, there is no protection

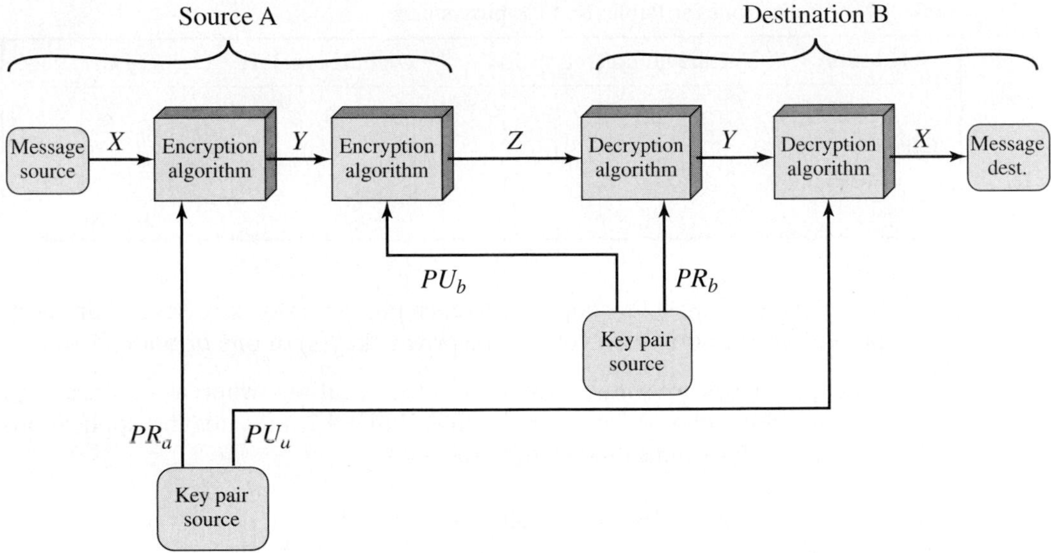

Figure 9.4 Public-Key Cryptosystem: Authentication and Secrecy

of confidentiality because any observer can decrypt the message by using the sender's public key.

It is, however, possible to provide both the authentication function and confidentiality by a double use of the public-key scheme (Figure 9.4):

$$Z = \mathrm{E}(PU_b, \mathrm{E}(PR_a, X))$$
$$X = \mathrm{D}(PU_a, \mathrm{D}(PR_b, Z))$$

In this case, we begin as before by encrypting a message, using the sender's private key. This provides the digital signature. Next, we encrypt again, using the receiver's public key. The final ciphertext can be decrypted only by the intended receiver, who alone has the matching private key. Thus, confidentiality is provided. The disadvantage of this approach is that the public-key algorithm, which is complex, must be exercised four times rather than two in each communication.

Applications for Public-Key Cryptosystems

Before proceeding, we need to clarify one aspect of public-key cryptosystems that is otherwise likely to lead to confusion. Public-key systems are characterized by the use of a cryptographic algorithm with two keys, one held private and one available publicly. Depending on the application, the sender uses either the sender's private key or the receiver's public key, or both, to perform some type of cryptographic function. In broad terms, we can classify the use of public-key cryptosystems into three categories:

- **Encryption/decryption:** The sender encrypts a message with the recipient's public key.
- **Digital signature:** The sender "signs" a message with its private key. Signing is achieved by a cryptographic algorithm applied to the message or to a small block of data that is a function of the message.

Table 9.2 Applications for Public-Key Cryptosystems

Algorithm	Encryption/Decryption	Digital Signature	Key Exchange
RSA	Yes	Yes	Yes
Elliptic Curve	Yes	Yes	Yes
Diffie-Hellman	No	No	Yes
DSS	No	Yes	No

- **Key exchange:** Two sides cooperate to exchange a session key. Several different approaches are possible, involving the private key(s) of one or both parties.

Some algorithms are suitable for all three applications, whereas others can be used only for one or two of these applications. Table 9.2 indicates the applications supported by the algorithms discussed in this book.

Requirements for Public-Key Cryptography

The cryptosystem illustrated in Figures 9.2 through 9.4 depends on a cryptographic algorithm based on two related keys. Diffie and Hellman postulated this system without demonstrating that such algorithms exist. However, they did lay out the conditions that such algorithms must fulfill [DIFF76b]:

1. It is computationally easy for a party B to generate a pair (public key PU_b, private key PR_b).
2. It is computationally easy for a sender A, knowing the public key and the message to be encrypted, M, to generate the corresponding ciphertext:

$$C = \mathrm{E}(PU_b, M)$$

3. It is computationally easy for the receiver B to decrypt the resulting ciphertext using the private key to recover the original message:

$$M = \mathrm{D}(PR_b, C) = \mathrm{D}[PR_b, \mathrm{E}(PU_b, M)]$$

4. It is computationally infeasible for an adversary, knowing the public key, PU_b, to determine the private key, PR_b.
5. It is computationally infeasible for an adversary, knowing the public key, PU_b, and a ciphertext, C, to recover the original message, M.

We can add a sixth requirement that, although useful, is not necessary for all public-key applications:

6. The two keys can be applied in either order:

$$M = \mathrm{D}[PU_b, \mathrm{E}(PR_b, M)] = \mathrm{D}[PR_b, \mathrm{E}(PU_b, M)]$$

These are formidable requirements, as evidenced by the fact that only a few algorithms (RSA, elliptic curve cryptography, Diffie-Hellman, DSS) have received widespread acceptance in the several decades since the concept of public-key cryptography was proposed.

Before elaborating on why the requirements are so formidable, let us first recast them. The requirements boil down to the need for a trap-door one-way function. A *one-way function*[3] is one that maps a domain into a range such that every function value has a unique inverse, with the condition that the calculation of the function is easy whereas the calculation of the inverse is infeasible:

$$Y = \mathrm{f}(X) \qquad \text{easy}$$
$$X = \mathrm{f}^{-1}(Y) \qquad \text{infeasible}$$

Generally, *easy* is defined to mean a problem that can be solved in polynomial time as a function of input length. Thus, if the length of the input is n bits, then the time to compute the function is proportional to n^a, where a is a fixed constant. Such algorithms are said to belong to the class **P**. The term *infeasible* is a much fuzzier concept. In general, we can say a problem is infeasible if the effort to solve it grows faster than polynomial time as a function of input size. For example, if the length of the input is n bits and the time to compute the function is proportional to 2^n, the problem is considered infeasible. Unfortunately, it is difficult to determine if a particular algorithm exhibits this complexity. Furthermore, traditional notions of computational complexity focus on the worst-case or average-case complexity of an algorithm. These measures are inadequate for cryptography, which requires that it be infeasible to invert a function for virtually all inputs, not for the worst case or even average case. A brief introduction to some of these concepts is provided in Appendix 9B.

We now turn to the definition of a *trap-door one-way function*, which is easy to calculate in one direction and infeasible to calculate in the other direction unless certain additional information is known. With the additional information the inverse can be calculated in polynomial time. We can summarize as follows: A trap-door one-way function is a family of invertible functions f_k, such that

$$Y = \mathrm{f}_k(X) \qquad \text{easy, if } k \text{ and } X \text{ are known}$$
$$X = \mathrm{f}_k^{-1}(Y) \qquad \text{easy, if } k \text{ and } Y \text{ are known}$$
$$X = \mathrm{f}_k^{-1}(Y) \qquad \text{infeasible, if } Y \text{ is known but } k \text{ is not known}$$

Thus, the development of a practical public-key scheme depends on discovery of a suitable trap-door one-way function.

Public-Key Cryptanalysis

As with symmetric encryption, a public-key encryption scheme is vulnerable to a brute-force attack. The countermeasure is the same: Use large keys. However, there is a tradeoff to be considered. Public-key systems depend on the use of some sort of invertible mathematical function. The complexity of calculating these functions may not scale linearly with the number of bits in the key but grow more rapidly than that. Thus, the key size must be large enough to make brute-force attack impractical but small enough for practical encryption and decryption. In practice, the key sizes that have been proposed do make brute-force attack impractical but result in encryption/decryption speeds that are too slow for general-purpose use. Instead, as was

[3]Not to be confused with a one-way hash function, which takes an arbitrarily large data field as its argument and maps it to a fixed output. Such functions are used for authentication (see Chapter 11).

mentioned earlier, public-key encryption is currently confined to key management and signature applications.

Another form of attack is to find some way to compute the private key given the public key. To date, it has not been mathematically proven that this form of attack is infeasible for a particular public-key algorithm. Thus, any given algorithm, including the widely used RSA algorithm, is suspect. The history of cryptanalysis shows that a problem that seems insoluble from one perspective can be found to have a solution if looked at in an entirely different way.

Finally, there is a form of attack that is peculiar to public-key systems. This is, in essence, a probable-message attack. Suppose, for example, that a message were to be sent that consisted solely of a 56-bit DES key. An adversary could encrypt all possible 56-bit DES keys using the public key and could discover the encrypted key by matching the transmitted ciphertext. Thus, no matter how large the key size of the public-key scheme, the attack is reduced to a brute-force attack on a 56-bit key. This attack can be thwarted by appending some random bits to such simple messages.

9.2 THE RSA ALGORITHM

The pioneering paper by Diffie and Hellman [DIFF76b] introduced a new approach to cryptography and, in effect, challenged cryptologists to come up with a cryptographic algorithm that met the requirements for public-key systems. One of the first of the responses to the challenge was developed in 1977 by Ron Rivest, Adi Shamir, and Len Adleman at MIT and first published in 1978 [RIVE78].[4] The Rivest-Shamir-Adleman (RSA) scheme has since that time reigned supreme as the most widely accepted and implemented general-purpose approach to public-key encryption.

The RSA scheme is a block cipher in which the plaintext and ciphertext are integers between 0 and $n - 1$ for some n. A typical size for n is 1024 bits, or 309 decimal digits. That is, n is less than 2^{1024}. We examine RSA in this section in some detail, beginning with an explanation of the algorithm. Then we examine some of the computational and cryptanalytical implications of RSA.

Description of the Algorithm

The scheme developed by Rivest, Shamir, and Adleman makes use of an expression with exponentials. Plaintext is encrypted in blocks, with each block having a binary value less than some number n. That is, the block size must be less than or equal to $\log_2(n)$; in practice, the block size is i bits, where $2^i < n \leq 2^{i+1}$. Encryption and decryption are of the following form, for some plaintext block M and ciphertext block C:

$$C = M^e \bmod n$$
$$M = C^d \bmod n = (M^e)^d \bmod n = M^{ed} \bmod n$$

Both sender and receiver must know the value of n. The sender knows the value of e, and only the receiver knows the value of d. Thus, this is a public-key encryption

[4]Apparently, the first workable public-key system for encryption/decryption was put forward by Clifford Cocks of Britain's CESG in 1973 [COCK73]; Cocks's method is virtually identical to RSA.

algorithm with a public key of $PU = \{e, n\}$ and a private key of $PR = \{d, n\}$. For this algorithm to be satisfactory for public-key encryption, the following requirements must be met:

1. It is possible to find values of e, d, n such that $M^{ed} \bmod n = M$ for all $M < n$.
2. It is relatively easy to calculate $M^e \bmod n$ and $C^d \bmod n$ for all values of $M < n$.
3. It is infeasible to determine d given e and n.

For now, we focus on the first requirement and consider the other questions later. We need to find a relationship of the form

$$M^{ed} \bmod n = M$$

The preceding relationship holds if e and d are multiplicative inverses modulo $\phi(n)$, where $\phi(n)$ is the Euler totient function. It is shown in Chapter 8 that for p, q prime, $\phi(pq) = (p - 1)(q - 1)$. The relationship between e and d can be expressed as

$$ed \bmod \phi(n) = 1 \tag{9.1}$$

This is equivalent to saying

$$ed \equiv 1 \bmod \phi(n)$$
$$d \equiv e^{-1} \bmod \phi(n)$$

That is, e and d are multiplicative inverses mod $\phi(n)$. Note that, according to the rules of modular arithmetic, this is true only if d (and therefore e) is relatively prime to $\phi(n)$. Equivalently, $\gcd(\phi(n), d) = 1$. See Appendix 9A for a proof that Equation (9.1) satisfies the requirement for RSA.

We are now ready to state the RSA scheme. The ingredients are the following:

p, q, two prime numbers	(private, chosen)
$n = pq$	(public, calculated)
e, with $\gcd(\phi(n), e) = 1; 1 < e < \phi(n)$	(public, chosen)
$d \equiv e^{-1}(\bmod\ \phi(n))$	(private, calculated)

The private key consists of $\{d, n\}$ and the public key consists of $\{e, n\}$. Suppose that user A has published its public key and that user B wishes to send the message M to A. Then B calculates $C = M^e \bmod n$ and transmits C. On receipt of this ciphertext, user A decrypts by calculating $M = C^d \bmod n$.

Figure 9.5 summarizes the RSA algorithm. An example, from [SING99], is shown in Figure 9.6. For this example, the keys were generated as follows:

1. Select two prime numbers, $p = 17$ and $q = 11$.
2. Calculate $n = pq = 17 \times 11 = 187$.

Key Generation	
Select p, q	p and q both prime, $p \neq q$
Calculate $n = p \times q$	
Calculate $\phi(n) = (p-1)(q-1)$	
Select integer e	$\gcd(\phi(n), e) = 1;\ 1 < e < \phi(n)$
Calculate d	$d \equiv e^{-1} \pmod{\phi(n)}$
Public key	$PU = \{e, n\}$
Private key	$PR = \{d, n\}$

Encryption	
Plaintext:	$M < n$
Ciphertext:	$C = M^e \bmod n$

Decryption	
Ciphertext:	C
Plaintext:	$M = C^d \bmod n$

Figure 9.5 The RSA Algorithm

3. Calculate $\phi(n) = (p - 1)(q - 1) = 16 \times 10 = 160$.
4. Select e such that e is relatively prime to $\phi(n) = 160$ and less than $\phi(n)$; we choose $e = 7$.
5. Determine d such that $de \equiv 1 \pmod{160}$ and $d < 160$. The correct value is $d = 23$, because $23 \times 7 = 161 = 10 \times 160 + 1$; d can be calculated using the extended Euclid's algorithm (Chapter 4).

The resulting keys are public key $PU = \{7, 187\}$ and private key $PR = \{23, 187\}$. The example shows the use of these keys for a plaintext input of

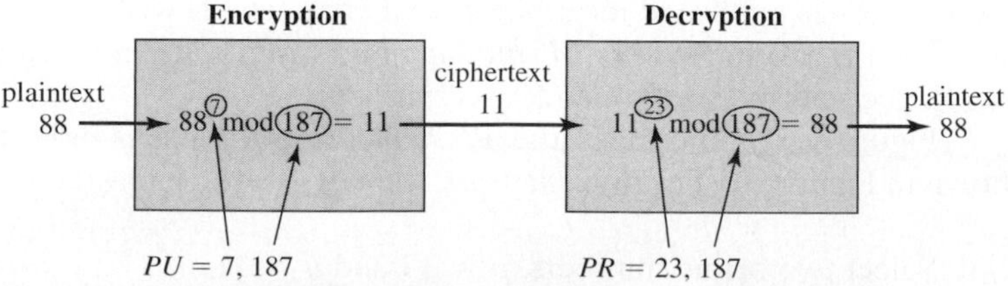

Figure 9.6 Example of RSA Algorithm

$M = 88$. For encryption, we need to calculate $C = 88^7 \bmod 187$. Exploiting the properties of modular arithmetic, we can do this as follows:

$$\begin{aligned}
88^7 \bmod 187 &= [(88^4 \bmod 187) \times (88^2 \bmod 187) \times (88^1 \bmod 187)] \bmod 187 \\
88^1 \bmod 187 &= 88 \\
88^2 \bmod 187 &= 7744 \bmod 187 = 77 \\
88^4 \bmod 187 &= 59{,}969{,}536 \bmod 187 = 132 \\
88^7 \bmod 187 &= (88 \times 77 \times 132) \bmod 187 = 894{,}432 \bmod 187 = 11
\end{aligned}$$

For decryption, we calculate $M = 11^{23} \bmod 187$:

$$\begin{aligned}
11^{23} \bmod 187 &= [(11^1 \bmod 187) \times (11^2 \bmod 187) \times (11^4 \bmod 187) \times \\
&\quad (11^8 \bmod 187) \times (11^8 \bmod 187)] \bmod 187 \\
11^1 \bmod 187 &= 11 \\
11^2 \bmod 187 &= 121 \\
11^4 \bmod 187 &= 14{,}641 \bmod 187 = 55 \\
11^8 \bmod 187 &= 214{,}358{,}881 \bmod 187 = 33 \\
11^{23} \bmod 187 &= (11 \times 121 \times 55 \times 33 \times 33) \bmod 187 = 79{,}720{,}245 \bmod 187 = 88
\end{aligned}$$

Computational Aspects

We now turn to the issue of the complexity of the computation required to use RSA. There are actually two issues to consider: encryption/decryption and key generation. Let us look first at the process of encryption and decryption and then consider key generation.

Exponentiation in Modular Arithmetic Both encryption and decryption in RSA involve raising an integer to an integer power, mod n. If the exponentiation is done over the integers and then reduced modulo n, the intermediate values would be gargantuan. Fortunately, as the preceding example shows, we can make use of a property of modular arithmetic:

$$[(a \bmod n) \times (b \bmod n)] \bmod n = (a \times b) \bmod n$$

Thus, we can reduce intermediate results modulo n. This makes the calculation practical.

Another consideration is the efficiency of exponentiation, because with RSA we are dealing with potentially large exponents. To see how efficiency might be increased, consider that we wish to compute x^{16}. A straightforward approach requires 15 multiplications:

$$x^{16} = x \times x \times x \times x \times x \times x \times x \times x \times x \times x \times x \times x \times x \times x \times x \times x$$

However, we can achieve the same final result with only four multiplications if we repeatedly take the square of each partial result, successively forming x^2, x^4, x^8, x^{16}. As another example, suppose we wish to calculate $x^{11} \bmod n$ for some integers x and n. Observe that $x^{11} = x^{1+2+8} = (x)(x^2)(x^8)$. In this case we compute $x \bmod n$,

```
c ← 0; f ← 1
for i ← k downto 0
    do  c ← 2 × c
        f ← (f × f) mod n
    if  bi = 1
        then c ← c + 1
             f ← (f × a) mod n
return f
```

Note: The integer b is expressed as a binary number $b_k b_{k-1} \ldots b_0$

Figure 9.7 Algorithm for Computing $a^b \bmod n$

$x^2 \bmod n$, $x^4 \bmod n$, and $x^8 \bmod n$ and then calculate $[(x \bmod n) \times (x^2 \bmod n) \times (x^8 \bmod n)] \bmod n$.

More generally, suppose we wish to find the value a^b, with a and b positive integers. If we express b as a binary number $b_k b_{k-1} \ldots b_0$, then we have

$$b = \sum_{b_i \neq 0} 2^i$$

Therefore,

$$a^b = a^{\left(\sum_{b_i \neq 0} 2^i\right)} = \prod_{b_i \neq 0} a^{(2^i)}$$

$$a^b \bmod n = \left[\prod_{b_i \neq 0} a^{(2^i)}\right] \bmod n = \left(\prod_{b_i \neq 0}\left[a^{(2^i)} \bmod n\right]\right) \bmod n$$

We can therefore develop the algorithm[5] for computing $a^b \bmod n$, shown in Figure 9.7. Table 9.3 shows an example of the execution of this algorithm. Note that the variable c is not needed; it is included for explanatory purposes. The final value of c is the value of the exponent.

Table 9.3 Result of the Fast Modular Exponentiation Algorithm for $a^b \bmod n$, where $a = 7, b = 560 = 1000110000, n = 561$

i	9	8	7	6	5	4	3	2	1	0
b_i	1	0	0	0	1	1	0	0	0	0
c	1	2	4	8	17	35	70	140	280	560
f	7	49	157	526	160	241	298	166	67	1

[5]The algorithm has a long history; this particular pseudocode expression is from [CORM01].

Efficient Operation Using the Public Key To speed up the operation of the RSA algorithm using the public key, a specific choice of e is usually made. The most common choice is 65537 ($2^{16} - 1$); two other popular choices are 3 and 17. Each of these choices has only two 1 bits and so the number of multiplications required to perform exponentiation is minimized.

However, with a very small public key, such as $e = 3$, RSA becomes vulnerable to a simple attack. Suppose we have three different RSA users who all use the value $e = 3$ but have unique values of n, namely n_1, n_2, n_3. If user A sends the same encrypted message M to all three users, then the three ciphertexts are $C_1 = M^3 \bmod n_1$; $C_2 = M^3 \bmod n_2$; $C_3 = M^3 \bmod n_3$. It is likely that n_1, n_2, and n_3 are pairwise relatively prime. Therefore, one can use the Chinese remainder theorem (CRT) to compute $M^3 \bmod (n_1 n_2 n_3)$. By the rules of the RSA algorithm, M is less than each of the n_i; therefore $M^3 < n_1 n_2 n_3$. Accordingly, the attacker need only compute the cube root of M^3. This attack can be countered by adding a unique pseudorandom bit string as padding to each instance of M to be encrypted. This approach is discussed subsequently.

The reader may have noted that the definition of the RSA algorithm (Figure 9.5) requires that during key generation the user selects a value of e that is relatively prime to $\phi(n)$. Thus, for example, if a user has preselected $e = 65537$ and then generated primes p and q, it may turn out that $\gcd(\phi(n), e) \neq 1$, Thus, the user must reject any value of p or q that is not congruent to 1 (mod 65537).

Efficient Operation Using the Private Key We cannot similarly choose a small constant value of d for efficient operation. A small value of d is vulnerable to a brute-force attack and to other forms of cryptanalysis [WIEN90]. However, there is a way to speed up computation using the CRT. We wish to compute the value $M = C^d \bmod n$. Let us define the following intermediate results:

$$V_p = C^d \bmod p \qquad V_q = C^d \bmod q$$

Following the CRT, Equation (8.8), define the quantities:

$$X_p = q \times (q^{-1} \bmod p) \qquad X_q = p \times (p^{-1} \bmod q)$$

The CRT then shows, using Equation (8.9), that

$$M = (V_p X_p + V_q X_q) \bmod n$$

Further, we can simplify the calculation of V_p and V_q using Fermat's theorem, which states that $a^{p-1} \equiv 1 \pmod p$ if p and a are relatively prime. Some thought should convince you that the following are valid:

$$V_p = C^d \bmod p = C^{d \bmod (p-1)} \bmod p \qquad V_q = C^d \bmod q = C^{d \bmod (q-1)} \bmod q$$

The quantities $d \bmod (p - 1)$ and $d \bmod (q - 1)$ can be precalculated. The end result is that the calculation is approximately four times as fast as evaluating $M = C^d \bmod n$ directly [BONE02].

Key Generation Before the application of the public-key cryptosystem, each participant must generate a pair of keys. This involves the following tasks:

- Determining two prime numbers, p and q
- Selecting either e or d and calculating the other

First, consider the selection of p and q. Because the value of $n = pq$ will be known to any potential adversary, to prevent the discovery of p and q by exhaustive methods, these primes must be chosen from a sufficiently large set (i.e., p and q must be large numbers). On the other hand, the method used for finding large primes must be reasonably efficient.

At present, there are no useful techniques that yield arbitrarily large primes, so some other means of tackling the problem is needed. The procedure that is generally used is to pick at random an odd number of the desired order of magnitude and test whether that number is prime. If not, pick successive random numbers until one is found that tests prime.

A variety of tests for primality have been developed (e.g., see [KNUT98] for a description of a number of such tests). Almost invariably, the tests are probabilistic. That is, the test will merely determine that a given integer is *probably* prime. Despite this lack of certainty, these tests can be run in such a way as to make the probability as close to 1.0 as desired. As an example, one of the more efficient and popular algorithms, the Miller-Rabin algorithm, is described in Chapter 8. With this algorithm and most such algorithms, the procedure for testing whether a given integer n is prime is to perform some calculation that involves n and a randomly chosen integer a. If n "fails" the test, then n is not prime. If n "passes" the test, then n may be prime or nonprime. If n passes many such tests with many different randomly chosen values for a, then we can have high confidence that n is, in fact, prime.

In summary, the procedure for picking a prime number is as follows.

1. Pick an odd integer n at random (e.g., using a pseudorandom number generator).
2. Pick an integer $a < n$ at random.
3. Perform the probabilistic primality test, such as Miller-Rabin, with a as a parameter. If n fails the test, reject the value n and go to step 1.
4. If n has passed a sufficient number of tests, accept n; otherwise, go to step 2.

This is a somewhat tedious procedure. However, remember that this process is performed relatively infrequently: only when a new pair (PU, PR) is needed.

It is worth noting how many numbers are likely to be rejected before a prime number is found. A result from number theory, known as the prime number theorem, states that the primes near N are spaced on the average one every ($\ln N$) integers. Thus, on average, one would have to test on the order of $\ln(N)$ integers before a prime is found. Actually, because all even integers can be immediately rejected, the correct figure is $\ln(N)/2$. For example, if a prime on the order of magnitude of 2^{200} were sought, then about $\ln(2^{200})/2 = 70$ trials would be needed to find a prime.

Having determined prime numbers p and q, the process of key generation is completed by selecting a value of e and calculating d or, alternatively, selecting a value of d and calculating e. Assuming the former, then we need to select an e such that $\gcd(\phi(n), e) = 1$ and then calculate $d \equiv e^{-1}(\bmod \phi(n))$. Fortunately, there is a single algorithm that will, at the same time, calculate the greatest common divisor of two integers and, if the gcd is 1, determine the inverse of one of the integers modulo the other. The algorithm, referred to as the extended Euclid's algorithm, is explained in Chapter 8. Thus, the procedure is to generate a series of random numbers, testing each against $\phi(n)$ until a number relatively prime to $\phi(n)$ is found. Again, we can ask the question: How many random numbers must we test to find a usable number, that is, a number relatively prime to $\phi(n)$? It can be shown easily that the probability that two random numbers are relatively prime is about 0.6; thus, very few tests would be needed to find a suitable integer (see Problem 8.2).

The Security of RSA

Four possible approaches to attacking the RSA algorithm are as follows:

- **Brute force:** This involves trying all possible private keys.
- **Mathematical attacks:** There are several approaches, all equivalent in effort to factoring the product of two primes.
- **Timing attacks:** These depend on the running time of the decryption algorithm.
- **Chosen ciphertext attacks:** This type of attack exploits properties of the RSA algorithm.

The defense against the brute-force approach is the same for RSA as for other cryptosystems, namely, use a large key space. Thus, the larger the number of bits in d, the better. However, because the calculations involved, both in key generation and in encryption/decryption, are complex, the larger the size of the key, the slower the system will run.

In this subsection, we provide an overview of mathematical and timing attacks.

The Factoring Problem

We can identify three approaches to attacking RSA mathematically:

- Factor n into its two prime factors. This enables calculation of $\phi(n) = (p - 1) \times (q - 1)$, which, in turn, enables determination of $d \equiv e^{-1} \pmod{\phi(n)}$.
- Determine $\phi(n)$ directly, without first determining p and q. Again, this enables determination of $d \equiv e^{-1} \pmod{\phi(n)}$.
- Determine d directly, without first determining $\phi(n)$.

Most discussions of the cryptanalysis of RSA have focused on the task of factoring n into its two prime factors. Determining $\phi(n)$ given n is equivalent to factoring n [RIBE96]. With presently known algorithms, determining d given e and n appears to be at least as time-consuming as the factoring problem [KALI95]. Hence, we can use factoring performance as a benchmark against which to evaluate the security of RSA.

For a large n with large prime factors, factoring is a hard problem, but not as hard as it used to be. A striking illustration of this is the following. In 1977, the three inventors of RSA dared *Scientific American* readers to decode a cipher they printed in Martin Gardner's "Mathematical Games" column [GARD77]. They offered a $100 reward for the return of a plaintext sentence, an event they predicted might not occur for some 40 quadrillion years. In April of 1994, a group working over the Internet claimed the prize after only eight months of work [LEUT94]. This challenge used a public key size (length of n) of 129 decimal digits, or around 428 bits. In the meantime, just as they had done for DES, RSA Laboratories had issued challenges for the RSA cipher with key sizes of 100, 110, 120, and so on, digits. The latest challenge to be met is the RSA-200 challenge with a key length of 200 decimal digits, or about 663 bits.

Table 9.4 Progress in Factorization

Number of Decimal Digits	Approximate Number of Bits	Date Achieved	MIPS-years	Algorithm
100	332	April 1991	7	Quadratic sieve
110	365	April 1992	75	Quadratic sieve
120	398	June 1993	830	Quadratic sieve
129	428	April 1994	5000	Quadratic sieve
130	431	April 1996	1000	Generalized number field sieve
140	465	February 1999	2000	Generalized number field sieve
155	512	August 1999	8000	Generalized number field sieve
160	530	April 2003	—	Lattice sieve
174	576	December 2003	—	Lattice sieve
200	663	May 2005	—	Lattice sieve

Table 9.4 shows the results to date. The level of effort is measured in MIPS-years: a million-instructions-per-second processor running for one year, which is about 3×10^{13} instructions executed. A 1 GHz Pentium is about a 250-MIPS machine.

A striking fact about Table 9.4 concerns the method used. Until the mid-1990s, factoring attacks were made using an approach known as the quadratic sieve. The attack on RSA-130 used a newer algorithm, the generalized number field sieve (GNFS), and was able to factor a larger number than RSA-129 at only 20% of the computing effort.

The threat to larger key sizes is twofold: the continuing increase in computing power, and the continuing refinement of factoring algorithms. We have seen that the move to a different algorithm resulted in a tremendous speedup. We can expect further refinements in the GNFS, and the use of an even better algorithm is also a possibility. In fact, a related algorithm, the special number field sieve (SNFS), can factor numbers with a specialized form considerably faster than the generalized number field sieve. Figure 9.8 compares the performance of the two algorithms. It is reasonable to expect a breakthrough that would enable a general factoring performance in about the same time as SNFS, or even better [ODLY95]. Thus, we need to be careful in choosing a key size for RSA. For the near future, a key size in the range of 1024 to 2048 bits seems reasonable.

In addition to specifying the size of n, a number of other constraints have been suggested by researchers. To avoid values of n that may be factored more easily, the algorithm's inventors suggest the following constraints on p and q:

1. p and q should differ in length by only a few digits. Thus, for a 1024-bit key (309 decimal digits), both p and q should be on the order of magnitude of 10^{75} to 10^{100}.
2. Both $(p - 1)$ and $(q - 1)$ should contain a large prime factor.
3. $\gcd(p - 1, q - 1)$ should be small.

In addition, it has been demonstrated that if $e < n$ and $d < n^{1/4}$, then d can be easily determined [WIEN90].

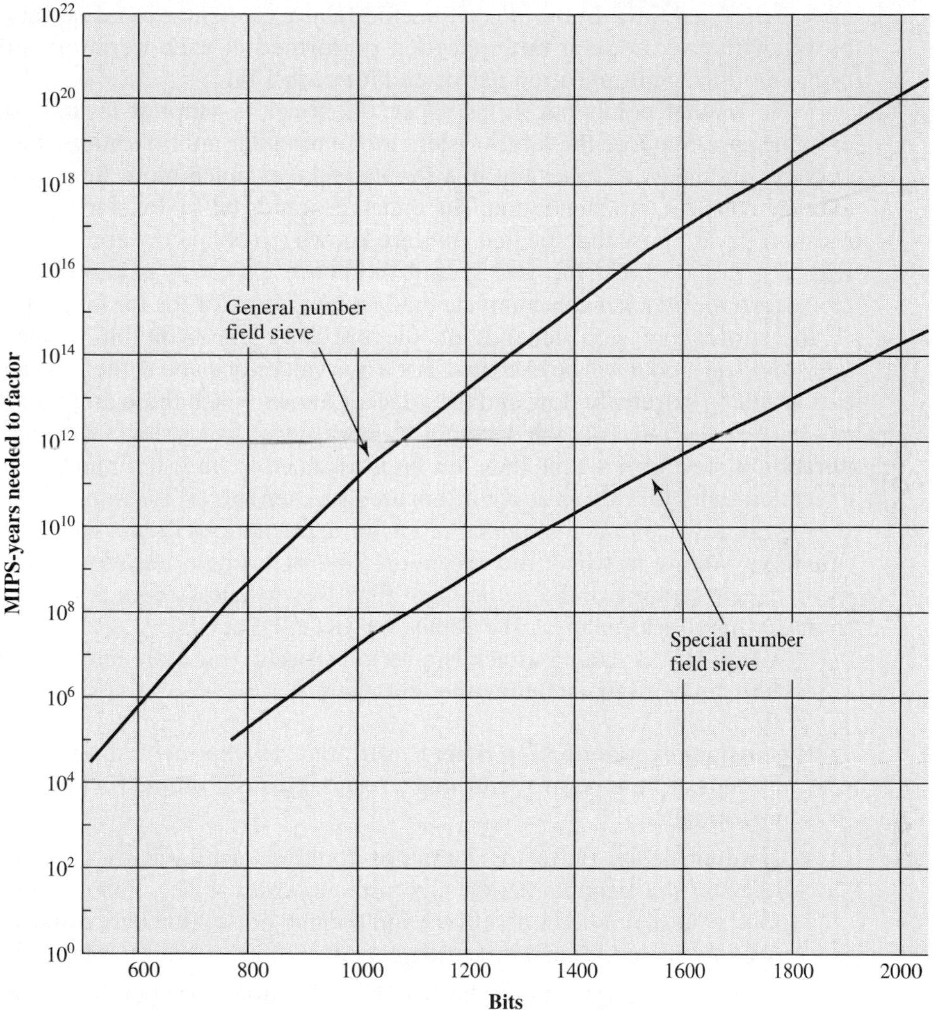

Figure 9.8 MIPS-years Needed to Factor

Timing Attacks If one needed yet another lesson about how difficult it is to assess the security of a cryptographic algorithm, the appearance of timing attacks provides a stunning one. Paul Kocher, a cryptographic consultant, demonstrated that a snooper can determine a private key by keeping track of how long a computer takes to decipher messages [KOCH96, KALI96b]. Timing attacks are applicable not just to RSA, but to other public-key cryptography systems. This attack is alarming for two reasons: It comes from a completely unexpected direction and it is a ciphertext-only attack.

A timing attack is somewhat analogous to a burglar guessing the combination of a safe by observing how long it takes for someone to turn the dial from number to number. We can explain the attack using the modular exponentiation algorithm of Figure 9.7, but the attack can be adapted to work with any implementation that does not run in fixed time. In this algorithm, modular exponentiation is accomplished bit by bit, with one modular multiplication performed at each iteration and an additional modular multiplication performed for each 1 bit.

As Kocher points out in his paper, the attack is simplest to understand in an extreme case. Suppose the target system uses a modular multiplication function that is very fast in almost all cases but in a few cases takes much more time than an entire average modular exponentiation. The attack proceeds bit-by-bit starting with the leftmost bit, b_k. Suppose that the first j bits are known (to obtain the entire exponent, start with $j = 0$ and repeat the attack until the entire exponent is known). For a given ciphertext, the attacker can complete the first j iterations of the **for** loop. The operation of the subsequent step depends on the unknown exponent bit. If the bit is set, $d \leftarrow (d \times a) \bmod n$ will be executed. For a few values of a and d, the modular multiplication will be extremely slow, and the attacker knows which these are. Therefore, if the observed time to execute the decryption algorithm is always slow when this particular iteration is slow with a 1 bit, then this bit is assumed to be 1. If a number of observed execution times for the entire algorithm are fast, then this bit is assumed to be 0.

In practice, modular exponentiation implementations do not have such extreme timing variations, in which the execution time of a single iteration can exceed the mean execution time of the entire algorithm. Nevertheless, there is enough variation to make this attack practical. For details, see [KOCH96].

Although the timing attack is a serious threat, there are simple countermeasures that can be used, including the following:

- **Constant exponentiation time:** Ensure that all exponentiations take the same amount of time before returning a result. This is a simple fix but does degrade performance.
- **Random delay:** Better performance could be achieved by adding a random delay to the exponentiation algorithm to confuse the timing attack. Kocher points out that if defenders don't add enough noise, attackers could still succeed by collecting additional measurements to compensate for the random delays.
- **Blinding:** Multiply the ciphertext by a random number before performing exponentiation. This process prevents the attacker from knowing what ciphertext bits are being processed inside the computer and therefore prevents the bit-by-bit analysis essential to the timing attack.

RSA Data Security incorporates a blinding feature into some of its products. The private-key operation $M = C^d \bmod n$ is implemented as follows:

1. Generate a secret random number r between 0 and $n - 1$.
2. Compute $C' = C(r^e) \bmod n$, where e is the public exponent.
3. Compute $M' = (C')^d \bmod n$ with the ordinary RSA implementation.
4. Compute $M = M'r^{-1} \bmod n$. In this equation, r^{-1} is the multiplicative inverse of $r \bmod n$; see Chapter 8 for a discussion of this concept. It can be demonstrated that this is the correct result by observing that $r^{ed} \bmod n = r \bmod n$.

RSA Data Security reports a 2 to 10% performance penalty for blinding.

Chosen Ciphertext Attack and Optimal Asymmetric Encryption Padding The basic RSA algorithm is vulnerable to a chosen ciphertext attack (CCA). CCA is defined as an attack in which adversary chooses a number of ciphertexts and is then given the corresponding plaintexts, decrypted with the target's private key. Thus, the adversary could select a plaintext, encrypt it with the target's public key and then be able to get the plaintext back by having it decrypted with the private key. Clearly, this provides the adversary with no new information. Instead, the adversary exploits properties of RSA and selects blocks of data that, when processed using the target's private key, yield information needed for cryptanalysis.

A simple example of a CCA against RSA takes advantage of the following property of RSA:

$$\text{E}(PU, M_1) \times \text{E}(PU, M_2) = \text{E}(PU, [M_1 \times M_2]) \tag{9.2}$$

We can decrypt $C = M^e \bmod n$ using a CCA as follows.

1. Compute $X = (C \times 2^e) \bmod n$.
2. Submit X as a chosen ciphertext and receive back $Y = X^d \bmod n$.

But now note the following:

$$\begin{aligned} X &= (C \bmod n) \times (2^e \bmod n) \\ &= (M^e \bmod n) \times (2^e \bmod n) \\ &= (2M)^e \bmod n \end{aligned}$$

Therefore, $Y = (2M) \bmod n$. From this, we can deduce M. To overcome this simple attack, practical RSA-based cryptosystems randomly pad the plaintext prior to encryption. This randomizes the ciphertext so that Equation (9.2) no longer holds. However, more sophisticated CCAs are possible and a simple padding with a random value has been shown to be insufficient to provide the desired security. To counter such attacks RSA Security Inc., a leading RSA vendor and former holder of the RSA patent, recommends modifying the plaintext using a procedure known as optimal asymmetric encryption padding (OAEP). A full discussion of the threats and OAEP are beyond our scope; see [POIN02] for an introduction and [BELL94a] for a thorough analysis. Here, we simply summarize the OAEP procedure.

Figure 9.9 depicts OAEP encryption. As a first step the message M to be encrypted is padded. A set of optional parameters P is passed through a hash function H.[6] The output is then padded with zeros to get the desired length in the overall data block (DB). Next, a random seed is generated and passed through another hash function, called the mask generating function (MGF). The resulting hash value is bit-by-bit XORed with DB to produce a maskedDB. The maskedDB is in turn passed through

[6]A hash function maps a variable-length data block or message into a fixed-length value called a hash code. Hash functions are discussed in depth in Chapters 11 and 12.

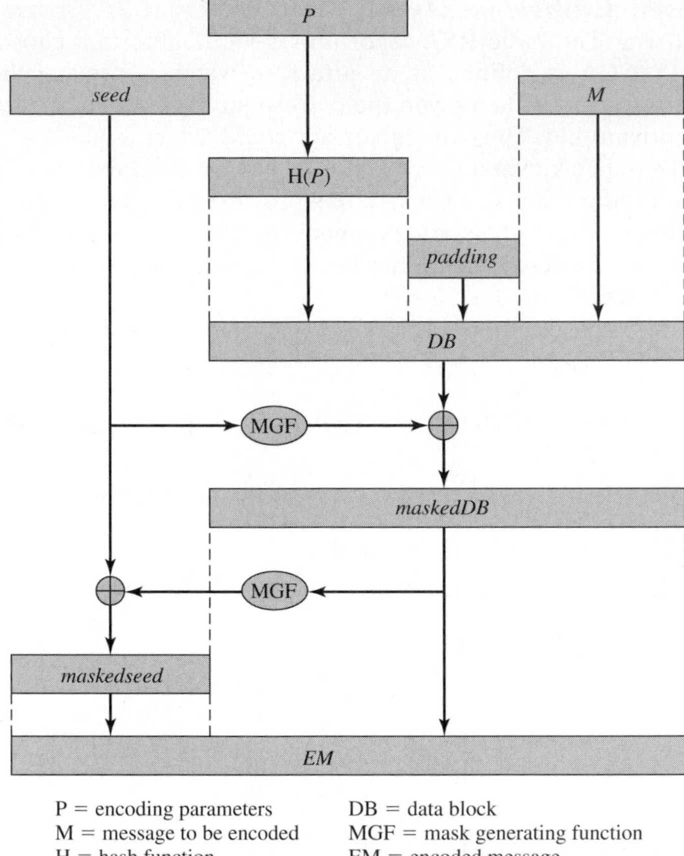

P = encoding parameters
M = message to be encoded
H = hash function
DB = data block
MGF = mask generating function
EM = encoded message

Figure 9.9 Encryption Using Optimal Assymetric Encryption Padding (OAEP)

the MGF to form a hash that is XORed with the seed to produce the masked seed. The concatenation of the maskedseed and the maskedDB forms the encoded message EM. Note that the EM includes the padded message, masked by the seed, and the seed, masked by the maskedDB. The EM is then encrypted using RSA.

9.3 RECOMMENDED READING AND WEB SITES

The recommended treatments of encryption listed in Chapter 3 cover public-key as well as symmetric encryption.

[DIFF88] describes in detail the several attempts to devise secure two-key cryptoalgorithms and the gradual evolution of a variety of protocols based on them. [CORM01] provides a concise but complete and readable summary of all of the algorithms relevant to the verification, computation, and cryptanalysis of RSA. [BONE99] discusses various cryptanalytic attacks on RSA. A more recent discussion is [SHAM03].

BONE99 Boneh, D. "Twenty Years of Attacks on the RSA Cryptosystem." *Notices of the American Mathematical Society*, February 1999.

CORM01 Cormen, T.; Leiserson, C.; Rivest, R.; and Stein, C. *Introduction to Algorithms.* Cambridge, MA: MIT Press, 2001.

DIFF88 Diffie, W. "The First Ten Years of Public-Key Cryptography." *Proceedings of the IEEE*, May 1988. Reprinted in [SIMM92].

SHAM03 Shamir, A., and Tromer, E. "On the Cost of Factoring RSA-1024." *CryptoBytes*, Summer 2003. **http://www.rsasecurity.com/rsalabs**

Recommended Web Site:

- **RSA Laboratories:** Extensive collection of technical material on RSA and other topics in cryptography

9.4 KEY TERMS, REVIEW QUESTIONS, AND PROBLEMS

Key Terms

chosen ciphertext attack (CCA)	private key	RSA
digital signature	public key	time complexity
key exchange	public key cryptography	timing attack
one-way function	public key cryptosystems	trapdoor one-way function
optimal asymmetric encryption padding (OAEP)	public key encryption	

Review Questions

9.1 What are the principal elements of a public-key cryptosystem?

9.2 What are the roles of the public and private key?

9.3 What are three broad categories of applications of public-key cryptosystems?

9.4 What requirements must a public key cryptosystems fulfill to be a secure algorithm?

9.5 What is a one-way function?

9.6 What is a trapdoor one-way function?

9.7 Describe in general terms an efficient procedure for picking a prime number.

Problems

9.1 Prior to the discovery of any specific public-key schemes, such as RSA, an existence proof was developed whose purpose was to demonstrate that public-key encryption is possible in theory. Consider the functions $f_1(x_1) = z_1$; $f_2(x_2, y_2) = z_2$; $f_3(x_3, y_3) = z_3$, where all values are integers with $1 \le x_i, y_i, z_i \le N$. Function f_1 can be represented by a vector M1 of length N, in which the kth entry is the value of $f_1(k)$. Similarly, f_2 and f_3 can be represented by $N \times N$ matrices M2 and M3. The intent is to represent the encryption/decryption process by table look-ups for tables with very large values of N. Such tables would be impractically huge but could, in principle, be constructed. The scheme works as follows: construct M1 with a random permutation of all integers between 1 and N; that is, each integer appears exactly once in M1. Construct M2 so that each row contains a random permutation of the first N integers. Finally, fill in M3 to satisfy the following condition:

$$f_3(f_2(f_1(k), p), k) = p \qquad \text{for all } k, p \text{ with } 1 \leq k, p \leq N$$

In words,

1. M1 takes an input k and produces an output x.
2. M2 takes inputs x and p giving output z.
3. M3 takes inputs z and k and produces p.

The three tables, once constructed, are made public.

a. It should be clear that it is possible to construct M3 to satisfy the preceding condition. As an example, fill in M3 for the following simple case:

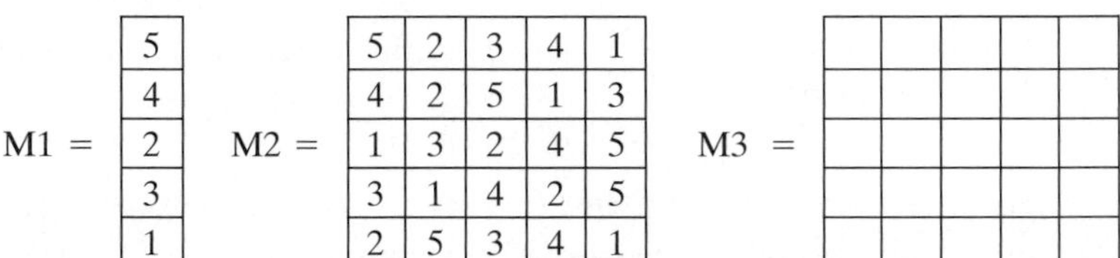

M1 =
5
4
2
3
1
M2 =
5 2 3 4 1
4 2 5 1 3
1 3 2 4 5
3 1 4 2 5
2 5 3 4 1
M3 =

Convention: The ith element of M1 corresponds to $k = i$. The ith row of M2 corresponds to $x = i$; the jth column of M2 corresponds to $p = j$. The ith row of M3 corresponds to $z = i$; the jth column of M3 corresponds to $k = j$.

b. Describe the use of this set of tables to perform encryption and decryption between two users.

c. Argue that this is a secure scheme.

9.2 Perform encryption and decryption using the RSA algorithm, as in Figure 9.6, for the following:

a. $p = 3; q = 11, e = 7; M = 5$
b. $p = 5; q = 11, e = 3; M = 9$
c. $p = 7; q = 11, e = 17; M = 8$
d. $p = 11; q = 13, e = 11; M = 7$
e. $p = 17; q = 31, e = 7; M = 2$. *Hint:* Decryption is not as hard as you think; use some finesse.

9.3 In a public-key system using RSA, you intercept the ciphertext $C = 10$ sent to a user whose public key is $e = 5, n = 35$. What is the plaintext M?

9.4 In an RSA system, the public key of a given user is $e = 31, n = 3599$. What is the private key of this user? *Hint:* First use trail and error to determine p and q; then use the extended Euclidean algorithm to find the multiplicative inverse of 31 modulo $\phi(n)$.

9.5 In using the RSA algorithm, if a small number of repeated encodings give back the plaintext, what is the likely cause?

9.6 Suppose we have a set of blocks encoded with the RSA algorithm and we don't have the private key. Assume $n = pq$, e is the public key. Suppose also someone tells us they know one of the plaintext blocks has a common factor with n. Does this help us in any way?

9.7 In the RSA public-key encryption scheme, each user has a public key, e, and a private key, d. Suppose Bob leaks his private key. Rather than generating a new modulus, he decides to generate a new public and a new private key. Is this safe?

9.8 Suppose Bob uses the RSA cryptosystem with a very large modulus n for which the factorization cannot be found in a reasonable amount of time. Suppose Alice sends a message to Bob by representing each alphabetic character as an integer between 0 and

25 ($A \rightarrow 0, \ldots, Z \rightarrow 25$), and then encrypting each number separately using RSA with large e and large n. Is this method secure? If not, describe the most efficient attack against this encryption method.

9.9 Using a spreadsheet (such as Excel), or a calculator, perform the described below operations. Document results of all intermediate modular multiplications. Determine a number of modular multiplications per each major transformation (such as encryption, decryption, primality testing, etc.).

a. Test all odd numbers in the range from 233 to 241 for primality using the Miller-Rabin test with base 2.

b. Encrypt the message block $M = 2$ using RSA with the following parameters: $e = 23$ and $n = 233 \times 241$.

c. Compute a private key (d, p, q) corresponding to the given above public key (e, n).

d. Perform the decryption of the obtained ciphertext using two different methods:

1. without using the Chinese Remainder Theorem,
2. using the Chinese Remainder Theorem.

9.10 Assume that you generate an authenticated and encrypted message by first applying the RSA transformation determined by your private key, and then enciphering the message using recipient's public key (note that you do NOT use hash function before the first transformation). Will this scheme work correctly [i.e., give the possibility to reconstruct the original message at the recipient's side, for all possible relations between the sender's modulus n_S and the recipient's modulus n_R $(n_S > n_R, n_S < n_R, n_S = n_R)$]? Explain your answer. In case your answer is "no," how would you correct this scheme?

9.11 "I want to tell you, Holmes," Dr. Watson's voice was enthusiastic, "that your recent activities in network security have increased my interest in cryptography. And just yesterday I found a way to make one-time pad encryption practical."

"Oh, really?" Holmes' face lost its sleepy look.

"Yes, Holmes. The idea is quite simple. For a given one-way function F, I generate a long pseudorandom sequence of elements by applying F to some standard sequence of arguments. The cryptanalyst is assumed to know F and the general nature of the sequence, which may be as simple as S, S + 1, S + 2, . . . , but not secret S. And due to the one-way nature of F no one is able to extract S given F(S + i) for some i, thus even if he somehow obtains a certain segment of the sequence, he will not be able to determine the rest."

"I am afraid, Watson, that your proposal isn't without flaws and at least it needs some additional conditions to be satisfied by F. Let's consider, for instance, the RSA encryption function, that is $F(M) = M^K \bmod N$, K is secret. This function is believed to be one-way, but I wouldn't recommend its use, for example, on the sequence $M = 2, 3, 4, 5, 6, \ldots$"

"But why, Holmes?" Dr. Watson apparently didn't understand. "Why do you think that the resulting sequence $2^K \bmod N, 3^K \bmod N, 4^K \bmod N, \ldots$ is not appropriate for one-time pad encryption if K is kept secret?"

"Because it is—at least partially—predictable, dear Watson, even if K is kept secret. You have said that the cryptanalyst is assumed to know F and the general nature of the sequence. Now let's assume that he will obtain somehow a short segment of the output sequence. In crypto circles this assumption is generally considered to be a viable one. And for this output sequence, knowledge of just the first two elements will allow him to predict quite a lot of the next elements of the sequence, even if not all of them, thus this sequence can't be considered to be cryptographically strong. And with the knowledge of a longer segment he could predict even more of the next elements of the sequence. Look, knowing the general nature of the sequence and its first two elements $2^K \bmod N$ and $3^K \bmod N$, you can easily compute its following elements."

Show how this can be done.

9.12 Show how RSA can be represented by matrices M1, M2, and M3 of Problem 9.1.

9.13 Consider the following scheme:

1. Pick an odd number, E.
2. Pick two prime numbers, P and Q, where $(P - 1)(Q - 1) - 1$ is evenly divisible by E.
3. Multiply P and Q to get N.
4. Calculate $D = \frac{(P - 1)(Q - 1)(E - 1) + 1}{E}$.

Is this scheme equivalent to RSA? Show why or why not.

9.14 Consider the following scheme by which B encrypts a message for A.

1. A chooses two large primes P and Q that are also relatively prime to $(P - 1)$ and $(Q - 1)$.
2. A publishes $N = PQ$ as its public key.
3. A calculates P' and Q' such that $PP' \equiv 1 \pmod{Q - 1}$ and $QQ' \equiv 1 \pmod{P - 1}$.
4. B encrypts message M as $C = M^N \bmod N$.
5. A finds M by solving $M \equiv C^{P'} \pmod{Q}$ and $M \equiv C^{Q'} \pmod{P}$.

a. Explain how this scheme works.
b. How does it differ from RSA?
c. Is there any particular advantage to RSA compared to this scheme?
d. Show how this scheme can be represented by matrices M1, M2, and M3 of Problem 9.1.

9.15 "This is a very interesting case, Watson," Holmes said. "The young man loves a girl and she loves him too. However, her father is a strange fellow who insists that his would-be son in law must design a simple and secure protocol for an appropriate public-key cryptosystem he could use in his company's computer network. The young man came up with the following protocol for communication between two parties, for example, user A wishing to send message M to user B: (messages exchanged are in the format (sender's name, text, receiver's name)."

1. A sends B the following block: $(A, \mathrm{E}(PU_b, [M, A]), B)$.
2. B acknowledges receipt by sending to A the following block: $(B, \mathrm{E}(PU_a, [M, B]), A)$.

"You can see that the protocol is really simple. But the girl's father claims that the young man has not satisfied his call for a simple protocol, because the proposal contains a certain redundancy and can be further simplified to the following:"

1. A sends B the block: $(A, \mathrm{E}(PU_b, M), B)$.
2. B acknowledges receipt by sending to A the block: $(B, \mathrm{E}(PU_a, M), A)$.

"On the basis of that, the girl's father refuses to allow his daughter to marry the young man, thus making them both unhappy. The young man was just here to ask me for help."

"Hmm, I don't see how you can help him." Watson was visibly unhappy with the idea that the sympathetic young man has to lose his love.

"Well, I think I could help. You know, Watson, redundancy is sometimes good to ensure the security of protocol. Thus, the simplification the girl's father has proposed could make the new protocol vulnerable to an attack the original protocol was able to resist," mused Holmes. "Yes, it is so, Watson. Look, all an adversary needs is to be one of the users of the network and to be able to intercept messages exchanged between A and B. Being a user of the network, he has his own public encryption key and is able to send his own messages to A or to B and to receive theirs. With the help of the simplified protocol, he could then obtain message M user A has previously sent to B using the following procedure:"

Complete the description.

9.16 Use the fast exponentiation algorithm of Figure 9.7 to determine $5^{596} \bmod 1234$. Show the steps involved in the computation.

9.17 Here is another realization of the fast exponentiation algorithm. Demonstrate that it is equivalent to the one in Figure 9.7.

1. f ← 1; T ← a; E ← b
2. **if** odd(e) **then** f ← f × T
3. E ← ⌊E/2⌋
4. T ← T × T
5. **if** E > 0 **then goto** 2
6. **output** f

9.18 The problem illustrates a simple application of the chosen ciphertext attack. Bob intercepts a ciphertext C intended for Alice and encrypted with Alice's public key e. Bob want to obtain the original message $M = C^d \bmod n$. Bob chooses a random value r less than n and computes

$$Z = r^e \bmod n$$
$$X = ZC \bmod n$$
$$t = r^{-1} \bmod n$$

Next, Bob gets Alice to authenticate (sign) X with her private key (as in Figure 9.3), thereby decrypting X. Alice returns $Y = X^d \bmod n$. Show how Bob can use the information now available to him to determine M.

9.19 Show the OAEP decoding operation, used for decryption, that corresponds to the encoding operation of Figure 9.9.

9.20 Improve on algorithm P1 in Appendix 9B.

a. Develop an algorithm that requires $2n$ multiplications and $n + 1$ additions. *Hint:* $x^{i+1} = x^i \times x$.

b. Develop an algorithm that requires only $n + 1$ multiplications and $n + 1$ additions. *Hint:* $\mathrm{P}(x) = a_0 + x \times q(x)$, where $q(x)$ is a polynomial of degree $(n - 1)$.

Note: The remaining problems concern the knapsack public-key algorithm described in Appendix F.

9.21 What items are in the knapsack in Figure F.1?

9.22 Perform encryption and decryption using the knapsack algorithm for the following:

a. $\mathbf{a}' = (1, 3, 5, 10); w = 7; m = 20; \mathbf{x} = 1101$

b. $\mathbf{a}' = (1, 3, 5, 11, 23, 46, 136, 263)); w = 203; m = 491; \mathbf{x} = 11101000$

c. $\mathbf{a}' = (2, 3, 6, 12, 25); w = 46; m = 53; \mathbf{x} = 11101$

d. $\mathbf{a}' = (15, 92, 108, 279, 563, 1172, 2243, 4468); w = 2393; m = 9291; \mathbf{x} = 10110001$

9.23 Why is it a requirement that $m > \sum_{1=1}^{n} a_i'$?

APPENDIX 9A PROOF OF THE RSA ALGORITHM

The basic elements of the RSA algorithm can be summarized as follows. Given two prime numbers p and q, with $n = pq$ and a message block $M < n$, two integers e and d are chosen such that

$$M^{ed} \bmod n = M$$

We state in Section 9.2, that the preceding relationship holds if e and d are multiplicative inverses modulo $\phi(n)$, where $\phi(n)$ is the Euler totient function. It is shown in Chapter 8 that for p, q prime, $\phi(pq) = (p - 1)(q - 1)$. The relationship between e and d can be expressed as

$$ed \bmod \phi(n) = 1$$

Another way to state this is that there is an integer k such that $ed = k\phi(n) + 1$. Thus, we must show that

$$M^{k\phi(n)+1} \bmod n = M^{k(p-1)(q-1)+1} \bmod n = M \tag{9.3}$$

Basic Results

Before proving Equation (9.3), we summarize some basic results. In Chapter 4, we showed that a property of modular arithmetic is the following:

$$[(a \bmod n) \times (b \bmod n)] \bmod n = (a \times b) \bmod n$$

From this, it should be easy to see that if we have $x \bmod n = 1$, then $x^2 \bmod n = 1$ and for any integer y, we have $x^y \bmod n = 1$. Similarly, if we have $x \bmod n = 0$, for any integer y, we have $x^y \bmod n = 0$.

Another property of modular arithmetic is

$$[(a \bmod n) - (b \bmod n)] \bmod n = (a - b) \bmod n$$

The other result we need is Euler's theorem, which was developed in Chapter 8. If integers a and n are relatively prime, than $a^{\phi(n)} \bmod n = 1$.

Proof

First we show that $M^{k(p-1)(q-1)+1} \bmod p = M \bmod p$. There are two cases to consider.

Case 1: M and p are not relatively prime; that is, p divides M. In this case $M \bmod p = 0$ and therefore $M^{k(p-1)(q-1)+1} \bmod p = 0$. Thus, $M^{k(p-1)(q-1)+1} \bmod p = M \bmod p$.

Case 2: If M and p are relatively prime, by Euler's theorem, $M^{\phi(p)} \bmod p = 1$. We proceed as follows:

$$\begin{aligned}
M^{k(p-1)(q-1)+1} \bmod p &= [(M)M^{k(p-1)(q-1)}] \bmod p \\
&= [(M)(M^{(p-1)})^{k(q-1)}] \bmod p \\
&= [(M)(M^{\phi(p)})^{k(q-1)}] \bmod p \\
&= (M \bmod p) \times [(M^{\phi(p)}) \bmod p]^{k(q-1)} \\
&= (M \bmod p) \times (1)^{k(q-1)} \qquad \text{(by Euler's theorem)} \\
&= M \bmod p
\end{aligned}$$

We now observe that

$$[M^{k(p-1)(q-1)+1} - M] \bmod p = [M^{k(p-1)(q-1)+1} \bmod p] - [M \bmod p] = 0$$

Thus, p divides $[M^{k(p-1)(q-1)+1} - M]$. By the same reasoning, we can show that q divides $[M^{k(p-1)(q-1)+1} - M]$. Because p and q are distinct primes, there must exist an integer r that satisfies

$$[M^{k(p-1)(q-1)+1} - M] = (pq)r = nr$$

Therefore, p divides $[M^{k(p-1)(q-1)+1} - M]$, and so $M^{k\phi(n)+1} \bmod n = M^{k(p-1)(q-1)+1} \bmod n = M$.

APPENDIX 9B THE COMPLEXITY OF ALGORITHMS

The central issue in assessing the resistance of an encryption algorithm to cryptanalysis is the amount of time that a given type of attack will take. Typically, one cannot be sure that one has found the most efficient attack algorithm. The most that one can say is that for a particular algorithm, the level of effort for an attack is of a particular order of magnitude. One can then compare that order of magnitude to the speed of current or predicted processors to determine the level of security of a particular algorithm.

A common measure of the efficiency of an algorithm is its time complexity. We define the **time complexity** of an algorithm to be f(n) if, for all n and all inputs of length n, the execution of the algorithm takes at most f(n) steps. Thus, for a given size of input and a given processor speed, the time complexity is an upper bound on the execution time.

There are several ambiguities here. First, the definition of a step is not precise. A step could be a single operation of a Turing machine, a single processor machine instruction, a single high-level language machine instruction, and so on. However, these various definitions of step should all be related by simple multiplicative constants. For very large values of n, these constants are not important. What is important is how fast the relative execution time is growing. For example, if we are concerned about whether to use 50-digit ($n = 10^{50}$) or 100-digit ($n = 10^{100}$) keys for RSA, it is not necessary (or really possible) to know exactly how long it would take to break each size of key. Rather, we are interested in ballpark figures for level of effort and in knowing how much extra relative effort is required for the larger key size.

A second issue is that, generally speaking, we cannot pin down an exact formula for f(n). We can only approximate it. But again, we are primarily interested in the rate of change of f(n) as n becomes very large.

There is a standard mathematical notation, known as the "big-O" notation, for characterizing the time complexity of algorithms that is useful in this context. The definition is as follows: $f(n) = O(g(n))$ if and only if there exist two numbers a and M such that

$$|f(n)| \leq a \times |g(n)|, \qquad n \geq M \tag{9.4}$$

An example helps clarify the use of this notation. Suppose we wish to evaluate a general polynomial of the form

$$P(x) = a_n x^n + a_{n-1} x^{n-1} + \ldots + a_1 x + a_0$$

The following simple-minded algorithm is from [POHL81]:

```
algorithm P1;
    n, i, j: integer; x, polyval: real;
    a, S: array [0..100] of real;
    begin
        read(x, n);
        for i := 0 upto n do
        begin
            S[i] := 1; read(a[i]);
            for j := 1 upto i do S[i] := x × S[i];
            S[i] := a[i] × S[i]
        end;
        polyval := 0;
        for i := 0 upto n do polyval := polyval + S[i];
        write ('value at', x, 'is', polyval)
    end.
```

In this algorithm, each subexpression is evaluated separately. Each S[i] requires $(i + 1)$ multiplications: i multiplications to compute S[i] and one to multiply by a[i]. Computing all n terms requires

$$\sum_{i=0}^{n} (i + 1) = \frac{(n + 2)(n + 1)}{2}$$

multiplications. There are also $(n + 1)$ additions, which we can ignore relative to the much larger number of multiplications. Thus, the time complexity of this algorithm is $f(n) = (n + 2)(n + 1)/2$. We now show that $f(n) = O(n^2)$. From the definition of Equation (9.4), we want to show that for $a = 1$ and $M = 4$, the relationship holds for $g(n) = n^2$. We do this by induction on n. The relationship holds for $n = 4$ because $(4 + 2)(4 + 1)/2 = 15 < 4^2 = 16$. Now assume that it holds for all values of n up to k [i.e., $(k + 2)(k + 1)/2 < k^2$]. Then, with $n = k + 1$,

$$\begin{aligned}\frac{(n+2)(n+1)}{2} &= \frac{(k+3)(k+2)}{2} \\ &= \frac{(k+2)(k+1)}{2} + k + 2 \\ &\le k^2 + k + 2 \\ &\le k^2 + 2k + 1 = (k+1)^2 = n^2\end{aligned}$$

Therefore, the result is true for $n = k + 1$.

In general, the big-O notation makes use of the term that grows the fastest. For example,

1. $O[ax^7 + 3x^3 + \sin(x)] = O(ax^7) = O(x^7)$
2. $O(e^n + an^{10}) = O(e^n)$
3. $O(n! + n^{50}) = O(n!)$

There is much more to the big-O notation, with fascinating ramifications. For the interested reader, two of the best accounts are in [GRAH94] and [KNUT97].

An algorithm with an input of size n is said to be

- **Linear:** If the running time is $O(n)$
- **Polynomial:** If the running time is $O(n^t)$ for some constant t
- **Exponential:** If the running time is $O(t^{h(n)})$ for some constant t and polynomial $h(n)$

Generally, a problem that can be solved in polynomial time is considered feasible, whereas anything worse than polynomial time, especially exponential time, is considered infeasible. But you must be careful with these terms. First, if the size of the input is small enough, even very complex algorithms become feasible. Suppose, for example, that you have a system that can execute 10^{12} operations per unit time. Table 9.5 shows the size of input that can be handled in one time unit for algorithms of various complexities. For algorithms of exponential or factorial time, only very small inputs can be accommodated.

The second thing to be careful about is the way in which the input is characterized. For example, the complexity of cryptanalysis of an encryption algorithm can be characterized equally well in terms of the number of possible keys or the length of the key. For the Advanced Encryption Standard (AES), for example, the number of possible keys is 2^{128}, and the length of the key is 128 bits. If we consider a single encryption to be a "step" and the number of possible keys to be $N = 2^n$, then the time complexity of the algorithm is linear in terms of the number of keys [$O(N)$] but exponential in terms of the length of the key [$O(2^n)$].

Table 9.5 Level of Effort for Various Levels of Complexity

Complexity	Size	Operations
$\log_2 n$	$2^{10^{12}} = 10^{3\times10^{11}}$	10^{12}
N	10^{12}	10^{12}
n^2	10^6	10^{12}
n^6	10^2	10^{12}
2^n	39	10^{12}
$n!$	15	10^{12}

Key Management; Other Public-Key Cryptosystems

No Singhalese, whether man or woman, would venture out of the house without a bunch of keys in his hand, for without such a talisman he would fear that some devil might take advantage of his weak state to slip into his body.

—*The Golden Bough*, Sir James George Frazer

KEY POINTS

- Public-key encryption schemes are secure only if the authenticity of the public key is assured. A public-key certificate scheme provides the necessary security.
- A simple public-key algorithm is Diffie-Hellman key exchange. This protocol enables two users to establish a secret key using a public-key scheme based on discrete logarithms. The protocol is secure only if the authenticity of the two participants can be established.
- Elliptic curve arithmetic can be used to develop a variety of elliptic curve cryptography (ECC) schemes, including key exchange, encryption, and digital signature.
- For purposes of ECC, elliptic curve arithmetic involves the use of an elliptic curve equation defined over a finite field. The coefficients and variables in the equation are elements of a finite field. Schemes using Z_p and $GF(2^m)$ have been developed.

This chapter continues our overview of public-key encryption. We examine key distribution and management for public-key systems, including a discussion of Diffie-Hellman key exchange. Finally, we provide an introduction to elliptic curve cryptography.

10.1 KEY MANAGEMENT

In Chapter 7, we examined the problem of the distribution of secret keys. One of the major roles of public-key encryption has been to address the problem of key distribution. There are actually two distinct aspects to the use of public-key cryptography in this regard:

- The distribution of public keys
- The use of public-key encryption to distribute secret keys

We examine each of these areas in turn.

Distribution of Public Keys

Several techniques have been proposed for the distribution of public keys. Virtually all these proposals can be grouped into the following general schemes:

- Public announcement
- Publicly available directory
- Public-key authority
- Public-key certificates

Public Announcement of Public Keys On the face of it, the point of public-key encryption is that the public key is public. Thus, if there is some broadly accepted public-key algorithm, such as RSA, any participant can send his or her public key to any other participant or broadcast the key to the community at large (Figure 10.1). For example, because of the growing popularity of PGP (pretty good privacy, discussed in Chapter 15), which makes use of RSA, many PGP users have adopted the practice of appending their public key to messages that they send to public forums, such as USENET newsgroups and Internet mailing lists.

Although this approach is convenient, it has a major weakness. Anyone can forge such a public announcement. That is, some user could pretend to be user A and send a public key to another participant or broadcast such a public key. Until such time as user A discovers the forgery and alerts other participants, the forger is able to read all encrypted messages intended for A and can use the forged keys for authentication (see Figure 9.3).

Publicly Available Directory A greater degree of security can be achieved by maintaining a publicly available dynamic directory of public keys. Maintenance and distribution of the public directory would have to be the responsibility of some trusted entity or organization (Figure 10.2). Such a scheme would include the following elements:

1. The authority maintains a directory with a {name, public key} entry for each participant.
2. Each participant registers a public key with the directory authority. Registration would have to be in person or by some form of secure authenticated communication.

Figure 10.1 Uncontrolled Public-Key Distribution

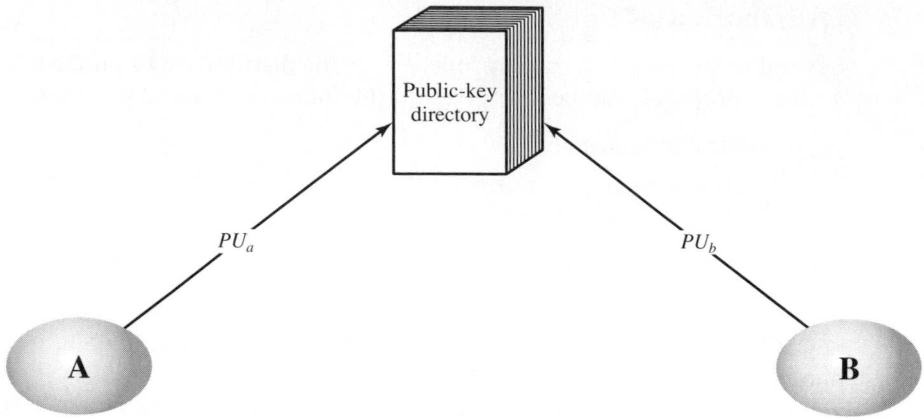

Figure 10.2 Public-Key Publication

3. A participant may replace the existing key with a new one at any time, either because of the desire to replace a public key that has already been used for a large amount of data, or because the corresponding private key has been compromised in some way.
4. Participants could also access the directory electronically. For this purpose, secure, authenticated communication from the authority to the participant is mandatory.

This scheme is clearly more secure than individual public announcements but still has vulnerabilities. If an adversary succeeds in obtaining or computing the private key of the directory authority, the adversary could authoritatively pass out counterfeit public keys and subsequently impersonate any participant and eavesdrop on messages sent to any participant. Another way to achieve the same end is for the adversary to tamper with the records kept by the authority.

Public-Key Authority Stronger security for public-key distribution can be achieved by providing tighter control over the distribution of public keys from the directory. A typical scenario is illustrated in Figure 10.3, which is based on a figure in [POPE79]. As before, the scenario assumes that a central authority maintains a dynamic directory of public keys of all participants. In addition, each participant reliably knows a public key for the authority, with only the authority knowing the corresponding private key. The following steps (matched by number to Figure 10.3) occur:

1. A sends a timestamped message to the public-key authority containing a request for the current public key of B.
2. The authority responds with a message that is encrypted using the authority's private key, PR_{auth}. Thus, A is able to decrypt the message using the authority's public key. Therefore, A is assured that the message originated with the authority. The message includes the following:
   - B's public key, PU_b, which A can use to encrypt messages destined for B
   - The original request, to enable A to match this response with the corresponding earlier request and to verify that the original request was not altered before reception by the authority

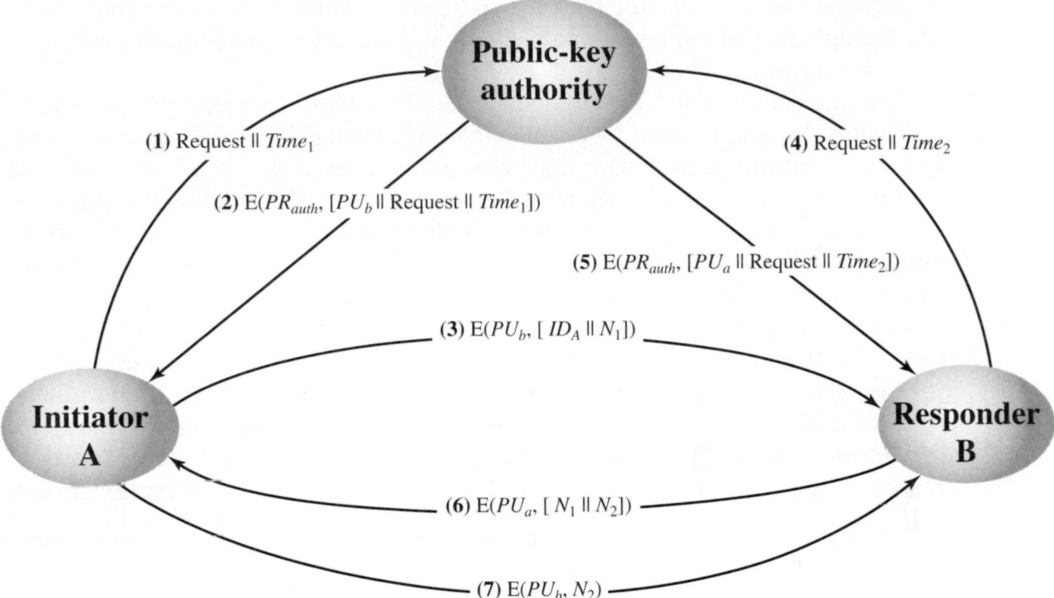

Figure 10.3 Public-Key Distribution Scenario

- The original timestamp, so A can determine that this is not an old message from the authority containing a key other than B's current public key

3. A stores B's public key and also uses it to encrypt a message to B containing an identifier of A (ID_A) and a nonce (N_1), which is used to identify this transaction uniquely.

4, 5. B retrieves A's public key from the authority in the same manner as A retrieved B's public key.

At this point, public keys have been securely delivered to A and B, and they may begin their protected exchange. However, two additional steps are desirable:

6. B sends a message to A encrypted with PU_a and containing A's nonce (N_1) as well as a new nonce generated by B (N_2). Because only B could have decrypted message (3), the presence of N_1 in message (6) assures A that the correspondent is B.
7. A returns N_2, encrypted using B's public key, to assure B that its correspondent is A.

Thus, a total of seven messages are required. However, the initial four messages need be used only infrequently because both A and B can save the other's public key for future use, a technique known as caching. Periodically, a user should request fresh copies of the public keys of its correspondents to ensure currency.

Public-Key Certificates

The scenario of Figure 10.3 is attractive, yet it has some drawbacks. The public-key authority could be somewhat of a bottleneck in the system, for a user must appeal to the authority for a public key for every other user that it wishes to contact. As before, the directory of names and public keys maintained by the authority is vulnerable to tampering.

An alternative approach, first suggested by Kohnfelder [KOHN78], is to use **certificates** that can be used by participants to exchange keys without contacting a public-key authority, in a way that is as reliable as if the keys were obtained directly from a public-key authority. In essence, a certificate consists of a public key plus an identifier of the key owner, with the whole block signed by a trusted third party. Typically, the third party is a certificate authority, such as a government agency or a financial institution, that is trusted by the user community. A user can present his or her public key to the authority in a secure manner, and obtain a certificate. The user can then publish the certificate. Anyone needed this user's public key can obtain the certificate and verify that it is valid by way of the attached trusted signature. A participant can also convey its key information to another by transmitting its certificate. Other participants can verify that the certificate was created by the authority. We can place the following requirements on this scheme:

1. Any participant can read a certificate to determine the name and public key of the certificate's owner.
2. Any participant can verify that the certificate originated from the certificate authority and is not counterfeit.
3. Only the certificate authority can create and update certificates.

These requirements are satisfied by the original proposal in [KOHN78]. Denning [DENN83] added the following additional requirement:

4. Any participant can verify the currency of the certificate.

A certificate scheme is illustrated in Figure 10.4. Each participant applies to the certificate authority, supplying a public key and requesting a certificate.

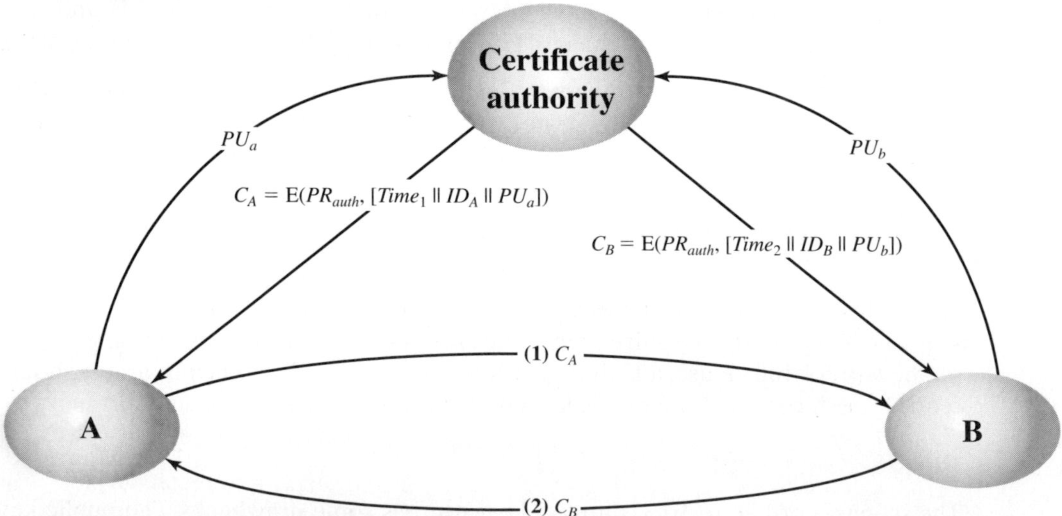

Figure 10.4 Exchange of Public-Key Certificates

Application must be in person or by some form of secure authenticated communication. For participant A, the authority provides a certificate of the form

$$C_A = \mathrm{E}(PR_{auth}, [T \| ID_A \| PU_a])$$

where PR_{auth} is the private key used by the authority and T is a timestamp. A may then pass this certificate on to any other participant, who reads and verifies the certificate as follows:

$$\mathrm{D}(PU_{auth}, C_A) = \mathrm{D}(PU_{auth}, \mathrm{E}(PR_{auth}, [T \| ID_A \| PU_a])) = (T \| ID_A \| PU_a)$$

The recipient uses the authority's public key, PU_{auth}, to decrypt the certificate. Because the certificate is readable only using the authority's public key, this verifies that the certificate came from the certificate authority. The elements ID_A and PU_a provide the recipient with the name and public key of the certificate's holder. The timestamp T validates the currency of the certificate. The timestamp counters the following scenario. A's private key is learned by an adversary. A generates a new private/public key pair and applies to the certificate authority for a new certificate. Meanwhile, the adversary replays the old certificate to B. If B then encrypts messages using the compromised old public key, the adversary can read those messages.

In this context, the compromise of a private key is comparable to the loss of a credit card. The owner cancels the credit card number but is at risk until all possible communicants are aware that the old credit card is obsolete. Thus, the timestamp serves as something like an expiration date. If a certificate is sufficiently old, it is assumed to be expired.

One scheme has become universally accepted for formatting public-key certificates: the X.509 standard. X.509 certificates are used in most network security applications, including IP security, secure sockets layer (SSL), secure electronic transactions (SET), and S/MIME, all of which are discussed in Part Two. X.509 is examined in detail in Chapter 14.

Distribution of Secret Keys Using Public-Key Cryptography

Once public keys have been distributed or have become accessible, secure communication that thwarts eavesdropping (Figure 9.2), tampering (Figure 9.3), or both (Figure 9.4) is possible. However, few users will wish to make exclusive use of public-key encryption for communication because of the relatively slow data rates that can be achieved. Accordingly, public-key encryption provides for the distribution of secret keys to be used for conventional encryption.

Simple Secret Key Distribution An extremely simple scheme was put forward by Merkle [MERK79], as illustrated in Figure 10.5. If A wishes to communicate with B, the following procedure is employed:

1. A generates a public/private key pair $\{PU_a, PR_a\}$ and transmits a message to B consisting of PU_a and an identifier of A, ID_A.
2. B generates a secret key, K_s, and transmits it to A, encrypted with A's public key.
3. A computes $\mathrm{D}(PR_a, \mathrm{E}(PU_a, K_s))$ to recover the secret key. Because only A can decrypt the message, only A and B will know the identity of K_s.
4. A discards PU_a and PR_a and B discards PU_a.

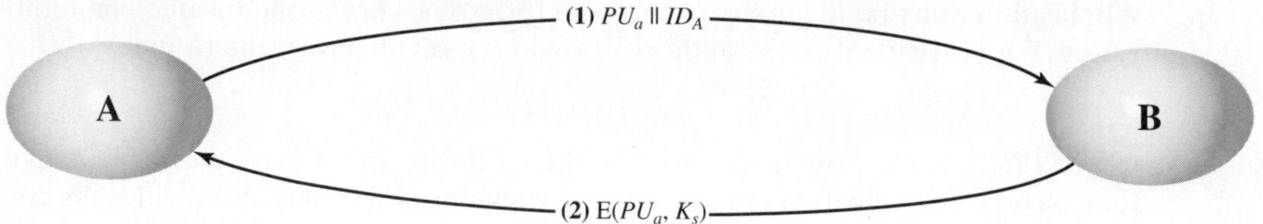

Figure 10.5 Simple Use of Public-Key Encryption to Establish a Session Key

A and B can now securely communicate using conventional encryption and the session key K_s. At the completion of the exchange, both A and B discard K_s. Despite its simplicity, this is an attractive protocol. No keys exist before the start of the communication and none exist after the completion of communication. Thus, the risk of compromise of the keys is minimal. At the same time, the communication is secure from eavesdropping.

The protocol depicted in Figure 10.5 is insecure against an adversary who can intercept messages and then either relay the intercepted message or substitute another message (see Figure 1.4c). Such an attack is known as a **man-in-the-middle attack** [RIVE84]. In this case, if an adversary, E, has control of the intervening communication channel, then E can compromise the communication in the following fashion without being detected:

1. A generates a public/private key pair $\{PU_a, PR_a\}$ and transmits a message intended for B consisting of PU_a and an identifier of A, ID_A.
2. E intercepts the message, creates its own public/private key pair $\{PU_e, PR_e\}$ and transmits $PU_e \| ID_A$ to B.
3. B generates a secret key, K_s, and transmits $E(PU_e, K_s)$.
4. E intercepts the message, and learns K_s by computing $D(PR_e, E(PU_e, K_s))$.
5. E transmits $E(PU_a, K_s)$ to A.

The result is that both A and B know K_s and are unaware that K_s has also been revealed to E. A and B can now exchange messages using K_s. E no longer actively interferes with the communications channel but simply eavesdrops. Knowing K_s, E can decrypt all messages, and both A and B are unaware of the problem. Thus, this simple protocol is only useful in an environment where the only threat is eavesdropping.

Secret Key Distribution with Confidentiality and Authentication

Figure 10.6, based on an approach suggested in [NEED78], provides protection against both active and passive attacks. We begin at a point when it is assumed that A and B have exchanged public keys by one of the schemes described earlier in this section. Then the following steps occur:

1. A uses B's public key to encrypt a message to B containing an identifier of A (ID_A) and a nonce (N_1), which is used to identify this transaction uniquely.
2. B sends a message to A encrypted with PU_a and containing A's nonce (N_1) as well as a new nonce generated by B (N_2). Because only B could have

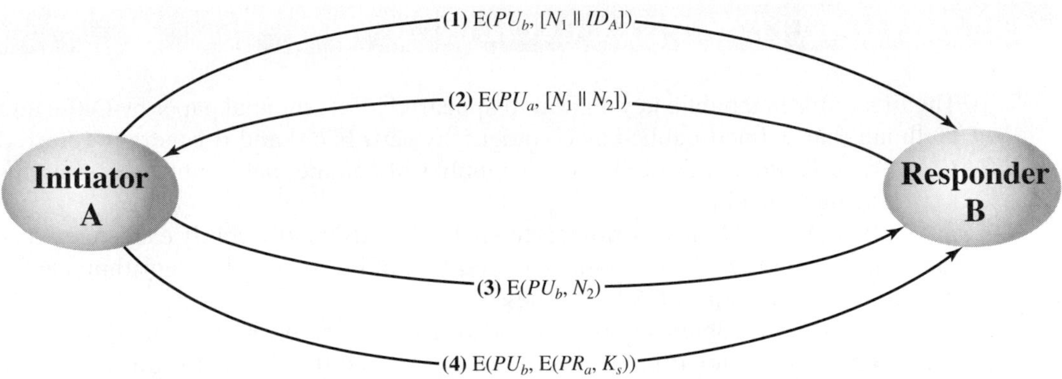

Figure 10.6 Public-Key Distribution of Secret Keys

decrypted message (1), the presence of N_1 in message (2) assures A that the correspondent is B.

3. A returns N_2, encrypted using B's public key, to assure B that its correspondent is A.
4. A selects a secret key K_s and sends $M = \text{E}(PU_b, \text{E}(PR_a, K_s))$ to B. Encryption of this message with B's public key ensures that only B can read it; encryption with A's private key ensures that only A could have sent it.
5. B computes $\text{D}(PU_a, \text{D}(PR_b, M))$ to recover the secret key.

Notice that the first three steps of this scheme are the same as the last three steps of Figure 10.3. The result is that this scheme ensures both confidentiality and authentication in the exchange of a secret key.

A Hybrid Scheme Yet another way to use public-key encryption to distribute secret keys is a hybrid approach in use on IBM mainframes [LE93]. This scheme retains the use of a key distribution center (KDC) that shares a secret master key with each user and distributes secret session keys encrypted with the master key. A public key scheme is used to distribute the master keys. The following rationale is provided for using this three-level approach:

- **Performance:** There are many applications, especially transaction-oriented applications, in which the session keys change frequently. Distribution of session keys by public-key encryption could degrade overall system performance because of the relatively high computational load of public-key encryption and decryption. With a three-level hierarchy, public-key encryption is used only occasionally to update the master key between a user and the KDC.
- **Backward compatibility:** The hybrid scheme is easily overlaid on an existing KDC scheme, with minimal disruption or software changes.

The addition of a public-key layer provides a secure, efficient means of distributing master keys. This is an advantage in a configuration in which a single KDC serves a widely distributed set of users.

10.2 DIFFIE-HELLMAN KEY EXCHANGE

The first published public-key algorithm appeared in the seminal paper by Diffie and Hellman that defined public-key cryptography [DIFF76b] and is generally referred to as Diffie-Hellman key exchange.[1] A number of commercial products employ this key exchange technique.

The purpose of the algorithm is to enable two users to securely exchange a key that can then be used for subsequent encryption of messages. The algorithm itself is limited to the exchange of secret values.

The Diffie-Hellman algorithm depends for its effectiveness on the difficulty of computing discrete logarithms. Briefly, we can define the discrete logarithm in the following way. First, we define a primitive root of a prime number p as one whose powers modulo p generate all the integers from 1 to $p - 1$. That is, if a is a primitive root of the prime number p, then the numbers

$$a \bmod p, a^2 \bmod p, \ldots, a^{p-1} \bmod p$$

are distinct and consist of the integers from 1 through $p - 1$ in some permutation.

For any integer b and a primitive root a of prime number p, we can find a unique exponent i such that

$$b \equiv a^i \pmod{p} \qquad \text{where } 0 \le i \le (p - 1)$$

The exponent i is referred to as the discrete logarithm of b for the base a, mod p. We express this value as $\mathrm{dlog}_{a,p}(b)$. See Chapter 8 for an extended discussion of discrete logarithms.

The Algorithm

Figure 10.7 summarizes the Diffie-Hellman key exchange algorithm. For this scheme, there are two publicly known numbers: a prime number q and an integer α that is a primitive root of q. Suppose the users A and B wish to exchange a key. User A selects a random integer $X_A < q$ and computes $Y_A = \alpha^{X_A} \bmod q$. Similarly, user B independently selects a random integer $X_B < q$ and computes $Y_B = \alpha^{X_B} \bmod q$. Each side keeps the X value private and makes the Y value available publicly to the other side. User A computes the key as $K = (Y_B)^{X_A} \bmod q$ and user B computes the key as $K = (Y_A)^{X_B} \bmod q$. These two calculations produce identical results:

$$\begin{aligned} K &= (Y_B)^{X_A} \bmod q \\ &= (\alpha^{X_B} \bmod q)^{X_A} \bmod q \\ &= (\alpha^{X_B})^{X_A} \bmod q \qquad \text{by the rules of modular arithmetic} \\ &= \alpha^{X_B X_A} \bmod q \\ &= (\alpha^{X_A})^{X_B} \bmod q \\ &= (\alpha^{X_A} \bmod q)^{X_B} \bmod q \\ &= (Y_A)^{X_B} \bmod q \end{aligned}$$

[1]Williamson of Britain's CESG published the identical scheme a few months earlier in a classified document [WILL76] and claims to have discovered it several years prior to that; see [ELLI99] for a discussion.

Global Public Elements	
q	prime number
α	$\alpha < q$ and α a primitive root of q

User A Key Generation	
Select private X_A	$X_A < q$
Calculate public Y_A	$Y_A = \alpha^{X_A} \bmod q$

User B Key Generation	
Select private X_B	$X_B < q$
Calculate public Y_B	$Y_B = \alpha^{X_B} \bmod q$

Calculation of Secret Key by User A
$K = (Y_B)^{X_A} \bmod q$

Calculation of Secret Key by User B
$K = (Y_A)^{X_B} \bmod q$

Figure 10.7 The Diffie-Hellman Key Exchange Algorithm

The result is that the two sides have exchanged a secret value. Furthermore, because X_A and X_B are private, an adversary only has the following ingredients to work with: q, α, Y_A, and Y_B. Thus, the adversary is forced to take a discrete logarithm to determine the key. For example, to determine the private key of user B, an adversary must compute

$$X_B = \text{dlog}_{\alpha,q}(Y_B)$$

The adversary can then calculate the key K in the same manner as user B calculates it.

The security of the Diffie-Hellman key exchange lies in the fact that, while it is relatively easy to calculate exponentials modulo a prime, it is very difficult to calculate discrete logarithms. For large primes, the latter task is considered infeasible.

Here is an example. Key exchange is based on the use of the prime number $q = 353$ and a primitive root of 353, in this case $\alpha = 3$. A and B select secret keys $X_A = 97$ and $X_B = 233$, respectively. Each computes its public key:

$$\text{A computes } Y_A = 3^{97} \bmod 353 = 40.$$
$$\text{B computes } Y_B = 3^{233} \bmod 353 = 248.$$

After they exchange public keys, each can compute the common secret key:

$$\text{A computes } K = (Y_B)^{X_A} \bmod 353 = 248^{97} \bmod 353 = 160.$$
$$\text{B computes } K = (Y_A)^{X_B} \bmod 353 = 40^{233} \bmod 353 = 160.$$

We assume an attacker would have available the following information:

$$q = 353; \alpha = 3; Y_A = 40; Y_B = 248$$

In this simple example, it would be possible by brute force to determine the secret key 160. In particular, an attacker E can determine the common key by discovering a solution to the equation $3^a \bmod 353 = 40$ or the equation $3^b \bmod 353 = 248$. The brute-force approach is to calculate powers of 3 modulo 353, stopping when the result equals either 40 or 248. The desired answer is reached with the exponent value of 97, which provides $3^{97} \bmod 353 = 40$.

With larger numbers, the problem becomes impractical.

Key Exchange Protocols

Figure 10.8 shows a simple protocol that makes use of the Diffie-Hellman calculation. Suppose that user A wishes to set up a connection with user B and use a secret key to encrypt messages on that connection. User A can generate a one-time private key X_A, calculate Y_A, and send that to user B. User B responds by generating a private value X_B, calculating Y_B, and sending Y_B to user A. Both users can now calculate the key. The necessary public values q and α would need to be known ahead of time. Alternatively, user A could pick values for q and α and include those in the first message.

As an example of another use of the Diffie-Hellman algorithm, suppose that a group of users (e.g., all users on a LAN) each generate a long-lasting private value X_i (for user i) and calculate a public value Y_i. These public values, together with global public values for q and α, are stored in some central directory. At any time, user j can access user i's public value, calculate a secret key, and use that to send an encrypted message to user A. If the central directory is trusted, then this form of communication

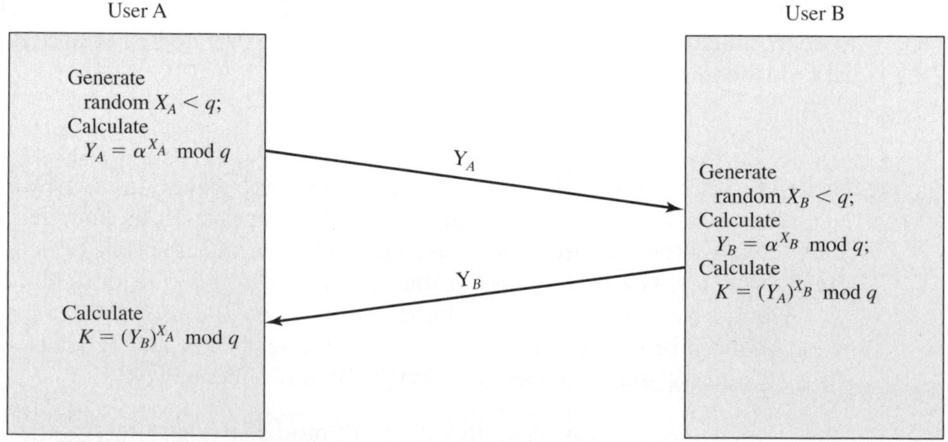

Figure 10.8 Diffie-Hellman Key Exchange

provides both confidentiality and a degree of authentication. Because only i and j can determine the key, no other user can read the message (confidentiality). Recipient i knows that only user j could have created a message using this key (authentication). However, the technique does not protect against replay attacks.

Man-in-the-Middle Attack

The protocol depicted in Figure 10.8 is insecure against a man-in-the-middle attack. Suppose Alice and Bob wish to exchange keys, and Darth is the adversary. The attack proceeds as follows:

1. Darth prepares for the attack by generating two random private keys X_{D1} and X_{D2}, and then computing the corresponding public keys Y_{D1} and Y_{D2}.
2. Alice transmits Y_A to Bob.
3. Darth intercepts Y_A and transmits Y_{D1} to Bob. Darth also calculates $K2 = (Y_A)^{X_{D2}} \bmod q$.
4. Bob receives Y_{D1} and calculates $K1 = (Y_{D1})^{X_B} \bmod q$.
5. Bob transmits X_A to Alice.
6. Darth intercepts X_A and transmits Y_{D2} to Alice. Darth calculates $K1 = (Y_B)^{X_{D1}} \bmod q$.
7. Alice receives Y_{D2} and calculates $K2 = (Y_{D2})^{X_A} \bmod q$.

At this point, Bob and Alice think that they share a secret key, but instead Bob and Darth share secret key $K1$ and Alice and Darth share secret key $K2$. All future communication between Bob and Alice is compromised in the following way:

1. Alice sends an encrypted message M: E($K2$, M).
2. Darth intercepts the encrypted message and decrypts it, to recover M.
3. Darth sends Bob E($K1$, M) or E($K1$, M'), where M' is any message. In the first case, Darth simply wants to eavesdrop on the communication without altering it. In the second case, Darth wants to modify the message going to Bob.

The key exchange protocol is vulnerable to such an attack because it does not authenticate the participants. This vulnerability can be overcome with the use of digital signatures and public-key certificates; these topics are explored in Chapters 13 and 14.

10.3 ELLIPTIC CURVE ARITHMETIC

Most of the products and standards that use public-key cryptography for encryption and digital signatures use RSA. As we have seen, the key length for secure RSA use has increased over recent years, and this has put a heavier processing load on applications using RSA. This burden has ramifications, especially for electronic commerce sites that conduct large numbers of secure transactions. Recently, a competing system has begun to challenge RSA: elliptic curve cryptography (ECC). Already, ECC is showing up in standardization efforts, including the IEEE P1363 Standard for Public-Key Cryptography.

The principal attraction of ECC, compared to RSA, is that it appears to offer equal security for a far smaller key size, thereby reducing processing overhead. On the other hand, although the theory of ECC has been around for some time, it is only recently that products have begun to appear and that there has been sustained cryptanalytic interest in probing for weaknesses. Accordingly, the confidence level in ECC is not yet as high as that in RSA.

ECC is fundamentally more difficult to explain than either RSA or Diffie-Hellman, and a full mathematical description is beyond the scope of this book. This section and the next give some background on elliptic curves and ECC. We begin with a brief review of the concept of abelian group. Next, we examine the concept of elliptic curves defined over the real numbers. This is followed by a look at elliptic curves defined over finite fields. Finally, we are able to examine elliptic curve ciphers.

The reader may wish to review the material on finite fields in Chapter 4 before proceeding.

Abelian Groups

Recall from Chapter 4, that an abelian **group** G, sometimes denoted by $\{G, \bullet\}$, is a set of elements with a binary operation, denoted by $\bullet$, that associates to each ordered pair (a, b) of elements in G an element $(a \bullet b)$ in G, such that the following axioms are obeyed:[2]

(A1) Closure:	If a and b belong to G, then $a \bullet b$ is also in G.
(A2) Associative:	$a \bullet (b \bullet c) = (a \bullet b) \bullet c$ for all a, b, c in G.
(A3) Identity element:	There is an element e in G such that $a \bullet \mathrm{e} = \mathrm{e} \bullet a = a$ for all a in G.
(A4) Inverse element:	For each a in G there is an element a' in G such that $a \bullet a' = a' \bullet a = \mathrm{e}$.
(A5) Commutative:	$a \bullet b = b \bullet a$ for all a, b in G.

A number of public-key ciphers are based on the use of an abelian group. For example, Diffie-Hellman key exchange involves multiplying pairs of nonzero integers modulo a prime number q. Keys are generated by exponentiation over the group, with exponentiation defined as repeated multiplication. For example, $a^k \bmod q = \underbrace{(a \times a \times \ldots \times a)}_{k \text{ times}} \bmod q$. To attack Diffie-Hellman, the attacker must determine k given a and a^k; this is the discrete log problem.

For elliptic curve cryptography, an operation over elliptic curves, called addition, is used. Multiplication is defined by repeated addition. For example, $a \times k = \underbrace{(a + a + \ldots + a)}_{k \text{ times}}$, where the addition is performed over an elliptic curve. Cryptanalysis involves determining k given a and $(a \times k)$.

---

[2]The operator $\bullet$ is generic and can refer to addition, multiplication, or some other mathematical operation.

An elliptic curve is defined by an equation in two variables, with coefficients. For cryptography, the variables and coefficients are restricted to elements in a finite field, which results in the definition of a finite abelian group. Before looking at this, we first look at elliptic curves in which the variables and coefficients are real numbers. This case is perhaps easier to visualize.

Elliptic Curves over Real Numbers

Elliptic curves are not ellipses. They are so named because they are described by cubic equations, similar to those used for calculating the circumference of an ellipse. In general, cubic equations for elliptic curves take the form

$$y^2 + axy + by = x^3 + cx^2 + dx + e$$

where a, b, c, d, and e are real numbers and x and y take on values in the real numbers.[3] For our purpose, it is sufficient to limit ourselves to equations of the form

$$y^2 = x^3 + ax + b \tag{10.1}$$

Such equations are said to be cubic, or of degree 3, because the highest exponent they contain is a 3. Also included in the definition of an elliptic curve is a single element denoted O and called the *point at infinity* or the *zero point*, which we discuss subsequently. To plot such a curve, we need to compute

$$y = \sqrt{x^3 + ax + b}$$

For given values of a and b, the plot consists of positive and negative values of y for each value of x. Thus each curve is symmetric about $y = 0$. Figure 10.9 shows two examples of elliptic curves. As you can see, the formula sometimes produces weird-looking curves.

Now, consider the set of points E(a, b) consisting of all of the points (x, y) that satisfy Equation (10.1) together with the element O. Using a different value of the pair (a, b) results in a different set E(a, b). Using this terminology, the two curves in Figure 10.9 depict the sets E(-1, 0) and E(1, 1), respectively.

Geometric Description of Addition It can be shown that a group can be defined based on the set E(a, b) for specific values of a and b in Equation (10.1), provided the following condition is met:

$$4a^3 + 27b^2 \neq 0 \tag{10.2}$$

To define the group, we must define an operation, called addition and denoted by +, for the set E(a, b), where a and b satisfy Equation (10.2). In geometric terms, the rules for addition can be stated as follows: If three points on an elliptic curve lie on a straight line, their sum is O. From this definition, we can define the rules of addition over an elliptic curve:

1. O serves as the additive identity. Thus $O = -O$; for any point P on the elliptic curve, $P + O = P$. In what follows, we assume $P \neq O$ and $Q \neq O$.

[3]Note that x and y are true variables, which take on values. This is in contrast to our discussion of polynomial rings and fields in Chapter 4, where x was treated as an indeterminate.

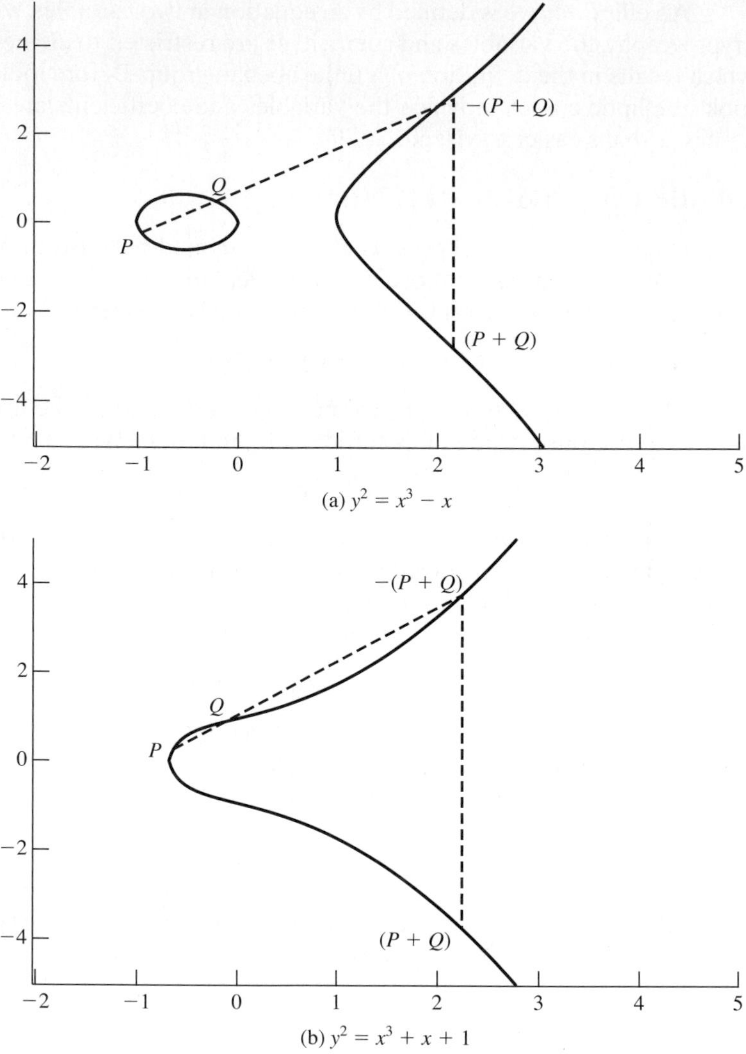

Figure 10.9 Example of Elliptic Curves

2. The negative of a point P is the point with the same x coordinate but the negative of the y coordinate; that is, if $P = (x, y)$, then $-P = (x, -y)$. Note that these two points can be joined by a vertical line. Note that $P + (-P) = P - P = O$.
3. To add two points P and Q with different x coordinates, draw a straight line between them and find the third point of intersection R. It is easily seen that there is a unique point R that is the point of intersection (unless the line is tangent to the curve at either P or Q, in which case we take $R = P$ or $R = Q$, respectively). To form a group structure, we need to define addition on these three points as follows: $P + Q = -R$. That is, we define $P + Q$ to be the mirror image (with respect to the x axis) of the third point of intersection. Figure 10.9 illustrates this construction.

4. The geometric interpretation of the preceding item also applies to two points, P and $-P$, with the same x coordinate. The points are joined by a vertical line, which can be viewed as also intersecting the curve at the infinity point. We therefore have $P + (-P) = O$, consistent with item (2).
5. To double a point Q, draw the tangent line and find the other point of intersection S. Then $Q + Q = 2Q = -S$.

With the preceding list of rules, it can be shown that the set $E(a, b)$ is an abelian group.

Algebraic Description of Addition In this subsection we present some results that enable calculation of additions over elliptic curves.[4] For two distinct points $P = (x_P, y_P)$ and $Q = (x_Q, y_Q)$ that are not negatives of each other, the slope of the line l that joins them is $\Delta = (y_Q - y_P)/(x_Q - x_P)$. There is exactly one other point where l intersects the elliptic curve, and that is the negative of the sum of P and Q. After some algebraic manipulation, we can express the sum $R = P + Q$ as follows:

$$\begin{aligned} x_R &= \Delta^2 - x_P - x_Q \\ y_R &= -y_P + \Delta(x_P - x_R) \end{aligned} \tag{10.3}$$

We also need to be able to add a point to itself: $P + P = 2P = R$. When $y_P \neq 0$, the expressions are

$$\begin{aligned} x_R &= \left(\frac{3x_P^2 + a}{2y_P}\right)^2 - 2x_P \\ y_R &= \left(\frac{3x_P^2 + a}{2y_P}\right)(x_P - x_R) - y_P \end{aligned} \tag{10.4}$$

Elliptic Curves over Z_p

Elliptic curve cryptography makes use of elliptic curves in which the variables and coefficients are all restricted to elements of a finite field. Two families of elliptic curves are used in cryptographic applications: prime curves over Z_p and binary curves over $GF(2^m)$. For a **prime curve** over Z_p, we use a cubic equation in which the variables and coefficients all take on values in the set of integers from 0 through $p - 1$ and in which calculations are performed modulo p. For a **binary curve** defined over $GF(2^m)$, the variables and coefficients all take on values in $GF(2^n)$ and in calculations are performed over $GF(2^n)$. [FERN99] points out that prime curves are best for software applications, because the extended bit-fiddling operations needed by binary curves are not required; and that binary curves are best for hardware applications, where it takes remarkably few logic gates to create a powerful, fast cryptosystem. We examine these two families in this section and the next.

There is no obvious geometric interpretation of elliptic curve arithmetic over finite fields. The algebraic interpretation used for elliptic curve arithmetic over real numbers does readily carry over, and this is the approach we take.

[4] For derivations of these results, see [KOBL94] or other mathematical treatments of elliptic curves.

For elliptic curves over Z_p, as with real numbers, we limit ourselves to equations of the form of Equation (10.1), but in this case with coefficients and variables limited to Z_p:

$$y^2 \bmod p = (x^3 + ax + b) \bmod p \tag{10.5}$$

For example, Equation (10.5) is satisfied for $a = 1, b = 1, x = 9, y = 7, p = 23$:

$$\begin{aligned} 7^2 \bmod 23 &= (9^3 + 9 + 1) \bmod 23 \\ 49 \bmod 23 &= 739 \bmod 23 \\ 3 &= 3 \end{aligned}$$

Now consider the set $E_p(a, b)$ consisting of all pairs of integers (x, y) that satisfy Equation (10.5), together with a point at infinity O. The coefficients a and b and the variables x and y are all elements of Z_p.

For example, let $p = 23$ and consider the elliptic curve $y^2 = x^3 + x + 1$. In this case, $a = b = 1$. Note that this equation is the same as that of Figure 10.9b. The figure shows a continuous curve with all of the real points that satisfy the equation. For the set $E_{23}(1, 1)$, we are only interested in the nonnegative integers in the quadrant from $(0, 0)$ through $(p - 1, p - 1)$ that satisfy the equation mod p. Table 10.1 lists the points (other than O) that are part of $E_{23}(1, 1)$. Figure 10.10 plots the points of $E_{23}(1, 1)$; note that the points, with one exception, are symmetric about $y = 11.5$.

It can be shown that a finite abelian group can be defined based on the set $E_p(a, b)$ provided that $(x^3 + ax + b) \bmod p$ has no repeated factors. This is equivalent to the condition

$$(4a^3 + 27b^2) \bmod p \neq 0 \bmod p \tag{10.6}$$

Note that Equation (10.6) has the same form as Equation (10.2).

The rules for addition over $E_p(a, b)$ correspond to the algebraic technique described for elliptic curves defined over real number. For all points $P, Q \in E_p(a, b)$:

1. $P + O = P$.
2. If $P = (x_P, y_P)$, then $P + (x_P, -y_P) = O$. The point $(x_P, -y_P)$ is the negative of P, denoted as $-P$. For example, in $E_{23}(1, 1)$, for $P = (13, 7)$, we have $-P = (13, -7)$. But $-7 \bmod 23 = 16$. Therefore, $-P = (13, 16)$, which is also in $E_{23}(1, 1)$.

Table 10.1 Points on the Elliptic Curve $E_{23}(1, 1)$

(0, 1)	(6, 4)	(12, 19)
(0, 22)	(6, 19)	(13, 7)
(1, 7)	(7, 11)	(13, 16)
(1, 16)	(7, 12)	(17, 3)
(3, 10)	(9, 7)	(17, 20)
(3, 13)	(9, 16)	(18, 3)
(4, 0)	(11, 3)	(18, 20)
(5, 4)	(11, 20)	(19, 5)
(5, 19)	(12, 4)	(19, 18)

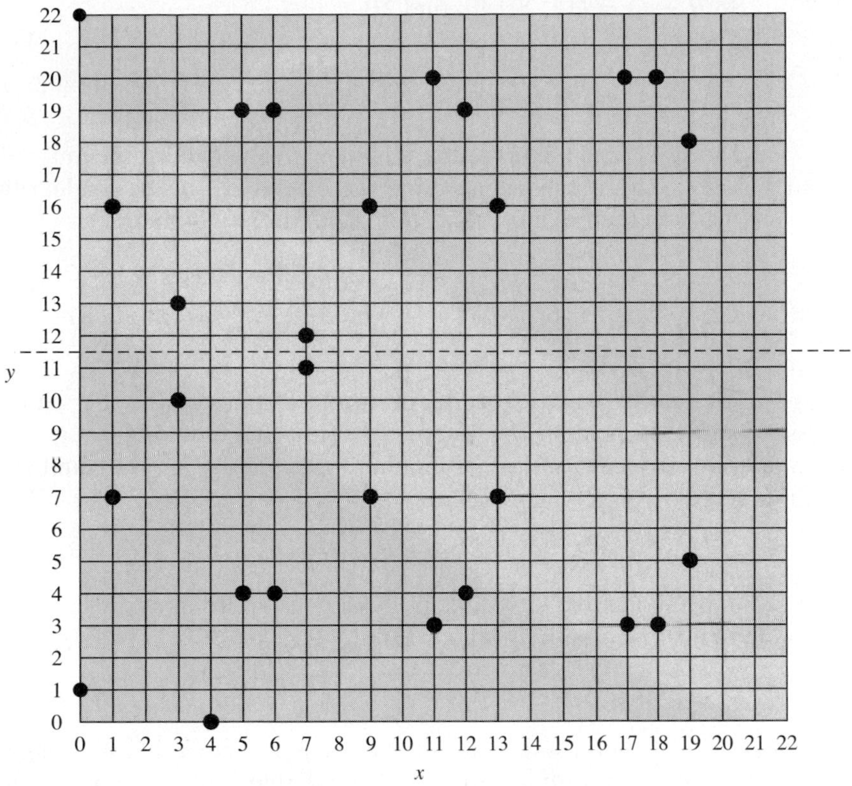

Figure 10.10 The Elliptic Curve $E_{23}(1, 1)$

3. If $P = (x_P, y_P)$ and $Q = (x_Q, y_Q)$ with $P \neq -Q$, then $R = P + Q = (x_R, y_R)$ is determined by the following rules:

$$x_R = (\lambda^2 - x_P - x_Q) \bmod p$$
$$y_R = (\lambda(x_P - x_R) - y_P) \bmod p$$

where

$$\lambda = \begin{cases} \left(\dfrac{y_Q - y_P}{x_Q - x_P}\right) \bmod p & \text{if } P \neq Q \\ \left(\dfrac{3x_P^2 + a}{2y_P}\right) \bmod p & \text{if } P = Q \end{cases}$$

4. Multiplication is defined as repeated addition; for example, $4P = P + P + P + P$.

For example, let $P = (3, 10)$ and $Q = (9, 7)$ in $E_{23}(1, 1)$. Then

$$\lambda = \left(\frac{7 - 10}{9 - 3}\right) \bmod 23 = \left(\frac{-3}{6}\right) \bmod 23 = \left(\frac{-1}{2}\right) \bmod 23 = 11$$
$$x_R = (11^2 - 3 - 9) \bmod 23 = 109 \bmod 23 = 17$$
$$y_R = (11(3 - 17) - 10) \bmod 23 = -164 \bmod 23 = 20$$

So $P + Q = (17, 20)$. To find $2P$,

$$\lambda = \left(\frac{3(3^2) + 1}{2 \times 10}\right) \bmod 23 = \left(\frac{5}{20}\right) \bmod 23 = \left(\frac{1}{4}\right) \bmod 23 = 6$$

The last step in the preceding equation involves taking the multiplicative inverse of 4 in Z_{23}. This can be done using the extended Euclidean algorithm defined in Section 4.4. To confirm, note that $(6 \times 4) \bmod 23 = 24 \bmod 23 = 1$.

$$x_R = (6^2 - 3 - 3) \bmod 23 = 30 \bmod 23 = 7$$
$$y_R = (6(3 - 7) - 10) \bmod 23 = (-34) \bmod 23 = 12$$

and $2P = (7, 12)$.

For determining the security of various elliptic curve ciphers, it is of some interest to know the number the number of points in a finite abelian group defined over an elliptic curve. In the case of the finite group $E_p(a, b)$, the number of points N is bounded by

$$p + 1 - 2\sqrt{p} \leq N \leq p + 1 + 2\sqrt{p}$$

Note that the number of points in $E_p(a, b)$ is approximately equal to the number of elements in Z_p, namely p elements.

Elliptic Curves over GF(2^m)

Recall from Chapter 4 that a finite field GF(2^m) consists of 2^m elements, together with addition and multiplication operations that can be defined over polynomials. For elliptic curves over GF(2^m), we use a cubic equation in which the variables and coefficients all take on values in GF(2^m), for some number m, and in which calculations are performed using the rules of arithmetic in GF(2^m).

It turns out that the form of cubic equation appropriate for cryptographic applications for elliptic curves is somewhat different for GF(2^m) than for Z_p. The form is

$$y^2 + xy = x^3 + ax^2 + b \tag{10.7}$$

where it is understood that the variables x and y and the coefficients a and b are elements of GF(2^m) and that calculations are performed in GF(2^m).

Now consider the set $E_{2^m}(a, b)$ consisting of all pairs of integers (x, y) that satisfy Equation (10.7), together with a point at infinity O.

For example, let us use the finite field GF(2^4) with the irreducible polynomial $f(x) = x^4 + x + 1$. This yields a generator that satisfies $f(g) = 0$, with a value of $g^4 = g + 1$, or in binary 0010. We can develop the powers of g as follows:

$g^0 = 0001$	$g^4 = 0011$	$g^8 = 0101$	$g^{12} = 1111$
$g^1 = 0010$	$g^5 = 0110$	$g^9 = 1010$	$g^{13} = 1101$
$g^2 = 0100$	$g^6 = 1100$	$g^{10} = 0111$	$g^{14} = 1001$
$g^3 = 1000$	$g^7 = 1011$	$g^{11} = 1110$	$g^{15} = 0001$

For example, $g^5 = (g^4)(g) = g^2 + g = 0110$.

Table 10.2 Points on the Elliptic Curve $E_{2^4}(g^4, 1)$

$(0, 1)$	(g^5, g^3)	(g^9, g^{13})
$(1, g^6)$	(g^5, g^{11})	(g^{10}, g)
$(1, g^{13})$	(g^6, g^8)	(g^{10}, g^8)
(g^3, g^8)	(g^6, g^{14})	$(g^{12}, 0)$
(g^3, g^{13})	(g^9, g^{10})	(g^{12}, g^{12})

Now consider the elliptic curve $y^2 + xy = x^3 + g^4x^2 + 1$. In this case $a = g^4$ and $b = g^0 = 1$. One point that satisfies this equation is (g^5, g^3):

$$(g^3)^2 + (g^5)(g^3) = (g^5)^3 + (g^4)(g^5)^2 + 1$$
$$g^6 + g^8 = g^{15} + g^{14} + 1$$
$$1100 + 0101 = 0001 + 1001 + 0001$$
$$1001 = 1001$$

Table 10.2 lists the points (other than O) that are part of $E_{2^4}(g^4, 1)$. Figure 10.11 plots the points of $E_{2^4}(g^4, 1)$.

It can be shown that a finite abelian group can be defined based on the set $E_{2^m}(a, b)$, provided that $b \neq 0$. The rules for addition can be stated as follows. For all points $P, Q \in E_{2^m}(a, b)$:

1. $P + O = P$.
2. If $P = (x_P, y_P)$, then $P + (x_P, x_P + y_P) = O$. The point $(x_P, x_P + y_P)$ is the negative of P, denoted as $-P$.

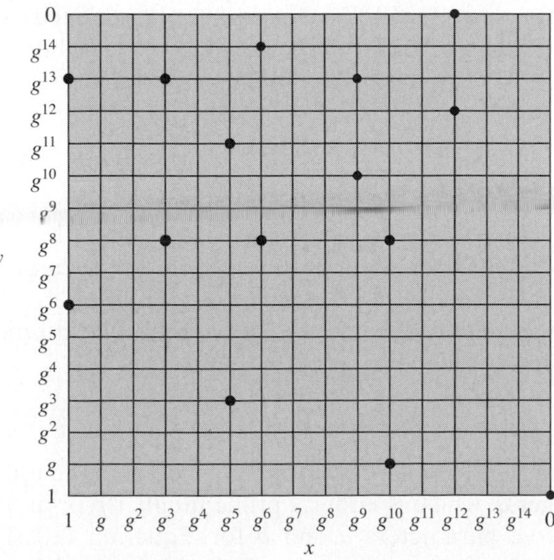

Figure 10.11 The Elliptic Curve $E_{2^4}(g^4, 1)$

3. If $P = (x_P, y_P)$ and $Q = (x_Q, y_Q)$ with $P \neq -Q$ and $P \neq Q$, then $R = P + Q = (x_R, y_R)$ is determined by the following rules:

$$x_R = \lambda^2 + \lambda + x_P + x_Q + a$$
$$y_R = \lambda(x_P + x_R) + x_R + y_P$$

where

$$\lambda = \frac{y_Q + y_P}{x_Q + x_P}$$

4. If $P = (x_P, y_P)$ then $R = 2P = (x_R, y_R)$ is determined by the following rules:

$$x_R = \lambda^2 + \lambda + a$$
$$y_R = x_P^2 + (\lambda + 1)x_R$$

where

$$\lambda = x_P + \frac{y_P}{x_P}$$

10.4 ELLIPTIC CURVE CRYPTOGRAPHY

The addition operation in ECC is the counterpart of modular multiplication in RSA, and multiple addition is the counterpart of modular exponentiation. To form a cryptographic system using elliptic curves, we need to find a "hard problem" corresponding to factoring the product of two primes or taking the discrete logarithm.

Consider the equation $Q = kP$ where $Q, P \in E_p(a, b)$ and $k < p$. It is relatively easy to calculate Q given k and P, but it is relatively hard to determine k given Q and P. This is called the discrete logarithm problem for elliptic curves.

We give an example taken from the Certicom Web site (**www.certicom.com**). Consider the group $E_{23}(9, 17)$. This is the group defined by the equation $y^2 \bmod 23 = (x^3 + 9x + 17) \bmod 23$. What is the discrete logarithm k of $Q = (4, 5)$ to the base $P = (16, 5)$? The brute-force method is to compute multiples of P until Q is found. Thus

$$P = (16, 5); 2P = (20, 20); 3P = (14, 14); 4P = (19, 20); 5P = (13, 10);$$
$$6P = (7, 3); 7P = (8, 7); 8P = (12, 17); 9P = (4, 5).$$

Because $9P = (4, 5) = Q$, the discrete logarithm $Q = (4, 5)$ to the base $P = (16, 5)$ is $k = 9$. In a real application, k would be so large as to make the brute-force approach infeasible.

In the remainder of this section, we show two approaches to ECC that give the flavor of this technique.

Analog of Diffie-Hellman Key Exchange

Key exchange using elliptic curves can be done in the following manner. First pick a large integer q, which is either a prime number p or an integer of the form 2^m and elliptic curve parameters a and b for Equation (10.5) or Equation (10.7). This defines the elliptic group of points $E_q(a, b)$. Next, pick a *base point* $G = (x_1, y_1)$ in $E_p(a, b)$ whose order is a very large value n. The **order** n of a point G on an elliptic curve is the smallest positive integer n such that $nG = O$. $E_q(a, b)$ and G are parameters of the cryptosystem known to all participants.

A key exchange between users A and B can be accomplished as follows (Figure 10.12):

1. A selects an integer n_A less than n. This is A's private key. A then generates a public key $P_A = n_A \times G$; the public key is a point in $E_q(a, b)$.
2. B similarly selects a private key n_B and computes a public key P_B.
3. A generates the secret key $K = n_A \times P_B$. B generates the secret key $K = n_B \times P_A$.

The two calculations in step 3 produce the same result because

$$n_A \times P_B = n_A \times (n_B \times G) = n_B \times (n_A \times G) = n_B \times P_A$$

To break this scheme, an attacker would need to be able to compute k given G and kG, which is assumed hard.

Global Public Elements

$E_q(a, b)$	elliptic curve with parameters a, b, and q, where q is a prime or an integer of the form 2^m
G	point on elliptic curve whose order is large value n

User A Key Generation

Select private n_A	$n_A < n$
Calculate public P_A	$P_A = n_A \times G$

User B Key Generation

Select private n_B	$n_A < n$
Calculate public P_B	$P_B = n_B \times G$

Calculation of Secret Key by User A

$K = n_A \times P_B$

Calculation of Secret Key by User B

$K = n_B \times P_A$

Figure 10.12 ECC Diffie-Hellman Key Exchange

As an example,[5] take $p = 211$; $E_p(0, -4)$, which is equivalent to the curve $y^2 = x^3 - 4$; and $G = (2, 2)$. One can calculate that $240G = O$. A's private key is $n_A = 121$, so A's public key is $P_A = 121(2, 2) = (115, 48)$. B's private key is $n_B = 203$, so B's public key is $203(2, 2) = (130, 203)$. The shared secret key is $121(130, 203) = 203(115, 48) = (161, 69)$.

Note that the secret key is a pair of numbers. If this key is to be used as a session key for conventional encryption, then a single number must be generated. We could simply use the x coordinates or some simple function of the x coordinate.

Elliptic Curve Encryption/Decryption

Several approaches to encryption/decryption using elliptic curves have been analyzed in the literature. In this subsection we look at perhaps the simplest. The first task in this system is to encode the plaintext message m to be sent as an x-y point P_m. It is the point P_m that will be encrypted as a ciphertext and subsequently decrypted. Note that we cannot simply encode the message as the x or y coordinate of a point, because not all such coordinates are in $E_q(a, b)$; for example, see Table 10.1. Again, there are several approaches to this encoding, which we will not address here, but suffice it to say that there are relatively straightforward techniques that can be used.

As with the key exchange system, an encryption/decryption system requires a point G and an elliptic group $E_q(a, b)$ as parameters. Each user A selects a private key n_A and generates a public key $P_A = n_A \times G$.

To encrypt and send a message P_m to B, A chooses a random positive integer k and produces the ciphertext C_m consisting of the pair of points:

$$C_m = \{kG, P_m + kP_B\}$$

Note that A has used B's public key P_B. To decrypt the ciphertext, B multiplies the first point in the pair by B's secret key and subtracts the result from the second point:

$$P_m + kP_B - n_B(kG) = P_m + k(n_BG) - n_B(kG) = P_m$$

A has masked the message P_m by adding kP_B to it. Nobody but A knows the value of k, so even though P_B is a public key, nobody can remove the mask kP_B. However, A also includes a "clue," which is enough to remove the mask if one knows the private key n_B. For an attacker to recover the message, the attacker would have to compute k given G and kG, which is assumed hard.

As an example of the encryption process (taken from [KOBL94]), take $p = 751$; $E_p(-1, 188)$, which is equivalent to the curve $y^2 = x^3 - x + 188$; and $G = (0, 376)$. Suppose that A wishes to send a message to B that is encoded in the elliptic point $P_m = (562, 201)$ and that A selects the random number $k = 386$. B's public key is $P_B = (201, 5)$. We have $386(0, 376) = (676, 558)$, and $(562, 201) + 386(201, 5) = (385, 328)$. Thus A sends the cipher text $\{(676, 558), (385, 328)\}$.

Security of Elliptic Curve Cryptography

The security of ECC depends on how difficult it is to determine k given kP and P. This is referred to as the elliptic curve logarithm problem. The fastest known technique for taking the elliptic curve logarithm is known as the Pollard rho method. Table 10.3 com-

[5]Provided by Ed Schaefer of Santa Clara University.

Table 10.3 Comparable Key Sizes in Terms of Computational Effort for Cryptanalysis

Symmetric Scheme (key size in bits)	ECC-Based Scheme (size of n in bits)	RSA/DSA (modulus size in bits)
56	112	512
80	160	1024
112	224	2048
128	256	3072
92	384	7680
256	512	15360

Source: Certicom

pares various algorithms by showing comparable key sizes in terms of computational effort for cryptanalysis. As can be seen, a considerably smaller key size can be used for ECC compared to RSA. Furthermore, for equal key lengths, the computational effort required for ECC and RSA is comparable [JURI97]. Thus, there is a computational advantage to using ECC with a shorter key length than a comparably secure RSA.

10.5 RECOMMENDED READING AND WEB SITES

A quite readable treatment of elliptic curve cryptography is [ROSI99]; the emphasis is on software implementation. Another readable, but rigorous, book is [HANK04]. Two other good treatments, both of which contain some rather stiff mathematics, are [BLAK99] and [ENGE99]. There are also good but more concise descriptions in [KUMA98], [STIN02], and [KOBL94]. Two interesting survey treatments are [FERN99] and [JURI97].

BLAK99 Blake, I.; Seroussi, G.; and Smart, N. *Elliptic Curves in Cryptography.* Cambridge: Cambridge University Press, 1999.

ENGE99 Enge, A. *Elliptic Curves and Their Applications to Cryptography.* Norwell, MA: Kluwer Academic Publishers, 1999.

FERN99 Fernandes, A. "Elliptic Curve Cryptography." *Dr. Dobb's Journal*, December 1999.

HANK04 Hankerson, D.; Menezes, A.; and Vanstone, S. *Guide to Elliptic Curve Cryptography.* New York: Springer, 2004.

JURI97 Jurisic, A., and Menezes, A. "Elliptic Curves and Cryptography." *Dr. Dobb's Journal*, April 1997.

KOBL94 Koblitz, N. *A Course in Number Theory and Cryptography.* New York: Springer-Verlag, 1994.

KUMA98 Kumanduri, R., and Romero, C. *Number Theory with Computer Applications.* Upper Saddle River, NJ: Prentice Hall, 1998.

ROSI99 Rosing, M. *Implementing Elliptic Curve Cryptography.* Greeenwich, CT: Manning Publications, 1999.

STIN02 Stinson, D. *Cryptography: Theory and Practice.* Boca Raton, FL: CRC Press, 2002.

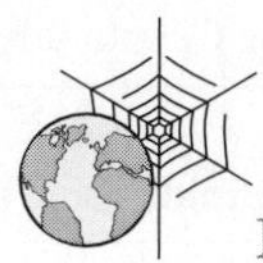

Recommended Web Site:

- **Certicom:** Extensive collection of technical material on elliptic curve cryptography and other topics in cryptography

10.6 KEY TERMS, REVIEW QUESTIONS, AND PROBLEMS

Key Terms

abelian group	elliptic curve arithmetic	prime curve
binary curve	elliptic curve cryptography	primitive root
cubic equation	finite field	public-key certificate
Diffie-Hellman key exchange	key distribution	public-key directory
discrete logarithm	key management	zero point
elliptic curve	man-the-middle attack	

Review Questions

10.1 What are two different uses of public-key cryptography related to key distribution?

10.2 List four general categories of schemes for the distribution of public keys.

10.3 What are the essential ingredients of a public-key directory?

10.4 What is a public-key certificate?

10.5 What are the requirements for the use of a public-key certificate scheme?

10.6 Briefly explain Diffie-Hellman key exchange.

10.7 What is an elliptic curve?

10.8 What is the zero point of an elliptic curve?

10.9 What is the sum of three points on an elliptic curve that lie on a straight line?

Problems

10.1 Users A and B use the Diffie-Hellman key exchange technique with a common prime $q = 71$ and a primitive root $\alpha = 7$.

a. If user A has private key $X_A = 5$, what is A's public key Y_A?

b. If user B has private key $X_B = 12$, what is B's public key Y_B?

c. What is the shared secret key?

10.2 Consider a Diffie-Hellman scheme with a common prime $q = 11$ and a primitive root $\alpha = 2$.

a. Show that 2 is a primitive root of 11.

b. If user A has public key $Y_A = 9$, what is A's private key X_A?

c. If user B has public key $Y_B = 3$, what is the shared secret key K, shared with A?

10.3 In the Diffie-Hellman protocol, each participant selects a secret number x and sends the other participant $\alpha^x \bmod q$ for some public number α. What would happen if the participants sent each other x^α for some public number α instead? Give at least one method Alice and Bob could use to agree on a key. Can Eve break your system without finding the secret numbers? Can Eve find the secret numbers?

10.4 This problem illustrates the point that the Diffie-Hellman protocol is not secure without the step where you take the modulus; i.e. the "Indiscrete Log Problem" is not a hard problem! You are Eve, and have captured Alice and Bob and imprisoned them. You overhear the following dialog.

Bob: Oh, let's not bother with the prime in the Diffie-Hellman protocol, it will make things easier.
Alice: Okay, but we still need a base α to raise things to. How about g = 3?
Bob: All right, then my result is 27.
Alice: And mine is 243.

What is Bob's secret X_B and Alice's secret X_A? What is their secret combined key? (Don't forget to show your work.)

10.5 Section 10.2 describes a man-in-the-middle attack on the Diffie-Hellman key exchange protocol in which the adversary generates two public-private key pairs for the attack. Could the same attack be accomplished with one pair? Explain.

10.6 In 1985, T. ElGamal announced a public-key scheme based on discrete logarithms, closely related to the Diffie-Hellman technique. As with Diffie-Hellman, the global elements of the ElGamal scheme are a prime number q and α, a primitive root of q. A user A selects a private key X_A and calculates a public key Y_A as in Diffie-Hellman. User A encrypts a plaintext $M < q$ intended for user B as follows:

1. Choose a random integer k such that $1 \leq k \leq q - 1$.
2. Compute $K = (Y_B)^k \bmod q$.
3. Encrypt M as the pair of integers (C_1, C_2) where

$$C_1 = \alpha^k \bmod q \quad C_2 = KM \bmod q$$

User B recovers the plaintext as follows:

1. Compute $K = (C_1)^{X_B} \bmod q$.
2. Compute $M = (C_2K^{-1}) \bmod q$.

Show that the system works; that is, show that the decryption process does recover the plaintext.

10.7 Consider an ElGamal scheme with a common prime $q = 71$ and a primitive root $\alpha = 7$.

a. If B has public key $Y_B = 3$ and A chose the random integer $k = 2$, what is the ciphertext of $M = 30$?
b. If A now chooses a different value of k, so that the encoding of $M = 30$ is $C = (59, C_2)$, what is the integer C_2?

10.8 Rule (5) for doing arithmetic in elliptic curves over real numbers states that to double a point Q, draw the tangent line and find the other point of intersection S. Then $Q + Q = 2Q = -S$. If the tangent line is not vertical, there will be exactly one point of intersection. However, suppose the tangent line is vertical? In that case, what is the value $2Q$? What is the value $3Q$?

10.9 Demonstrate that the two elliptic curves of Figure 10.9 each satisfy the conditions for a group over the real numbers.

10.10 Is (4,7) a point on the elliptic curve $y^2 = x^3 - 5x + 5$ over real numbers?

10.11 On the elliptic curve over the real numbers $y^2 = x^3 - 36x$, let $P = (-3.5, 9.5)$ and $Q = (-2.5, 8.5)$. Find $P + Q$ and $2P$.

10.12 Does the elliptic curve equation $y^2 = x^3 + 10x + 5$ define a group over Z_{17}?

10.13 Consider the elliptic curve $E_{11}(1, 6)$; that is, the curve is defined by $y^2 = x^3 + x + 6$ with a modulus of $p = 11$. Determine all of the points in $E_{11}(1, 6)$. *Hint:* Start by calculating the right-hand side of the equation for all values of x.

10.14 What are the negatives of the following elliptic curve points over Z_{17}? P = (5, 8); Q = (3, 0); R = (0, 6).

10.15 For $E_{11}(1, 6)$, consider the point $G = (2, 7)$. Compute the multiples of G from $2G$ through $13G$.

10.16 This problem performs elliptic curve encryption/decryption using the scheme outlined in Section 10.4. The cryptosystem parameters are $E_{11}(1, 6)$ and $G = (2, 7)$. B's secret key is $n_B = 7$.

a. Find B's public key P_B.

b. A wishes to encrypt the message $P_m = (10, 9)$ and chooses the random value $k = 3$. Determine the ciphertext C_m.

c. Show the calculation by which B recovers P_m from C_m.

10.17 The following is a first attempt at an Elliptic Curve signature scheme. We have a global elliptic curve, prime p, and "generator" G. Alice picks a private signing key X_A and forms the public verifying key $Y_A = X_A G$. To sign a message M:

- Alice picks a value k.
- Alice sends Bob M, k and the signature $S = M - kX_A G$.
- Bob verifies that $M = S + kY_A$

a. Show that this scheme works. That is, show that the verification process produces an equality if the signature is valid.

b. Show that the scheme is unacceptable by describing a simple technique for forging a user's signature on an arbitrary message.

10.18 Here is an improved version of the scheme given in the previous problem. As before, we have a global elliptic curve, prime p, and "generator" G. Alice picks a private signing key X_A and forms the public verifying key $Y_A = X_A G$. To sign a message M,

- Bob picks a value k.
- Bob sends Alice $C_1 = kG$.
- Alice sends Bob M and the signature $S = M - X_A C_1$.
- Bob verifies that $M = S + kY_A$

a. Show that this scheme works. That is, show that the verification process produces an equality if the signature is valid.

b. Show that forging a message in this scheme is as hard as breaking (ElGamal) Elliptic Curve Cryptography. (Or find an easier way to forge a message?)

c. This scheme has an extra "pass" compared to other cryptosystems and signature schemes we have looked at. What are some drawbacks to this?

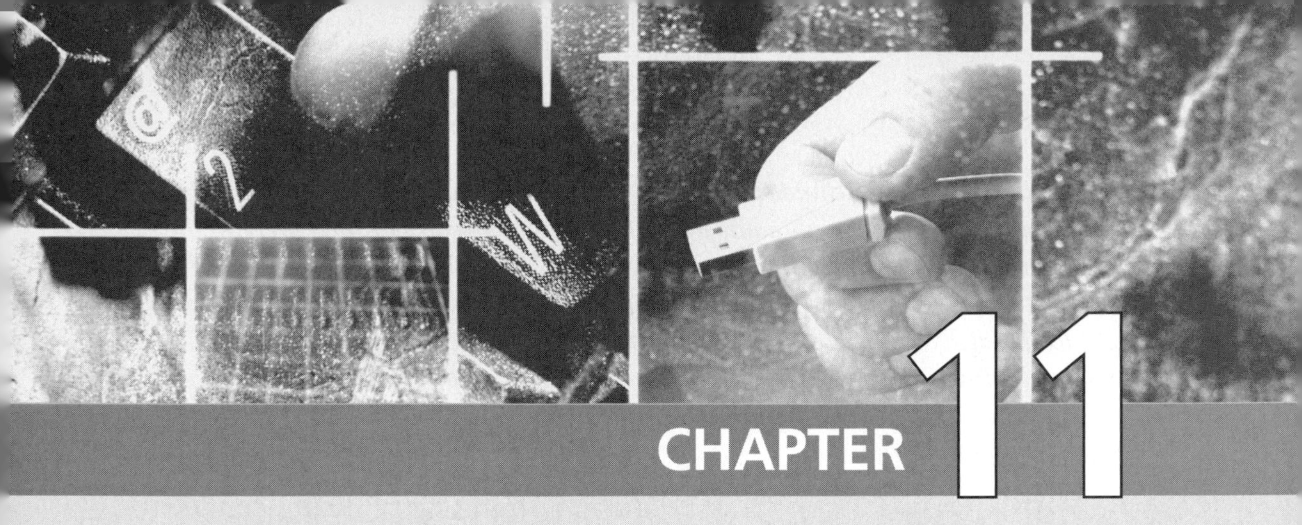

Message Authentication and Hash Functions

At cats' green on the Sunday he took the message from the inside of the pillar and added Peter Moran's name to the two names already printed there in the "Brontosaur" code. The message now read: "Leviathan to Dragon: Martin Hillman, Trevor Allan, Peter Moran: observe and tail." What was the good of it John hardly knew. He felt better, he felt that at last he had made an attack on Peter Moran instead of waiting passively and effecting no retaliation. Besides, what was the use of being in possession of the key to the codes if he never took advantage of it?

—*Talking to Strange Men*, Ruth Rendell

KEY POINTS

- Message authentication is a mechanism or service used to verify the integrity of a message. Message authentication assures that data received are exactly as sent by (i.e., contain no modification, insertion, deletion, or replay) and that the purported identity of the sender is valid.
- Symmetric encryption provides authentication among those who share the secret key. Encryption of a message by a sender's private key also provides a form of authentication.
- The two most common cryptographic techniques for message authentication are a message authentication code (MAC) and a secure hash function.
- A MAC is an algorithm that requires the use of a secret key. A MAC takes a variable-length message and a secret key as input and produces an authentication code. A recipient in possession of the secret key can generate an authentication code to verify the integrity of the message.
- A hash function maps a variable-length message into a fixed length hash value, or message digest. For message authentication, a secure hash function must be combined in some fashion with a secret key.

Perhaps the most confusing area of network security is that of message authentication and the related topic of digital signatures. The attacks and countermeasures become so convoluted that practitioners in this area begin to remind one of the astronomers of old, who built epicycles on top of epicycles in an attempt to account for all contingencies. Fortunately, it appears that today's designers of cryptographic protocols, unlike those long-forgotten astronomers, are working from a fundamentally sound model.

It would be impossible, in anything less than book length, to exhaust all the cryptographic functions and protocols that have been proposed or implemented for message authentication and digital signatures. Instead, the purpose of this chapter and the next two is to provide a broad overview of the subject and to develop a systematic means of describing the various approaches.

This chapter begins with an introduction to the requirements for authentication and digital signature and the types of attacks to be countered. Then the basic approaches are surveyed, including the increasingly important area of secure hash functions. Specific hash functions are examined in Chapter 12.

11.1 AUTHENTICATION REQUIREMENTS

In the context of communications across a network, the following attacks can be identified:

1. **Disclosure:** Release of message contents to any person or process not possessing the appropriate cryptographic key.
2. **Traffic analysis:** Discovery of the pattern of traffic between parties. In a connection-oriented application, the frequency and duration of connections could be determined. In either a connection-oriented or connectionless environment, the number and length of messages between parties could be determined.
3. **Masquerade:** Insertion of messages into the network from a fraudulent source. This includes the creation of messages by an opponent that are purported to come from an authorized entity. Also included are fraudulent acknowledgments of message receipt or nonreceipt by someone other than the message recipient.
4. **Content modification:** Changes to the contents of a message, including insertion, deletion, transposition, and modification.
5. **Sequence modification:** Any modification to a sequence of messages between parties, including insertion, deletion, and reordering.
6. **Timing modification:** Delay or replay of messages. In a connection-oriented application, an entire session or sequence of messages could be a replay of some previous valid session, or individual messages in the sequence could be delayed or replayed. In a connectionless application, an individual message (e.g., datagram) could be delayed or replayed.
7. **Source repudiation:** Denial of transmission of message by source.
8. **Destination repudiation:** Denial of receipt of message by destination.

Measures to deal with the first two attacks are in the realm of message confidentiality and are dealt with in Part One. Measures to deal with items 3 through 6 in the foregoing list are generally regarded as message authentication. Mechanisms for dealing specifically with item 7 come under the heading of digital signatures. Generally, a digital signature technique will also counter some or all of the attacks listed under items 3 through 6. Dealing with item 8 may require a combination of the use of digital signatures and a protocol designed to counter this attack.

In summary, message authentication is a procedure to verify that received messages come from the alleged source and have not been altered. Message authentication may also verify sequencing and timeliness. A digital signature is an authentication technique that also includes measures to counter repudiation by the source.

11.2 AUTHENTICATION FUNCTIONS

Any message authentication or digital signature mechanism has two levels of functionality. At the lower level, there must be some sort of function that produces an authenticator: a value to be used to authenticate a message. This lower-level function is then used as a primitive in a higher-level authentication protocol that enables a receiver to verify the authenticity of a message.

This section is concerned with the types of functions that may be used to produce an authenticator. These may be grouped into three classes, as follows:

- **Message encryption:** The ciphertext of the entire message serves as its authenticator
- **Message authentication code (MAC):** A function of the message and a secret key that produces a fixed-length value that serves as the authenticator
- **Hash function:** A function that maps a message of any length into a fixed-length hash value, which serves as the authenticator

We now briefly examine each of these topics; MACs and hash functions are then examined in greater detail in Sections 11.3 and 11.4.

Message Encryption

Message encryption by itself can provide a measure of authentication. The analysis differs for symmetric and public-key encryption schemes.

Symmetric Encryption Consider the straightforward use of symmetric encryption (Figure 11.1a). A message M transmitted from source A to destination B is encrypted using a secret key K shared by A and B. If no other party knows the key, then confidentiality is provided: No other party can recover the plaintext of the message.

In addition, we may say that B is assured that the message was generated by A. Why? The message must have come from A because A is the only other party that possesses K and therefore the only other party with the information necessary to construct ciphertext that can be decrypted with K. Furthermore, if M is recovered, B knows that none of the bits of M have been altered, because an opponent that does not know K would not know how to alter bits in the ciphertext to produce desired changes in the plaintext.

So we may say that symmetric encryption provides authentication as well as confidentiality. However, this flat statement needs to be qualified. Consider exactly what is happening at B. Given a decryption function D and a secret key K, the destination will accept *any* input X and produce output $Y = D(K, X)$. If X is the ciphertext of a legitimate message M produced by the corresponding encryption function, then Y is some plaintext message M. Otherwise, Y will likely be a meaningless sequence of bits. There may need to be some automated means of determining at B whether Y is legitimate plaintext and therefore must have come from A.

The implications of the line of reasoning in the preceding paragraph are profound from the point of view of authentication. Suppose the message M can be any arbitrary bit pattern. In that case, there is no way to determine automatically, at the

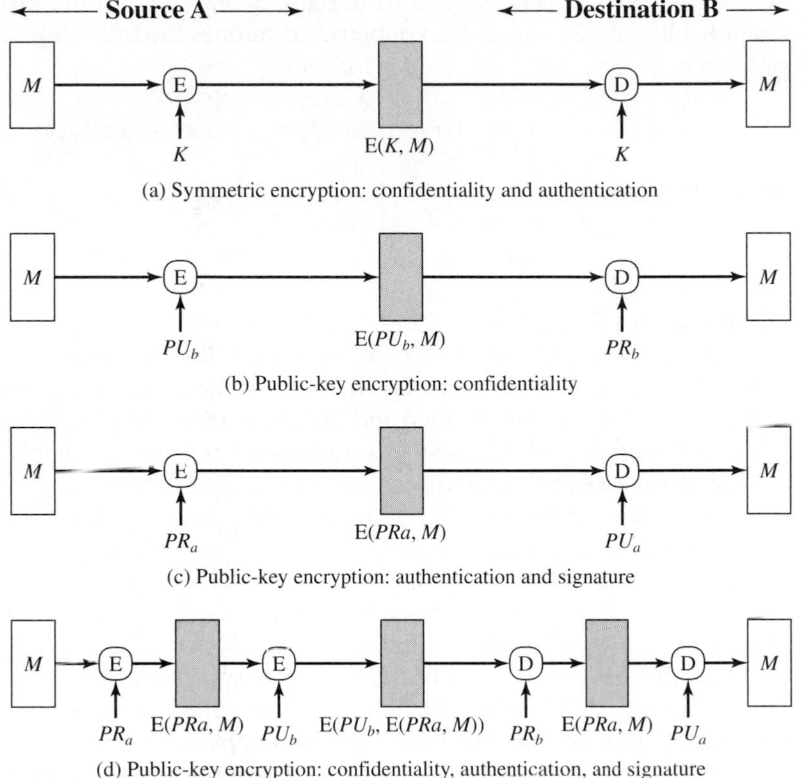

Figure 11.1 Basic Uses of Message Encryption

destination, whether an incoming message is the ciphertext of a legitimate message. This conclusion is incontrovertible: If M can be any bit pattern, then regardless of the value of X, the value $Y = \mathrm{D}(K, X)$ is *some* bit pattern and therefore must be accepted as authentic plaintext.

Thus, in general, we require that only a small subset of all possible bit patterns be considered legitimate plaintext. In that case, any spurious ciphertext is unlikely to produce legitimate plaintext. For example, suppose that only one bit pattern in 10^6 is legitimate plaintext. Then the probability that any randomly chosen bit pattern, treated as ciphertext, will produce a legitimate plaintext message is only 10^{-6}.

For a number of applications and encryption schemes, the desired conditions prevail as a matter of course. For example, suppose that we are transmitting English-language messages using a Caesar cipher with a shift of one ($K = 1$). A sends the following legitimate ciphertext:

```
nbsftfbupbutboeepftfbupbutboemjuumfmbnctfbujwz
```

B decrypts to produce the following plaintext:

```
mareseatoatsanddoeseatoatsandlittlelambseativy
```

A simple frequency analysis confirms that this message has the profile of ordinary English. On the other hand, if an opponent generates the following random sequence of letters:

```
zuvrsoevgqxlzwigamdvnmhpmccxiuureosfbcebtqxsxq
```

this decrypts to:

```
ytuqrndufpwkyvhfzlcumlgolbbwhttqdnreabdaspwrwp
```

which does not fit the profile of ordinary English.

It may be difficult to determine *automatically* if incoming ciphertext decrypts to intelligible plaintext. If the plaintext is, say, a binary object file or digitized X-rays, determination of properly formed and therefore authentic plaintext may be difficult. Thus, an opponent could achieve a certain level of disruption simply by issuing messages with random content purporting to come from a legitimate user.

One solution to this problem is to force the plaintext to have some structure that is easily recognized but that cannot be replicated without recourse to the encryption function. We could, for example, append an error-detecting code, also known as a frame check sequence (FCS) or checksum, to each message before encryption, as illustrated in Figure 11.2a. A prepares a plaintext message M and then provides this as input to a function F that produces an FCS. The FCS is appended to M and the entire block is then encrypted. At the destination, B decrypts the incoming block and treats the results as a message with an appended FCS. B applies the same function F to attempt to reproduce the FCS. If the calculated FCS is equal to the incoming FCS, then the message is considered authentic. It is unlikely that any random sequence of bits would exhibit the desired relationship.

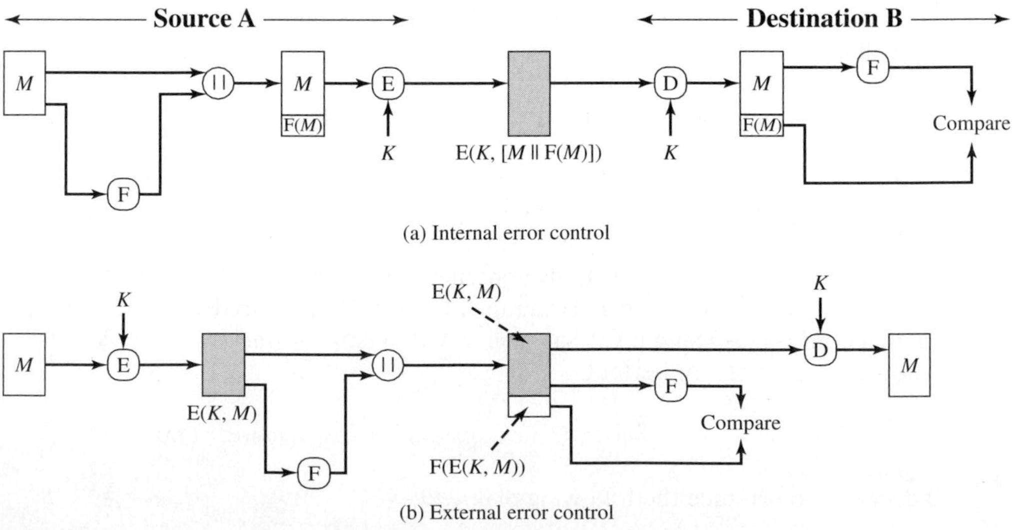

Figure 11.2 Internal and External Error Control

Note that the order in which the FCS and encryption functions are performed is critical. The sequence illustrated in Figure 11.2a is referred to in [DIFF79] as internal error control, which the authors contrast with external error control (Figure 11.2b). With internal error control, authentication is provided because an opponent would have difficulty generating ciphertext that, when decrypted, would have valid error control bits. If instead the FCS is the outer code, an opponent can construct messages with valid error-control codes. Although the opponent cannot know what the decrypted plaintext will be, he or she can still hope to create confusion and disrupt operations.

An error-control code is just one example; in fact, any sort of structuring added to the transmitted message serves to strengthen the authentication capability. Such structure is provided by the use of a communications architecture consisting of layered protocols. As an example, consider the structure of messages transmitted using the TCP/IP protocol architecture. Figure 11.3 shows the format of a TCP segment, illustrating the TCP header. Now suppose that each pair of hosts shared a unique secret key, so that all exchanges between a pair of hosts used the same key, regardless of application. Then we could simply encrypt all of the datagram except the IP header (see Figure 7.5). Again, if an opponent substituted some arbitrary bit pattern for the encrypted TCP segment, the resulting plaintext would not include a meaningful header. In this case, the header includes not only a checksum (which covers the header) but also other useful information, such as the sequence number. Because successive TCP segments on a given connection are numbered sequentially, encryption assures that an opponent does not delay, misorder, or delete any segments.

Public-Key Encryption The straightforward use of public-key encryption (Figure 11.1b) provides confidentiality but not authentication. The source (A) uses the public key PU_b of the destination (B) to encrypt M. Because only B has the corresponding private key PR_b, only B can decrypt the message. This scheme provides no authentication because any opponent could also use B's public key to encrypt a message, claiming to be A.

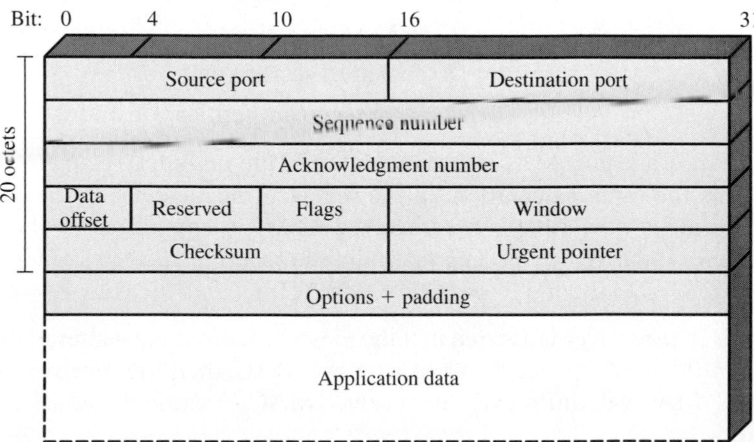

Figure 11.3 TCP Segment

To provide authentication, A uses its private key to encrypt the message, and B uses A's public key to decrypt (Figure 11.1c). This provides authentication using the same type of reasoning as in the symmetric encryption case: The message must have come from A because A is the only party that possesses PR_a and therefore the only party with the information necessary to construct ciphertext that can be decrypted with PU_a. Again, the same reasoning as before applies: There must be some internal structure to the plaintext so that the receiver can distinguish between well-formed plaintext and random bits.

Assuming there is such structure, then the scheme of Figure 11.1c does provide authentication. It also provides what is known as digital signature.[1] Only A could have constructed the ciphertext because only A possesses PR_a. Not even B, the recipient, could have constructed the ciphertext. Therefore, if B is in possession of the ciphertext, B has the means to prove that the message must have come from A. In effect, A has "signed" the message by using its private key to encrypt. Note that this scheme does not provide confidentiality. Anyone in possession of A's public key can decrypt the ciphertext.

To provide both confidentiality and authentication, A can encrypt M first using its private key, which provides the digital signature, and then using B's public key, which provides confidentiality (Figure 11.1d). The disadvantage of this approach is that the public-key algorithm, which is complex, must be exercised four times rather than two in each communication.

Table 11.1 summarizes the confidentiality and authentication implications of these various approaches to message encryption.

Message Authentication Code

An alternative authentication technique involves the use of a secret key to generate a small fixed-size block of data, known as a cryptographic checksum or MAC that is appended to the message. This technique assumes that two communicating parties, say A and B, share a common secret key K. When A has a message to send to B, it calculates the MAC as a function of the message and the key: $\text{MAC} = \text{C}(K, M)$, where

$$\begin{aligned} M &= \text{input message} \\ \text{C} &= \text{MAC function} \\ K &= \text{shared secret key} \\ \text{MAC} &= \text{message authentication code} \end{aligned}$$

The message plus MAC are transmitted to the intended recipient. The recipient performs the same calculation on the received message, using the same secret key, to generate a new MAC. The received MAC is compared to the calculated MAC (Figure 11.4a). If we assume that only the receiver and the sender know the identity of the secret key, and if the received MAC matches the calculated MAC, then

1. The receiver is assured that the message has not been altered. If an attacker alters the message but does not alter the MAC, then the receiver's calculation of the MAC will differ from the received MAC. Because the attacker is assumed not to

[1] This is not the way in which digital signatures are constructed, as we shall see, but the principle is the same.

Table 11.1 Confidentiality and Authentication Implications of Message Encryption (see Figure 11.1)

A → B: E(K, M)

- Provides confidentiality
  —Only A and B share K
- Provides a degree of authentication
  —Could come only from A
  —Has not been altered in transit
  —Requires some formatting/redundancy
- Does not provide signature
  —Receiver could forge message
  —Sender could deny message

(a) Symmetric encryption

A → B: E(PU_b, M)

- Provides confidentiality
  —Only B has PR_b to decrypt
- Provides no authentication
  —Any party could use PU_b to encrypt message and claim to be A

(b) Public-key (asymmetric) encryption: confidentiality

A → B: E(PR_a, M)

- Provides authentication and signature
  —Only A has PR_a to encrypt
  —Has not been altered in transit
  —Requires some formatting/redundancy
  —Any party can use PU_a to verify signature

(c) Public-key encryption: authentication and signature

A → B: E(PU_b, E(PR_a, M))

- Provides confidentiality because of PU_b
- Provides authentication and signature because of PR_a

(d) Public-key encryption: confidentiality, authentication, and signature

know the secret key, the attacker cannot alter the MAC to correspond to the alterations in the message.

2. The receiver is assured that the message is from the alleged sender. Because no one else knows the secret key, no one else could prepare a message with a proper MAC.
3. If the message includes a sequence number (such as is used with HDLC, X.25, and TCP), then the receiver can be assured of the proper sequence because an attacker cannot successfully alter the sequence number.

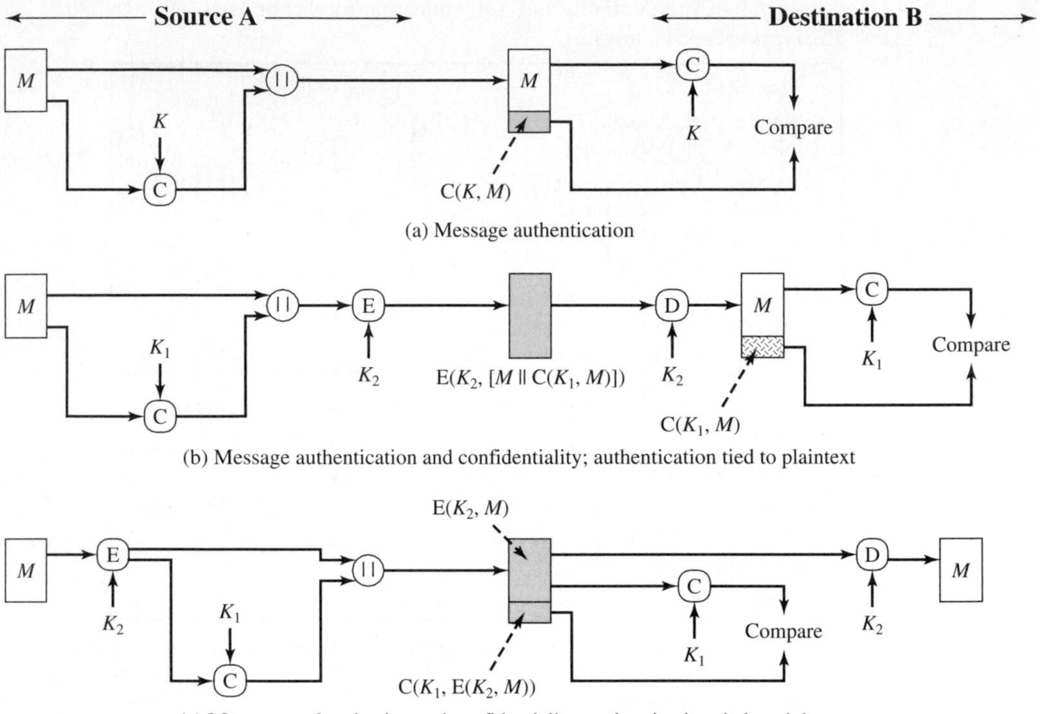

Figure 11.4 Basic Uses of Message Authentication Code (MAC)

A MAC function is similar to encryption. One difference is that the MAC algorithm need not be reversible, as it must for decryption. In general, the MAC function is a many-to-one function. The domain of the function consists of messages of some arbitrary length, whereas the range consists of all possible MACs and all possible keys. If an n-bit MAC is used, then there are 2^n possible MACs, whereas there are N possible messages with $N \gg 2^n$. Furthermore, with a k-bit key, there are 2^k possible keys.

For example, suppose that we are using 100-bit messages and a 10-bit MAC. Then, there are a total of 2^{100} different messages but only 2^{10} different MACs. So, on average, each MAC value is generated by a total of $2^{100}/2^{10} = 2^{90}$ different messages. If a 5-bit key is used, then there are $2^5 = 32$ different mappings from the set of messages to the set of MAC values.

It turns out that because of the mathematical properties of the authentication function, it is less vulnerable to being broken than encryption.

The process depicted in Figure 11.4a provides authentication but not confidentiality, because the message as a whole is transmitted in the clear. Confidentiality can be provided by performing message encryption either after (Figure 11.4b) or before (Figure 11.4c) the MAC algorithm. In both these cases, two separate keys are needed, each of which is shared by the sender and the receiver. In the first case, the MAC is calculated with the message as input and is then concatenated to the message. The entire block is then encrypted. In the second case, the message is encrypted first.

Then the MAC is calculated using the resulting ciphertext and is concatenated to the ciphertext to form the transmitted block. Typically, it is preferable to tie the authentication directly to the plaintext, so the method of Figure 11.4b is used.

Because symmetric encryption will provide authentication and because it is widely used with readily available products, why not simply use this instead of a separate message authentication code? [DAVI89] suggests three situations in which a message authentication code is used:

1. There are a number of applications in which the same message is broadcast to a number of destinations. Examples are notification to users that the network is now unavailable or an alarm signal in a military control center. It is cheaper and more reliable to have only one destination responsible for monitoring authenticity. Thus, the message must be broadcast in plaintext with an associated message authentication code. The responsible system has the secret key and performs authentication. If a violation occurs, the other destination systems are alerted by a general alarm.
2. Another possible scenario is an exchange in which one side has a heavy load and cannot afford the time to decrypt all incoming messages. Authentication is carried out on a selective basis, messages being chosen at random for checking.
3. Authentication of a computer program in plaintext is an attractive service. The computer program can be executed without having to decrypt it every time, which would be wasteful of processor resources. However, if a message authentication code were attached to the program, it could be checked whenever assurance was required of the integrity of the program.

Three other rationales may be added, as follows:

4. For some applications, it may not be of concern to keep messages secret, but it is important to authenticate messages. An example is the Simple Network Management Protocol Version 3 (SNMPv3), which separates the functions of confidentiality and authentication. For this application, it is usually important for a managed system to authenticate incoming SNMP messages, particularly if the message contains a command to change parameters at the managed system. On the other hand, it may not be necessary to conceal the SNMP traffic.
5. Separation of authentication and confidentiality functions affords architectural flexibility. For example, it may be desired to perform authentication at the application level but to provide confidentiality at a lower level, such as the transport layer.
6. A user may wish to prolong the period of protection beyond the time of reception and yet allow processing of message contents. With message encryption, the protection is lost when the message is decrypted, so the message is protected against fraudulent modifications only in transit but not within the target system.

Finally, note that the MAC does not provide a digital signature because both sender and receiver share the same key.

Table 11.2 summarizes the confidentiality and authentication implications of the approaches illustrated in Figure 11.4.

Table 11.2 Basic Uses of Message Authentication Code C (see Figure 11.4)

$A \rightarrow B: M \| C(K, M)$
• Provides authentication —Only A and B share K

(a) Message authentication

$A \rightarrow B: E(K_2, [M \| C(K, M)])$
• Provides authentication —Only A and B share K_1
• Provides confidentiality —Only A and B share K_2

(b) Message authentication and confidentiality: authentication tied to plaintext

$A \rightarrow B: E(K_2, M) \| C(K_1, E(K_2, M))$
• Provides authentication —Using K_1
• Provides confidentiality —Using K_2

(c) Message authentication and confidentiality: authentication tied to ciphertext

Hash Function

A variation on the message authentication code is the one-way hash function. As with the message authentication code, a hash function accepts a variable-size message M as input and produces a fixed-size output, referred to as a **hash code** H(M). Unlike a MAC, a hash code does not use a key but is a function only of the input message. The hash code is also referred to as a **message digest** or **hash value**. The hash code is a function of all the bits of the message and provides an error-detection capability: A change to any bit or bits in the message results in a change to the hash code.

Figure 11.5 illustrates a variety of ways in which a hash code can be used to provide message authentication, as follows:

a. The message plus concatenated hash code is encrypted using symmetric encryption. This is identical in structure to the internal error control strategy shown in Figure 11.2a. The same line of reasoning applies: Because only A and B share the secret key, the message must have come from A and has not been altered. The hash code provides the structure or redundancy required to achieve authentication. Because encryption is applied to the entire message plus hash code, confidentiality is also provided.

b. Only the hash code is encrypted, using symmetric encryption. This reduces the processing burden for those applications that do not require confidentiality.

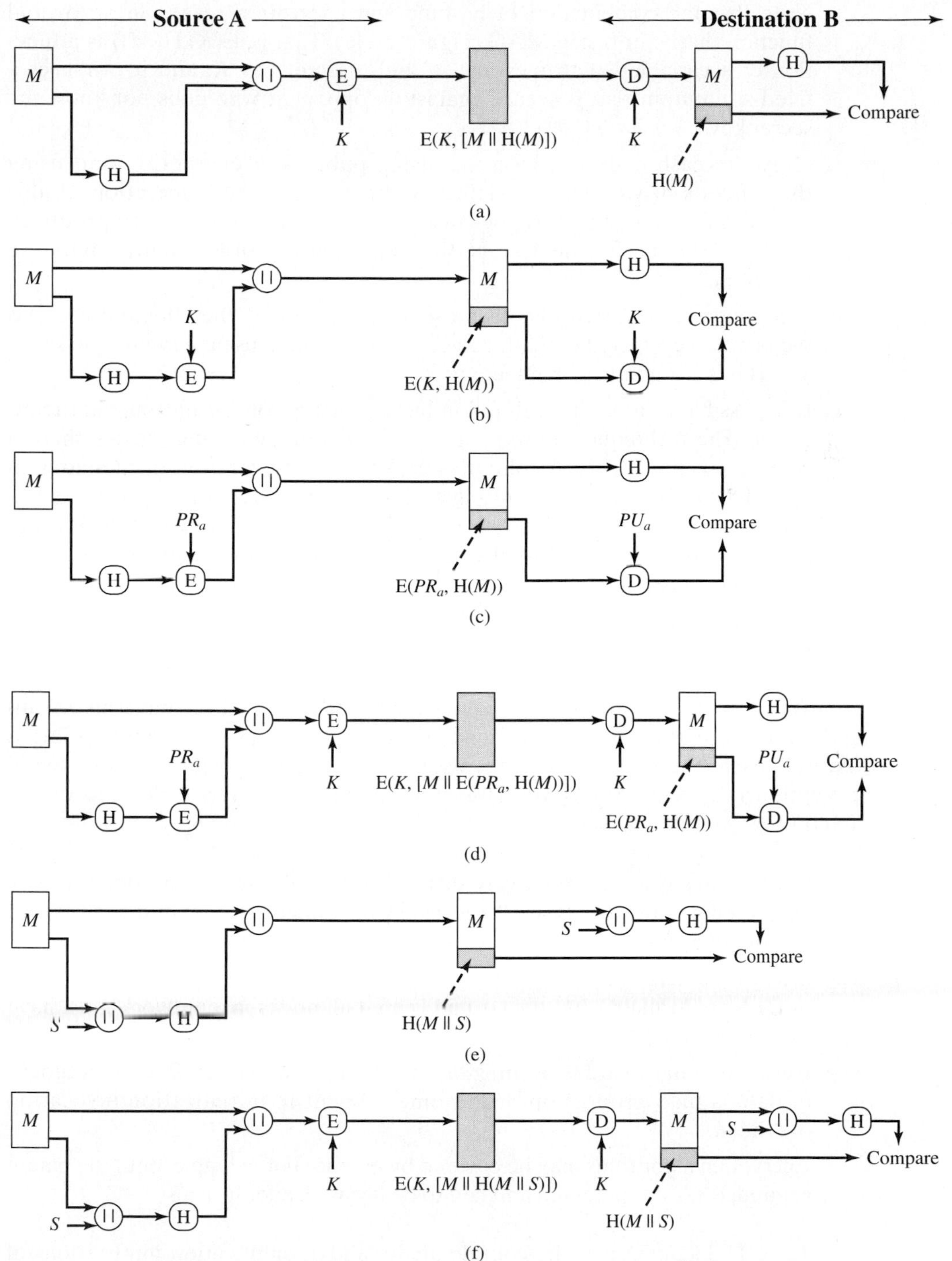

Figure 11.5 Basic Uses of Hash Function

Note that the combination of hashing and encryption results in an overall function that is, in fact, a MAC (Figure 11.4a). That is, E(K, H(M)) is a function of a variable-length message M and a secret key K, and it produces a fixed-size output that is secure against an opponent who does not know the secret key.

c. Only the hash code is encrypted, using public-key encryption and using the sender's private key. As with (b), this provides authentication. It also provides a digital signature, because only the sender could have produced the encrypted hash code. In fact, this is the essence of the digital signature technique.

d. If confidentiality as well as a digital signature is desired, then the message plus the private-key-encrypted hash code can be encrypted using a symmetric secret key. This is a common technique.

e. It is possible to use a hash function but no encryption for message authentication. The technique assumes that the two communicating parties share a common secret value S. A computes the hash value over the concatenation of M and S and appends the resulting hash value to M. Because B possesses S, it can recompute the hash value to verify. Because the secret value itself is not sent, an opponent cannot modify an intercepted message and cannot generate a false message.

f. Confidentiality can be added to the approach of (e) by encrypting the entire message plus the hash code.

When confidentiality is not required, methods (b) and (c) have an advantage over those that encrypt the entire message in that less computation is required. Nevertheless, there has been growing interest in techniques that avoid encryption (Figure 11.5e). Several reasons for this interest are pointed out in [TSUD92]:

- Encryption software is relatively slow. Even though the amount of data to be encrypted per message is small, there may be a steady stream of messages into and out of a system.
- Encryption hardware costs are not negligible. Low-cost chip implementations of DES are available, but the cost adds up if all nodes in a network must have this capability.
- Encryption hardware is optimized toward large data sizes. For small blocks of data, a high proportion of the time is spent in initialization/invocation overhead.
- Encryption algorithms may be covered by patents. For example, until the patent expired, RSA was patented and had to be licensed, adding a cost.

Table 11.3 summarizes the confidentiality and authentication implications of the approaches illustrated in Figure 11.5. We next examine MACs and hash codes in more detail.

Table 11.3 Basic Uses of Hash Function H (see Figure 11.5)

A → B: E(K, [M‖H(M)]) • Provides confidentiality —Only A and B share K • Provides authentication —H(M) is cryptographically protected	A → B: E(K, [M‖E(PR_a, H(M))]) • Provides authentication and digital signature • Provides confidentiality —Only A and B share K
(a) Encrypt message plus hash code	(d) Encrypt result of (c)—shared secret key
A → B: M‖E(K, H(M)) • Provides authentication —H(M) is cryptographically protected	A → B: M‖H(M‖S) • Provides authentication —Only A and B share S
(b) Encrypt hash code—shared secret key	(e) Compute hash code of message plus secret value
A → B: M‖E(PR_a, H(M)) • Provides authentication and digital signature —H(M) is cryptographically protected —Only A could create E(PR_a, H(M))	A → B: E(K, [M‖H(M‖S]) • Provides authentication —Only A and B share S • Provides confidentiality —Only A and B share K
(c) Encrypt hash code—sender's private *key*	(f) Encrypt result of (e)

11.3 MESSAGE AUTHENTICATION CODES

A MAC, also known as a cryptographic checksum, is generated by a function C of the form

$$\text{MAC} = \text{C}(K, M)$$

where M is a variable-length message, K is a secret key shared only by sender and receiver, and C(K, M) is the fixed-length authenticator. The MAC is appended to the message at the source at a time when the message is assumed or known to be correct. The receiver authenticates that message by recomputing the MAC.

In this section, we review the requirements for the function C and then examine a specific example. Other examples are discussed in Chapter 12.

Requirements for MACs

When an entire message is encrypted for confidentiality, using either symmetric or asymmetric encryption, the security of the scheme generally depends on the bit length of the key. Barring some weakness in the algorithm, the opponent must resort to a brute-force attack using all possible keys. On average, such an attack will require $2^{(k-1)}$ attempts for a k-bit key. In particular, for a ciphertext-only attack, the opponent, given ciphertext C, would perform $P_i = \text{D}(K_i, C)$ for all possible key values K_i until a P_i was produced that matched the form of acceptable plaintext.

In the case of a MAC, the considerations are entirely different. In general, the MAC function is a many-to-one function, due to the many-to-one nature of the function. Using brute-force methods, how would an opponent attempt to discover a key? If confidentiality is not employed, the opponent has access to plaintext messages and their associated MACs. Suppose $k > n$; that is, suppose that the key size is greater than the MAC size. Then, given a known M_1 and MAC_1, with $MAC_1 = \mathrm{C}(K, M_1)$, the cryptanalyst can perform $MAC_i = \mathrm{C}(K_i, M_1)$ for all possible key values K_i. At least one key is guaranteed to produce a match of $MAC_i = MAC_1$. Note that a total of 2^k MACs will be produced, but there are only $2^n < 2^k$ different MAC values. Thus, a number of keys will produce the correct MAC and the opponent has no way of knowing which is the correct key. On average, a total of $2^k/2^n = 2^{(k-n)}$ keys will produce a match. Thus, the opponent must iterate the attack:

- **Round 1**

  Given: M_1, $MAC_1 = \mathrm{C}(K, M_1)$

  Compute $MAC_i = \mathrm{C}(K_i, M_1)$ for all 2^k keys

  Number of matches $\approx 2^{(k-n)}$

- **Round 2**

  Given: M_2, $MAC_2 = \mathrm{C}(K, M_2)$

  Compute $MAC_i = \mathrm{C}(K_i, M_2)$ for the $2^{(k-n)}$ keys resulting from Round 1

  Number of matches $\approx 2^{(k-2\times n)}$

and so on. On average, α rounds will be needed if $k = \alpha \times n$. For example, if an 80-bit key is used and the MAC is 32 bits long, then the first round will produce about 2^{48} possible keys. The second round will narrow the possible keys to about 2^{16} possibilities. The third round should produce only a single key, which must be the one used by the sender.

If the key length is less than or equal to the MAC length, then it is likely that a first round will produce a single match. It is possible that more than one key will produce such a match, in which case the opponent would need to perform the same test on a new (message, MAC) pair.

Thus, a brute-force attempt to discover the authentication key is no less effort and may be more effort than that required to discover a decryption key of the same length. However, other attacks that do not require the discovery of the key are possible.

Consider the following MAC algorithm. Let $M = (X_1 \| X_2 \| \ldots \| X_m)$ be a message that is treated as a concatenation of 64-bit blocks X_i. Then define

$$\Delta(M) = X_1 \oplus X_2 \oplus \cdots \oplus X_m$$
$$\mathrm{C}(K, M) = \mathrm{E}(K, \Delta(M))$$

where $\oplus$ is the exclusive-OR (XOR) operation and the encryption algorithm is DES in electronic codebook mode. Thus, the key length is 56 bits and the MAC length is 64 bits. If an opponent observes $\{M \| \mathrm{C}(K, M)\}$, a brute-force attempt to determine K will require at least 2^{56} encryptions. But the opponent can attack the system by replacing X_1 through X_{m-1} with any desired values Y_1 through Y_{m-1} and replacing X_m with Y_m, where Y_m is calculated as follows:

$$Y_m = Y_1 \oplus Y_2 \oplus \ldots \oplus Y_{m-1} \oplus \Delta(M)$$

The opponent can now concatenate the new message, which consists of Y_1 through Y_m, with the original MAC to form a message that will be accepted as authentic by the receiver. With this tactic, any message of length $64 \times (m - 1)$ bits can be fraudulently inserted.

Thus, in assessing the security of a MAC function, we need to consider the types of attacks that may be mounted against it. With that in mind, let us state the requirements for the function. Assume that an opponent knows the MAC function C but does not know K. Then the MAC function should satisfy the following requirements:

1. If an opponent observes M and $\mathrm{C}(K, M)$, it should be computationally infeasible for the opponent to construct a message M' such that $\mathrm{C}(K, M') = \mathrm{C}(K, M)$.
2. $\mathrm{C}(K, M)$ should be uniformly distributed in the sense that for randomly chosen messages, M and M', the probability that $\mathrm{C}(K, M) = \mathrm{C}(K, M')$ is 2^{-n}, where n is the number of bits in the MAC.
3. Let M' be equal to some known transformation on M. That is, $M' = \mathrm{f}(M)$. For example, f may involve inverting one or more specific bits. In that case, $\Pr[\mathrm{C}(K, M) = \mathrm{C}(K, M')] = 2^{-n}$.

The first requirement speaks to the earlier example, in which an opponent is able to construct a new message to match a given MAC, even though the opponent does not know and does not learn the key. The second requirement deals with the need to thwart a brute-force attack based on chosen plaintext. That is, if we assume that the opponent does not know K but does have access to the MAC function and can present messages for MAC generation, then the opponent could try various messages until finding one that matches a given MAC. If the MAC function exhibits uniform distribution, then a brute-force method would require, on average, $2^{(n-1)}$ attempts before finding a message that fits a given MAC.

The final requirement dictates that the authentication algorithm should not be weaker with respect to certain parts or bits of the message than others. If this were not the case, then an opponent who had M and $\mathrm{C}(K, M)$ could attempt variations on M at the known "weak spots" with a likelihood of early success at producing a new message that matched the old MAC.

Message Authentication Code Based on DES

The Data Authentication Algorithm, based on DES, has been one of the most widely used MACs for a number of years. The algorithm is both a FIPS publication (FIPS PUB 113) and an ANSI standard (X9.17). However, as we discuss in Chapter 12, security weaknesses in this algorithm have been discovered and it is being replaced by newer and stronger algorithms.

The algorithm can be defined as using the cipher block chaining (CBC) mode of operation of DES (Figure 6.4) with an initialization vector of zero. The data (e.g., message, record, file, or program) to be authenticated are grouped into contiguous 64-bit blocks: $D_1, D_2, \ldots, D_N$. If necessary, the final block is padded on the right with zeroes

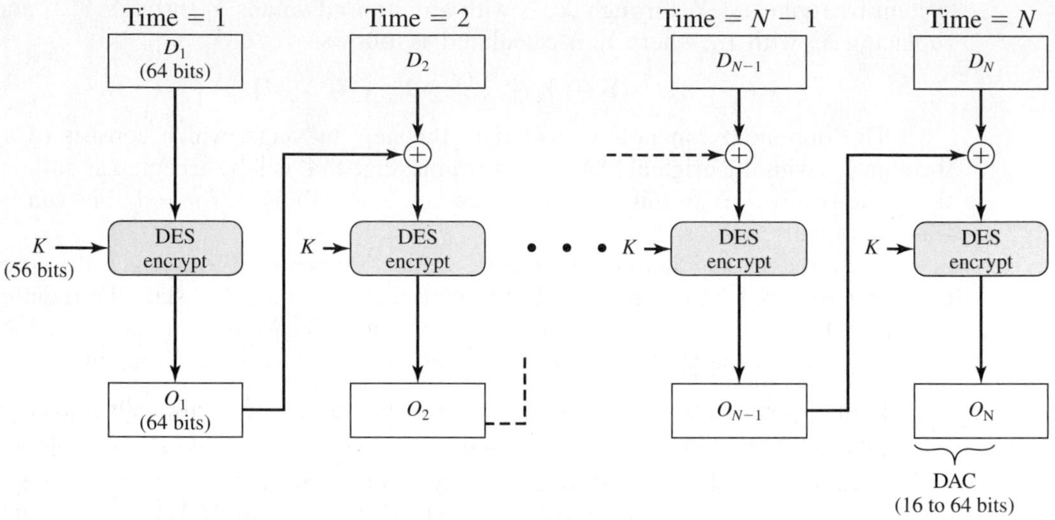

Figure 11.6 Data Authentication Algorithm (FIPS PUB 113)

to form a full 64-bit block. Using the DES encryption algorithm, E, and a secret key, K, a data authentication code (DAC) is calculated as follows (Figure 11.6):

$$
\begin{aligned}
O_1 &= \mathrm{E}(K, D_1) \\
O_2 &= \mathrm{E}(K, [D_2 \oplus O_1]) \\
O_3 &= \mathrm{E}(K, [D_3 \oplus O_2]) \\
&\cdot \\
&\cdot \\
&\cdot \\
O_N &= \mathrm{E}(K, [D_N \oplus O_{N-1}])
\end{aligned}
$$

The DAC consists of either the entire block O_N or the leftmost M bits of the block, with $16 \leq M \leq 64$.

11.4 HASH FUNCTIONS

A hash value h is generated by a function H of the form

$$h = \mathrm{H}(M)$$

where M is a variable-length message and $\mathrm{H}(M)$ is the fixed-length hash value. The hash value is appended to the message at the source at a time when the message is assumed or known to be correct. The receiver authenticates that message by recomputing the hash value. Because the hash function itself is not considered to be secret, some means is required to protect the hash value (Figure 11.5).

We begin by examining the requirements for a hash function to be used for message authentication. Because hash functions are typically quite complex, it is useful to examine some very simple hash functions to get a feel for the issues involved. We then look at several approaches to hash function design.

Requirements for a Hash Function

The purpose of a hash function is to produce a "fingerprint" of a file, message, or other block of data. To be useful for message authentication, a hash function H must have the following properties (adapted from a list in [NECH92]):

1. H can be applied to a block of data of any size.
2. H produces a fixed-length output.
3. $H(x)$ is relatively easy to compute for any given x, making both hardware and software implementations practical.
4. For any given value h, it is computationally infeasible to find x such that $H(x) = h$. This is sometimes referred to in the literature as the **one-way property**.
5. For any given block x, it is computationally infeasible to find $y \neq x$ such that $H(y) = H(x)$. This is sometimes referred to as **weak collision resistance**.
6. It is computationally infeasible to find any pair (x, y) such that $H(x) = H(y)$. This is sometimes referred to as **strong collision resistance**.[2]

The first three properties are requirements for the practical application of a hash function to message authentication.

The fourth property, the one-way property, states that it is easy to generate a code given a message but virtually impossible to generate a message given a code. This property is important if the authentication technique involves the use of a secret value (Figure 11.5e). The secret value itself is not sent; however, if the hash function is not one way, an attacker can easily discover the secret value: If the attacker can observe or intercept a transmission, the attacker obtains the message M and the hash code $C = H(S_{AB} \| M)$. The attacker then inverts the hash function to obtain $S_{AB} \| M = H^{-1}(C)$. Because the attacker now has both M and $S_{AB} \| M$, it is a trivial matter to recover S_{AB}.

The fifth property guarantees that an alternative message hashing to the same value as a given message cannot be found. This prevents forgery when an encrypted hash code is used (Figures 11.5b and c). For these cases, the opponent can read the message and therefore generate its hash code. However, because the opponent does not have the secret key, the opponent should not be able to alter the message without detection. If this property were not true, an attacker would be capable of the following sequence: First, observe or intercept a message plus its encrypted hash code; second, generate an unencrypted hash code from the message; third, generate an alternate message with the same hash code.

The sixth property refers to how resistant the hash function is to a type of attack known as the birthday attack, which we examine shortly.

---

[2]Unfortunately, these terms are not used consistently. Alternate terms used in the literature include *one-way hash function*: (properties 4 and 5); *collision-resistant hash function*: (properties 4, 5, and 6); *weak one-way hash function*: (properties 4 and 5); *strong one-way hash function*: (properties 4, 5, and 6). The reader must take care in reading the literature to determine the meaning of the particular terms used.

Simple Hash Functions

All hash functions operate using the following general principles. The input (message, file, etc.) is viewed as a sequence of n-bit blocks. The input is processed one block at a time in an iterative fashion to produce an n-bit hash function.

One of the simplest hash functions is the bit-by-bit exclusive-OR (XOR) of every block. This can be expressed as follows:

$$C_i = b_{i1} \oplus b_{i2} \oplus \cdots \oplus b_{im}$$

where

$$\begin{aligned} C_i &= i\text{th bit of the hash code, } 1 \le i \le \text{n} \\ m &= \text{number of } n\text{-bit blocks in the input} \\ b_{ij} &= i\text{th bit in } j\text{th block} \\ \oplus &= \text{XOR operation} \end{aligned}$$

This operation produces a simple parity for each bit position and is known as a longitudinal redundancy check. It is reasonably effective for random data as a data integrity check. Each n-bit hash value is equally likely. Thus, the probability that a data error will result in an unchanged hash value is 2^{-n}. With more predictably formatted data, the function is less effective. For example, in most normal text files, the high-order bit of each octet is always zero. So if a 128-bit hash value is used, instead of an effectiveness of 2^{-128}, the hash function on this type of data has an effectiveness of 2^{-112}.

A simple way to improve matters is to perform a one-bit circular shift, or rotation, on the hash value after each block is processed. The procedure can be summarized as follows:

1. Initially set the n-bit hash value to zero.
2. Process each successive n-bit block of data as follows:
   a. Rotate the current hash value to the left by one bit.
   b. XOR the block into the hash value.

This has the effect of "randomizing" the input more completely and overcoming any regularities that appear in the input. Figure 11.7 illustrates these two types of hash functions for 16-bit hash values.

Although the second procedure provides a good measure of data integrity, it is virtually useless for data security when an encrypted hash code is used with a plaintext message, as in Figures 11.5b and c. Given a message, it is an easy matter to produce a new message that yields that hash code: Simply prepare the desired alternate message and then append an n-bit block that forces the new message plus block to yield the desired hash code.

Although a simple XOR or rotated XOR (RXOR) is insufficient if only the hash code is encrypted, you may still feel that such a simple function could be useful when the message as well as the hash code are encrypted (Figure 11.5a). But you must be careful. A technique originally proposed by the National Bureau of Standards used the simple XOR applied to 64-bit blocks of the message and then an encryption of the

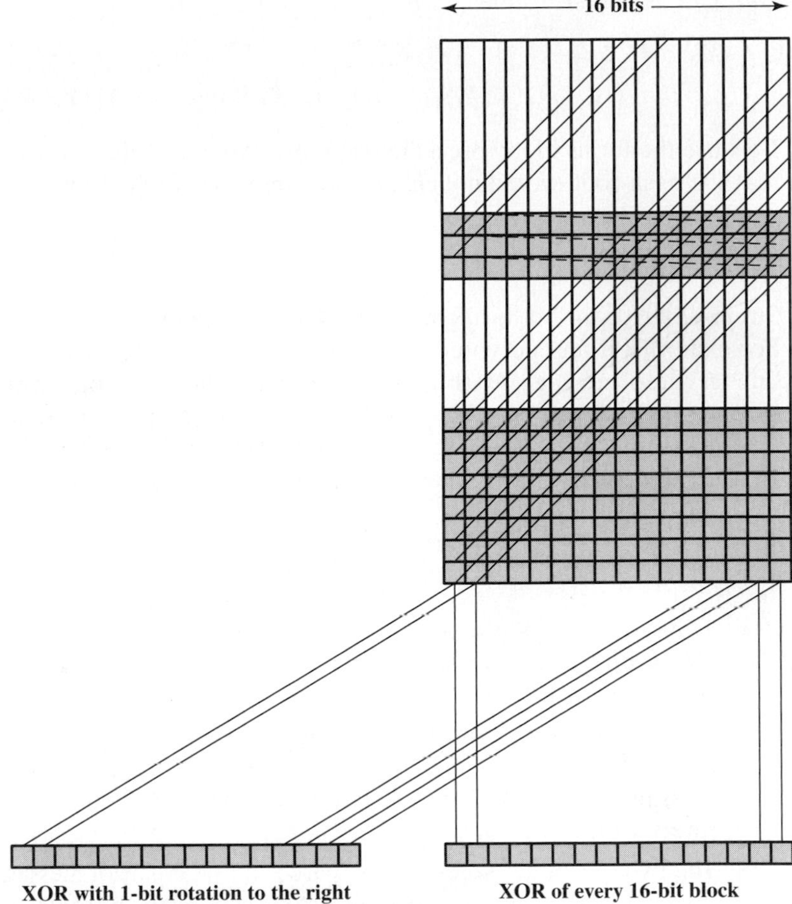

Figure 11.7 Two Simple Hash Functions

entire message that used the cipher block chaining (CBC) mode. We can define the scheme as follows: Given a message consisting of a sequence of 64-bit blocks $X_1, X_2, \ldots, X_N$, define the hash code C as the block-by-block XOR of all blocks and append the hash code as the final block:

$$C = X_{N+1} = X_1 \oplus X_2 \oplus \ldots \oplus X_N$$

Next, encrypt the entire message plus hash code, using CBC mode to produce the encrypted message $Y_1, Y_2, \ldots, Y_{N+1}$. [JUEN85] points out several ways in which the ciphertext of this message can be manipulated in such a way that it is not detectable by the hash code. For example, by the definition of CBC (Figure 6.4), we have

$$\begin{aligned} X_1 &= IV \oplus \mathrm{D}(K, Y_1) \\ X_i &= Y_{i-1} \oplus \mathrm{D}(K, Y_i) \\ X_{N+1} &= Y_N \oplus \mathrm{D}(K, Y_{N+1}) \end{aligned}$$

But X_{N+1} is the hash code:

$$X_{N+1} = X_1 \oplus X_2 \oplus \cdots \oplus X_N$$
$$= [IV \oplus \mathrm{D}(K, Y_1)] \oplus [Y_1 \oplus \mathrm{D}(K, Y_2)] \oplus \cdots \oplus [Y_{N-1} \oplus \mathrm{D}(K, Y_N)]$$

Because the terms in the preceding equation can be XORed in any order, it follows that the hash code would not change if the ciphertext blocks were permuted.

Birthday Attacks

Suppose that a 64-bit hash code is used. One might think that this is quite secure. For example, if an encrypted hash code C is transmitted with the corresponding unencrypted message M (Figure 11.5b or c), then an opponent would need to find an M' such that $\mathrm{H}(M') = \mathrm{H}(M)$ to substitute another message and fool the receiver. On average, the opponent would have to try about 2^{63} messages to find one that matches the hash code of the intercepted message [see Appendix 11A, Equation (11.1)].

However, a different sort of attack is possible, based on the birthday paradox (Appendix 11A). Yuval proposed the following strategy [YUVA79]:

1. The source, A, is prepared to "sign" a message by appending the appropriate m-bit hash code and encrypting that hash code with A's private key (Figure 11.5c).
2. The opponent generates $2^{m/2}$ variations on the message, all of which convey essentially the same meaning. The opponent prepares an equal number of messages, all of which are variations on the fraudulent message to be substituted for the real one.
3. The two sets of messages are compared to find a pair of messages that produces the same hash code. The probability of success, by the birthday paradox, is greater than 0.5. If no match is found, additional valid and fraudulent messages are generated until a match is made.
4. The opponent offers the valid variation to A for signature. This signature can then be attached to the fraudulent variation for transmission to the intended recipient. Because the two variations have the same hash code, they will produce the same signature; the opponent is assured of success even though the encryption key is not known.

Thus, if a 64-bit hash code is used, the level of effort required is only on the order of 2^{32} [see Appendix 11A, Equation (11.7)].

The generation of many variations that convey the same meaning is not difficult. For example, the opponent could insert a number of "space-space-backspace" character pairs between words throughout the document. Variations could then be generated by substituting "space-backspace-space" in selected instances. Alternatively, the opponent could simply reword the message but retain the meaning. Figure 11.8 [DAVI89] provides an example.

The conclusion to be drawn from this is that the length of the hash code should be substantial. We discuss this further in Section 11.5.

Dear Anthony,

{This letter is / I am writing} to introduce {you to / to you} {Mr. / --} Alfred {P. / --}

Barton, the {new / newly appointed} {chief / senior} jewellery buyer for {our / the}

Northern {European / Europe} {area / division}. He {will take / has taken} over {the / --}

responsibility for {all / the whole of} our interests in {watches and jewellery / jewellery and watches}

in the {area / region}. Please {afford / give} him {every / all the} help he {may need / needs}

to {seek out / find} the most {modern / up to date} lines for the {top / high} end of the

market. He is {empowered / authorized} to receive on our behalf {samples / specimens} of the

{latest / newest} {watch and jewellery / jewellery and watch} products, {up / subject} to a {limit / maximum}

of ten thousand dollars. He will {carry / hold} a signed copy of this {letter / document}

as proof of identity. An order with his signature, which is {appended / attached}

{authorizes / allows} you to charge the cost to this company at the {above / head office}

address. We {fully / --} expect that our {level / volume} of orders will increase in

the {following / next} year and {trust / hope} that the new appointment will {be / prove}

{advantageous / an advantage} to both our companies.

Figure 11.8 A Letter in 2^{37} Variations [DAVI89]

Block Chaining Techniques

A number of proposals have been made for hash functions based on using a cipher block chaining technique, but without the secret key. One of the first such proposals was that of Rabin [RABI78]. Divide a message M into fixed-size blocks $M_1, M_2, \ldots, M_N$ and use a symmetric encryption system such as DES to compute the hash code G as follows:

$$H_0 = \text{initial value}$$
$$H_i = \text{E}(M_i, H_{i-1})$$
$$G = H_N$$

This is similar to the CBC technique, but in this case there is no secret key. As with any hash code, this scheme is subject to the birthday attack, and if the encryption algorithm is DES and only a 64-bit hash code is produced, then the system is vulnerable.

Furthermore, another version of the birthday attack can be used even if the opponent has access to only one message and its valid signature and cannot obtain multiple signings. Here is the scenario; we assume that the opponent intercepts a message with a signature in the form of an encrypted hash code and that the unencrypted hash code is m bits long:

1. Use the algorithm defined at the beginning of this subsection to calculate the unencrypted hash code G.
2. Construct any desired message in the form $Q_1, Q_2, \ldots, Q_{N-2}$.
3. Compute $H_i = \mathrm{E}(Q_i, H_{i-1})$ for $1 \leq i \leq (N - 2)$.
4. Generate $2^{m/2}$ random blocks; for each block X, compute $\mathrm{E}(X, H_{N-2})$. Generate an additional $2^{m/2}$ random blocks; for each block Y, compute D(Y, G), where D is the decryption function corresponding to E.
5. Based on the birthday paradox, with high probability there will be an X and Y such that $\mathrm{E}(X, H_{N-2}) = \mathrm{D}(Y, G)$.
6. Form the message $Q_1, Q_2, \ldots, Q_{N-2}, X, Y$. This message has the hash code G and therefore can be used with the intercepted encrypted signature.

This form of attack is known as a **meet-in-the-middle attack**. A number of researchers have proposed refinements intended to strengthen the basic block chaining approach. For example, Davies and Price [DAVI89] describe the following variation:

$$H_i = \mathrm{E}(M_i, H_{i-1}) \oplus H_{i-1}$$

Another variation, proposed in [MEYE88],

$$H_i = \mathrm{E}(H_{i-1}, M_i) \oplus M_i$$

However, both of these schemes have been shown to be vulnerable to a variety of attacks [MIYA90]. More generally, it can be shown that some form of birthday attack will succeed against any hash scheme involving the use of cipher block chaining without a secret key provided that either the resulting hash code is small enough (e.g., 64 bits or less) or that a larger hash code can be decomposed into independent subcodes [JUEN87].

Thus, attention has been directed at finding other approaches to hashing. Many of these have also been shown to have weaknesses [MITC92]. We examine two strong hash functions in Chapter 12.

11.5 SECURITY OF HASH FUNCTIONS AND MACS

Just as with symmetric and public-key encryption, we can group attacks on hash functions and MACs into two categories: brute-force attacks and cryptanalysis.

Brute-Force Attacks

The nature of brute-force attacks differs somewhat for hash functions and MACs.

Hash Functions The strength of a hash function against brute-force attacks depends solely on the length of the hash code produced by the algorithm. Recall from our discussion of hash functions that there are three desirable properties:

- **One-way:** For any given code h, it is computationally infeasible to find x such that $H(x) = h$.
- **Weak collision resistance:** For any given block x, it is computationally infeasible to find $y \neq x$ with $H(y) = H(x)$.
- **Strong collision resistance:** It is computationally infeasible to find any pair (x, y) such that $H(x) = H(y)$.

For a hash code of length n, the level of effort required, as we have seen is proportional to the following:

One way	2^n
Weak collision resistance	2^n
Strong collision resistance	$2^{n/2}$

If strong collision resistance is required (and this is desirable for a general-purpose secure hash code), then the value $2^{n/2}$ determines the strength of the hash code against brute-force attacks. Oorschot and Wiener [VANO94] presented a design for a $10 million collision search machine for MD5, which has a 128-bit hash length, that could find a collision in 24 days. Thus a 128-bit code may be viewed as inadequate. The next step up, if a hash code is treated as a sequence of 32 bits, is a 160-bit hash length. With a hash length of 160 bits, the same search machine would require over four thousand years to find a collision. However, even 160 bits is now considered weak. We return to this topic in Chapter 12.

Message Authentication Codes A brute-force attack on a MAC is a more difficult undertaking because it requires known message-MAC pairs. Let us see why this is so. To attack a hash code, we can proceed in the following way. Given a fixed message x with n-bit hash code $h = H(x)$, a brute-force method of finding a collision is to pick a random bit string y and check if $H(y) = H(x)$. The attacker can do this repeatedly off line. Whether an off-line attack can be used on a MAC algorithm depends on the relative size of the key and the MAC.

To proceed, we need to state the desired security property of a MAC algorithm, which can be expressed as follows:

- **Computation resistance:** Given one or more text-MAC pairs $[x_i, C(K, x_i)]$, it is computationally infeasible to compute any text-MAC pair $[x, C(K, x)]$ for any new input $x \neq x_i$.

In other words, the attacker would like to come up with the valid MAC code for a given message x. There are two lines of attack possible: Attack the key space and attack the MAC value. We examine each of these in turn.

If an attacker can determine the MAC key, then it is possible to generate a valid MAC value for any input x. Suppose the key size is k bits and that the attacker has one known text-MAC pair. Then the attacker can compute the n-bit MAC on the known text for all possible keys. At least one key is guaranteed to produce the correct MAC, namely, the valid key that was initially used to produce the known text-MAC pair. This phase of the attack takes a level of effort proportional to 2^k (that is, one operation for each of the 2^k possible key values). However, as was described earlier, because the MAC is a many-to-one mapping, there may be other keys that produce the correct value. Thus, if more than one key is found to produce the correct value, additional text-MAC pairs must be tested. It can be shown that the level of effort drops off rapidly with each additional text-MAC pair and that the overall level of effort is roughly 2^k [MENE97].

An attacker can also work on the MAC value without attempting to recover the key. Here, the objective is to generate a valid MAC value for a given message or to find a message that matches a given MAC value. In either case, the level of effort is comparable to that for attacking the one-way or weak collision resistant property of a hash code, or 2^n. In the case of the MAC, the attack cannot be conducted off line without further input; the attacker will require chosen text-MAC pairs or knowledge of the key.

To summarize, the level of effort for brute-force attack on a MAC algorithm can be expressed as $\min(2^k, 2^n)$. The assessment of strength is similar to that for symmetric encryption algorithms. It would appear reasonable to require that the key length and MAC length satisfy a relationship such as $\min(k, n) \geq N$, where N is perhaps in the range of 128 bits.

Cryptanalysis

As with encryption algorithms, cryptanalytic attacks on hash functions and MAC algorithms seek to exploit some property of the algorithm to perform some attack other than an exhaustive search. The way to measure the resistance of a hash or MAC algorithm to cryptanalysis is to compare its strength to the effort required for a brute-force attack. That is, an ideal hash or MAC algorithm will require a cryptanalytic effort greater than or equal to the brute-force effort.

Hash Functions In recent years, there has been considerable effort, and some successes, in developing cryptanalytic attacks on hash functions. To understand these, we need to look at the overall structure of a typical secure hash function, indicated in Figure 11.9. This structure, referred to as an iterated hash function, was proposed by Merkle [MERK79, MERK89] and is the structure of most hash functions in use today, including SHA and Whirlpool, which are discussed in Chapter 12. The hash function takes an input message and partitions it into L fixed-sized blocks of b bits each. If necessary, the final block is padded to b bits. The final block also includes the value of the total length of the input to the hash function. The inclusion of the length makes the job of the opponent more difficult. Either the opponent must find two messages of equal length that hash to the same value or two messages of differing lengths that, together with their length values, hash to the same value.

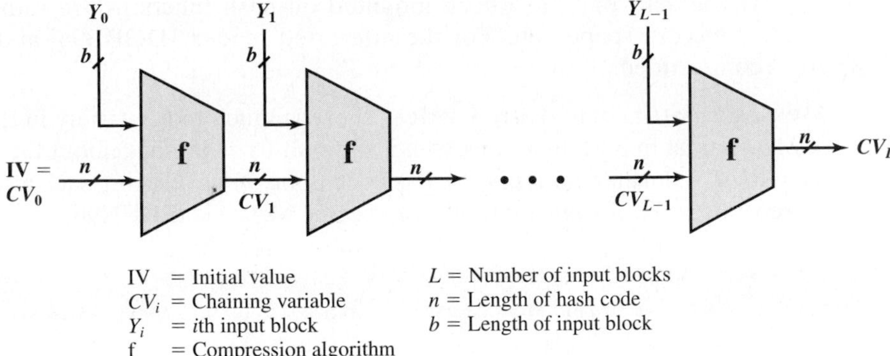

IV = Initial value
CV_i = Chaining variable
Y_i = ith input block
f = Compression algorithm
L = Number of input blocks
n = Length of hash code
b = Length of input block

Figure 11.9 General Structure of Secure Hash Code

The hash algorithm involves repeated use of a **compression function**, f, that takes two inputs (an n-bit input from the previous step, called the *chaining variable*, and a b-bit block) and produces an n-bit output. At the start of hashing, the chaining variable has an initial value that is specified as part of the algorithm. The final value of the chaining variable is the hash value. Often, $b > n$; hence the term *compression*. The hash function can be summarized as follows:

$$\begin{aligned} CV_0 &= IV = \text{initial } n\text{-bit value} \\ CV_i &= \mathrm{f}(CV_{i-1}, Y_{i-1}) \qquad 1 \leq i \leq L \\ \mathrm{H}(M) &= CV_L \end{aligned}$$

where the input to the hash function is a message M consisting of the blocks $Y_0, Y_1, \ldots, Y_{L-1}$.

The motivation for this iterative structure stems from the observation by Merkle [MERK89] and Damgard [DAMG89] that if the compression function is collision resistant, then so is the resultant iterated hash function.[3] Therefore, the structure can be used to produce a secure hash function to operate on a message of any length. The problem of designing a secure hash function reduces to that of designing a collision-resistant compression function that operates on inputs of some fixed size.

Cryptanalysis of hash functions focuses on the internal structure of f and is based on attempts to find efficient techniques for producing collisions for a single execution of f. Once that is done, the attack must take into account the fixed value of IV. The attack on f depends on exploiting its internal structure. Typically, as with symmetric block ciphers, f consists of a series of rounds of processing, so that the attack involves analysis of the pattern of bit changes from round to round.

Keep in mind that for any hash function there must exist collisions, because we are mapping a message of length at least equal to twice the block size b (because we must append a length field) into a hash code of length n, where $b \geq n$. What is required is that it is computationally infeasible to find collisions.

---

[3]The converse is not necessarily true.

The attacks that have been mounted on hash functions are rather complex and beyond our scope here. For the interested reader, [DOBB96] and [BELL97] are recommended.

Message Authentication Codes There is much more variety in the structure of MACs than in hash functions, so it is difficult to generalize about the cryptanalysis of MACs. Further, far less work has been done on developing such attacks. A useful recent survey of some methods for specific MACs is [PREN96].

11.6 RECOMMENDED READING

[JUEN85] and [JUEN87] provide a good background on message authentication, with a focus on cryptographic MACs and hash functions. Solid treatments of hash functions and message authentication codes are found in [STIN02] and [MENE97]. A good recent survey is [PREN99].

JUEN85 Jueneman, R.; Matyas, S.; and Meyer, C. "Message Authentication." *IEEE Communications Magazine*, September 1988.

JUEN87 Jueneman, R. "Electronic Document Authentication." *IEEE Network Magazine*, April 1987.

MENE97 Menezes, A.; Oorshcot, P.; and Vanstone, S. *Handbook of Applied Cryptography.* Boca Raton, FL: CRC Press, 1997.

PREN99 Preneel, B. "The State of Cryptographic Hash Functions." *Proceedings, EUROCRYPT '96*, 1996; published by Springer-Verlag.

STIN02 Stinson, D. *Cryptography: Theory and Practice.* Boca Raton, FL: CRC Press, 2002.

11.7 KEY TERMS, REVIEW QUESTIONS, AND PROBLEMS

Key Terms

authenticator	hash function	message digest
birthday attack	hash value	one-way hash function
birthday paradox	message authentication	strong collision resistance
compression function	message authentication code (MAC)	weak collision resistance
cryptographic checksum		
hash code		

Review Questions

11.1 What types of attacks are addressed by message authentication?

11.2 What two levels of functionality comprise a message authentication or digital signature mechanism?

11.3 What are some approaches to producing message authentication?

11.4 When a combination of symmetric encryption and an error control code is used for message authentication, in what order must the two functions be performed?

11.5 What is a message authentication code?

11.6 What is the difference between a message authentication code and a one-way hash function?

11.7 In what ways can a hash value be secured so as to provide message authentication?

11.8 Is it necessary to recover the secret key in order to attack a MAC algorithm?

11.9 What characteristics are needed in a secure hash function?

11.10 What is the difference between weak and strong collision resistance?

11.11 What is the role of a compression function in a hash function?

Problems

11.1 If F is an error-detection function, either internal or external use (Figure 11.2) will provide error-detection capability. If any bit of the transmitted message is altered, this will be reflected in a mismatch of the received FCS and the calculated FCS, whether the FCS function is performed inside or outside the encryption function. Some codes also provide an error-correction capability. Depending on the nature of the function, if one or a small number of bits is altered in transit, the error-correction code contains sufficient redundant information to determine the errored bit or bits and correct them. Clearly, an error-correction code will provide error correction capability when used external to the encryption function. Will it also provide this capability if used internal to the encryption function?

11.2 The data authentication algorithm, described in Section 11.3, can be defined as using the cipher block chaining (CBC) mode of operation of DES with an initialization vector of zero (Figure 11.6). Show that the same result can be produced using the cipher feedback mode.

11.3 The high-speed transport protocol XTP (Xpress Transfer Protocol) uses a 32-bit checksum function defined as the concatenation of two 16-bit functions: XOR and RXOR, defined in Section 11.4 as "two simple hash functions" and illustrated in Figure 11.7.

a. Will this checksum detect all errors caused by an odd number of error bits? Explain.

b. Will this checksum detect all errors caused by an even number of error bits? If not, characterize the error patterns that will cause the checksum to fail.

c. Comment on the effectiveness of this function for use as a hash function for authentication.

11.4 a. Consider the Davies and Price hash code scheme described in Section 11.4 and assume that DES is used as the encryption algorithm:

$$H_i = H_{i-1} \oplus \mathrm{E}(M_i, H_{i-1})$$

and recall the complementarity property of DES (Problem 3.14): If $Y = \mathrm{E}(K, X)$, then $Y' = \mathrm{E}(K', X')$. Use this property to show how a message consisting of blocks $M_1, M_2, \ldots, M_N$ can be altered without altering its hash code.

b. Show that a similar attack will succeed against the scheme proposed in [MEYE88]:

$$H_i = M_i \oplus \mathrm{E}(H_{i-1}, M_i)$$

11.5 a. Consider the following hash function. Messages are in the form of a sequence of decimal numbers, $M = (a_1, a_2, \ldots, a_t)$. The hash value h is calculated as $\left(\sum_{i=1}^{t} a_i\right) \bmod n$, for some predefined value n. Does this hash function satisfy any of the requirements for a hash function listed in Section 11.4? Explain your answer.

b. Repeat part (a) for the hash function $h = \left(\sum_{i=1}^{t} (a_i)^2\right) \bmod n$.

c. Calculate the hash function of part (b) for $M = (189, 632, 900, 722, 349)$ and $n = 989$.

11.6 It is possible to use a hash function to construct a block cipher with a structure similar to DES. Because a hash function is one way and a block cipher must be reversible (to decrypt), how is it possible?

11.7 Now consider the opposite problem: using an encryption algorithm to construct a one-way hash function. Consider using RSA with a known key. Then process a message consisting of a sequence of blocks as follows: Encrypt the first block, XOR the result with the second block and encrypt again, etc. Show that this scheme is not secure by solving the following problem. Given a two-block message B1, B2, and its hash

$$\text{RSAH(B1, B2)} = \text{RSA(RSA(B1)} \oplus \text{B2)}$$

Given an arbitrary block C1, choose C2 so that RSAH(C1, C2) = RSAH(B1, B2). Thus, the hash function does not satisfy weak collision resistance.

11.8 Suppose H(m) is a collision resistant hash function that maps a message of arbitrary bit length into an n-bit hash value. Is it true that, for all messages x, x' with $x \neq x'$, we have $H(x) \neq H(x')$? Explain your answer.

APPENDIX 11A MATHEMATICAL BASIS OF THE BIRTHDAY ATTACK

In this appendix, we derive the mathematical justification for the birthday attack. We begin with a related problem and then look at the problem from which the name "birthday attack" is derived.

Related Problem

A general problem relating to hash functions is the following. Given a hash function H, with n possible outputs and a specific value H(x), if H is applied to k random inputs, what must be the value of k so that the probability that at least one input y satisfies $H(y) = H(x)$ is 0.5?

For a single value of y, the probability that $H(y) = H(x)$ is just $1/n$. Conversely, the probability that $H(y) \neq H(x)$ is $[1 - (1/n)]$. If we generate k random values of y, then the probability that none of them match is just the product of the probabilities that each individual value does not match, or $[1 - (1/n)]^k$. Thus, the probability that there is at least one match is $1 - [1 - (1/n)]^k$.

The binomial theorem can be stated as follows:

$$(1 - a)^k = 1 - ka + \frac{k(k-1)}{2!}a^2 - \frac{k(k-1)(k-2)}{3!}a^3 \ldots$$

For very small values of a, this can be approximated as $(1 - ka)$. Thus, the probability of at least one match is approximated as $1 - [1 - (1/n)]^k \approx 1 - [1 - (k/n)] = k/n$. For a probability of 0.5, we have $k = n/2$.

In particular, for an m-bit hash code, the number of possible codes is 2^m and the value of k that produces a probability of one-half is

$$k = 2^{(m-1)} \qquad \textbf{(11.1)}$$

The Birthday Paradox

The birthday paradox is often presented in elementary probability courses to demonstrate that probability results are sometimes counterintuitive. The problem can be stated as follows: What is the minimum value of k such that the probability is greater than 0.5 that at least two people in a group of k people have the same birthday? Ignore February 29 and assume that each birthday is equally likely. To answer, let us define

$$\text{P}(n, k) = \text{Pr[at least one duplicate in } k \text{ items, with each item able to take on one of } n \text{ equally likely values between 1 and } n]$$

Thus, we are looking for the smallest value of k such that $\text{P}(365, k) \geq 0.5$. It is easier first to derive the probability that there are no duplicates, which we designate as $\text{Q}(365, k)$. If $k > 365$, then it is impossible for all values to be different. So we assume $k \leq 365$. Now consider the number of different ways, N, that we can have k values with no duplicates. We may choose any of the 365 values for the first item, any of the remaining 364 numbers for the second item, and so on. Hence, the number of different ways is

$$N = 365 \times 364 \times \ldots (365 - k + 1) = \frac{365!}{(365 - k)!} \qquad \textbf{(11.2)}$$

If we remove the restriction that there are no duplicates, then each item can be any of 365 values, and the total number of possibilities is 365^k. So the probability of no duplicates is simply the fraction of sets of values that have no duplicates out of all possible sets of values:

$$\text{Q}(365, k) = \frac{365!/(365 - k)!}{(365)^k} = \frac{365!}{(365 - k)!(365)^k}$$

and

$$\text{P}(365, k) = 1 - \text{Q}(365, k) = 1 - \frac{365!}{(365 - k)!(365)^k} \qquad \textbf{(11.3)}$$

This function is plotted in Figure 11.10. The probabilities may seem surprisingly large to anyone who has not considered the problem before. Many people would guess that to have a probability greater than 0.5 that there is at least one duplicate, the number of people in the group would have to be about 100. In fact, the number is 23, with $\text{P}(365, 23) = 0.5073$. For $k = 100$, the probability of at least one duplicate is 0.9999997.

Perhaps the reason that the result seems so surprising is that if you consider a particular person in a group, the probability that some other person in the group has the same birthday is small. But the probability that we are concerned with is the probability that *any* pair of people in the group has the same birthday. In a group of 23, there are $(23(23 - 1))/2 = 253$ different pairs of people. Hence the high probabilities.

Useful Inequality

Before developing a generalization of the birthday problem, we derive an inequality that will be needed:

$$(1 - x) \leq e^{-x} \quad \text{for all } x \geq 0 \qquad \textbf{(11.4)}$$

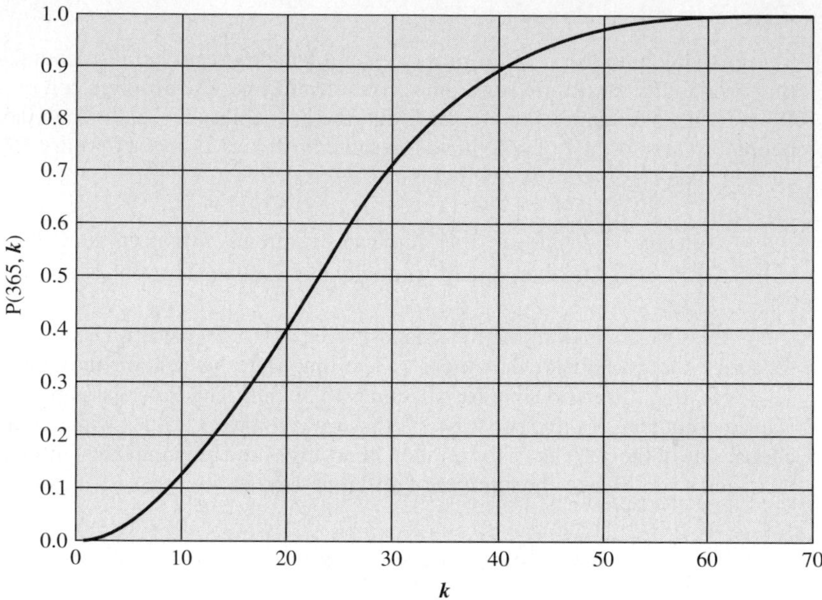

Figure 11.10 The Birthday Paradox

Figure 11.11 illustrates the inequality. To see that the inequality holds, note that the lower line is the tangent to e^{-x} at $x = 0$. The slope of that line is just the derivative of e^{-x} at $x = 0$:

$$f(x) = e^{-x}$$

$$f'(x) = \frac{d}{dx}e^{-x} = -e^{-x}$$

$$f'(0) = -1$$

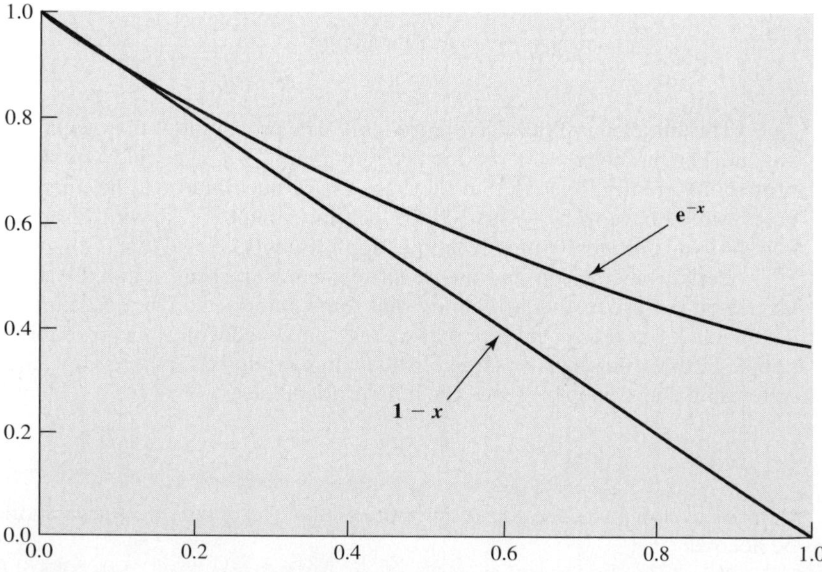

Figure 11.11 A Useful Inequality

The tangent is a straight line of the form $ax + b$, with $a = -1$, and the tangent at $x = 0$ must equal $e^{-0} = 1$. Thus, the tangent is the function $(1 - x)$, confirming the inequality of Equation (11.4). Further, note that for small x, we have $(1 - x) \approx e^{-x}$.

The General Case of Duplications

The birthday problem can be generalized to the following problem: Given a random variable that is an integer with uniform distribution between 1 and n and a selection of k instances $(k \leq n)$ of the random variable, what is the probability, $P(n, k)$, that there is at least one duplicate? The birthday problem is just the special case with $n = 365$. By the same reasoning as before, we have the following generalization of Equation (11.3):

$$P(n, k) = 1 - \frac{n!}{(n - k)!n^k} \qquad \textbf{(11.5)}$$

We can rewrite as

$$\begin{aligned} P(n, k) &= 1 - \frac{n \times (n - 1) \times \ldots \times (n - k + 1)}{n^k} \\ &= 1 - \left[\frac{n - 1}{n} \times \frac{n - 2}{n} \times \ldots \times \frac{n - k + 1}{n}\right] \\ &= 1 - \left[\left(1 - \frac{1}{n}\right) \times \left(1 - \frac{2}{n}\right) \times \ldots \times \left(1 - \frac{k - 1}{n}\right)\right] \end{aligned}$$

Using the inequality of Equation (11.4):

$$\begin{aligned} P(n, k) &> 1 - \left[(e^{-1/n}) \times (e^{-2/n}) \times \ldots \times (e^{-(k-1)/n})\right] \\ &> 1 - e^{-[(1/n)+(2/n)+\ldots+((k-1)/n)]} \\ &> 1 - e^{-(k\times(k-1))/2n} \end{aligned}$$

Now let us pose the question: What value of k is required such that $P(n, k) > 0.5$? To satisfy the requirement, we have

$$\begin{aligned} 1/2 &= 1 - e^{-(k\times(k-1))/2n} \\ 2 &= e^{(k\times(k-1))/2n} \\ \ln 2 &= \frac{k \times (k - 1)}{2n} \end{aligned}$$

For large k, we can replace $k \times (k - 1)$ by k^2, and we get

$$k = \sqrt{2(\ln 2)n} = 1.18\sqrt{n} \approx \sqrt{n} \qquad \textbf{(11.6)}$$

As a reality check, for $n = 365$, we get $k = 1.18 \times \sqrt{365} = 22.54$, which is very close to the correct answer of 23.

We can now state the basis of the birthday attack in the following terms. Suppose we have a function H, with 2^m possible outputs (i.e., an m-bit output). If H is applied to k random inputs, what must be the value of k so that there is the probability of at least one duplicate [i.e., $H(x) = H(y)$ for some inputs x, y)]? Using the approximation in Equation (11.6):

$$k = \sqrt{2^m} = 2^{m/2} \qquad \textbf{(11.7)}$$

Overlap between Two Sets

There is a problem related to the general case of duplications that is also of relevance for our discussions. The problem is this: Given an integer random variable with uniform distribution between 1 and n and two sets of k instances ($k \le n$) of the random variable, what is the probability, $R(n, k)$, that the two sets are not disjoint; that is, what is the probability that there is at least one value found in both sets?

Let us call the two sets X and Y, with elements $\{x_1, x_2, \dots, x_k\}$ and $\{y_1, y_2, \dots, y_k\}$, respectively. Given the value of x_1, the probability that $y_1 = x_1$ is just $1/n$, and therefore probability that y_1 does not match x_1 is $[1 - (1/n)]$. If we generate the k random values in Y, the probability that none of these values is equal to x_1 is $[1 - (1/n)]^k$. Thus, the probability that there is at least one match to x_1 is $1 - [1 - (1/n)]^k$.

To proceed, let us make the assumption that all the elements of X are distinct. If n is large and if k is also large (e.g., on the order of $\sqrt{n}$), then this is a good approximation. In fact, there may be a few duplications, but most of the values will be distinct. With that assumption, we can make the following derivation:

$$\Pr[\text{no match in } Y \text{ to } x_1] = \left(1 - \frac{1}{n}\right)^k$$

$$\Pr[\text{no match in } Y \text{ to } X] = \left(\left(1 - \frac{1}{n}\right)^k\right)^k = \left(1 - \frac{1}{n}\right)^{k^2}$$

$$R(n, k) = \Pr[\text{at least one match in } Y \text{ to } X] = 1 - \left(1 - \frac{1}{n}\right)^{k^2}$$

Using the inequality of Equation (11.4):

$$R(n, k) > 1 - (e^{-1/n})^{k^2}$$
$$R(n, k) > 1 - (e^{-k^2/n})$$

Let us pose the question: What value of k is required such that $R(n, k) > 0.5$? To satisfy the requirement, we have

$$1/2 = 1 - (e^{-k^2/n})$$
$$2 = e^{k^2/n}$$
$$\ln(2) = \frac{k^2}{n}$$
$$k = \sqrt{(\ln(2))n} = 0.83\sqrt{n} \approx \sqrt{n} \qquad \textbf{(11.8)}$$

We can state this in terms related to birthday attacks as follows. Suppose we have a function H, with 2^m possible outputs (i.e., an m-bit output). Apply H to k random inputs to produce the set X and again to k additional random inputs to produce the set Y. What must be the value of k so that there is the probability of at least 0.5 that there is a match between the two sets (i.e., $H(x) = H(y)$ for some inputs $x \in X, y \in Y$)? Using the approximation in Equation (11.8):

$$k = \sqrt{2^m} = 2^{m/2}$$

CHAPTER 12

Hash and MAC Algorithms

Each of the messages, like each one he had ever read of Stern's commands, began with a number and ended with a number or row of numbers. No efforts on the part of Mungo or any of his experts had been able to break Stern's code, nor was there any clue as to what the preliminary number and those ultimate numbers signified.

—*Talking to Strange Men,* Ruth Rendell

The Douglas Squirrel has a distinctive eating habit. It usually eats pine cones from the bottom end up. Partially eaten cones can indicate the presence of these squirrels if they have been attacked from the bottom first. If, instead, the cone has been eaten from the top end down, it is more likely to have been a crossbill finch that has been doing the dining.

—*Squirrels: A Wildlife Handbook*, Kim Long

KEY POINTS

- Virtually all secure hash algorithms have the general structure shown in Figure 11.9.
- The compression function used in secure hash algorithms falls into one of two categories: a function specifically designed for the hash function or a symmetric block cipher. SHA and Whirlpool are examples of these two approaches, respectively.
- Message authentication codes also fall into two categories; those based on the use of a secure hash algorithm and those based on the use of a symmetric block cipher. HMAC and CMAC are examples of these two approaches, respectively.

In this chapter, we look at important examples of both secure hash algorithms and message authentication codes (MACs). Most important modern hash functions follow the basic structure of Figure 11.9. This has proved to be a fundamentally sound structure, and newer designs simply refine the structure and add to the hash code length. Within this basic structure, two approaches have been followed in the design of the compression function, which is the basic building block of the hash function. Traditionally, most hash functions that have achieved widespread use rely on a compression function specifically designed for the hash function. Typically, the compression function makes use of modular arithmetic and logical binary operations. Another approach is to use a symmetric block cipher as the compression function. In this chapter, we examine perhaps the most important example of each approach: the Secure Hash Algorithm (SHA) and Whirlpool.

MACs also conveniently fall into two categories based on their fundamental building block. One popular approach is to use a hash algorithm such as SHA as the core of the MAC algorithm. Another approach is to use a symmetric block cipher in a cipher block chaining mode. Again, we look at perhaps the most important example of each approach: HMAC and CMAC.

12.1 SECURE HASH ALGORITHM

The Secure Hash Algorithm (SHA) was developed by the National Institute of Standards and Technology (NIST) and published as a federal information processing standard (FIPS 180) in 1993; a revised version was issued as FIPS 180-1 in 1995 and is generally referred to as SHA-1. The actual standards document is entitled Secure Hash Standard. SHA is based on the hash function MD4 and its design closely models MD4. SHA-1 is also specified in RFC 3174, which essentially duplicates the material in FIPS 180-1, but adds a C code implementation.

SHA-1 produces a hash value of 160 bits. In 2002, NIST produced a revised version of the standard, FIPS 180-2, that defined three new versions of SHA, with hash value lengths of 256, 384, and 512 bits, known as SHA-256, SHA-384, and SHA-512 (Table 12.1). These new versions have the same underlying structure and use the same types of modular arithmetic and logical binary operations as SHA-1. In 2005, NIST announced the intention to phase out approval of SHA-1 and move to a reliance on the other SHA versions by 2010. Shortly thereafter, a research team described an attack in which two separate messages could be found that deliver the same SHA-1 hash using 2^{69} operations, far fewer than the 2^{80} operations previously thought needed to find a collision with an SHA-1 hash [WANG05]. This result should hasten the transition to the other versions of SHA.

In this section, we provide a description of SHA-512. The other versions are quite similar.

SHA-512 Logic

The algorithm takes as input a message with a maximum length of less than 2^{128} bits and produces as output a 512-bit message digest. The input is processed in 1024-bit blocks. Figure 12.1 depicts the overall processing of a message to produce a digest.

Table 12.1 Comparison of SHA Parameters

	SHA-1	SHA-256	SHA-384	SHA-512
Message digest size	160	256	384	512
Message size	$<2^{64}$	$<2^{64}$	$<2^{128}$	$<2^{128}$
Block size	512	512	1024	1024
Word size	32	32	64	64
Number of steps	80	64	80	80
Security	80	128	192	256

Notes: 1. All sizes are measured in bits.

2. Security refers to the fact that a birthday attack on a message digest of size n produces a collision with a workfactor of approximately $2^{n/2}$.

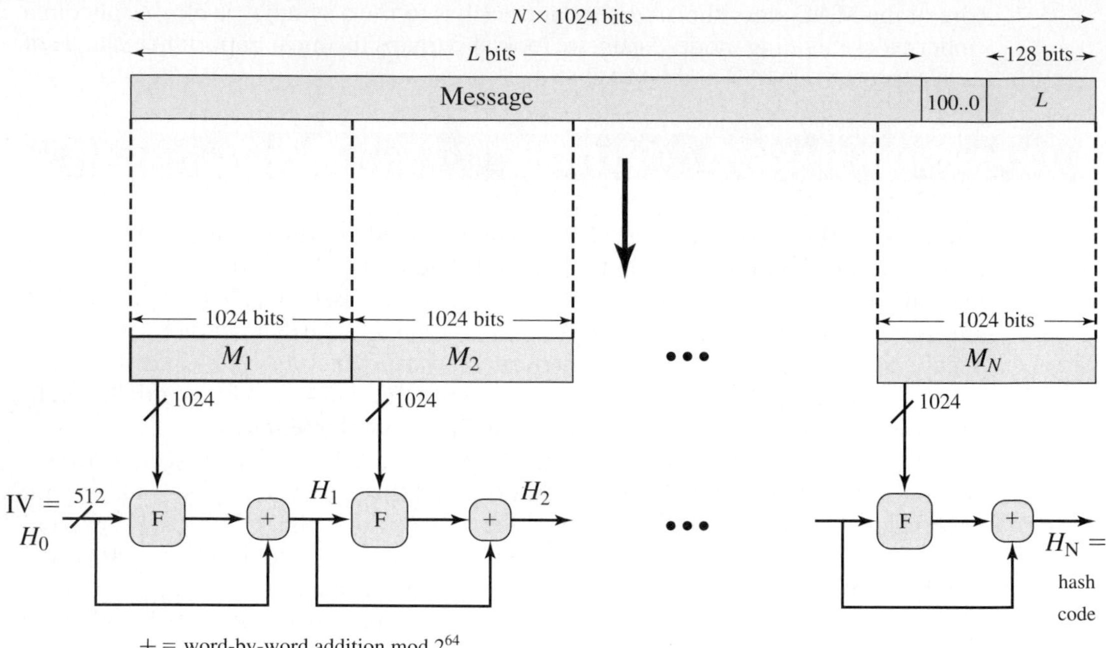

Figure 12.1 Message Digest Generation Using SHA-512

This follows the general structure depicted in Figure 11.9. The processing consists of the following steps:

- **Step 1: Append padding bits.** The message is padded so that its length is congruent to 896 modulo 1024 [length $\equiv$ 896 (mod 1024)]. Padding is always added, even if the message is already of the desired length. Thus, the number of padding bits is in the range of 1 to 1024. The padding consists of a single 1-bit followed by the necessary number of 0-bits.
- **Step 2: Append length.** A block of 128 bits is appended to the message. This block is treated as an unsigned 128-bit integer (most significant byte first) and contains the length of the original message (before the padding).

  The outcome of the first two steps yields a message that is an integer multiple of 1024 bits in length. In Figure 12.1, the expanded message is represented as the sequence of 1024-bit blocks $M_1, M_2, \ldots, M_N$, so that the total length of the expanded message is $N \times 1024$ bits.
- **Step 3: Initialize hash buffer.** A 512-bit buffer is used to hold intermediate and final results of the hash function. The buffer can be represented as eight 64-bit registers (a, b, c, d, e, f, g, h). These registers are initialized to the following 64-bit integers (hexadecimal values):

a = 6A09E667F3BCC908	e = 510E527FADE682D1
b = BB67AE8584CAA73B	f = 9B05688C2B3E6C1F
c = 3C6EF372FE94F82B	g = 1F83D9ABFB41BD6B
c = A54FF53A5F1D36F1	h = 5BE0CDI9137E2179

These values are stored in big-endian format, which is the most significant byte of a word in the low-address (leftmost) byte position. These words were obtained by taking the first sixty-four bits of the fractional parts of the square roots of the first eight prime numbers.

- **Step 4: Process message in 1024-bit (128-word) blocks.** The heart of the algorithm is a module that consists of 80 rounds; this module is labeled F in Figure 12.1. The logic is illustrated in Figure 12.2.

  Each round takes as input the 512-bit buffer value abcdefgh, and updates the contents of the buffer. At input to the first round, the buffer has the value of the intermediate hash value, H_{i-1}. Each round t makes use of a 64-bit value W_t, derived from the current 1024-bit block being processed (M_i). These values are derived using a message schedule described subsequently. Each round also makes use of an additive constant K_t, where $0 \leq t \leq 79$ indicates one of the 80 rounds. These words represent the first sixty-four bits of the fractional parts of the cube roots of the first eighty prime numbers. The constants provide a "randomized" set of 64-bit patterns, which should eliminate any regularities in the input data.

  The output of the eightieth round is added to the input to the first round (H_{i-1}) to produce H_i. The addition is done independently for each of the eight words in the buffer with each of the corresponding words in H_{i-1}, using addition modulo 2^{64}.

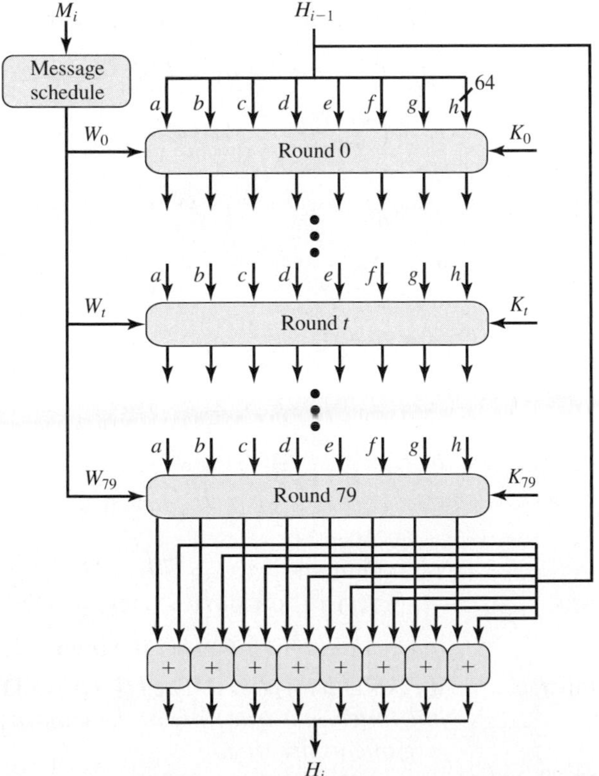

Figure 12.2 SHA-512 Processing of a Single 1024-Bit Block

- **Step 5: Output.** After all N 1024-bit blocks have been processed, the output from the Nth stage is the 512-bit message digest.

  We can summarize the behavior of SHA-512 as follows:

$$H_0 = \text{IV}$$
$$H_i = \text{SUM}_{64}(H_{i-1}, \text{abcdefgh}_i)$$
$$MD = H_N$$

where

IV	= initial value of the abcdefgh buffer, defined in step 3
abcdefgh_i	= the output of the last round of processing of the ith message block
N	= the number of blocks in the message (including padding and length fields)
SUM_{64}	= Addition modulo 2^{64} performed separately on each word of the pair of inputs
MD	= final message digest value

SHA-512 Round Function

Let us look in more detail at the logic in each of the 80 steps of the processing of one 512-bit block (Figure 12.3). Each round is defined by the following set of equations:

$$T_1 = h + \text{Ch}(e, f, g) + \left(\sum\nolimits_1^{512} e\right) + W_t + K_t$$
$$T_2 = \left(\sum\nolimits_0^{512} a\right) + \text{Maj}(a, b, c)$$
$$a = T_1 + T_2$$
$$b = a$$
$$c = b$$
$$d = c$$
$$e = d + T_1$$
$$f = e$$
$$g = f$$
$$h = g$$

where

t	= step number; $0 \le t \le 79$
$\text{Ch}(e, f, g)$	= $(e \text{ AND } f) \oplus (\text{NOT } e \text{ AND } g)$ *the conditional function*: *If e* then *f* else *g*
$\text{Maj}(a, b, c)$	= $(a \text{ AND } b) \oplus (a \text{ AND } c) \oplus (b \text{ AND } c)$ *the function is true only of the majority (two or three) of the arguments are true.*
$\left(\sum\nolimits_0^{512} a\right)$	= $\text{ROTR}^{28}(a) \oplus \text{ROTR}^{34}(a) \oplus \text{ROTR}^{39}(a)$

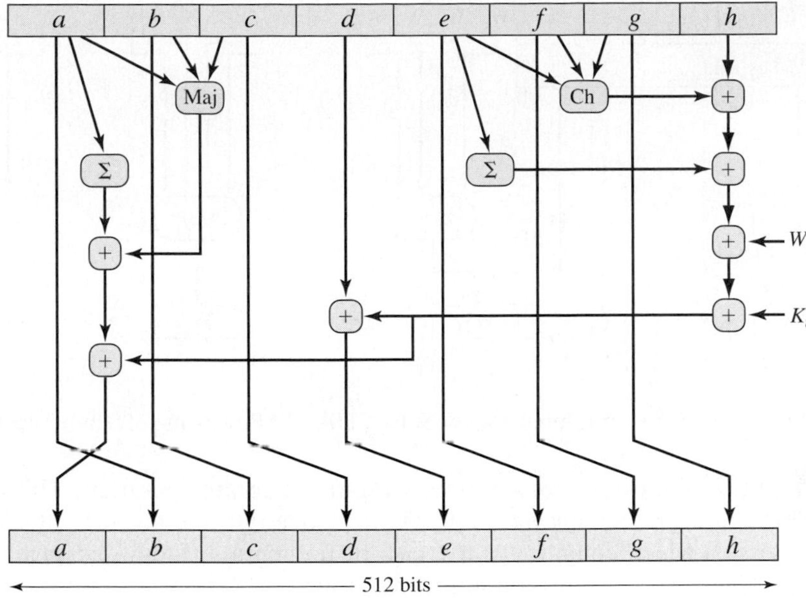

Figure 12.3 Elementary SHA-512 Operation (single round)

$$\left(\textstyle\sum_1^{512} e\right) = \text{ROTR}^{14}(e) \oplus \text{ROTR}^{18}(e) \oplus \text{ROTR}^{41}(e)$$

$\text{ROTR}^n(x)$ = circular right shift (rotation) of the 64-bit argument x by n bits

W_t = a 64-bit word derived from the current 512-bit input block

K_t = a 64-bit additive constant

$+$ = addition modulo 2^{64}

It remains to indicate how the 64-bit word values W_t are derived from the 1024-bit message. Figure 12.4 illustrates the mapping. The first 16 values of W_t are taken directly from the 16 words of the current block. The remaining values are defined as follows:

$$W_t = \sigma_1^{512}(W_{t-2}) + W_{t-7} + \sigma_0^{512}(W_{t-15}) + W_{t-16}$$

where

$\sigma_0^{512}(x)$ = $\text{ROTR}^1(x) \oplus \text{ROTR}^8(x) \oplus \text{SHR}^7(x)$

$\sigma_1^{512}(x)$ = $\text{ROTR}^{19}(x) \oplus \text{ROTR}^{61}(x) \oplus \text{SHR}^6(x)$

$\text{ROTR}^n(x)$ = circular right shift (rotation) of the 64-bit argument x by n bits

$\text{SHR}^n(x)$ = left shift of the 64-bit argument x by n bits with padding *by zeros on the right*

Thus, in the first 16 steps of processing, the value of W_t is equal to the corresponding word in the message block. For the remaining 64 steps, the value of W_t consists of the circular left shift by one bit of the XOR of four of the preceding values of

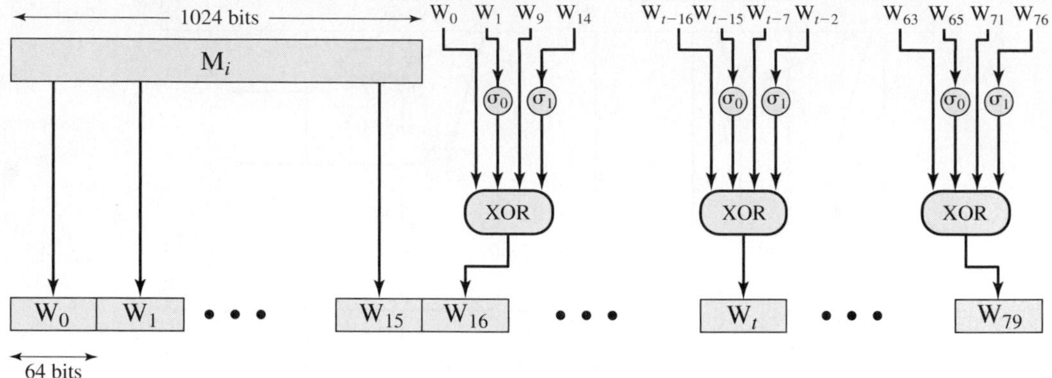

Figure 12.4 Creation of 80-word Input Sequence for SHA-512 Processing of Single Block

W_t, with two of those values subjected to shift and rotate operations. This introduces a great deal of redundancy and interdependence into the message blocks that are compressed, which complicates the task of finding a different message block that maps to the same compression function output.

12.2 WHIRLPOOL[1]

In this section, we examine the hash function Whirlpool [BARR03], one of whose designers is also co-inventor of Rijndael, adopted as the Advanced Encryption Standard (AES). Whirlpool is one of only two hash functions endorsed by NESSIE (New European Schemes for Signatures, Integrity, and Encryption).[2] The NESSIE project is a European Union–sponsored effort to put forward a portfolio of strong cryptographic primitives of various types.

Whirlpool is based on the use of a block cipher for the compression function. As was mentioned in Chapter 11, there has traditionally been little interest in the use of block-cipher-based hash functions because of the demonstrated security vulnerabilities of the structure. The following are potential drawbacks:

1. Block ciphers do not possess the properties of randomizing functions. For example, they are invertible. This lack of randomness may lead to weaknesses that can be exploited.
2. Block ciphers typically exhibit other regularities or weaknesses. For example, [MIYA90] demonstrates how to compromise many hash schemes based on properties of the underlying block cipher.
3. Typically, block-cipher-based hash functions are significantly slower than hash functions based on a compression function specifically designed for the hash function.
4. A principal measure of the strength of a hash function is the length of the hash code in bits. For block-cipher-based hash codes, proposed designs have a hash

[1]Most of the material in this section originally appeared in [STAL O6].

[2]The other endorsed scheme consists of three variants of SHA: SHA-256, SHA-384, and SHA-512.

code length equal to either the cipher block length or twice the cipher block length. Traditionally, cipher block length has been limited to 64 bits (e.g., DES, triple DES), resulting in a hash code of questionable strength.

However, since the adoption of AES, there has been renewed interested in developing a secure hash function based on a strong block cipher and exhibiting good performance. Whirlpool is a block-cipher-based hash function intended to provide security and performance that is comparable, if not better, than that found in non-block-cipher based hash functions, such as SHA. Whirlpool has the following features:

1. The hash code length is 512 bits, equaling the longest hash code available with SHA.
2. The overall structure of the hash function is one that has been shown to be resistant to the usual attacks on block-cipher-based hash codes.
3. The underlying block cipher is based on AES and is designed to provide for implementation in both software and hardware that is both compact and exhibits good performance.

The design of Whirlpool sets the following security goals: Assume we take as hash result the value of any n-bit substring of the full Whirlpool output.

- The expected workload of generating a collision is of the order of $2^{n/2}$ executions of Whirlpool.
- Given an n-bit value, the expected workload of finding a message that hashes to that value is of the order of 2^n executions of Whirlpool.
- Given a message and its n-bit hash result, the expected workload of finding a second message that hashes to the same value is of the order of 2^n executions of Whirlpool.
- It is infeasible to detect systematic correlations between any linear combination of input bits and any linear combination of bits of the hash result, or to predict what bits of the hash result will change value when certain input bits are flipped (this means resistance against linear and differential attacks).

The designers assert their confidence that these goals have been met with a considerable safety margin. However, the goals are not susceptible to a formal proof.

We begin with a discussion of the structure of the overall hash function, and then examine the block cipher used as the basic building block.

Whirlpool Hash Structure

Background The general iterated hash structure proposed by Merkle (Figure 11.9) is used in virtually all secure hash functions. However, as was pointed out, there are difficulties in designing a truly secure iterated hash function when the compression function is a block cipher. Preneel [PREN93a, PREN93b] performed a systematic analysis of block-cipher-based hash functions, using the model depicted in Figure 12.5. In this model, the hash code length equals the cipher block length. Additional security problems are introduced and the analysis is more difficult if the hash code length exceeds the cipher block length. Preneel devised 64 possible permutations of the basic model, based on which input served as the encryption key and which served as plaintext and

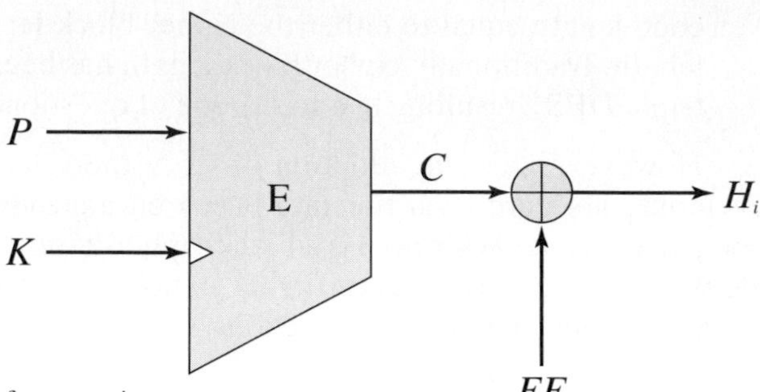

m_i = ith block of message input
H_i = ith intermediate hash value
P = plaintext; K = encryption key; C = ciphertext
FF = feed forward value
P, K, and FF can be chosen from the set $(0, m_i, H_{i-1}, m_i \oplus H_{i-1})$

Note: Triangular hatch indicates encryption key input.

Figure 12.5 Model of Single Iteration of Hash Function (hash code equals block length)

on what input, if any, was combined with the ciphertext to produce the intermediate hash code. Based on his analysis, he concluded that only schemes in which the plaintext was fed forward and combined with the ciphertext were secure. Such an arrangement makes the compression function difficult to invert. [BLAC02] confirmed these results, but pointed out the security problem of using an established block cipher such as AES: The 128-bit hash code value resulting from the use of AES or another scheme with the same block size may be inadequate for security.

Whirlpool Logic Given a message consisting of a sequence of blocks $m_1, m_2, \ldots, m_t$, the Whirlpool hash function is expressed as follows:

$$\begin{aligned} H_0 &= \text{initial value} \\ H_i &= \mathrm{E}(H_{i-1}, m_i) \oplus H_{i-1} \oplus m_i = \text{intermediate value} \\ H_t &= \text{hash code value} \end{aligned}$$

In terms of the model of Figure 12.5, the encryption key input for each iteration is the intermediate hash value from the previous iteration; the plaintext is the current message block; and the feedforward value is the bitwise XOR of the current message block and the intermediate hash value from the previous iteration.

The algorithm takes as input a message with a maximum length of less than 2^{256} bits and produces as output a 512-bit message digest. The input is processed in 512-bit blocks. Figure 12.6 depicts the overall processing of a message to produce a digest. This follows the general structure depicted in Figure 11.9. The processing consists of the following steps:

- **Step 1: Append padding bits.** The message is padded so that its length in bits is an odd multiple of 256. Padding is always added, even if the message is already of the desired length. For example, if the message is $256 \times 3 = 768$ bits long, it is padded by 512 bits to a length of $256 \times 5 = 1280$ bits. Thus, the number of padding bits is in the range of 1 to 512.

  The padding consists of a single 1-bit followed by the necessary number of 0-bits.

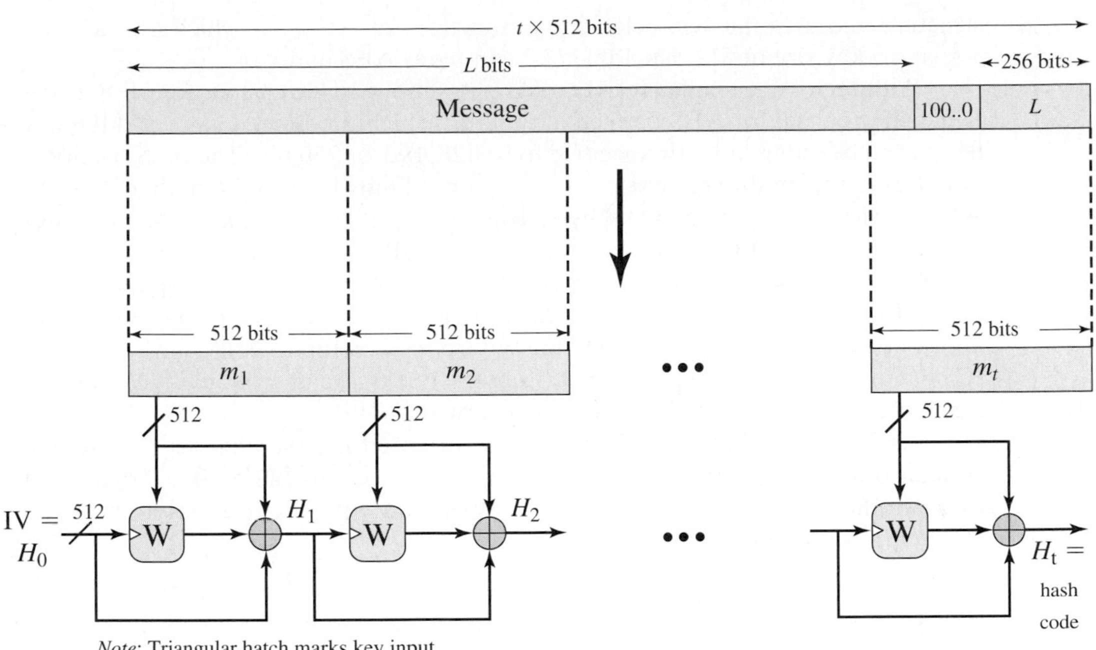

Figure 12.6 Message Digest Generation Using Whirlpool

- **Step 2: Append length.** A block of 256 bits is appended to the message. This block is treated as an unsigned 256-bit integer (most significant byte first) and contains the length in bits of the original message (before the padding).

  The outcome of the first two steps yields a message that is an integer multiple of 512 bits in length. In Figure 12.6, the expanded message is represented as the sequence of 512-bit blocks $m_1, m_2, \ldots, m_t$, so that the total length of the expanded message is $t \times 512$ bits. These blocks are viewed externally as arrays of bytes by sequentially grouping the bits in 8-bit chunks. However, internally, the hash state H_i is viewed as an 8×8 matrix of bytes. The transformation between the two is explained subsequently.
- **Step 3: Initialize hash matrix.** An 8×8 matrix of bytes is used to hold intermediate and final results of the hash function. The matrix is initialized as consisting of all 0-bits.
- **Step 4: Process message in 512-bit (64-byte) blocks.** The heart of the algorithm is the block cipher W.

Block Cipher W

Unlike virtually all other proposals for a block-cipher-based hash function, Whirlpool uses a block cipher that is specifically designed for use in the hash function and that is unlikely ever to be used as a standalone encryption function. The reason for this is that the designers wanted to make use of a block cipher with the security and efficiency of AES but with a hash length that provided a potential security equal to SHA-512. The result is the block cipher W, which has a similar structure and uses the same elementary functions as AES, but which uses a block size and a key size of 512 bits. Table 12.2 compares AES and W.

Although W is similar to AES, it is not simply an extension. Recall that the Rijndael proposal for AES defined a cipher in which the block length and the key length can be independently specified to be 128, 192, or 256 bits. The AES specification uses the same three key size alternatives but limits the block length to 128 bits. AES operates on a state of 4×4 bytes. Rijndael with block length 192 bits operates on a state of 4×6 bytes. Rijndael with block length 256 bits operates on a state of 4×8 bytes. W operates on a state of 8×8 bytes. The more the state representation differs from a square, the slower the diffusion goes and the more rounds the cipher needs. For a block length of 512 bits, the Whirlpool developers could have defined a Rijndael operating on a state of 4×16 bytes, but that cipher would have needed many rounds and it would have been very slow.

As Table 12.2 indicates, W uses a row-oriented matrix whereas AES uses a column-oriented matrix. There is no technical reason to prefer one orientation over another, because one can easily construct an equivalent description of the same cipher, exchanging rows with columns.

Overall Structure Figure 12.7 shows the overall structure of W. The encryption algorithm takes a 512-bit block of plaintext and a 512-bit key as input and produces a 512-bit block of ciphertext as output. The encryption algorithm involves the use of four different functions, or transformations: add key (AK), substitute bytes (SB), shift columns (SC), and mix rows (MR), whose operations are explained subsequently. W consists of a single application of AK followed by 10 rounds that involve all four functions. We can concisely express the operation of a round r as a round function RF that is a composition of functions:

$$\mathrm{RF}(\boldsymbol{K}_r) = \mathrm{AK}[\boldsymbol{K}_r] \circ \mathrm{MR} \circ \mathrm{SC} \circ \mathrm{SB} \qquad \textbf{(12.1)}$$

Table 12.2 Comparison of Whirlpool Block Cipher W and AES

	W	AES
Block size (bits)	512	128
Key size (bits)	512	128, 192, or 256
Matrix orientation	Input is mapped row-wise	Input is mapped column-wise
Number of rounds	10	10, 12, or 14
Key expansion	W round function	Dedicated expansion algorithm
GF(2^8) polynomial	$x^8 + x^4 + x^3 + x^2 + 1$ (011D)	$x^8 + x^4 + x^3 + x + 1$ (011B)
Origin of S-box	Recursive structure	Multiplicative inverse in GF(2^8) plus affine transformation
Origin of round constants	Successive entries of the S-box	Elements 2^i of GF(2^8)
Diffusion layer	Right multiplication by 8×8 circulant MDS matrix (1, 1, 4, 1, 8, 5, 2, 9) - mix rows	Left multiplication by 4×4 circulant MDS matrix (2, 3, 1, 1) - mix columns
Permutation	Shift columns	Shift rows

where $\boldsymbol{K}_r$ is the round key matrix for round r. The overall algorithm, with key input **K**, can be defined as follows:

$$W(K) = \left(\underset{r=1}{\overset{10}{\mathrm{O}}} \mathrm{RF}(\boldsymbol{K}_r) \right) \mathrm{o} \mathrm{AK}(\boldsymbol{K}_0)$$

where the large circle indicates iteration of the composition function with index r running from 1 through 10.

The plaintext input to W is a single 512-bit block. This block is treated as an 8×8 square matrix of bytes, labeled **CState**. Figure 12.8 illustrates that the ordering of bytes within a matrix is by row. So, for example, the first eight bytes of a 512-bit plaintext input to the encryption cipher occupy the first row of the internal matrix **CState**, the second eight bytes occupy the second row, and so on. The representation of the linear byte stream as a square matrix can be concisely expressed as a mapping function μ. For a linear byte array X with elements $x_k (0 \leq k \leq 63)$, the corresponding matrix **A** with elements $a_{i,j} (0 \leq i,j \leq 7)$, we have the following correspondence:

$$\mathbf{A} = \mu(\mathrm{X}) \Leftrightarrow a_{i,j} = x_{8i} + j$$

Similarly, the 512-bit key is depicted as a square matrix **KState** of bytes. This key is used as input to the initial AK function. The key is also expanded into a set of 10 round keys, as explained subsequently.

We now look at the individual functions that are part of W.

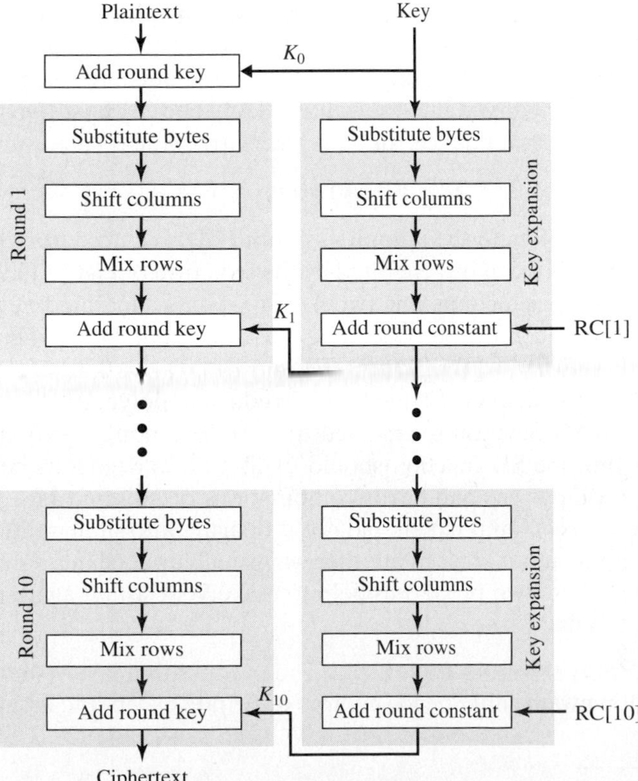

Figure 12.7 Whirlpool Cipher W

in_0	in_1	in_2	in_3	in_4	in_5	in_6	in_7
in_8	in_9	in_{10}	in_{11}	in_{12}	in_{13}	in_{14}	in_{15}
in_{16}	in_{17}	in_{18}	in_{19}	in_{20}	in_{21}	in_{22}	in_{23}
in_{24}	in_{25}	in_{26}	in_{27}	in_{28}	in_{29}	in_{30}	in_{31}
in_{32}	in_{33}	in_{34}	in_{35}	in_{36}	in_{37}	in_{38}	in_{39}
in_{40}	in_{41}	in_{42}	in_{43}	in_{44}	in_{45}	in_{46}	in_{47}
in_{48}	in_{49}	in_{50}	in_{51}	in_{52}	in_{53}	in_{54}	in_{55}
in_{56}	in_{57}	in_{58}	in_{59}	in_{60}	in_{61}	in_{62}	in_{63}

Input string of bytes

→

$a_{0,0}$	$a_{0,1}$	$a_{0,2}$	$a_{0,3}$	$a_{0,4}$	$a_{0,5}$	$a_{0,6}$	$a_{0,7}$
$a_{1,0}$	$a_{1,1}$	$a_{1,2}$	$a_{1,3}$	$a_{1,4}$	$a_{1,5}$	$a_{1,6}$	$a_{1,7}$
$a_{2,0}$	$a_{2,1}$	$a_{2,2}$	$a_{2,3}$	$a_{2,4}$	$a_{2,5}$	$a_{2,6}$	$a_{2,7}$
$a_{3,0}$	$a_{3,1}$	$a_{3,2}$	$a_{3,3}$	$a_{3,4}$	$a_{3,5}$	$a_{3,6}$	$a_{3,7}$
$a_{4,0}$	$a_{4,1}$	$a_{4,2}$	$a_{4,3}$	$a_{4,4}$	$a_{4,5}$	$a_{4,6}$	$a_{4,7}$
$a_{5,0}$	$a_{5,1}$	$a_{5,2}$	$a_{5,3}$	$a_{5,4}$	$a_{5,5}$	$a_{5,6}$	$a_{5,7}$
$a_{6,0}$	$a_{6,1}$	$a_{6,2}$	$a_{6,3}$	$a_{6,4}$	$a_{6,5}$	$a_{6,6}$	$a_{6,7}$
$a_{7,0}$	$a_{7,1}$	$a_{7,2}$	$a_{7,3}$	$a_{7,4}$	$a_{7,5}$	$a_{7,6}$	$a_{7,7}$

Internal cipher matrix **CState**

Figure 12.8 Whirlpool Matrix Structure

The Nonlinear Layer SB The substitute byte function (SB) is a simple table lookup that provides a nonlinear mapping. W defines a 16 × 16 matrix of byte values, called an S-box (Table 12.3), that contains a permutation of all possible 256 8-bit values. Each individual byte of **CState** is mapped into a new byte in the following way: The leftmost 4 bits of the byte are used as a row value and the rightmost 4 bits are used as a column value. These row and column values serve as indexes into the S-box to select a unique 8-bit output value. For example, the hexadecimal value[3] {95} references row 9, column 5 of the S-box, which contains the value {BA}. Accordingly, the value {95} is mapped into the value {BA}. The SB function can be expressed by the following correspondence, for an input matrix **A** and an output matrix **B**:

$$\mathbf{B} = \mathrm{SB}(\mathbf{A}) \Leftrightarrow b_{i,j} = \mathrm{S}[a_{i,j}], \quad 0 \leq i,j \leq 7$$

where S[x] refers to the mapping of input byte x into output byte S[x] by the S-box.

The S-box can be generated by the structure of Figure 12.9. It consists of two nonlinear layers, each containing two 4 × 4 S-boxes separated by a 4 × 4 randomly generated box. Each of the boxes maps a 4-bit input into a 4-bit output. The E box is defined as $\mathrm{E}(u) = \{\mathrm{B}\}^u$ if $u \neq \{\mathrm{F}\}$ and $\mathrm{E}(\{\mathrm{F}\}) = 0$, where arithmetic is performed over the finite field $\mathrm{GF}(2^4)$ with the irreducible polynomial $f(x) = x^4 + x + 1$.

The SB function is designed to introduce nonlinearity into the algorithm. This means that the SB function should exhibit no correlations between linear combinations of a input bits and linear combinations of a output bits. In addition, differences between sets of input bits should not propagate into similar differences among the corresponding output bits; put another way, small input changes should cause large output changes. These two properties help to make W resistant against linear and differential cryptanalysis.

The Permutation Layer SC The permutation layer (shift columns) causes a circular downward shift of each column of **CState** except the first column. For the second

[3]As we did for AES, a hexadecimal number is indicated by enclosing it in curly brackets when this is needed for clarity.

Table 12.3 Whirlpool S-Box

(a) S-box

	0	1	2	3	4	5	6	7	8	9	A	B	C	D	E	F
0	18	23	C6	E8	87	B8	01	4F	36	A6	D2	F5	79	6F	91	52
1	60	BC	9B	8E	A3	0C	7B	35	1D	E0	D7	C2	2E	4B	FE	57
2	15	77	37	E5	9F	F0	4A	CA	58	C9	29	0A	B1	A0	6B	85
3	BD	5D	10	F4	CB	3E	05	67	E4	27	41	8B	A7	7D	95	C8
4	FB	EE	7C	66	DD	17	47	9E	CA	2D	BF	07	AD	5A	83	33
5	63	02	AA	71	C8	19	49	C9	F2	E3	5B	88	9A	26	32	B0
6	E9	0F	D5	80	BE	CD	34	48	FF	7A	90	5F	20	68	1A	AE
7	B4	54	93	22	64	F1	73	12	40	08	C3	EC	DB	A1	8D	3D
8	97	00	CF	2B	76	82	D6	1B	B5	AF	6A	50	45	F3	30	EF
9	3F	55	A2	EA	65	BA	2F	C0	DE	1C	FD	4D	92	75	06	8A
A	B2	E6	0E	1F	62	D4	A8	96	F9	C5	25	59	84	72	39	4C
B	5E	78	38	8C	C1	A5	E2	61	B3	21	9C	1E	43	C7	FC	04
C	51	99	6D	0D	FA	DF	7E	24	3B	AB	CE	11	8F	4E	B7	EB
D	3C	81	94	F7	B9	13	2C	D3	E7	6E	C4	03	56	44	7F	A9
E	2A	BB	C1	53	DC	0B	9D	6C	31	74	F6	46	AC	89	14	E1
F	16	3A	69	09	70	B6	C0	ED	CC	42	98	A4	28	5C	F8	86

(b) E mini-box

u	0	1	2	3	4	5	6	7	8	9	A	B	C	D	E	F
E(u)	1	B	9	C	D	6	F	3	E	8	7	4	A	2	5	0

(c) E^{-1} mini-box

u	0	1	2	3	4	5	6	7	8	9	A	B	C	D	E	F
$E^{-1}(u)$	F	0	D	7	B	E	5	A	9	2	C	1	3	4	8	6

(d) R mini-box

u	0	1	2	3	4	5	6	7	8	9	A	B	C	D	E	F
R(u)	7	C	B	D	E	4	9	F	6	3	8	A	2	5	1	0

column, a 1-byte circular downward shift is performed; for the third column, a 2-byte circular downward shift is performed; and so on. The SC function can be expressed by the following correspondence, for an input matrix **A** and an output matrix **B**:

$$\mathbf{B} = \mathrm{SC}(\mathbf{A}) \Leftrightarrow b_{i,j} = a_{(i-j) \bmod 8, j} \quad 0 \le i, j \le 7$$

The shift column transformation is more substantial than it may first appear. This is because **CState** is treated as an array of eight 8-byte rows. Thus, on encryption, the first 8 bytes of the plaintext are copied to the first row of **CState**, and so on. A column shift moves an individual byte from one row to another, which is a linear distance of a multiple of 8 bytes. Also note that the transformation ensures that the 8 bytes of one row are spread out to eight different rows.

The Diffusion Layer MR Recall from Chapter 3 that for a function that exhibits diffusion, the statistical structure of the input is dissipated into long-range statistics of the output. This is achieved by having each input bit affect the value of many output

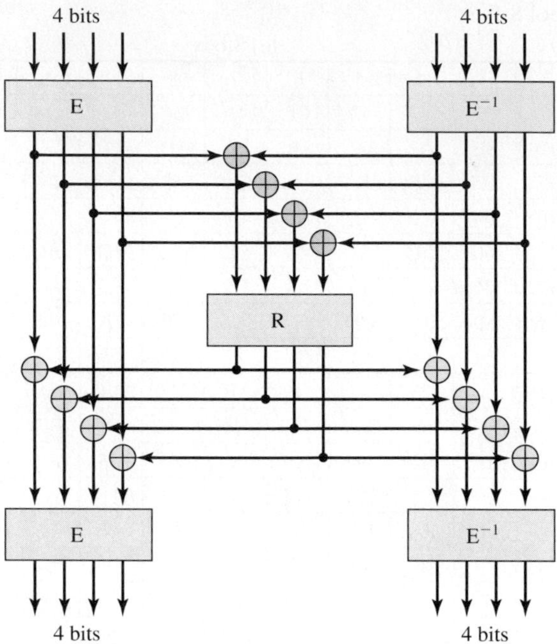

Figure 12.9 Implementation of Whirlpool S-Box

bits; generally, this results in each output bit being affected by many input bits. The diffusion layer (mix rows) achieves diffusion within each row individually. Each byte of a row is mapped into a new value that is a function of all eight bytes in that row. The transformation can be defined by the matrix multiplication: **B** = **AC**, where **A** is the input matrix, **B** is the output matrix, and **C** is the transformation matrix:

$$C = \begin{bmatrix} 01 & 01 & 04 & 01 & 08 & 05 & 02 & 09 \\ 09 & 01 & 01 & 04 & 01 & 08 & 05 & 02 \\ 02 & 09 & 01 & 01 & 04 & 01 & 08 & 05 \\ 05 & 02 & 09 & 01 & 01 & 04 & 01 & 08 \\ 08 & 05 & 02 & 09 & 01 & 01 & 04 & 01 \\ 01 & 08 & 05 & 02 & 09 & 01 & 01 & 04 \\ 04 & 01 & 08 & 05 & 02 & 09 & 01 & 01 \\ 01 & 04 & 01 & 08 & 05 & 02 & 09 & 01 \end{bmatrix}$$

Each element in the product matrix is the sum of products of elements of one row and one column. In this case, the individual additions and multiplications[4] are performed in GF(2^8) with the irreducible polynomial $f(x) = x^8 + x^4 + x^3 + x^2 + 1$. As an example of the matrix multiplication involved, the first element of the output matrix is

$$b_{0,0} = a_{0,0} \oplus (9 \cdot a_{0,1}) \oplus (2 \cdot a_{0,2}) \oplus (5 \cdot a_{0,3}) \oplus (8 \cdot a_{0,4}) \oplus a_{0,5} \oplus (4 \cdot a_{0,6}) \oplus a_{0,7}$$

[4]As we did for AES, we use the symbol • to indicate multiplication over the finite field GF(2^8) and $\oplus$ to indicate bitwise XOR, which corresponds to addition in GF(2^8).

Note that each row of **C** is constructed by means of a circular right shift of the preceding row. **C** is designed to be a **maximum distance separable** (MDS) matrix. In the field of error-correcting codes, an MDS code takes as input a fixed-length bit string and produces an expanded output string such that there is the maximum Hamming distance between pairs of output strings. With an MDS code, even multiple bit errors result in a code that is closer to the correct value than to some other value. In the context of block ciphers, a transformation matrix constructed using an MDS code provides a high degree of diffusion [JUNO04]. The use of MDS codes to provide high diffusion was first proposed in [RIJM96].

The matrix **C** is an MDS matrix that has as many 1-elements as possible (3 per row). Overall, the coefficients in **C** provide for efficient hardware implementation.

The Add Key Layer AK In the add key layer, the 512 bits of **CState** are bitwise XORed with the 512 bits of the round key. The AK function can be expressed by the following correspondence, for an input matrix **A**, an output matrix **B**, and a round key K_i:

$$\mathbf{B} = \text{AK}[K_i](\mathbf{A}) \Leftrightarrow b_{i,j} = a_{i,j} \oplus k_{i,j}, \quad 0 \le i, j \le 7$$

Key Expansion for the Block Cipher W As shown in Figure 12.7, key expansion is achieved by using the block cipher itself, with a round constant serving as the round key for the expansion. The round constant for round $r(1 \le r \le 10)$ is a matrix $\mathbf{RC}[r]$ in which only the first row is nonzero, and is defined as follows:

$$\begin{aligned} \text{rc}[r]_{0,j} &= S[8(r-1)+j], && 0 \le j \le 7, 1 \le r \le 10 \\ \text{rc}[r]_{i,j} &= 0, && 1 \le i \le 7, 0 \le j \le 7, 1 \le r \le 10 \end{aligned}$$

Each element of the first row is a mapping using the S-box. Thus, the first row of **RC**[1] is

S[0]	S[1]	S[2]	S[3]	S[4]	S[5]	S[6]	S[7]

=

18	23	C6	E8	87	B8	01	4F

Using the round constants, the key schedule expands the 512-bit cipher key ***K*** onto a sequence of round keys $\mathbf{K}_0, \mathbf{K}_1, \ldots, \mathbf{K}_{10}$:

$$\begin{aligned} K_0 &= K \\ K_r &= \text{RF}[\mathbf{RC}[r]](K_{r-1}) \end{aligned}$$

where RF is the round function defined in Equation (12.1). Note that for the AK phase of each round, only the first row of **KState** is altered.

Performance of Whirlpool

As yet, there has been little implementation experience with Whirlpool. Recall that the NIST evaluation of Rijndael determined that it exhibited good performance in both hardware and software and that it is well suited to restricted-space (low memory) requirements. These criteria were important in the selection of Rijndael for AES. Because Whirlpool uses the same functional building blocks as AES and has the same structure, we can expect similar performance and space characteristics.

One study that has been done is reported in [KITS04]. The authors compared Whirlpool with a number of other secure hash functions, including all of the versions of SHA. The authors developed multiple hardware implementations of each hash function and concluded that, compared to SHA-512, Whirlpool requires more hardware resources but performs much better in terms of throughput.

12.3 HMAC

In Chapter 11, we looked at an example of a message authentication code (MAC) based on the use of a symmetric block cipher, namely the Data Authentication Algorithm defined in FIPS PUB 113. This has traditionally been the most common approach to constructing a MAC. In recent years, there has been increased interest in developing a MAC derived from a cryptographic hash function. The motivations for this interest are

1. Cryptographic hash functions such as MD5 and SHA-1 generally execute faster in software than symmetric block ciphers such as DES.
2. Library code for cryptographic hash functions is widely available.

With the development of AES and the more widespread availability of code for encryption algorithms, these considerations are less significant, but hash-based MACs continue to be widely used.

A hash function such as SHA was not designed for use as a MAC and cannot be used directly for that purpose because it does not rely on a secret key. There have been a number of proposals for the incorporation of a secret key into an existing hash algorithm. The approach that has received the most support is HMAC [BELL96a, BELL96b]. HMAC has been issued as RFC 2104, has been chosen as the mandatory-to-implement MAC for IP security, and is used in other Internet protocols, such as SSL. HMAC has also been issued as a NIST standard (FIPS 198).

HMAC Design Objectives

RFC 2104 lists the following design objectives for HMAC:

- To use, without modifications, available hash functions. In particular, hash functions that perform well in software, and for which code is freely and widely available.
- To allow for easy replaceability of the embedded hash function in case faster or more secure hash functions are found or required.
- To preserve the original performance of the hash function without incurring a significant degradation.
- To use and handle keys in a simple way.
- To have a well understood cryptographic analysis of the strength of the authentication mechanism based on reasonable assumptions about the embedded hash function.

The first two objectives are important to the acceptability of HMAC. HMAC treats the hash function as a "black box." This has two benefits. First, an existing implementation of a hash function can be used as a module in implementing HMAC. In this way, the bulk of the HMAC code is prepackaged and ready to use without modification. Second, if it is ever desired to replace a given hash function in an HMAC implementation, all that is required is to remove the existing hash function module and drop in the new module. This could be done if a faster hash function were desired. More important, if the security of the embedded hash function were compromised, the security of HMAC could be retained simply by replacing the embedded hash function with a more secure one (e.g., replacing SHA with Whirlpool).

The last design objective in the preceding list is, in fact, the main advantage of HMAC over other proposed hash-based schemes. HMAC can be proven secure provided that the embedded hash function has some reasonable cryptographic strengths. We return to this point later in this section, but first we examine the structure of HMAC.

HMAC Algorithm

Figure 12.10 illustrates the overall operation of HMAC. Define the following terms:

H	=	embedded hash function (e.g., MD5, SHA-1, RIPEMD-160)
IV	=	initial value input to hash function
M	=	message input to HMAC(including the padding specified in the embedded hash function)
Y_i	=	ith block of M, $0 \le i \le (L - 1)$
L	=	number of blocks in M
b	=	number of bits in a block
n	=	length of hash code produced by embedded hash function
K	=	secret key recommended length is $\ge n$; if key length is greater than b; the key is input to the hash function to produce an n-bit key
K^+	=	K padded with zeros on the left so that the result is b bits in length
ipad	=	00110110 (36 in hexadecimal)repeated $b/8$ times
opad	=	01011100 (5C in hexadecimal)repeated $b/8$ times

Then HMAC can be expressed as follows:

$$\text{HMAC}(K, M) = \text{H}[(K^+ \oplus \text{opad}) \| \text{H}[(K^+ \oplus \text{ipad}) \| M]]$$

In words,

1. Append zeros to the left end of K to create a b-bit string K^+ (e.g., if K is of length 160 bits and $b = 512$, then K will be appended with 44 zero bytes 0×00).
2. XOR (bitwise exclusive-OR) K^+ with ipad to produce the b-bit block S_i.
3. Append M to S_i.
4. Apply H to the stream generated in step 3.
5. XOR K^+ with opad to produce the b-bit block S_o.
6. Append the hash result from step 4 to S_o.
7. Apply H to the stream generated in step 6 and output the result.

Note that the XOR with ipad results in flipping one-half of the bits of K. Similarly, the XOR with opad results in flipping one-half of the bits of K, but a different set of bits. In effect, by passing S_i and S_o through the compression function of the hash algorithm, we have pseudorandomly generated two keys from K.

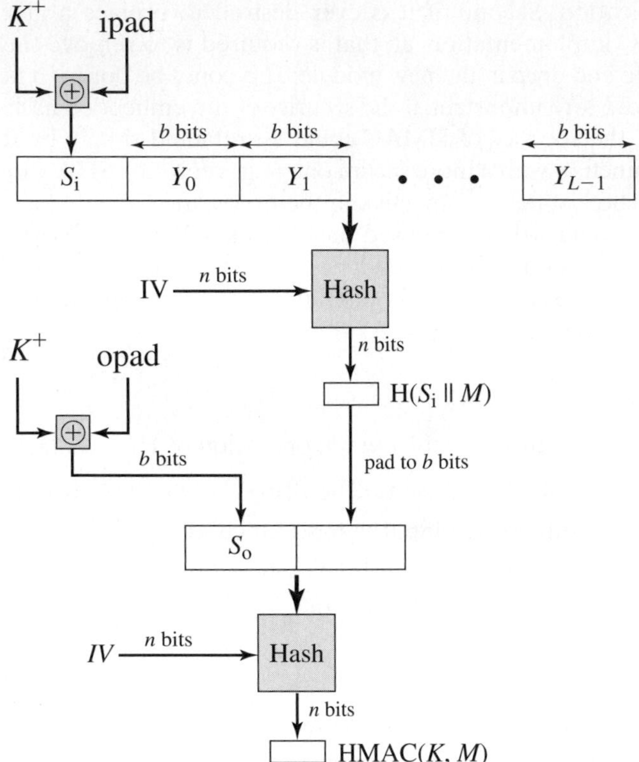

Figure 12.10 HMAC Structure

HMAC should execute in approximately the same time as the embedded hash function for long messages. HMAC adds three executions of the hash compression function (for S_i, S_o, and the block produced from the inner hash).

A more efficient implementation is possible, as shown in Figure 12.11. Two quantities are precomputed:

$$\mathrm{f}(\mathrm{IV}, (K^+ \oplus \mathrm{ipad}))$$
$$\mathrm{f}(\mathrm{IV}, (K^+ \oplus \mathrm{opad}))$$

where f(cv, block) is the compression function for the hash function, which takes as arguments a chaining variable of n bits and a block of b bits and produces a chaining variable of n bits. These quantities only need to be computed initially and every time the key changes. In effect, the precomputed quantities substitute for the initial value (IV) in the hash function. With this implementation, only one additional instance of the compression function is added to the processing normally produced by the hash function. This more efficient implementation is especially worthwhile if most of the messages for which a MAC is computed are short.

Security of HMAC

The security of any MAC function based on an embedded hash function depends in some way on the cryptographic strength of the underlying hash function. The appeal of HMAC is that its designers have been able to prove an exact relationship between the strength of the embedded hash function and the strength of HMAC.

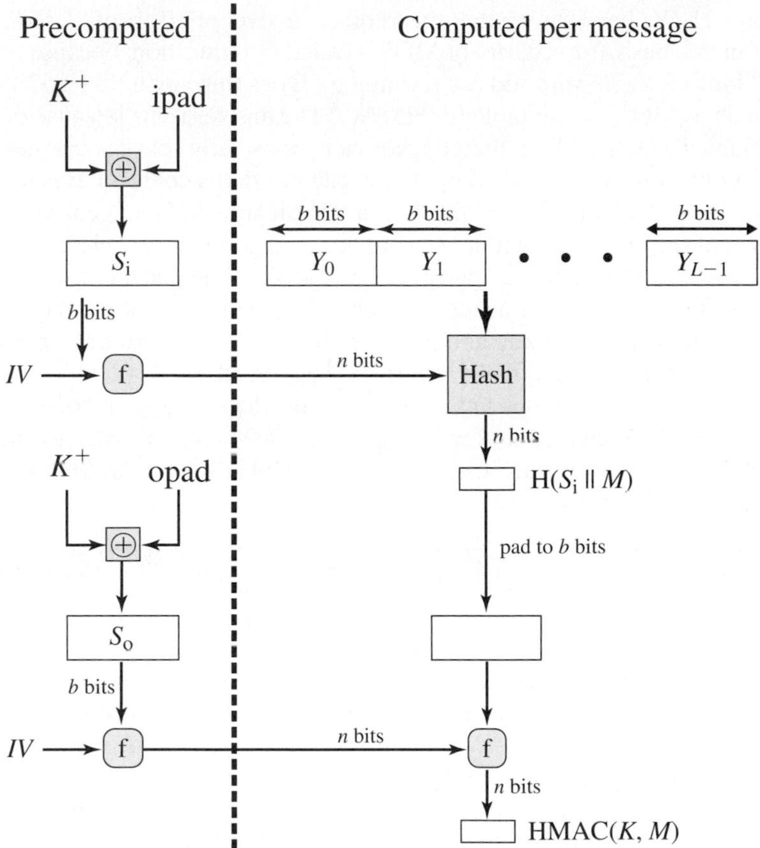

Figure 12.11 Efficient Implementation of HMAC

The security of a MAC function is generally expressed in terms of the probability of successful forgery with a given amount of time spent by the forger and a given number of message-MAC pairs created with the same key. In essence, it is proved in [BELL96a] that for a given level of effort (time, message-MAC pairs) on messages generated by a legitimate user and seen by the attacker, the probability of successful attack on HMAC is equivalent to one of the following attacks on the embedded hash function:

1. The attacker is able to compute an output of the compression function even with an IV that is random, secret, and unknown to the attacker.
2. The attacker finds collisions in the hash function even when the IV is random and secret.

In the first attack, we can view the compression function as equivalent to the hash function applied to a message consisting of a single b-bit block. For this attack, the IV of the hash function is replaced by a secret, random value of n bits. An attack on this hash function requires either a brute-force attack on the key, which is a level of effort on the order of 2^n, or a birthday attack, which is a special case of the second attack, discussed next.

In the second attack, the attacker is looking for two messages M and M' that produce the same hash: $H(M) = H(M')$. This is the birthday attack discussed in

Chapter 11. We have shown that this requires a level of effort of $2^{n/2}$ for a hash length of n. On this basis, the security of MD5 is called into question, because a level of effort of 2^{64} looks feasible with today's technology. Does this mean that a 128-bit hash function such as MD5 is unsuitable for HMAC? The answer is no, because of the following argument. To attack MD5, the attacker can choose any set of messages and work on these off line on a dedicated computing facility to find a collision. Because the attacker knows the hash algorithm and the default IV, the attacker can generate the hash code for each of the messages that the attacker generates. However, when attacking HMAC, the attacker cannot generate message/code pairs off line because the attacker does not know K. Therefore, the attacker must observe a sequence of messages generated by HMAC under the same key and perform the attack on these known messages. For a hash code length of 128 bits, this requires 2^{64} observed blocks (2^{72} bits) generated using the same key. On a 1-Gbps link, one would need to observe a continuous stream of messages with no change in key for about 150,000 years in order to succeed. Thus, if speed is a concern, it is fully acceptable to use MD5 rather than SHA-1 as the embedded hash function for HMAC.

12.4 CMAC

The Data Authentication Algorithm defined in FIPS PUB 113, also known as the CBC-MAC (cipher block chaining message authentication code), is described in Chapter 11. This cipher-based MAC has been widely adopted in government and industry. [BELL00] demonstrated that this MAC is secure under a reasonable set of security criteria, with the following restriction. Only messages of one fixed length of mn bits are processed, where n is the cipher block size and m is a fixed positive integer. As a simple example, notice that given the CBC MAC of a one-block message X, say $T = \text{MAC}(K, X)$, the adversary immediately knows the CBC MAC for the two-block message $X \| (X \oplus T)$ since this is once again T.

Black and Rogaway [BLAC00] demonstrated that this limitation could be overcome using three keys: one key of length k to be used at each step of the cipher block chaining and two keys of length n, where k is the key length and n is the cipher block length. This proposed construction was refined by Iwata and Kurosawa so that the two n-bit keys could be derived from the encryption key, rather than being provided separately [IWAT03]. This refinement has been adopted by NIST cipher-based message authentication code (CMAC) mode of operation, for use with AES and triple DES. It is specified in NIST Special Publication 800-38B.

First, let us consider the operation of CMAC when the message is an integer multiple n of the cipher block length b. For AES, $b = 128$ and for triple DES, $b = 64$. The message is divided into n blocks, $M_1, M_2, \ldots, M_n$. The algorithm makes use of a k-bit encryption key K and an n-bit constant K_1. For AES, the key size k is 128, 192, or 256 bits; for triple DES, the key size is 112 or 168 bits. CMAC is calculated as follows (Figure 12.12a):

$$C_1 = \text{E}(K, M_1)$$
$$C_2 = \text{E}(K, [M_2 \oplus C_1])$$
$$C_3 = \text{E}(K, [M_3 \oplus C_2])$$
$$\vdots$$

$$C_n = E(K, [M_N \oplus C_{n-1} \oplus K_1])$$
$$T = MSB_{Tlen}(C_n)$$

where

T = message authentication code, also referred to as the tag

$Tlen$ = bit length of T

$MSB_s(X)$ = the s leftmost bits of the bit string X

If the message is not an integer multiple of the cipher block length, then the final block is padded to the right (least significant bits) with a 1 and as many 0s as necessary so that the final block is also of length b. The CMAC operation then proceeds as before, except that a different n-bit key K_2 is used instead of K_1.

The two n-bit keys are derived from the k-bit encryption key as follows:

$$L = E(K, 0^n)$$
$$K_1 = L \cdot x$$
$$K_2 = L \cdot x^2 = (L \cdot x) \cdot x$$

where multiplication (•) is done in the finite field $GF(2^n)$ and x and x^2 are first and second order polynomials that are elements of $GF(2^n)$. Thus the binary representation of x consists of $n - 2$ zeros followed by 10; the binary representation of x^2 con-

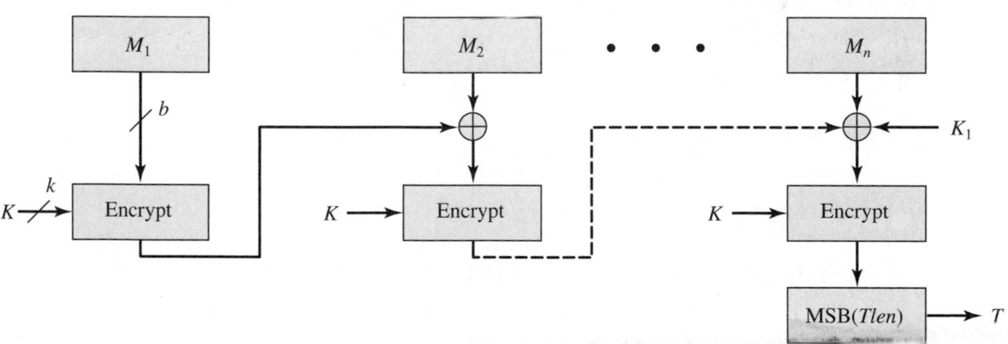

(a) Message length is integer multiple of block size

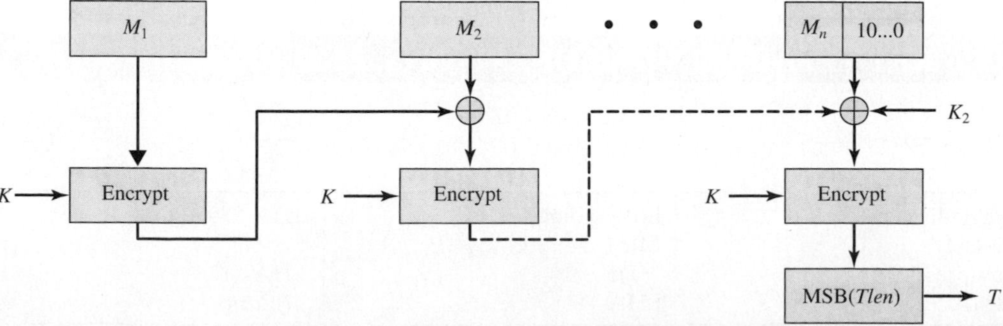

(b) Message length is not integer multiple of block size

Figure 12.12 Cipher-Based Message Authentication Code (CMAC)

sists of $n - 3$ zeros followed by 100. The finite field is defined with respect to an irreducible polynomial that is lexicographically first among all such polynomials with the minimum possible number of nonzero terms. For the two approved block sizes, the polynomials are $x^{64} + x^4 + x^3 + x + 1$ and $x^{128} + x^7 + x^2 + x + 1$.

To generate K_1 and K_2, the block cipher is applied to the block that consists entirely of 0 bits. The first subkey is derived from the resulting cipher text by a left shift of one bit, and, conditionally, by XORing a constant that depends on the block size. The second subkey is derived in the same manner from the first subkey. This property of finite fields of the form $GF(2^n)$ was explained in the discussion of MixColumns in Chapter 5.

12.5 RECOMMENDED READING AND WEB SITES

[GILB03] examines the security of SHA-256 through SHA-512. Overviews of HMAC can be found in [BELL96a] and [BELL96b].

BELL96a Bellare, M.; Canetti, R.; and Krawczyk, H. "Keying Hash Functions for Message Authentication." *Proceedings, CRYPTO '96*, August 1996; published by Springer-Verlag. An expanded version is available at **http://www-cse.ucsd.edu/users/mihir**.

BELL96b Bellare, M.; Canetti, R.; and Krawczyk, H. "The HMAC Construction." *CryptoBytes*, Spring 1996.

GILB03 Gilbert, H. and Handschuh, H. "Security Analysis of SHA-256 and Sisters." "*Proceedings, CRYPTO '03*, 2003; published by Springer-Verlag.

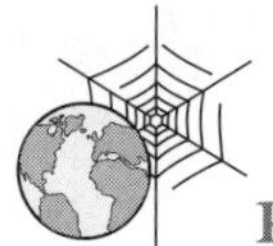

Recommended Web Sites:

- **NIST Secure Hashing Page:** SHA FIPS and related documents
- **Whirlpool:** Range of information on Whirlpool
- **Block cipher modes of operation:** NIST page with full information on CMAC

12.6 KEY TERMS, REVIEW QUESTIONS, AND PROBLEMS

Key Terms

big endian	little endian	SHA-256
CMAC	MD4	SHA-384
compression function	MD5	SHA-512
HMAC	SHA-1	Whirlpool

Review Questions

12.1 What is the difference between little-endian and big-endian format?

12.2 What basic arithmetical and logical functions are used in SHA?

12.3 What basic arithmetical and logical functions are used in Whirlpool?

12.4 Why has there been an interest in developing a message authentication code derived from a cryptographic hash function as opposed to one derived from a symmetric cipher?

12.5 What changes in HMAC are required in order to replace one underlying hash function with another?

Problems

12.1 In Figure 12.4, it is assumed that an array of 80 64-bit words is available to store the values of W_t, so that they can be precomputed at the beginning of the processing of a block. Now assume that space is at a premium. As an alternative, consider the use of a 16-word circular buffer that is initially loaded with W_0 through W_{15}. Design an algorithm that, for each step *t*, computes the required input value W_t.

12.2 For SHA-512, show the equations for the values of W_{16}, W_{17}, W_{18}, W_{19}.

12.3 Suppose $a_1\ a_2\ a_3\ a_4$ are the 4 bytes in a 32-bit word. Each a_i can be viewed as an integer in the range 0 to 255, represented in binary. In a big-endian architecture, this word represents the integer

$$a_1 2^{24} + a_2 2^{16} + a_3 2^8 + a_4$$

In a little-endian architecture, this word represents the integer

$$a_4 2^{24} + a_3 2^{16} + a_2 2^8 + a_1$$

a. Some hash functions, such as MD5, assume a little-endian architecture. It is important that the message digest be independent of the underlying architecture. Therefore, to perform the modulo 2 addition operation of MD5 or RIPEMD-160 on a big-endian architecture, an adjustment must be made. Suppose $X = x_1\ x_2\ x_3\ x_4$ and $Y = y_1\ y_2\ y_3\ y_4$. Show how the MD5 addition operation $(X + Y)$ would be carried out on a big-endian machine.

b. SHA assumes a big-endian architecture. Show how the operation $(X + Y)$ for SHA would be carried out on a little-endian machine.

12.4 This problem introduces a hash function similar in spirit to SHA that operates on letters instead of binary data. It is called the *toy tetragraph hash* (tth).[5] Given a message consisting of a sequence of letters, tth produces a hash value consisting of four letters. First, tth divides the message into blocks of 16 letters, ignoring spaces, punctuation, and capitalization. If the message length is not divisible by 16, it is padded out with nulls. A four-number running total is maintained that starts out with the value (0, 0, 0, 0); this is input to the compression function for processing the first block. The compression function consists of two rounds. **Round 1:** Get the next block of text and arrange it as a row-wise 4 × 4 block of text and convert it to numbers (A = 0, B = 1, etc.). For example, for the block ABCDEFGHIJKLMNOP, we have:

A	B	C	D
E	F	G	H
I	J	K	L
M	N	O	P

0	1	2	3
4	5	6	7
8	9	10	11
12	13	14	15

[5]I thank William K. Mason, of the magazine staff of *The Cryptogram*, for providing this example.

Then, add each column mod 26 and add the result to the running total, mod 26. In this example, the running total is (24, 2, 6, 10). **Round 2:** Using the matrix from round 1, rotate the first row left by 1, second row left by 2, third row left by 3 , and reverse the order of the fourth row. In our example:

B	C	D	A
G	H	E	F
L	I	J	K
P	O	N	M

1	2	3	0
6	7	4	5
11	8	9	10
15	14	13	12

Now, add each column mod 26 and add the result to the running total. The new running total is (5, 7, 9, 11). This running total is now the input into the first round of the compression function for the next block of text. After the final block is processed, convert the final running total to letters. For example, if the message is ABCDEFGHIJKLMNOP, then the hash is FHJL.

a. Draw figures comparable to Figures 12.1 and 12.2 to depict the overall tth logic and the compression function logic.

b. Calculate the hash function for the 48-letter message "I leave twenty million dollars to my friendly cousin Bill."

c. To demonstrate the weakness of tth, find a 48-letter block that produces the same hash as that just derived. *Hint:* Use lots of A's.

12.5 Develop a table similar to Table 4.8 for GF(2^8) with $m(x) = x^8 + x^4 + x^3 + x^2 + 1$.

12.6 Show the E and E^{-1} mini-boxes in Table 12.3 in the traditional S-box square matrix format, such as that of Table 5.4.

12.7 Verify that Figure 12.9 is a valid implementation of the S-box shown in Table 12.3a. Do this by showing the calculations involved for three input values: 00, 55, 1E.

12.8 Provide a Boolean expression that defines the S-box functionality of Figure 12.9.

12.9 Whirlpool makes use of the construction $H_i = E(H_{i-1}, M_i) \oplus H_{i-1} \oplus M_i$. Another construction that was shown by Preneel to be secure is $H_i = E(H_{i-1}, M_i) \oplus M_i$. Now notice that the key schedule for Whirlpool resembles encryption of the cipher key under a pseudo-key defined by the round constants, so that the core of the hashing process could be formally viewed as two interacting encryption lines. Consider the encryption $E(H_{i-1}, M_i)$. We could write the final round key for this block as $K_{10} = E(RC, H_{i-1})$. Now show that the two hash constructions are essentially equivalent because of the way that the key schedule is defined.

12.10 At the beginning of Section 12.4, it was noted that given the CBC MAC of a one-block message X, say $T = \text{MAC}(K, X)$, the adversary immediately knows the CBC MAC for the two-block message $X \| (X \oplus T)$ since this is once again T. Justify this statement.

12.11 In this problem, we demonstrate that for CMAC, a variant that XORs the second key after applying the final encryption doesn't work. Let us consider this for the case of the message being an integer multiple of the block size. Then the variant can be expressed as $\text{VMAC}(K, M) = \text{CBC}(K, M) \oplus K_1$. Now suppose an adversary is able to ask for the MACs of three messages: the message $\mathbf{0} = 0^n$, where n is the cipher block size; the message $\mathbf{1} = 1^n$, and the message $\mathbf{1} \| \mathbf{0}$. As a result of these three queries the adversary gets $T_0 = \text{CBC}(K, \mathbf{0}) \oplus K_1$; $T_1 = \text{CBC}(K, \mathbf{1}) \oplus K_1$, and $T_2 = \text{CBC}(K, [\text{CBC}(K, \mathbf{1})]) \oplus K_1$. Show that the adversary can compute the correct MAC for the (unqueried) message $\mathbf{0} \| (T_0 \oplus T_1)$.

12.12 In the discussion of subkey generation in CMAC, it states that the block cipher is applied to the block that consists entirely of 0 bits. The first subkey is derived from the resulting string by a left shift of one bit, and, conditionally, by XORing a constant that depends on the block size. The second subkey is derived in the same manner from the first subkey.

a. What constants are needed for block sizes of 64 and 128 bits?

b. Explain how the left shift and XOR accomplishes the desired result.

CHAPTER 13

Digital Signatures and Authentication Protocols

To guard against the baneful influence exerted by strangers is therefore an elementary dictate of savage prudence. Hence before strangers are allowed to enter a district, or at least before they are permitted to mingle freely with the inhabitants, certain ceremonies are often performed by the natives of the country for the purpose of disarming the strangers of their magical powers, or of disinfecting, so to speak, the tainted atmosphere by which they are supposed to be surrounded.

—*The Golden Bough*, Sir James George Frazer

KEY POINTS

- A digital signature is an authentication mechanism that enables the creator of a message to attach a code that acts as a signature. The signature is formed by taking the hash of the message and encrypting the message with the creator's private key. The signature guarantees the source and integrity of the message.
- Mutual authentication protocols enable communicating parties to satisfy themselves mutually about each other's identity and to exchange session keys.
- In one-way authentication, the recipient wants some assurance that a message is from the alleged sender.
- The digital signature standard (DSS) is an NIST standard that uses the secure hash algorithm (SHA).

The most important development from the work on public-key cryptography is the digital signature. The digital signature provides a set of security capabilities that would be difficult to implement in any other way. We begin this chapter with an overview of digital signatures. Then we look at authentication protocols, many of which depend on the use of the digital signature. Finally, we introduce the Digital Signature Standard (DSS).

13.1 DIGITAL SIGNATURES

Requirements

Message authentication protects two parties who exchange messages from any third party. However, it does not protect the two parties against each other. Several forms of dispute between the two are possible.

For example, suppose that John sends an authenticated message to Mary, using one of the schemes of Figure 11.4. Consider the following disputes that could arise:

1. Mary may forge a different message and claim that it came from John. Mary would simply have to create a message and append an authentication code using the key that John and Mary share.
2. John can deny sending the message. Because it is possible for Mary to forge a message, there is no way to prove that John did in fact send the message.

Both scenarios are of legitimate concern. Here is an example of the first scenario: An electronic funds transfer takes place, and the receiver increases the amount of funds transferred and claims that the larger amount had arrived from the sender. An example of the second scenario is that an electronic mail message contains instructions to a stockbroker for a transaction that subsequently turns out badly. The sender pretends that the message was never sent.

In situations where there is not complete trust between sender and receiver, something more than authentication is needed. The most attractive solution to this problem is the digital signature. The digital signature is analogous to the handwritten signature. It must have the following properties:

- It must verify the author and the date and time of the signature.
- It must to authenticate the contents at the time of the signature.
- It must be verifiable by third parties, to resolve disputes.

Thus, the digital signature function includes the authentication function.

On the basis of these properties, we can formulate the following requirements for a digital signature:

- The signature must be a bit pattern that depends on the message being signed.
- The signature must use some information unique to the sender, to prevent both forgery and denial.
- It must be relatively easy to produce the digital signature.
- It must be relatively easy to recognize and verify the digital signature.
- It must be computationally infeasible to forge a digital signature, either by constructing a new message for an existing digital signature or by constructing a fraudulent digital signature for a given message.
- It must be practical to retain a copy of the digital signature in storage.

A secure hash function, embedded in a scheme such as that of Figure 11.5c or d, satisfies these requirements.

A variety of approaches has been proposed for the digital signature function. These approaches fall into two categories: direct and arbitrated.

Direct Digital Signature

The direct digital signature involves only the communicating parties (source, destination). It is assumed that the destination knows the public key of the source. A digital signature may be formed by encrypting the entire message with the sender's private key (Figure 11.1c) or by encrypting a hash code of the message with the sender's private key (Figure 11.5c).

Confidentiality can be provided by further encrypting the entire message plus signature with either the receiver's public key (public-key encryption) or a shared secret key (symmetric encryption); for example, see Figures 11.1d and 11.5d. Note that it is important to perform the signature function first and then an outer confidentiality function. In case of dispute, some third party must view the message and its signature. If the signature is calculated on an encrypted message, then the third party also needs access to the decryption key to read the original message. However, if the signature is the inner operation, then the recipient can store the plaintext message and its signature for later use in dispute resolution.

All direct schemes described so far share a common weakness. The validity of the scheme depends on the security of the sender's private key. If a sender later wishes to deny sending a particular message, the sender can claim that the private key was lost or stolen and that someone else forged his or her signature. Administrative controls relating to the security of private keys can be employed to thwart or at least weaken this ploy, but the threat is still there, at least to some degree. One example is to require every signed message to include a timestamp (date and time) and to require prompt reporting of compromised keys to a central authority.

Another threat is that some private key might actually be stolen from X at time T. The opponent can then send a message signed with X's signature and stamped with a time before or equal to T.

Arbitrated Digital Signature

The problems associated with direct digital signatures can be addressed by using an arbiter.

As with direct signature schemes, there is a variety of arbitrated signature schemes. In general terms, they all operate as follows. Every signed message from a sender X to a receiver Y goes first to an arbiter A, who subjects the message and its signature to a number of tests to check its origin and content. The message is then dated and sent to Y with an indication that it has been verified to the satisfaction of the arbiter. The presence of A solves the problem faced by direct signature schemes: that X might disown the message.

The arbiter plays a sensitive and crucial role in this sort of scheme, and all parties must have a great deal of trust that the arbitration mechanism is working properly. The use of a trusted system, described in Chapter 20, might satisfy this requirement.

Table 13.1, based on scenarios described in [AKL83] and [MITC92], gives several examples of arbitrated digital signatures.[1] In the first, symmetric encryption is used. It is assumed that the sender X and the arbiter A share a secret key K_{xa} and that A and Y share secret key K_{ay}. X constructs a message M and computes its hash value H(M). Then X transmits the message plus a signature to A. The signature consists of an identifier ID_X of X plus the hash value, all encrypted using K_{xa}. A decrypts the signature and checks the hash value to validate the message. Then A transmits a message to Y,

[1]The following format is used. A communication step in which P sends a message M to Q is represented as P $\rightarrow$ Q: M.

Table 13.1 Arbitrated Digital Signature Techniques

(1) X → A: $M \| \mathrm{E}(K_{xa}, [ID_X \| \mathrm{H}(M)])$
(2) A → Y: $\mathrm{E}(K_{ay}, [ID_X \| M \| \mathrm{E}(K_{xa}, [ID_X \| \mathrm{H}(M)]) \| T])$

(a) Conventional Encryption, Arbiter Sees Message

(1) X → A: $ID_X \| \mathrm{E}(K_{xy}, M) \| \mathrm{E}(K_{xa}, [ID_X \| \mathrm{H}(\mathrm{E}(K_{xy}, M))])$
(2) A → Y: $\mathrm{E}(K_{ay}, [ID_X \| \mathrm{E}(K_{xy}, M)]) \| \mathrm{E}(K_{xa}, [ID_X \| \mathrm{H}(\mathrm{E}(K_{xy}, M)) \| T])$

(b) Conventional Encryption, Arbiter Does Not See Message

(1) X → A: $ID_X \| \mathrm{E}(PR_x, [ID_X \| \mathrm{E}(PU_y, \mathrm{E}(PR_x, M))])$
(2) A → Y: $\mathrm{E}(PR_a, [ID_X \| \mathrm{E}(PU_y, \mathrm{E}(PR_x, M)) \| T])$

(c) Public-Key Encryption, Arbiter Does Not See Message

Notation:

X = sender
Y = recipient
A = Arbiter
M = message
T = timestamp

encrypted with K_{ay}. The message includes ID_X, the original message from X, the signature, and a timestamp. Y can decrypt this to recover the message and the signature. The timestamp informs Y that this message is timely and not a replay. Y can store M and the signature. In case of dispute, Y, who claims to have received M from X, sends the following message to A:

$$\mathrm{E}(K_{ay}, [ID_X \| M \| \mathrm{E}(K_{xa}, [ID_X \| \mathrm{H}(M)])])$$

The arbiter uses K_{ay} to recover ID_X, M, and the signature, and then uses K_{xa} to decrypt the signature and verify the hash code. In this scheme, Y cannot directly check X's signature; the signature is there solely to settle disputes. Y considers the message from X authentic because it comes through A. In this scenario, both sides must have a high degree of trust in A:

- X must trust A not to reveal K_{xa} and not to generate false signatures of the form $\mathrm{E}(K_{xa}, [ID_X \| \mathrm{H}(M)])$.
- Y must trust A to send $\mathrm{E}(K_{ay}, [ID_X \| M \| \mathrm{E}(K_{xa}, [ID_X \| \mathrm{H}(M)]) \| T])$ only if the hash value is correct and the signature was generated by X.
- Both sides must trust A to resolve disputes fairly.

If the arbiter does live up to this trust, then X is assured that no one can forge his signature and Y is assured that X cannot disavow his signature.

The preceding scenario also implies that A is able to read messages from X to Y and, indeed, that any eavesdropper is able to do so. Table 13.1b shows a scenario that provides the arbitration as before but also assures confidentiality. In this case it is assumed that X and Y share the secret key K_{xy}. Now, X transmits an identifier, a copy of the message encrypted with K_{xy}, and a signature to A. The signature consists of the identifier plus the hash value of the encrypted message, all encrypted using K_{xa}. As before, A decrypts the signature and checks the hash value to validate the message. In this case, A is working only with the encrypted version of the message and is prevented from reading it. A then transmits everything that it received from X, plus a timestamp, all encrypted with K_{ay}, to Y.

Although unable to read the message, the arbiter is still in a position to prevent fraud on the part of either X or Y. A remaining problem, one shared with the first scenario, is that the arbiter could form an alliance with the sender to deny a signed message, or with the receiver to forge the sender's signature.

All the problems just discussed can be resolved by going to a public-key scheme, one version of which is shown in Table 13.1c. In this case, X double encrypts a message M first with X's private key, PR_x, and then with Y's public key, PU_y. This is a signed, secret version of the message. This signed message, together with X's identifier, is encrypted again with PR_x and, together with ID_X, is sent to A. The inner, double-encrypted message is secure from the arbiter (and everyone else except Y). However, A can decrypt the outer encryption to assure that the message must have come from X (because only X has PR_x). A checks to make sure that X's private/public key pair is still valid and, if so, verifies the message. Then A transmits a message to Y, encrypted with PR_a. The message includes ID_X, the double-encrypted message, and a timestamp.

This scheme has a number of advantages over the preceding two schemes. First, no information is shared among the parties before communication, preventing alliances to defraud. Second, no incorrectly dated message can be sent, even if PR_x is compromised, assuming that PR_a is not compromised. Finally, the content of the message from X to Y is secret from A and anyone else. However, this final scheme involves encryption of the message twice with a public-key algorithm. We discuss more practical approaches subsequently.

13.2 AUTHENTICATION PROTOCOLS

The basic tools described in Chapter 11 are used in a variety of applications, including the digital signature discussed in Section 13.1. Other uses are numerous and growing. In this section, we focus on two general areas (mutual authentication and one-way authentication) and examine some of the implications of authentication techniques in both.

Mutual Authentication

An important application area is that of mutual authentication protocols. Such protocols enable communicating parties to satisfy themselves mutually about each other's identity and to exchange session keys. This topic was examined in Section 7.3 (symmetric techniques) and Section 10.1 (public-key techniques). There, the focus was key distribution. We return to this topic here to consider the wider implications of authentication.

Central to the problem of authenticated key exchange are two issues: confidentiality and timeliness. To prevent masquerade and to prevent compromise of session keys, essential identification and session key information must be communicated in encrypted form. This requires the prior existence of secret or public keys that can be used for this purpose. The second issue, timeliness, is important because of the threat of message replays. Such replays, at worst, could allow an opponent to compromise a session key or successfully impersonate another party. At minimum, a successful replay can disrupt operations by presenting parties with messages that appear genuine but are not.

[GONG93] lists the following examples of replay attacks:

- **Simple replay:** The opponent simply copies a message and replays it later.
- **Repetition that can be logged:** An opponent can replay a timestamped message within the valid time window.
- **Repetition that cannot be detected:** This situation could arise because the original message could have been suppressed and thus did not arrive at its destination; only the replay message arrives.
- **Backward replay without modification:** This is a replay back to the message sender. This attack is possible if symmetric encryption is used and the sender cannot easily recognize the difference between messages sent and messages received on the basis of content.

One approach to coping with replay attacks is to attach a sequence number to each message used in an authentication exchange. A new message is accepted only if its sequence number is in the proper order. The difficulty with this approach is that it requires each party to keep track of the last sequence number for each claimant it has dealt with. Because of this overhead, sequence numbers are generally not used for authentication and key exchange. Instead, one of the following two general approaches is used:

- **Timestamps:** Party A accepts a message as fresh only if the message contains a timestamp that, in A's judgment, is close enough to A's knowledge of current time. This approach requires that clocks among the various participants be synchronized.
- **Challenge/response:** Party A, expecting a fresh message from B, first sends B a nonce (challenge) and requires that the subsequent message (response) received from B contain the correct nonce value.

It can be argued (e.g., [LAM92a]) that the timestamp approach should not be used for connection-oriented applications because of the inherent difficulties with this technique. First, some sort of protocol is needed to maintain synchronization among the various processor clocks. This protocol must be both fault tolerant, to cope with network errors, and secure, to cope with hostile attacks. Second, the opportunity for a successful attack will arise if there is a temporary loss of synchronization resulting from a fault in the clock mechanism of one of the parties. Finally, because of the variable and unpredictable nature of network delays, distributed clocks cannot be expected to maintain precise synchronization. Therefore, any timestamp-based procedure must allow for a window of time sufficiently large to accommodate network delays yet sufficiently small to minimize the opportunity for attack.

On the other hand, the challenge-response approach is unsuitable for a connectionless type of application because it requires the overhead of a handshake before any connectionless transmission, effectively negating the chief characteristic of a connectionless transaction. For such applications, reliance on some sort of secure time server and a consistent attempt by each party to keep its clocks in synchronization may be the best approach (e.g., [LAM92b]).

Symmetric Encryption Approaches As was discussed in Section 7.3, a two-level hierarchy of symmetric encryption keys can be used to provide confidentiality for communication in a distributed environment. In general, this strategy involves the use of a trusted key distribution center (KDC). Each party in the network shares a secret key, known as a master key, with the KDC. The KDC is responsible for generating keys to be used for a short time over a connection between two parties, known as session keys, and for distributing those keys using the master keys to protect the distribution. This approach is quite common. As an example, we look at the Kerberos system in Chapter 14. The discussion in this subsection is relevant to an understanding of the Kerberos mechanisms.

Figure 7.9 illustrates a proposal initially put forth by Needham and Schroeder [NEED78] for secret key distribution using a KDC that, as was mentioned in Chapter 7, includes authentication features. The protocol can be summarized as follows:

1. A → KDC: $ID_A \| ID_B \| N_1$
2. KDC → A: $E(K_a, [K_s \| ID_B \| N_1 \| E(K_b, [K_s \| ID_A])])$
3. A → B: $E(K_b, [K_s \| ID_A])$
4. B → A: $E(K_s, N_2)$
5. A → B: $E(K_s, f(N_2))$

Secret keys K_a and K_b are shared between A and the KDC and B and the KDC, respectively. The purpose of the protocol is to distribute securely a session key K_s to A and B. A securely acquires a new session key in step 2. The message in step 3 can be decrypted, and hence understood, only by B. Step 4 reflects B's knowledge of K_s, and step 5 assures B of A's knowledge of K_s and assures B that this is a fresh message because of the use of the nonce N_2. Recall from our discussion in Chapter 7 that the purpose of steps 4 and 5 is to prevent a certain type of replay attack. In particular, if an opponent is able to capture the message in step 3 and replay it, this might in some fashion disrupt operations at B.

Despite the handshake of steps 4 and 5, the protocol is still vulnerable to a form of replay attack. Suppose that an opponent, X, has been able to compromise an old session key. Admittedly, this is a much more unlikely occurrence than that an opponent has simply observed and recorded step 3. Nevertheless, it is a potential security risk. X can impersonate A and trick B into using the old key by simply replaying step 3. Unless B remembers indefinitely all previous session keys used with A, B will be unable to determine that this is a replay. If X can intercept the handshake message, step 4, then it can impersonate A's response, step 5. From this point on, X can send bogus messages to B that appear to B to come from A using an authenticated session key.

Denning [DENN81, DENN82] proposes to overcome this weakness by a modification to the Needham/Schroeder protocol that includes the addition of a timestamp to steps 2 and 3. Her proposal assumes that the master keys, K_a and K_b, are secure, and it consists of the following steps:

1. A → KDC: $ID_A \| ID_B$
2. KDC → A: $E(K_a, [K_s \| ID_B \| T \| E(K_b, [K_s \| ID_A \| T])])$
3. A → B: $E(K_b, [K_s \| ID_A \| T])$

4. B → A: $E(K_s, N_1)$
5. A → B: $E(K_s, f(N_1))$

T is a timestamp that assures A and B that the session key has only just been generated. Thus, both A and B know that the key distribution is a fresh exchange. A and B can verify timeliness by checking that

$$|\text{Clock} - T| < \Delta t_1 + \Delta t_2$$

where Δt_1 is the estimated normal discrepancy between the KDC's clock and the local clock (at A or B) and Δt_2 is the expected network delay time. Each node can set its clock against some standard reference source. Because the timestamp T is encrypted using the secure master keys, an opponent, even with knowledge of an old session key, cannot succeed because a replay of step 3 will be detected by B as untimely.

A final point: Steps 4 and 5 were not included in the original presentation [DENN81] but were added later [DENN82]. These steps confirm the receipt of the session key at B.

The Denning protocol seems to provide an increased degree of security compared to the Needham/Schroeder protocol. However, a new concern is raised: namely, that this new scheme requires reliance on clocks that are synchronized throughout the network. [GONG92] points out a risk involved. The risk is based on the fact that the distributed clocks can become unsynchronized as a result of sabotage on or faults in the clocks or the synchronization mechanism.[2] The problem occurs when a sender's clock is ahead of the intended recipient's clock. In this case, an opponent can intercept a message from the sender and replay it later when the timestamp in the message becomes current at the recipient's site. This replay could cause unexpected results. Gong refers to such attacks as **suppress-replay attacks**.

One way to counter suppress-replay attacks is to enforce the requirement that parties regularly check their clocks against the KDC's clock. The other alternative, which avoids the need for clock synchronization, is to rely on handshaking protocols using nonces. This latter alternative is not vulnerable to a suppress-replay attack because the nonces the recipient will choose in the future are unpredictable to the sender. The Needham/Schroeder protocol relies on nonces only but, as we have seen, has other vulnerabilities.

In [KEHN92], an attempt is made to respond to the concerns about suppress-replay attacks and at the same time fix the problems in the Needham/Schroeder protocol. Subsequently, an inconsistency in this latter protocol was noted and an improved strategy was presented in [NEUM93a].[3] The protocol is as follows:

1. A → B: $ID_A \| N_a$
2. B → KDC: $ID_B \| N_b \| E(K_b, [ID_A \| N_a \| T_b])$
3. KDC → A: $E(K_a, [ID_B \| N_a \| K_s \| T_b]) \| E(K_b, [ID_A \| K_s \| T_b]) \| N_b$
4. A → B: $E(K_b, [ID_A \| K_s \| T_b]) \| E(K_s, N_b)$

---

[2]Such things can and do happen. In recent years, flawed chips were used in a number of computers and other electronic systems to track the time and date. The chips had a tendency to skip forward one day [NEUM90].

[3]It really is hard to get these things right.

Let us follow this exchange step by step.

1. A initiates the authentication exchange by generating a nonce, N_a, and sending that plus its identifier to B in plaintext. This nonce will be returned to A in an encrypted message that includes the session key, assuring A of its timeliness.
2. B alerts the KDC that a session key is needed. Its message to the KDC includes its identifier and a nonce, N_b. This nonce will be returned to B in an encrypted message that includes the session key, assuring B of its timeliness. B's message to the KDC also includes a block encrypted with the secret key shared by B and the KDC. This block is used to instruct the KDC to issue credentials to A; the block specifies the intended recipient of the credentials, a suggested expiration time for the credentials, and the nonce received from A.
3. The KDC passes on to A B's nonce and a block encrypted with the secret key that B shares with the KDC. The block serves as a "ticket" that can be used by A for subsequent authentications, as will be seen. The KDC also sends to A a block encrypted with the secret key shared by A and the KDC. This block verifies that B has received A's initial message (ID_B) and that this is a timely message and not a replay (N_a), and it provides A with a session key (K_s) and the time limit on its use (T_b).
4. A transmits the ticket to B, together with the B's nonce, the latter encrypted with the session key. The ticket provides B with the secret key that is used to decrypt $\mathrm{E}(K_s, N_b)$ to recover the nonce. The fact that B's nonce is encrypted with the session key authenticates that the message came from A and is not a replay.

This protocol provides an effective, secure means for A and B to establish a session with a secure session key. Furthermore, the protocol leaves A in possession of a key that can be used for subsequent authentication to B, avoiding the need to contact the authentication server repeatedly. Suppose that A and B establish a session using the aforementioned protocol and then conclude that session. Subsequently, but within the time limit established by the protocol, A desires a new session with B. The following protocol ensues:

1. A → B: $\mathrm{E}(K_b, [ID_A \| K_s \| T_b]) \| N'_a$
2. B → A: $N'_b \| \mathrm{E}(K_s, N'_a)$
3. A → B: $\mathrm{E}(K_s, N'_b)$

When B receives the message in step 1, it verifies that the ticket has not expired. The newly generated nonces N'_a and N'_b assure each party that there is no replay attack.

In all the foregoing, the time specified in T_b is a time relative to B's clock. Thus, this timestamp does not require synchronized clocks because B checks only self-generated timestamps.

Public-Key Encryption Approaches In Chapter 10, we presented one approach to the use of public-key encryption for the purpose of session key distribution (Figure 10.6). This protocol assumes that each of the two parties is in possession of the current public key of the other. It may not be practical to require this assumption.

A protocol using timestamps is provided in [DENN81]:

1. A → AS: $ID_A \| ID_B$
2. AS → A: $E(PR_{as}, [ID_A \| PU_a \| T]) \| E(PR_{as}, [ID_B \| PU_b \| T])$
3. A → B: $E(PR_{as}, [ID_A \| PU_a \| T]) \| E(PR_{as}, [ID_B \| PU_b \| T])$
$\| E(PU_b, E(PR_a, [K_s \| T]))$

In this case, the central system is referred to as an authentication server (AS), because it is not actually responsible for secret key distribution. Rather, the AS provides public-key certificates. The session key is chosen and encrypted by A; hence, there is no risk of exposure by the AS. The timestamps protect against replays of compromised keys.

This protocol is compact but, as before, requires synchronization of clocks. Another approach, proposed by Woo and Lam [WOO92a], makes use of nonces. The protocol consists of the following steps:

1. A → KDC: $ID_A \| ID_B$
2. KDC → A: $E(PR_{auth}, [ID_B \| PU_b])$
3. A → B: $E(PU_b, [N_a \| ID_A])$
4. B → KDC: $ID_A \| ID_B \| E(PU_{auth}, N_a)$
5. KDC → B: $E(PR_{auth}, [ID_A \| PU_a]) \| E(PU_b, E(PR_{auth}, [N_a \| K_s \| ID_B]))$
6. B → A: $E(PU_a, E(PR_{auth}, [(N_a \| K_s \| ID_B) \| N_b]))$
7. A → B: $E(K_s, N_b)$

In step 1, A informs the KDC of its intention to establish a secure connection with B. The KDC returns to A a copy of B's public-key certificate (step 2). Using B's public key, A informs B of its desire to communicate and sends a nonce N_a (step 3). In step 4, B asks the KDC for A's public-key certificate and requests a session key; B includes A's nonce so that the KDC can stamp the session key with that nonce. The nonce is protected using the KDC's public key. In step 5, the KDC returns to B a copy of A's public-key certificate, plus the information $\{N_a, K_s, ID_B\}$. This information basically says that K_s is a secret key generated by the KDC on behalf of B and tied to N_a; the binding of K_s and N_a will assure A that K_s is fresh. This triple is encrypted, using the KDC's private key, to allow B to verify that the triple is in fact from the KDC. It is also encrypted using B's public key, so that no other entity may use the triple in an attempt to establish a fraudulent connection with A. In step 6, the triple $\{N_a, K_s, ID_B\}$, still encrypted with the KDC's private key, is relayed to A, together with a nonce N_b generated by B. All the foregoing are encrypted using A's public key. A retrieves the session key K_s and uses it to encrypt N_b and return it to B. This last message assures B of A's knowledge of the session key.

This seems to be a secure protocol that takes into account the various attacks. However, the authors themselves spotted a flaw and submitted a revised version of the algorithm in [WOO92b]:

1. A → KDC: $ID_A \| ID_B$
2. KDC → A: $E(PR_{auth}, [ID_B \| PU_b])$
3. A → B: $E(PU_b, [N_a \| ID_A])$

4. B → KDC: $ID_A \| ID_B \| \mathrm{E}(PU_{auth}, N_a)$
5. KDC → B: $\mathrm{E}(PR_{auth}, [ID_A \| PU_a]) \| \mathrm{E}(PU_b, \mathrm{E}(PR_{auth}, [N_a \| K_s \| ID_A \| ID_B]))$
6. B → A: $\mathrm{E}(PU_a, \mathrm{E}(PR_{auth}, [(N_a \| K_s \| ID_A \| ID_B) \| N_b]))$
7. A → B: $\mathrm{E}(K_s, N_b)$

The identifier of A, ID_A, is added to the set of items encrypted with the KDC's private key in steps 5 and 6. This binds the session key K_s to the identities of the two parties that will be engaged in the session. This inclusion of ID_A accounts for the fact that the nonce value N_a is considered unique only among all nonces generated by A, not among all nonces generated by all parties. Thus, it is the pair $\{ID_A, N_a\}$ that uniquely identifies the connection request of A.

In both this example and the protocols described earlier, protocols that appeared secure were revised after additional analysis. These examples highlight the difficulty of getting things right in the area of authentication.

One-Way Authentication

One application for which encryption is growing in popularity is electronic mail (e-mail). The very nature of electronic mail, and its chief benefit, is that it is not necessary for the sender and receiver to be online at the same time. Instead, the e-mail message is forwarded to the receiver's electronic mailbox, where it is buffered until the receiver is available to read it.

The "envelope" or header of the e-mail message must be in the clear, so that the message can be handled by the store-and-forward e-mail protocol, such as the Simple Mail Transfer Protocol (SMTP) or X.400. However, it is often desirable that the mail-handling protocol not require access to the plaintext form of the message, because that would require trusting the mail-handling mechanism. Accordingly, the e-mail message should be encrypted such that the mail-handling system is not in possession of the decryption key.

A second requirement is that of authentication. Typically, the recipient wants some assurance that the message is from the alleged sender.

Symmetric Encryption Approach Using symmetric encryption, the decentralized key distribution scenario illustrated in Figure 7.11 is impractical. This scheme requires the sender to issue a request to the intended recipient, await a response that includes a session key, and only then send the message.

With some refinement, the KDC strategy illustrated in Figure 7.9 is a candidate for encrypted electronic mail. Because we wish to avoid requiring that the recipient (B) be on line at the same time as the sender (A), steps 4 and 5 must be eliminated. For a message with content M, the sequence is as follows:

1. A → KDC: $ID_A \| ID_B \| N_1$
2. KDC → A: $\mathrm{E}(K_a, [K_s \| ID_B \| N_1 \| \mathrm{E}(K_b, [K_s \| ID_A])])$
3. A → B: $\mathrm{E}(K_b, [K_s \| ID_A]) \| \mathrm{E}(K_s, M)$

This approach guarantees that only the intended recipient of a message will be able to read it. It also provides a level of authentication that the sender is A. As specified, the protocol does not protect against replays. Some measure of defense could be provided by including a timestamp with the message. However, because of the potential delays in the e-mail process, such timestamps may have limited usefulness.

Public-Key Encryption Approaches We have already presented public-key encryption approaches that are suited to electronic mail, including the straightforward encryption of the entire message for confidentiality (Figure 11.1b), authentication (Figure 11.1c), or both (Figure 11.1d). These approaches require that either the sender know the recipient's public key (confidentiality) or the recipient know the sender's public key (authentication) or both (confidentiality plus authentication). In addition, the public-key algorithm must be applied once or twice to what may be a long message.

If confidentiality is the primary concern, then the following may be more efficient:

$$\mathrm{A} \rightarrow \mathrm{B}\colon \mathrm{E}(PU_b, K_s) \| \mathrm{E}(K_s, M)$$

In this case, the message is encrypted with a one-time secret key. A also encrypts this one-time key with B's public key. Only B will be able to use the corresponding private key to recover the one-time key and then use that key to decrypt the message. This scheme is more efficient than simply encrypting the entire message with B's public key.

If authentication is the primary concern, then a digital signature may suffice, as was illustrated in Figure 11.5c:

$$\mathrm{A} \rightarrow \mathrm{B}\colon M \| \mathrm{E}(PR_a, \mathrm{H}(M))$$

This method guarantees that A cannot later deny having sent the message. However, this technique is open to another kind of fraud. Bob composes a message to his boss Alice that contains an idea that will save the company money. He appends his digital signature and sends it into the e-mail system. Eventually, the message will get delivered to Alice's mailbox. But suppose that Max has heard of Bob's idea and gains access to the mail queue before delivery. He finds Bob's message, strips off his signature, appends his, and requeues the message to be delivered to Alice. Max gets credit for Bob's idea.

To counter such a scheme, both the message and signature can be encrypted with the recipient's public key:

$$\mathrm{A} \rightarrow \mathrm{B}\colon \mathrm{E}(PU_b, [M \| \mathrm{E}(PR_a, \mathrm{H}(M))])$$

The latter two schemes require that B know A's public key and be convinced that it is timely. An effective way to provide this assurance is the digital certificate, described in Chapter 10. Now we have

$$\mathrm{A} \rightarrow \mathrm{B}\colon M \| \mathrm{E}(PR_a, \mathrm{H}(M)) \| \mathrm{E}(PR_{as}, [T \| ID_A \| PU_a])$$

In addition to the message, A sends B the signature, encrypted with A's private key, and A's certificate, encrypted with the private key of the authentication server. The recipient of the message first uses the certificate to obtain the sender's public key and verify that it is authentic and then uses the public key to verify the message itself. If confidentiality is required, then the entire message can be encrypted with B's public key. Alternatively, the entire message can be encrypted with a one-time secret key; the secret key is also transmitted, encrypted with B's public key. This approach is explored in Chapter 15.

13.3 DIGITAL SIGNATURE STANDARD

The National Institute of Standards and Technology (NIST) has published Federal Information Processing Standard FIPS 186, known as the Digital Signature Standard (DSS). The DSS makes use of the Secure Hash Algorithm (SHA) described in Chapter 12 and presents a new digital signature technique, the Digital Signature Algorithm (DSA). The DSS was originally proposed in 1991 and revised in 1993 in response to public feedback concerning the security of the scheme. There was a further minor revision in 1996. In 2000, an expanded version of the standard was issued as FIPS 186-2. This latest version also incorporates digital signature algorithms based on RSA and on elliptic curve cryptography. In this section, we discuss the original DSS algorithm.

The DSS Approach

The DSS uses an algorithm that is designed to provide only the digital signature function. Unlike RSA, it cannot be used for encryption or key exchange. Nevertheless, it is a public-key technique.

Figure 13.1 contrasts the DSS approach for generating digital signatures to that used with RSA. In the RSA approach, the message to be signed is input to a hash function that produces a secure hash code of fixed length. This hash code is then encrypted using the sender's private key to form the signature. Both the message and the signature are then transmitted. The recipient takes the message and produces a hash code. The recipient also decrypts the signature using the sender's public key. If the calculated hash code matches the decrypted signature, the signature is accepted as valid. Because only the sender knows the private key, only the sender could have produced a valid signature.

The DSS approach also makes use of a hash function. The hash code is provided as input to a signature function along with a random number k generated for this particular signature. The signature function also depends on the sender's private key

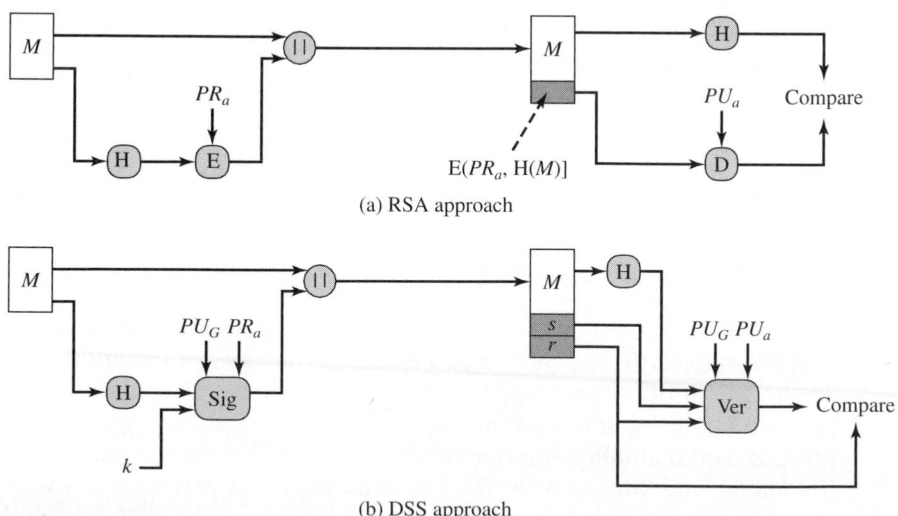

Figure 13.1 Two Approaches to Digital Signatures

(PR_a) and a set of parameters known to a group of communicating principals. We can consider this set to constitute a global public key (PU_G).[4] The result is a signature consisting of two components, labeled s and r.

At the receiving end, the hash code of the incoming message is generated. This plus the signature is input to a verification function. The verification function also depends on the global public key as well as the sender's public key (PU_a), which is paired with the sender's private key. The output of the verification function is a value that is equal to the signature component r if the signature is valid. The signature function is such that only the sender, with knowledge of the private key, could have produced the valid signature.

We turn now to the details of the algorithm.

The Digital Signature Algorithm

The DSA is based on the difficulty of computing discrete logarithms (see Chapter 8) and is based on schemes originally presented by ElGamal [ELGA85] and Schnorr [SCHN91].

Figure 13.2 summarizes the algorithm. There are three parameters that are public and can be common to a group of users. A 160-bit prime number q is chosen.

Global Public-Key Components

p prime number where $2^{L-1} < p < 2^L$ for $512 \le L \le 1024$ and L a multiple of 64; i.e., bit length of between 512 and 1024 bits in increments of 64 bits

q prime divisor of $(p - 1)$, where $2^{159} < q < 2^{160}$; i.e., bit length of 160 bits

g $= h^{(p-1)/q} \bmod p$, where h is any integer with $1 < h < (p - 1)$ such that $h^{(p-1)/q} \bmod p > 1$

User's Private Key

x random or pseudorandom integer with $0 < x < q$

User's Public Key

$y = g^x \bmod p$

User's Per-Message Secret Number

k = random or pseudorandom integer with $0 < k < q$

Signing

$r = (g^k \bmod p) \bmod q$

$s = [k^{-1} (H(M) + xr)] \bmod q$

Signature = (r, s)

Verifying

$w = (s')^{-1} \bmod q$

$u_1 = [H(M')w] \bmod q$

$u_2 = (r')w \bmod q$

$v = [(g^{u1} y^{u2}) \bmod p] \bmod q$

TEST: $v = r'$

M = message to be signed

$H(M)$ = hash of M using SHA-1

M', r', s' = received versions of M, r, s

Figure 13.2 The Digital Signature Algorithm (DSA)

---

[4]It is also possible to allow these additional parameters to vary with each user so that they are a part of a user's public key. In practice, it is more likely that a global public key will be used that is separate from each user's public key.

Next, a prime number p is selected with a length between 512 and 1024 bits such that q divides $(p - 1)$. Finally, g is chosen to be of the form $h^{(p-1)/q} \bmod p$ where h is an integer between 1 and $(p - 1)$ with the restriction that g must be greater than 1.[5]

With these numbers in hand, each user selects a private key and generates a public key. The private key x must be a number from 1 to $(q - 1)$ and should be chosen randomly or pseudorandomly. The public key is calculated from the private key as $y = g^x \bmod p$. The calculation of y given x is relatively straightforward. However, given the public key y, it is believed to be computationally infeasible to determine x, which is the discrete logarithm of y to the base g, mod p (see Chapter 8).

To create a signature, a user calculates two quantities, r and s, that are functions of the public key components (p, q, g), the user's private key (x), the hash code of the message, H(M), and an additional integer k that should be generated randomly or pseudorandomly and be unique for each signing.

At the receiving end, verification is performed using the formulas shown in Figure 13.2. The receiver generates a quantity v that is a function of the public key components, the sender's public key, and the hash code of the incoming message. If this quantity matches the r component of the signature, then the signature is validated.

Figure 13.3 depicts the functions of signing and verifying.

The structure of the algorithm, as revealed in Figure 13.3, is quite interesting. Note that the test at the end is on the value r, which does not depend on the

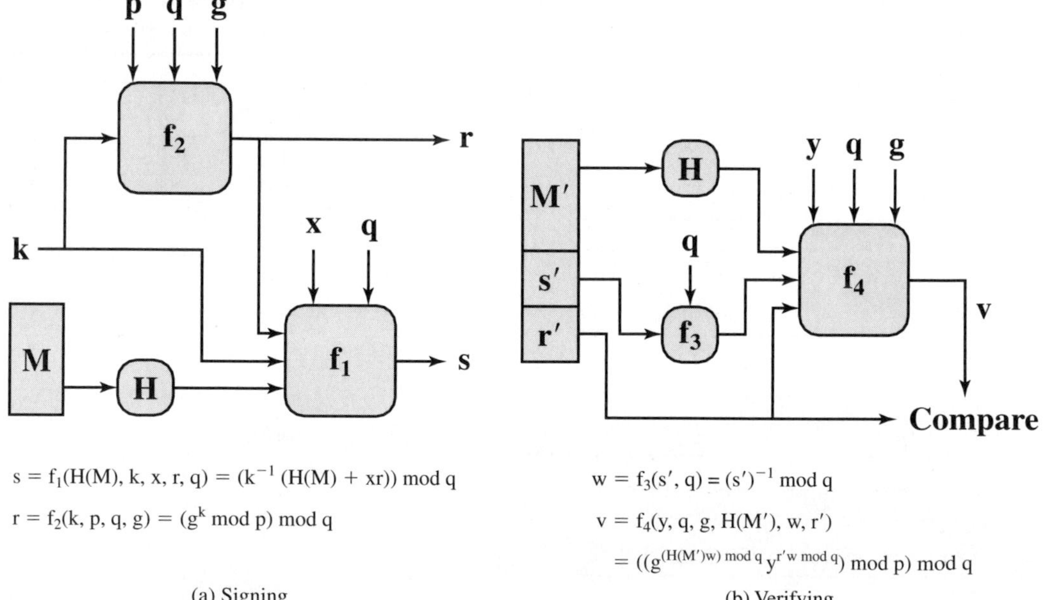

Figure 13.3 DSS Signing and Verifying

[5]In number-theoretic terms, g is of order q mod p; see Chapter 8.

message at all. Instead, r is a function of k and the three global public-key components. The multiplicative inverse of $k \pmod q$ is passed to a function that also has as inputs the message hash code and the user's private key. The structure of this function is such that the receiver can recover r using the incoming message and signature, the public key of the user, and the global public key. It is certainly not obvious from Figure 13.2 or Figure 13.3 that such a scheme would work. A proof is provided at this book's Web site.

Given the difficulty of taking discrete logarithms, it is infeasible for an opponent to recover k from r or to recover x from s.

Another point worth noting is that the only computationally demanding task in signature generation is the exponential calculation $g^k \bmod p$. Because this value does not depend on the message to be signed, it can be computed ahead of time. Indeed, a user could precalculate a number of values of r to be used to sign documents as needed. The only other somewhat demanding task is the determination of a multiplicative inverse, k^{-1}. Again, a number of these values can be precalculated.

13.4 RECOMMENDED READING AND WEB SITES

[AKL83] is the classic paper on digital signatures and is still highly relevant. A more recent, and excellent, survey is [MITC92].

AKL83 Akl, S. "Digital Signatures: A Tutorial Survey." *Computer*, February 1983.
MITC92 Mitchell, C.; Piper, F. ; and Wild, P. "Digital Signatures." In [SIMM92a].

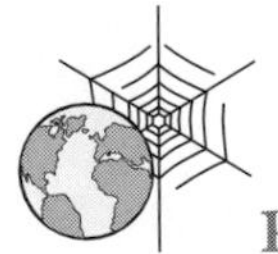

Recommended Web Sites:

- **Digital Signatures:** NIST page with information on NIST-approved digital signature options

13.5 KEY TERMS, REVIEW QUESTIONS, AND PROBLEMS

Key Terms

arbiter arbitrated digital signature direct digital signature digital signature	digital signature algorithm (DSA) digital signature standard (DSS) mutual authentication	nonce one-way authentication replay attack suppress-replay attack timestamp

Review Questions

13.1 List two disputes that can arise in the context of message authentication.

13.2 What are the properties a digital signature should have?

13.3 What requirements should a digital signature scheme satisfy?

13.4 What is the difference between direct and arbitrated digital signature?

13.5 In what order should the signature function and the confidentiality function be applied to a message, and why?

13.6 What are some threats associated with a direct digital signature scheme?

13.7 Give examples of replay attacks.

13.8 List three general approaches to dealing with replay attacks.

13.9 What is a suppress-replay attack?

Problems

13.1 Modify the digital signature techniques of Table 13.1a and b to enable the receiver to verify the signature.

13.2 Modify the digital signature technique of Table 13.1c to avoid triple encryption of the entire message.

13.3 In discussing Table 13.1c, it was stated that alliances to defraud were impossible. In fact, there is one possibility. Describe it and explain why it would have so little credibility that we can safely ignore it.

13.4 In Section 13.2, we outlined the public-key scheme proposed in [WOO92a] for the distribution of secret keys. The revised version includes ID_A in steps 5 and 6. What attack, specifically, is countered by this revision?

13.5 The protocol referred to in Problem 13.1 can be reduced from seven steps to five, having the following sequence:

(1) A → B:
(2) B → KDC:
(3) KDC → B:
(4) B → A:
(5) A → B:

Show the message transmitted at each step. *Hint:* The final message in this protocol is the same as the final message in the original protocol.

13.6 With reference to the suppress-replay attack described in Section 13.2:

a. Give an example of an attack when a party's clock is ahead of that of the KDC.
b. Give an example of an attack when a party's clock is ahead of that of another party.

13.7 There are three typical ways to use nonces as challenges. Suppose N_a is a nonce generated by A, A and B share key K, and f() is a function such as increment. The three usages are

Usage 1	Usage 2	Usage 3
(1) A → B: N_a	(1) A → B: E(K, N_a)	(1) A → B: E(K, N_a)
(2) B → A: E(K, N_a)	(2) B → A: N_a	(2) B → A: E(K, f(N_a))

Describe situations for which each usage is appropriate.

13.8 Dr. Watson patiently waited until Sherlock Holmes finished. "Some interesting problem to solve, Holmes?" he asked when Holmes finally logged out.

"Oh, not exactly. I merely checked my e-mail and then made a couple of network experiments instead of my usual chemical ones. I have only one client now and

I have already solved his problem. If I remember correctly, you once mentioned cryptology among your other hobbies, so it may interest you."

"Well, I am only an amateur cryptologist, Holmes. But of course I am interested in the problem. What is it about?"

"My client is Mr. Hosgrave, director of a small but progressive bank. The bank is fully computerized and of course uses network communications extensively. The bank already uses RSA to protect its data and to digitally sign documents that are communicated. Now the bank wants to introduce some changes in its procedures; in particular, it needs to digitally sign some documents by *two* signatories so that

1. The first signatory prepares the document, forms its signature, and passes the document to the second signatory.
2. The second signatory as a first step must verify that the document was really signed by the first signatory. She then incorporates her signature into the document's signature so that the recipient, as well as any member of the public, may verify that the document was indeed signed by both signatories. In addition only the second signatory has to be able to verify the document's signature after the step (1); that is the recipient (or any member of the public) should be able to verify only the complete document with signatures of both signatories, but not the document in its intermediate form where only one signatory has signed it. Moreover, the bank would like to make use of its existing modules that support RSA-style digital signatures."

"Hm, I understand how RSA can be used to digitally sign documents by *one* signatory, Holmes. I guess you have solved the problem of Mr. Hosgrave by appropriate generalization of RSA digital signatures."

"Exactly, Watson," nodded Sherlock Holmes. "Originally, the RSA digital signature was formed by encrypting the document by the signatory's private decryption key 'd', and the signature could be verified by anyone through its decryption using publicly known encryption key 'e'. One can verify that the signature S was formed by the person who knows d, which is supposed to be the only signatory. Now the problem of Mr. Hosgrave can be solved in the same way by slight generalization of the process, that is . . . "

Finish the explanation.

13.9 DSA specifies that if the signature generation process results in a value of $s = 0$, a new value of k should be generated and the signature should be recalculated. Why?

13.10 What happens if a k value used in creating a DSA signature is compromised?

13.11 The DSS document includes a recommended algorithm for testing a number for primality, as follows:

(1) **[Choose w]** Let w be a random odd integer. Then $(w - 1)$ is even and can be expressed in the form $2^a m$ with m odd. That is, 2^a is the largest power of 2 that divides $(w - 1)$.
(2) **[Generate b]** Let b be a random integer in the range $1 < b < w$.
(3) **[Exponentiate]** Set $j = 0$ and $z = b^m \bmod w$.
(4) **[Done?]** If $j = 0$ and $z = 1$, or if $z = w - 1$, then w passes the test and may be prime; go to step 8.
(5) **[Terminate?]** If $j > 0$ and $z = 1$, then w is not prime; terminate algorithm for this w.
(6) **[Increase j]** Set $j = j + 1$. If $j < a$, set $z = z^2 \bmod w$ and go to step 4.
(7) **[Terminate]** w is not prime; terminate algorithm for this w.
(8) **[Test again?]** If enough random values of b have been tested, then accept w as prime and terminate algorithm; otherwise, go to step 2.

a. Explain how the algorithm works.
b. Show that it is equivalent to the Miller-Rabin test described in Chapter 8.

13.12 With DSS, because the value of k is generated for each signature, even if the same message is signed twice on different occasions, the signatures will differ. This is not true of RSA signatures. What is the practical implication of this difference?

13.13 Consider the problem of creating domain parameters for DSA. Suppose we have already found primes p and q such that $q|(p-1)$. Now we need to find $g \in Z_p$ with g of order q mod p. Consider the following two algorithms:

Algorithm 1	Algorithm 2
repeat	**repeat**
select $g \in Z_p$	**select** $h \in Z_p$
$h \leftarrow g^q \bmod p$	$g \leftarrow h^{(p-1)/p} \bmod p$
until $(h = 1 \text{ and } g \neq 1)$	**until** $(g \neq 1)$
return g	**return** g

a. Prove that the value returned by Algorithm 1 has order q.
b. Prove that the value returned by Algorithm 1 has order q.
c. Suppose $p = 40193$ and $q = 157$. How many loop iterations do you expect Algorithm 1 to make before it finds a generator?
d. If p is 1024 bits and q is 160 bits, would you recommend using Algorithm 1 to find g? Explain.
e. Suppose $p = 40193$ and $q = 157$. What is the probability that Algorithm 2 computes a generator in its very first loop iteration? (if it is helpful, you may use the fact that $\sum_{d|n} \varphi(d) = n$ when answering this question).

13.14 It is tempting to try to develop a variation on Diffie-Hellman that could be used as a digital signature. Here is one that is simpler than DSA and that does not require a secret random number in addition to the private key.

Public elements:

q prime number
α $\alpha < q$ and α is a primitive root of q

Private key:

X $X < q$

Public key:

$$Y = \alpha^X \bmod q$$

To sign a message M, compute $h = \text{H}(M)$, the hash code of the message. We require that $\gcd(h, q-1) = 1$. If not, append the hash to the message and calculate a new hash. Continue this process until a hash code is produced that is relatively prime to $(q-1)$. Then calculate Z to satisfy $Z \times h \equiv X(\text{mod } q-1)$. The signature of the message is α^Z. To verify the signature, a user verifies that $Y = (\alpha^Z)^h = \alpha^X \bmod q$.

a. Show that this scheme works. That is, show that the verification process produces an equality if the signature is valid.
b. Show that the scheme is unacceptable by describing a simple technique for forging a user's signature on an arbitrary message.

13.15 An early proposal for a digital signature scheme using symmetric encryption is based on the following: To sign an n-bit message, the sender randomly generates in advance 2n 56-bit cryptographic keys:

$$k1, K1, k2, K2, \ldots, kn, Kn$$

which are kept secret. The sender prepares in advance two sets of corresponding nonsecret 64-bit validation parameters, which are made public:

$$u1, V1, u2, V2, \ldots, un, Vn \quad \text{and} \quad v1, V1, v2, V2, \ldots, vn, Vn$$

where

$$vi = \mathrm{E}(ki, ui), Vi = \mathrm{E}(ki, Ui)$$

The message M is signed as follows. For the ith bit of the message, either ki or Ki is attached to the message, depending on whether the message bit is 0 or 1. For example, if the first three bits of the message are 011, then the first three keys of the signature are $k1$, $K2$, $K3$.

a. How does the receiver validate the message?
b. Is the technique secure?
c. How many times can the same set of secret keys be safely used for different messages?
d. What, if any, practical problems does this scheme present?

PART THREE

Network Security Applications

In practice, the effectiveness of a countermeasure often depends on how it is used; the best safe in the world is worthless if no one remembers to close the door.

—*Computers at Risk: Safe Computing in the Information Age*, National Research Council, 1991

Increased use of computer and communications networks, computer literacy, and dependence on information technology heighten U.S. industry's risk of losing proprietary information to economic espionage. In part to reduce the risk, industry is more frequently using hardware and software with encryption capabilities.

—*Communications Privacy: Federal Policy and Actions*. General Accounting Office Report GAO/OSI-94-2, November 1993

In the first two parts, we examined various ciphers and their use for confidentiality, authentication, key exchange, and related functions. Part Three surveys important network security tools and applications that make use of these functions. These applications can be used across a single network, a corporate intranet, or the Internet.

ROAD MAP FOR PART THREE

Chapter 14: Authentication Applications

Chapter 14 is a survey of two of the most important authentication specifications in current use. Kerberos is an authentication protocol based on conventional encryption that has received widespread support and is used in a variety of systems X.509 specifies an authentication algorithm and defines a certificate facility. The latter enables users to obtain certificates of public keys so that a community of users can have confidence in the validity of the public keys. This facility is employed as a building block in a number of applications.

Chapter 15: Electronic Mail Security

The most heavily used distributed application is electronic mail, and there is increasing interest in providing authentication and confidentiality services as part of an electronic mail facility. Chapter 15 looks at the two approaches likely to dominate electronic mail security in the near future. Pretty Good Privacy (PGP) is a widely used scheme that does not depend on any organization or authority. Thus, it is as well suited to individual, personal use as it is to incorporation in network configurations operated by organizations. S/MIME (Secure/Multipurpose Internet Mail Extension) was developed specifically to be an Internet Standard.

Chapter 16: IP Security

The Internet Protocol (IP) is the central element in the Internet and private intranets. Security at the IP level, accordingly, is important to the design of any internetwork-based security scheme. Chapter 16 looks at the IP security scheme that has been developed to operate both with the current IP and the emerging next-generation IP, known as IPv6.

Chapter 17: Web Security

The explosive growth in the use of the World Wide Web for electronic commerce and to disseminate information has generated the need for strong Web-based security. Chapter 17 provides a survey of this important new security area and looks at two key standards: Secure Sockets Layer (SSL) and Secure Electronic Transaction (SET).

CHAPTER 14

AUTHENTICATION APPLICATIONS

We cannot enter into alliance with neighboring princes until we are acquainted with their designs.

—*The Art of War*, Sun Tzu

KEY POINTS

- Kerberos is an authentication service designed for use in a distributed environment.
- Kerberos makes use of a trusted third-part authentication service that enables clients and servers to establish authenticated communication.
- X.509 defines the format for public-key certificates. This format is widely used in a variety of applications.
- A public key infrastructure (PKI) is defined as the set of hardware, software, people, policies, and procedures needed to create, manage, store, distribute, and revoke digital certificates based on asymmetric cryptography.
- Typically, PKI implementations make use of X.509 certificates.

This chapter examines some of the authentication functions that have been developed to support application-level authentication and digital signatures.

We begin by looking at one of the earliest and also one of the most widely used services: Kerberos. Next, we examine the X.509 directory authentication service. This standard is important as part of the directory service that it supports, but is also a basic building block used in other standards, such as S/MIME, discussed in Chapter 15. Finally, this chapter examines the concept of a public-key infrastructure (PKI).

14.1 KERBEROS

Kerberos[1] is an authentication service developed as part of Project Athena at MIT. The problem that Kerberos addresses is this: Assume an open distributed environment in which users at workstations wish to access services on servers distributed throughout the network. We would like for servers to be able to restrict access to authorized users and to be able to authenticate requests for service. In this environment, a workstation cannot be trusted to identify its users correctly to network services. In particular, the following three threats exist:

- A user may gain access to a particular workstation and pretend to be another user operating from that workstation.

---

[1]"In Greek mythology, a many headed dog, commonly three, perhaps with a serpent's tail, the guardian of the entrance of Hades." From *Dictionary of Subjects and Symbols in Art*, by James Hall, Harper & Row, 1979. Just as the Greek Kerberos has three heads, the modern Kerberos was intended to have three components to guard a network's gate: authentication, accounting, and audit. The last two heads were never implemented.

- A user may alter the network address of a workstation so that the requests sent from the altered workstation appear to come from the impersonated workstation.
- A user may eavesdrop on exchanges and use a replay attack to gain entrance to a server or to disrupt operations.

In any of these cases, an unauthorized user may be able to gain access to services and data that he or she is not authorized to access. Rather than building in elaborate authentication protocols at each server, Kerberos provides a centralized authentication server whose function is to authenticate users to servers and servers to users. Unlike most other authentication schemes described in this book, Kerberos relies exclusively on symmetric encryption, making no use of public-key encryption.

Two versions of Kerberos are in common use. Version 4 [MILL88, STEI88] implementations still exist. Version 5 [KOHL94] corrects some of the security deficiencies of version 4 and has been issued as a proposed Internet Standard (RFC 1510).[2]

We begin this section with a brief discussion of the motivation for the Kerberos approach. Then, because of the complexity of Kerberos, it is best to start with a description of the authentication protocol used in version 4. This enables us to see the essence of the Kerberos strategy without considering some of the details required to handle subtle security threats. Finally, we examine version 5.

Motivation

If a set of users is provided with dedicated personal computers that have no network connections, then a user's resources and files can be protected by physically securing each personal computer. When these users instead are served by a centralized time-sharing system, the time-sharing operating system must provide the security. The operating system can enforce access control policies based on user identity and use the logon procedure to identify users.

Today, neither of these scenarios is typical. More common is a distributed architecture consisting of dedicated user workstations (clients) and distributed or centralized servers. In this environment, three approaches to security can be envisioned:

1. Rely on each individual client workstation to assure the identity of its user or users and rely on each server to enforce a security policy based on user identification (ID).
2. Require that client systems authenticate themselves to servers, but trust the client system concerning the identity of its user.
3. Require the user to prove his or her identity for each service invoked. Also require that servers prove their identity to clients.

In a small, closed environment, in which all systems are owned and operated by a single organization, the first or perhaps the second strategy may suffice.[3] But in a more open environment, in which network connections to other machines are supported, the third approach is needed to protect user information and resources

[2]Versions 1 through 3 were internal development versions. Version 4 is the "original" Kerberos.

[3]However, even a closed environment faces the threat of attack by a disgruntled employee.

housed at the server. Kerberos supports this third approach. Kerberos assumes a distributed client/server architecture and employs one or more Kerberos servers to provide an authentication service.

The first published report on Kerberos [STEI88] listed the following requirements:

- **Secure:** A network eavesdropper should not be able to obtain the necessary information to impersonate a user. More generally, Kerberos should be strong enough that a potential opponent does not find it to be the weak link.
- **Reliable:** For all services that rely on Kerberos for access control, lack of availability of the Kerberos service means lack of availability of the supported services. Hence, Kerberos should be highly reliable and should employ a distributed server architecture, with one system able to back up another.
- **Transparent:** Ideally, the user should not be aware that authentication is taking place, beyond the requirement to enter a password.
- **Scalable:** The system should be capable of supporting large numbers of clients and servers. This suggests a modular, distributed architecture.

To support these requirements, the overall scheme of Kerberos is that of a trusted third-party authentication service that uses a protocol based on that proposed by Needham and Schroeder [NEED78], which was discussed in Chapter 7. It is trusted in the sense that clients and servers trust Kerberos to mediate their mutual authentication. Assuming the Kerberos protocol is well designed, then the authentication service is secure if the Kerberos server itself is secure.[4]

Kerberos Version 4

Version 4 of Kerberos makes use of DES, in a rather elaborate protocol, to provide the authentication service. Viewing the protocol as a whole, it is difficult to see the need for the many elements contained therein. Therefore, we adopt a strategy used by Bill Bryant of Project Athena [BRYA88] and build up to the full protocol by looking first at several hypothetical dialogues. Each successive dialogue adds additional complexity to counter security vulnerabilities revealed in the preceding dialogue.

After examining the protocol, we look at some other aspects of version 4.

A Simple Authentication Dialogue In an unprotected network environment, any client can apply to any server for service. The obvious security risk is that of impersonation. An opponent can pretend to be another client and obtain unauthorized privileges on server machines. To counter this threat, servers must be able to confirm the identities of clients who request service. Each server can be required

[4]Remember that the security of the Kerberos server should not automatically be assumed but must be guarded carefully (e.g., in a locked room). It is well to remember the fate of the Greek Kerberos, whom Hercules was ordered by Eurystheus to capture as his Twelfth Labor: "Hercules found the great dog on its chain and seized it by the throat. At once the three heads tried to attack, and Kerberos lashed about with his powerful tail. Hercules hung on grimly, and Kerberos relaxed into unconsciousness. Eurystheus may have been surprised to see Hercules alive—when he saw the three slavering heads and the huge dog they belonged to he was frightened out of his wits, and leapt back into the safety of his great bronze jar." From *The Hamlyn Concise Dictionary of Greek and Roman Mythology*, by Michael Stapleton, Hamlyn, 1982.

to undertake this task for each client/server interaction, but in an open environment, this places a substantial burden on each server.

An alternative is to use an authentication server (AS) that knows the passwords of all users and stores these in a centralized database. In addition, the AS shares a unique secret key with each server. These keys have been distributed physically or in some other secure manner. Consider the following hypothetical dialogue:[5]

(1) C → AS: $ID_C \| P_C \| ID_V$

(2) AS → C: *Ticket*

(3) C → V: $ID_C \| Ticket$

$$Ticket = \mathrm{E}(K_v, [ID_C \| AD_C \| ID_V])$$

where

C = client

AS = authentication server

V = server

ID_C = identifier of user on C

ID_V = identifier of V

P_C = password of user on C

AD_C = network address of C

K_v = secret encryption key shared by AS and V

In this scenario, the user logs on to a workstation and requests access to server V. The client module C in the user's workstation requests the user's password and then sends a message to the AS that includes the user's ID, the server's ID, and the user's password. The AS checks its database to see if the user has supplied the proper password for this user ID and whether this user is permitted access to server V. If both tests are passed, the AS accepts the user as authentic and must now convince the server that this user is authentic. To do so, the AS creates a ticket that contains the user's ID and network address and the server's ID. This ticket is encrypted using the secret key shared by the AS and this server. This ticket is then sent back to C. Because the ticket is encrypted, it cannot be altered by C or by an opponent.

With this ticket, C can now apply to V for service. C sends a message to V containing C's ID and the ticket. V decrypts the ticket and verifies that the user ID in the ticket is the same as the unencrypted user ID in the message. If these two match, the server considers the user authenticated and grants the requested service.

Each of the ingredients of message (3) is significant. The ticket is encrypted to prevent alteration or forgery. The server's ID (ID_V) is included in the ticket so that the server can verify that it has decrypted the ticket properly. ID_C is included in the ticket to indicate that this ticket has been issued on behalf of C. Finally, AD_C serves to counter the following threat. An opponent could capture the ticket transmitted in message (2), then use the name ID_C and transmit a message of form (3) from another

[5]The portion to the left of the colon indicates the sender and receiver; the portion to the right indicates the contents of the message, the symbol ‖ indicates concatenation.

workstation. The server would receive a valid ticket that matches the user ID and grant access to the user on that other workstation. To prevent this attack, the AS includes in the ticket the network address from which the original request came. Now the ticket is valid only if it is transmitted from the same workstation that initially requested the ticket.

A More Secure Authentication Dialogue Although the foregoing scenario solves some of the problems of authentication in an open network environment, problems remain. Two in particular stand out. First, we would like to minimize the number of times that a user has to enter a password. Suppose each ticket can be used only once. If user C logs on to a workstation in the morning and wishes to check his or her mail at a mail server, C must supply a password to get a ticket for the mail server. If C wishes to check the mail several times during the day, each attempt requires reentering the password. We can improve matters by saying that tickets are reusable. For a single logon session, the workstation can store the mail server ticket after it is received and use it on behalf of the user for multiple accesses to the mail server.

However, under this scheme it remains the case that a user would need a new ticket for every different service. If a user wished to access a print server, a mail server, a file server, and so on, the first instance of each access would require a new ticket and hence require the user to enter the password.

The second problem is that the earlier scenario involved a plaintext transmission of the password [message (1)]. An eavesdropper could capture the password and use any service accessible to the victim.

To solve these additional problems, we introduce a scheme for avoiding plaintext passwords and a new server, known as the ticket-granting server (TGS). The new but still hypothetical scenario is as follows:

Once per user logon session:

(1) C $\rightarrow$ AS: $ID_C \| ID_{tgs}$

(2) AS $\rightarrow$ C: $E(K_c, Ticket_{tgs})$

Once per type of service:

(3) C $\rightarrow$ TGS: $ID_C \| ID_V \| Ticket_{tgs}$

(4) TGS $\rightarrow$ C: $Ticket_v$

Once per service session:

(5) C $\rightarrow$ V: $ID_C \| Ticket_v$

$$Ticket_{tgs} = E(K_{tgs}, [ID_C \| AD_C \| ID_{tgs} \| TS_1 \| Lifetime_1])$$
$$Ticket_v = E(K_v, [ID_C \| AD_C \| ID_v \| TS_2 \| Lifetime_2])$$

The new service, TGS, issues tickets to users who have been authenticated to AS. Thus, the user first requests a ticket-granting ticket ($Ticket_{tgs}$) from the AS. The client module in the user workstation saves this ticket. Each time the user requires access to a new service, the client applies to the TGS, using the ticket to authenticate itself. The TGS then grants a ticket for the particular service. The client saves each service-granting ticket and uses it to authenticate its user to a server each time a particular service is requested. Let us look at the details of this scheme:

1. The client requests a ticket-granting ticket on behalf of the user by sending its user's ID and password to the AS, together with the TGS ID, indicating a request to use the TGS service.
2. The AS responds with a ticket that is encrypted with a key that is derived from the user's password. When this response arrives at the client, the client prompts the user for his or her password, generates the key, and attempts to decrypt the incoming message. If the correct password is supplied, the ticket is successfully recovered.

Because only the correct user should know the password, only the correct user can recover the ticket. Thus, we have used the password to obtain credentials from Kerberos without having to transmit the password in plaintext. The ticket itself consists of the ID and network address of the user, and the ID of the TGS. This corresponds to the first scenario. The idea is that the client can use this ticket to request multiple service-granting tickets. So the ticket-granting ticket is to be reusable. However, we do not wish an opponent to be able to capture the ticket and use it. Consider the following scenario: An opponent captures the login ticket and waits until the user has logged off his or her workstation. Then the opponent either gains access to that workstation or configures his workstation with the same network address as that of the victim. The opponent would be able to reuse the ticket to spoof the TGS. To counter this, the ticket includes a timestamp, indicating the date and time at which the ticket was issued, and a lifetime, indicating the length of time for which the ticket is valid (e.g., eight hours). Thus, the client now has a reusable ticket and need not bother the user for a password for each new service request. Finally, note that the ticket-granting ticket is encrypted with a secret key known only to the AS and the TGS. This prevents alteration of the ticket. The ticket is reencrypted with a key based on the user's password. This assures that the ticket can be recovered only by the correct user, providing the authentication.

Now that the client has a ticket-granting ticket, access to any server can be obtained with steps 3 and 4:

1. The client requests a service-granting ticket on behalf of the user. For this purpose, the client transmits a message to the TGS containing the user's ID, the ID of the desired service, and the ticket-granting ticket.
2. The TGS decrypts the incoming ticket and verifies the success of the decryption by the presence of its ID. It checks to make sure that the lifetime has not expired. Then it compares the user ID and network address with the incoming information to authenticate the user. If the user is permitted access to the server V, the TGS issues a ticket to grant access to the requested service.

The service-granting ticket has the same structure as the ticket-granting ticket. Indeed, because the TGS is a server, we would expect that the same elements are needed to authenticate a client to the TGS and to authenticate a client to an application server. Again, the ticket contains a timestamp and lifetime. If the user wants access to the same service at a later time, the client can simply use the previously acquired service-granting ticket and need not bother the user for a password. Note that the ticket is encrypted with a secret key (K_v) known only to the TGS and the server, preventing alteration.

Finally, with a particular service-granting ticket, the client can gain access to the corresponding service with step 5:

5. The client requests access to a service on behalf of the user. For this purpose, the client transmits a message to the server containing the user's ID and the service-granting ticket. The server authenticates by using the contents of the ticket.

This new scenario satisfies the two requirements of only one password query per user session and protection of the user password.

The Version 4 Authentication Dialogue Although the foregoing scenario enhances security compared to the first attempt, two additional problems remain. The heart of the first problem is the lifetime associated with the ticket-granting ticket. If this lifetime is very short (e.g., minutes), then the user will be repeatedly asked for a password. If the lifetime is long (e.g., hours), then an opponent has a greater opportunity for replay. An opponent could eavesdrop on the network and capture a copy of the ticket-granting ticket and then wait for the legitimate user to log out. Then the opponent could forge the legitimate user's network address and send the message of step (3) to the TGS. This would give the opponent unlimited access to the resources and files available to the legitimate user.

Similarly, if an opponent captures a service-granting ticket and uses it before it expires, the opponent has access to the corresponding service.

Thus, we arrive at an additional requirement. A network service (the TGS or an application service) must be able to prove that the person using a ticket is the same person to whom that ticket was issued.

The second problem is that there may be a requirement for servers to authenticate themselves to users. Without such authentication, an opponent could sabotage the configuration so that messages to a server were directed to another location. The false server would then be in a position to act as a real server and capture any information from the user and deny the true service to the user.

We examine these problems in turn and refer to Table 14.1, which shows the actual Kerberos protocol.

First, consider the problem of captured ticket-granting tickets and the need to determine that the ticket presenter is the same as the client for whom the ticket was issued. The threat is that an opponent will steal the ticket and use it before it expires. To get around this problem, let us have the AS provide both the client and the TGS with a secret piece of information in a secure manner. Then the client can prove its identity to the TGS by revealing the secret information, again in a secure manner. An efficient way of accomplishing this is to use an encryption key as the secure information; this is referred to as a session key in Kerberos.

Table 14.1a shows the technique for distributing the session key. As before, the client sends a message to the AS requesting access to the TGS. The AS responds with a message, encrypted with a key derived from the user's password (K_c), that contains the ticket. The encrypted message also contains a copy of the session key, $K_{c,tgs}$, where the subscripts indicate that this is a session key for C and TGS. Because this session key is

Table 14.1 Summary of Kerberos Version 4 Message Exchanges

(1) C → AS $ID_c \| ID_{tgs} \| TS_1$

(2) AS → C $E(K_c, [K_{c,tgs} \| ID_{tgs} \| TS_2 \| Lifetime_2 \| Ticket_{tgs}])$

$$Ticket_{tgs} = \mathrm{E}(\mathrm{K}_{tgs}, [\mathrm{K}_{c,tgs} \| \mathrm{ID}_C \| \mathrm{AD}_C \| \mathrm{ID}_{tgs} \| \mathrm{TS}_2 \| \mathrm{Lifetime}_2])$$

(a) Authentication Service Exchange to obtain ticket-granting ticket

(3) C → TGS $ID_v \| Ticket_{tgs} \| Authenticator_c$

(4) TGS → C $E(K_{c,tgs}, [K_{c,v} \| ID_v \| TS_4 \| Ticket_v])$

$$Ticket_{tgs} = \mathrm{E}(\mathrm{K}_{tgs}, [\mathrm{K}_{c,tgs} \| \mathrm{ID}_C \| \mathrm{AD}_C \| \mathrm{ID}_{tgs} \| \mathrm{TS}_2 \| \mathrm{Lifetime}_2])$$

$$Ticket_v = \mathrm{E}(\mathrm{K}_v, [\mathrm{K}_{c,v} \| \mathrm{ID}_C \| \mathrm{AD}_C \| \mathrm{ID}_v \| \mathrm{TS}_4 \| \mathrm{Lifetime}_4])$$

$$Authenticator_c = \mathrm{E}(\mathrm{K}_{c,tgs}, [\mathrm{ID}_C \| \mathrm{AD}_C \| \mathrm{TS}_3])$$

(b) Ticket-Granting Service Exchange to obtain service-granting ticket

(5) C → V $Ticket_v \| Authenticator_c$

(6) V → C $E(K_{c,v}, [TS_5 + 1])$ (for mutual authentication)

$$Ticket_v = \mathrm{E}(\mathrm{K}_v, [\mathrm{K}_{c,v} \| \mathrm{ID}_C \| \mathrm{AD}_C \| \mathrm{ID}_v \| \mathrm{TS}_4 \| \mathrm{Lifetime}_4])$$

$$Authenticator_c = \mathrm{E}(\mathrm{K}_{c,v}, [\mathrm{ID}_C \| \mathrm{AD}_C \| \mathrm{TS}_5])$$

(c) Client/Server Authentication Exchange to obtain service

inside the message encrypted with K_c, only the user's client can read it. The same session key is included in the ticket, which can be read only by the TGS. Thus, the session key has been securely delivered to both C and the TGS.

Note that several additional pieces of information have been added to this first phase of the dialogue. Message (1) includes a timestamp, so that the AS knows that the message is timely. Message (2) includes several elements of the ticket in a form accessible to C. This enables C to confirm that this ticket is for the TGS and to learn its expiration time.

Armed with the ticket and the session key, C is ready to approach the TGS. As before, C sends the TGS a message that includes the ticket plus the ID of the requested service (message (3) in Table 14.1b). In addition, C transmits an authenticator, which includes the ID and address of C's user and a timestamp. Unlike the ticket, which is reusable, the authenticator is intended for use only once and has a very short lifetime. The TGS can decrypt the ticket with the key that it shares with the AS. This ticket indicates that user C has been provided with the session key $K_{c,tgs}$. In effect, the ticket says, "Anyone who uses $K_{c,tgs}$ must be C." The TGS uses the session key to decrypt the authenticator. The TGS can then check the name and address from the authenticator with that of the ticket and with the network address of the incoming message. If all match, then the TGS is assured that the sender of the ticket is indeed the ticket's real owner. In effect, the authenticator says, "At time TS_3, I hereby use $K_{c,tgs}$." Note that the ticket does not prove anyone's identity but is a way to distribute keys securely. It is the authenticator that proves the client's identity. Because the authenticator can be used only once and has a short lifetime, the threat of an opponent stealing both the ticket and the authenticator for presentation later is countered.

The reply from the TGS, in message (4), follows the form of message (2). The message is encrypted with the session key shared by the TGS and C and includes a session key to be shared between C and the server V, the ID of V, and the timestamp of the ticket. The ticket itself includes the same session key.

C now has a reusable service-granting ticket for V. When C presents this ticket, as shown in message (5), it also sends an authenticator. The server can decrypt the ticket, recover the session key, and decrypt the authenticator.

If mutual authentication is required, the server can reply as shown in message (6) of Table 14.1. The server returns the value of the timestamp from the authenticator, incremented by 1, and encrypted in the session key. C can decrypt this message to recover the incremented timestamp. Because the message was encrypted by the session key, C is assured that it could have been created only by V. The contents of the message assure C that this is not a replay of an old reply.

Finally, at the conclusion of this process, the client and server share a secret key. This key can be used to encrypt future messages between the two or to exchange a new random session key for that purpose.

Table 14.2 summarizes the justification for each of the elements in the Kerberos protocol, and Figure 14.1 provides a simplified overview of the action.

Kerberos Realms and Multiple Kerberi A full-service Kerberos environment consisting of a Kerberos server, a number of clients, and a number of application servers requires the following:

1. The Kerberos server must have the user ID and hashed passwords of all participating users in its database. All users are registered with the Kerberos server.
2. The Kerberos server must share a secret key with each server. All servers are registered with the Kerberos server.

Such an environment is referred to as a **Kerberos realm**. The concept of *realm* can be explained as follows. A Kerberos realm is a set of managed nodes that share the same Kerberos database. The Kerberos database resides on the Kerberos master computer system, which should be kept in a physically secure room. A read-only copy of the Kerberos database might also reside on other Kerberos computer systems. However, all changes to the database must be made on the master computer system. Changing or accessing the contents of a Kerberos database requires the Kerberos master password. A related concept is that of a **Kerberos principal**, which is a service or user that is known to the Kerberos system. Each Kerberos principal is identified by its principal name. Principal names consist of three parts: a service or user name, an instance name, and a realm name

Networks of clients and servers under different administrative organizations typically constitute different realms. That is, it generally is not practical, or does not conform to administrative policy, to have users and servers in one administrative domain registered with a Kerberos server elsewhere. However, users in one realm may need access to servers in other realms, and some servers may be willing to provide service to users from other realms, provided that those users are authenticated.

Table 14.2 Rationale for the Elements of the Kerberos Version 4 Protocol

Message (1)	Client requests ticket-granting ticket
ID_C	Tells AS identity of user from this client
ID_{tgs}	Tells AS that user requests access to TGS
TS_1	Allows AS to verify that client's clock is synchronized with that of AS
Message (2)	AS returns ticket-granting ticket
K_c	Encryption is based on user's password, enabling AS and client to verify password, and protecting contents of message (2)
$K_{c,tgs}$	Copy of session key accessible to client created by AS to permit secure exchange between client and TGS without requiring them to share a permanent key
ID_{tgs}	Confirms that this ticket is for the TGS
TS_2	Informs client of time this ticket was issued
$Lifetime_2$	Informs client of the lifetime of this ticket
$Ticket_{tgs}$	Ticket to be used by client to access TGS

(a) Authentication Service Exchange

Message (3)	Client requests service-granting ticket
ID_V	Tells TGS that user requests access to server V
$Ticket_{tgs}$	Assures TGS that this user has been authenticated by AS
$Authenticator_c$	Generated by client to validate ticket
Message (4)	TGS returns service-granting ticket
$K_{c,tgs}$	Key shared only by C and TGS protects contents of message (4)
$K_{c,v}$	Copy of session key accessible to client created by TGS to permit secure exchange between client and server without requiring them to share a permanent key
ID_V	Confirms that this ticket is for server V
TS_4	Informs client of time this ticket was issued
$Ticket_V$	Ticket to be used by client to access server V
$Ticket_{tgs}$	Reusable so that user does not have to reenter password
K_{tgs}	Ticket is encrypted with key known only to AS and TGS, to prevent tampering
$K_{c,tgs}$	Copy of session key accessible to TGS used to decrypt authenticator, thereby authenticating ticket
ID_C	Indicates the rightful owner of this ticket
AD_C	Prevents use of ticket from workstation other than one that initially requested the ticket
ID_{tgs}	Assures server that it has decrypted ticket properly
TS_2	Informs TGS of time this ticket was issued
$Lifetime_2$	Prevents replay after ticket has expired
$Authenticator_c$	Assures TGS that the ticket presenter is the same as the client for whom the ticket was issued has very short lifetime to prevent replay
$K_{c,tgs}$	Authenticator is encrypted with key known only to client and TGS, to prevent tamperig

ID_C	Must match ID in ticket to authenticate ticket
AD_C	Must match address in ticket to authenticate ticket
TS_3	Informs TGS of time this authenticator was generated

(b) Ticket-Granting Service Exchange

Message (5)	Client requests service
$Ticket_V$	Assures server that this user has been authenticated by AS
$Authenticator_c$	Generated by client to validate ticket
Message (6)	Optional authentication of server to client
$K_{c,v}$	Assures C that this message is from V
$TS_5 + 1$	Assures C that this is not a replay of an old reply
$Ticket_v$	Reusable so that client does not need to request a new ticket from TGS for each access to the same server
K_v	Ticket is encrypted with key known only to TGS and server, to prevent tampering
$K_{c,v}$	Copy of session key accessible to client; used to decrypt authenticator, thereby authenticating ticket
ID_C	Indicates the rightful owner of this ticket
AD_C	Prevents use of ticket from workstation other than one that initially requested the ticket
ID_V	Assures server that it has decrypted ticket properly
TS_4	Informs server of time this ticket was issued
$Lifetime_4$	Prevents replay after ticket has expired
$Authenticator_c$	Assures server that the ticket presenter is the same as the client for whom the ticket was issued; has very short lifetime to prevent replay
$K_{c,v}$	Authenticator is encrypted with key known only to client and server, to prevent tampering
ID_C	Must match ID in ticket to authenticate ticket
AD_c	Must match address in ticket to authenticate ticket
TS_5	Informs server of time this authenticator was generated

(c) Client/Server Authentication Exchange

Kerberos provides a mechanism for supporting such interrealm authentication. For two realms to support interrealm authentication, a third requirement is added:

3. The Kerberos server in each interoperating realm shares a secret key with the server in the other realm. The two Kerberos servers are registered with each other.

The scheme requires that the Kerberos server in one realm trust the Kerberos server in the other realm to authenticate its users. Furthermore, the participating servers in the second realm must also be willing to trust the Kerberos server in the first realm.

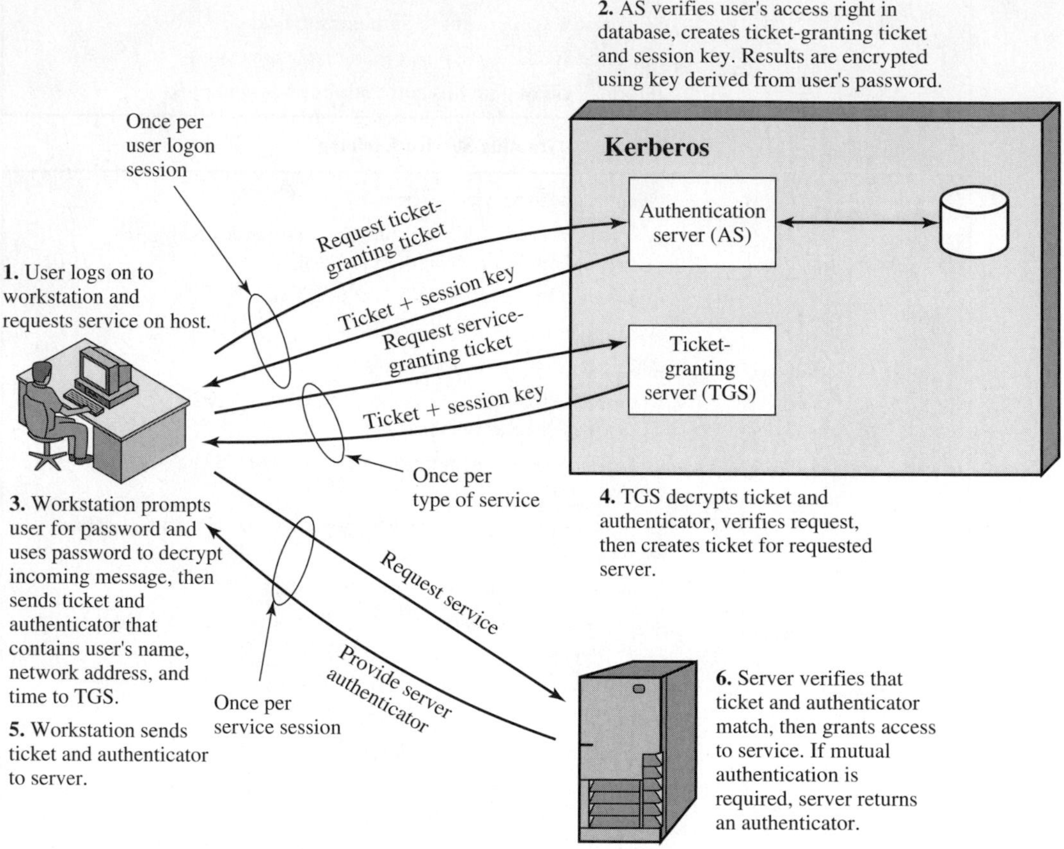
2. AS verifies user's access right in database, creates ticket-granting ticket and session key. Results are encrypted using key derived from user's password.
Once per user logon session
Kerberos
Authentication server (AS)
Request ticket-granting ticket
Ticket + session key
1. User logs on to workstation and requests service on host.
Request service-granting ticket
Ticket-granting server (TGS)
Ticket + session key
Once per type of service
3. Workstation prompts user for password and uses password to decrypt incoming message, then sends ticket and authenticator that contains user's name, network address, and time to TGS.
4. TGS decrypts ticket and authenticator, verifies request, then creates ticket for requested server.
Request service
Provide server authenticator
Once per service session
5. Workstation sends ticket and authenticator to server.
6. Server verifies that ticket and authenticator match, then grants access to service. If mutual authentication is required, server returns an authenticator.

Figure 14.1 Overview of Kerberos

With these ground rules in place, we can describe the mechanism as follows (Figure 14.2): A user wishing service on a server in another realm needs a ticket for that server. The user's client follows the usual procedures to gain access to the local TGS and then requests a ticket-granting ticket for a remote TGS (TGS in another realm). The client can then apply to the remote TGS for a service-granting ticket for the desired server in the realm of the remote TGS.

The details of the exchanges illustrated in Figure 14.2 are as follows (compare Table 14.1):

(1) C → AS: $ID_c \| ID_{tgs} \| TS_1$

(2) AS → C: $\mathrm{E}(K_c, [K_{c,tgs} \| ID_{tgs} \| TS_2 \| Lifetime_2 \| Ticket_{tgs}])$

(3) C → TGS: $ID_{tgsrem} \| Ticket_{tgs} \| Authenticator_c$

(4) TGS → C: $\mathrm{E}(K_{c,tgs}, [K_{c,tgsrem} \| ID_{tgsrem} \| TS_4 \| Ticket_{tgsrem}])$

(5) C → $\mathrm{TGS_{rem}}$: $ID_{vrem} \| Ticket_{tgsrem} \| Authenticator_c$

(6) $\mathrm{TGS_{rem}}$ → C: $\mathrm{E}(K_{c,tgsrem}, [K_{c,vrem} \| ID_{vrem} \| TS_6 \| Ticket_{vrem}])$

(7) C → $\mathrm{V_{rem}}$: $Ticket_{vrem} \| Authenticator_c$

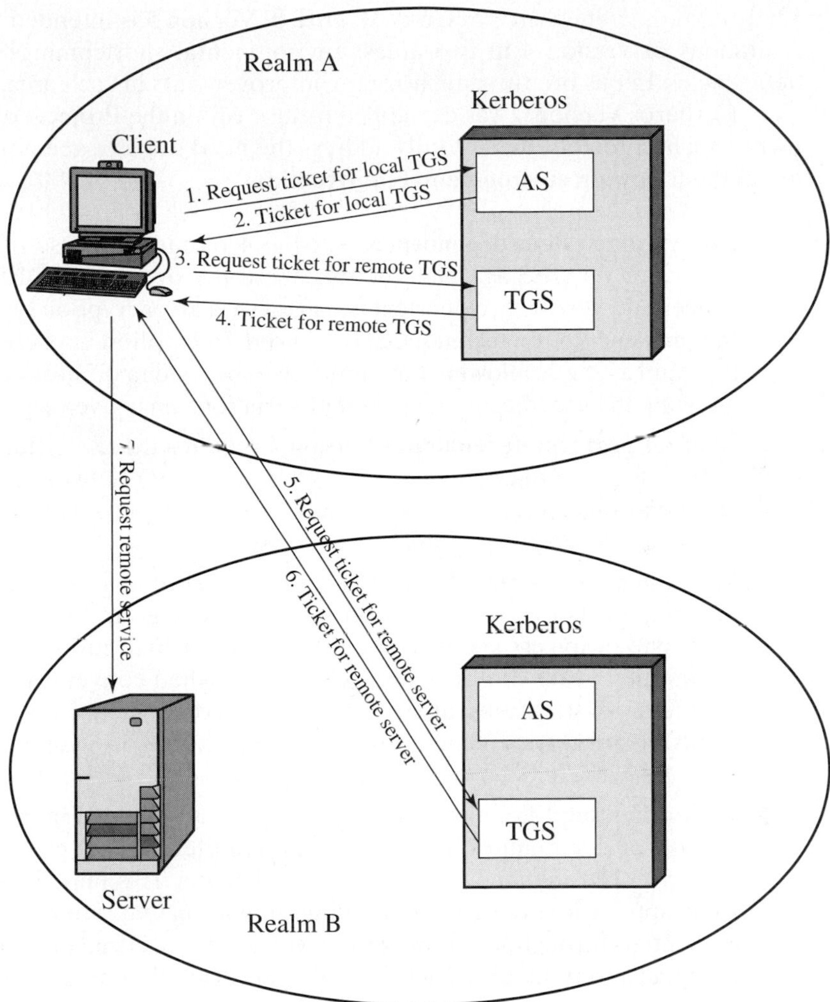

Figure 14.2 Request for Service in Another Realm

The ticket presented to the remote server (V_{rem}) indicates the realm in which the user was originally authenticated. The server chooses whether to honor the remote request.

One problem presented by the foregoing approach is that it does not scale well to many realms. If there are N realms, then there must be $N(N - 1)/2$ secure key exchanges so that each Kerberos realm can interoperate with all other Kerberos realms.

Kerberos Version 5

Kerberos Version 5 is specified in RFC 1510 and provides a number of improvements over version 4 [KOHL94]. To begin, we provide an overview of the changes from version 4 to version 5 and then look at the version 5 protocol.

Differences between Versions 4 and 5 Version 5 is intended to address the limitations of version 4 in two areas: environmental shortcomings and technical deficiencies. Let us briefly summarize the improvements in each area.[6]

Kerberos Version 4 was developed for use within the Project Athena environment and, accordingly, did not fully address the need to be of general purpose. This led to the following **environmental shortcomings:**

1. **Encryption system dependence:** Version 4 requires the use of DES. Export restriction on DES as well as doubts about the strength of DES were thus of concern. In version 5, ciphertext is tagged with an encryption type identifier so that any encryption technique may be used. Encryption keys are tagged with a type and a length, allowing the same key to be used in different algorithms and allowing the specification of different variations on a given algorithm.
2. **Internet protocol dependence:** Version 4 requires the use of Internet Protocol (IP) addresses. Other address types, such as the ISO network address, are not accommodated. Version 5 network addresses are tagged with type and length, allowing any network address type to be used.
3. **Message byte ordering:** In version 4, the sender of a message employs a byte ordering of its own choosing and tags the message to indicate least significant byte in lowest address or most significant byte in lowest address. This techniques works but does not follow established conventions. In version 5, all message structures are defined using Abstract Syntax Notation One (ASN.1) and Basic Encoding Rules (BER), which provide an unambiguous byte ordering.
4. **Ticket lifetime:** Lifetime values in version 4 are encoded in an 8-bit quantity in units of five minutes. Thus, the maximum lifetime that can be expressed is $2^8 \times 5 = 1280$ minutes, or a little over 21 hours. This may be inadequate for some applications (e.g., a long-running simulation that requires valid Kerberos credentials throughout execution). In version 5, tickets include an explicit start time and end time, allowing tickets with arbitrary lifetimes.
5. **Authentication forwarding:** Version 4 does not allow credentials issued to one client to be forwarded to some other host and used by some other client. This capability would enable a client to access a server and have that server access another server on behalf of the client. For example, a client issues a request to a print server that then accesses the client's file from a file server, using the client's credentials for access. Version 5 provides this capability.
6. **Interrealm authentication:** In version 4, interoperability among N realms requires on the order of N^2 Kerberos-to-Kerberos relationships, as described earlier. Version 5 supports a method that requires fewer relationships, as described shortly.

Apart from these environmental limitations, there are **technical deficiencies** in the version 4 protocol itself. Most of these deficiencies were documented

[6]The following discussion follows the presentation in [KOHL94].

in [BELL90], and version 5 attempts to address these. The deficiencies are the following:

1. **Double encryption:** Note in Table 14.1 [messages (2) and (4)] that tickets provided to clients are encrypted twice, once with the secret key of the target server and then again with a secret key known to the client. The second encryption is not necessary and is computationally wasteful.
2. **PCBC encryption:** Encryption in version 4 makes use of a nonstandard mode of DES known as propagating cipher block chaining (PCBC).[7] It has been demonstrated that this mode is vulnerable to an attack involving the interchange of ciphertext blocks [KOHL89]. PCBC was intended to provide an integrity check as part of the encryption operation. Version 5 provides explicit integrity mechanisms, allowing the standard CBC mode to be used for encryption. In particular, a checksum or hash code is attached to the message prior to encryption using CBC.
3. **Session keys:** Each ticket includes a session key that is used by the client to encrypt the authenticator sent to the service associated with that ticket. In addition, the session key may subsequently be used by the client and the server to protect messages passed during that session. However, because the same ticket may be used repeatedly to gain service from a particular server, there is the risk that an opponent will replay messages from an old session to the client or the server. In version 5, it is possible for a client and server to negotiate a subsession key, which is to be used only for that one connection. A new access by the client would result in the use of a new subsession key.
4. **Password attacks:** Both versions are vulnerable to a password attack. The message from the AS to the client includes material encrypted with a key based on the client's password.[8] An opponent can capture this message and attempt to decrypt it by trying various passwords. If the result of a test decryption is of the proper form, then the opponent has discovered the client's password and may subsequently use it to gain authentication credentials from Kerberos. This is the same type of password attack described in Chapter 18, with the same kinds of countermeasures being applicable. Version 5 does provide a mechanism known as preauthentication, which should make password attacks more difficult, but it does not prevent them.

The Version 5 Authentication Dialogue Table 14.3 summarizes the basic version 5 dialogue. This is best explained by comparison with version 4 (Table 14.1).

First, consider the **authentication service exchange**. Message (1) is a client request for a ticket-granting ticket. As before, it includes the ID of the user and the TGS. The following new elements are added:

- **Realm:** Indicates realm of user
- **Options:** Used to request that certain flags be set in the returned ticket

---

[7]This is described in Appendix 14A.

[8]Appendix 14A describes the mapping of passwords to encryption keys.

Table 14.3 Summary of Kerberos Version 5 Message Exchanges

(1) C → AS Options $\| ID_c \| Realm_c \| ID_{tgs} \| Times \| Nonce_1$

(2) AS → C $Realm_c \| ID_C \| Ticket_{tgs} \| E(K_c, [K_{c,tgs} \| Times \| Nonce_1 \| Realm_{tgs} \| ID_{tgs}])$

$$Ticket_{tgs} = E(K_{tgs}, [Flags \| K_{c,tgs} \| Realm_c \| ID_C \| AD_C \| Times])$$

(a) Authentication Service Exchange to obtain ticket-granting ticket

(3) C → TGS Options $\| ID_v \| Times \|\| Nonce_2 \| Ticket_{tgs} \| Authenticator_c$

(4) TGS → C $Realm_c \| ID_C \| Ticket_v \| E(K_{c,tgs}, [K_{c,v} \| Times \| Nonce_2 \| Realm_v \| ID_v])$

$$Ticket_{tgs} = E(K_{tgs}, [Flags \| K_{c,tgs} \| Realm_c \| ID_C \| AD_C \| Times])$$

$$Ticket_v = E(K_v, [Flags \| K_{c,v} \| Realm_c \| ID_C \| AD_C \| Times])$$

$$Authenticator_c = E(K_{c,tgs}, [ID_C \| Realm_c \| TS_1])$$

(b) Ticket-Granting Service Exchange to obtain service-granting ticket

(5) C → V Options $\| Ticket_v \| Authenticator_c$

(6) V → C $E_{K_{c,v}}[TS_2 \| Subkey \| Seq\#]$

$$Ticket_v = E(K_v, [Flags \| K_{c,v} \| Realm_c \| ID_C \| AD_C \| Times])$$

$$Authenticator_c = E(K_{c,v}, [ID_C \| Realm_c \| TS_2 \| Subkey \| Seq\#])$$

(c) Client/Server Authentication Exchange to obtain service

- **Times:** Used by the client to request the following time settings in the ticket:
  —from: the desired start time for the requested ticket
  —till: the requested expiration time for the requested ticket
  —rtime: requested renew-till time
- **Nonce:** A random value to be repeated in message (2) to assure that the response is fresh and has not been replayed by an opponent

Message (2) returns a ticket-granting ticket, identifying information for the client, and a block encrypted using the encryption key based on the user's password. This block includes the session key to be used between the client and the TGS, times specified in message (1), the nonce from message (1), and TGS identifying information. The ticket itself includes the session key, identifying information for the client, the requested time values, and flags that reflect the status of this ticket and the requested options. These flags introduce significant new functionality to version 5. For now, we defer a discussion of these flags and concentrate on the overall structure of the version 5 protocol.

Let us now compare the **ticket-granting service exchange** for versions 4 and 5. We see that message (3) for both versions includes an authenticator, a ticket, and the name of the requested service. In addition, version 5 includes requested times and options for the ticket and a nonce, all with functions similar to those of message (1). The authenticator itself is essentially the same as the one used in version 4.

Message (4) has the same structure as message (2), returning a ticket plus information needed by the client, the latter encrypted with the session key now shared by the client and the TGS.

Finally, for the **client/server authentication exchange**, several new features appear in version 5. In message (5), the client may request as an option that mutual authentication is required. The authenticator includes several new fields as follows:

- **Subkey:** The client's choice for an encryption key to be used to protect this specific application session. If this field is omitted, the session key from the ticket ($K_{c,v}$) is used.
- **Sequence number:** An optional field that specifies the starting sequence number to be used by the server for messages sent to the client during this session. Messages may be sequence numbered to detect replays.

If mutual authentication is required, the server responds with message (6). This message includes the timestamp from the authenticator. Note that in version 4, the timestamp was incremented by one. This is not necessary in version 5 because the nature of the format of messages is such that it is not possible for an opponent to create message (6) without knowledge of the appropriate encryption keys. The subkey field, if present, overrides the subkey field, if present, in message (5). The optional sequence number field specifies the starting sequence number to be used by the client.

Ticket Flags The flags field included in tickets in version 5 supports expanded functionality compared to that available in version 4. Table 14.4 summarizes the flags that may be included in a ticket.

The INITIAL flag indicates that this ticket was issued by the AS, not by the TGS. When a client requests a service-granting ticket from the TGS, it presents a

Table 14.4 Kerberos Version 5 Flags

INITIAL	This ticket was issued using the AS protocol and not issued based on a ticket-granting ticket.
PRE-AUTHENT	During initial authentication, the client was authenticated by the KDC before a ticket was issued.
HW-AUTHENT	The protocol employed for initial authentication required the use of hardware expected to be possessed solely by the named client.
RENEWABLE	Tells TGS that this ticket can be used to obtain a replacement ticket that expires at a later date.
MAY-POSTDATE	Tells TGS that a postdated ticket may be issued based on this ticket-granting ticket.
POSTDATED	Indicates that this ticket has been postdated; the end server can check the authtime field to see when the original authentication occurred.
INVALID	This ticket is invalid and must be validated by the KDC before use.
PROXIABLE	Tells TGS that a new service-granting ticket with a different network address may be issued based on the presented ticket.
PROXY	Indicates that this ticket is a proxy.
FORWARDABLE	Tells TGS that a new ticket-granting ticket with a different network address may be issued based on this ticket-granting ticket.
FORWARDED	Indicates that this ticket has either been forwarded or was issued based on authentication involving a forwarded ticket-granting ticket.

ticket-granting ticket obtained from the AS. In version 4, this was the only way to obtain a service-granting ticket. Version 5 provides the additional capability that the client can get a service-granting ticket directly from the AS. The utility of this is as follows: A server, such as a password-changing server, may wish to know that the client's password was recently tested.

The PRE-AUTHENT flag, if set, indicates that when the AS received the initial request [message (1)], it authenticated the client before issuing a ticket. The exact form of this preauthentication is left unspecified. As an example, the MIT implementation of version 5 has encrypted timestamp preauthentication, enabled by default. When a user wants to get a ticket, it has to send to the AS a preauthentication block containing a random confounder, a version number, and a timestamp, encrypted in the client's password-based key. The AS decrypts the block and will not send a ticket-granting ticket back unless the timestamp in the preauthentication block is within the allowable time skew (time interval to account for clock drift and network delays). Another possibility is the use of a smart card that generates continually changing passwords that are included in the preauthenticated messages. The passwords generated by the card can be based on a user's password but be transformed by the card so that, in effect, arbitrary passwords are used. This prevents an attack based on easily guessed passwords. If a smart card or similar device was used, this is indicated by the HW-AUTHENT flag.

When a ticket has a long lifetime, there is the potential for it to be stolen and used by an opponent for a considerable period. If a short lifetime is used to lessen the threat, then overhead is involved in acquiring new tickets. In the case of a ticket-granting ticket, the client would either have to store the user's secret key, which is clearly risky, or repeatedly ask the user for a password. A compromise scheme is the use of renewable tickets. A ticket with the RENEWABLE flag set includes two expiration times: one for this specific ticket and one that is the latest permissible value for an expiration time. A client can have the ticket renewed by presenting it to the TGS with a requested new expiration time. If the new time is within the limit of the latest permissible value, the TGS can issue a new ticket with a new session time and a later specific expiration time. The advantage of this mechanism is that the TGS may refuse to renew a ticket reported as stolen.

A client may request that the AS provide a ticket-granting ticket with the MAY-POSTDATE flag set. The client can then use this ticket to request a ticket that is flagged as POSTDATED and INVALID from the TGS. Subsequently, the client may submit the postdated ticket for validation. This scheme can be useful for running a long batch job on a server that requires a ticket periodically. The client can obtain a number of tickets for this session at once, with spread-out time values. All but the first ticket are initially invalid. When the execution reaches a point in time when a new ticket is required, the client can get the appropriate ticket validated. With this approach, the client does not have to repeatedly use its ticket-granting ticket to obtain a service-granting ticket.

In version 5 it is possible for a server to act as a proxy on behalf of a client, in effect adopting the credentials and privileges of the client to request a service from another server. If a client wishes to use this mechanism, it requests a ticket-granting ticket with the PROXIABLE flag set. When this ticket is presented to the TGS, the TGS is permitted to issue a service-granting ticket with a different network address; this latter ticket will have its PROXY flag set. An application receiving such a ticket may accept it or require additional authentication to provide an audit trail.[9]

The proxy concept is a limited case of the more powerful forwarding procedure. If a ticket is set with the FORWARDABLE flag, a TGS can issue to the requestor a ticket-granting ticket with a different network address and the FORWARDED flag set. This ticket can then be presented to a remote TGS. This capability allows a client to gain access to a server on another realm without requiring that each Kerberos maintain a secret key with Kerberos servers in every other realm. For example, realms could be structured hierarchically. Then a client could walk up the tree to a common node and then back down to reach a target realm. Each step of the walk would involve forwarding a ticket-granting ticket to the next TGS in the path.

14.2 X.509 AUTHENTICATION SERVICE

ITU-T recommendation X.509 is part of the X.500 series of recommendations that define a directory service. The directory is, in effect, a server or distributed set of servers that maintains a database of information about users. The information includes a mapping from user name to network address, as well as other attributes and information about the users.

X.509 defines a framework for the provision of authentication services by the X.500 directory to its users. The directory may serve as a repository of public-key certificates of the type discussed in Chapter 9. Each certificate contains the public key of a user and is signed with the private key of a trusted certification authority. In addition, X.509 defines alternative authentication protocols based on the use of public-key certificates.

X.509 is an important standard because the certificate structure and authentication protocols defined in X.509 are used in a variety of contexts. For example, the X.509 certificate format is used in S/MIME (Chapter 15), IP Security (Chapter 16), and SSL/TLS and SET (Chapter 17).

X.509 was initially issued in 1988. The standard was subsequently revised to address some of the security concerns documented in [IANS90] and [MITC90]; a revised recommendation was issued in 1993. A third version was issued in 1995 and revised in 2000.

X.509 is based on the use of public-key cryptography and digital signatures. The standard does not dictate the use of a specific algorithm but recommends RSA. The digital signature scheme is assumed to require the use of a hash function. Again, the standard does not dictate a specific hash algorithm. The 1988 recommendation included the description of a recommended hash algorithm; this algorithm has since been shown to be insecure and was dropped from the 1993 recommendation. Figure 14.3 illustrates the generation of a public-key certificate.

---

[9]For a discussion of some of the possible uses of the proxy capability, see [NEUM93b].

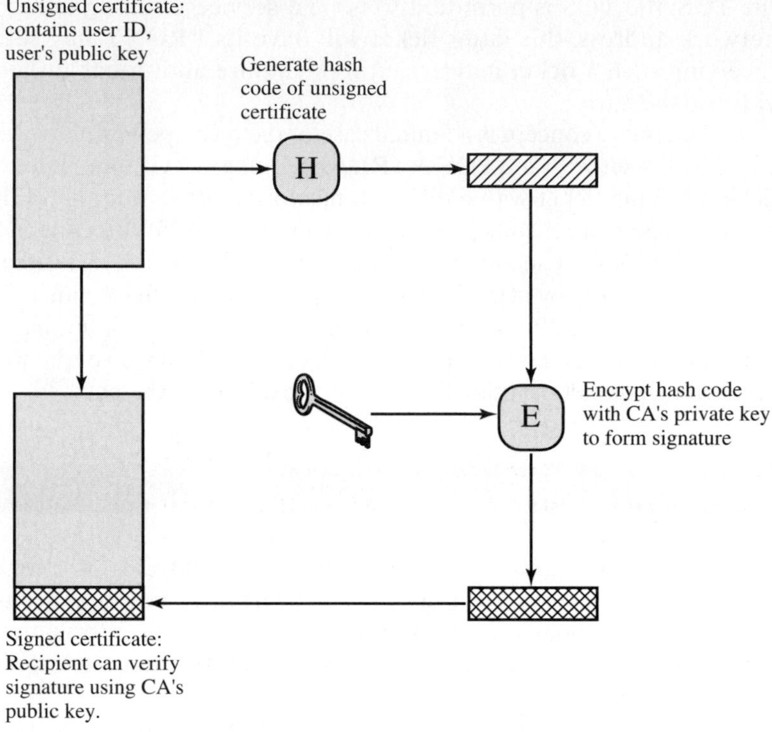
Unsigned certificate:
contains user ID,
user's public key
Generate hash
code of unsigned
certificate
H
E
Encrypt hash code
with CA's private key
to form signature
Signed certificate:
Recipient can verify
signature using CA's
public key.

Figure 14.3 Public-Key Certificate Use

Certificates

The heart of the X.509 scheme is the public-key certificate associated with each user. These user certificates are assumed to be created by some trusted certification authority (CA) and placed in the directory by the CA or by the user. The directory server itself is not responsible for the creation of public keys or for the certification function; it merely provides an easily accessible location for users to obtain certificates.

Figure 14.4a shows the general format of a certificate, which includes the following elements:

- **Version:** Differentiates among successive versions of the certificate format; the default is version 1. If the Issuer Unique Identifier or Subject Unique Identifier are present, the value must be version 2. If one or more extensions are present, the version must be version 3.
- **Serial number:** An integer value, unique within the issuing CA, that is unambiguously associated with this certificate.
- **Signature algorithm identifier:** The algorithm used to sign the certificate, together with any associated parameters. Because this information is repeated in the Signature field at the end of the certificate, this field has little, if any, utility.
- **Issuer name:** X.500 name of the CA that created and signed this certificate.

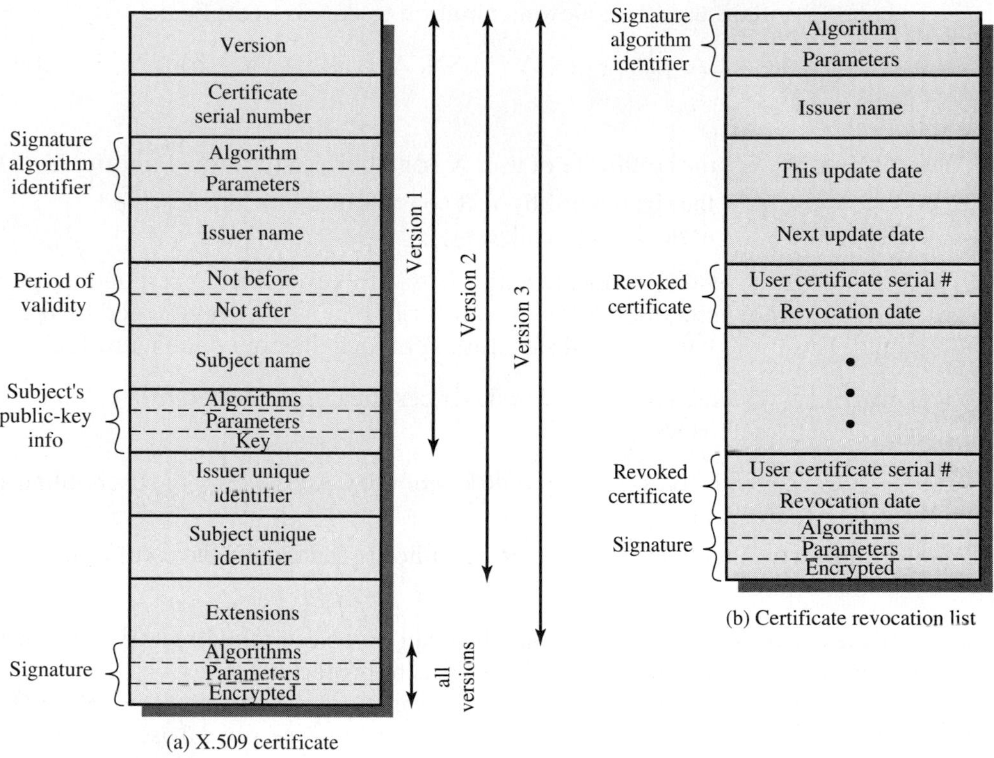

Figure 14.4 X.509 Formats

- **Period of validity:** Consists of two dates: the first and last on which the certificate is valid.
- **Subject name:** The name of the user to whom this certificate refers. That is, this certificate certifies the public key of the subject who holds the corresponding private key.
- **Subject's public-key information:** The public key of the subject, plus an identifier of the algorithm for which this key is to be used, together with any associated parameters.
- **Issuer unique identifier:** An optional bit string field used to identify uniquely the issuing CA in the event the X.500 name has been reused for different entities.
- **Subject unique identifier:** An optional bit string field used to identify uniquely the subject in the event the X.500 name has been reused for different entities.
- **Extensions:** A set of one or more extension fields. Extensions were added in version 3 and are discussed later in this section.
- **Signature:** Covers all of the other fields of the certificate; it contains the hash code of the other fields, encrypted with the CA's private key. This field includes the signature algorithm identifier.

The unique identifier fields were added in version 2 to handle the possible reuse of subject and/or issuer names over time. These fields are rarely used.

The standard uses the following notation to define a certificate:

$$CA \ll A \gg = CA\ \{V, SN, AI, CA, T_A, A, Ap\}$$

where

$Y \ll X \gg$ = the certificate of user X issued by certification authority Y

Y {I} = the signing of I by Y. It consists of I with an encrypted hash code appended

The CA signs the certificate with its private key. If the corresponding public key is known to a user, then that user can verify that a certificate signed by the CA is valid. This is the typical digital signature approach illustrated in Figure 11.5c.

Obtaining a User's Certificate User certificates generated by a CA have the following characteristics:

- Any user with access to the public key of the CA can verify the user public key that was certified.
- No party other than the certification authority can modify the certificate without this being detected.

Because certificates are unforgeable, they can be placed in a directory without the need for the directory to make special efforts to protect them.

If all users subscribe to the same CA, then there is a common trust of that CA. All user certificates can be placed in the directory for access by all users. In addition, a user can transmit his or her certificate directly to other users. In either case, once B is in possession of A's certificate, B has confidence that messages it encrypts with A's public key will be secure from eavesdropping and that messages signed with A's private key are unforgeable.

If there is a large community of users, it may not be practical for all users to subscribe to the same CA. Because it is the CA that signs certificates, each participating user must have a copy of the CA's own public key to verify signatures. This public key must be provided to each user in an absolutely secure (with respect to integrity and authenticity) way so that the user has confidence in the associated certificates. Thus, with many users, it may be more practical for there to be a number of CAs, each of which securely provides its public key to some fraction of the users.

Now suppose that A has obtained a certificate from certification authority X_1 and B has obtained a certificate from CA X_2. If A does not securely know the public key of X_2, then B's certificate, issued by X_2, is useless to A. A can read B's certificate, but A cannot verify the signature. However, if the two CAs have securely exchanged their own public keys, the following procedure will enable A to obtain B's public key:

1. A obtains, from the directory, the certificate of X_2 signed by X_1. Because A securely knows X_1's public key, A can obtain X_2's public key from its certificate and verify it by means of X_1's signature on the certificate.
2. A then goes back to the directory and obtains the certificate of B signed by X_2. Because A now has a trusted copy of X_2's public key, A can verify the signature and securely obtain B's public key.

A has used a chain of certificates to obtain B's public key. In the notation of X.509, this chain is expressed as

$$X_1 \ll X_2 \gg X_2 \ll B \gg$$

In the same fashion, B can obtain A's public key with the reverse chain:

$$X_2 \ll X_1 \gg X_1 \ll A \gg$$

This scheme need not be limited to a chain of two certificates. An arbitrarily long path of CAs can be followed to produce a chain. A chain with N elements would be expressed as

$$X_1 \ll X_2 \gg X_2 \ll X_3 \gg \cdots X_N \ll B \gg$$

In this case, each pair of CAs in the chain (X_i, X_{i+1}) must have created certificates for each other.

All these certificates of CAs by CAs need to appear in the directory, and the user needs to know how they are linked to follow a path to another user's public-key certificate. X.509 suggests that CAs be arranged in a hierarchy so that navigation is straightforward.

Figure 14.5, taken from X.509, is an example of such a hierarchy. The connected circles indicate the hierarchical relationship among the CAs; the associated boxes indicate certificates maintained in the directory for each CA entry. The directory entry for each CA includes two types of certificates:

- **Forward certificates:** Certificates of X generated by other CAs
- **Reverse certificates:** Certificates generated by X that are the certificates of other CAs

In this example, user A can acquire the following certificates from the directory to establish a certification path to B:

$$X \ll W \gg W \ll V \gg V \ll Y \gg Y \ll Z \gg Z \ll B \gg$$

When A has obtained these certificates, it can unwrap the certification path in sequence to recover a trusted copy of B's public key. Using this public key, A can send encrypted messages to B. If A wishes to receive encrypted messages back from B, or to sign messages sent to B, then B will require A's public key, which can be obtained from the following certification path:

$$Z \ll Y \gg Y \ll V \gg V \ll W \gg W \ll X \gg X \ll A \gg$$

B can obtain this set of certificates from the directory, or A can provide them as part of its initial message to B.

Revocation of Certificates Recall from Figure 14.4 that each certificate includes a period of validity, much like a credit card. Typically, a new certificate is issued just before the expiration of the old one. In addition, it may be desirable on occasion to revoke a certificate before it expires, for one of the following reasons:

1. The user's private key is assumed to be compromised.
2. The user is no longer certified by this CA.
3. The CA's certificate is assumed to be compromised.

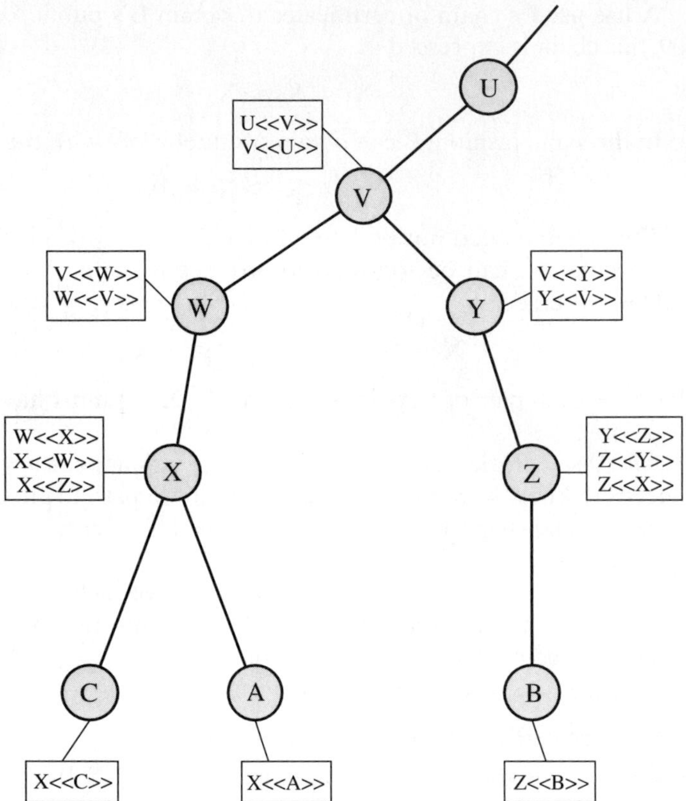

Figure 14.5 X.509 Hierarchy: A Hypothetical Example

Each CA must maintain a list consisting of all revoked but not expired certificates issued by that CA, including both those issued to users and to other CAs. These lists should also be posted on the directory.

Each certificate revocation list (CRL) posted to the directory is signed by the issuer and includes (Figure 14.4b) the issuer's name, the date the list was created, the date the next CRL is scheduled to be issued, and an entry for each revoked certificate. Each entry consists of the serial number of a certificate and revocation date for that certificate. Because serial numbers are unique within a CA, the serial number is sufficient to identify the certificate.

When a user receives a certificate in a message, the user must determine whether the certificate has been revoked. The user could check the directory each time a certificate is received. To avoid the delays (and possible costs) associated with directory searches, it is likely that the user would maintain a local cache of certificates and lists of revoked certificates.

Authentication Procedures

X.509 also includes three alternative authentication procedures that are intended for use across a variety of applications. All these procedures make use of public-key

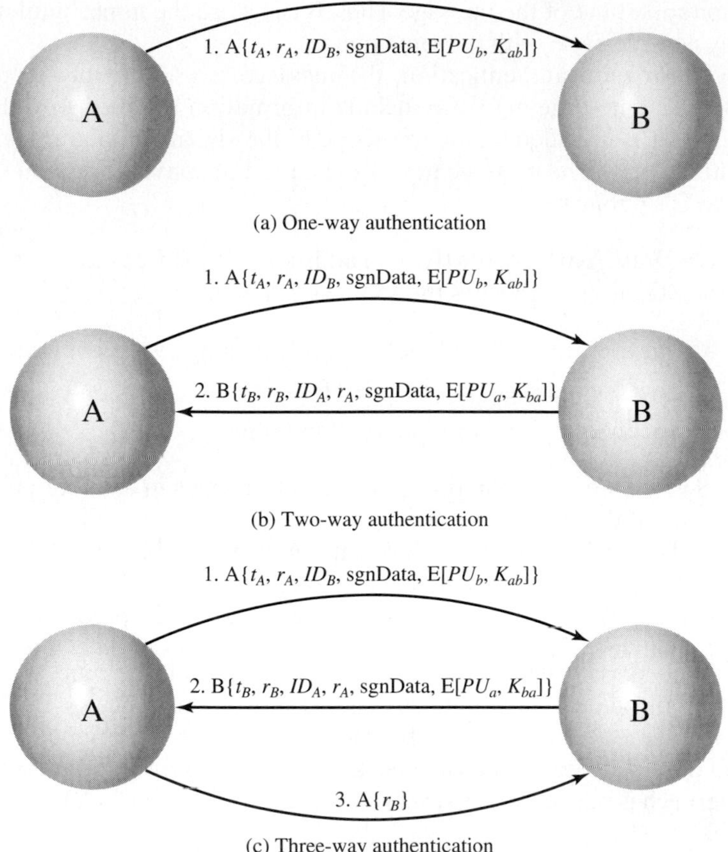

Figure 14.6 X.509 Strong Authentication Procedures

signatures. It is assumed that the two parties know each other's public key, either by obtaining each other's certificates from the directory or because the certificate is included in the initial message from each side.

Figure 14.6 illustrates the three procedures.

One-Way Authentication One way authentication involves a single transfer of information from one user (A) to another (B), and establishes the following:

1. The identity of A and that the message was generated by A
2. That the message was intended for B
3. The integrity and originality (it has not been sent multiple times) of the message

Note that only the identity of the initiating entity is verified in this process, not that of the responding entity.

At a minimum, the message includes a timestamp t_A, a nonce r_A, and the identity of B and is signed with A's private key. The timestamp consists of an optional generation time and an expiration time. This prevents delayed delivery of messages. The nonce can be used to detect replay attacks. The nonce value must be unique within the expiration time of the message. Thus, B can store the nonce until it expires and reject any new messages with the same nonce.

For pure authentication, the message is used simply to present credentials to B. The message may also include information to be conveyed. This information, sgnData, is included within the scope of the signature, guaranteeing its authenticity and integrity. The message may also be used to convey a session key to B, encrypted with B's public key.

Two-Way Authentication In addition to the three elements just listed, two-way authentication establishes the following elements:

4. The identity of B and that the reply message was generated by B
5. That the message was intended for A
6. The integrity and originality of the reply

Two-way authentication thus permits both parties in a communication to verify the identity of the other.

The reply message includes the nonce from A, to validate the reply. It also includes a timestamp and nonce generated by B. As before, the message may include signed additional information and a session key encrypted with A's public key.

Three-Way Authentication In three-way authentication, a final message from A to B is included, which contains a signed copy of the nonce r_B. The intent of this design is that timestamps need not be checked: Because both nonces are echoed back by the other side, each side can check the returned nonce to detect replay attacks. This approach is needed when synchronized clocks are not available.

X.509 Version 3

The X.509 version 2 format does not convey all of the information that recent design and implementation experience has shown to be needed. [FORD95] lists the following requirements not satisfied by version 2:

1. The Subject field is inadequate to convey the identity of a key owner to a public-key user. X.509 names may be relatively short and lacking in obvious identification details that may be needed by the user.
2. The Subject field is also inadequate for many applications, which typically recognize entities by an Internet e-mail address, a URL, or some other Internet-related identification.
3. There is a need to indicate security policy information. This enables a security application or function, such as IPSec, to relate an X.509 certificate to a given policy.
4. There is a need to limit the damage that can result from a faulty or malicious CA by setting constraints on the applicability of a particular certificate.
5. It is important to be able to identify different keys used by the same owner at different times. This feature supports key life cycle management, in particular the ability to update key pairs for users and CAs on a regular basis or under exceptional circumstances.

Rather than continue to add fields to a fixed format, standards developers felt that a more flexible approach was needed. Thus, version 3 includes a number of optional extensions that may be added to the version 2 format. Each extension consists of an extension identifier, a criticality indicator, and an extension value. The criticality indicator indicates whether an extension can be safely ignored. If the indicator has a value of TRUE and an implementation does not recognize the extension, it must treat the certificate as invalid.

The certificate extensions fall into three main categories: key and policy information, subject and issuer attributes, and certification path constraints.

Key and Policy Information These extensions convey additional information about the subject and issuer keys, plus indicators of certificate policy. A certificate policy is a named set of rules that indicates the applicability of a certificate to a particular community and/or class of application with common security requirements. For example, a policy might be applicable to the authentication of electronic data interchange (EDI) transactions for the trading of goods within a given price range.

This area includes the following:

- **Authority key identifier:** Identifies the public key to be used to verify the signature on this certificate or CRL. Enables distinct keys of the same CA to be differentiated. One use of this field is to handle CA key pair updating.
- **Subject key identifier:** Identifies the public key being certified. Useful for subject key pair updating. Also, a subject may have multiple key pairs and, correspondingly, different certificates for different purposes (e.g., digital signature and encryption key agreement).
- **Key usage:** Indicates a restriction imposed as to the purposes for which, and the policies under which, the certified public key may be used. May indicate one or more of the following: digital signature, nonrepudiation, key encryption, data encryption, key agreement, CA signature verification on certificates, CA signature verification on CRLs.
- **Private-key usage period:** Indicates the period of use of the private key corresponding to the public key. Typically, the private key is used over a different period from the validity of the public key. For example, with digital signature keys, the usage period for the signing private key is typically shorter than that for the verifying public key.
- **Certificate policies:** Certificates may be used in environments where multiple policies apply. This extension lists policies that the certificate is recognized as supporting, together with optional qualifier information.
- **Policy mappings:** Used only in certificates for CAs issued by other CAs. Policy mappings allow an issuing CA to indicate that one or more of that issuer's policies can be considered equivalent to another policy used in the subject CA's domain.

Certificate Subject and Issuer Attributes These extensions support alternative names, in alternative formats, for a certificate subject or certificate issuer and can convey additional information about the certificate subject, to increase a certificate user's confidence that the certificate subject is a particular person or entity. For example, information such as postal address, position within a corporation, or picture image may be required.

The extension fields in this area include the following:

- **Subject alternative name:** Contains one or more alternative names, using any of a variety of forms. This field is important for supporting certain applications, such as electronic mail, EDI, and IPSec, which may employ their own name forms.
- **Issuer alternative name:** Contains one or more alternative names, using any of a variety of forms.
- **Subject directory attributes:** Conveys any desired X.500 directory attribute values for the subject of this certificate.

Certification Path Constraints These extensions allow constraint specifications to be included in certificates issued for CAs by other CAs. The constraints may restrict the types of certificates that can be issued by the subject CA or that may occur subsequently in a certification chain.

The extension fields in this area include the following:

- **Basic constraints:** Indicates if the subject may act as a CA. If so, a certification path length constraint may be specified.
- **Name constraints:** Indicates a name space within which all subject names in subsequent certificates in a certification path must be located.
- **Policy constraints:** Specifies constraints that may require explicit certificate policy identification or inhibit policy mapping for the remainder of the certification path.

14.3 PUBLIC-KEY INFRASTRUCTURE

RFC 2822 (*Internet Security Glossary*) defines public-key infrastructure (PKI) as the set of hardware, software, people, policies, and procedures needed to create, manage, store, distribute, and revoke digital certificates based on asymmetric cryptography. The principal objective for developing a PKI is to enable secure, convenient, and efficient acquisition of public keys. The Internet Engineering Task Force (IETF) Public Key Infrastructure X.509 (PKIX) working group has been the driving force behind setting up a formal (and generic) model based on X.509 that is suitable for deploying a certificate-based architecture on the Internet. This section describes the PKIX model.

Figure 14.7 shows the interrelationship among the key elements of the PKIX model. These elements are

- **End entity:** A generic term used to denote end users, devices (e.g., servers, routers), or any other entity that can be identified in the subject field of a public key certificate. End entities typically consume and/or support PKI-related services.

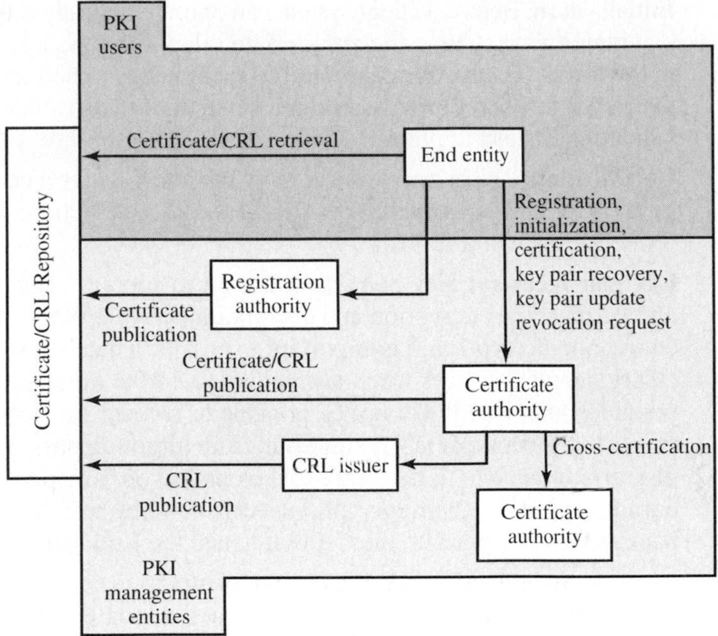

Figure 14.7 PKIX Architectural Model

- **Certification authority (CA):** The issuer of certificates and (usually) certificate revocation lists (CRLs). It may also support a variety of administrative functions, although these are often delegated to one or more Registration Authorities.
- **Registration authority (RA):** An optional component that can assume a number of administrative functions from the CA. The RA is often associated with the End Entity registration process, but can assist in a number of other areas as well.
- **CRL issuer:** An optional component that a CA can delegate to publish CRLs.
- **Repository:** A generic term used to denote any method for storing certificates and CRLs so that they can be retrieved by End Entities.

PKIX Management Functions

PKIX identifies a number of management functions that potentially need to be supported by management protocols. These are indicated in Figure 14.7 and include the following:

- **Registration:** This is the process whereby a user first makes itself known to a CA (directly, or through an RA), prior to that CA issuing a certificate or certificates for that user. Registration begins the process of enrolling in a PKI. Registration usually involves some offline or online procedure for mutual authentication. Typically, the end entity is issued one or more shared secret keys used for subsequent authentication.

- **Initialization:** Before a client system can operate securely, it is necessary to install key materials that have the appropriate relationship with keys stored elsewhere in the infrastructure. For example, the client needs to be securely initialized with the public key and other assured information of the trusted CA(s), to be used in validating certificate paths.
- **Certification:** This is the process in which a CA issues a certificate for a user's public key, and returns that certificate to the user's client system and/or posts that certificate in a repository.
- **Key pair recovery:** Key pairs can be used to support digital signature creation and verification, encryption and decryption, or both. When a key pair is used for encryption/decryption, it is important to provide a mechanism to recover the necessary decryption keys when normal access to the keying material is no longer possible, otherwise it will not be possible to recover the encrypted data. Loss of access to the decryption key can result from forgotten passwords/PINs, corrupted disk drives, damage to hardware tokens, and so on. Key pair recovery allows end entities to restore their encryption/decryption key pair from an authorized key backup facility (typically, the CA that issued the End Entity's certificate).
- **Key pair update:** All key pairs need to be updated regularly (i.e., replaced with a new key pair) and new certificates issued. Update is required when the certificate lifetime expires and as a result of certificate revocation.
- **Revocation request:** An authorized person advises a CA of an abnormal situation requiring certificate revocation. Reasons for revocation include private key compromise, change in affiliation, and name change.
- **Cross certification:** Two CAs exchange information used in establishing a cross-certificate. A cross-certificate is a certificate issued by one CA to another CA that contains a CA signature key used for issuing certificates.

PKIX Management Protocols

The PKIX working group has defines two alternative management protocols between PKIX entities that support the management functions listed in the preceding subsection. RFC 2510 defines the certificate management protocols (CMP). Within CMP, each of the management functions is explicitly identified by specific protocol exchanges. CMP is designed to be a flexible protocol able to accommodate a variety of technical, operational, and business models.

RFC 2797 defines certificate management messages over CMS (CMC), where CMS refers to RFC 2630, cryptographic message syntax. CMC is built on earlier work and is intended to leverage existing implementations. Although all of the PKIX functions are supported, the functions do not all map into specific protocol exchanges.

14.4 RECOMMENDED READING AND WEB SITES

A painless way to get a grasp of Kerberos concepts is found in [BRYA88]. One of the best treatments of Kerberos is [KOHL94]. [TUNG99] describes Kerberos from a user's point of view.

[PERL99] reviews various trust models that can be used in a PKI. [GUTM02] highlights difficulties in PKI use and recommends approaches for an effective PKI.

BRYA88 Bryant, W. *Designing an Authentication System: A Dialogue in Four Scenes*. Project Athena document, February 1988. Available at **http://web.mit.edu/kerberos/www/dialogue.html**.

GUTM02 Gutmann, P. "PKI: It's Not Dead, Just Resting." *Computer*, August 2002.

KOHL94 Kohl, J.; Neuman, B.; and Ts'o, T. "The Evolution of the Kerberos Authentication Service." in Brazier, F., and Johansen, D. *Distributed Open Systems*. Los Alamitos, CA: IEEE Computer Society Press, 1994. Available at **http://web.mit.edu/kerberos/www/papers. html**.

PERL99 Perlman, R. "An Overview of PKI Trust Models." *IEEE Network*, November/December 1999.

TUNG99 Tung, B. *Kerberos: A Network Authentication System*. Reading, MA: Addison-Wesley, 1999.

Recommended Web Sites:

- **MIT Kerberos Site:** Information about Kerberos, including the FAQ, papers and documents, and pointers to commercial product sites
- **USC/ISI Kerberos Page:** Another good source of Kerberos material
- **Kerberos Working Group:** IETF group developing standards based on Kerberos
- **Public-Key Infrastructure Working Group:** IETF group developing standards based on X.509v3
- **Verisign:** A leading commercial vendor of X.509-related products; white papers and other worthwhile material at this site
- **NIST PKI Program:** Good source of information

14.5 KEY TERMS, REVIEW QUESTIONS, AND PROBLEMS

Key Terms

authentication	nonce	sequence number
authentication server	propagating cipher block chaining (PCBC) mode	subkey
Kerberos	public-key certificate	ticket
Kerberos realm	realm	ticket-granting server (TGS)
lifetime		X.509 certificate

Review Questions

14.1 What problem was Kerberos designed to address?

14.2 What are three threats associated with user authentication over a network or Internet?

14.3 List three approaches to secure user authentication in a distributed environment.

14.4 What four requirements were defined for Kerberos?

14.5 What entities constitute a full-service Kerberos environment?
14.6 In the context of Kerberos, what is a realm?
14.7 What are the principal differences between version 4 and version 5 of Kerberos?
14.8 What is the purpose of the X.509 standard?
14.9 What is a chain of certificates?
14.10 How is an X.509 certificate revoked?

Problems

14.1 Show that a random error in one block of ciphertext is propagated to all subsequent blocks of plaintext in PCBC mode (Figure 14.9).

14.2 Suppose that, in PCBC mode, blocks C_i and C_{i+1} are interchanged during transmission. Show that this affects only the decrypted blocks P_i and P_{i+1} but not subsequent blocks.

14.3 The original three-way authentication procedure for X.509 illustrated in Figure 14.6c contains a security flaw. The essence of the protocol is as follows:

A → B: A $\{t_A, r_A, ID_B\}$
B → A: B $\{t_B, r_B, ID_A, r_A\}$
A → B: A $\{r_B\}$

The text of X.509 states that checking timestamps t_A and t_B is optional for three-way authentication. But consider the following example: Suppose A and B have used the preceding protocol on some previous occasion, and that opponent C has intercepted the preceding three messages. In addition, suppose that timestamps are not used and are all set to 0. Finally, suppose C wishes to impersonate A to B. C initially sends the first captured message to B:

C → B: A $\{0, r_A, ID_B\}$

B responds, thinking it is talking to A but is actually talking to C:

B → C: B $\{0, r'_B, ID_A, r_A\}$

C meanwhile causes A to initiate authentication with C by some means. As a result, A sends C the following:

A → C: A $\{0, r'_A, ID_C\}$

C responds to A using the same nonce provided to C by B.

C → A: C $\{0, r'_B, ID_A, r'_A\}$

A responds with

A → C: A $\{r'_B\}$

This is exactly what C needs to convince B that it is talking to A, so C now repeats the incoming message back out to B.

C → B: A $\{r'_B\}$

So B will believe it is talking to A whereas it is actually talking to C. Suggest a simple solution to this problem that does not involve the use of timestamps.

14.4 The 1988 version of X.509 lists properties that RSA keys must satisfy to be secure, given current knowledge about the difficulty of factoring large numbers. The discussion concludes with a constraint on the public exponent and the modulus n:

> It must be ensured that $e > \log_2(n)$ to prevent attack by taking the eth root mod n to disclose the plaintext.

Although the constraint is correct, the reason given for requiring it is incorrect. What is wrong with the reason given and what is the correct reason?

APPENDIX 14A KERBEROS ENCRYPTION TECHNIQUES

Kerberos includes an encryption library that supports various encryption-related operations. These were included in the Kerberos 5 specification and are common in commercial implementations. In February 2005, IETF issued RFCs 3961 and 3962, which expand the options of cryptographic techniques. In this appendix, we describe the RFC 1510 techniques.

Password-to-Key Transformation

In Kerberos, passwords are limited to the use of the characters that can be represented in a 7-bit ASCII format. This password, of arbitrary length, is converted into an encryption key that is stored in the Kerberos database. Figure 14.8 illustrates the procedure.

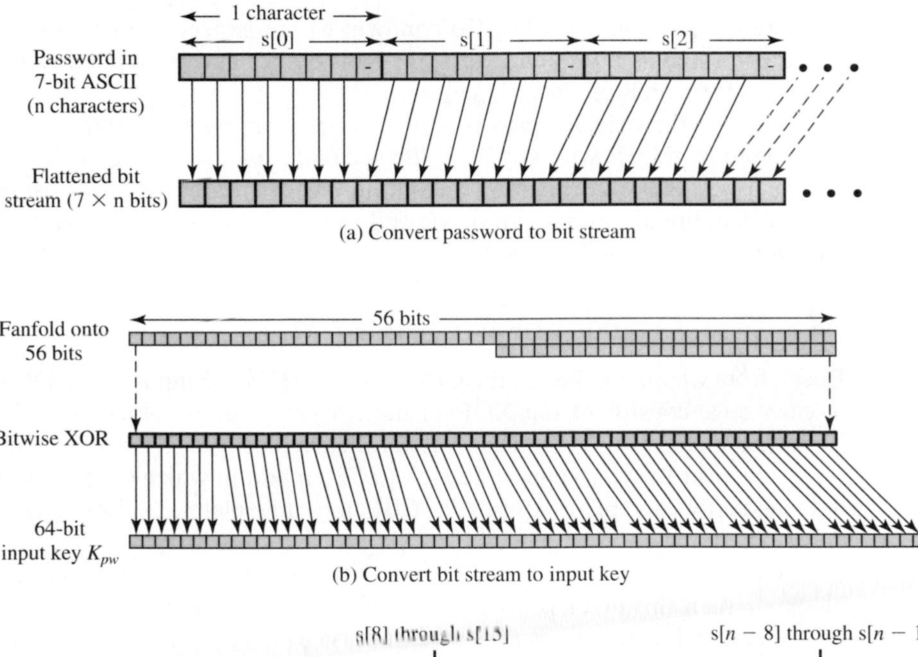

(a) Convert password to bit stream

(b) Convert bit stream to input key

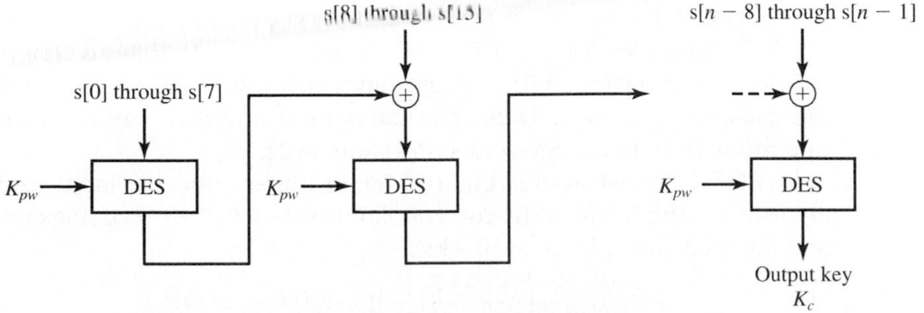

(c) Generate DES CBC checksum of password

Figure 14.8 Generation of Encryption Key from Password

First, the character string, s, is packed into a bit string, b, such that the first character is stored in the first 7 bits, the second character in the second 7 bits, and so on. This can be expressed as

b[0] = bit 0 of s[0]
...
b[6] = bit 6 of s[0]
b[7] = bit 0 of s[1]
...
b[7i + m] = bit m of s[i] $0 \le m \le 6$

Next, the bit string is compacted to 56 bits by aligning the bits in "fanfold" fashion and performing a bitwise XOR. For example, if the bit string is of length 59, then

$$b[55] = b[55] \oplus b[56]$$
$$b[54] = b[54] \oplus b[57]$$
$$b[53] = b[53] \oplus b[58]$$

This creates a 56-bit DES key. To conform to the expected 64-bit key format, the string is treated as a sequence of eight 7-bit blocks and is mapped into eight 8-bit blocks to form an input key K_{pw}.

Finally, the original password is encrypted using the cipher block chaining (CBC) mode of DES with key K_{pw}. The last 64-bit block returned from this process, known as the CBC checksum, is the output key associated with this password.

The entire algorithm can be viewed as a hash function that maps an arbitrary password into a 64-bit hash code.

Propagating Cipher Block Chaining Mode

Recall from Chapter 6 that, in the CBC mode of DES, the input to the DES algorithm at each stage consists of the XOR of the current plaintext block and the preceding ciphertext block, with the same key used for each block (Figure 6.4). The advantage of this mode over the electronic codebook (ECB) mode, in which each plaintext block is independently encrypted, is this: With CBC, the same plaintext block, if repeated, produces different ciphertext blocks.

CBC has the property that if an error occurs in transmission of ciphertext block C_I, then this error propagates to the recovered plaintext blocks P_I and P_{I+1}.

Version 4 of Kerberos uses an extension to CBC, called the propagating CBC (PCBC) mode [MEYE82]. This mode has the property that an error in one ciphertext block is propagated to all subsequent decrypted blocks of the message, rendering each block useless. Thus, data encryption and integrity are combined in one operation. (For an exception, see Problem 14.2).

PCBC is illustrated in Figure 14.9. In this scheme, the input to the encryption algorithm is the XOR of the current plaintext block, the preceding cipher text block, and the preceding plaintext block:

$$C_n = E(K, [C_{n-1} \oplus P_{n-1} \oplus P_n])$$

On decryption, each ciphertext block is passed through the decryption algorithm. Then the output is XORed with the preceding ciphertext block and

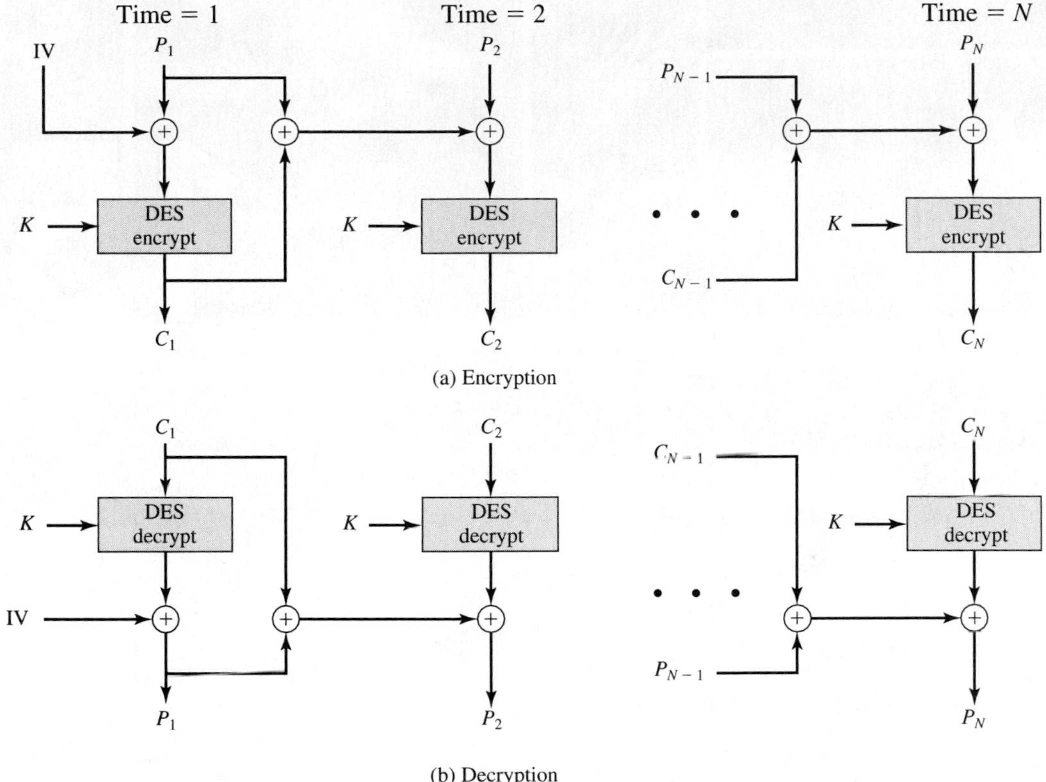

Figure 14.9 Propagating Cipher Block Chaining (PCBC) Mode

the preceding plaintext block. We can demonstrate that this scheme works, as follows:

$$\mathrm{D}(K, C_n) = \mathrm{D}(K, \mathrm{E}(K, [C_{n-1} \oplus P_{n-1} \oplus P_n]))$$
$$\mathrm{D}(K, C_n) = C_{n-1} \oplus P_{n-1} \oplus P_n$$
$$C_{n-1} \oplus P_{n-1} \oplus \mathrm{D}(K, C_n) = P_n$$

CHAPTER 15

Electronic Mail Security

Despite the refusal of VADM Poindexter and LtCol North to appear, the Board's access to other sources of information filled much of this gap. The FBI provided documents taken from the files of the National Security Advisor and relevant NSC staff members, including messages from the PROF system between VADM Poindexter and LtCol North. The PROF messages were conversations by computer, written at the time events occurred and presumed by the writers to be protected from disclosure. In this sense, they provide a first-hand, contemporaneous account of events.

—The Tower Commission Report to President Reagan
on the Iran-Contra Affair, 1987

Bless the man who made it,
And pray that he ain't dead.
He could've made a million
If he'd sold it to the feds,
But he was hot for freedom;
He gave it out for free.
Now every common citizen's got PGP.

—From the song "P.G.P."
by Leslie Fish

KEY POINTS

- PGP is an open-source freely available software package for e-mail security. It provides authentication through the use of digital signature; confidentiality through the use of symmetric block encryption; compression using the ZIP algorithm; e-mail compatibility using the radix-64 encoding scheme; and segmentation and reassembly to accommodate long e-mails.
- PGP incorporates tools for developing a public-key trust model and public-key certificate management.
- S/MIME is an Internet standard approach to e-mail security that incorporates the same functionality as PGP.

In virtually all distributed environments, electronic mail is the most heavily used network-based application. It is also the only distributed application that is widely used across all architectures and vendor platforms. Users expect to be able to, and do, send mail to others who are connected directly or indirectly to the Internet, regardless of host operating system or communications suite.

With the explosively growing reliance on electronic mail for every conceivable purpose, there grows a demand for authentication and confidentiality services. Two schemes stand out as approaches that enjoy widespread use: Pretty Good Privacy (PGP) and S/MIME. Both are examined in this chapter.

15.1 PRETTY GOOD PRIVACY

PGP is a remarkable phenomenon. Largely the effort of a single person, Phil Zimmermann, PGP provides a confidentiality and authentication service that can be used for electronic mail and file storage applications. In essence, Zimmermann has done the following:

1. Selected the best available cryptographic algorithms as building blocks
2. Integrated these algorithms into a general-purpose application that is independent of operating system and processor and that is based on a small set of easy-to-use commands
3. Made the package and its documentation, including the source code, freely available via the Internet, bulletin boards, and commercial networks such as AOL (America On Line)
4. Entered into an agreement with a company (Viacrypt, now Network Associates) to provide a fully compatible, low-cost commercial version of PGP

PGP has grown explosively and is now widely used. A number of reasons can be cited for this growth:

1. It is available free worldwide in versions that run on a variety of platforms, including Windows, UNIX, Macintosh, and many more. In addition, the commercial version satisfies users who want a product that comes with vendor support.
2. It is based on algorithms that have survived extensive public review and are considered extremely secure. Specifically, the package includes RSA, DSS, and Diffie-Hellman for public-key encryption; CAST-128, IDEA, and 3DES for symmetric encryption; and SHA-1 for hash coding.
3. It has a wide range of applicability, from corporations that wish to select and enforce a standardized scheme for encrypting files and messages to individuals who wish to communicate securely with others worldwide over the Internet and other networks.
4. It was not developed by, nor is it controlled by, any governmental or standards organization. For those with an instinctive distrust of "the establishment," this makes PGP attractive.
5. PGP is now on an Internet standards track (RFC 3156). Nevertheless, PGP still has an aura of an antiestablishment endeavor.

We begin with an overall look at the operation of PGP. Next, we examine how cryptographic keys are created and stored. Then, we address the vital issue of public key management.

Notation

Most of the notation used in this chapter has been used before, but a few terms are new. It is perhaps best to summarize those at the beginning. The following symbols are used:

K_s = session key used in symmetric encryption scheme
PR_a = private key of user A, used in public-key encryption scheme
PU_a = public key of user A, used in public-key encryption scheme
EP = public-key encryption
DP = public-key decryption
EC = symmetric encryption
DC = symmetric decryption
H = hash function
$\|$ = concatenation
Z = compression using ZIP algorithm
R64 = conversion to radix 64 ASCII format

The PGP documentation often uses the term *secret key* to refer to a key paired with a public key in a public-key encryption scheme. As was mentioned earlier, this practice risks confusion with a secret key used for symmetric encryption. Hence, we will use the term *private key* instead.

Operational Description

The actual operation of PGP, as opposed to the management of keys, consists of five services: authentication, confidentiality, compression, e-mail compatibility, and segmentation (Table 15.1). We examine each of these in turn.

Authentication Figure 15.1a illustrates the digital signature service provided by PGP. This is the digital signature scheme discussed in Chapter 13 and illustrated in Figure 11.5c. The sequence is as follows:

1. The sender creates a message.
2. SHA-1 is used to generate a 160-bit hash code of the message.
3. The hash code is encrypted with RSA using the sender's private key, and the result is prepended to the message.
4. The receiver uses RSA with the sender's public key to decrypt and recover the hash code.
5. The receiver generates a new hash code for the message and compares it with the decrypted hash code. If the two match, the message is accepted as authentic.

The combination of SHA-1 and RSA provides an effective digital signature scheme. Because of the strength of RSA, the recipient is assured that only the possessor of the matching private key can generate the signature. Because of the strength of SHA-1, the recipient is assured that no one else could generate a new message that matches the hash code and, hence, the signature of the original message.

Table 15.1 Summary of PGP Services

Function	Algorithms Used	Description
Digital signature	DSS/SHA or RSA/SHA	A hash code of a message is created using SHA-1. This message digest is encrypted using DSS or RSA with the sender's private key and included with the message.
Message encryption	CAST or IDEA or Three-key Triple DES with Diffie-Hellman or RSA	A message is encrypted using CAST-128 or IDEA or 3DES with a one-time session key generated by the sender. The session key is encrypted using Diffie-Hellman or RSA with the recipient's public key and included with the message.
Compression	ZIP	A message may be compressed, for storage or transmission, using ZIP.
Email compatibility	Radix 64 conversion	To provide transparency for email applications, an encrypted message may be converted to an ASCII string using radix 64 conversion.
Segmentation	—	To accommodate maximum message size limitations, PGP performs segmentation and reassembly.

As an alternative, signatures can be generated using DSS/SHA-1.

Although signatures normally are found attached to the message or file that they sign, this is not always the case: Detached signatures are supported. A detached signature may be stored and transmitted separately from the message it signs. This is useful in several contexts. A user may wish to maintain a separate signature log of all messages sent or received. A detached signature of an executable program can detect subsequent virus infection. Finally, detached signatures can be used when more than one party must sign a document, such as a legal contract. Each person's signature is independent and therefore is applied only to the document. Otherwise, signatures would have to be nested, with the second signer signing both the document and the first signature, and so on.

Confidentiality Another basic service provided by PGP is confidentiality, which is provided by encrypting messages to be transmitted or to be stored locally as files. In both cases, the symmetric encryption algorithm CAST-128 may be used. Alternatively, IDEA or 3DES may be used. The 64-bit cipher feedback (CFB) mode is used.

As always, one must address the problem of key distribution. In PGP, each symmetric key is used only once. That is, a new key is generated as a random 128-bit number for each message. Thus, although this is referred to in the documentation as a session key, it is in reality a one-time key. Because it is to be used only once, the session key is bound to the message and transmitted with it. To protect the key, it is encrypted with the receiver's public key. Figure 15.1b illustrates the sequence, which can be described as follows:

1. The sender generates a message and a random 128-bit number to be used as a session key for this message only.

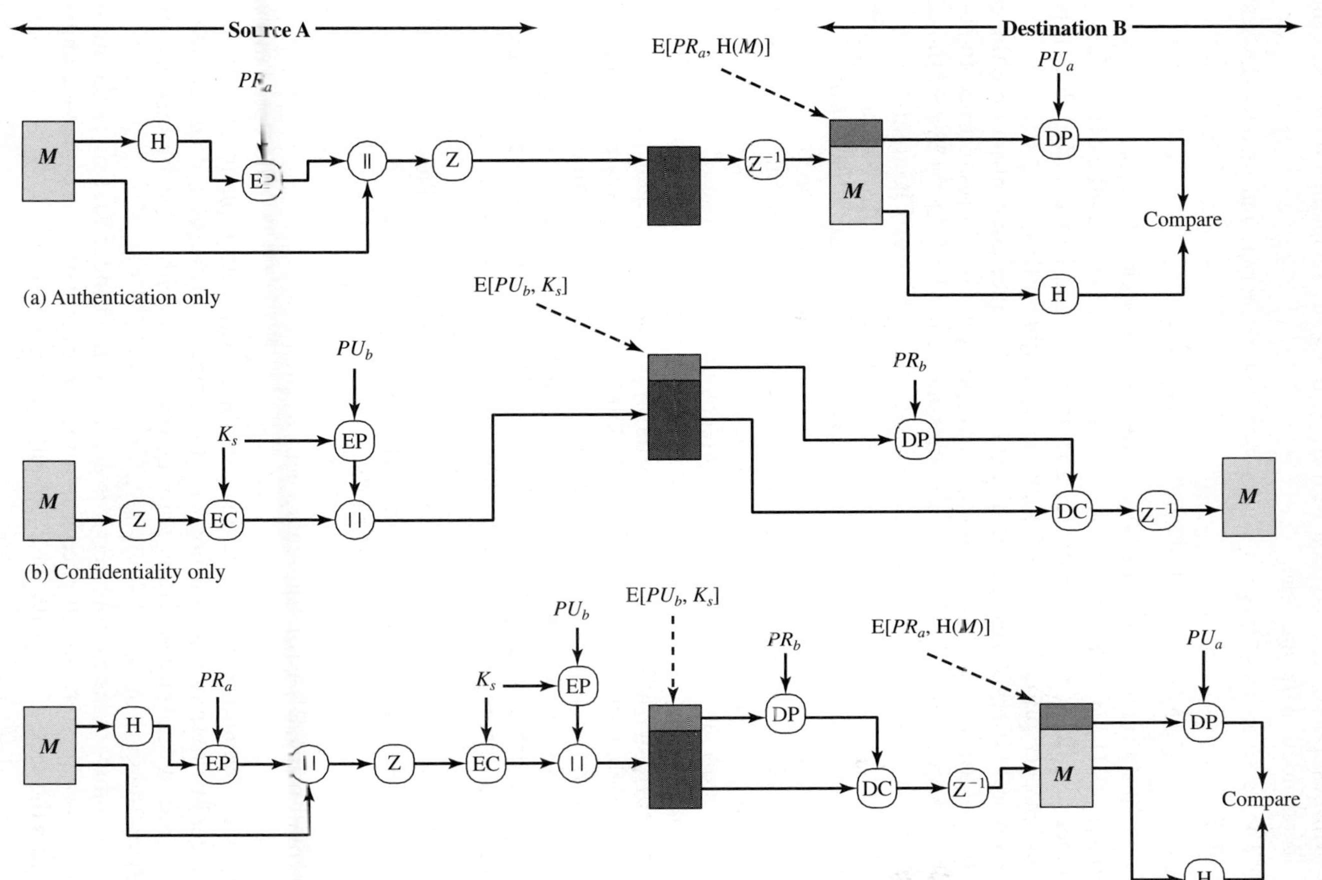

Figure 15.1 PGP Cryptographic Functions

2. The message is encrypted, using CAST-128 (or IDEA or 3DES) with the session key.
3. The session key is encrypted with RSA, using the recipient's public key, and is prepended to the message.
4. The receiver uses RSA with its private key to decrypt and recover the session key.
5. The session key is used to decrypt the message.

As an alternative to the use of RSA for key encryption, PGP provides an option referred to as *Diffie-Hellman*. As was explained in Chapter 10, Diffie-Hellman is a key exchange algorithm. In fact, PGP uses a variant of Diffie-Hellman that does provide encryption/decryption, known as ElGamal (see Problem 10.6).

Several observations may be made. First, to reduce encryption time the combination of symmetric and public-key encryption is used in preference to simply using RSA or ElGamal to encrypt the message directly: CAST-128 and the other symmetric algorithms are substantially faster than RSA or ElGamal. Second, the use of the public-key algorithm solves the session key distribution problem, because only the recipient is able to recover the session key that is bound to the message. Note that we do not need a session key exchange protocol of the type discussed in Chapter 10, because we are not beginning an ongoing session. Rather, each message is a one-time independent event with its own key. Furthermore, given the store-and-forward nature of electronic mail, the use of handshaking to assure that both sides have the same session key is not practical. Finally, the use of one-time symmetric keys strengthens what is already a strong symmetric encryption approach. Only a small amount of plaintext is encrypted with each key, and there is no relationship among the keys. Thus, to the extent that the public-key algorithm is secure, the entire scheme is secure. To this end, PGP provides the user with a range of key size options from 768 to 3072 bits (the DSS key for signatures is limited to 1024 bits).

Confidentiality and Authentication As Figure 15.1c illustrates, both services may be used for the same message. First, a signature is generated for the plaintext message and prepended to the message. Then the plaintext message plus signature is encrypted using CAST-128 (or IDEA or 3DES), and the session key is encrypted using RSA (or ElGamal). This sequence is preferable to the opposite: encrypting the message and then generating a signature for the encrypted message. It is generally more convenient to store a signature with a plaintext version of a message. Furthermore, for purposes of third-party verification, if the signature is performed first, a third party need not be concerned with the symmetric key when verifying the signature.

In summary, when both services are used, the sender first signs the message with its own private key, then encrypts the message with a session key, and then encrypts the session key with the recipient's public key.

Compression As a default, PGP compresses the message after applying the signature but before encryption. This has the benefit of saving space both for e-mail transmission and for file storage.

The placement of the compression algorithm, indicated by Z for compression and Z^{-1} for decompression in Figure 15.1, is critical:

1. The signature is generated before compression for two reasons:
   a. It is preferable to sign an uncompressed message so that one can store only the uncompressed message together with the signature for future verification. If one signed a compressed document, then it would be necessary either to store a compressed version of the message for later verification or to recompress the message when verification is required.
   b. Even if one were willing to generate dynamically a recompressed message for verification, PGP's compression algorithm presents a difficulty. The algorithm is not deterministic; various implementations of the algorithm achieve different tradeoffs in running speed versus compression ratio and, as a result, produce different compressed forms. However, these different compression algorithms are interoperable because any version of the algorithm can correctly decompress the output of any other version. Applying the hash function and signature after compression would constrain all PGP implementations to the same version of the compression algorithm.
2. Message encryption is applied after compression to strengthen cryptographic security. Because the compressed message has less redundancy than the original plaintext, cryptanalysis is more difficult.

The compression algorithm used is ZIP, which is described in Appendix 15A.

E-mail Compatibility When PGP is used, at least part of the block to be transmitted is encrypted. If only the signature service is used, then the message digest is encrypted (with the sender's private key). If the confidentiality service is used, the message plus signature (if present) are encrypted (with a one-time symmetric key). Thus, part or all of the resulting block consists of a stream of arbitrary 8-bit octets. However, many electronic mail systems only permit the use of blocks consisting of ASCII text. To accommodate this restriction, PGP provides the service of converting the raw 8-bit binary stream to a stream of printable ASCII characters.

The scheme used for this purpose is radix-64 conversion. Each group of three octets of binary data is mapped into four ASCII characters. This format also appends a CRC to detect transmission errors. See Appendix 15B for a description.

The use of radix 64 expands a message by 33%. Fortunately, the session key and signature portions of the message are relatively compact, and the plaintext message has been compressed. In fact, the compression should be more than enough to compensate for the radix-64 expansion. For example, [HELD96] reports an average compression ratio of about 2.0 using ZIP. If we ignore the relatively small signature and key components, the typical overall effect of compression and expansion of a file of length X would be $1.33 \times 0.5 \times X = 0.665 \times X$. Thus, there is still an overall compression of about one-third.

One noteworthy aspect of the radix-64 algorithm is that it blindly converts the input stream to radix-64 format regardless of content, even if the input happens to be ASCII text. Thus, if a message is signed but not encrypted and the conversion is applied to the entire block, the output will be unreadable to the casual observer, which provides a certain level of confidentiality. As an option, PGP can be configured to convert to radix-64 format only the signature portion of signed plaintext messages. This enables the human recipient to read the message without using PGP. PGP would still have to be used to verify the signature.

Figure 15.2 shows the relationship among the four services so far discussed. On transmission, if it is required, a signature is generated using a hash code of the uncompressed plaintext. Then the plaintext, plus signature if present, is compressed. Next, if confidentiality is required, the block (compressed plaintext or compressed signature plus plaintext) is encrypted and prepended with the public-key-encrypted symmetric encryption key. Finally, the entire block is converted to radix-64 format.

On reception, the incoming block is first converted back from radix-64 format to binary. Then, if the message is encrypted, the recipient recovers the session key and decrypts the message. The resulting block is then decompressed. If the message is signed, the recipient recovers the transmitted hash code and compares it to its own calculation of the hash code.

Segmentation and Reassembly E-mail facilities often are restricted to a maximum message length. For example, many of the facilities accessible through the Internet impose a maximum length of 50,000 octets. Any message longer than that must be broken up into smaller segments, each of which is mailed separately.

To accommodate this restriction, PGP automatically subdivides a message that is too large into segments that are small enough to send via e-mail. The segmentation is done after all of the other processing, including the radix-64 conversion. Thus, the session key component and signature component appear only once, at the beginning of the first segment. At the receiving end, PGP must strip off all e-mail headers and reassemble the entire original block before performing the steps illustrated in Figure 15.2b.

Cryptographic Keys and Key Rings

PGP makes use of four types of keys: one-time session symmetric keys, public keys, private keys, and passphrase-based symmetric keys (explained subsequently). Three separate requirements can be identified with respect to these keys:

1. A means of generating unpredictable session keys is needed.
2. We would like to allow a user to have multiple public-key/private-key pairs. One reason is that the user may wish to change his or her key pair from time to time. When this happens, any messages in the pipeline will be constructed with an obsolete key. Furthermore, recipients will know only the old public key until an update reaches them. In addition to the need to change keys over time, a user may wish to have multiple key pairs at a given time to interact with different groups of correspondents or simply to enhance security by limiting the amount of material encrypted with any one key. The upshot of all this is that there is not a one-to-one correspondence between users and their public keys. Thus, some means is needed for identifying particular keys.
3. Each PGP entity must maintain a file of its own public/private key pairs as well as a file of public keys of correspondents.

We examine each of these requirements in turn.

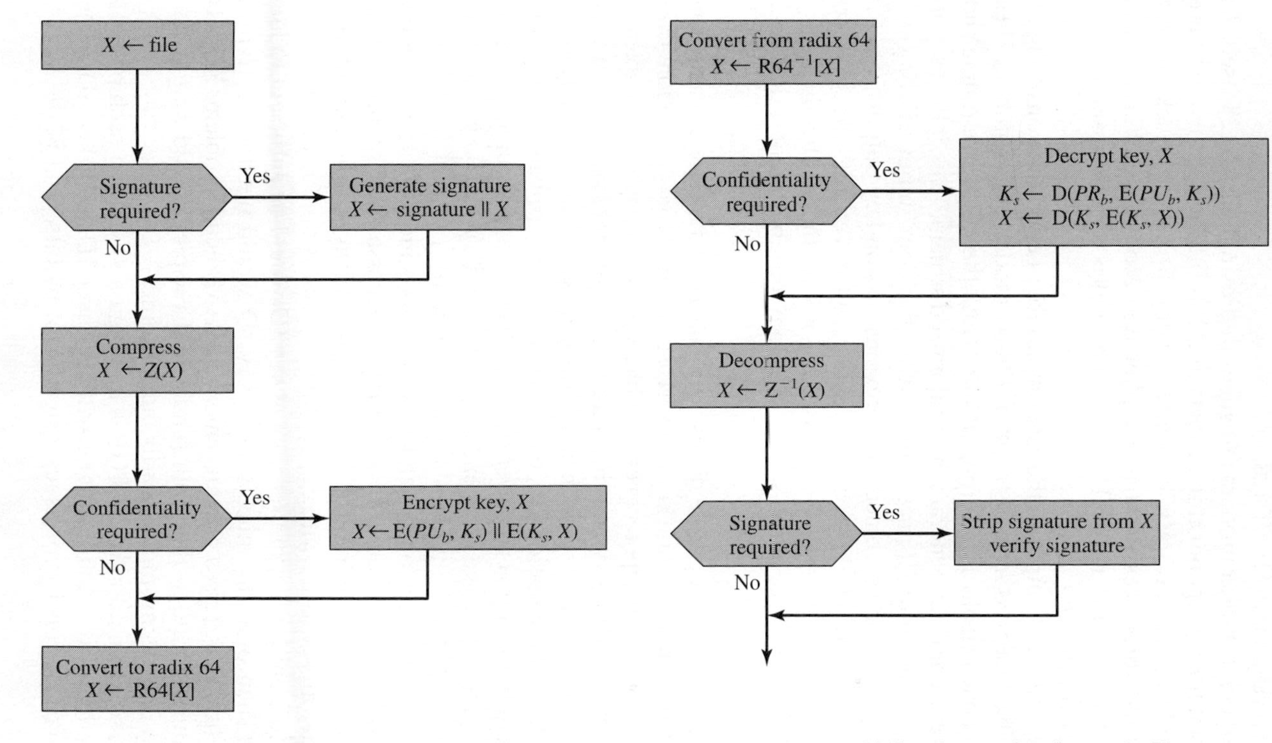

(a) Generic transmission diagram (from A)

(b) Generic reception diagram (to B)

Figure 15.2 Transmission and Reception of PGP Messages

Session Key Generation Each session key is associated with a single message and is used only for the purpose of encrypting and decrypting that message. Recall that message encryption/decryption is done with a symmetric encryption algorithm. CAST-128 and IDEA use 128-bit keys; 3DES uses a 168-bit key. For the following discussion, we assume CAST-128.

Random 128-bit numbers are generated using CAST-128 itself. The input to the random number generator consists of a 128-bit key and two 64-bit blocks that are treated as plaintext to be encrypted. Using cipher feedback mode, the CAST-128 encrypter produces two 64-bit cipher text blocks, which are concatenated to form the 128-bit session key. The algorithm that is used is based on the one specified in ANSI X12.17.

The "plaintext" input to the random number generator, consisting of two 64-bit blocks, is itself derived from a stream of 128-bit randomized numbers. These numbers are based on keystroke input from the user. Both the keystroke timing and the actual keys struck are used to generate the randomized stream. Thus, if the user hits arbitrary keys at his or her normal pace, a reasonably "random" input will be generated. This random input is also combined with previous session key output from CAST-128 to form the key input to the generator. The result, given the effective scrambling of CAST-128, is to produce a sequence of session keys that is effectively unpredictable.

Appendix 15C discusses PGP random number generation techniques in more detail.

Key Identifiers As we have discussed, an encrypted message is accompanied by an encrypted form of the session key that was used for message encryption. The session key itself is encrypted with the recipient's public key. Hence, only the recipient will be able to recover the session key and therefore recover the message. If each user employed a single public/private key pair, then the recipient would automatically know which key to use to decrypt the session key: the recipient's unique private key. However, we have stated a requirement that any given user may have multiple public/private key pairs.

How, then, does the recipient know which of its public keys was used to encrypt the session key? One simple solution would be to transmit the public key with the message. The recipient could then verify that this is indeed one of its public keys, and proceed. This scheme would work, but it is unnecessarily wasteful of space. An RSA public key may be hundreds of decimal digits in length. Another solution would be to associate an identifier with each public key that is unique at least within one user. That is, the combination of user ID and key ID would be sufficient to identify a key uniquely. Then only the much shorter key ID would need to be transmitted. This solution, however, raises a management and overhead problem: Key IDs must be assigned and stored so that both sender and recipient could map from key ID to public key. This seems unnecessarily burdensome.

The solution adopted by PGP is to assign a key ID to each public key that is, with very high probability, unique within a user ID.[1] The key ID associated with each public key consists of its least significant 64 bits. That is, the key ID of public

[1]We have seen this introduction of probabilistic concepts before, in Section 8.3, for determining whether a number is prime. It is often the case in designing algorithms that the use of probabilistic techniques results in a less time-consuming or less complex solution, or both.

key PU_a is (PU_a mod 2^{64}). This is a sufficient length that the probability of duplicate key IDs is very small.

A key ID is also required for the PGP digital signature. Because a sender may use one of a number of private keys to encrypt the message digest, the recipient must know which public key is intended for use. Accordingly, the digital signature component of a message includes the 64-bit key ID of the required public key. When the message is received, the recipient verifies that the key ID is for a public key that it knows for that sender and then proceeds to verify the signature.

Now that the concept of key ID has been introduced, we can take a more detailed look at the format of a transmitted message, which is shown in Figure 15.3. A message consists of three components: the message component, a signature (optional), and a session key component (optional).

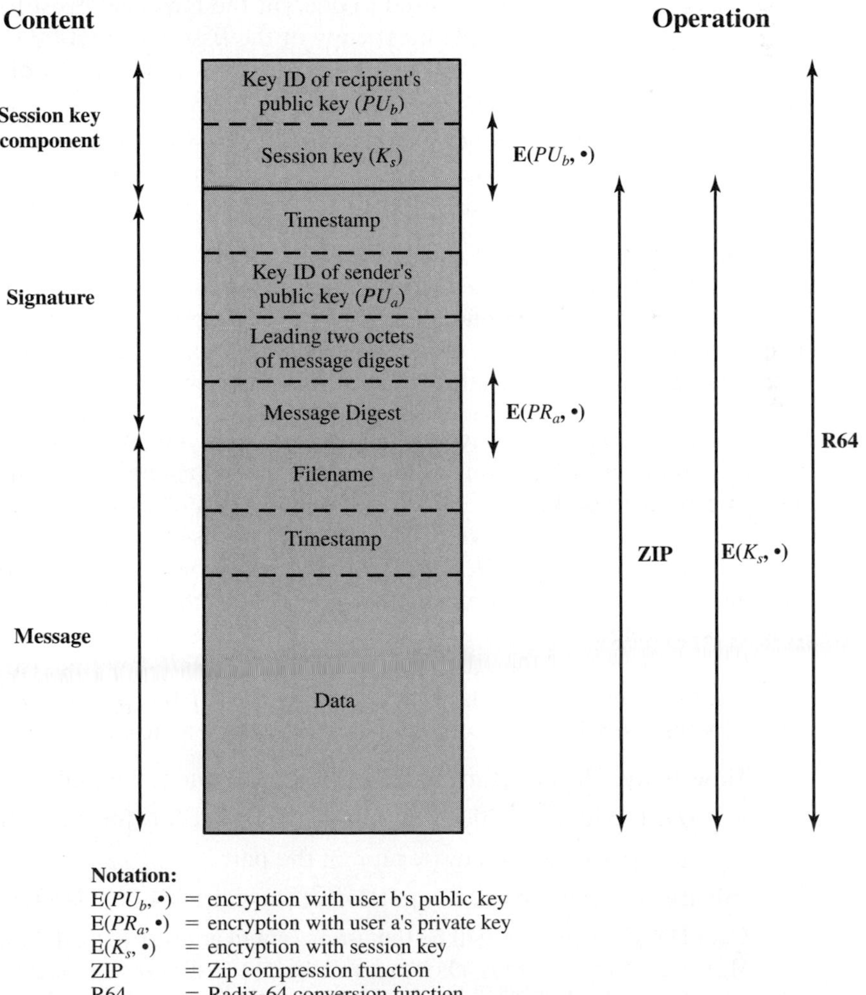

Notation:
E(PU_b, •) = encryption with user b's public key
E(PR_a, •) = encryption with user a's private key
E(K_s, •) = encryption with session key
ZIP = Zip compression function
R64 = Radix-64 conversion function

Figure 15.3 General Format of PGP Message (from A to B)

The **message component** includes the actual data to be stored or transmitted, as well as a filename and a timestamp that specifies the time of creation.

The **signature component** includes the following:

- **Timestamp:** The time at which the signature was made.
- **Message digest:** The 160-bit SHA-1 digest, encrypted with the sender's private signature key. The digest is calculated over the signature timestamp concatenated with the data portion of the message component. The inclusion of the signature timestamp in the digest assures against replay types of attacks. The exclusion of the filename and timestamp portions of the message component ensures that detached signatures are exactly the same as attached signatures prefixed to the message. Detached signatures are calculated on a separate file that has none of the message component header fields.
- **Leading two octets of message digest:** To enable the recipient to determine if the correct public key was used to decrypt the message digest for authentication, by comparing this plaintext copy of the first two octets with the first two octets of the decrypted digest. These octets also serve as a 16-bit frame check sequence for the message.
- **Key ID of sender's public key:** Identifies the public key that should be used to decrypt the message digest and, hence, identifies the private key that was used to encrypt the message digest.

The message component and optional signature component may be compressed using ZIP and may be encrypted using a session key.

The **session key component** includes the session key and the identifier of the recipient's public key that was used by the sender to encrypt the session key.

The entire block is usually encoded with radix-64 encoding.

Key Rings We have seen how key IDs are critical to the operation of PGP and that two key IDs are included in any PGP message that provides both confidentiality and authentication. These keys need to be stored and organized in a systematic way for efficient and effective use by all parties. The scheme used in PGP is to provide a pair of data structures at each node, one to store the public/private key pairs owned by that node and one to store the public keys of other users known at this node. These data structures are referred to, respectively, as the private-key ring and the public-key ring.

Figure 15.4 shows the general structure of a **private-key ring**. We can view the ring as a table, in which each row represents one of the public/private key pairs owned by this user. Each row contains the following entries:

- **Timestamp:** The date/time when this key pair was generated.
- **Key ID:** The least significant 64 bits of the public key for this entry.
- **Public key:** The public-key portion of the pair.
- **Private key:** The private-key portion of the pair; this field is encrypted.
- **User ID:** Typically, this will be the user's e-mail address (e.g., **stallings@acm.org**). However, the user may choose to associate a different name with each pair (e.g., Stallings, WStallings, WilliamStallings, etc.) or to reuse the same User ID more than once.

Private-Key Ring

Timestamp	Key ID*	Public Key	Encrypted Private Key	User ID*
⋮	⋮	⋮	⋮	⋮
T_i	PU_i mod 2^{64}	PU_i	$E(H(P_i), PR_i)$	User i
⋮	⋮	⋮	⋮	⋮

Public-Key Ring

Timestamp	Key ID*	Public Key	Owner Trust	User ID*	Key Legitimacy	Signature(s)	Signature Trust(s)
⋮	⋮	⋮	⋮	⋮	⋮	⋮	⋮
T_i	PU_i mod 2^{64}	PU_i	trust_flag$_i$	User i	trust_flag$_i$		
⋮	⋮	⋮	⋮	⋮	⋮	⋮	⋮

* = field used to index table

Figure 15.4 General Structure of Private- and Public-Key Rings

The private-key ring can be indexed by either User ID or Key ID; later we will see the need for both means of indexing.

Although it is intended that the private-key ring be stored only on the machine of the user that created and owns the key pairs, and that it be accessible only to that user, it makes sense to make the value of the private key as secure as possible. Accordingly, the private key itself is not stored in the key ring. Rather, this key is encrypted using CAST-128 (or IDEA or 3DES). The procedure is as follows:

1. The user selects a passphrase to be used for encrypting private keys.
2. When the system generates a new public/private key pair using RSA, it asks the user for the passphrase. Using SHA-1, a 160-bit hash code is generated from the passphrase, and the passphrase is discarded.
3. The system encrypts the private key using CAST-128 with the 128 bits of the hash code as the key. The hash code is then discarded, and the encrypted private key is stored in the private-key ring.

Subsequently, when a user accesses the private-key ring to retrieve a private key, he or she must supply the passphrase. PGP will retrieve the encrypted private key, generate the hash code of the passphrase, and decrypt the encrypted private key using CAST-128 with the hash code.

This is a very compact and effective scheme. As in any system based on passwords, the security of this system depends on the security of the password. To avoid the temptation to write it down, the user should use a passphrase that is not easily guessed but that is easily remembered.

Figure 15.4 also shows the general structure of a **public-key ring**. This data structure is used to store public keys of other users that are known to this user. For the moment, let us ignore some fields shown in the table and describe the following fields:

- **Timestamp:** The date/time when this entry was generated.
- **Key ID:** The least significant 64 bits of the public key for this entry.
- **Public Key:** The public key for this entry.
- **User ID:** Identifies the owner of this key. Multiple user IDs may be associated with a single public key.

The public-key ring can be indexed by either User ID or Key ID; we will see the need for both means of indexing later.

We are now in a position to show how these key rings are used in message transmission and reception. For simplicity, we ignore compression and radix-64 conversion in the following discussion. First consider message transmission (Figure 15.5) and

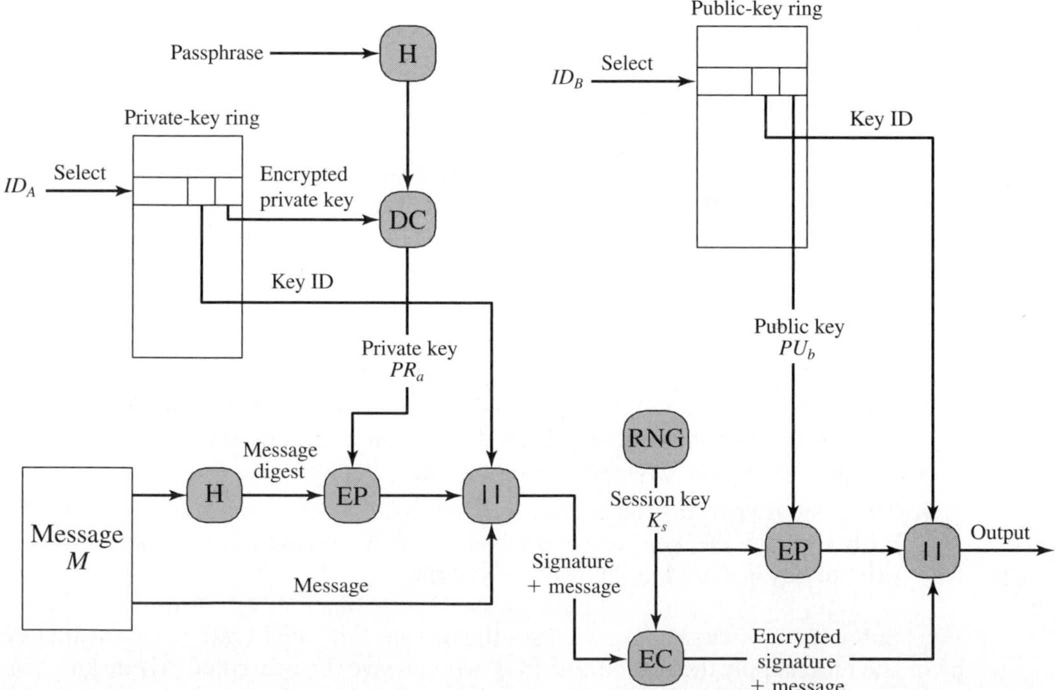

Figure 15.5 PGP Message Generation (from User A to User B; no compression or radix 64 conversion)

assume that the message is to be both signed and encrypted. The sending PGP entity performs the following steps:

1. Signing the message
   a. PGP retrieves the sender's private key from the private-key ring using your_userid as an index. If your_userid was not provided in the command, the first private key on the ring is retrieved.
   b. PGP prompts the user for the passphrase to recover the unencrypted private key.
   c. The signature component of the message is constructed.
2. Encrypting the message
   a. PGP generates a session key and encrypts the message.
   b. PGP retrieves the recipient's public key from the public-key ring using her_userid as an index.
   c. The session key component of the message is constructed.

The receiving PGP entity performs the following steps (Figure 15.6):

1. Decrypting the message
   a. PGP retrieves the receiver's private key from the private-key ring, using the Key ID field in the session key component of the message as an index.

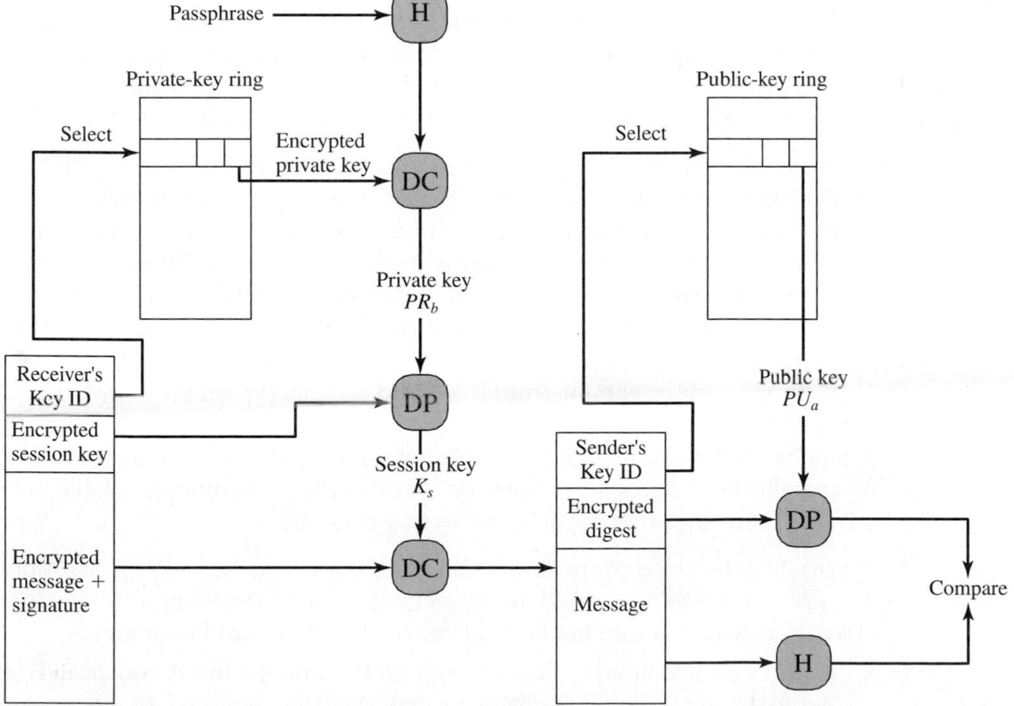

Figure 15.6 PGP Message Reception (from User A to User B; no compression or radix 64 conversion)

   b. PGP prompts the user for the passphrase to recover the unencrypted private key.
   c. PGP then recovers the session key and decrypts the message.
2. Authenticating the message
   a. PGP retrieves the sender's public key from the public-key ring, using the Key ID field in the signature key component of the message as an index.
   b. PGP recovers the transmitted message digest.
   c. PGP computes the message digest for the received message and compares it to the transmitted message digest to authenticate.

Public-Key Management

As can be seen from the discussion so far, PGP contains a clever, efficient, interlocking set of functions and formats to provide an effective confidentiality and authentication service. To complete the system, one final area needs to be addressed, that of public-key management. The PGP documentation captures the importance of this area:

> This whole business of protecting public keys from tampering is the single most difficult problem in practical public key applications. It is the "Achilles heel" of public key cryptography, and a lot of software complexity is tied up in solving this one problem.

PGP provides a structure for solving this problem, with several suggested options that may be used. Because PGP is intended for use in a variety of formal and informal environments, no rigid public-key management scheme is set up, such as we will see in our discussion of S/MIME later in this chapter.

Approaches to Public-Key Management The essence of the problem is this: User A must build up a public-key ring containing the public keys of other users to interoperate with them using PGP. Suppose that A's key ring contains a public key attributed to B but that the key is, in fact, owned by C. This could happen if, for example, A got the key from a bulletin board system (BBS) that was used by B to post the public key but that has been compromised by C. The result is that two threats now exist. First, C can send messages to A and forge B's signature, so that A will accept the message as coming from B. Second, any encrypted message from A to B can be read by C.

A number of approaches are possible for minimizing the risk that a user's public-key ring contains false public keys. Suppose that A wishes to obtain a reliable public key for B. The following are some approaches that could be used:

1. Physically get the key from B. B could store her public key (PU_b) on a floppy disk and hand it to A. A could then load the key into his system from the floppy disk. This is a very secure method but has obvious practical limitations.
2. Verify a key by telephone. If A can recognize B on the phone, A could call B and ask her to dictate the key, in radix-64 format, over the phone. As a more practical alternative, B could transmit her key in an e-mail message to A. A could have PGP generate a 160-bit SHA-1 digest of the key and display it in hexadecimal

format; this is referred to as the "fingerprint" of the key. A could then call B and ask her to dictate the fingerprint over the phone. If the two fingerprints match, the key is verified.

3. Obtain B's public key from a mutual trusted individual D. For this purpose, the introducer, D, creates a signed certificate. The certificate includes B's public key, the time of creation of the key, and a validity period for the key. D generates an SHA-1 digest of this certificate, encrypts it with her private key, and attaches the signature to the certificate. Because only D could have created the signature, no one else can create a false public key and pretend that it is signed by D. The signed certificate could be sent directly to A by B or D, or could be posted on a bulletin board.
4. Obtain B's public key from a trusted certifying authority. Again, a public key certificate is created and signed by the authority. A could then access the authority, providing a user name and receiving a signed certificate.

For cases 3 and 4, A would already have to have a copy of the introducer's public key and trust that this key is valid. Ultimately, it is up to A to assign a level of trust to anyone who is to act as an introducer.

The Use of Trust Although PGP does not include any specification for establishing certifying authorities or for establishing trust, it does provide a convenient means of using trust, associating trust with public keys, and exploiting trust information.

The basic structure is as follows. Each entry in the public-key ring is a public-key certificate, as described in the preceding subsection. Associated with each such entry is a **key legitimacy field** that indicates the extent to which PGP will trust that this is a valid public key for this user; the higher the level of trust, the stronger is the binding of this user ID to this key. This field is computed by PGP. Also associated with the entry are zero or more signatures that the key ring owner has collected that sign this certificate. In turn, each signature has associated with it a **signature trust field** that indicates the degree to which this PGP user trusts the signer to certify public keys. The key legitimacy field is derived from the collection of signature trust fields in the entry. Finally, each entry defines a public key associated with a particular owner, and an **owner trust field** is included that indicates the degree to which this public key is trusted to sign other public-key certificates; this level of trust is assigned by the user. We can think of the signature trust fields as cached copies of the owner trust field from another entry.

The three fields mentioned in the previous paragraph are each contained in a structure referred to as a trust flag byte. The content of this trust flag for each of these three uses is shown in Table 15.2. Suppose that we are dealing with the public-key ring of user A. We can describe the operation of the trust processing as follows:

1. When A inserts a new public key on the public-key ring, PGP must assign a value to the trust flag that is associated with the owner of this public key. If the owner is A, and therefore this public key also appears in the private-key ring, then a value of *ultimate trust* is automatically assigned to the trust field. Otherwise, PGP asks A for his assessment of the trust to be assigned to the owner of this key, and A must enter the desired level. The user can specify that this owner is unknown, untrusted, marginally trusted, or completely trusted.

Table 15.2 Contents of Trust Flag Byte

(a) Trust Assigned to Public-Key Owner (appears after key packet; user defined)	**(b) Trust Assigned to Public Key/User ID Pair (appears after User ID packet; computed by PGP)**	**(c) Trust Assigned to Signature (appears after signature packet; cached copy of OWNERTRUST for this signator)**
OWNERTRUST Field —undefined trust —unknown user —usually not trusted to sign other keys —usually trusted to sign other keys —always trusted to sign other keys —this key is present in secret key ring (ultimate trust) BUCKSTOP bit —set if this key appears in secret key ring	KEYLEGIT Field —unknown or undefined trust —key ownership not trusted —marginal trust in key ownership —complete trust in key ownership WARNONLY bit —set if user wants only to be warned when key that is not fully validated is used for encryption	SIGTRUST Field —undefined trust —unknown user —usually not trusted to sign other keys —usually trusted to sign other keys —always trusted to sign other keys —this key is present in secret key ring (ultimate trust) CONTIG bit —set if signature leads up a contiguous trusted certification path back to the ultimately trusted key ring owner

2. When the new public key is entered, one or more signatures may be attached to it. More signatures may be added later. When a signature is inserted into the entry, PGP searches the public-key ring to see if the author of this signature is among the known public-key owners. If so, the OWNERTRUST value for this owner is assigned to the SIGTRUST field for this signature. If not, an *unknown user* value is assigned.
3. The value of the key legitimacy field is calculated on the basis of the signature trust fields present in this entry. If at least one signature has a signature trust value of *ultimate*, then the key legitimacy value is set to complete. Otherwise, PGP computes a weighted sum of the trust values. A weight of $1/X$ is given to signatures that are always trusted and $1/Y$ to signatures that are usually trusted, where X and Y are user-configurable parameters. When the total of weights of the introducers of a key/UserID combination reaches 1, the binding is considered to be trustworthy, and the key legitimacy value is set to complete. Thus, in the absence of ultimate trust, at least X signatures that are always trusted or Y signatures that are usually trusted or some combination is needed.

Periodically, PGP processes the public-key ring to achieve consistency. In essence, this is a top-down process. For each OWNERTRUST field, PGP scans the ring for all signatures authored by that owner and updates the SIGTRUST field to equal the OWNERTRUST field. This process starts with keys for which there is ultimate trust. Then all KEYLEGIT fields are computed on the basis of the attached signatures.

Figure 15.7 provides an example of the way in which signature trust and key legitimacy are related.[2] The figure shows the structure of a public-key ring. The user has acquired a number of public keys, some directly from their owners and some from a third party such as a key server.

The node labeled "You" refers to the entry in the public-key ring corresponding to this user. This key is legitimate and the OWNERTRUST value is ultimate trust. Each other node in the key ring has an OWNERTRUST value of undefined unless some other value is assigned by the user. In this example, this user has specified that it always trusts the following users to sign other keys: D, E, F, L. This user partially trusts users A and B to sign other keys.

So the shading, or lack thereof, of the nodes in Figure 15.7 indicates the level of trust assigned by this user. The tree structure indicates which keys have been signed by which other users. If a key is signed by a user whose key is also in this key ring, the arrow joins the signed key to the signatory. If the key is signed by a user whose key is not present in this key ring, the arrow joins the signed key to a question mark, indicating that the signatory is unknown to this user.

Several points are illustrated in this Figure 15.7:

1. Note that all keys whose owners are fully or partially trusted by this user have been signed by this user, with the exception of node L. Such a user signature is not always necessary, as the presence of node L indicates, but in practice, most

[2]Figure provided to the author by Phil Zimmermann.

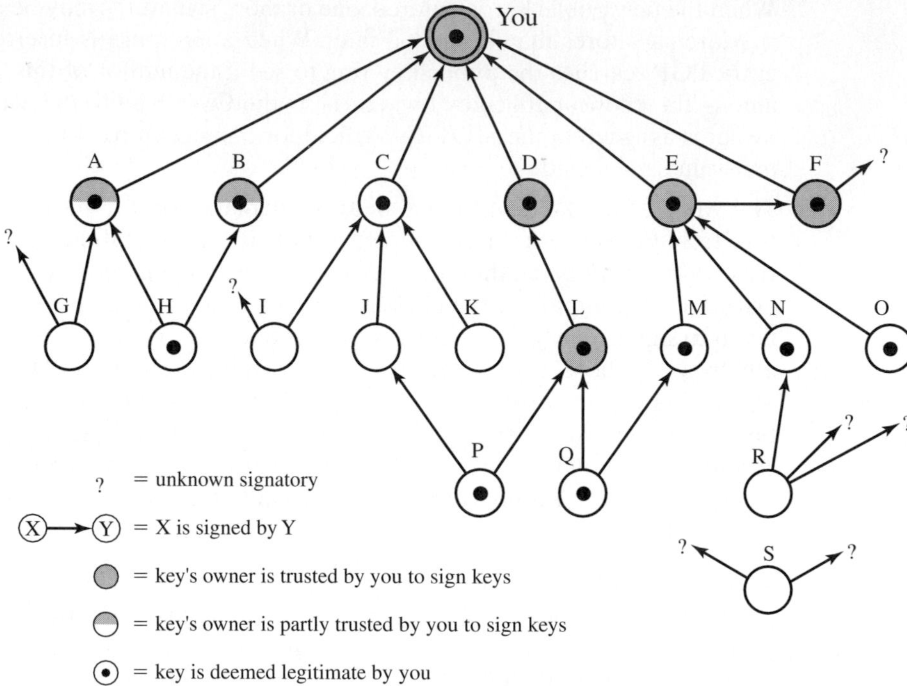

Figure 15.7 PGP Trust Model Example

users are likely to sign the keys for most owners that they trust. So, for example, even though E's key is already signed by trusted introducer F, the user chose to sign E's key directly.

2. We assume that two partially trusted signatures are sufficient to certify a key. Hence, the key for user H is deemed legitimate by PGP because it is signed by A and B, both of whom are partially trusted.
3. A key may be determined to be legitimate because it is signed by one fully trusted or two partially trusted signatories, but its user may not be trusted to sign other keys. For example, N's key is legitimate because it is signed by E, whom this user trusts, but N is not trusted to sign other keys because this user has not assigned N that trust value. Therefore, although R's key is signed by N, PGP does not consider R's key legitimate. This situation makes perfect sense. If you wish to send a private message to some individual, it is not necessary that you trust that individual in any respect. It is only necessary that you are sure that you have the correct public key for that individual.
4. Figure 15.7 also shows an example of a detached "orphan" node S, with two unknown signatures. Such a key may have been acquired from a key server. PGP cannot assume that this key is legitimate simply because it came from a reputable server. The user must declare the key legitimate by signing it or by telling PGP that it is willing to trust fully one of the key's signatories.

A final point: Earlier it was mentioned that multiple user IDs may be associated with a single public key on the public-key ring. This could be because a person has changed names or has been introduced via signature under multiple names, indicating different e-mail addresses for the same person, for example. So we can think of a public key as the root of a tree. A public key has a number of user IDs associating with it, with a number of signatures below each user ID. The binding of a particular user ID to a key depends on the signatures associated with that user ID and that key, whereas the level of trust in this key (for use in signing other keys) is a function of all the dependent signatures.

Revoking Public Keys A user may wish to revoke his or her current public key either because compromise is suspected or simply to avoid the use of the same key for an extended period. Note that a compromise would require that an opponent somehow had obtained a copy of your unencrypted private key or that the opponent had obtained both the private key from your private-key ring and your passphrase.

The convention for revoking a public key is for the owner to issue a key revocation certificate, signed by the owner. This certificate has the same form as a normal signature certificate but includes an indicator that the purpose of this certificate is to revoke the use of this public key. Note that the corresponding private key must be used to sign a certificate that revokes a public key. The owner should then attempt to disseminate this certificate as widely and as quickly as possible to enable potential correspondents to update their public-key rings.

Note that an opponent who has compromised the private key of an owner can also issue such a certificate. However, this would deny the opponent as well as the legitimate owner the use of the public key, and therefore it seems a much less likely threat than the malicious use of a stolen private key.

15.2 S/MIME

S/MIME (Secure/Multipurpose Internet Mail Extension) is a security enhancement to the MIME Internet e-mail format standard, based on technology from RSA Data Security. Although both PGP and S/MIME are on an IETF standards track, it appears likely that S/MIME will emerge as the industry standard for commercial and organizational use, while PGP will remain the choice for personal e-mail security for many users. S/MIME is defined in a number of documents, most importantly RFCs 3369, 3370, 3850 and 3851.

To understand S/MIME, we need first to have a general understanding of the underlying e-mail format that it uses, namely MIME. But to understand the significance of MIME, we need to go back to the traditional e-mail format standard, RFC 822, which is still in common use. Accordingly, this section first provides an introduction to these two earlier standards and then moves on to a discussion of S/MIME.

RFC 822

RFC 822 defines a format for text messages that are sent using electronic mail. It has been the standard for Internet-based text mail message and remains in common use.

In the RFC 822 context, messages are viewed as having an envelope and contents. The envelope contains whatever information is needed to accomplish transmission and delivery. The contents compose the object to be delivered to the recipient. The RFC 822 standard applies only to the contents. However, the content standard includes a set of header fields that may be used by the mail system to create the envelope, and the standard is intended to facilitate the acquisition of such information by programs.

The overall structure of a message that conforms to RFC 822 is very simple. A message consists of some number of header lines (*the header*) followed by unrestricted text (*the body*). The header is separated from the body by a blank line. Put differently, a message is ASCII text, and all lines up to the first blank line are assumed to be header lines used by the user agent part of the mail system.

A header line usually consists of a keyword, followed by a colon, followed by the keyword's arguments; the format allows a long line to be broken up into several lines. The most frequently used keywords are *From*, *To*, *Subject*, and *Date*. Here is an example message:

```
Date: Tue, 16 Jan 1998 10:37:17 (EST)
From: "William Stallings" <ws@shore.net>
Subject: The Syntax in RFC 822
To: Smith@Other-host.com
Cc: Jones@Yet-Another-Host.com

Hello. This section begins the actual
message body, which is delimited from the
message heading by a blank line.
```

Another field that is commonly found in RFC 822 headers is *Message-ID*. This field contains a unique identifier associated with this message.

Multipurpose Internet Mail Extensions

MIME is an extension to the RFC 822 framework that is intended to address some of the problems and limitations of the use of SMTP (Simple Mail Transfer Protocol) or some other mail transfer protocol and RFC 822 for electronic mail. [RODR02] lists the following limitations of the SMTP/822 scheme:

1. SMTP cannot transmit executable files or other binary objects. A number of schemes are in use for converting binary files into a text form that can be used by SMTP mail systems, including the popular UNIX UUencode/UUdecode scheme. However, none of these is a standard or even a de facto standard.
2. SMTP cannot transmit text data that includes national language characters because these are represented by 8-bit codes with values of 128 decimal or higher, and SMTP is limited to 7-bit ASCII.
3. SMTP servers may reject mail message over a certain size.

4. SMTP gateways that translate between ASCII and the character code EBCDIC do not use a consistent set of mappings, resulting in translation problems.
5. SMTP gateways to X.400 electronic mail networks cannot handle nontextual data included in X.400 messages.
6. Some SMTP implementations do not adhere completely to the SMTP standards defined in RFC 821. Common problems include:
   - Deletion, addition, or reordering of carriage return and linefeed
   - Truncating or wrapping lines longer than 76 characters
   - Removal of trailing white space (tab and space characters)
   - Padding of lines in a message to the same length
   - Conversion of tab characters into multiple space characters

MIME is intended to resolve these problems in a manner that is compatible with existing RFC 822 implementations. The specification is provided in RFCs 2045 through 2049.

Overview The MIME specification includes the following elements:

1. Five new message header fields are defined, which may be included in an RFC 822 header. These fields provide information about the body of the message.
2. A number of content formats are defined, thus standardizing representations that support multimedia electronic mail.
3. Transfer encodings are defined that enable the conversion of any content format into a form that is protected from alteration by the mail system.

In this subsection, we introduce the five message header fields. The next two subsections deal with content formats and transfer encodings.

The five header fields defined in MIME are as follows:

- **MIME-Version:** Must have the parameter value 1.0. This field indicates that the message conforms to RFCs 2045 and 2046.
- **Content-Type:** Describes the data contained in the body with sufficient detail that the receiving user agent can pick an appropriate agent or mechanism to represent the data to the user or otherwise deal with the data in an appropriate manner.
- **Content-Transfer-Encoding:** Indicates the type of transformation that has been used to represent the body of the message in a way that is acceptable for mail transport.
- **Content-ID:** Used to identify MIME entities uniquely in multiple contexts.
- **Content-Description:** A text description of the object with the body; this is useful when the object is not readable (e.g., audio data).

Any or all of these fields may appear in a normal RFC 822 header. A compliant implementation must support the MIME-Version, Content-Type, and

Content-Transfer-Encoding fields; the Content-ID and Content-Description fields are optional and may be ignored by the recipient implementation.

MIME Content Types The bulk of the MIME specification is concerned with the definition of a variety of content types. This reflects the need to provide standardized ways of dealing with a wide variety of information representations in a multimedia environment.

Table 15.3 lists the content types specified in RFC 2046. There are seven different major types of content and a total of 15 subtypes. In general, a content type declares the general type of data, and the subtype specifies a particular format for that type of data.

For the **text type** of body, no special software is required to get the full meaning of the text, aside from support of the indicated character set. The primary subtype is *plain text*, which is simply a string of ASCII characters or ISO 8859 characters. The *enriched* subtype allows greater formatting flexibility.

The **multipart type** indicates that the body contains multiple, independent parts. The Content-Type header field includes a parameter, called boundary, that defines the delimiter between body parts. This boundary should not appear in any parts of the message. Each boundary starts on a new line and consists of two hyphens followed by the boundary value. The final boundary, which indicates the end of the last part, also has a suffix of two hyphens. Within each part, there may be an optional ordinary MIME header.

Here is a simple example of a multipart message, containing two parts both consisting of simple text (taken from RFC 2046):

```
From: Nathaniel Borenstein <nsb@bellcore.com>
To:  Ned Freed <ned@innosoft.com>
Subject: Sample message
MIME-Version: 1.0
Content-type: multipart/mixed; boundary="simple
boundary"
This is the preamble.  It is to be ignored, though it
 is a handy place for mail composers to include an
explanatory note to non-MIME conformant readers.
—simple boundary
This is implicitly typed plain ASCII text. It does NOT
end with a linebreak.
—simple boundary
Content-type: text/plain; charset=us-ascii
This is explicitly typed plain ASCII text. It DOES end
with a linebreak.
—simple boundary—
This is the epilogue.  It is also to be ignored.
```

There are four subtypes of the multipart type, all of which have the same overall syntax. The **multipart/mixed subtype** is used when there are multiple independent

Table 15.3 MIME Content Types

Type	Subtype	Description
Text	Plain	Unformatted text; may be ASCII or ISO 8859.
	Enriched	Provides greater format flexibility.
Multipart	Mixed	The different parts are independent but are to be transmitted together. They should be presented to the receiver in the order that they appear in the mail message.
	Parallel	Differs from Mixed only in that no order is defined for delivering the parts to the receiver.
	Alternative	The different parts are alternative versions of the same information. They are ordered in increasing faithfulness to the original, and the recipient's mail system should display the "best" version to the user.
	Digest	Similar to Mixed, but the default type/subtype of each part is message/rfc822.
Message	rfc822	The body is itself an encapsulated message that conforms to RFC 822.
	Partial	Used to allow fragmentation of large mail items, in a way that is transparent to the recipient.
	External-body	Contains a pointer to an object that exists elsewhere.
Image	jpeg	The image is in JPEG format, JFIF encoding.
	gif	The image is in GIF format.
Video	mpeg	MPEG format.
Audio	Basic	Single-channel 8-bit ISDN mu-law encoding at a sample rate of 8 kHz.
Application	PostScript	Adobe Postscript.
	octet-stream	General binary data consisting of 8-bit bytes.

body parts that need to be bundled in a particular order. For the **multipart/parallel subtype**, the order of the parts is not significant. If the recipient's system is appropriate, the multiple parts can be presented in parallel. For example, a picture or text part could be accompanied by a voice commentary that is played while the picture or text is displayed.

For the **multipart/alternative subtype**, the various parts are different representations of the same information. The following is an example:

```
From:  Nathaniel Borenstein <nsb@bellcore.com>
To: Ned Freed <ned@innosoft.com>
Subject: Formatted text mail
MIME-Version: 1.0
Content-Type: multipart/alternative;
boundary=boundary42
--boundary42
Content-Type: text/plain; charset=us-ascii
   ...plain text version of message goes here....
--boundary42
Content-Type: text/enriched
   ....RFC 1896 text/enriched version of same message
goes here...
—boundary42—
```

In this subtype, the body parts are ordered in terms of increasing preference. For this example, if the recipient system is capable of displaying the message in the text/enriched format, this is done; otherwise, the plain text format is used.

The **multipart/digest subtype** is used when each of the body parts is interpreted as an RFC 822 message with headers. This subtype enables the construction of a message whose parts are individual messages. For example, the moderator of a group might collect e-mail messages from participants, bundle these messages, and send them out in one encapsulating MIME message.

The **message type** provides a number of important capabilities in MIME. The **message/rfc822 subtype** indicates that the body is an entire message, including header and body. Despite the name of this subtype, the encapsulated message may be not only a simple RFC 822 message, but also any MIME message.

The **message/partial subtype** enables fragmentation of a large message into a number of parts, which must be reassembled at the destination. For this subtype, three parameters are specified in the Content-Type: Message/Partial field: an *id* common to all fragments of the same message, a *sequence number* unique to each fragment, and the *total* number of fragments.

The **message/external-body subtype** indicates that the actual data to be conveyed in this message are not contained in the body. Instead, the body contains the information needed to access the data. As with the other message types, the message/external-body subtype has an outer header and an encapsulated message with its own header. The only necessary field in the outer header is the Content-Type field, which identifies this as a message/external-body subtype. The inner header is the message header for the encapsulated message. The Content-Type field in the outer header must include an access-type parameter, which indicates the method of access, such as FTP (file transfer protocol).

The **application type** refers to other kinds of data, typically either uninterpreted binary data or information to be processed by a mail-based application.

MIME Transfer Encodings The other major component of the MIME specification, in addition to content type specification, is a definition of transfer encodings for message bodies. The objective is to provide reliable delivery across the largest range of environments.

The MIME standard defines two methods of encoding data. The Content-Transfer-Encoding field can actually take on six values, as listed in Table 15.4. However, three of these values (7bit, 8bit, and binary) indicate that no encoding has been done but provide some information about the nature of the data. For SMTP transfer, it is safe to use the 7bit form. The 8bit and binary forms may be usable in other mail transport contexts. Another Content-Transfer-Encoding value is x-token, which indicates that some other encoding scheme is used, for which a name is to be supplied. This could be a vendor-specific or application-specific scheme. The two actual encoding schemes defined are quoted-printable and base64. Two schemes are defined to provide a choice between a transfer technique that is essentially human readable and one that is safe for all types of data in a way that is reasonably compact.

The **quoted-printable** transfer encoding is useful when the data consists largely of octets that correspond to printable ASCII characters. In essence, it represents nonsafe characters by the hexadecimal representation of their code and introduces reversible (soft) line breaks to limit message lines to 76 characters.

The **base64 transfer encoding**, also known as radix-64 encoding, is a common one for encoding arbitrary binary data in such a way as to be invulnerable to the processing by mail transport programs. It is also used in PGP and is described in Appendix 15B.

A Multipart Example Figure 15.8, taken from RFC 2045, is the outline of a complex multipart message. The message has five parts to be displayed serially: two introductory plain text parts, an embedded multipart message, a richtext part, and a

Table 15.4 MIME Transfer Encodings

7bit	The data are all represented by short lines of ASCII characters.
8bit	The lines are short, but there may be non-ASCII characters (octets with the high-order bit set).
binary	Not only may non-ASCII characters be present but the lines are not necessarily short enough for SMTP transport.
quoted-printable	Encodes the data in such a way that if the data being encoded are mostly ASCII text, the encoded form of the data remains largely recognizable by humans.
base64	Encodes data by mapping 6-bit blocks of input to 8-bit blocks of output, all of which are printable ASCII characters.
x-token	A named nonstandard encoding.

```
MIME-Version: 1.0
From: Nathaniel Borenstein <nsb@bellcore.com>
To: Ned Freed <ned@innosoft.com>
Subject: A multipart example
Content-Type: multipart/mixed;
   boundary=unique-boundary-1

This is the preamble area of a multipart message. Mail readers that understand multipart format should ignore
this preamble. If you are reading this text, you might want to consider changing to a mail reader that understands
how to properly display multipart messages.

--unique-boundary-1

   ...Some text appears here...
[Note that the preceding blank line means no header fields were given and this is text, with charset US ASCII.
It could have been done with explicit typing as in the next part.]

--unique-boundary-1
Content-type: text/plain; charset=US-ASCII

This could have been part of the previous part, but illustrates explicit versus implicit typing of body parts.

--unique-boundary-1
Content-Type: multipart/parallel;   boundary=unique-boundary-2

--unique-boundary-2
Content-Type: audio/basic
Content-Transfer-Encoding: base64

   ... base64-encoded 8000 Hz single-channel mu-law-format audio data goes here....

--unique-boundary-2
Content-Type: image/jpeg
Content-Transfer-Encoding: base64

   ... base64-encoded image data goes here....

--unique-boundary-2--

--unique-boundary-1
Content-type: text/enriched

This is <bold><italic>richtext.</italic></bold> <smaller>as defined in RFC 1896</smaller>

Isn't it <bigger><bigger>cool?</bigger></bigger>

--unique-boundary-1
Content-Type: message/rfc822

From: (mailbox in US-ASCII)
To: (address in US-ASCII)
Subject: (subject in US-ASCII)
Content-Type: Text/plain; charset=ISO-8859-1
Content-Transfer-Encoding: Quoted-printable

   ... Additional text in ISO-8859-1 goes here ...

--unique-boundary-1--
```

Figure 15.8 Example MIME Message Structure

closing encapsulated text message in a non-ASCII character set. The embedded multipart message has two parts to be displayed in parallel, a picture and an audio fragment.

Canonical Form An important concept in MIME and S/MIME is that of canonical form. Canonical form is a format, appropriate to the content type, that is standardized for use between systems. This is in contrast to native form, which is a format that may be peculiar to a particular system. Table 15.5, from RFC 2049, should help clarify this matter.

S/MIME Functionality

In terms of general functionality, S/MIME is very similar to PGP. Both offer the ability to sign and/or encrypt messages. In this subsection, we briefly summarize S/MIME capability. We then look in more detail at this capability by examining message formats and message preparation.

Functions S/MIME provides the following functions:

- **Enveloped data:** This consists of encrypted content of any type and encrypted-content encryption keys for one or more recipients.
- **Signed data:** A digital signature is formed by taking the message digest of the content to be signed and then encrypting that with the private key of the signer. The content plus signature are then encoded using base64 encoding. A signed data message can only be viewed by a recipient with S/MIME capability.
- **Clear-signed data:** As with signed data, a digital signature of the content is formed. However, in this case, only the digital signature is encoded using base64. As a result, recipients without S/MIME capability can view the message content, although they cannot verify the signature.
- **Signed and enveloped data:** Signed-only and encrypted-only entities may be nested, so that encrypted data may be signed and signed data or clear-signed data may be encrypted.

Table 15.5 Native and Canonical Form

Native Form	The body to be transmitted is created in the system's native format. The native character set is used and, where appropriate, local end-of-line conventions are used as well. The body may be a UNIX-style text file, or a Sun raster image, or a VMS indexed file, or audio data in a system-dependent format stored only in memory, or anything else that corresponds to the local model for the representation of some form of information. Fundamentally, the data is created in the "native" form that corresponds to the type specified by the media type.
Canonical Form	The entire body, including "out-of-band" information such as record lengths and possibly file attribute information, is converted to a universal canonical form. The specific media type of the body as well as its associated attributes dictate the nature of the canonical form that is used. Conversion to the proper canonical form may involve character set conversion, transformation of audio data, compression, or various other operations specific to the various media types. If character set conversion is involved, however, care must be taken to understand the semanties of the media type, which may have strong implications for any character set conversion (e.g. with regard to syntactically meaningful characters in a text subtype other than "plain").

Table 15.6 Cryptographic Algorithms Used in S/MIME

Function	Requirement
Create a message digest to be used in forming a digital signature. Encrypt message digest to form digital signature.	MUST support SHA-1. Receiver SHOULD support MD5 for backward compatibility. Sending and receiving agents MUST support DSS. Sending agents SHOULD support RSA encryption. Receiving agents SHOULD support verification of RSA signatures with key sizes 512 bits to 1024 bits.
Encrypt session key for transmission with message.	Sending and receiving agents SHOULD support Diffie-Hellman. Sending and receiving agents MUST support RSA encryption with key sizes 512 bits to 1024 bits.
Encrypt message for transmission with one-time session key.	Sending and receiving agents MUST support encryption with triple DES Sending agents SHOULD support encryption with AES. Sending agents SHOULD support encryption with RC2/40.
Create a message authentication code	Receiving agents MUST support HMAC with SHA-1. Receiving agents SHOULD support HMAC with SHA-1.

Cryptographic Algorithms Table 15.6 summarizes the cryptographic algorithms used in S/MIME. S/MIME uses the following terminology, taken from RFC 2119 to specify the requirement level:

- **Must:** The definition is an absolute requirement of the specification. An implementation must include this feature or function to be in conformance with the specification.
- **Should:** There may exist valid reasons in particular circumstances to ignore this feature or function, but it is recommended that an implementation include the feature or function.

S/MIME incorporates three public-key algorithms. The Digital Signature Standard (DSS) described in Chapter 13 is the preferred algorithm for digital signature. S/MIME lists Diffie-Hellman as the preferred algorithm for encrypting session keys; in fact, S/MIME uses a variant of Diffie-Hellman that does provide encryption/decryption, known as ElGamal (see Problem 10.6). As an alternative, RSA, described in Chapter 9, can be used for both signatures and session key encryption. These are the same algorithms used in PGP and provide a high level of security. For the hash function used to create the digital signature, the specification requires the 160-bit SHA-1 but recommends receiver support for the 128-bit MD5 for backward compatibility with older versions of S/MIME. As we discussed in Chapter 12, there is justifiable concern about the security of MD5, so SHA-1 is clearly the preferred alternative.

For message encryption, three-key triple DES (tripleDES) is recommended, but compliant implementations must support 40-bit RC2. The latter is a weak encryption algorithm but allows compliance with U.S. export controls.

The S/MIME specification includes a discussion of the procedure for deciding which content encryption algorithm to use. In essence, a sending agent has two decisions to make. First, the sending agent must determine if the receiving agent is capable of decrypting using a given encryption algorithm. Second, if the receiving agent is only capable of accepting weakly encrypted content, the sending agent must decide if it is acceptable to send using weak encryption. To support this decision process, a sending agent may announce its decrypting capabilities in order of preference any message that it sends out. A receiving agent may store that information for future use.

The following rules, in the following order, should be followed by a sending agent:

1. If the sending agent has a list of preferred decrypting capabilities from an intended recipient, it SHOULD choose the first (highest preference) capability on the list that it is capable of using.
2. If the sending agent has no such list of capabilities from an intended recipient but has received one or more messages from the recipient, then the outgoing message SHOULD use the same encryption algorithm as was used on the last signed and encrypted message received from that intended recipient.
3. If the sending agent has no knowledge about the decryption capabilities of the intended recipient and is willing to risk that the recipient may not be able to decrypt the message, then the sending agent SHOULD use tripleDES.
4. If the sending agent has no knowledge about the decryption capabilities of the intended recipient and is not willing to risk that the recipient may not be able to decrypt the message, then the sending agent MUST use RC2/40.

If a message is to be sent to multiple recipients and a common encryption algorithm cannot be selected for all, then the sending agent will need to send two messages. However, in that case, it is important to note that the security of the message is made vulnerable by the transmission of one copy with lower security.

S/MIME Messages

S/MIME makes use of a number of new MIME content types, which are shown in Table 15.7. All of the new application types use the designation PKCS. This refers to a set of public-key cryptography specifications issued by RSA Laboratories and made available for the S/MIME effort.

We examine each of these in turn after first looking at the general procedures for S/MIME message preparation.

Securing a MIME Entity S/MIME secures a MIME entity with a signature, encryption, or both. A MIME entity may be an entire message (except for the RFC 822 headers), or if the MIME content type is multipart, then a MIME entity is one or more of the subparts of the message. The MIME entity is prepared according to the normal rules for MIME message preparation. Then the MIME entity plus some security-related data, such as algorithm identifiers and certificates, are processed by S/MIME to

Table 15.7 S/MIME Content Types

Type	Subtype	smime Parameter	Description
Multipart	Signed		A clear-signed message in two parts: one is the message and the other is the signature.
Application	pkcs 7-mime	signedData	A signed S/MIME entity.
	pkcs 7-mime	envelopedData	An encrypted S/MIME entity.
	pkcs 7-mime	degenerate signedData	An entity containing only public-key certificates.
	pkcs 7-mime	CompressedData	A compressed S/MIME entity
	pkcs 7-signature	signedData	The content type of the signature subpart of a multipart/signed message.

produce what is known as a PKCS object. A PKCS object is then treated as message content and wrapped in MIME (provided with appropriate MIME headers). This process should become clear as we look at specific objects and provide examples.

In all cases, the message to be sent is converted to canonical form. In particular, for a given type and subtype, the appropriate canonical form is used for the message content. For a multipart message, the appropriate canonical form is used for each subpart.

The use of transfer encoding requires special attention. For most cases, the result of applying the security algorithm will be to produce an object that is partially or totally represented in arbitrary binary data. This will then be wrapped in an outer MIME message and transfer encoding can be applied at that point, typically base64. However, in the case of a multipart signed message, described in more detail later, the message content in one of the subparts is unchanged by the security process. Unless that content is 7bit, it should be transfer encoded using base64 or quoted-printable, so that there is no danger of altering the content to which the signature was applied.

We now look at each of the S/MIME content types.

EnvelopedData An application/pkcs7-mime subtype is used for one of four categories of S/MIME processing, each with a unique smime-type parameter. In all cases, the resulting entity, referred to as an *object*, is represented in a form known as Basic Encoding Rules (BER), which is defined in ITU-T Recommendation X.209. The BER format consists of arbitrary octet strings and is therefore binary data. Such an object should be transfer encoded with base64 in the outer MIME message. We first look at envelopedData.

The steps for preparing an envelopedData MIME entity are as follows:

1. Generate a pseudorandom session key for a particular symmetric encryption algorithm (RC2/40 or tripleDES).
2. For each recipient, encrypt the session key with the recipient's public RSA key.
3. For each recipient, prepare a block known as RecipientInfo that contains an identifier of the recipient's public-key certificate,[3] an identifier of

[3]This is an X.509 certificate, discussed later in this section.

the algorithm used to encrypt the session key, and the encrypted session key.

4. Encrypt the message content with the session key.

The RecipientInfo blocks followed by the encrypted content constitute the envelopedData. This information is then encoded into base64. A sample message (excluding the RFC 822 headers) is the following:

```
Content-Type: application/pkcs7-mime; smime-type=enveloped-
      data; name=smime.p7m
Content-Transfer-Encoding: base64
Content-Disposition: attachment; filename=smime.p7m
rfvbnj75.6tbBghyHhHUujhJhjH77n8HHGT9HG4VQpfyF467GhIGfHfYT6
7n8HHGghyHhHUujhJh4VQpfyF467GhIGfHfYGTrfvbnjT6jH7756tbB9H
f8HHGTrfvhJhjH776tbB9HG4VQbnj7567GhIGfHfYT6ghyHhHUujpfyF4
0GhIGfHfQbnj756YT64V
```

To recover the encrypted message, the recipient first strips off the base64 encoding. Then the recipient's private key is used to recover the session key. Finally, the message content is decrypted with the session key.

SignedData The signedData smime-type can actually be used with one or more signers. For clarity, we confine our description to the case of a single digital signature. The steps for preparing a signedData MIME entity are as follows:

1. Select a message digest algorithm (SHA or MD5).
2. Compute the message digest, or hash function, of the content to be signed.
3. Encrypt the message digest with the signer's private key.
4. Prepare a block known as SignerInfo that contains the signer's public-key certificate, an identifier of the message digest algorithm, an identifier of the algorithm used to encrypt the message digest, and the encrypted message digest.

The signedData entity consists of a series of blocks, including a message digest algorithm identifier, the message being signed, and SignerInfo. The signedData entity may also include a set of public-key certificates sufficient to constitute a chain from a recognized root or top-level certification authority to the signer. This information is then encoded into base64. A sample message (excluding the RFC 822 headers) is the following:

```
Content-Type: application/pkcs7-mime; smime-type=signed-data;
      name=smime.p7m
Content-Transfer-Encoding: base64
Content-Disposition: attachment; filename=smime.p7m
567GhIGfHfYT6ghyHhHUujpfyF4f8HHGTrfvhJhjH776tbB9HG4VQbnj7
77n8HHGT9HG4VQpfyF467GhIGfHfYT6rfvbnj756tbBghyHhHUujhJhjH
HUujhJh4VQpfyF467GhIGfHfYGTrfvbnjT6jH7756tbB9H7n8HHGghyHh
6YT64V0GhIGfHfQbnj75
```

To recover the signed message and verify the signature, the recipient first strips off the base64 encoding. Then the signer's public key is used to decrypt the message digest. The recipient independently computes the message digest and compares it to the decrypted message digest to verify the signature.

Clear Signing Clear signing is achieved using the multipart content type with a signed subtype. As was mentioned, this signing process does not involve transforming the message to be signed, so that the message is sent "in the clear." Thus, recipients with MIME capability but not S/MIME capability are able to read the incoming message.

A multipart/signed message has two parts. The first part can be any MIME type but must be prepared so that it will not be altered during transfer from source to destination. This means that if the first part is not 7bit, then it needs to be encoded using base64 or quoted-printable. Then this part is processed in the same manner as signedData, but in this case an object with signedData format is created that has an empty message content field. This object is a detached signature. It is then transfer encoded using base64 to become the second part of the multipart/signed message. This second part has a MIME content type of application and a subtype of pkcs7-signature. Here is a sample message:

```
Content-Type: multipart/signed;
   protocol="application/pkcs7-signature";
   micalg=sha1; boundary=boundary42
—boundary42
Content-Type: text/plain
This is a clear-signed message.
—boundary42
Content-Type: application/pkcs7-signature; name=smime.p7s
Content-Transfer-Encoding: base64
Content-Disposition: attachment; filename=smime.p7s
ghyHhHUujhJhjH77n8HHGTrfvbnj756tbB9HG4VQpfyF467GhIGfHfYT6
4VQpfyF467GhIGfHfYT6jH77n8HHGghyHhHUujhJh756tbB9HGTrfvbnj
n8HHGTrfvhJhjH776tbB9HG4VQbnj7567GhIGfHfYT6ghyHhHUujpfyF4
7GhIGfHfYT64VQbnj756
—boundary42—
```

The protocol parameter indicates that this is a two-part clear-signed entity. The micalg parameter indicates the type of message digest used. The receiver can verify the signature by taking the message digest of the first part and comparing this to the message digest recovered from the signature in the second part.

Registration Request Typically, an application or user will apply to a certification authority for a public-key certificate. The application/pkcs10 S/MIME entity is used to transfer a certification request. The certification request includes certificationRequestInfo block, followed by an identifier of the public-key encryption algorithm, followed by the signature of the certificationRequestInfo block, made using the sender's private key. The certificationRequestInfo block includes a name of the certificate subject (the entity whose public key is to be certified) and a bit-string representation of the user's public key.

Certificates-Only Message A message containing only certificates or a certificate revocation list (CRL) can be sent in response to a registration request. The message is an application/pkcs7-mime type/subtype with an smime-type parameter of degenerate. The steps involved are the same as those for creating a signedData message, except that there is no message content and the signerInfo field is empty.

S/MIME Certificate Processing

S/MIME uses public-key certificates that conform to version 3 of X.509 (see Chapter 14). The key-management scheme used by S/MIME is in some ways a hybrid between a strict X.509 certification hierarchy and PGP's web of trust. As with the PGP model, S/MIME managers and/or users must configure each client with a list of trusted keys and with certificate revocation lists. That is, the responsibility is local for maintaining the certificates needed to verify incoming signatures and to encrypt outgoing messages. On the other hand, the certificates are signed by certification authorities.

User Agent Role An S/MIME user has several key-management functions to perform:

- **Key generation:** The user of some related administrative utility (e.g., one associated with LAN management) MUST be capable of generating separate Diffie-Hellman and DSS key pairs and SHOULD be capable of generating RSA key pairs. Each key pair MUST be generated from a good source of nondeterministic random input and be protected in a secure fashion. A user agent SHOULD generate RSA key pairs with a length in the range of 768 to 1024 bits and MUST NOT generate a length of less than 512 bits.
- **Registration:** A user's public key must be registered with a certification authority in order to receive an X.509 public-key certificate.
- **Certificate storage and retrieval:** A user requires access to a local list of certificates in order to verify incoming signatures and to encrypt outgoing messages. Such a list could be maintained by the user or by some local administrative entity on behalf of a number of users.

VeriSign Certificates There are several companies that provide certification authority (CA) services. For example, Nortel has designed an enterprise CA solution and can provide S/MIME support within an organization. There are a number of Internet-based CAs, including VeriSign, GTE, and the U.S. Postal Service. Of these, the most widely used is the VeriSign CA service, a brief description of which we now provide.

VeriSign provides a CA service that is intended to be compatible with S/MIME and a variety of other applications. VeriSign issues X.509 certificates with the product name VeriSign Digital ID. As of early 1998, over 35,000 commercial Web sites were using VeriSign Server Digital IDs, and over a million consumer Digital IDs had been issued to users of Netscape and Microsoft browsers.

The information contained in a Digital ID depends on the type of Digital ID and its use. At a minimum, each Digital ID contains

- Owner's public key
- Owner's name or alias
- Expiration date of the Digital ID
- Serial number of the Digital ID
- Name of the certification authority that issued the Digital ID
- Digital signature of the certification authority that issued the Digital ID

Digital IDs can also contain other user-supplied information, including

- Address
- E-mail address
- Basic registration information (country, zip code, age, and gender)

VeriSign provides three levels, or classes, of security for public-key certificates, as summarized in Table 15.8. A user requests a certificate online at VeriSign's Web site or other participating Web sites. Class 1 and Class 2 requests are processed on line, and in most cases take only a few seconds to approve. Briefly, the following procedures are used:

- For Class 1 Digital IDs, VeriSign confirms the user's e-mail address by sending a PIN and Digital ID pick-up information to the e-mail address provided in the application.
- For Class 2 Digital IDs, VeriSign verifies the information in the application through an automated comparison with a consumer database in addition to performing all of the checking associated with a Class 1 Digital ID. Finally, confirmation is sent to the specified postal address alerting the user that a Digital ID has been issued in his or her name.
- For Class 3 Digital IDs, VeriSign requires a higher level of identity assurance. An individual must prove his or her identity by providing notarized credentials or applying in person.

Enhanced Security Services

As of this writing, three enhanced security services have been proposed in an Internet draft. The details of these may change, and additional services may be added. The three services are as follows:

- **Signed receipts:** A signed receipt may be requested in a SignedData object. Returning a signed receipt provides proof of delivery to the originator of a message and allows the originator to demonstrate to a third party that the recipient received the message. In essence, the recipient signs the entire original message plus original (sender's) signature and appends the new signature to form a new S/MIME message.
- **Security labels:** A security label may be included in the authenticated attributes of a SignedData object. A security label is a set of security information regarding

Table 15.8 VeriSign Public-Key Certificate Classes

	Summary of Confirmation of Identity	IA Private Key Protection	Certificate Applicant and Subscriber Private Key Protection	Applications implemented or contemplated by Users
Class 1	Automated unambiguous name and e-mail address search	PCA: trustworthy hardware; CA: trust-worthy software or trustworthy hardware	Encryption software (PIN protected) recommended but not required	Web-browsing and certain e-mail usage
Class 2	Same as Class 1, plus automated enrollment information check plus automated address check	PCA and CA: trustworthy hardware	Encryption software (PIN protected) required	Individual and intra and inter-company E-mail, online subscriptions, password replacement, and software validation
Class 3	Same as Class 1, plus personal presence and ID documents plus Class 2 automated ID check for individuals; business records (or filings) for organizations	PCA and CA: trustworthy hardware	Encryption software (PIN protected) required; hardware token recommended but not required	E-banking, corp, database access, personal banking, membership-based online services, content integrity services, e-commerce server, software validation; authentication of LRAAs; and strong encryption for certain servers

IA Issuing Authority
CA Certification Authority
PCA VeriSign public primary certification authority
PIN Personal Identification Number
LRAA Local Registration Authority Administrator

the sensitivity of the content that is protected by S/MIME encapsulation. The labels may be used for access control, by indicating which users are permitted access to an object. Other uses include priority (secret, confidential, restricted, and so on) or role based, describing which kind of people can see the information (e.g., patient's health-care team, medical billing agents, etc.).

- **Secure mailing lists:** When a user sends a message to multiple recipients, a certain amount of per-recipient processing is required, including the use of each recipient's public key. The user can be relieved of this work by employing the services of an S/MIME Mail List Agent (MLA). An MLA can take a single incoming message, perform the recipient-specific encryption for each recipient, and forward the message. The originator of a message need only send the message to the MLA, with encryption performed using the MLA's public key.

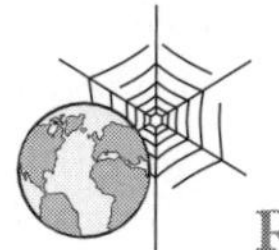

Recommended Web Sites:

- **PGP Home Page:** PGP Web site by PGP Corp., the leading PGP commercial vendor.
- **International PGP Home Page:** Designed to promote worldwide use of PGP. Contains documents and links of interest.
- **MIT Distribution Site for PGP:** Leading distributor of freeware PGP. Contains FAQ, other information, and links to other PGP sites.
- **PGP Charter:** Latest RFCs and Internet drafts for Open Specification PGP.
- **S/MIME Charter:** Latest RFCs and Internet drafts for S/MIME.

15.3 KEY TERMS, REVIEW QUESTIONS, AND PROBLEMS

Key Terms

detached signature	Pretty Good Privacy (PGP)	trust
electronic mail	radix 64	ZIP
Multipurpose Internet Mail Extensions (MIME)	session key	
	S/MIME	

Review Questions

15.1 What are the five principal services provided by PGP?
15.2 What is the utility of a detached signature?
15.3 Why does PGP generate a signature before applying compression?
15.4 What is R64 conversion?
15.5 Why is R64 conversion useful for an e-mail application?
15.6 Why is the segmentation and reassembly function in PGP needed?
15.7 How does PGP use the concept of trust?
15.8 What is RFC 822?
15.9 What is MIME?
15.10 What is S/MIME?

Problems

15.1 PGP makes use of the cipher feedback (CFB) mode of CAST-128, whereas most symmetric encryption applications (other than key encryption) use the cipher block chaining (CBC) mode. We have

$$\text{CBC:} \quad C_i = \mathrm{E}(K, [C_{i-1} \oplus P_i]); \quad P_i = C_{i-1} \oplus D(K, C_i)$$
$$CFB\text{:} \quad C_i = P_i \oplus E(K, C_{i-1}); \quad P_i = C_i \oplus E(K, C_{i-1})$$

These two appear to provide equal security. Suggest a reason why PGP uses the CFB mode.

15.2 In the PGP scheme, what is the expected number of session keys generated before a previously created key is produced?

15.3 In PGP, what is the probability that a user with N public keys will have at least one duplicate key ID?

15.4 The first 16 bits of the message digest in a PGP signature are translated in the clear.
  a. To what extent does this compromise the security of the hash algorithm?
  b. To what extent does it in fact perform its intended function, namely, to help determine if the correct RSA key was used to decrypt the digest?

15.5 In Figure 15.4, each entry in the public-key ring contains an owner trust field that indicates the degree of trust associated with this public-key owner. Why is that not enough? That is, if this owner is trusted and this is supposed to be the owner's public key, why is not that trust enough to permit PGP to use this public key?

15.6 Consider radix-64 conversion as a form of encryption. In this case, there is no key. But suppose that an opponent knew only that some form of substitution algorithm was being used to encrypt English text and did not guess it was R64. How effective would this algorithm be against cryptanalysis?

15.7 Phil Zimmermann chose IDEA, three-key triple DES, and CAST-128 as symmetric encryption algorithms for PGP. Give reasons why each of the following symmetric encryption algorithms described in this book is suitable or unsuitable for PGP: DES, two-key triple DES, and AES.

APPENDIX 15A DATA COMPRESSION USING ZIP

PGP makes use of a compression package called ZIP, written by Jean-lup Gailly, Mark Adler, and Richard Wales. ZIP is a freeware package written in C that runs as a utility on UNIX and some other systems. ZIP is functionally equivalent to PKZIP, a widely available shareware package for Windows systems developed by PKWARE, Inc. The zip algorithm is perhaps the most commonly used cross-platform compression technique; freeware and shareware versions are available for Macintosh and other systems as well as Windows and UNIX systems.

Zip and similar algorithms stem from research by Jacob Ziv and Abraham Lempel. In 1977, they described a technique based on a sliding window buffer that holds the most recently processed text [ZIV77]. This algorithm is generally referred to as LZ77. A version of this algorithm is used in the zip compression scheme (PKZIP, gzip, zipit, etc.).

LZ77 and its variants exploit the fact that words and phrases within a text stream (image patterns in the case of GIF) are likely to be repeated. When a repetition occurs, the repeated sequence can be replaced by a short code. The compression program scans for such repetitions and develops codes on the fly to replace the repeated sequence. Over time, codes are reused to capture new sequences. The algorithm must be defined in such a way that the decompression program is able to deduce the current mapping between codes and sequences of source data.

Before looking at the details of LZ77, let us look at a simple example.[4] Consider the nonsense phrase

`the brown fox jumped over the brown foxy jumping frog`

which is 53 octets = 424 bits long. The algorithm processes this text from left to right. Initially, each character is mapped into a 9-bit pattern consisting of a binary 1 followed by the 8-bit ASCII representation of the character. As the processing proceeds, the algorithm looks for repeated sequences. When a repetition is encountered, the algorithm continues scanning until the repetition ends. In other words, each time a repetition occurs, the algorithm includes as many characters as possible. The first such sequence encountered is **`the brown fox`**. This sequence is replaced by a pointer to the prior sequence and the length of the sequence. In this case the prior sequence of **`the brown fox`** occurs 26 character positions before and the length of the sequence is 13 characters. For this example, assume two options for encoding; an 8-bit pointer and a 4-bit length, or a 12-bit pointer and a 6-bit length; a 2-bit header indicates which option is chosen, with 00 indicating the first option and 01 the second option. Thus, the second occurrence of **`the brown fox`** is encoded as $<00_b><26_d><13_d>$, or 00 00011010 1101.

The remaining parts of the compressed message are the letter **`y`**; the sequence $<00_b><27_d><5_d>$, which replaces the sequence consisting of the space character followed by **`jump`**; and the character sequence **`ing frog`**.

Figure 15.9 illustrates the compression mapping. The compressed message consists of 35 9-bit characters and two codes, for a total of $35 \times 9 + 2 \times 14 = 343$ bits. This compares with 424 bits in the uncompressed message for a compression ratio of 1.24.

Compression Algorithm

The compression algorithm for LZ77 and its variants makes use of two buffers. A **sliding history buffer** contains the last *N* characters of source that have been processed, and a **look-ahead buffer** contains the next *L* characters to be processed (Figure 15.10a). The algorithm attempts to match two or more characters from the

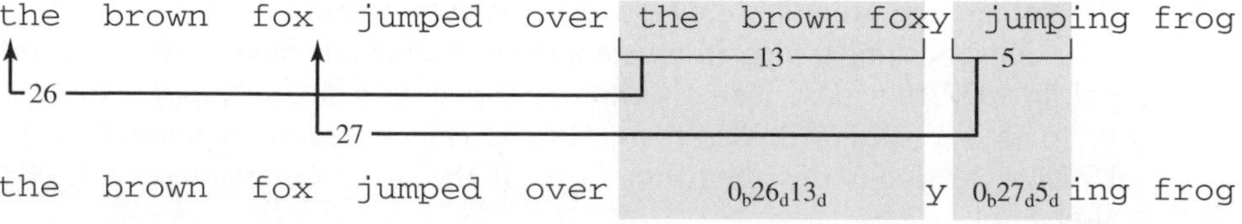

Figure 15.9 Example of LZ77 Scheme

[4]Based on an example in [WEIS93].

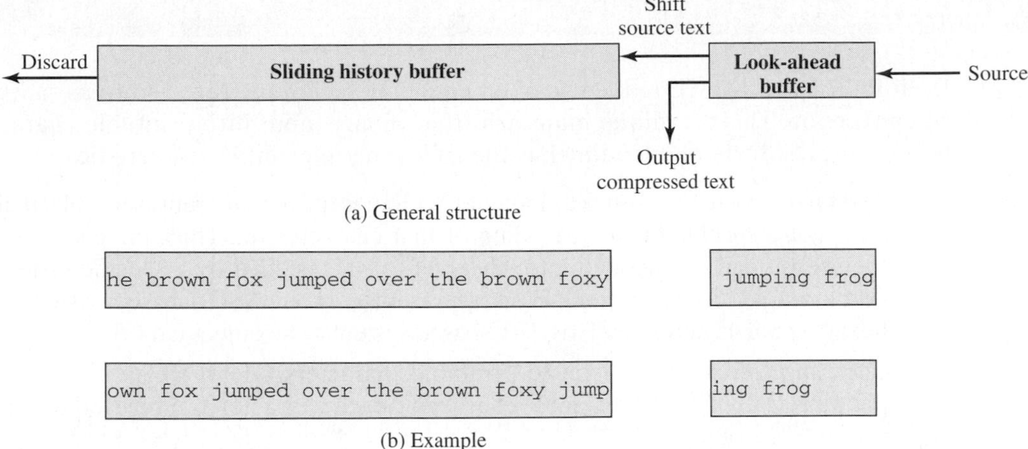

Figure 15.10 LZ77 Scheme

beginning of the look-ahead buffer to a string in the sliding history buffer. If no match is found, the first character in the look-ahead buffer is output as a 9-bit character and is also shifted into the sliding window, with the oldest character in the sliding window shifted out. If a match is found, the algorithm continues to scan for the longest match. Then the matched string is output as a triplet (indicator, pointer, length). For a *K*-character string, the *K* oldest characters in the sliding window are shifted out, and the *K* characters of the encoded string are shifted into the window.

Figure 15.10b shows the operation of this scheme on our example sequence. The illustration assumes a 39-character sliding window and a 13-character look-ahead buffer. In the upper part of the example, the first 40 characters have been processed and the uncompressed version of the most recent 39 of these characters is in the sliding window. The remaining source is in the look-ahead window. The compression algorithm determines the next match, shifts 5 characters from the look-ahead buffer into the sliding window, and outputs the code for this string. The state of the buffer after these operations is shown in the lower part of the example.

While LZ77 is effective and does adapt to the nature of the current input, it has some drawbacks. The algorithm uses a finite window to look for matches in previous text. For a very long block of text, compared to the size of the window, many potential matches are eliminated. The window size can be increased, but this imposes two penalties: (1) The processing time of the algorithm increases because it must perform a string comparison against the look-ahead buffer for every position in the sliding window, and (2) the <pointer> field must be larger to accommodate the longer jumps.

Decompression Algorithm

Decompression of LZ77-compressed text is simple. The decompression algorithm must save the last *N* characters of decompressed output. When an encoded string is encountered, the decompression algorithm uses the <pointer> and <length> fields to replace the code with the actual text string.

APPENDIX 15B RADIX-64 CONVERSION

Both PGP and S/MIME make use of an encoding technique referred to as radix-64 conversion. This technique maps arbitrary binary input into printable character output. The form of encoding has the following relevant characteristics:

1. The range of the function is a character set that is universally representable at all sites, not a specific binary encoding of that character set. Thus, the characters themselves can be encoded into whatever form is needed by a specific system. For example, the character "E" is represented in an ASCII-based system as hexadecimal 45 and in an EBCDIC-based system as hexadecimal C5.
2. The character set consists of 65 printable characters, one of which is used for padding. With $2^6 = 64$ available characters, each character can be used to represent 6 bits of input.
3. No control characters are included in the set. Thus, a message encoded in radix 64 can traverse mail-handling systems that scan the data stream for control characters.
4. The hyphen character ("−") is not used. This character has significance in the RFC 822 format and should therefore be avoided.

Table 15.9 shows the mapping of 6-bit input values to characters. The character set consists of the alphanumeric characters plus "+" and "/". The "=" character is used as the padding character.

Table 15.9 Radix-64 Encoding

6-Bit Value	Character Encoding	6-Bit Value	Character Encoding	6-Bit Value	Character Encoding	6-Bit Value	Character Encoding
0	A	16	Q	32	g	48	w
1	B	17	R	33	h	49	x
2	C	18	S	34	i	50	y
3	D	19	T	35	j	51	z
4	E	20	U	36	k	52	0
5	F	21	V	37	l	53	1
6	G	22	W	38	m	54	2
7	H	23	X	39	n	55	3
8	I	24	Y	40	o	56	4
9	J	25	Z	41	p	57	5
10	K	26	a	42	q	58	6
11	L	27	b	43	r	59	7
12	M	28	c	44	s	60	8
13	N	29	d	45	t	61	9
14	O	30	e	46	u	62	+
15	P	31	f	47	v	63	/
						(pad)	=

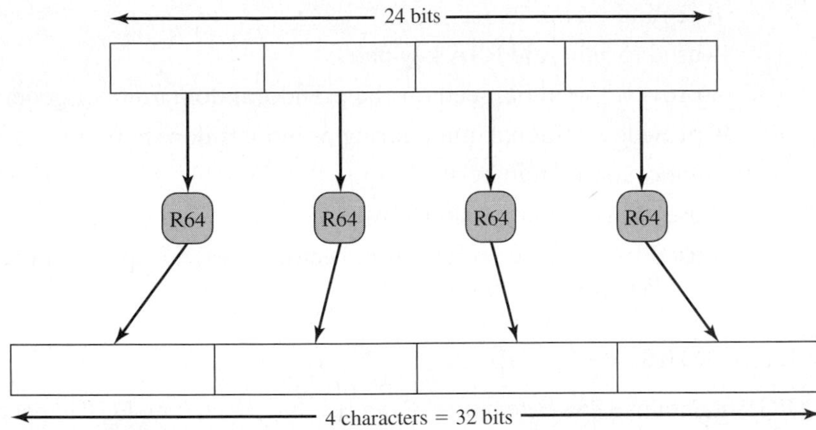

Figure 15.11 Printable Encoding of Binary Data into Radix-64 Format

Figure 15.11 illustrates the simple mapping scheme. Binary input is processed in blocks of 3 octets, or 24 bits. Each set of 6 bits in the 24-bit block is mapped into a character. In the figure, the characters are shown encoded as 8-bit quantities. In this typical case, each 24-bit input is expanded to 32 bits of output.

For example, consider the 24-bit raw text sequence 00100011 01011100 10010001, which can be expressed in hexadecimal as 235C91. We arrange this input in blocks of 6 bits:

001000 110101 110010 010001

The extracted 6-bit decimal values are 8, 53, 50, 17. Looking these up in Table 15.9 yields the radix-64 encoding as the following characters: I1yR. If these characters are stored in 8-bit ASCII format with parity bit set to zero, we have

01001001 00110001 01111001 01010010

In hexadecimal, this is 49317952. To summarize,

Input Data	
Binary representation	00100011 01011100 10010001
Hexadecimal representation	235C91
Radix-64 Encoding of Input Data	
Character representation	I1yR
ASCII code (8 bit, zero parity)	01001001 00110001 01111001 01010010
Hexadecimal representation	49317952

APPENDIX 15C PGP RANDOM NUMBER GENERATION

PGP uses a complex and powerful scheme for generating random numbers and pseudorandom numbers, for a variety of purposes. PGP generates random numbers from the content and timing of user keystrokes, and pseudorandom numbers using an algorithm based on the one in ANSI X9.17. PGP uses these numbers for the following purposes:

- True random numbers:
  —used to generate RSA key pairs
  —provide the initial seed for the pseudorandom number generator
  —provide additional input during pseudorandom number generation
- Pseudorandom numbers:
  —used to generate session keys
  —used to generate initialization vectors (IVs) for use with the session key in CFB mode encryption

True Random Numbers

PGP maintains a 256-byte buffer of random bits. Each time PGP expects a keystroke, it records the time, in 32-bit format, at which it starts waiting. When it receives the keystroke, it records the time the key was pressed and the 8-bit value of the keystroke. The time and keystroke information are used to generate a key, which is, in turn, used to encrypt the current value of the random-bit buffer.

Pseudorandom Numbers

Pseudorandom number generation makes use of a 24-octet seed and produces a 16-octet session key, an 8-octet initialization vector, and a new seed to be used for the next pseudorandom number generation. The algorithm is based on the X9.17 algorithm described in Chapter 7 (see Figure 7.14) but uses CAST-128 instead of triple DES for encryption. The algorithm uses the following data structures:

1. Input

   —randseed.bin (24 octets): If this file is empty, it is filled with 24 true random octets.

   —message: The session key and IV that will be used to encrypt a message are themselves a function of that message. This further contributes to the randomness of the key and IV, and if an opponent already knows the plaintext content of the message, there is no apparent need for capturing the one-time session key.

2. Output

   —K (24 octets): The first 16 octets, K[0..15], contain a session key, and the last eight octets, K[16..23], contain an IV.

   —randseed.bin (24 octets): A new seed value is placed in this file.

3. Internal data structures

   —dtbuf (8 octets): The first 4 octets, dtbuf[0..3], are initialized with the current date/time value. This buffer is equivalent to the DT variable in the X12.17 algorithm.

   —rkey (16 octets): CAST-128 encryption key used at all stages of the algorithm.

   —rseed (8 octets): Equivalent to the X12.17 V_i variable.

—rbuf (8 octets): A pseudorandom number generated by the algorithm. This buffer is equivalent to the X12.17 R_i variable.

—K′ (24 octets): Temporary buffer for the new value of randseed.bin.

The algorithm consists of nine steps, G1 through G9. The first and last steps are obfuscation steps, intended to reduce the value of a captured randseed.bin file to an opponent. The remaining steps are essentially equivalent to three iterations of the X12.17 algorithm and are illustrated in Figure 15.12 (compare Figure 7.14). To summarize,

G1. [Prewash previous seed]

a. Copy randseed.bin to K[0..23].

b. Take the hash of the message (this has already been generated if the message is being signed; otherwise the first 4K octets of the message are used). Use the result as a key, use a null IV, and encrypt K in CFB mode; store result back in K.

G2. [Set initial seed]

a. Set dtbuf[0..3] to the 32-bit local time. Set dtbuf[4..7] to all zeros. Copy rkey ← K[0..15]. Copy rseed ← K[16..23].

b. Encrypt the 64-bit dtbuf using the 128-bit rkey in ECB mode; store the result back in dtbuf.

G3. [Prepare to generate random octets] Set rcount ← 0 and k ← 23. The loop of steps G4-G7 will be executed 24 times (k = 23...0), once for each random octet produced and placed in K. The variable rcount is the number of unused random octets in rbuf. It will count down from 8 to 0 three times to generate the 24 octets.

G4. [Bytes available?] If rcount = 0 goto G5 else goto G7. Steps G5 and G6 perform one instance of the X12.17 algorithm to generate a new batch of eight random octets.

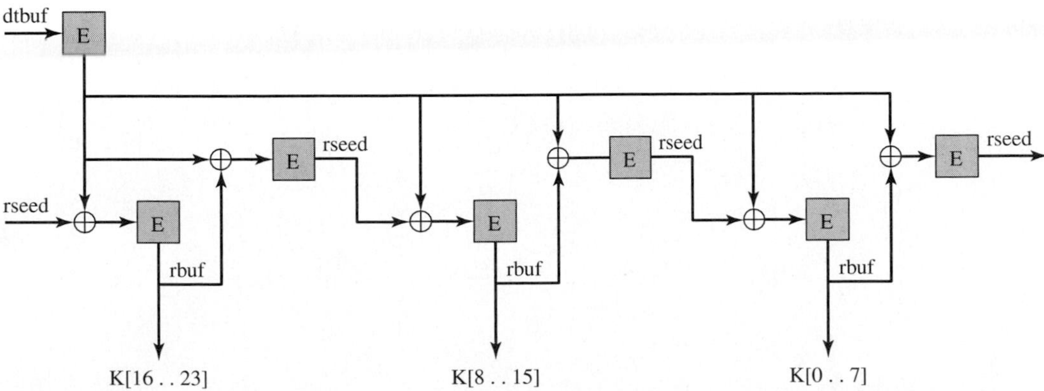

Figure 15.12 PGP Session Key and IV Generation (steps G2 through G8)

```
G5. [Generate new random octets]
    a. rseed ← rseed ⊕ dtbuf
    b. rbuf ← E_rkey[rseed]        in ECB mode
G6. [Generate next seed]
    a.rseed ← rbuf ⊕ dtbuf
    b. rseed ← E_rkey[rseed]        in ECB mode
    c. Set rcount ← 8
G7. [Transfer one byte at a time from rbuf to K]
    a. Set rcount ← rcount - 1
    b. Generate a true random byte b, and set K[k] ←
    rbuf[rcount] ⊕ b
G8. [Done?] If k = 0 goto G9 else set k ← k - 1 and goto G4
G9. [Postwash seed and return result]
    a. Generate 24 more bytes by the method of steps G4-G7,
       except do not XOR in a random byte in G7. Place the
       result in buffer K'
    b. Encrypt K' with key K[0..15] and IV K[16..23] in CFB
       mode; store result in randseed.bin
    c. Return K
```

It should not be possible to determine the session key from the 24 new octets generated in step G9.a. However, to make sure that the stored randseed.bin file provides no information about the most recent session key, the 24 new octets are encrypted and the result is stored as the new seed.

This elaborate algorithm should provide cryptographically strong pseudorandom numbers.

16

CHAPTER

IP SECURITY

If a secret piece of news is divulged by a spy before the time is ripe, he must be put to death, together with the man to whom the secret was told.

—*The Art of War*, Sun Tzu

KEY POINTS

- IP security (IPSec) is a capability that can be added to either current version of the Internet Protocol (IPv4 or IPv6), by means of additional headers.
- IPSec encompasses three functional areas: authentication, confidentiality, and key management.
- Authentication makes use of the HMAC message authentication code. Authentication can be applied to the entire original IP packet (tunnel mode) or to all of the packet except for the IP header (transport mode).
- Confidentiality is provided by an encryption format known as encapsulating security payload. Both tunnel and transport modes can be accommodated.
- IPSec defines a number of techniques for key management.

The Internet community has developed application-specific security mechanisms in a number of application areas, including electronic mail (S/MIME, PGP), client/server (Kerberos), Web access (Secure Sockets Layer), and others. However, users have some security concerns that cut across protocol layers. For example, an enterprise can run a secure, private TCP/IP network by disallowing links to untrusted sites, encrypting packets that leave the premises, and authenticating packets that enter the premises. By implementing security at the IP level, an organization can ensure secure networking not only for applications that have security mechanisms but also for the many security-ignorant applications.

IP-level security encompasses three functional areas: authentication, confidentiality, and key management. The authentication mechanism assures that a received packet was, in fact, transmitted by the party identified as the source in the packet header. In addition, this mechanism assures that the packet has not been altered in transit. The confidentiality facility enables communicating nodes to encrypt messages to prevent eavesdropping by third parties. The key management facility is concerned with the secure exchange of keys.

We begin this chapter with an overview of IP security (IPSec) and an introduction to the IPSec architecture. We then look at each of the three functional areas in detail. The appendix to this chapter reviews internet protocols.

16.1 IP SECURITY OVERVIEW

In response to these issues, the IAB included authentication and encryption as necessary security features in the next-generation IP, which has been issued as IPv6. Fortunately, these security capabilities were designed to be usable both with the current IPv4 and the future IPv6. This means that vendors can begin offering these features now, and many vendors do now have some IPSec capability in their products.

Applications of IPSec

IPSec provides the capability to secure communications across a LAN, across private and public WANs, and across the Internet. Examples of its use include the following:

- **Secure branch office connectivity over the Internet:** A company can build a secure virtual private network over the Internet or over a public WAN. This enables a business to rely heavily on the Internet and reduce its need for private networks, saving costs and network management overhead.
- **Secure remote access over the Internet:** An end user whose system is equipped with IP security protocols can make a local call to an Internet service provider (ISP) and gain secure access to a company network. This reduces the cost of toll charges for traveling employees and telecommuters.
- **Establishing extranet and intranet connectivity with partners:** IPSec can be used to secure communication with other organizations, ensuring authentication and confidentiality and providing a key exchange mechanism.
- **Enhancing electronic commerce security:** Even though some Web and electronic commerce applications have built-in security protocols, the use of IPSec enhances that security.

The principal feature of IPSec that enables it to support these varied applications is that it can encrypt and/or authenticate *all* traffic at the IP level. Thus, all distributed applications, including remote logon, client/server, e-mail, file transfer, Web access, and so on, can be secured.

Figure 16.1 is a typical scenario of IPSec usage. An organization maintains LANs at dispersed locations. Nonsecure IP traffic is conducted on each LAN. For traffic offsite, through some sort of private or public WAN, IPSec protocols are used. These protocols operate in networking devices, such as a router or firewall, that connect each LAN to the outside world. The IPSec networking device will typically encrypt and compress all traffic going into the WAN, and decrypt and decompress traffic coming from the WAN; these operations are transparent to workstations and servers on the LAN. Secure transmission is also possible with individual users who dial into the WAN. Such user workstations must implement the IPSec protocols to provide security.

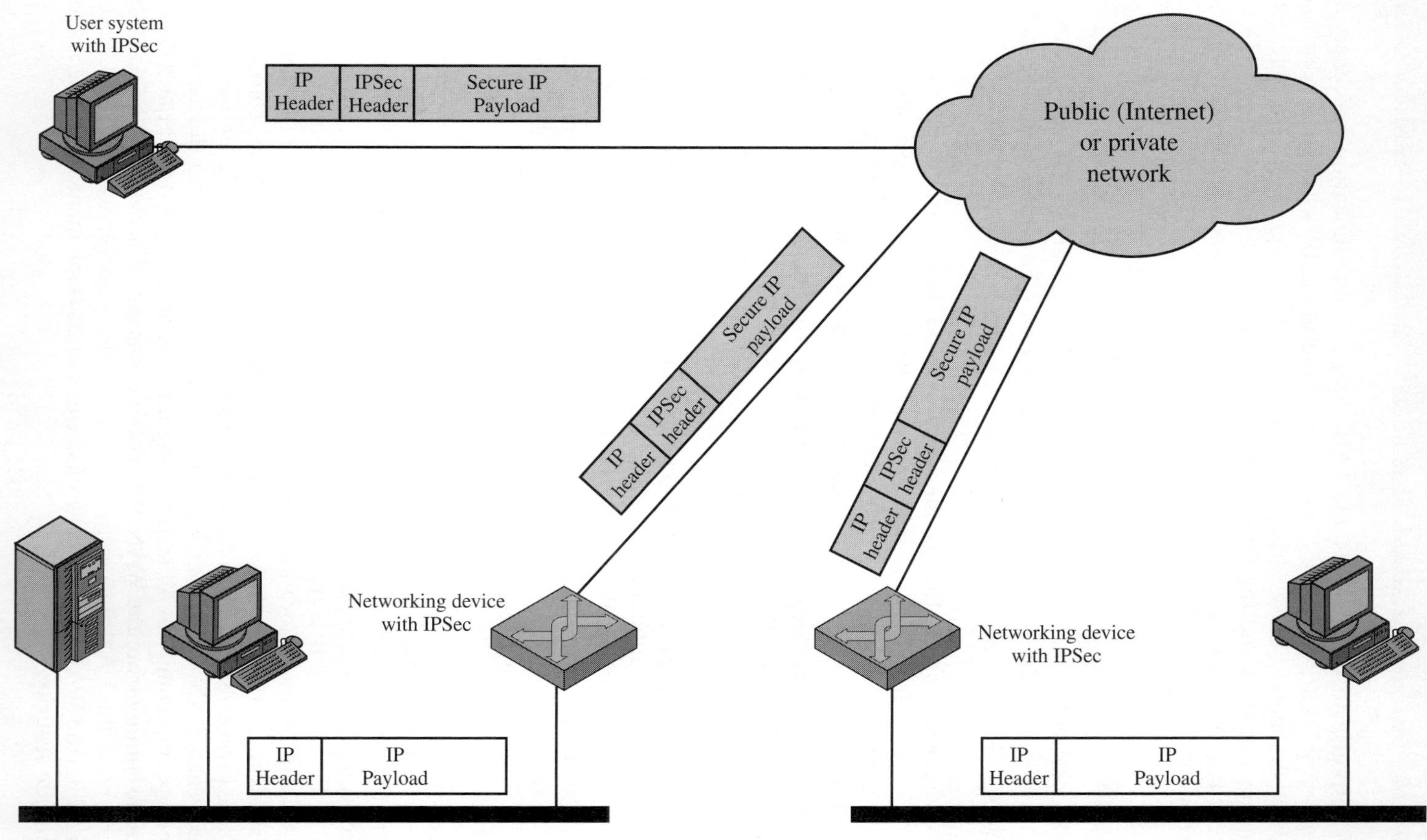

Figure 16.1 An IP Security Scenario

Benefits of IPSec

[MARK97] lists the following benefits of IPSec:

- When IPSec is implemented in a firewall or router, it provides strong security that can be applied to all traffic crossing the perimeter. Traffic within a company or workgroup does not incur the overhead of security-related processing.
- IPSec in a firewall is resistant to bypass if all traffic from the outside must use IP, and the firewall is the only means of entrance from the Internet into the organization.
- IPSec is below the transport layer (TCP, UDP) and so is transparent to applications. There is no need to change software on a user or server system when IPSec is implemented in the firewall or router. Even if IPSec is implemented in end systems, upper-layer software, including applications, is not affected.
- IPSec can be transparent to end users. There is no need to train users on security mechanisms, issue keying material on a per-user basis, or revoke keying material when users leave the organization.
- IPSec can provide security for individual users if needed. This is useful for offsite workers and for setting up a secure virtual subnetwork within an organization for sensitive applications.

Routing Applications

In addition to supporting end users and protecting premises systems and networks, IPSec can play a vital role in the routing architecture required for internetworking. [HUIT98] lists the following examples of the use of IPSec. IPSec can assure that

- A router advertisement (a new router advertises its presence) comes from an authorized router
- A neighbor advertisement (a router seeks to establish or maintain a neighbor relationship with a router in another routing domain) comes from an authorized router.
- A redirect message comes from the router to which the initial packet was sent.
- A routing update is not forged.

Without such security measures, an opponent can disrupt communications or divert some traffic. Routing protocols such as OSPF should be run on top of security associations between routers that are defined by IPSec.

16.2 IP SECURITY ARCHITECTURE

The IPSec specification has become quite complex. To get a feel for the overall architecture, we begin with a look at the documents that define IPSec. Then we discuss IPSec services and introduce the concept of security association.

IPSec Documents

The IPSec specification consists of numerous documents. The most important of these, issued in November of 1998, are RFCs 2401, 2402, 2406, and 2408:

- RFC 2401: An overview of a security architecture
- RFC 2402: Description of a packet authentication extension to IPv4 and IPv6
- RFC 2406: Description of a packet encryption extension to IPv4 and IPv6
- RFC 2408: Specification of key management capabilities

Support for these features is mandatory for IPv6 and optional for IPv4. In both cases, the security features are implemented as extension headers that follow the main IP header. The extension header for authentication is known as the Authentication header; that for encryption is known as the Encapsulating Security Payload (ESP) header.

In addition to these four RFCs, a number of additional drafts have been published by the IP Security Protocol Working Group set up by the IETF. The documents are divided into seven groups, as depicted in Figure 16.2 (RFC 2401):

- **Architecture:** Covers the general concepts, security requirements, definitions, and mechanisms defining IPSec technology.

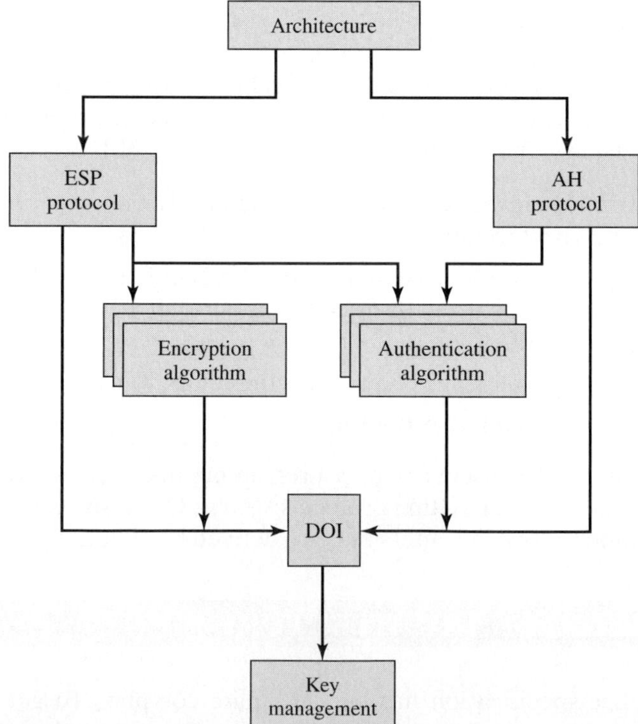

Figure 16.2 IPSec Document Overview

- **Encapsulating Security Payload (ESP):** Covers the packet format and general issues related to the use of the ESP for packet encryption and, optionally, authentication.
- **Authentication Header (AH):** Covers the packet format and general issues related to the use of AH for packet authentication.
- **Encryption Algorithm:** A set of documents that describe how various encryption algorithms are used for ESP.
- **Authentication Algorithm:** A set of documents that describe how various authentication algorithms are used for AH and for the authentication option of ESP.
- **Key Management:** Documents that describe key management schemes.
- **Domain of Interpretation (DOI):** Contains values needed for the other documents to relate to each other. These include identifiers for approved encryption and authentication algorithms, as well as operational parameters such as key lifetime.

IPSec Services

IPSec provides security services at the IP layer by enabling a system to select required security protocols, determine the algorithm(s) to use for the service(s), and put in place any cryptographic keys required to provide the requested services. Two protocols are used to provide security: an authentication protocol designated by the header of the protocol, Authentication Header (AH); and a combined encryption/authentication protocol designated by the format of the packet for that protocol, Encapsulating Security Payload (ESP). The services are

- Access control
- Connectionless integrity
- Data origin authentication
- Rejection of replayed packets (a form of partial sequence integrity)
- Confidentiality (encryption)
- Limited traffic flow confidentiality

Table 16.1 shows which services are provided by the AH and ESP protocols. For ESP, there are two cases: with and without the authentication option. Both AH and ESP are vehicles for access control, based on the distribution of cryptographic keys and the management of traffic flows relative to these security protocols.

Security Associations

A key concept that appears in both the authentication and confidentiality mechanisms for IP is the security association (SA). An association is a one-way relationship between a sender and a receiver that affords security services to the traffic carried on it. If a peer relationship is needed, for two-way secure exchange, then two security associations are required. Security services are afforded to an SA for the use of AH or ESP, but not both.

Table 16.1 IPSec Services

	AH	ESP (encryption only)	ESP (encryption plus authentication)
Access control	✔	✔	✔
Connectionless integrity	✔		✔
Data origin authentication	✔		✔
Rejection of replayed packets	✔	✔	✔
Confidentiality		✔	✔
Limited traffic flow confidentiality		✔	✔

A security association is uniquely identified by three parameters:

- **Security Parameters Index (SPI):** A bit string assigned to this SA and having local significance only. The SPI is carried in AH and ESP headers to enable the receiving system to select the SA under which a received packet will be processed.
- **IP Destination Address:** Currently, only unicast addresses are allowed; this is the address of the destination endpoint of the SA, which may be an end user system or a network system such as a firewall or router.
- **Security Protocol Identifier:** This indicates whether the association is an AH or ESP security association.

Hence, in any IP packet,[1] the security association is uniquely identified by the Destination Address in the IPv4 or IPv6 header and the SPI in the enclosed extension header (AH or ESP).

SA Parameters In each IPSec implementation, there is a nominal[2] Security Association Database that defines the parameters associated with each SA. A security association is normally defined by the following parameters:

- **Sequence Number Counter:** A 32-bit value used to generate the Sequence Number field in AH or ESP headers, described in Section 16.3 (required for all implementations).
- **Sequence Counter Overflow:** A flag indicating whether overflow of the Sequence Number Counter should generate an auditable event and prevent further transmission of packets on this SA (required for all implementations).
- **Anti-Replay Window:** Used to determine whether an inbound AH or ESP packet is a replay, described in Section 16.3 (required for all implementations).
- **AH Information:** Authentication algorithm, keys, key lifetimes, and related parameters being used with AH (required for AH implementations).

[1]In this chapter, the term *IP packet* refers to either an IPv4 datagram or an IPv6 packet.

[2]Nominal in the sense that the functionality provided by a Security Association Database must be present in any IPSec implementation, but the way in which that functionality is provided is up to the implementer.

- **ESP Information:** Encryption and authentication algorithm, keys, initialization values, key lifetimes, and related parameters being used with ESP (required for ESP implementations).
- **Lifetime of This Security Association:** A time interval or byte count after which an SA must be replaced with a new SA (and new SPI) or terminated, plus an indication of which of these actions should occur (required for all implementations).
- **IPSec Protocol Mode:** Tunnel, transport, or wildcard (required for all implementations). These modes are discussed later in this section.
- **Path MTU:** Any observed path maximum transmission unit (maximum size of a packet that can be transmitted without fragmentation) and aging variables (required for all implementations).

The key management mechanism that is used to distribute keys is coupled to the authentication and privacy mechanisms only by way of the Security Parameters Index. Hence, authentication and privacy have been specified independent of any specific key management mechanism.

SA Selectors IPSec provides the user with considerable flexibility in the way in which IPSec services are applied to IP traffic. As we will see later, SAs can be combined in a number of ways to yield the desired user configuration. Furthermore, IPSec provides a high degree of granularity in discriminating between traffic that is afforded IPSec protection and traffic that is allowed to bypass IPSec, in the former case relating IP traffic to specific SAs.

The means by which IP traffic is related to specific SAs (or no SA in the case of traffic allowed to bypass IPSec) is the nominal Security Policy Database (SPD). In its simplest form, an SPD contains entries, each of which defines a subset of IP traffic and points to an SA for that traffic. In more complex environments, there may be multiple entries that potentially relate to a single SA or multiple SAs associated with a single SPD entry. The reader is referred to the relevant IPSec documents for a full discussion.

Each SPD entry is defined by a set of IP and upper-layer protocol field values, called *selectors*. In effect, these selectors are used to filter outgoing traffic in order to map it into a particular SA. Outbound processing obeys the following general sequence for each IP packet:

1. Compare the values of the appropriate fields in the packet (the selector fields) against the SPD to find a matching SPD entry, which will point to zero or more SAs.
2. Determine the SA if any for this packet and its associated SPI.
3. Do the required IPSec processing (i.e., AH or ESP processing).

The following selectors determine an SPD entry:

- **Destination IP Address:** This may be a single IP address, an enumerated list or range of addresses, or a wildcard (mask) address. The latter two are required to support more than one destination system sharing the same SA (e.g., behind a firewall).

- **Source IP Address:** This may be a single IP address, an enumerated list or range of addresses, or a wildcard (mask) address. The latter two are required to support more than one source system sharing the same SA (e.g., behind a firewall).
- **UserID:** A user identifier from the operating system. This is not a field in the IP or upper-layer headers but is available if IPSec is running on the same operating system as the user.
- **Data Sensitivity Level:** Used for systems providing information flow security (e.g., Secret or Unclassified).
- **Transport Layer Protocol:** Obtained from the IPv4 Protocol or IPv6 Next Header field. This may be an individual protocol number, a list of protocol numbers, or a range of protocol numbers.
- **Source and Destination Ports:** These may be individual TCP or UDP port values, an enumerated list of ports, or a wildcard port.

Transport and Tunnel Modes

Both AH and ESP support two modes of use: transport and tunnel mode. The operation of these two modes is best understood in the context of a description of AH and ESP, which are covered in Sections 16.3 and 16.4, respectively. Here we provide a brief overview.

Transport Mode Transport mode provides protection primarily for upper-layer protocols. That is, transport mode protection extends to the payload of an IP packet. Examples include a TCP or UDP segment or an ICMP packet, all of which operate directly above IP in a host protocol stack. Typically, transport mode is used for end-to-end communication between two hosts (e.g., a client and a server, or two workstations). When a host runs AH or ESP over IPv4, the payload is the data that normally follow the IP header. For IPv6, the payload is the data that normally follow both the IP header and any IPv6 extensions headers that are present, with the possible exception of the destination options header, which may be included in the protection.

ESP in transport mode encrypts and optionally authenticates the IP payload but not the IP header. AH in transport mode authenticates the IP payload and selected portions of the IP header.

Tunnel Mode Tunnel mode provides protection to the entire IP packet. To achieve this, after the AH or ESP fields are added to the IP packet, the entire packet plus security fields is treated as the payload of new "outer" IP packet with a new outer IP header. The entire original, or inner, packet travels through a "tunnel" from one point of an IP network to another; no routers along the way are able to examine the inner IP header. Because the original packet is encapsulated, the new, larger packet may have totally different source and destination addresses, adding to the security. Tunnel mode is used when one or both ends of an SA are a security gateway, such as a firewall or router that implements IPSec. With tunnel mode, a number of hosts on networks behind firewalls may engage in secure communications without implementing IPSec. The unprotected packets generated by such hosts are tunneled through external networks by tunnel mode

Table 16.2 Tunnel Mode and Transport Mode Functionality

	Transport Mode SA	Tunnel Mode SA
AH	Authenticates IP payload and selected portions of IP header and IPv6 extension headers.	Authenticates entire inner IP packet (inner header plus IP payload) plus selected portions of outer IP header and outer IPv6 extension headers.
ESP	Encrypts IP payload and any IPv6 extension headers following the ESP header.	Encrypts entire inner IP packet.
ESP with Authentication	Encrypts IP payload and any IPv6 extension headers following the ESP header. Authenticates IP payload but not IP header.	Encrypts entire inner IP packet. Authenticates inner IP packet.

SAs set up by the IPSec software in the firewall or secure router at the boundary of the local network.

Here is an example of how tunnel mode IPSec operates. Host A on a network generates an IP packet with the destination address of host B on another network. This packet is routed from the originating host to a firewall or secure router at the boundary of A's network. The firewall filters all outgoing packets to determine the need for IPSec processing. If this packet from A to B requires IPSec, the firewall performs IPSec processing and encapsulates the packet with an outer IP header. The source IP address of this outer IP packet is this firewall, and the destination address may be a firewall that forms the boundary to B's local network. This packet is now routed to B's firewall, with intermediate routers examining only the outer IP header. At B's firewall, the outer IP header is stripped off, and the inner packet is delivered to B.

ESP in tunnel mode encrypts and optionally authenticates the entire inner IP packet, including the inner IP header. AH in tunnel mode authenticates the entire inner IP packet and selected portions of the outer IP header.

Table 16.2 summarizes transport and tunnel mode functionality.

16.3 AUTHENTICATION HEADER

The Authentication Header provides support for data integrity and authentication of IP packets. The data integrity feature ensures that undetected modification to a packet's content in transit is not possible. The authentication feature enables an end system or network device to authenticate the user or application and filter traffic accordingly; it also prevents the address spoofing attacks observed in today's Internet. The AH also guards against the replay attack described later in this section.

Authentication is based on the use of a message authentication code (MAC), as described in Chapter 11; hence the two parties must share a secret key.

The Authentication Header consists of the following fields (Figure 16.3):

- **Next Header (8 bits):** Identifies the type of header immediately following this header.
- **Payload Length (8 bits):** Length of Authentication Header in 32-bit words, minus 2. For example, the default length of the authentication data field is 96 bits, or three 32-bit words. With a three-word fixed header, there are a total of six words in the header, and the Payload Length field has a value of 4.
- **Reserved (16 bits):** For future use.
- **Security Parameters Index (32 bits):** Identifies a security association.
- **Sequence Number (32 bits):** A monotonically increasing counter value, discussed later.
- **Authentication Data (variable):** A variable-length field (must be an integral number of 32-bit words) that contains the Integrity Check Value (ICV), or MAC, for this packet, discussed later.

Anti-Replay Service

A replay attack is one in which an attacker obtains a copy of an authenticated packet and later transmits it to the intended destination. The receipt of duplicate, authenticated IP packets may disrupt service in some way or may have some other undesired consequence. The Sequence Number field is designed to thwart such attacks. First, we discuss sequence number generation by the sender, and then we look at how it is processed by the recipient.

When a new SA is established, the **sender** initializes a sequence number counter to 0. Each time that a packet is sent on this SA, the sender increments the counter and places the value in the Sequence Number field. Thus, the first value to be used is 1. If anti-replay is enabled (the default), the sender must not allow the sequence number to cycle past $2^{32} - 1$ back to zero. Otherwise, there would be multiple valid packets with the same sequence number. If the limit of $2^{32} - 1$ is reached, the sender should terminate this SA and negotiate a new SA with a new key.

Because IP is a connectionless, unreliable service, the protocol does not guarantee that packets will be delivered in order and does not guarantee that all packets

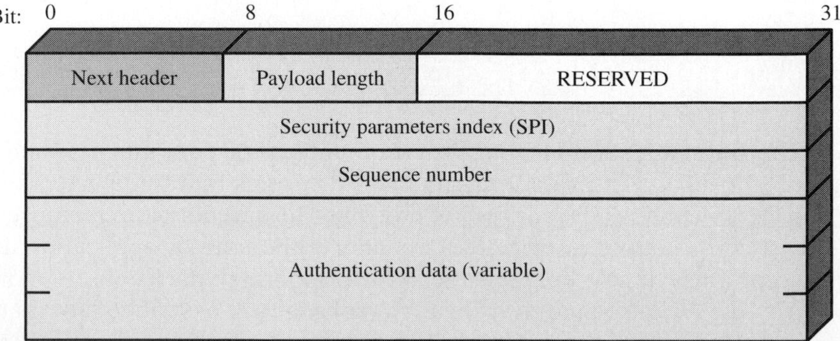

Figure 16.3 IPSec Authentication Header

will be delivered. Therefore, the IPSec authentication document dictates that the **receiver** should implement a window of size W, with a default of $W = 64$. The right edge of the window represents the highest sequence number, N, so far received for a valid packet. For any packet with a sequence number in the range from $N - W + 1$ to N that has been correctly received (i.e., properly authenticated), the corresponding slot in the window is marked (Figure 16.4). Inbound processing proceeds as follows when a packet is received:

1. If the received packet falls within the window and is new, the MAC is checked. If the packet is authenticated, the corresponding slot in the window is marked.
2. If the received packet is to the right of the window and is new, the MAC is checked. If the packet is authenticated, the window is advanced so that this sequence number is the right edge of the window, and the corresponding slot in the window is marked.
3. If the received packet is to the left of the window, or if authentication fails, the packet is discarded; this is an auditable event.

Integrity Check Value

The Authentication Data field holds a value referred to as the Integrity Check Value. The ICV is a message authentication code or a truncated version of a code produced by a MAC algorithm. The current specification dictates that a compliant implementation must support

- HMAC-MD5-96
- HMAC-SHA-1-96

Both of these use the HMAC algorithm , the first with the MD5 hash code and the second with the SHA-1 hash code (all of these algorithms are described in Chapter 12). In both cases, the full HMAC value is calculated but then truncated by using the first 96 bits, which is the default length for the Authentication Data field.

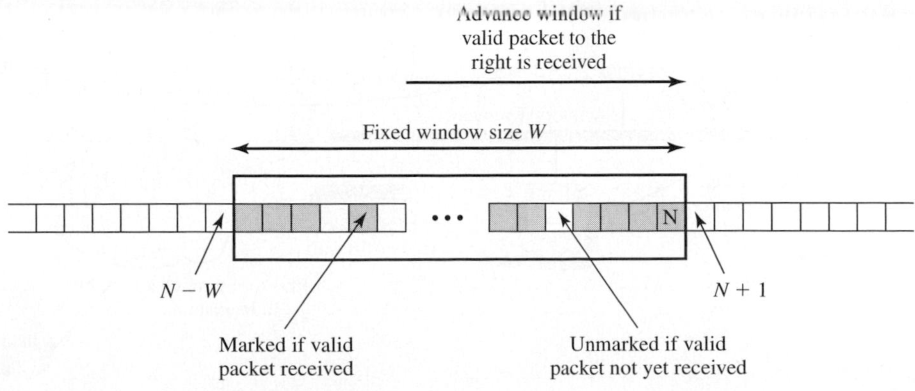

Figure 16.4 Antireplay Mechanism

The MAC is calculated over

- IP header fields that either do not change in transit (immutable) or that are predictable in value upon arrival at the endpoint for the AH SA. Fields that may change in transit and whose value on arrival are unpredictable are set to zero for purposes of calculation at both source and destination.
- The AH header other than the Authentication Data field. The Authentication Data field is set to zero for purposes of calculation at both source and destination.
- The entire upper-level protocol data, which is assumed to be immutable in transit (e.g., a TCP segment or an inner IP packet in tunnel mode).

For IPv4, examples of immutable fields are Internet Header Length and Source Address. An example of a mutable but predictable field is the Destination Address (with loose or strict source routing). Examples of mutable fields that are zeroed prior to ICV calculation are the Time to Live and Header Checksum fields. Note that both source and destination address fields are protected, so that address spoofing is prevented.

For IPv6, examples in the base header are Version (immutable), Destination Address (mutable but predictable), and Flow Label (mutable and zeroed for calculation).

Transport and Tunnel Modes

Figure 16.5 shows two ways in which the IPSec authentication service can be used. In one case, authentication is provided directly between a server and client workstations; the workstation can be either on the same network as the server or on an external network. As long as the workstation and the server share a protected secret key, the authentication process is secure. This case uses a transport mode SA. In the other case, a remote workstation authenticates itself to the corporate firewall, either for access to the entire internal network or because the requested server does not support the authentication feature. This case uses a tunnel mode SA.

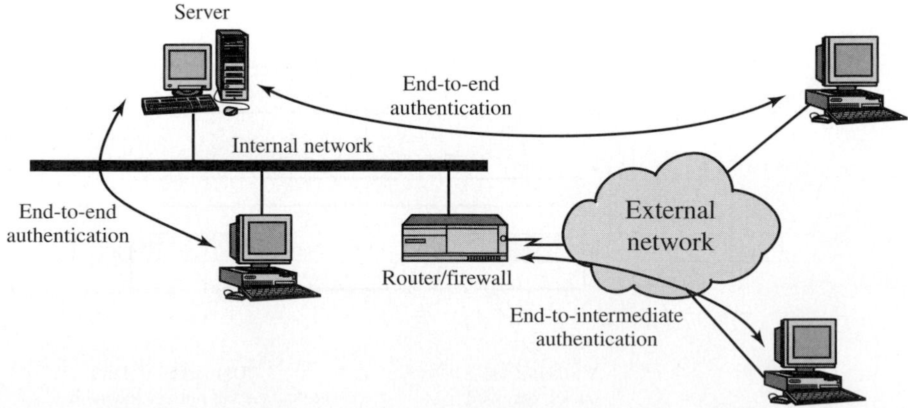

Figure 16.5 End-to-End versus End-to-Intermediate Authentication

In this subsection, we look at the scope of authentication provided by AH and the authentication header location for the two modes. The considerations are somewhat different for IPv4 and IPv6. Figure 16.6a shows typical IPv4 and IPv6 packets. In this case, the IP payload is a TCP segment; it could also be a data unit for any other protocol that uses IP, such as UDP or ICMP.

For **transport mode AH** using IPv4, the AH is inserted after the original IP header and before the IP payload (e.g., a TCP segment); this is shown in the upper part of Figure 16.6b. Authentication covers the entire packet, excluding mutable fields in the IPv4 header that are set to zero for MAC calculation.

In the context of IPv6, AH is viewed as an end-to-end payload; that is, it is not examined or processed by intermediate routers. Therefore, the AH appears after the

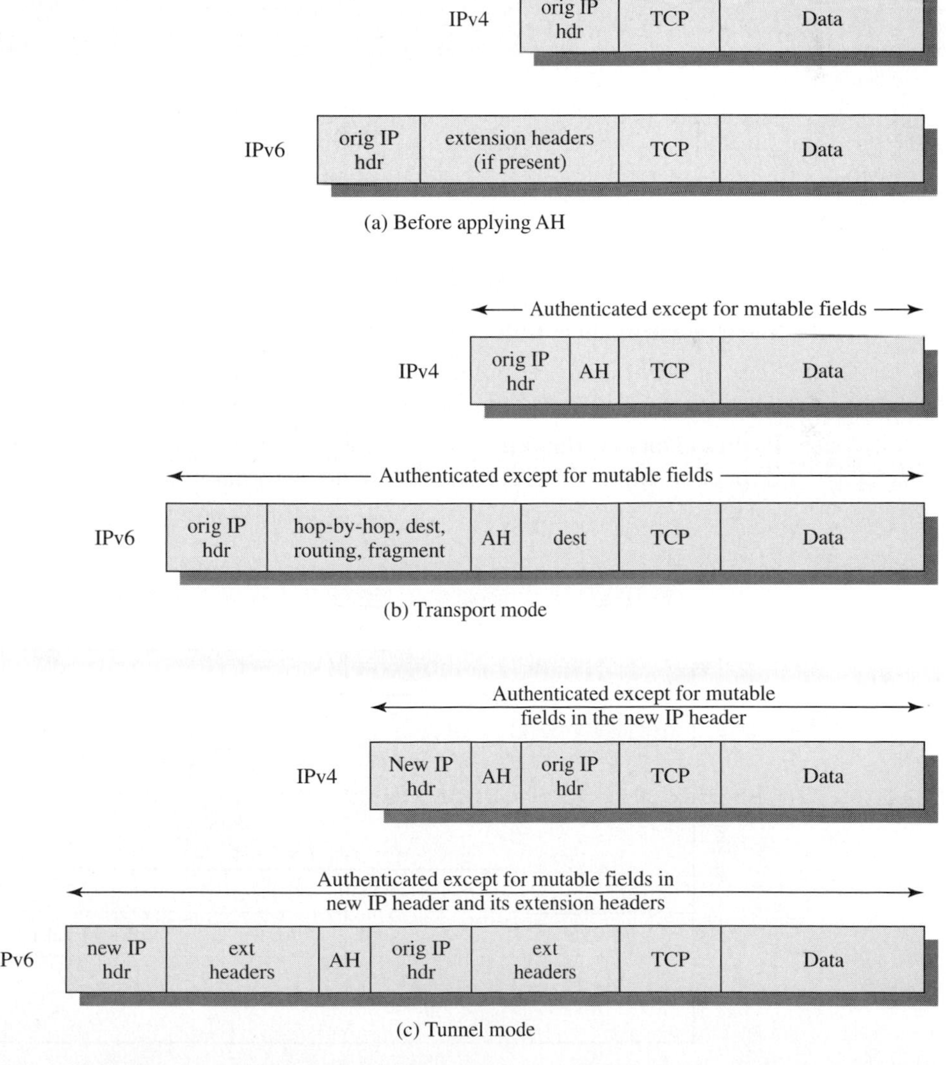

Figure 16.6 Scope of AH Authentication

IPv6 base header and the hop-by-hop, routing, and fragment extension headers. The destination options extension header could appear before or after the AH header, depending on the semantics desired. Again, authentication covers the entire packet, excluding mutable fields that are set to zero for MAC calculation.

For **tunnel mode AH**, the entire original IP packet is authenticated, and the AH is inserted between the original IP header and a new outer IP header (Figure 16.6c). The inner IP header carries the ultimate source and destination addresses, while an outer IP header may contain different IP addresses (e.g., addresses of firewalls or other security gateways).

With tunnel mode, the entire inner IP packet, including the entire inner IP header is protected by AH. The outer IP header (and in the case of IPv6, the outer IP extension headers) is protected except for mutable and unpredictable fields.

16.4 ENCAPSULATING SECURITY PAYLOAD

The Encapsulating Security Payload provides confidentiality services, including confidentiality of message contents and limited traffic flow confidentiality. As an optional feature, ESP can also provide an authentication service.

ESP Format

Figure 16.7 shows the format of an ESP packet. It contains the following fields:

- **Security Parameters Index (32 bits):** Identifies a security association.
- **Sequence Number (32 bits):** A monotonically increasing counter value; this provides an anti-replay function, as discussed for AH.
- **Payload Data (variable):** This is a transport-level segment (transport mode) or IP packet (tunnel mode) that is protected by encryption.

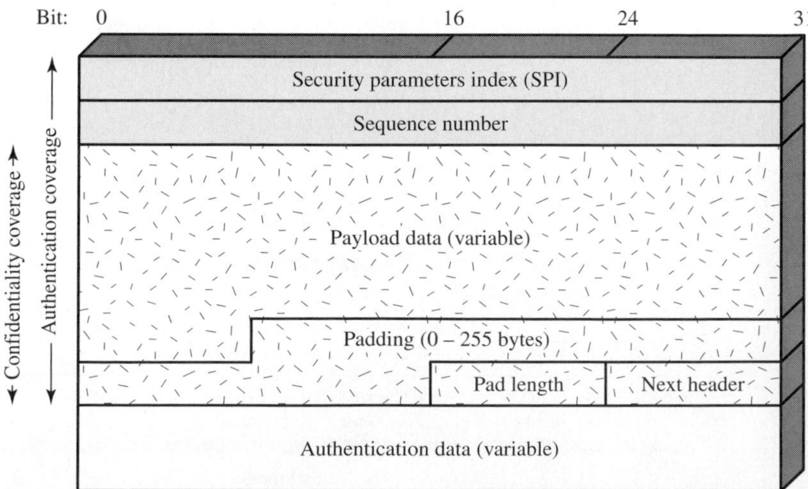

Figure 16.7 IPSec ESP format

- **Padding (0–255 bytes):** The purpose of this field is discussed later.
- **Pad Length (8 bits):** Indicates the number of pad bytes immediately preceding this field.
- **Next Header (8 bits):** Identifies the type of data contained in the payload data field by identifying the first header in that payload (for example, an extension header in IPv6, or an upper-layer protocol such as TCP).
- **Authentication Data (variable):** A variable-length field (must be an integral number of 32-bit words) that contains the Integrity Check Value computed over the ESP packet minus the Authentication Data field.

Encryption and Authentication Algorithms

The Payload Data, Padding, Pad Length, and Next Header fields are encrypted by the ESP service. If the algorithm used to encrypt the payload requires cryptographic synchronization data, such as an initialization vector (IV), then these data may be carried explicitly at the beginning of the Payload Data field. If included, an IV is usually not encrypted, although it is often referred to as being part of the ciphertext.

The current specification dictates that a compliant implementation must support DES in cipher block chaining (CBC) mode (described in Chapter 3). A number of other algorithms have been assigned identifiers in the DOI document and could therefore easily be used for encryption; these include

- Three-key triple DES
- RC5
- IDEA
- Three-key triple IDEA
- CAST
- Blowfish

Many of these algorithms are described in Chapter 6.

As with AH, ESP supports the use of a MAC with a default length of 96 bits. Also as with AH, the current specification dictates that a compliant implementation must support HMAC-MD5-96 and HMAC-SHA-1-96.

Padding

The Padding field serves several purposes:

- If an encryption algorithm requires the plaintext to be a multiple of some number of bytes (e.g., the multiple of a single block for a block cipher), the Padding field is used to expand the plaintext (consisting of the Payload Data, Padding, Pad Length, and Next Header fields) to the required length.
- The ESP format requires that the Pad Length and Next Header fields be right aligned within a 32-bit word. Equivalently, the ciphertext must be an integer multiple of 32 bits. The Padding field is used to assure this alignment.
- Additional padding may be added to provide partial traffic flow confidentiality by concealing the actual length of the payload.

Transport and Tunnel Modes

Figure 16.8 shows two ways in which the IPSec ESP service can be used. In the upper part of the figure, encryption (and optionally authentication) is provided directly between two hosts. Figure 16.8b shows how tunnel mode operation can be used to set up a *virtual private network*. In this example, an organization has four private networks interconnected across the Internet. Hosts on the internal networks use the Internet for transport of data but do not interact with other Internet-based hosts. By terminating the tunnels at the security gateway to each internal network, the configuration allows the hosts to avoid implementing the security capability. The former technique is support by a transport mode SA, while the latter technique uses a tunnel mode SA.

In this section, we look at the scope of ESP for the two modes. The considerations are somewhat different for IPv4 and IPv6. As with our discussion of AH scope, we will use the packet formats of Figure 16.6a as a starting point.

Transport Mode ESP Transport mode ESP is used to encrypt and optionally authenticate the data carried by IP (e.g., a TCP segment), as shown in Figure 16.9a. For this mode using IPv4, the ESP header is inserted into the IP packet immediately

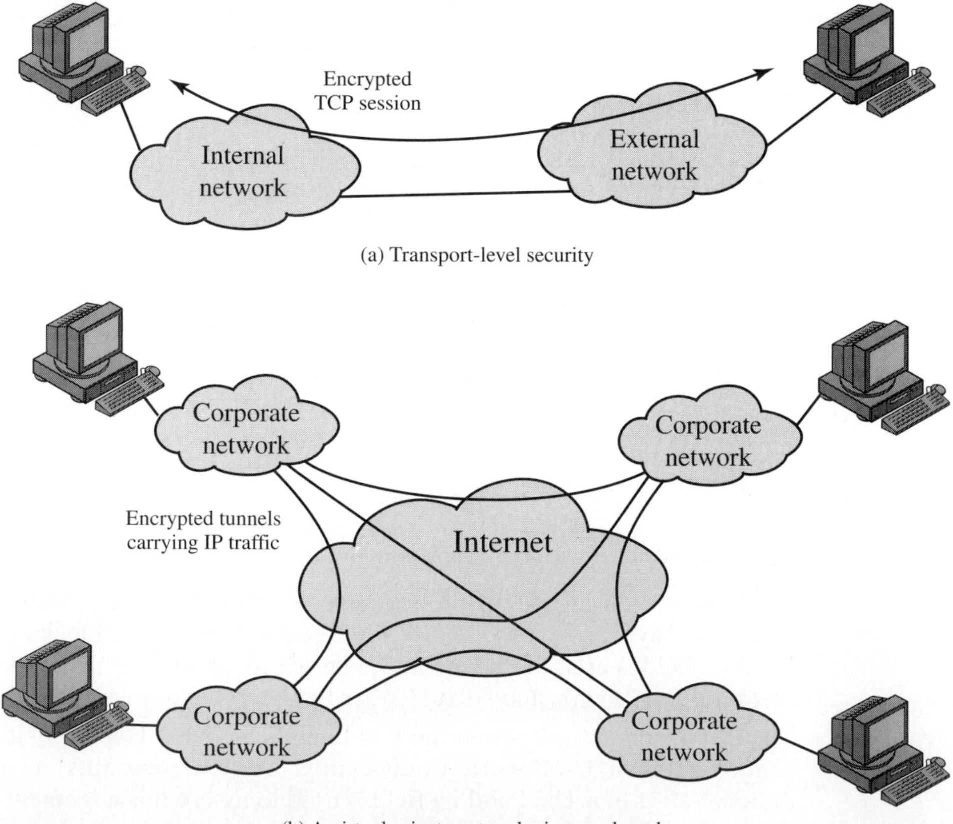

Figure 16.8 Transport-Mode vs. Tunnel-Mode Encryption

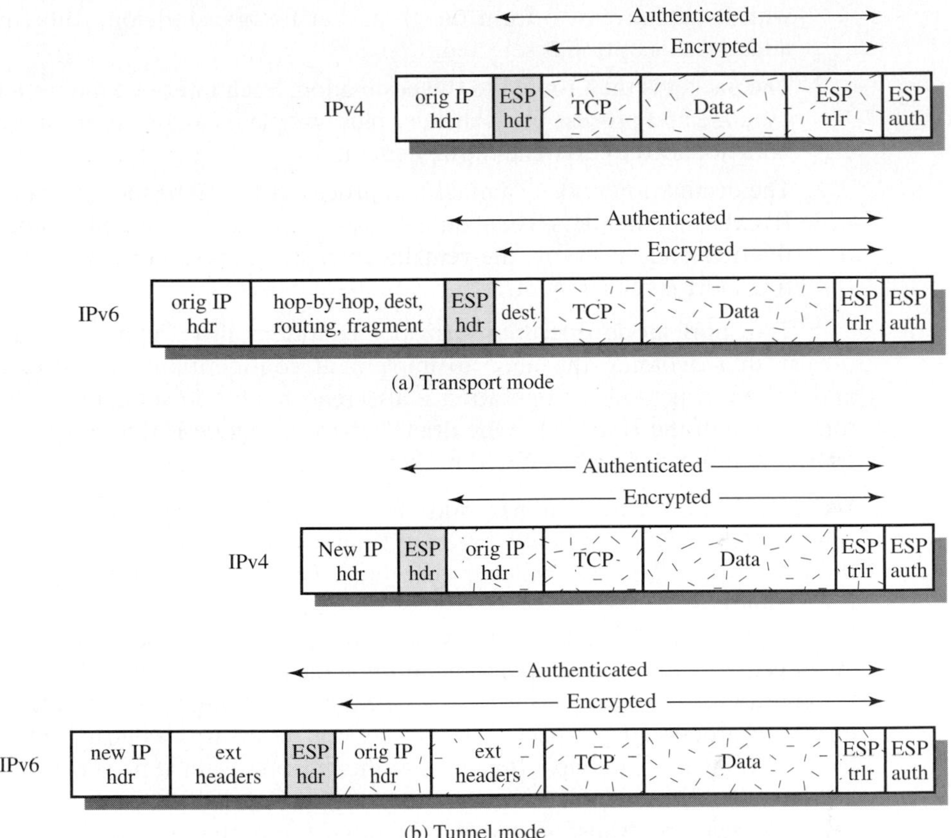

Figure 16.9 Scope of ESP Encryption and Authentication

prior to the transport-layer header (e.g., TCP, UDP, ICMP) and an ESP trailer (Padding, Pad Length, and Next Header fields) is placed after the IP packet; if authentication is selected, the ESP Authentication Data field is added after the ESP trailer. The entire transport-level segment plus the ESP trailer are encrypted. Authentication covers all of the ciphertext plus the ESP header.

In the context of IPv6, ESP is viewed as an end-to-end payload; that is, it is not examined or processed by intermediate routers. Therefore, the ESP header appears after the IPv6 base header and the hop-by-hop, routing, and fragment extension headers. The destination options extension header could appear before or after the ESP header, depending on the semantics desired. For IPv6, encryption covers the entire transport-level segment plus the ESP trailer plus the destination options extension header if it occurs after the ESP header. Again, authentication covers the ciphertext plus the ESP header.

Transport mode operation may be summarized as follows:

1. At the source, the block of data consisting of the ESP trailer plus the entire transport-layer segment is encrypted and the plaintext of this block is replaced

with its ciphertext to form the IP packet for transmission. Authentication is added if this option is selected.

2. The packet is then routed to the destination. Each intermediate router needs to examine and process the IP header plus any plaintext IP extension headers but does not need to examine the ciphertext.
3. The destination node examines and processes the IP header plus any plaintext IP extension headers. Then, on the basis of the SPI in the ESP header, the destination node decrypts the remainder of the packet to recover the plaintext transport-layer segment.

Transport mode operation provides confidentiality for any application that uses it, thus avoiding the need to implement confidentiality in every individual application. This mode of operation is also reasonably efficient, adding little to the total length of the IP packet. One drawback to this mode is that it is possible to do traffic analysis on the transmitted packets.

Tunnel Mode ESP Tunnel mode ESP is used to encrypt an entire IP packet (Figure 16.9b). For this mode, the ESP header is prefixed to the packet and then the packet plus the ESP trailer is encrypted. This method can be used to counter traffic analysis.

Because the IP header contains the destination address and possibly source routing directives and hop-by-hop option information, it is not possible simply to transmit the encrypted IP packet prefixed by the ESP header. Intermediate routers would be unable to process such a packet. Therefore, it is necessary to encapsulate the entire block (ESP header plus ciphertext plus Authentication Data, if present) with a new IP header that will contain sufficient information for routing but not for traffic analysis.

Whereas the transport mode is suitable for protecting connections between hosts that support the ESP feature, the tunnel mode is useful in a configuration that includes a firewall or other sort of security gateway that protects a trusted network from external networks. In this latter case, encryption occurs only between an external host and the security gateway or between two security gateways. This relieves hosts on the internal network of the processing burden of encryption and simplifies the key distribution task by reducing the number of needed keys. Further, it thwarts traffic analysis based on ultimate destination.

Consider a case in which an external host wishes to communicate with a host on an internal network protected by a firewall, and in which ESP is implemented in the external host and the firewalls. The following steps occur for transfer of a transport-layer segment from the external host to the internal host:

1. The source prepares an inner IP packet with a destination address of the target internal host. This packet is prefixed by an ESP header; then the packet and ESP trailer are encrypted and Authentication Data may be added. The resulting block is encapsulated with a new IP header (base header plus optional extensions such as routing and hop-by-hop options for IPv6) whose destination address is the firewall; this forms the outer IP packet.
2. The outer packet is routed to the destination firewall. Each intermediate router needs to examine and process the outer IP header plus any outer IP extension headers but does not need to examine the ciphertext.

3. The destination firewall examines and processes the outer IP header plus any outer IP extension headers. Then, on the basis of the SPI in the ESP header, the destination node decrypts the remainder of the packet to recover the plaintext inner IP packet. This packet is then transmitted in the internal network.
4. The inner packet is routed through zero or more routers in the internal network to the destination host.

16.5 COMBINING SECURITY ASSOCIATIONS

An individual SA can implement either the AH or ESP protocol but not both. Sometimes a particular traffic flow will call for the services provided by both AH and ESP. Further, a particular traffic flow may require IPSec services between hosts and, for that same flow, separate services between security gateways, such as firewalls. In all of these cases, multiple SAs must be employed for the same traffic flow to achieve the desired IPSec services. The term *security association bundle* refers to a sequence of SAs through which traffic must be processed to provide a desired set of IPSec services. The SAs in a bundle may terminate at different endpoints or at the same endpoints.

Security associations may be combined into bundles in two ways:

- **Transport adjacency:** Refers to applying more than one security protocol to the same IP packet, without invoking tunneling. This approach to combining AH and ESP allows for only one level of combination; further nesting yields no added benefit since the processing is performed at one IPsec instance: the (ultimate) destination.
- **Iterated tunneling:** Refers to the application of multiple layers of security protocols effected through IP tunneling. This approach allows for multiple levels of nesting, since each tunnel can originate or terminate at a different IPsec site along the path.

The two approaches can be combined, for example, by having a transport SA between hosts travel part of the way through a tunnel SA between security gateways.

One interesting issue that arises when considering SA bundles is the order in which authentication and encryption may be applied between a given pair of endpoints and the ways of doing so. We examine that issue next. Then we look at combinations of SAs that involve at least one tunnel.

Authentication Plus Confidentiality

Encryption and authentication can be combined in order to transmit an IP packet that has both confidentiality and authentication between hosts. We look at several approaches.

ESP with Authentication Option This approach is illustrated in Figure 16.9. In this approach, the user first applies ESP to the data to be protected and then appends the authentication data field. There are actually two subcases:

- **Transport mode ESP:** Authentication and encryption apply to the IP payload delivered to the host, but the IP header is not protected.

- **Tunnel mode ESP:** Authentication applies to the entire IP packet delivered to the outer IP destination address (e.g., a firewall), and authentication is performed at that destination. The entire inner IP packet is protected by the privacy mechanism, for delivery to the inner IP destination.

For both cases, authentication applies to the ciphertext rather than the plaintext.

Transport Adjacency Another way to apply authentication after encryption is to use two bundled transport SAs, with the inner being an ESP SA and the outer being an AH SA. In this case ESP is used without its authentication option. Because the inner SA is a transport SA, encryption is applied to the IP payload. The resulting packet consists of an IP header (and possibly IPv6 header extensions) followed by an ESP. AH is then applied in transport mode, so that authentication covers the ESP plus the original IP header (and extensions) except for mutable fields. The advantage of this approach over simply using a single ESP SA with the ESP authentication option is that the authentication covers more fields, including the source and destination IP addresses. The disadvantage is the overhead of two SAs versus one SA.

Transport-Tunnel Bundle The use of authentication prior to encryption might be preferable for several reasons. First, because the authentication data are protected by encryption, it is impossible for anyone to intercept the message and alter the authentication data without detection. Second, it may be desirable to store the authentication information with the message at the destination for later reference. It is more convenient to do this if the authentication information applies to the unencrypted message; otherwise the message would have to be reencrypted to verify the authentication information.

One approach to applying authentication before encryption between two hosts is to use a bundle consisting of an inner AH transport SA and an outer ESP tunnel SA. In this case, authentication is applied to the IP payload plus the IP header (and extensions) except for mutable fields. The resulting IP packet is then processed in tunnel mode by ESP; the result is that the entire, authenticated inner packet is encrypted and a new outer IP header (and extensions) is added.

Basic Combinations of Security Associations

The IPSec Architecture document lists four examples of combinations of SAs that must be supported by compliant IPSec hosts (e.g., workstation, server) or security gateways (e.g. firewall, router). These are illustrated in Figure 16.10. The lower part of each case in the figure represents the physical connectivity of the elements; the upper part represents logical connectivity via one or more nested SAs. Each SA can be either AH or ESP. For host-to-host SAs, the mode may be either transport or tunnel; otherwise it must be tunnel mode.

In **Case 1**, all security is provided between end systems that implement IPSec. For any two end systems to communicate via an SA, they must share the appropriate secret keys. Among the possible combinations:

a. AH in transport mode
b. ESP in transport mode
c. ESP followed by AH in transport mode (an ESP SA inside an AH SA)
d. Any one of a, b, or c inside an AH or ESP in tunnel mode

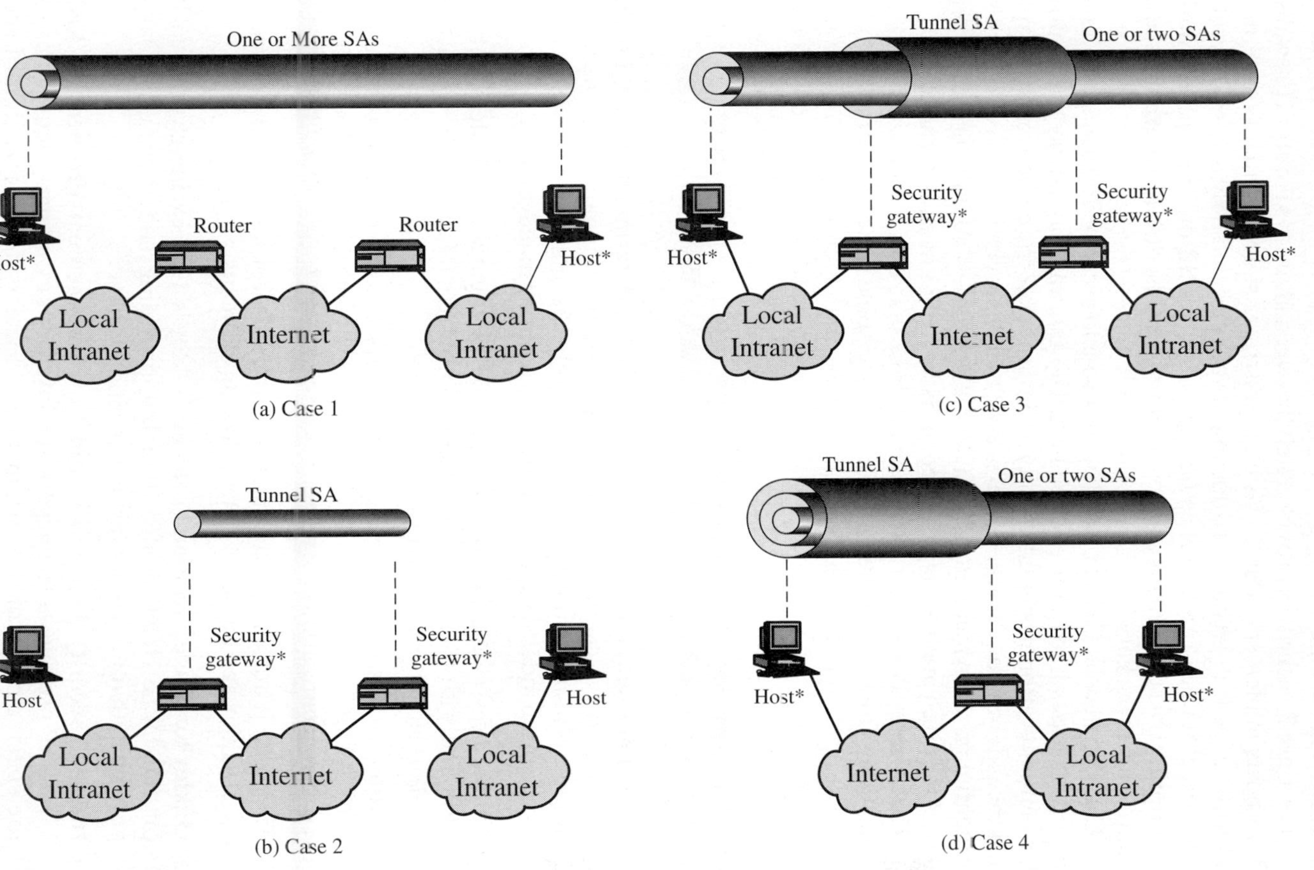

Figure 16.10 Basic Combinations of Security Associations

We have already discussed how these various combinations can be used to support authentication, encryption, authentication before encryption, and authentication after encryption.

For **Case 2**, security is provided only between gateways (routers, firewalls, etc.) and no hosts implement IPSec. This case illustrates simple virtual private network support. The security architecture document specifies that only a single tunnel SA is needed for this case. The tunnel could support AH, ESP, or ESP with the authentication option. Nested tunnels are not required because the IPSec services apply to the entire inner packet.

Case 3 builds on Case 2 by adding end-to-end security. The same combinations discussed for cases 1 and 2 are allowed here. The gateway-to-gateway tunnel provides either authentication or confidentiality or both for all traffic between end systems. When the gateway-to-gateway tunnel is ESP, it also provides a limited form of traffic confidentiality. Individual hosts can implement any additional IPSec services required for given applications or given users by means of end-to-end SAs.

Case 4 provides support for a remote host that uses the Internet to reach an organization's firewall and then to gain access to some server or workstation behind the firewall. Only tunnel mode is required between the remote host and the firewall. As in Case 1, one or two SAs may be used between the remote host and the local host.

16.6 KEY MANAGEMENT

The key management portion of IPSec involves the determination and distribution of secret keys. A typical requirement is four keys for communication between two applications: transmit and receive pairs for both AH and ESP. The IPSec Architecture document mandates support for two types of key management:

- **Manual:** A system administrator manually configures each system with its own keys and with the keys of other communicating systems. This is practical for small, relatively static environments.
- **Automated:** An automated system enables the on-demand creation of keys for SAs and facilitates the use of keys in a large distributed system with an evolving configuration.

The default automated key management protocol for IPSec is referred to as ISAKMP/Oakley and consists of the following elements:

- **Oakley Key Determination Protocol:** Oakley is a key exchange protocol based on the Diffie-Hellman algorithm but providing added security. Oakley is generic in that it does not dictate specific formats.
- **Internet Security Association and Key Management Protocol (ISAKMP):** ISAKMP provides a framework for Internet key management and provides the specific protocol support, including formats, for negotiation of security attributes.

ISAKMP by itself does not dictate a specific key exchange algorithm; rather, ISAKMP consists of a set of message types that enable the use of a variety of key exchange algorithms. Oakley is the specific key exchange algorithm mandated for use with the initial version of ISAKMP.

We begin with an overview of Oakley and then look at ISAKMP.

Oakley Key Determination Protocol

Oakley is a refinement of the Diffie-Hellman key exchange algorithm. Recall that Diffie-Hellman involves the following interaction between users A and B. There is prior agreement on two global parameters: q, a large prime number; and α, a primitive root of q. A selects a random integer X_A as its private key, and transmits to B its public key $Y_A = \alpha^{X_A} \bmod q$. Similarly, B selects a random integer X_B as its private key and transmits to A its public key $Y_B = \alpha^{X_B} \bmod q$. Each side can now compute the secret session key:

$$K = (Y_B)^{X_A} \bmod q = (Y_A)^{X_B} \bmod q = \alpha^{X_A X_B} \bmod q$$

The Diffie-Hellman algorithm has two attractive features:

- Secret keys are created only when needed. There is no need to store secret keys for a long period of time, exposing them to increased vulnerability.
- The exchange requires no preexisting infrastructure other than an agreement on the global parameters.

However, there are a number of weaknesses to Diffie-Hellman, as pointed out in [HUIT98]:

- It does not provide any information about the identities of the parties.
- It is subject to a man-in-the-middle attack, in which a third party C impersonates B while communicating with A and impersonates A while communicating with B. Both A and B end up negotiating a key with C, which can then listen to and pass on traffic. The man-in-the-middle attack proceeds as follows:
  1. B sends his public key Y_B in a message addressed to A (see Figure 10.8).
  2. The enemy (E) intercepts this message. E saves B's public key and sends a message to A that has B's User ID but E's public key Y_E. This message is sent in such a way that it appears as though it was sent from B's host system. A receives E's message and stores E's public key with B's User ID. Similarly, E sends a message to B with E's public key, purporting to come from A.
  3. B computes a secret key K_1 based on B's private key and Y_E. A computes a secret key K_2 based on A's private key and Y_E. E computes K_1 using E's secret key X_E and Y_B and computer K_2 using X_E and Y_A.
  4. From now on E is able to relay messages from A to B and from B to A, appropriately changing their encipherment en route in such a way that neither A nor B will know that they share their communication with E.
- It is computationally intensive. As a result, it is vulnerable to a clogging attack, in which an opponent requests a high number of keys. The victim spends considerable computing resources doing useless modular exponentiation rather than real work.

Oakley is designed to retain the advantages of Diffie-Hellman while countering its weaknesses.

Features of Oakley The Oakley algorithm is characterized by five important features:

1. It employs a mechanism known as cookies to thwart clogging attacks.
2. It enables the two parties to negotiate a *group*; this, in essence, specifies the global parameters of the Diffie-Hellman key exchange.
3. It uses nonces to ensure against replay attacks.
4. It enables the exchange of Diffie-Hellman public key values.
5. It authenticates the Diffie-Hellman exchange to thwart man-in-the-middle attacks.

We have already discussed Diffie-Hellman. Let us look the remainder of these elements in turn. First, consider the problem of clogging attacks. In this attack, an opponent forges the source address of a legitimate user and sends a public Diffie-Hellman key to the victim. The victim then performs a modular exponentiation to compute the secret key. Repeated messages of this type can *clog* the victim's system with useless work. The **cookie exchange** requires that each side send a pseudorandom number, the cookie, in the initial message, which the other side acknowledges. This acknowledgment must be repeated in the first message of the Diffie-Hellman key exchange. If the source address was forged, the opponent gets no answer. Thus, an opponent can only force a user to generate acknowledgments and not to perform the Diffie-Hellman calculation.

ISAKMP mandates that cookie generation satisfy three basic requirements:

1. The cookie must depend on the specific parties. This prevents an attacker from obtaining a cookie using a real IP address and UDP port and then using it to swamp the victim with requests from randomly chosen IP addresses or ports.
2. It must not be possible for anyone other than the issuing entity to generate cookies that will be accepted by that entity. This implies that the issuing entity will use local secret information in the generation and subsequent verification of a cookie. It must not be possible to deduce this secret information from any particular cookie. The point of this requirement is that the issuing entity need not save copies of its cookies, which are then more vulnerable to discovery, but can verify an incoming cookie acknowledgment when it needs to.
3. The cookie generation and verification methods must be fast to thwart attacks intended to sabotage processor resources.

The recommended method for creating the cookie is to perform a fast hash (e.g., MD5) over the IP Source and Destination addresses, the UDP Source and Destination ports, and a locally generated secret value.

Oakley supports the use of different **groups** for the Diffie-Hellman key exchange. Each group includes the definition of the two global parameters and the identity of the algorithm. The current specification includes the following groups:

- Modular exponentiation with a 768-bit modulus
  $q = 2^{768} - 2^{704} - 1 + 2^{64} \times (\lfloor 2^{638} \times \pi \rfloor + 149686)$
  $\alpha = 2$
- Modular exponentiation with a 1024-bit modulus
  $q = 2^{1024} - 2^{960} - 1 + 2^{64} \times (\lfloor 2^{894} \times \pi \rfloor + 129093)$
  $\alpha = 2$
- Modular exponentiation with a 1536-bit modulus
  —Parameters to be determined
- Elliptic curve group over 2^{155}
  —Generator (hexadecimal): X = 7B, Y = 1C8
  —Elliptic curve parameters (hexadecimal): A = 0, Y = 7338F
- Elliptic curve group over 2^{185}
  —Generator (hexadecimal): X = 18, Y = D
  —Elliptic curve parameters (hexadecimal): A = 0, Y = 1EE9

The first three groups are the classic Diffie-Hellman algorithm using modular exponentiation. The last two groups use the elliptic curve analog to Diffie-Hellman, which was described in Chapter 10.

Oakley employs **nonces** to ensure against replay attacks. Each nonce is a locally generated pseudorandom number. Nonces appear in responses and are encrypted during certain portions of the exchange to secure their use.

Three different **authentication** methods can be used with Oakley:

- **Digital signatures:** The exchange is authenticated by signing a mutually obtainable hash; each party encrypts the hash with its private key. The hash is generated over important parameters, such as user IDs and nonces.
- **Public-key encryption:** The exchange is authenticated by encrypting parameters such as IDs and nonces with the sender's private key.
- **Symmetric-key encryption:** A key derived by some out-of-band mechanism can be used to authenticate the exchange by symmetric encryption of exchange parameters.

Oakley Exchange Example The Oakley specification includes a number of examples of exchanges that are allowable under the protocol. To give a flavor of Oakley, we present one example, called aggressive key exchange in the specification, so called because only three messages are exchanged.

Figure 16.11 shows the aggressive key exchange protocol. In the first step, the initiator (I) transmits a cookie, the group to be used, and I's public Diffie-Hellman key for this exchange. I also indicates the offered public-key encryption, hash, and authentication algorithms to be used in this exchange. Also included in

I → R: CKY_I, OK_KEYX, GRP, g^x, EHAO, NIDP, ID_I, ID_R, N_I, $S_{KI}[ID_I \| ID_R \| N_I \| GRP \| g^x \| EHAO]$

R → I: CKY_R, CKY_I, OK_KEYX, GRP, g^y, EHAS, NIDP, ID_R, ID_I, N_R, N_I, $S_{KR}[ID_R \| ID_I \| N_R \| N_I \| GRP \| g^y \| g^x \| EHAS]$

I → R: CKY_I, CKY_R, OK_KEYX, GRP, g^x, EHAS, NIDP, ID_I, ID_R, N_I, N_R, $S_{KI}[ID_I \| ID_R \| N_I \| N_R \| GRP \| g^x \| g^y \| EHAS]$

Notation:

I	=	Initiator
R	=	Responder
CKY_I, CKY_R	=	Initiator, responder cookies
OK_KEYX	=	Key exchange message type
GRP	=	Name of Diffie-Hellman group for this exchange
g^x,g^y	=	Public key of initiator, responder; g^{xy} = session key from this exchange
EHAO, EHAS	=	Encryption, hash authentication functions, offered and selected
NIDP	=	Indicates encryption is not used for remainder of this message
ID_I, ID_R	=	Identifier for initiator, responder
N_I, N_R	=	Random nonce supplied by initiator, responder for this exchange
$S_{KI}[X]$, $S_{KR}[X]$	=	Indicates the signature over X using the private key (signing key) of intiator, responder

Figure 16.11 Example of Aggressive Oakley Key Exchange

this message are the identifiers of I and the responder (R) and I's nonce for this exchange. Finally, I appends a signature using I's private key that signs the two identifiers, the nonce, the group, the Diffie-Hellman public key, and the offered algorithms.

When R receives the message, R verifies the signature using I's public signing key. R acknowledges the message by echoing back I's cookie, identifier, and nonce, as well as the group. R also includes in the message a cookie, R's Diffie-Hellman public key, the selected algorithms (which must be among the offered algorithms), R's identifier, and R's nonce for this exchange. Finally, R appends a signature using R's private key that signs the two identifiers, the two nonces, the group, the two Diffie-Hellman public keys, and the selected algorithms.

When I receives the second message, I verifies the signature using R's public key. The nonce values in the message assure that this is not a replay of an old message. To complete the exchange, I must send a message back to R to verify that I has received R's public key.

ISAKMP

ISAKMP defines procedures and packet formats to establish, negotiate, modify, and delete security associations. As part of SA establishment, ISAKMP defines payloads for exchanging key generation and authentication data. These payload formats provide a consistent framework independent of the specific key exchange protocol, encryption algorithm, and authentication mechanism.

ISAKMP Header Format An ISAKMP message consists of an ISAKMP header followed by one or more payloads. All of this is carried in a transport protocol. The specification dictates that implementations must support the use of UDP for the transport protocol.

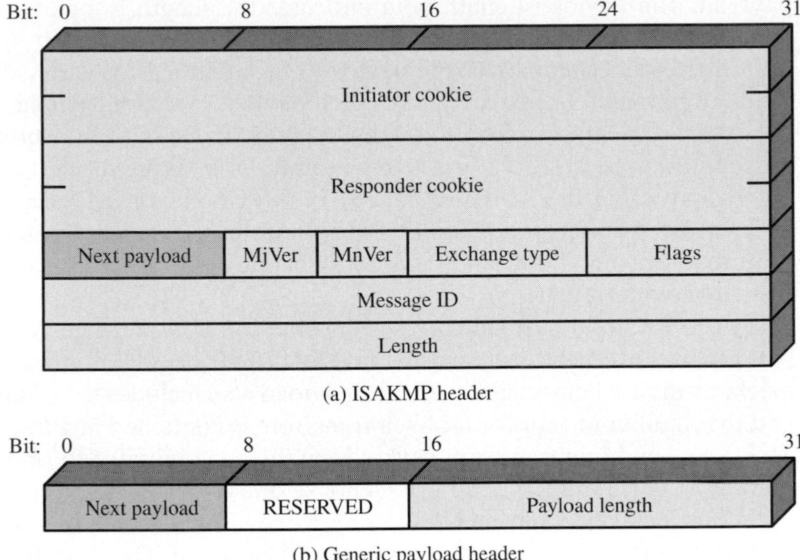

Figure 16.12 ISAKMP Formats

Figure 16.12a shows the header format for an ISAKMP message. It consists of the following fields:

- **Initiator Cookie (64 bits):** Cookie of entity that initiated SA establishment, SA notification, or SA deletion.
- **Responder Cookie (64 bits):** Cookie of responding entity; null in first message from initiator.
- **Next Payload (8 bits):** Indicates the type of the first payload in the message; payloads are discussed in the next subsection.
- **Major Version (4 bits):** Indicates major version of ISAKMP in use.
- **Minor Version (4 bits):** Indicates minor version in use.
- **Exchange Type (8 bits):** Indicates the type of exchange; these are discussed later in this section.
- **Flags (8 bits):** Indicates specific options set for this ISAKMP exchange. Two bits so far defined: The Encryption bit is set if all payloads following the header are encrypted using the encryption algorithm for this SA. The Commit bit is used to ensure that encrypted material is not received prior to completion of SA establishment.
- **Message ID (32 bits):** Unique ID for this message.
- **Length (32 bits):** Length of total message (header plus all payloads) in octets.

ISAKMP Payload Types All ISAKMP payloads begin with the same generic payload header shown in Figure 16.12b. The Next Payload field has a value of 0 if this is the last payload in the message; otherwise its value is the type of the next payload. The Payload Length field indicates the length in octets of this payload, including the generic payload header.

Table 16.3 summarizes the payload types defined for ISAKMP, and lists the fields, or parameters, that are part of each payload. The **SA payload** is used to begin the establishment of an SA. In this payload, the Domain of Interpretation parameter identifies the DOI under which negotiation is taking place. The IPSec DOI is one example, but ISAKMP can be used in other contexts. The Situation parameter defines the security policy for this negotiation; in essence, the levels of security required for encryption and confidentiality are specified (e.g., sensitivity level, security compartment).

The **Proposal payload** contains information used during SA negotiation. The payload indicates the protocol for this SA (ESP or AH) for which services and mechanisms are being negotiated. The payload also includes the sending entity's SPI and the number of transforms. Each transform is contained in a transform payload. The use of multiple transform payloads enables the initiator to offer several possibilities, of which the responder must choose one or reject the offer.

The **Transform payload** defines a security transform to be used to secure the communications channel for the designated protocol. The Transform # parameter serves to identify this particular payload so that the responder may use it to indicate acceptance of this transform. The Transform-ID and Attributes fields identify a specific transform (e.g., 3DES for ESP, HMAC-SHA-1-96 for AH) with its associated attributes (e.g., hash length).

The **Key Exchange payload** can be used for a variety of key exchange techniques, including Oakley, Diffie-Hellman, and the RSA-based key exchange used by PGP. The Key Exchange data field contains the data required to generate a session key and is dependent on the key exchange algorithm used.

The **Identification payload** is used to determine the identity of communicating peers and may be used for determining authenticity of information. Typically the ID Data field will contain an IPv4 or IPv6 address.

The **Certificate payload** transfers a public-key certificate. The Certificate Encoding field indicates the type of certificate or certificate-related information, which may include the following:

- PKCS #7 wrapped X.509 certificate
- PGP certificate
- DNS signed key
- X.509 certificate—signature
- X.509 certificate—key exchange
- Kerberos tokens
- Certificate Revocation List (CRL)
- Authority Revocation List (ARL)
- SPKI certificate

At any point in an ISAKMP exchange, the sender may include a **Certificate Request** payload to request the certificate of the other communicating entity.

Table 16.3 ISAKMP Payload Types

Type	Parameters	Description
Security Association (SA)	Domain of Interpretation, Situation	Used to negotiate security attributes and indicate the DOI and Situation under which negotiation is taking place.
Proposal (P)	Proposal #, Protocol-ID, SPI Size, # of Transforms, SPI	Used during SA negotiation; indicates protocol to be used and number of transforms.
Transform (T)	Transform #, Transform-ID, SA Attributes	Used during SA negotiation; indicates transform and related SA attributes.
Key Exchange (KE)	Key Exchange Data	Supports a variety of key exchange techniques.
Identification (ID)	ID Type, ID Data	Used to exchange identification information.
Certificate (CERT)	Cert Encoding, Certificate Data	Used to transport certificates and other certificate-related information.
Certificate Request (CR)	# Cert Types, Certificate Types, # Cert Auths, Certificate Authorities	Used to request certificates; indicates the types of certificates requested and the acceptable certificate authorities.
Hash (HASH)	Hash Data	Contains data generated by a hash function.
Signature (SIG)	Signature Data	Contains data generated by a digital signature function.
Nonce (NONCE)	Nonce Data	Contains a nonce.
Notification (N)	DOI, Protocol-ID, SPI Size, Notify Message Type, SPI, Notification Data	Used to transmit notification data, such as an error condition.
Delete (D)	DOI, Protocol-ID, SPI Size, # of SPIs, SPI (one or more)	Indicates an SA that is no longer valid.

The payload may list more than one certificate type that is acceptable and more than one certificate authority that is acceptable.

The **Hash payload** contains data generated by a hash function over some part of the message and/or ISAKMP state. This payload may be used to verify the integrity of the data in a message or to authenticate negotiating entities.

The **Signature payload** contains data generated by a digital signature function over some part of the message and/or ISAKMP state. This payload is used to verify the integrity of the data in a message and may be used for nonrepudiation services.

The **Nonce payload** contains random data used to guarantee liveness during an exchange and protect against replay attacks.

The **Notification payload** contains either error or status information associated with this SA or this SA negotiation. The following ISAKMP error messages have been defined:

Invalid Payload Type	Invalid Protocol ID	Invalid Cert Encoding
DOI Not Supported	Invalid SPI	Invalid Certificate
Situation Not Supported	Invalid Transform ID	Bad Cert Request Syntax
Invalid Cookie	Attributes Not Supported	Invalid Cert Authority
Invalid Major Version	No Proposal Chosen	Invalid Hash Information
Invalid Minor Version	Bad Proposal Syntax	Authentication Failed
Invalid Exchange Type	Payload Malformed	Invalid Signature
Invalid Flags	Invalid Key Information	Address Notification
Invalid Message ID		

The only ISAKMP status message so far defined is Connected. In addition to these ISAKMP notifications, DOI-specific notifications are used. For IPSec, the following additional status messages are defined:

- **Responder-Lifetime:** Communicates the SA lifetime chosen by the responder.
- **Replay-Status:** Used for positive confirmation of the responder's election of whether or not the responder will perform anti-replay detection.
- **Initial-Contact:** Informs the other side that this is the first SA being established with the remote system. The receiver of this notification might then delete any existing SA's it has for the sending system under the assumption that the sending system has rebooted and no longer has access to those SAs.

The **Delete payload** indicates one or more SAs that the sender has deleted from its database and that therefore are no longer valid.

ISAKMP Exchanges ISAKMP provides a framework for message exchange, with the payload types serving as the building blocks. The specification identifies five default exchange types that should be supported; these are summarized in Table 16.4. In the table, SA refers to an SA payload with associated Protocol and Transform payloads.

Table 16.4 ISAKMP Exchange Types

Exchange	Note
(a) Base Exchange	
(1) **I → R:** SA; NONCE	Begin ISAKMP-SA negotiation
(2) **R → I:** SA; NONCE	Basic SA agreed upon
(3) **I → R:** KE; ID_I; AUTH	Key generated; Initiator identity verified by responder
(4) **R → I:** KE; ID_R; AUTH	Responder identity verified by initiator; Key generated; SA established
(b) Identity Protection Exchange	
(1) **I → R:** SA	Begin ISAKMP-SA negotiation
(2) **R → I:** SA	Basic SA agreed upon
(3) **I → R:** KE; NONCE	Key generated
(4) **R → I:** KE; NONCE	Key generated
(5)* **I → R:** ID_I; AUTH	Initiator identity verified by responder
(6)* **R → I:** ID_R; AUTH	Responder identity verified by initiator; SA established
(c) Authentication Only Exchange	
(1) **I → R:** SA; NONCE	Begin ISAKMP-SA negotiation
(2) **R → I:** SA; NONCE; ID_R; AUTH	Basic SA agreed upon; Responder identity verified by initiator
(3) **I → R:** ID_I; AUTH	Initiator identity verified by responder; SA established
(d) Aggressive Exchange	
(1) **I → R:** SA; KE; NONCE; ID_I	Begin ISAKMP-SA negotiation and key exchange
(2) **R → I:** SA; KE; NONCE; ID_R; AUTH	Initiator identity verified by responder; Key generated; Basic SA agreed upon
(3)* **I → R:** AUTH	Responder identity verified by initiator; SA established
(e) Informational Exchange	
(1)* **I → R:** N/D	Error or status notification, or deletion

Notation:

I = initiator
R = responder
* = signifies payload encryption after the ISAKMP header
AUTH = authentication mechanism used

The **Base Exchange** allows key exchange and authentication material to be transmitted together. This minimizes the number of exchanges at the expense of not providing identity protection. The first two messages provide cookies and establish an SA with agreed protocol and transforms; both sides use a nonce to ensure against replay attacks. The last two messages exchange the key material and user IDs, with an authentication mechanism used to authenticate keys, identities, and the nonces from the first two messages.

The **Identity Protection Exchange** expands the Base Exchange to protect the users' identities. The first two messages establish the SA. The next two messages perform key exchange, with nonces for replay protection. Once the session key has been computed, the two parties exchange encrypted messages that contain authentication information, such as digital signatures and optionally certificates validating the public keys.

The **Authentication Only Exchange** is used to perform mutual authentication, without a key exchange. The first two messages establish the SA. In addition, the responder uses the second message to convey its ID and uses authentication to protect the message. The initiator sends the third message to transmit its authenticated ID.

The **Aggressive Exchange** minimizes the number of exchanges at the expense of not providing identity protection. In the first message, the initiator proposes an SA with associated offered protocol and transform options. The initiator also begins the key exchange and provides its ID. In the second message, the responder indicates its acceptance of the SA with a particular protocol and transform, completes the key exchange, and authenticates the transmitted information. In the third message, the initiator transmits an authentication result that covers the previous information, encrypted using the shared secret session key.

The **Informational Exchange** is used for one-way transmittal of information for SA management.

16.7 RECOMMENDED READING AND WEB SITE

IPv6 and IPv4 are covered in more detail in [STAL04]. [CHEN98] provides a good discussion of an IPSec design. [FRAN01] and [DORA99] are more comprehensive treatments of IPSec.

CHEN98 Cheng, P., et al. "A Security Architecture for the Internet Protocol." *IBM Systems Journal,* Number 1, 1998.

DORA03 Doraswamy, N., and Harkins, D. *IPSec.* Upper Saddle River, NJ: Prentice Hall, 2003.

FRAN01 Frankel, S. *Demystifying the IPSec Puzzle.* Boston: Artech House, 2001.

STAL04 Stallings, W. *Computer Networking with Internet Protocols and Technology.* Upper Saddle River, NJ: Prentice Hall, 2004.

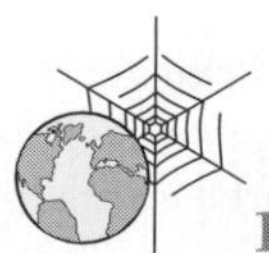

Recommended Web Site:

- **NIST IPSEC Project:** Contains papers, presentations, and reference implementations

16.8 KEY TERMS, REVIEW QUESTIONS, AND PROBLEMS

Key Terms

anti-replay service authentication header (AH) encapsulating security payload (ESP) Internet Security Association and Key Management Protocol (ISAKMP)	IP Security (IPSec) IPv4 IPv6 Oakley key determination protocol	replay attack security association (SA) transport mode tunnel mode

Review Questions

16.1 Give examples of applications of IPSec.

16.2 What services are provided by IPSec?

16.3 What parameters identify an SA and what parameters characterize the nature of a particular SA?

16.4 What is the difference between transport mode and tunnel mode?

16.5 What is a replay attack?

16.6 Why does ESP include a padding field?

16.7 What are the basic approaches to bundling SAs?

16.8 What are the roles of the Oakley key determination protocol and ISAKMP in IPSec?

Problems

16.1 In discussing AH processing, it was mentioned that not all of the fields in an IP header are included in MAC calculation.

  a. For each of the fields in the IPv4 header, indicate whether the field is immutable, mutable but predictable, or mutable (zeroed prior to ICV calculation).
  b. Do the same for the IPv6 header.
  c. Do the same for the IPv6 extension headers.

  In each case, justify your decision for each field.

16.2 When tunnel mode is used, a new outer IP header is constructed. For both IPv4 and IPv6, indicate the relationship of each outer IP header field and each extension header in the outer packet to the corresponding field or extension header of the inner IP packet. That is, indicate which outer values are derived from inner values and which are constructed independently of the inner values.

16.3 End-to-end authentication and encryption are desired between two hosts. Draw figures similar to Figures 16.6 and 16.9 that show

  a. Transport adjacency, with encryption applied before authentication
  b. A transport SA bundled inside a tunnel SA, with encryption applied before authentication
  c. A transport SA bundled inside a tunnel SA, with authentication applied before encryption

16.4 The IPSec architecture document states that when two transport mode SA's are bundled to allow both AH and ESP protocols on the same end-to-end flow, only onc ordering of security protocols seems appropriate: performing the ESP protocol before performing the AH protocol. Why is this approach recommended rather than authentication before encryption?

16.5 a. Which of the ISAKMP Exchange Types (Table 16.4) corresponds to the aggressive Oakley key exchange (Figure 16.11)?

b. For the Oakley aggressive key exchange, indicate which parameters in each message go in which ISAKMP payload types.

APPENDIX 16A INTERNETWORKING AND INTERNET PROTOCOLS

This appendix provides an overview of Internet protocols. We begin with a summary of the role of an internet protocol in providing internetworking. Then the two main internet protocols, IPv4 and IPv6, are introduced.

The Role of an Internet Protocol

An internet protocol (IP) provides the functionality for interconnecting end systems across multiple networks. For this purpose, IP is implemented in each end system and in routers, which are devices that provide connection between networks. Higher-level data at a source end system are encapsulated in an IP protocol data unit (PDU) for transmission. This PDU is then passed through one or more networks and connecting routers to reach the destination end system.

The router must be able to cope with a variety of differences among networks, including

- **Addressing schemes:** The networks may use different schemes for assigning addresses to devices. For example, an IEEE 802 LAN uses either 16-bit or 48-bit binary addresses for each attached device; an X.25 public packet-switching network uses 12-digit decimal addresses (encoded as 4 bits per digit for a 48-bit address). Some form of global network addressing must be provided, as well as a directory service.
- **Maximum packet sizes:** Packets from one network may have to be broken into smaller pieces to be transmitted on another network, a process known as **fragmentation**. For example, Ethernet imposes a maximum packet size of 1500 bytes; a maximum packet size of 1000 bytes is common on X.25 networks. A packet that is transmitted on an Ethernet system and picked up by a router for retransmission on an X.25 network may have to fragment the incoming packet into two smaller ones.
- **Interfaces:** The hardware and software interfaces to various networks differ. The concept of a router must be independent of these differences.
- **Reliability:** Various network services may provide anything from a reliable end-to-end virtual circuit to an unreliable service. The operation of the routers should not depend on an assumption of network reliability.

The operation of the router, as Figure 16.13 indicates, depends on an internet protocol. In this example, the Internet Protocol (IP) of the TCP/IP protocol suite per-

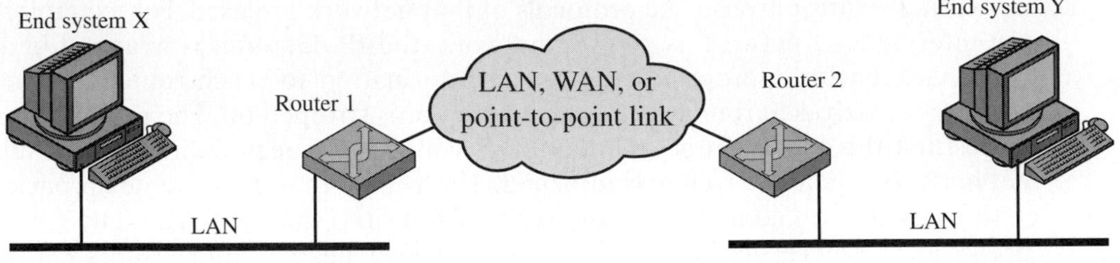

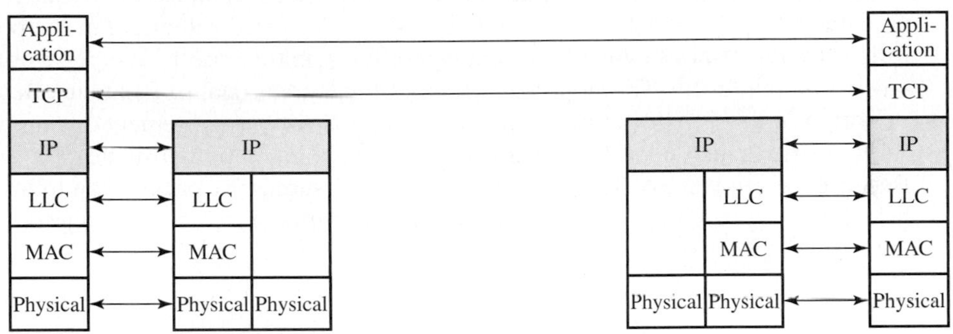

Figure 16.13 Configuration for TCP/IP Example

forms that function. IP must be implemented in all end systems on all networks as well as on the routers. In addition, each end system must have compatible protocols above IP to communicate successfully. The intermediate routers need only have up through IP.

Consider the transfer of a block of data from end system *X* to end system *Y* in Figure 16.13. The IP layer at *X* receives blocks of data to be sent to *Y* from TCP in *X*. The IP layer attaches a header that specifies the global internet address of *Y*. That address is in two parts: network identifier and end system identifier. Let us refer to this block as the IP packet. Next, IP recognizes that the destination (*Y*) is on another subnetwork. So the first step is to send the packet to a router, in this case router 1. To accomplish this, IP hands its data unit down to LLC with the appropriate addressing information. LLC creates an LLC PDU, which is handed down to the MAC layer. The MAC layer constructs a MAC packet whose header contains the address of router 1.

Next, the packet travels through LAN to router 1. The router removes the packet and LLC headers and trailers and analyzes the IP header to determine the ultimate destination of the data, in this case *Y*. The router must now make a routing decision. There are two possibilities:

1. The destination end system *Y* is connected directly to one of the subnetworks to which the router is attached.
2. To reach the destination, one or more additional routers must be traversed.

In this example, the packet must be routed through router 2 before reaching the destination. So router 1 passes the IP packet to router 2 via the intermediate network. For this purpose, the protocols of that network are used. For example, if the intermediate network is an X.25 network, the IP data unit is wrapped in an X.25 packet with appropriate addressing information to reach router 2. When this packet arrives at router 2, the packet header is stripped off. The router determines that this IP packet is destined for *Y*, which is connected directly to a subnetwork to which the router is attached. The router therefore creates a packet with a destination address of *Y* and sends it out onto the LAN. The data finally arrive at *Y*, where the packet, LLC, and internet headers and trailers can be stripped off.

This service offered by IP is an unreliable one. That is, IP does not guarantee that all data will be delivered or that the data that are delivered will arrive in the proper order. It is the responsibility of the next higher layer, in this case TCP, to recover from any errors that occur. This approach provides for a great deal of flexibility. Because delivery is not guaranteed, there is no particular reliability requirement on any of the subnetworks. Thus, the protocol will work with any combination of subnetwork types. Because the sequence of delivery is not guaranteed, successive packets can follow different paths through the internet. This allows the protocol to react to congestion and failure in the internet by changing routes.

IPv4

For decades, the keystone of the TCP/IP protocol architecture has been the Internet Protocol (IP) version 4. Figure 16.14a shows the IP header format, which is a minimum of 20 octets, or 160 bits. The fields are as follows:

- **Version (4 bits):** Indicates version number, to allow evolution of the protocol; the value is 4.
- **Internet Header Length (IHL) (4 bits):** Length of header in 32-bit words. The minimum value is five, for a minimum header length of 20 octets.
- **DS/ECN (8 bits):** Prior to the introduction of differentiated services, this field was referred to as the **Type of Service** field and specified reliability, precedence, delay, and throughput parameters. This interpretation has now been superseded. The first 6 bits of the TOS field are now referred to as the DS (Differentiated Services) field. The remaining 2 bits are reserved for an ECN (Explicit Congestion Notification) field.
- **Total Length (16 bits):** Total IP packet length, in octets.
- **Identification (16 bits):** A sequence number that, together with the source address, destination address, and user protocol, is intended to identify a packet uniquely. Thus, this number should be unique for the packet's source address, destination address, and user protocol for the time during which the packet will remain in the internet.
- **Flags (3 bits):** Only two of the bits are currently defined. When a packet is fragmented, the More bit indicates whether this is the last fragment in the original packet. The Don't Fragment bit prohibits fragmentation when set. This bit may be useful if it is known that the destination does not have the capability to reassemble fragments. However, if this bit is set, the packet will be discarded if it

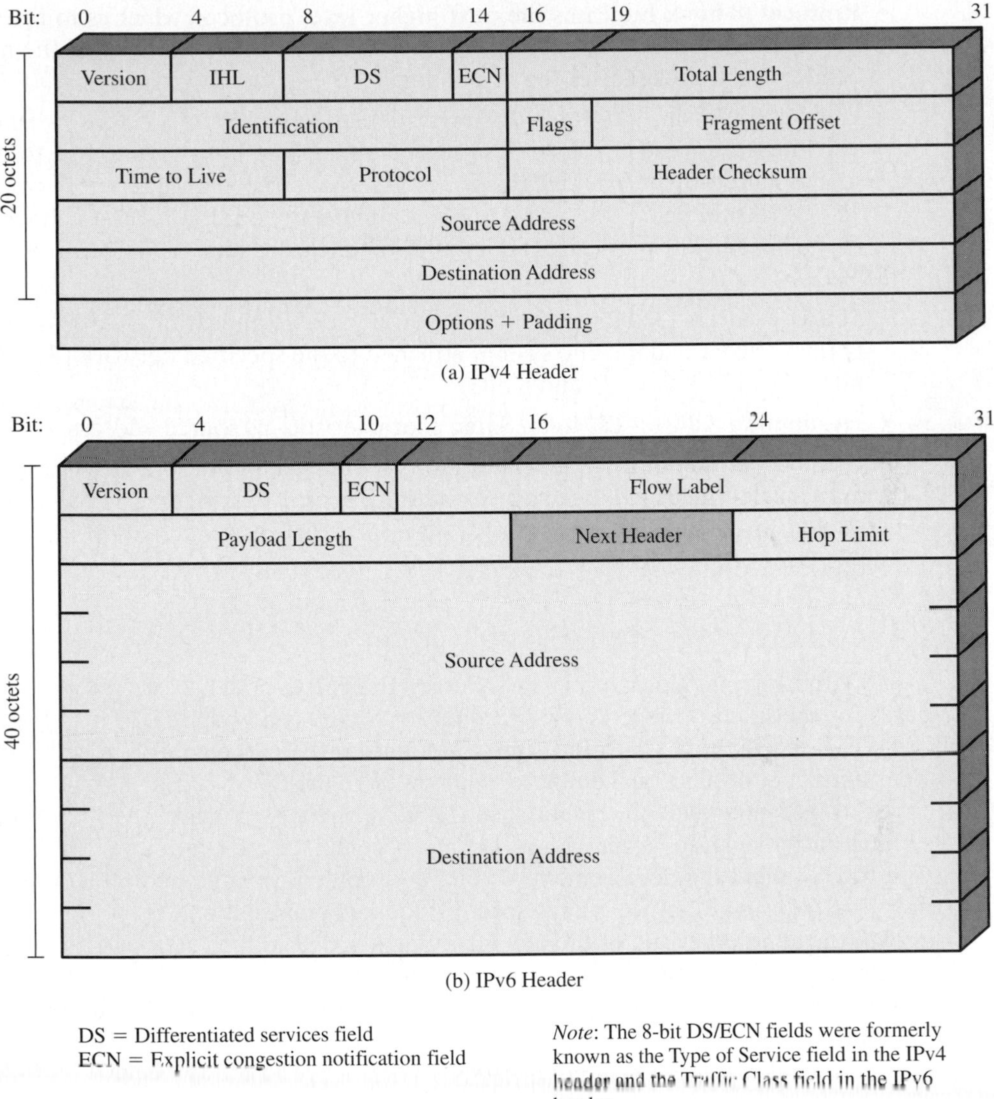

Figure 16.14 IP Headers

exceeds the maximum size of an en route subnetwork. Therefore, if the bit is set, it may be advisable to use source routing to avoid subnetworks with small maximum packet size.

- **Fragment Offset (13 bits):** Indicates where in the original packet this fragment belongs, measured in 64-bit units. This implies that fragments other than the last fragment must contain a data field that is a multiple of 64 bits in length.
- **Time to Live (8 bits):** Specifies how long, in seconds, a packet is allowed to remain in the internet. Every router that processes a packet must decrease the TTL by at least one, so the TTL is somewhat similar to a hop count.

- **Protocol (8 bits):** Indicates the next higher level protocol, which is to receive the data field at the destination; thus, this field identifies the type of the next header in the packet after the IP header.
- **Header Checksum (16 bits):** An error-detecting code applied to the header only. Because some header fields may change during transit (e.g., time to live, segmentation-related fields), this is reverified and recomputed at each router. The checksum field is the 16-bit one's complement addition of all 16-bit words in the header. For purposes of computation, the checksum field is itself initialized to a value of zero.
- **Source Address (32 bits):** Coded to allow a variable allocation of bits to specify the network and the end system attached to the specified network (7 and 24 bits, 14 and 16 bits, or 21 and 8 bits).
- **Destination Address (32 bits):** Same characteristics as source address.
- **Options (variable):** Encodes the options requested by the sending user; these may include security label, source routing, record routing, and timestamping.
- **Padding (variable):** Used to ensure that the packet header is a multiple of 32 bits in length.

IPv6

In 1995, the Internet Engineering Task Force (IETF), which develops protocol standards for the Internet, issued a specification for a next-generation IP, known then as IPng. This specification was turned into a standard in 1996 known as IPv6. IPv6 provides a number of functional enhancements over the existing IP (known as IPv4), designed to accommodate the higher speeds of today's networks and the mix of data streams, including graphic and video, that are becoming more prevalent. But the driving force behind the development of the new protocol was the need for more addresses. IPv4 uses a 32-bit address to specify a source or destination. With the explosive growth of the Internet and of private networks attached to the Internet, this address length became insufficient to accommodate all systems needing addresses. As Figure 16.14b shows, IPv6 includes 128-bit source and destination address fields. Ultimately, all installations using TCP/IP are expected to migrate from the current IP to IPv6, but this process will take many years, if not decades.

IPv6 Header The IPv6 header has a fixed length of 40 octets, consisting of the following fields (Figure 16.14b):

- **Version (4 bits):** Internet Protocol version number; the value is 6.
- **DS/ECN (8 bits):** Prior to the introduction of differentiated services, this field was referred to as the **Traffic Class** field and was reserved for use by originating nodes and/or forwarding routers to identify and distinguish between different classes or priorities of IPv6 packets. The first six bits of the Traffic Class field are now referred to as the DS (Differentiated Services) field. The remaining 2 bits are reserved for an ECN (Explicit Congestion Notification) field.
- **Flow Label (20 bits):** May be used by a host to label those packets for which it is requesting special handling by routers within a network. Flow labeling may assist resource reservation and real-time traffic processing.

- **Payload Length (16 bits):** Length of the remainder of the IPv6 packet following the header, in octets. In other words, this is the total length of all of the extension headers plus the transport-level PDU.
- **Next Header (8 bits):** Identifies the type of header immediately following the IPv6 header; this will either be an IPv6 extension header or a higher-layer header, such as TCP or UDP.
- **Hop Limit (8 bits):** The remaining number of allowable hops for this packet. The hop limit is set to some desired maximum value by the source and decremented by 1 by each node that forwards the packet. The packet is discarded if Hop Limit is decremented to zero.
- **Source Address (128 bits):** The address of the originator of the packet.
- **Destination Address (128 bits):** The address of the intended recipient of the packet. This may not in fact be the intended ultimate destination if a Routing extension header is present, as explained later.

Although the IPv6 header is longer than the mandatory portion of the IPv4 header (40 octets versus 20 octets), it contains fewer fields (8 versus 12). Thus, routers have less processing to do per header, which should speed up routing.

IPv6 Extension Headers An IPv6 packet includes the IPv6 header, just discussed, and zero or more extension headers. Outside of IPSec, the following extension headers have been defined:

- **Hop-by-Hop Options Header:** Defines special options that require hop-by-hop processing
- **Routing Header:** Provides extended routing, similar to IPv4 source routing
- **Fragment Header:** Contains fragmentation and reassembly information
- **Authentication Header:** Provides packet integrity and authentication
- **Encapsulating Security Payload Header:** Provides privacy
- **Destination Options Header:** Contains optional information to be examined by the destination node

The IPv6 standard recommends that, when multiple extension headers are used, the IPv6 headers appear in the following order:

1. IPv6 header: Mandatory, must always appear first
2. Hop-by-Hop Options header
3. Destination Options header: For options to be processed by the first destination that appears in the IPv6 Destination Address field plus subsequent destinations listed in the Routing header
4. Routing header
5. Fragment header
6. Authentication header
7. Encapsulating Security Payload header

8. Destination Options header: For options to be processed only by the final destination of the packet

Figure 16.15 shows an example of an IPv6 packet that includes an instance of each nonsecurity header. Note that the IPv6 header and each extension header include a Next Header field. This field identifies the type of the immediately following header. If the next header is an extension header, then this field contains the type identifier of that header. Otherwise, this field contains the protocol identifier of the upper-layer protocol using IPv6 (typically a transport-level protocol), using the same values as the IPv4 Protocol field. In the figure, the upper-layer protocol is TCP, so the upper-layer data carried by the IPv6 packet consist of a TCP header followed by a block of application data.

The **Hop-by-Hop Options header** carries optional information that, if present, must be examined by every router along the path. The header consists of the following fields:

- **Next Header (8 bits):** Identifies the type of header immediately following this header.

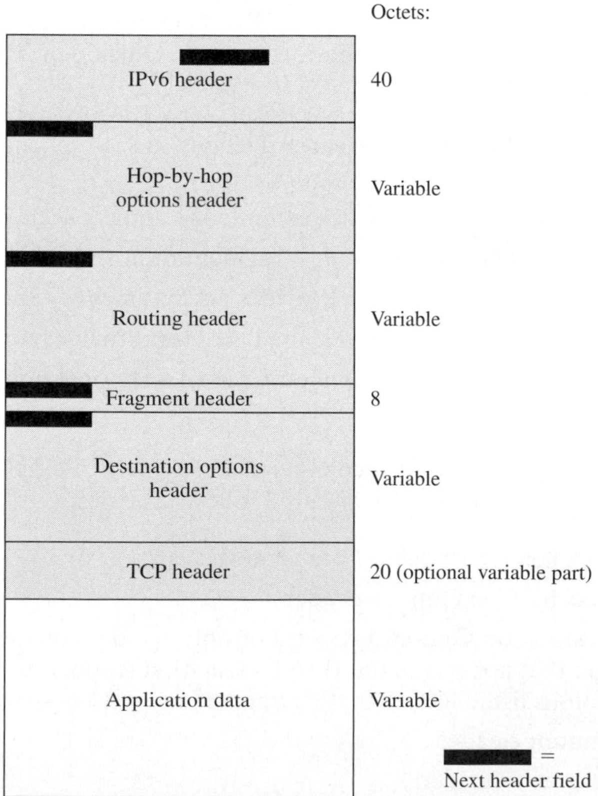

Figure 16.15 Ipv6 Packet with Extension Headers (containing a TCP segment)

- **Header Extension Length (8 bits):** Length of this header in 64-bit units, not including the first 64 bits.
- **Options:** Contains one or more options. Each option consists of three subfields: a tag, indicating the option type; a length, and a value.

Only one option has so far been defined: the Jumbo Payload option, used to send IPv6 packets with payloads longer than $2^{16} - 1 = 65{,}535$ octets. The Option Data field of this option is 32 bits long and gives the length of the packet in octets, excluding the IPv6 header. For such packets, the Payload Length field in the IPv6 header must be set to zero, and there must be no Fragment header. With this option, IPv6 supports packet sizes up to more than 4 billion octets. This facilitates the transmission of large video packets and enables IPv6 to make the best use of available capacity over any transmission medium.

The **Routing header** contains a list of one or more intermediate nodes to be visited on the way to a packet's destination. All routing headers start with a 32-bit block consisting of four 8-bit fields, followed by routing data specific to a given routing type. The four 8-bit fields are Next Header, Header Extension Length, and

- **Routing Type:** Identifies a particular Routing header variant. If a router does not recognize the Routing Type value, it must discard the packet.
- **Segments Left:** Number of explicitly listed intermediate nodes still to be visited before reaching the final destination.

In addition to this general header definition, the IPv6 specification defines the Type 0 Routing header. When using the Type 0 Routing header, the source node does not place the ultimate destination address in the IPv6 header. Instead, that address is the last address listed in the Routing header, and the IPv6 header contains the destination address of the first desired router on the path. The Routing header will not be examined until the packet reaches the node identified in the IPv6 header. At that point, the IPv6 and Routing header contents are updated and the packet is forwarded. The update consists of placing the next address to be visited in the IPv6 header and decrementing the Segments Left field in the Routing header.

IPv6 requires an IPv6 node to reverse routes in a packet it receives containing a Routing header, to return a packet to the sender.

The **Fragment header** is used by a source when fragmentation is required. In IPv6, fragmentation may only be performed by source nodes, not by routers along a packet's delivery path. To take full advantage of the internetworking environment, a node must perform a path discovery algorithm that enables it to learn the smallest maximum transmission unit (MTU) supported by any subnetwork on the path. In other words, the path discovery algorithm enables a node to learn the MTU of the "bottleneck" subnetwork on the path. With this knowledge, the source node will fragment, as required, for each given destination address. Otherwise the source must limit all packets to 1280 octets, which is the minimum MTU that must be supported by each subnetwork.

In addition to the Next Header field, the fragment header includes the following fields:

- **Fragment Offset (13 bits):** Indicates where in the original packet the payload of this fragment belongs. It is measured in 64-bit units. This implies that fragments (other than the last fragment) must contain a data field that is a multiple of 64 bits long.

- **Res (2 bits):** Reserved for future use.
- **M Flag (1 bit):** 1 = more fragments; 0 = last fragment.
- **Identification (32 bits):** Intended to identify uniquely the original packet. The identifier must be unique for the packet's source address and destination address for the time during which the packet will remain in the internet. All fragments with the same identifier, source address, and destination address are reassembled to form the original packet.

The **Destination Options header** carries optional information that, if present, is examined only by the packet's destination node. The format of this header is the same as that of the Hop-by-Hop Options header.

CHAPTER 17

Web Security

Use your mentality
Wake up to reality

—From the song, "I've Got You under My Skin"
by Cole Porter

KEY POINTS

- Secure socket layer (SSL) provides security services between TCP and applications that use TCP. The Internet standard version is called transport layer service (TLS).
- SSL/TLS provides confidentiality using symmetric encryption and message integrity using a message authentication code.
- SSL/TLS includes protocol mechanisms to enable two TCP users to determine the security mechanisms and services they will use.
- Secure electronic transaction (SET) is an open encryption and security specification designed to protect credit card transactions on the Internet.

Virtually all businesses, most government agencies, and many individuals now have Web sites. The number of individuals and companies with Internet access is expanding rapidly and all of these have graphical Web browsers. As a result, businesses are enthusiastic about setting up facilities on the Web for electronic commerce. But the reality is that the Internet and the Web are extremely vulnerable to compromises of various sorts. As businesses wake up to this reality, the demand for secure Web services grows.

The topic of Web security is a broad one and can easily fill a book (several are recommended at the end of this chapter). In this chapter, we begin with a discussion of the general requirements for Web security and then focus on two standardized schemes that are becoming increasingly important as part of Web commerce: SSL/TLS and SET.

17.1 WEB SECURITY CONSIDERATIONS

The World Wide Web is fundamentally a client/server application running over the Internet and TCP/IP intranets. As such, the security tools and approaches discussed so far in this book are relevant to the issue of Web security. But, as pointed out in [GARF97], the Web presents new challenges not generally appreciated in the context of computer and network security:

- The Internet is two way. Unlike traditional publishing environments, even electronic publishing systems involving teletext, voice response, or fax-back, the Web is vulnerable to attacks on the Web servers over the Internet.
- The Web is increasingly serving as a highly visible outlet for corporate and product information and as the platform for business transactions. Reputations can be damaged and money can be lost if the Web servers are subverted.

- Although Web browsers are very easy to use, Web servers are relatively easy to configure and manage, and Web content is increasingly easy to develop, the underlying software is extraordinarily complex. This complex software may hide many potential security flaws. The short history of the Web is filled with examples of new and upgraded systems, properly installed, that are vulnerable to a variety of security attacks.
- A Web server can be exploited as a launching pad into the corporation's or agency's entire computer complex. Once the Web server is subverted, an attacker may be able to gain access to data and systems not part of the Web itself but connected to the server at the local site.
- Casual and untrained (in security matters) users are common clients for Web-based services. Such users are not necessarily aware of the security risks that exist and do not have the tools or knowledge to take effective countermeasures.

Web Security Threats

Table 17.1 provides a summary of the types of security threats faced in using the Web. One way to group these threats is in terms of passive and active attacks. Passive attacks include eavesdropping on network traffic between browser and server and gaining access to information on a Web site that is supposed to be restricted. Active attacks include impersonating another user, altering messages in transit between client and server, and altering information on a Web site.

Another way to classify Web security threats is in terms of the location of the threat: Web server, Web browser, and network traffic between browser and server. Issues of server and browser security fall into the category of computer system security; Part Four of this book addresses the issue of system security in general but is also applicable to Web system security. Issues of traffic security fall into the category of network security and are addressed in this chapter.

Web Traffic Security Approaches

A number of approaches to providing Web security are possible. The various approaches that have been considered are similar in the services they provide and, to some extent, in the mechanisms that they use, but they differ with respect to their scope of applicability and their relative location within the TCP/IP protocol stack.

Figure 17.1 illustrates this difference. One way to provide Web security is to use IP Security (Figure 17.1a). The advantage of using IPSec is that it is transparent to end users and applications and provides a general-purpose solution. Further, IPSec includes a filtering capability so that only selected traffic need incur the overhead of IPSec processing.

Another relatively general-purpose solution is to implement security just above TCP (Figure 17.1b). The foremost example of this approach is the Secure Sockets Layer (SSL) and the follow-on Internet standard known as Transport Layer Security (TLS). At this level, there are two implementation choices. For full generality, SSL (or TLS) could be provided as part of the underlying protocol suite and therefore be transparent to applications. Alternatively, SSL can be embedded in specific packages.

Table 17.1 A Comparison of Threats on the Web [RUBI97]

	Threats	Consequences	Countermeasures
Integrity	• Modification of user data • Trojan horse browser • Modification of memory • Modification of message traffic in transit	• Loss of information • Compromise of machine • Vulnerabilty to all other threats	Cryptographic checksums
Confidentiality	• Eavesdropping on the Net • Theft of info from server • Theft of data from client • Info about network configuration • Info about which client talks to server	• Loss of information • Loss of privacy	Encryption, web proxies
Denial of Service	• Killing of user threads • Flooding machine with bogus requests • Filling up disk or memory • Isolating machine by DNS attacks	• Disruptive • Annoying • Prevent user from getting work done	Difficult to prevent
Authentication	• Impersonation of legitimate users • Data forgery	• Misrepresentation of user • Belief that false information is valid	Cryptographic techniques

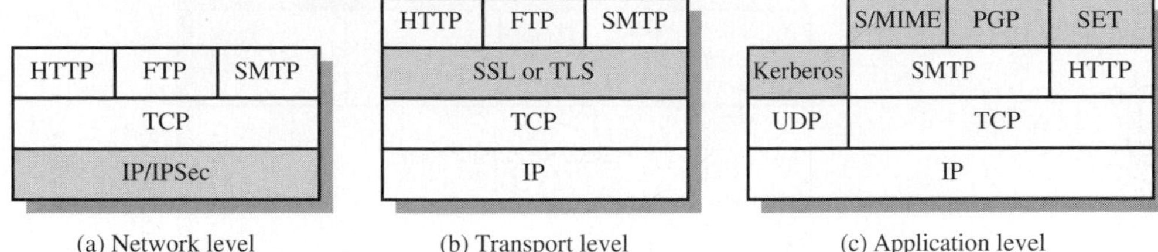

(a) Network level (b) Transport level (c) Application level

Figure 17.1 Relative Location of Security Facilities in the TCP/IP Protocol Stack

For example, Netscape and Microsoft Explorer browsers come equipped with SSL, and most Web servers have implemented the protocol.

Application-specific security services are embedded within the particular application. Figure 17.1c shows examples of this architecture. The advantage of this approach is that the service can be tailored to the specific needs of a given application. In the context of Web security, an important example of this approach is Secure Electronic Transaction (SET).[1]

The remainder of this chapter is devoted to a discussion of SSL/TLS and SET.

17.2 SECURE SOCKET LAYER AND TRANSPORT LAYER SECURITY

Netscape originated SSL. Version 3 of the protocol was designed with public review and input from industry and was published as an Internet draft document. Subsequently, when a consensus was reached to submit the protocol for Internet standardization, the TLS working group was formed within IETF to develop a common standard. This first published version of TLS can be viewed as essentially an SSLv3.1 and is very close to and backward compatible with SSLv3.

The bulk of this section is devoted to a discussion of SSLv3. At the end of the section, the principal differences between SSLv3 and TLS are described.

SSL Architecture

SSL is designed to make use of TCP to provide a reliable end-to-end secure service. SSL is not a single protocol but rather two layers of protocols, as illustrated in Figure 17.2.

The SSL Record Protocol provides basic security services to various higher-layer protocols. In particular, the Hypertext Transfer Protocol (HTTP), which provides the transfer service for Web client/server interaction, can operate on top of SSL. Three higher-layer protocols are defined as part of SSL: the Handshake Protocol, The Change Cipher Spec Protocol, and the Alert Protocol. These SSL-specific protocols are used in the management of SSL exchanges and are examined later in this section.

[1]Figure 17.1c shows SET on top of HTTP; this is a common implementation. In some implementations, SET makes use of TCP directly.

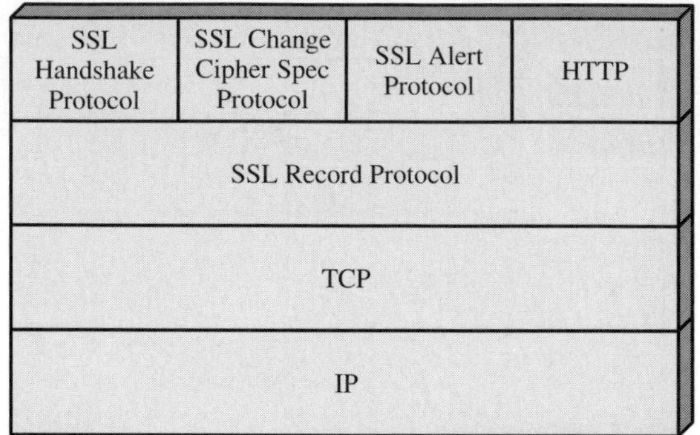

Figure 17.2 SSL Protocol Stack

Two important SSL concepts are the SSL session and the SSL connection, which are defined in the specification as follows:

- **Connection:** A connection is a transport (in the OSI layering model definition) that provides a suitable type of service. For SSL, such connections are peer-to-peer relationships. The connections are transient. Every connection is associated with one session.
- **Session:** An SSL session is an association between a client and a server. Sessions are created by the Handshake Protocol. Sessions define a set of cryptographic security parameters, which can be shared among multiple connections. Sessions are used to avoid the expensive negotiation of new security parameters for each connection.

Between any pair of parties (applications such as HTTP on client and server), there may be multiple secure connections. In theory, there may also be multiple simultaneous sessions between parties, but this feature is not used in practice.

There are actually a number of states associated with each session. Once a session is established, there is a current operating state for both read and write (i.e., receive and send). In addition, during the Handshake Protocol, pending read and write states are created. Upon successful conclusion of the Handshake Protocol, the pending states become the current states.

A session state is defined by the following parameters (definitions taken from the SSL specification):

- **Session identifier:** An arbitrary byte sequence chosen by the server to identify an active or resumable session state.
- **Peer certificate:** An X509.v3 certificate of the peer. This element of the state may be null.
- **Compression method:** The algorithm used to compress data prior to encryption.
- **Cipher spec:** Specifies the bulk data encryption algorithm (such as null, AES, etc.) and a hash algorithm (such as MD5 or SHA-1) used for

MAC calculation. It also defines cryptographic attributes such as the hash_size.

- **Master secret:** 48-byte secret shared between the client and server.
- **Is resumable:** A flag indicating whether the session can be used to initiate new connections.

A connection state is defined by the following parameters:

- **Server and client random:** Byte sequences that are chosen by the server and client for each connection.
- **Server write MAC secret:** The secret key used in MAC operations on data sent by the server.
- **Client write MAC secret:** The secret key used in MAC operations on data sent by the client.
- **Server write key:** The conventional encryption key for data encrypted by the server and decrypted by the client.
- **Client write key:** The conventional encryption key for data encrypted by the client and decrypted by the server.
- **Initialization vectors:** When a block cipher in CBC mode is used, an initialization vector (IV) is maintained for each key. This field is first initialized by the SSL Handshake Protocol. Thereafter the final ciphertext block from each record is preserved for use as the IV with the following record.
- **Sequence numbers:** Each party maintains separate sequence numbers for transmitted and received messages for each connection. When a party sends or receives a change cipher spec message, the appropriate sequence number is set to zero. Sequence numbers may not exceed $2^{64} - 1$.

SSL Record Protocol

The SSL Record Protocol provides two services for SSL connections:

- **Confidentiality:** The Handshake Protocol defines a shared secret key that is used for conventional encryption of SSL payloads.
- **Message Integrity:** The Handshake Protocol also defines a shared secret key that is used to form a message authentication code (MAC).

Figure 17.3 indicates the overall operation of the SSL Record Protocol. The Record Protocol takes an application message to be transmitted, fragments the data into manageable blocks, optionally compresses the data, applies a MAC, encrypts, adds a header, and transmits the resulting unit in a TCP segment. Received data are decrypted, verified, decompressed, and reassembled and then delivered to higher-level users.

The first step is **fragmentation**. Each upper-layer message is fragmented into blocks of 2^{14} bytes (16384 bytes) or less. Next, **compression** is optionally applied. Compression must be lossless and may not increase the content length by more

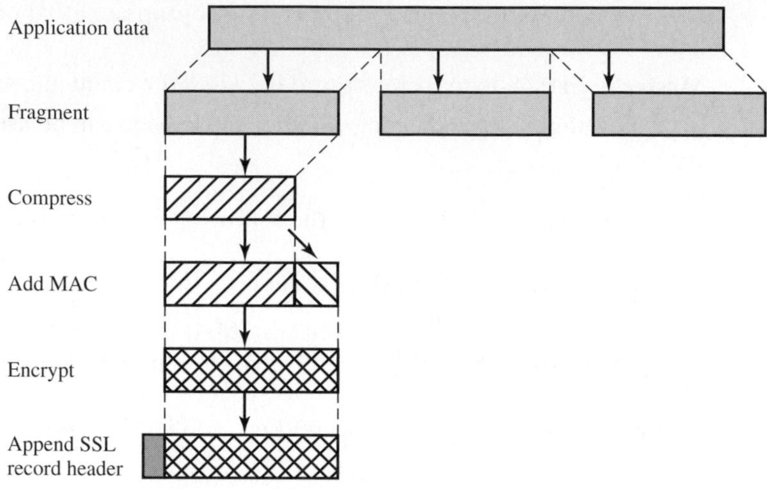

Figure 17.3 SSL Record Protocol Operation

than 1024 bytes.[2] In SSLv3 (as well as the current version of TLS), no compression algorithm is specified, so the default compression algorithm is null.

The next step in processing is to compute a **message authentication code** over the compressed data. For this purpose, a shared secret key is used. The calculation is defined as

```
hash(MAC_write_secret || pad_2 ||
     hash(MAC_write_secret || pad_1 || seq_num ||
     SSLCompressed.type ||
     SSLCompressed.length || SSLCompressed.fragment))
```

where

||	= concatenation
MAC_write_secret	= shared secret key
hash	= cryptographic hash algorithm; either MD5 or SHA-1
pad_1	= the byte 0x36 (0011 0110) repeated 48 times (384 bits) for MD5 and 40 times (320 bits) for SHA-1
pad_2	= the byte 0x5C (0101 1100) repeated 48 times for MD5 and 40 times for SHA-1
seq_num	= the sequence number for this message

[2]Of course, one hopes that compression shrinks rather than expands the data. However, for very short blocks, it is possible, because of formatting conventions, that the compression algorithm will actually provide output that is longer than the input.

SSLCompressed.type = the higher-level protocol used to process this fragment

SSLCompressed.length = the length of the compressed fragment

SSLCompressed.fragment = the compressed fragment (if compression is not used, the plaintext fragment)

Note that this is very similar to the HMAC algorithm defined in Chapter 12. The difference is that the two pads are concatenated in SSLv3 and are XORed in HMAC. The SSLv3 MAC algorithm is based on the original Internet draft for HMAC, which used concatenation. The final version of HMAC, defined in RFC 2104, uses the XOR.

Next, the compressed message plus the MAC are **encrypted** using symmetric encryption. Encryption may not increase the content length by more than 1024 bytes, so that the total length may not exceed $2^{14} + 2048$. The following encryption algorithms are permitted:

Block Cipher		Stream Cipher	
Algorithm	**Key Size**	**Algorithm**	**Key Size**
AES	128, 256	RC4-40	40
IDEA	128	RC4-128	128
RC2-40	40		
DES-40	40		
DES	56		
3DES	168		
Fortezza	80		

Fortezza can be used in a smart card encryption scheme.

For stream encryption, the compressed message plus the MAC are encrypted. Note that the MAC is computed before encryption takes place and that the MAC is then encrypted along with the plaintext or compressed plaintext.

For block encryption, padding may be added after the MAC prior to encryption. The padding is in the form of a number of padding bytes followed by a one-byte indication of the length of the padding. The total amount of padding is the smallest amount such that the total size of the data to be encrypted (plaintext plus MAC plus padding) is a multiple of the cipher's block length. An example is a plaintext (or compressed text if compression is used) of 58 bytes, with a MAC of 20 bytes (using SHA-1), that is encrypted using a block length of 8 bytes (e.g., DES). With the padding.length byte, this yields a total of 79 bytes. To make the total an integer multiple of 8, one byte of padding is added.

The final step of SSL Record Protocol processing is to prepend a header, consisting of the following fields:

- **Content Type (8 bits):** The higher layer protocol used to process the enclosed fragment.
- **Major Version (8 bits):** Indicates major version of SSL in use. For SSLv3, the value is 3.

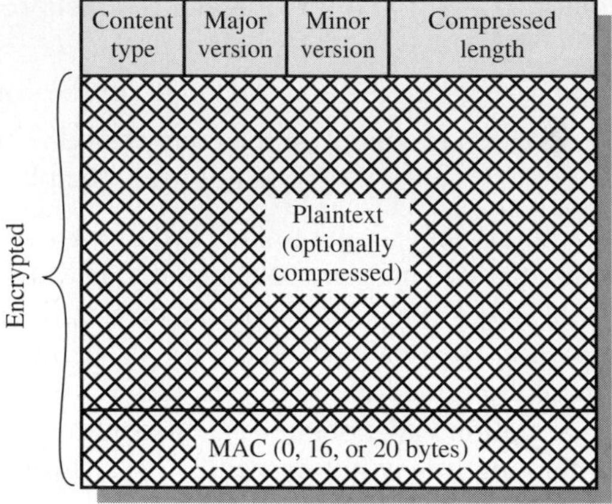

Figure 17.4 SSL Record Format

- **Minor Version (8 bits):** Indicates minor version in use. For SSLv3, the value is 0.
- **Compressed Length (16 bits):** The length in bytes of the plaintext fragment (or compressed fragment if compression is used). The maximum value is $2^{14} + 2048$.

The content types that have been defined are change_cipher_spec, alert, handshake, and application_data. The first three are the SSL-specific protocols, discussed next. Note that no distinction is made among the various applications (e.g., HTTP) that might use SSL; the content of the data created by such applications is opaque to SSL.

Figure 17.4 illustrates the SSL record format.

Change Cipher Spec Protocol

The Change Cipher Spec Protocol is one of the three SSL-specific protocols that use the SSL Record Protocol, and it is the simplest. This protocol consists of a single message (Figure 17.5a), which consists of a single byte with the value 1. The sole purpose

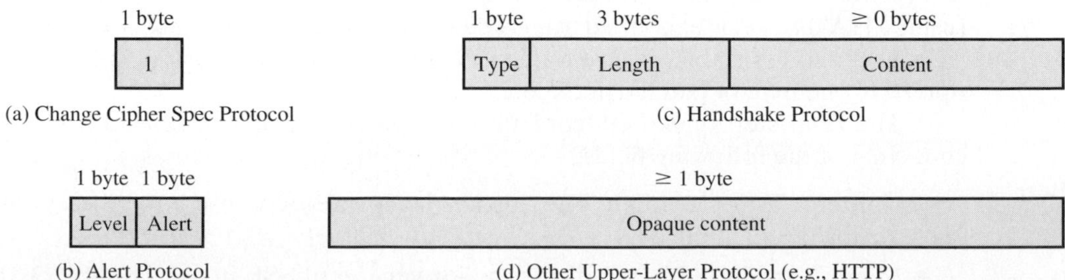

Figure 17.5 SSL Record Protocol Payload

of this message is to cause the pending state to be copied into the current state, which updates the cipher suite to be used on this connection.

Alert Protocol

The Alert Protocol is used to convey SSL-related alerts to the peer entity. As with other applications that use SSL, alert messages are compressed and encrypted, as specified by the current state.

Each message in this protocol consists of two bytes (Figure 17.5b). The first byte takes the value warning(1) or fatal(2) to convey the severity of the message. If the level is fatal, SSL immediately terminates the connection. Other connections on the same session may continue, but no new connections on this session may be established. The second byte contains a code that indicates the specific alert. First, we list those alerts that are always fatal (definitions from the SSL specification):

- **unexpected_message:** An inappropriate message was received.
- **bad_record_mac:** An incorrect MAC was received.
- **decompression_failure:** The decompression function received improper input (e.g., unable to decompress or decompress to greater than maximum allowable length).
- **handshake_failure:** Sender was unable to negotiate an acceptable set of security parameters given the options available.
- **illegal_parameter:** A field in a handshake message was out of range or inconsistent with other fields.

The remainder of the alerts are the following:

- **close_notify:** Notifies the recipient that the sender will not send any more messages on this connection. Each party is required to send a close_notify alert before closing the write side of a connection.
- **no_certificate:** May be sent in response to a certificate request if no appropriate certificate is available.
- **bad_certificate:** A received certificate was corrupt (e.g., contained a signature that did not verify).
- **unsupported_certificate:** The type of the received certificate is not supported.
- **certificate_revoked:** A certificate has been revoked by its signer.
- **certificate_expired:** A certificate has expired.
- **certificate_unknown:** Some other unspecified issue arose in processing the certificate, rendering it unacceptable.

Handshake Protocol

The most complex part of SSL is the Handshake Protocol. This protocol allows the server and client to authenticate each other and to negotiate an encryption and MAC algorithm and cryptographic keys to be used to protect data sent in an SSL record. The Handshake Protocol is used before any application data is transmitted.

Table 17.2 SSL Handshake Protocol Message Types

Message Type	Parameters
hello_request	null
client_hello	version, random, session id, cipher suite, compression method
server_hello	version, random, session id, cipher suite, compression method
certificate	chain of X.509v3 certificates
server_key_exchange	parameters, signature
certificate_request	type, authorities
server_done	null
certificate_verify	signature
client_key_exchange	parameters, signature
finished	hash value

The Handshake Protocol consists of a series of messages exchanged by client and server. All of these have the format shown in Figure 17.5c. Each message has three fields:

- **Type (1 byte):** Indicates one of 10 messages. Table 17.2 lists the defined message types.
- **Length (3 bytes):** The length of the message in bytes.
- **Content** (**≥0 bytes**)**:** The parameters associated with this message; these are listed in Table 17.2.

Figure 17.6 shows the initial exchange needed to establish a logical connection between client and server. The exchange can be viewed as having four phases.

Phase 1. Establish Security Capabilities This phase is used to initiate a logical connection and to establish the security capabilities that will be associated with it. The exchange is initiated by the client, which sends a **client_hello message** with the following parameters:

- **Version:** The highest SSL version understood by the client.
- **Random:** A client-generated random structure, consisting of a 32-bit timestamp and 28 bytes generated by a secure random number generator. These values serve as nonces and are used during key exchange to prevent replay attacks.
- **Session ID:** A variable-length session identifier. A nonzero value indicates that the client wishes to update the parameters of an existing connection or create a new connection on this session. A zero value indicates that the client wishes to establish a new connection on a new session.
- **CipherSuite:** This is a list that contains the combinations of cryptographic algorithms supported by the client, in decreasing order of preference. Each element of the list (each cipher suite) defines both a key exchange algorithm and a CipherSpec; these are discussed subsequently.
- **Compression Method:** This is a list of the compression methods the client supports.

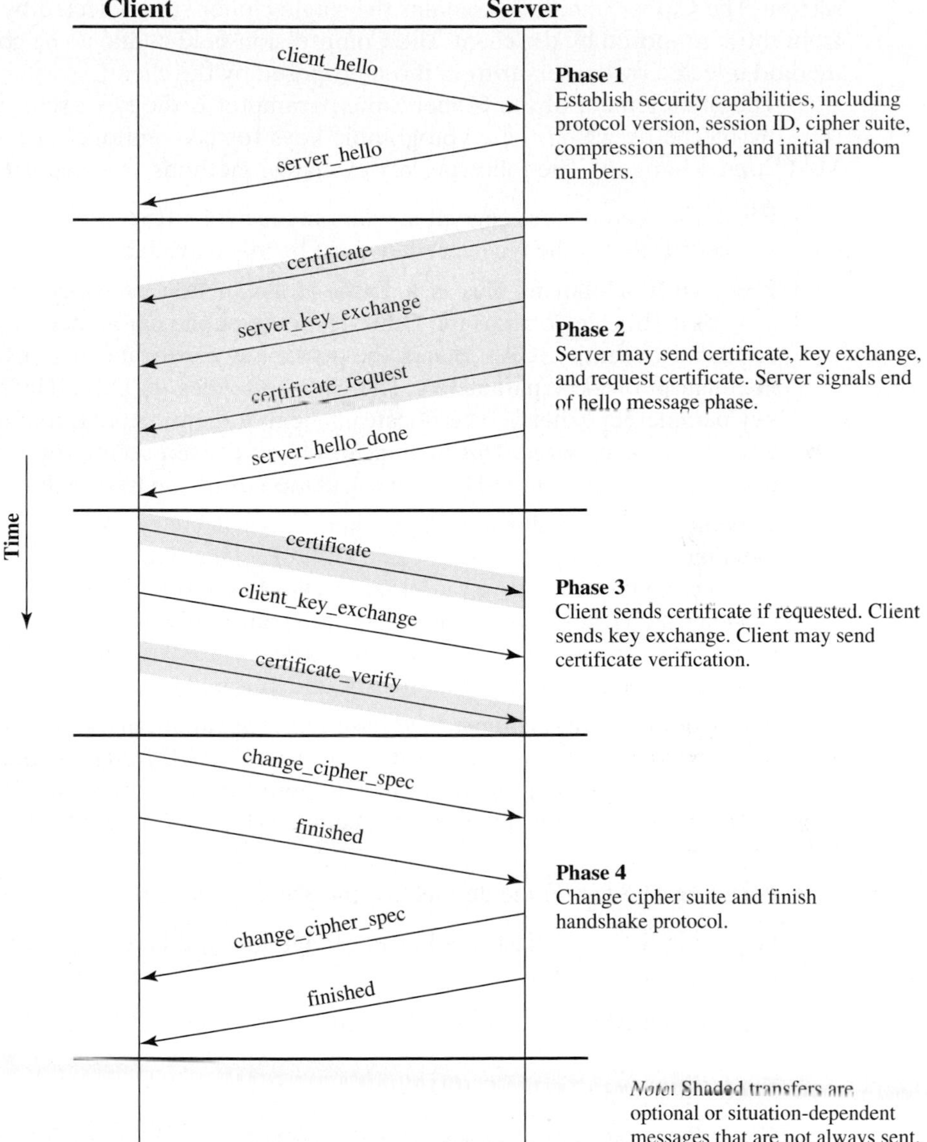

Figure 17.6 Handshake Protocol Action

After sending the client_hello message, the client waits for the **server_hello message**, which contains the same parameters as the client_hello message. For the server_hello message, the following conventions apply. The Version field contains the lower of the version suggested by the client and the highest supported by the server. The Random field is generated by the server and is independent of the client's Random field. If the SessionID field of the client was nonzero, the same value is used by the server; otherwise the server's SessionID field contains the value for a new session. The CipherSuite field contains the single cipher suite selected by the server from those proposed by the client. The Compression field contains the compression method selected by the server from those proposed by the client.

The first element of the Cipher Suite parameter is the key exchange method (i.e., the means by which the cryptographic keys for conventional encryption and MAC are exchanged). The following key exchange methods are supported:

- **RSA:** The secret key is encrypted with the receiver's RSA public key. A public-key certificate for the receiver's key must be made available.
- **Fixed Diffie-Hellman:** This is a Diffie-Hellman key exchange in which the server's certificate contains the Diffie-Hellman public parameters signed by the certificate authority (CA). That is, the public-key certificate contains the Diffie-Hellman public-key parameters. The client provides its Diffie-Hellman public key parameters either in a certificate, if client authentication is required, or in a key exchange message. This method results in a fixed secret key between two peers, based on the Diffie-Hellman calculation using the fixed public keys.
- **Ephemeral Diffie-Hellman:** This technique is used to create ephemeral (temporary, one-time) secret keys. In this case, the Diffie-Hellman public keys are exchanged, signed using the sender's private RSA or DSS key. The receiver can use the corresponding public key to verify the signature. Certificates are used to authenticate the public keys. This would appear to be the most secure of the three Diffie-Hellman options because it results in a temporary, authenticated key.
- **Anonymous Diffie-Hellman:** The base Diffie-Hellman algorithm is used, with no authentication. That is, each side sends its public Diffie-Hellman parameters to the other, with no authentication. This approach is vulnerable to man-in-the-middle attacks, in which the attacker conducts anonymous Diffie-Hellman with both parties.
- **Fortezza:** The technique defined for the Fortezza scheme.

Following the definition of a key exchange method is the CipherSpec, which includes the following fields:

- **CipherAlgorithm:** Any of the algorithms mentioned earlier: RC4, RC2, DES, 3DES, DES40, IDEA, Fortezza
- **MACAlgorithm:** MD5 or SHA-1
- **CipherType:** Stream or Block
- **IsExportable:** True or False
- **HashSize:** 0, 16 (for MD5), or 20 (for SHA-1) bytes
- **Key Material:** A sequence of bytes that contain data used in generating the write keys
- **IV Size:** The size of the Initialization Value for Cipher Block Chaining (CBC) encryption

Phase 2. Server Authentication and Key Exchange The server begins this phase by sending its certificate, if it needs to be authenticated; the message contains one or a chain of X.509 certificates. The **certificate message** is required for any agreed-on key exchange method except anonymous Diffie-Hellman. Note that if fixed Diffie-Hellman is used, this certificate message functions as the server's key exchange message because it contains the server's public Diffie-Hellman parameters.

Next, a **server_key_exchange message** may be sent if it is required. It is not required in two instances: (1) The server has sent a certificate with fixed Diffie-Hellman parameters, or (2) RSA key exchange is to be used. The server_key_exchange message is needed for the following:

- **Anonymous Diffie-Hellman:** The message content consists of the two global Diffie-Hellman values (a prime number and a primitive root of that number) plus the server's public Diffie-Hellman key (see Figure 10.7).
- **Ephemeral Diffie-Hellman:** The message content includes the three Diffie-Hellman parameters provided for anonymous Diffie-Hellman, plus a signature of those parameters.
- **RSA key exchange, in which the server is using RSA but has a signature-only RSA key:** Accordingly, the client cannot simply send a secret key encrypted with the server's public key. Instead, the server must create a temporary RSA public/private key pair and use the server_key_exchange message to send the public key. The message content includes the two parameters of the temporary RSA public key (exponent and modulus; see Figure 9.5) plus a signature of those parameters.
- **Fortezza**

Some further details about the signatures are warranted. As usual, a signature is created by taking the hash of a message and encrypting it with the sender's private key. In this case the hash is defined as

```
hash(ClientHello.random || ServerHello.random || ServerParams)
```

So the hash covers not only the Diffie-Hellman or RSA parameters, but also the two nonces from the initial hello messages. This ensures against replay attacks and misrepresentation. In the case of a DSS signature, the hash is performed using the SHA-1 algorithm. In the case of an RSA signature, both an MD5 and an SHA-1 hash are calculated, and the concatenation of the two hashes (36 bytes) is encrypted with the server's private key.

Next, a nonanonymous server (server not using anonymous Diffie-Hellman) can request a certificate from the client. The **certificate_request message** includes two parameters: certificate_type and certificate_authorities. The certificate type indicates the public-key algorithm and its use:

- RSA, signature only
- DSS, signature only
- RSA for fixed Diffie-Hellman; in this case the signature is used only for authentication, by sending a certificate signed with RSA
- DSS for fixed Diffie-Hellman; again, used only for authentication

- RSA for ephemeral Diffie-Hellman
- DSS for ephemeral Diffie-Hellman
- Fortezza

The second parameter in the certificate_request message is a list of the distinguished names of acceptable certificate authorities.

The final message in Phase 2, and one that is always required, is the **server_done message**, which is sent by the server to indicate the end of the server hello and associated messages. After sending this message, the server will wait for a client response. This message has no parameters.

Phase 3. Client Authentication and Key Exchange Upon receipt of the server_done message, the client should verify that the server provided a valid certificate if required and check that the server_hello parameters are acceptable. If all is satisfactory, the client sends one or more messages back to the server.

If the server has requested a certificate, the client begins this phase by sending a **certificate message**. If no suitable certificate is available, the client sends a no_certificate alert instead.

Next is the **client_key_exchange message**, which must be sent in this phase. The content of the message depends on the type of key exchange, as follows:

- **RSA:** The client generates a 48-byte *pre-master secret* and encrypts with the public key from the server's certificate or temporary RSA key from a server_key_exchange message. Its use to compute a *master secret* is explained later.
- **Ephemeral or Anonymous Diffie-Hellman:** The client's public Diffie-Hellman parameters are sent.
- **Fixed Diffie-Hellman:** The client's public Diffie-Hellman parameters were sent in a certificate message, so the content of this message is null.
- **Fortezza:** The client's Fortezza parameters are sent.

Finally, in this phase, the client may send a **certificate_verify message** to provide explicit verification of a client certificate. This message is only sent following any client certificate that has signing capability (i.e., all certificates except those containing fixed Diffie-Hellman parameters). This message signs a hash code based on the preceding messages, defined as follows:

```
CertificateVerify.signature.md5_hash
     MD5(master_secret || pad_2 || MD5(handshake_messages ||
         master_secret || pad_1));
Certificate.signature.sha_hash
      SHA(master_secret || pad_2 || SHA(handshake_messages ||
          master_secret || pad_1));
```

where pad_1 and pad_2 are the values defined earlier for the MAC, handshake_messages refers to all Handshake Protocol messages sent or received starting at client_hello but not including this message, and master_secret is the calculated secret whose construction is explained later in this section. If the user's private key is DSS, then it is used to encrypt the SHA-1 hash. If the user's private key is RSA, it is used to encrypt the concatenation of the MD5 and SHA-1 hashes. In either case, the purpose is to verify the client's ownership of the private key for the client certificate. Even if someone is misusing the client's certificate, he or she would be unable to send this message.

Phase 4. Finish This phase completes the setting up of a secure connection. The client sends a **change_cipher_spec message** and copies the pending CipherSpec into the current CipherSpec. Note that this message is not considered part of the Handshake Protocol but is sent using the Change Cipher Spec Protocol. The client then immediately sends the **finished message** under the new algorithms, keys, and secrets. The finished message verifies that the key exchange and authentication processes were successful. The content of the finished message is the concatenation of two hash values:

```
MD5(master_secret || pad2 || MD5(handshake_messages ||
    Sender || master_secret || pad1))
SHA(master_secret || pad2 || SHA(handshake_messages ||
    Sender || master_secret || pad1))
```

where Sender is a code that identifies that the sender is the client and handshake_messages is all of the data from all handshake messages up to but not including this message.

In response to these two messages, the server sends its own change_cipher_spec message, transfers the pending to the current CipherSpec, and sends its finished message. At this point the handshake is complete and the client and server may begin to exchange application layer data.

Cryptographic Computations

Two further items are of interest: the creation of a shared master secret by means of the key exchange, and the generation of cryptographic parameters from the master secret.

Master Secret Creation The shared master secret is a one-time 48-byte value (384 bits) generated for this session by means of secure key exchange. The creation is in two stages. First, a pre_master_secret is exchanged. Second, the master_secret is calculated by both parties. For pre_master_secret exchange, there are two possibilities:

- **RSA:** A 48-byte pre_master_secret is generated by the client, encrypted with the server's public RSA key, and sent to the server. The server decrypts the ciphertext using its private key to recover the pre_master_secret.
- **Diffie-Hellman:** Both client and server generate a Diffie-Hellman public key. After these are exchanged, each side performs the Diffie-Hellman calculation to create the shared pre_master_secret.

Both sides now compute the master_secret as follows:

```
master_secret = MD5(pre_master_secret || SHA('A' ||
                    pre_master_secret ||ClientHello.random ||
                    ServerHello.random)) ||
                MD5(pre_master_secret || SHA('BB' ||
                    pre_master_secret || ClientHello.random ||
                    ServerHello.random)) ||
                MD5(pre_master_secret || SHA('CCC' ||
                    pre_master_secret || ClientHello.random ||
                    ServerHello.random))
```

where ClientHello.random and ServerHello.random are the two nonce values exchanged in the initial hello messages.

Generation of Cryptographic Parameters CipherSpecs require a client write MAC secret, a server write MAC secret, a client write key, a server write key, a client write IV, and a server write IV, which are generated from the master secret in that order. These parameters are generated from the master secret by hashing the master secret into a sequence of secure bytes of sufficient length for all needed parameters.

The generation of the key material from the master secret uses the same format for generation of the master secret from the pre-master secret:

```
key_block = MD5(master_secret || SHA('A' || master_secret ||
                ServerHello.random || ClientHello.random)) ||
            MD5(master_secret || SHA('BB' || master_secret ||
                ServerHello.random || ClientHello.random)) ||
            MD5(master_secret || SHA('CCC' || master_
                secret || ServerHello.random ||
                ClientHello.random)) || . . .
```

until enough output has been generated. The result of this algorithmic structure is a pseudorandom function. We can view the master_secret as the pseudorandom seed value to the function. The client and server random numbers can be viewed as salt values to complicate cryptanalysis (see Chapter 18 for a discussion of the use of salt values).

Transport Layer Security

TLS is an IETF standardization initiative whose goal is to produce an Internet standard version of SSL. TLS is defined as a Proposed Internet Standard in RFC 2246. RFC 2246 is very similar to SSLv3. In this section, we highlight the differences.

Version Number The TLS Record Format is the same as that of the SSL Record Format (Figure 17.4), and the fields in the header have the same meanings. The one difference is in version values. For the current version of TLS, the Major Version is 3 and the Minor Version is 1.

Message Authentication Code There are two differences between the SSLv3 and TLS MAC schemes: the actual algorithm and the scope of the MAC calculation. TLS makes use of the HMAC algorithm defined in RFC 2104. Recall from Chapter 12 that HMAC is defined as follows:

$$\text{HMAC}_K(M) = \text{H}[(K^+ \oplus \text{opad}) \| \text{H}[(K^+ \oplus \text{ipad}) \| M]]$$

where

H = embedded hash function (for TLS, either MD5 or SHA-1)

M = message input to HMAC

K^+ = secret key padded with zeros on the left so that the result is equal to the block length of the hash code(for MD5 and SHA-1, block length = 512 bits)

ipad = 00110110 (36 in hexadecimal) repeated 64 times (512 bits)

opad = 01011100 (5C in hexadecimal) repeated 64 times (512 bits)

SSLv3 uses the same algorithm, except that the padding bytes are concatenated with the secret key rather than being XORed with the secret key padded to the block length. The level of security should be about the same in both cases.

For TLS, the MAC calculation encompasses the fields indicated in the following expression:

```
HMAC_hash(MAC_write_secret, seq_num || TLSCompressed.type ||
          TLSCompressed.version || TLSCompressed.length ||
          TLSCompressed.fragment)
```

The MAC calculation covers all of the fields covered by the SSLv3 calculation, plus the field TLSCompressed.version, which is the version of the protocol being employed.

Pseudorandom Function TLS makes use of a pseudorandom function referred to as PRF to expand secrets into blocks of data for purposes of key generation or validation. The objective is to make use of a relatively small shared secret value but to generate longer blocks of data in a way that is secure from the kinds of attacks made on hash functions and MACs. The PRF is based on the following data expansion function (Figure 17.7):

```
P_hash(secret, seed) = HMAC_hash(secret, A(1) || seed) ||
                       HMAC_hash(secret, A(2) || seed) ||
                       HMAC_hash(secret, A(3) || seed) || ...
```

where A() is defined as

$$\text{A}(0) = \text{seed}$$
$$\text{A}(i) = \text{HMAC\_hash (secret, A}(i - 1))$$

The data expansion function makes use of the HMAC algorithm, with either MD5 or SHA-1 as the underlying hash function. As can be seen, P_hash can be iterated as

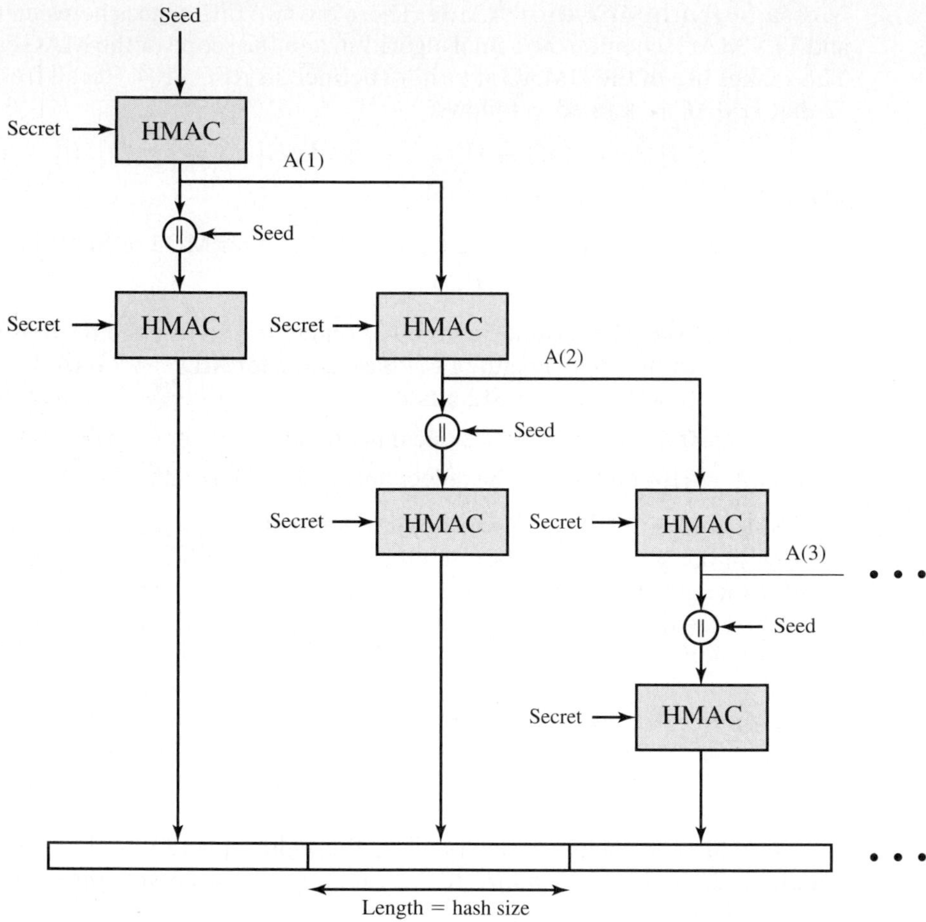

Figure 17.7 TLS Function P_hash (secret, seed)

many times as necessary to produce the required quantity of data. For example, if P_SHA-1 was used to generate 64 bytes of data, it would have to be iterated four times, producing 80 bytes of data, of which the last 16 would be discarded. In this case, P_MD5 would also have to be iterated four times, producing exactly 64 bytes of data. Note that each iteration involves two executions of HMAC, each of which in turn involves two executions of the underlying hash algorithm.

To make PRF as secure as possible, it uses two hash algorithms in a way that should guarantee its security if either algorithm remains secure. PRF is defined as

```
PRF(secret, label, seed) = P_MD5(S1, label || seed) ⊕
                           P_SHA-1(S2, label || seed)
```

PRF takes as input a secret value, an identifying label, and a seed value and produces an output of arbitrary length. The output is created by splitting the secret value into two halves (S1 and S2) and performing P_hash on each half, using MD5 on one half and SHA-1 on the other half. The two results are exclusive-ORed to produce the output; for this purpose, P_MD5 will generally have to be iterated more times than P_SHA-1 to produce an equal amount of data for input to the exclusive-OR function.

Alert Codes TLS supports all of the alert codes defined in SSLv3 with the exception of no_certificate. A number of additional codes are defined in TLS; of these, the following are always fatal:

- **decryption_failed:** A ciphertext decrypted in an invalid way; either it was not an even multiple of the block length or its padding values, when checked, were incorrect.
- **record_overflow:** A TLS record was received with a payload (ciphertext) whose length exceeds $2^{14} + 2048$ bytes, or the ciphertext decrypted to a length of greater than $2^{14} + 1024$ bytes.
- **unknown_ca:** A valid certificate chain or partial chain was received, but the certificate was not accepted because the CA certificate could not be located or could not be matched with a known, trusted CA.
- **access_denied:** A valid certificate was received, but when access control was applied, the sender decided not to proceed with the negotiation.
- **decode_error:** A message could not be decoded because a field was out of its specified range or the length of the message was incorrect.
- **export_restriction:** A negotiation not in compliance with export restrictions on key length was detected.
- **protocol_version:** The protocol version the client attempted to negotiate is recognized but not supported.
- **insufficient_security:** Returned instead of handshake_failure when a negotiation has failed specifically because the server requires ciphers more secure than those supported by the client.
- **internal_error:** An internal error unrelated to the peer or the correctness of the protocol makes it impossible to continue.

The remainder of the new alerts include the following:

- **decrypt_error:** A handshake cryptographic operation failed, including being unable to verify a signature, decrypt a key exchange, or validate a finished message.
- **user_canceled:** This handshake is being canceled for some reason unrelated to a protocol failure.
- **no_renegotiation:** Sent by a client in response to a hello request or by the server in response to a client hello after initial handshaking. Either of these messages would normally result in renegotiation, but this alert indicates that the sender is not able to renegotiate. This message is always a warning.

Cipher Suites There are several small differences between the cipher suites available under SSLv3 and under TLS:

- **Key Exchange:** TLS supports all of the key exchange techniques of SSLv3 with the exception of Fortezza.
- **Symmetric Encryption Algorithms:** TLS includes all of the symmetric encryption algorithms found in SSLv3, with the exception of Fortezza.

Client Certificate Types TLS defines the following certificate types to be requested in a certificate_request message: rsa_sign, dss_sign, rsa_fixed_dh, and dss_fixed_dh. These are all defined in SSLv3. In addition, SSLv3 includes rsa_ephemeral_dh, dss_ephemeral_dh, and fortezza_kea. Ephemeral Diffie-Hellman involves signing the Diffie-Hellman parameters with either RSA or DSS; for TLS, the rsa_sign and dss_sign types are used for that function; a separate signing type is not needed to sign Diffie-Hellman parameters. TLS does not include the Fortezza scheme.

Certificate_Verify and Finished Messages In the TLS certificate_verify message, the MD5 and SHA-1 hashes are calculated only over handshake_messages. Recall that for SSLv3, the hash calculation also included the master secret and pads. These extra fields were felt to add no additional security.

As with the finished message in SSLv3, the finished message in TLS is a hash based on the shared master_secret, the previous handshake messages, and a label that identifies client or server. The calculation is somewhat different. For TLS, we have

```
PRF(master_secret, finished_label, MD5(handshake_messages)||
    SHA-1(handshake_messages))
```

where finished_label is the string "client finished" for the client and "server finished" for the server.

Cryptographic Computations The pre_master_secret for TLS is calculated in the same way as in SSLv3. As in SSLv3, the master_secret in TLS is calculated as a hash function of the pre_master_secret and the two hello random numbers. The form of the TLS calculation is different from that of SSLv3 and is defined as follows:

```
master_secret = PRF(pre_master_secret, "master secret",
                    ClientHello.random || ServerHello.random)
```

The algorithm is performed until 48 bytes of pseudorandom output are produced. The calculation of the key block material (MAC secret keys, session encryption keys, and IVs) is defined as follows:

```
key_block = PRF(master_secret, "key expansion",
                SecurityParameters.server_random ||
                SecurityParameters.client_random)
```

until enough output has been generated. As with SSLv3, the key_block is a function of the master_secret and the client and server random numbers, but for TLS the actual algorithm is different.

Padding In SSL, the padding added prior to encryption of user data is the minimum amount required so that the total size of the data to be encrypted is a multiple of the cipher's block length. In TLS, the padding can be any amount that results in a total that is a multiple of the cipher's block length, up to a maximum of 255 bytes. For example, if the plaintext (or compressed text if compression is used) plus MAC plus padding.length byte is 79 bytes long, then the padding length, in bytes, can be 1, 9, 17, and so on, up to 249. A variable padding length may be used to frustrate attacks based on an analysis of the lengths of exchanged messages.

17.3 SECURE ELECTRONIC TRANSACTION

SET is an open encryption and security specification designed to protect credit card transactions on the Internet. The current version, SETv1, emerged from a call for security standards by MasterCard and Visa in February 1996. A wide range of companies were involved in developing the initial specification, including IBM, Microsoft, Netscape, RSA, Terisa, and Verisign. Beginning in 1996, there have been numerous tests of the concept, and by 1998 the first wave of SET-compliant products was available.

SET is not itself a payment system. Rather it is a set of security protocols and formats that enables users to employ the existing credit card payment infrastructure on an open network, such as the Internet, in a secure fashion. In essence, SET provides three services:

- Provides a secure communications channel among all parties involved in a transaction
- Provides trust by the use of X.509v3 digital certificates
- Ensures privacy because the information is only available to parties in a transaction when and where necessary

SET is a complex specification defined in three books issued in May of 1997:

- **Book 1:** Business Description (80 pages)
- **Book 2:** Programmer's Guide (629 pages)
- **Book 3:** Formal Protocol Definition (262 pages)

This is a total of 971 pages of specification. In contrast, the SSLv3 specification is 63 pages long and the TLS specification is 80 pages long. Accordingly, only a summary of this many-faceted specification is provided in this section.

SET Overview

A good way to begin our discussion of SET is to look at the business requirements for SET, its key features, and the participants in SET transactions.

Requirements Book 1 of the SET specification lists the following business requirements for secure payment processing with credit cards over the Internet and other networks:

- **Provide confidentiality of payment and ordering information:** It is necessary to assure cardholders that this information is safe and accessible only to the intended recipient. Confidentiality also reduces the risk of fraud by either party to the transaction or by malicious third parties. SET uses encryption to provide confidentiality.
- **Ensure the integrity of all transmitted data:** That is, ensure that no changes in content occur during transmission of SET messages. Digital signatures are used to provide integrity.
- **Provide authentication that a cardholder is a legitimate user of a credit card account:** A mechanism that links a cardholder to a specific account number reduces the incidence of fraud and the overall cost of payment processing. Digital signatures and certificates are used to verify that a cardholder is a legitimate user of a valid account.
- **Provide authentication that a merchant can accept credit card transactions through its relationship with a financial institution:** This is the complement to the preceding requirement. Cardholders need to be able to identify merchants with whom they can conduct secure transactions. Again, digital signatures and certificates are used.
- **Ensure the use of the best security practices and system design techniques to protect all legitimate parties in an electronic commerce transaction:** SET is a well-tested specification based on highly secure cryptographic algorithms and protocols.
- **Create a protocol that neither depends on transport security mechanisms nor prevents their use:** SET can securely operate over a "raw" TCP/IP stack. However, SET does not interfere with the use of other security mechanisms, such as IPSec and SSL/TLS.
- **Facilitate and encourage interoperability among software and network providers:** The SET protocols and formats are independent of hardware platform, operating system, and Web software.

Key Features of SET

To meet the requirements just outlined, SET incorporates the following features:

- **Confidentiality of information:** Cardholder account and payment information is secured as it travels across the network. An interesting and important feature of SET is that it prevents the merchant from learning the cardholder's credit card number; this is only provided to the issuing bank. Conventional encryption by DES is used to provide confidentiality.
- **Integrity of data:** Payment information sent from cardholders to merchants includes order information, personal data, and payment instructions. SET guarantees that these message contents are not altered in transit. RSA digital

signatures, using SHA-1 hash codes, provide message integrity. Certain messages are also protected by HMAC using SHA-1.

- **Cardholder account authentication:** SET enables merchants to verify that a cardholder is a legitimate user of a valid card account number. SET uses X.509v3 digital certificates with RSA signatures for this purpose.
- **Merchant authentication:** SET enables cardholders to verify that a merchant has a relationship with a financial institution allowing it to accept payment cards. SET uses X.509v3 digital certificates with RSA signatures for this purpose.

Note that unlike IPSec and SSL/TLS, SET provides only one choice for each cryptographic algorithm. This makes sense, because SET is a single application with a single set of requirements, whereas IPSec and SSL/TLS are intended to support a range of applications.

SET Participants Figure 17.8 indicates the participants in the SET system, which include the following:

- **Cardholder:** In the electronic environment, consumers and corporate purchasers interact with merchants from personal computers over the Internet. A cardholder is an authorized holder of a payment card (e.g., MasterCard, Visa) that has been issued by an issuer.
- **Merchant:** A merchant is a person or organization that has goods or services to sell to the cardholder. Typically, these goods and services are offered via a Web site or by electronic mail. A merchant that accepts payment cards must have a relationship with an acquirer.

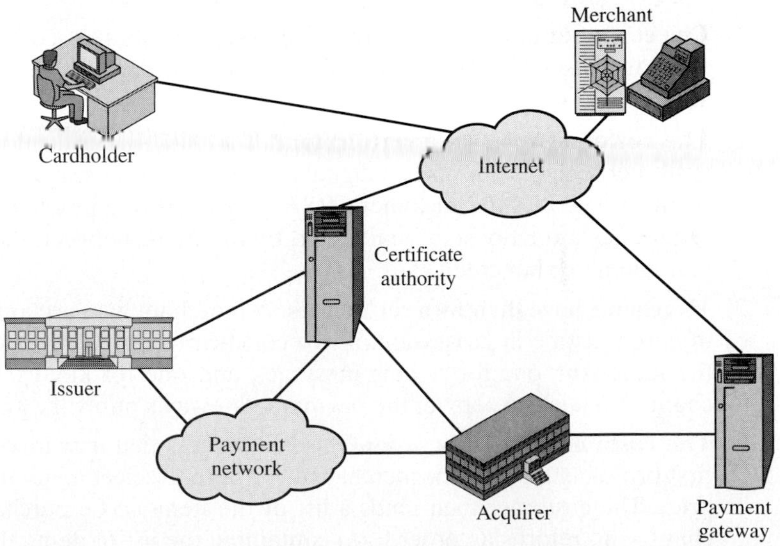

Figure 17.8 Secure Electronic Commerce Components

- **Issuer:** This is a financial institution, such as a bank, that provides the cardholder with the payment card. Typically, accounts are applied for and opened by mail or in person. Ultimately, it is the issuer that is responsible for the payment of the debt of the cardholder.
- **Acquirer:** This is a financial institution that establishes an account with a merchant and processes payment card authorizations and payments. Merchants will usually accept more than one credit card brand but do not want to deal with multiple bankcard associations or with multiple individual issuers. The acquirer provides authorization to the merchant that a given card account is active and that the proposed purchase does not exceed the credit limit. The acquirer also provides electronic transfer of payments to the merchant's account. Subsequently, the acquirer is reimbursed by the issuer over some sort of payment network for electronic funds transfer.
- **Payment gateway:** This is a function operated by the acquirer or a designated third party that processes merchant payment messages. The payment gateway interfaces between SET and the existing bankcard payment networks for authorization and payment functions. The merchant exchanges SET messages with the payment gateway over the Internet, while the payment gateway has some direct or network connection to the acquirer's financial processing system.
- **Certification authority (CA):** This is an entity that is trusted to issue X.509v3 public-key certificates for cardholders, merchants, and payment gateways. The success of SET will depend on the existence of a CA infrastructure available for this purpose. As was discussed in previous chapters, a hierarchy of CAs is used, so that participants need not be directly certified by a root authority.

We now briefly describe the sequence of events that are required for a transaction. We will then look at some of the cryptographic details.

1. **The customer opens an account.** The customer obtains a credit card account, such as MasterCard or Visa, with a bank that supports electronic payment and SET.
2. **The customer receives a certificate.** After suitable verification of identity, the customer receives an X.509v3 digital certificate, which is signed by the bank. The certificate verifies the customer's RSA public key and its expiration date. It also establishes a relationship, guaranteed by the bank, between the customer's key pair and his or her credit card.
3. **Merchants have their own certificates.** A merchant who accepts a certain brand of card must be in possession of two certificates for two public keys owned by the merchant: one for signing messages, and one for key exchange. The merchant also needs a copy of the payment gateway's public-key certificate.
4. **The customer places an order.** This is a process that may involve the customer first browsing through the merchant's Web site to select items and determine the price. The customer then sends a list of the items to be purchased to the merchant, who returns an order form containing the list of items, their price, a total price, and an order number.

5. **The merchant is verified.** In addition to the order form, the merchant sends a copy of its certificate, so that the customer can verify that he or she is dealing with a valid store.
6. **The order and payment are sent.** The customer sends both order and payment information to the merchant, along with the customer's certificate. The order confirms the purchase of the items in the order form. The payment contains credit card details. The payment information is encrypted in such a way that it cannot be read by the merchant. The customer's certificate enables the merchant to verify the customer.
7. **The merchant requests payment authorization.** The merchant sends the payment information to the payment gateway, requesting authorization that the customer's available credit is sufficient for this purchase.
8. **The merchant confirms the order.** The merchant sends confirmation of the order to the customer.
9. **The merchant provides the goods or service.** The merchant ships the goods or provides the service to the customer.
10. **The merchant requests payment.** This request is sent to the payment gateway, which handles all of the payment processing.

Dual Signature

Before looking at the details of the SET protocol, let us discuss an important innovation introduced in SET: the dual signature. The purpose of the dual signature is to link two messages that are intended for two different recipients. In this case, the customer wants to send the order information (OI) to the merchant and the payment information (PI) to the bank. The merchant does not need to know the customer's credit card number, and the bank does not need to know the details of the customer's order. The customer is afforded extra protection in terms of privacy by keeping these two items separate. However, the two items must be linked in a way that can be used to resolve disputes if necessary. The link is needed so that the customer can prove that this payment is intended for this order and not for some other goods or service.

To see the need for the link, suppose that the customers send the merchant two messages: a signed OI and a signed PI, and the merchant passes the PI on to the bank. If the merchant can capture another OI from this customer, the merchant could claim that this OI goes with the PI rather than the original OI. The linkage prevents this.

Figure 17.9 shows the use of a dual signature to meet the requirement of the preceding paragraph. The customer takes the hash (using SHA-1) of the PI and the hash of the OI. These two hashes are then concatenated and the hash of the result is taken. Finally, the customer encrypts the final hash with his or her private signature key, creating the dual signature. The operation can be summarized as

$$\mathrm{DS} = \mathrm{E}(PR_c, [\mathrm{H}(\mathrm{H}(\mathrm{PI}) \| \mathrm{H}(\mathrm{OI}))])$$

where PR_c is the customer's private signature key. Now suppose that the merchant is in possession of the dual signature (DS), the OI, and the message digest for the

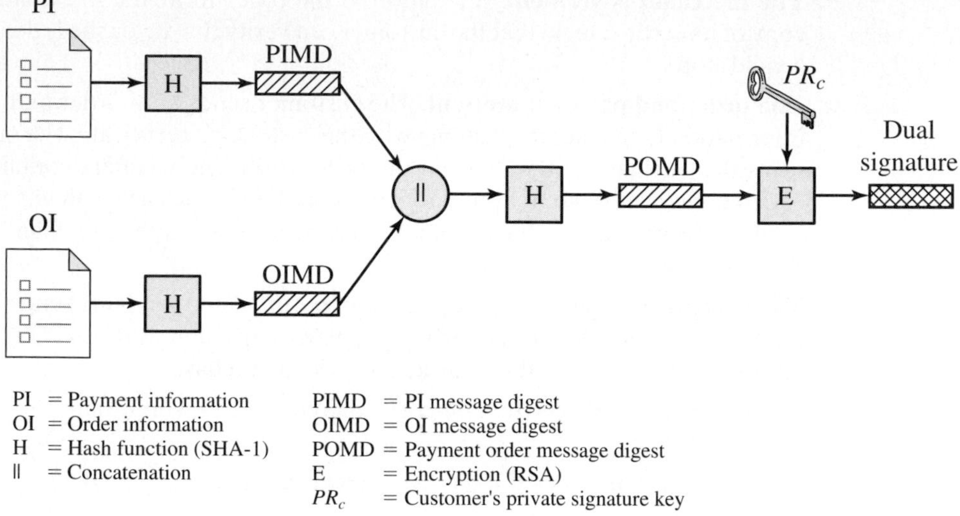

Figure 17.9 Construction of Dual Signature

PI (PIMD). The merchant also has the public key of the customer, taken from the customer's certificate. Then the merchant can compute the quantities

$$H(PIMS \| H[OI]);\ D(PU_c, DS)$$

where PU_c is the customer's public signature key. If these two quantities are equal, then the merchant has verified the signature. Similarly, if the bank is in possession of DS, PI, the message digest for OI (OIMD), and the customer's public key, then the bank can compute

$$H(H[OI] \| OIMD);\ D(PU_c, DS)$$

Again, if these two quantities are equal, then the bank has verified the signature. In summary,

1. The merchant has received OI and verified the signature.
2. The bank has received PI and verified the signature.
3. The customer has linked the OI and PI and can prove the linkage.

For example, suppose the merchant wishes to substitute another OI in this transaction, to its advantage. It would then have to find another OI whose hash matches the existing OIMD. With SHA-1, this is deemed not to be feasible. Thus, the merchant cannot link another OI with this PI.

Payment Processing

Table 17.3 lists the transaction types supported by SET. In what follows we look in some detail at the following transactions:

- Purchase request
- Payment authorization
- Payment capture

Table 17.3 SET Transaction Types

Cardholder registration	Cardholders must register with a CA before they can send SET messages to merchants.
Merchant registration	Merchants must register with a CA before they can exchange SET messages with customers and payment gateways.
Purchase request	Message from customer to merchant containing OI for merchant and PI for bank.
Payment authorization	Exchange between merchant and payment gateway to authorize a given amount for a purchase on a given credit card account.
Payment capture	Allows the merchant to request payment from the payment gateway.
Certificate inquiry and status	If the CA is unable to complete the processing of a certificate request quickly, it will send a reply to the cardholder or merchant indicating that the requester should check back later. The cardholder or merchant sends the *Certificate Inquiry* message to determine the status of the certificate request and to receive the certificate if the request has been approved.
Purchase inquiry	Allows the cardholder to check the status of the processing of an order after the purchase response has been received. Note that this message does not include information such as the status of back ordered goods, but does indicate the status of authorization, capture and credit processing.
Authorization reversal	Allows a merchant to correct previous authorization requests. If the order will not be completed, the merchant reverses the entire authorization. If part of the order will not be completed (such as when goods are back ordered), the merchant reverses part of the amount of the authorization.
Capture reversal	Allows a merchant to correct errors in capture requests such as transaction amounts that were entered incorrectly by a clerk.
Credit	Allows a merchant to issue a credit to a cardholder's account such as when goods are returned or were damaged during shipping. Note that the SET *Credit* message is always initiated by the merchant, not the cardholder. All communications between the cardholder and merchant that result in a credit being processed happen outside of SET.
Credit reversal	Allows a merchant to correct a previously request credit.
Payment gateway certificate request	Allows a merchant to query the payment gateway and receive a copy of the gateway's current key-exchange and signature certificates.
Batch administration	Allows a merchant to communicate information to the payment gateway regarding merchant batches.
Error message	Indicates that a responder rejects a message because it fails format or content verification tests.

Purchase Request Before the Purchase Request exchange begins, the cardholder has completed browsing, selecting, and ordering. The end of this preliminary phase occurs when the merchant sends a completed order form to the customer. All of the preceding occurs without the use of SET.

The purchase request exchange consists of four messages: Initiate Request, Initiate Response, Purchase Request, and Purchase Response.

In order to send SET messages to the merchant, the cardholder must have a copy of the certificates of the merchant and the payment gateway. The customer requests the certificates in the **Initiate Request** message, sent to the merchant. This message includes the brand of the credit card that the customer is using. The message also includes an ID assigned to this request/response pair by the customer and a nonce used to ensure timeliness.

The merchant generates a response and signs it with its private signature key. The response includes the nonce from the customer, another nonce for the customer to return in the next message, and a transaction ID for this purchase transaction. In addition to the signed response, the **Initiate Response** message includes the merchant's signature certificate and the payment gateway's key exchange certificate.

The cardholder verifies the merchant and gateway certificates by means of their respective CA signatures and then creates the OI and PI. The transaction ID assigned by the merchant is placed in both the OI and PI. The OI does not contain explicit order data such as the number and price of items. Rather, it contains an order reference generated in the exchange between merchant and customer during the shopping phase before the first SET message. Next, the cardholder prepares the **Purchase Request** message (Figure 17.10). For this purpose, the cardholder generates a one-time symmetric encryption key, K_s. The message includes the following:

1. **Purchase-related information.** This information will be forwarded to the payment gateway by the merchant and consists of

   —The PI

   —The dual signature, calculated over the PI and OI, signed with the customer's private signature key

   —The OI message digest (OIMD)

   The OIMD is needed for the payment gateway to verify the dual signature, as explained previously. All of these items are encrypted with K_s. The final item is

   —The digital envelope. This is formed by encrypting K_s with the payment gateway's public key-exchange key. It is called a digital envelope because this envelope must be opened (decrypted) before the other items listed previously can be read.

   The value of K_s is not made available to the merchant. Therefore, the merchant cannot read any of this payment-related information.

2. **Order-related information.** This information is needed by the merchant and consists of

   —The OI

   —The dual signature, calculated over the PI and OI, signed with the customer's private signature key

   —The PI message digest (PIMD)

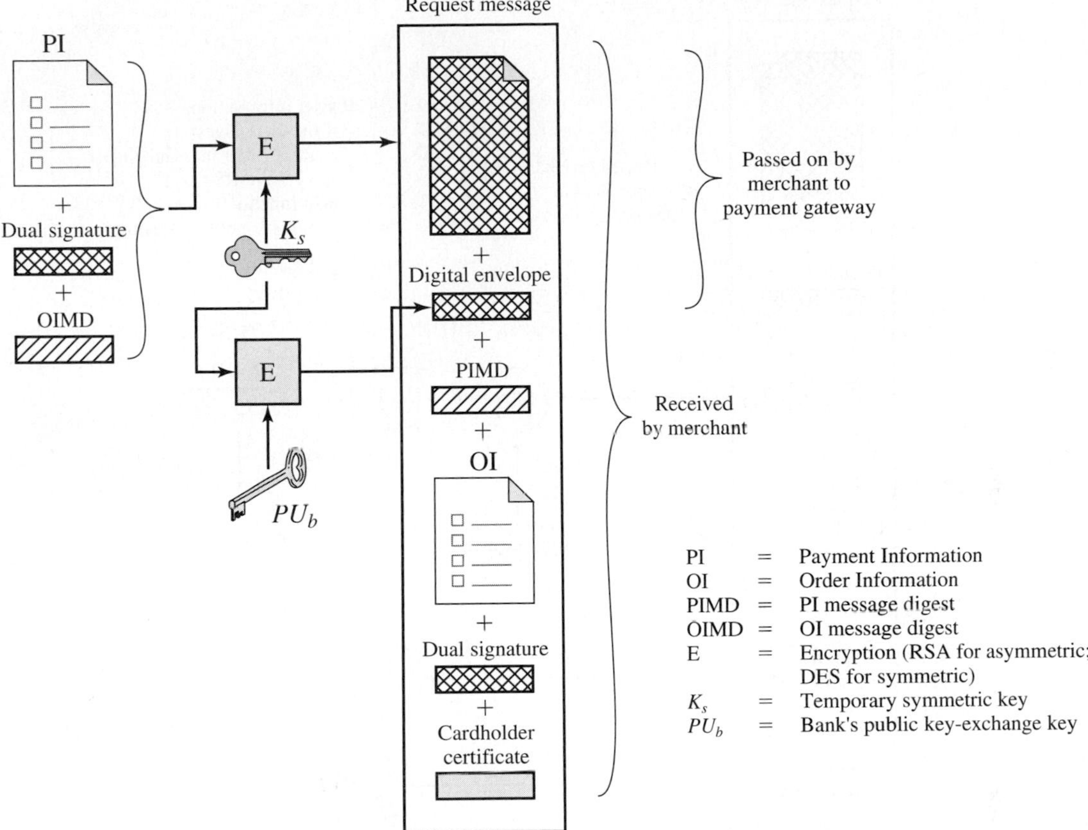

Figure 17.10 Cardholder Sends Purchase Request

The PIMD is needed for the merchant to verify the dual signature. Note that the OI is sent in the clear.

3. **Cardholder certificate.** This contains the cardholder's public signature key. It is needed by the merchant and by the payment gateway.

When the merchant receives the Purchase Request message, it performs the following actions (Figure 17.11):

1. Verifies the cardholder certificates by means of its CA signatures.
2. Verifies the dual signature using the customer's public signature key. This ensures that the order has not been tampered with in transit and that it was signed using the cardholder's private signature key.
3. Processes the order and forwards the payment information to the payment gateway for authorization (described later).
4. Sends a purchase response to the cardholder.

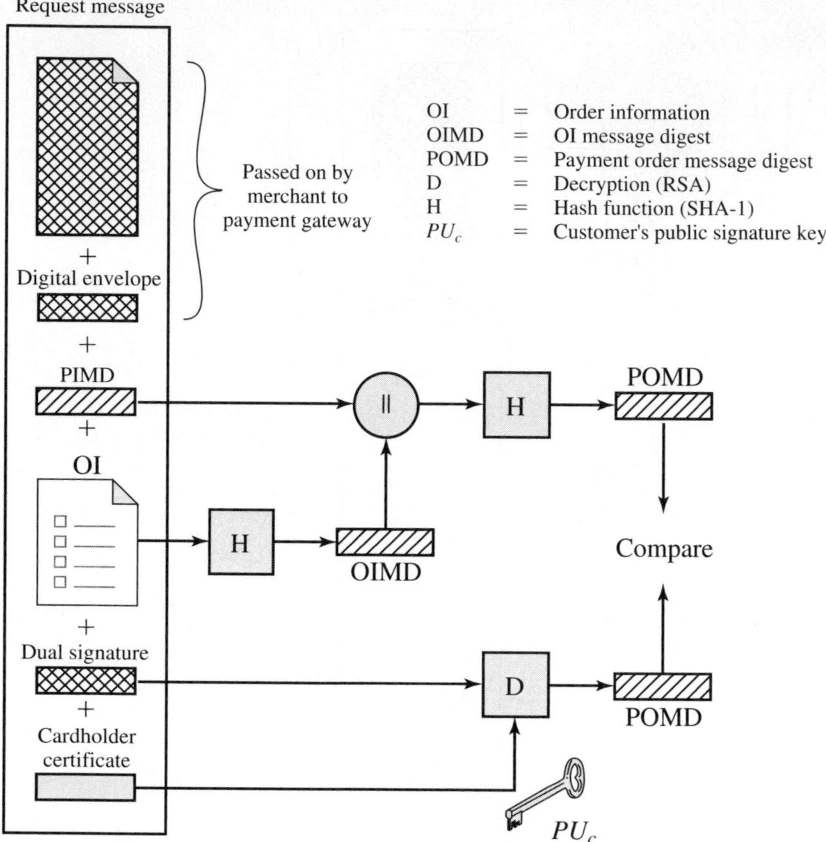

Figure 17.11 Merchant Verifies Customer Purchase Request

The **Purchase Response** message includes a response block that acknowledges the order and references the corresponding transaction number. This block is signed by the merchant using its private signature key. The block and its signature are sent to the customer, along with the merchant's signature certificate.

When the cardholder software receives the purchase response message, it verifies the merchant's certificate and then verifies the signature on the response block. Finally, it takes some action based on the response, such as displaying a message to the user or updating a database with the status of the order.

Payment Authorization During the processing of an order from a cardholder, the merchant authorizes the transaction with the payment gateway. The payment authorization ensures that the transaction was approved by the issuer. This authorization guarantees that the merchant will receive payment; the merchant can therefore provide the services or goods to the customer. The payment authorization exchange consists of two messages: Authorization Request and Authorization response.

The merchant sends an **Authorization Request** message to the payment gateway consisting of the following:

1. **Purchase-related information.** This information was obtained from the customer and consists of
   —The PI
   —The dual signature, calculated over the PI and OI, signed with the customer's private signature key
   —The OI message digest (OIMD)
   —The digital envelope
2. **Authorization-related information.** This information is generated by the merchant and consists of
   —An authorization block that includes the transaction ID, signed with the merchant's private signature key and encrypted with a one-time symmetric key generated by the merchant
   —A digital envelope. This is formed by encrypting the one-time key with the payment gateway's public key-exchange key.
3. **Certificates.** The merchant includes the cardholder's signature key certificate (used to verify the dual signature), the merchant's signature key certificate (used to verify the merchant's signature), and the merchant's key-exchange certificate (needed in the payment gateway's response).

The payment gateway performs the following tasks:

1. Verifies all certificates
2. Decrypts the digital envelope of the authorization block to obtain the symmetric key and then decrypts the authorization block
3. Verifies the merchant's signature on the authorization block
4. Decrypts the digital envelope of the payment block to obtain the symmetric key and then decrypts the payment block
5. Verifies the dual signature on the payment block
6. Verifies that the transaction ID received from the merchant matches that in the PI received (indirectly) from the customer
7. Requests and receives an authorization from the issuer

Having obtained authorization from the issuer, the payment gateway returns an **Authorization Response** message to the merchant. It includes the following elements:

1. **Authorization-related information.** Includes an authorization block, signed with the gateway's private signature key and encrypted with a one-time symmetric key generated by the gateway. Also includes a digital envelope that contains the one-time key encrypted with the merchants public key-exchange key.

2. **Capture token information.** This information will be used to effect payment later. This block is of the same form as (1), namely, a signed, encrypted capture token together with a digital envelope. This token is not processed by the merchant. Rather, it must be returned, as is, with a payment request.
3. **Certificate.** The gateway's signature key certificate.

With the authorization from the gateway, the merchant can provide the goods or service to the customer.

Payment Capture To obtain payment, the merchant engages the payment gateway in a payment capture transaction, consisting of a capture request and a capture response message.

For the **Capture Request** message, the merchant generates, signs, and encrypts a capture request block, which includes the payment amount and the transaction ID. The message also includes the encrypted capture token received earlier (in the Authorization Response) for this transaction, as well as the merchant's signature key and key-exchange key certificates.

When the payment gateway receives the capture request message, it decrypts and verifies the capture request block and decrypts and verifies the capture token block. It then checks for consistency between the capture request and capture token. It then creates a clearing request that is sent to the issuer over the private payment network. This request causes funds to be transferred to the merchant's account.

The gateway then notifies the merchant of payment in a **Capture Response** message. The message includes a capture response block that the gateway signs and encrypts. The message also includes the gateway's signature key certificate. The merchant software stores the capture response to be used for reconciliation with payment received from the acquirer.

17.4 RECOMMENDED READING AND WEB SITES

[RESC01] is a good detailed treatment of SSL and TLS.

The best-detailed overview of SET is in Book 1 of the specification, available at the MasterCard SET Web site. Another excellent overview is [MACG97]. [DREW99] is also a good source.

DREW99 Drew, G. *Using SET for Secure Electronic Commerce.* Upper Saddle River, NJ: Prentice Hall, 1999.

MACG97 Macgregor, R.; Ezvan, C.; Liguori, L.; and Han, J. *Secure Electronic Transactions: Credit Card Payment on the Web in Theory and Practice.* IBM RedBook SG24-4978-00, 1997. Available at **www.redbooks.ibm.com.**

RESC01 Rescorla, E. *SSL and TLS: Designing and Building Secure Systems.* Reading, MA: Addison-Wesley, 2001.

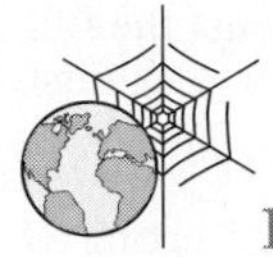

Recommended Web Sites:

- **Netscape's SSL Page:** Contains the SSL specification.
- **Transport Layer Security Charter:** Latest RFCs and Internet drafts for TLS.
- **OpenSSL Project:** Project to develop open-source SSL and TLS software. Site includes documents and links.

17.5 KEY TERMS, REVIEW QUESTIONS, AND PROBLEMS

Key Terms

acquirer cardholder certification authority (CA) dual signature issuer	merchant payment gateway Secure Electronic Transaction (SET)	Secure Socket Layer (SSL) Transport Layer Security (TLS)

Review Questions

17.1 What are the advantages of each of the three approaches shown in Figure 17.1?
17.2 What protocols comprise SSL?
17.3 What is the difference between an SSL connection and an SSL session?
17.4 List and briefly define the parameters that define an SSL session state.
17.5 List and briefly define the parameters that define an SSL session connection.
17.6 What services are provided by the SSL Record Protocol?
17.7 What steps are involved in the SSL Record Protocol transmission?
17.8 List and briefly define the principal categories of SET participants.
17.9 What is a dual signature and what is its purpose?

Problems

17.1 In SSL and TLS, why is there a separate Change Cipher Spec Protocol, rather than including a change_cipher_spec message in the Handshake Protocol?

17.2 Consider the following threats to Web security and describe how each is countered by a particular feature of SSL.

a. Brute-Force Cryptanalytic Attack: An exhaustive search of the key space for a conventional encryption algorithm.

b. Known Plaintext Dictionary Attack: Many messages will contain predictable plaintext, such as the HTTP GET command. An attacker constructs a dictionary containing every possible encryption of the known-plaintext message. When an encrypted message is intercepted, the attacker takes the portion containing the encrypted known plaintext and looks up the ciphertext in the dictionary. The ciphertext should match against an entry that was encrypted with the same secret key. If there are several matches, each of these can be tried against the full ciphertext to determine the right one. This attack is especially effective against small key sizes (e.g., 40-bit keys).

c. Replay Attack: Earlier SSL handshake messages are replayed.
d. Man-in-the-Middle Attack: An attacker interposes during key exchange, acting as the client to the server and as the server to the client.
e. Password Sniffing: Passwords in HTTP or other application traffic are eavesdropped.
f. IP Spoofing: Uses forged IP addresses to fool a host into accepting bogus data.
g. IP Hijacking: An active, authenticated connection between two hosts is disrupted and the attacker takes the place of one of the hosts.
h. SYN Flooding: An attacker sends TCP SYN messages to request a connection but does not respond to the final message to establish the connection fully. The attacked TCP module typically leaves the "half-open connection" around for a few minutes. Repeated SYN messages can clog the TCP module.

17.3 Based on what you have learned in this chapter, is it possible in SSL for the receiver to reorder SSL record blocks that arrive out of order? If so, explain how it can be done. If not, why not?

PART FOUR

System Security

Security is a concern of organizations with assets that are controlled by computer systems. By accessing or altering data, an attacker can steal tangible assets or lead an organization to take actions it would not otherwise take. By merely examining data, an attacker can gain a competitive advantage, without the owner of the data being any the wiser.

—*Computers at Risk: Safe Computing in the Information Age,*
National Research Council, 1991

The developers of secure software cannot adopt the various probabilistic measures of quality that developers of other software often can. For many applications, it is quite reasonable to tolerate a flaw that is rarely exposed and to assume that its having occurred once does not increase the likelihood that it will occur again. It is also reasonable to assume that logically independent failures will be statistically independent and not happen in concert. In contrast, a security vulnerability, once discovered, will be rapidly disseminated among a community of attackers and can be expected to be exploited on a regular basis until it is fixed.

—*Computers at Risk: Safe Computing in the Information Age,*
National Research Council, GAO/OSI-94-2, November 1993

Part Four looks at system-level security issues, including the threat of and countermeasures for intruders and viruses and the use of firewalls and trusted systems.

ROAD MAP FOR PART FOUR

Chapter 18: Intruders

Chapter 18 examines a variety of information access and service threats presented by hackers that exploit vulnerabilities in network-based computing systems. The chapter begins with a discussion of the types of attacks that can be made by unauthorized users, or intruders, and analyzes various approaches to prevention and detection. This chapter also covers the related issue of password management.

Chapter 19: Malicious Software

Chapter 19 examines software threats to systems, with a special emphasis on viruses and worms. The chapter begins with a survey of various types of malicious software, with a more detailed look at the nature of viruses and worms. The chapter then looks at countermeasures. Finally, this chapter deals with distributed denial of service attacks.

Chapter 20: Firewalls

A standard approach to the protection of local computer assets from external threats is the use of a firewall. Chapter 20 discusses the principles of firewall design and looks at specific techniques. This chapter also covers the related issue of trusted systems.

CHAPTER 18

INTRUDERS

They agreed that Graham should set the test for Charles Mabledene. It was neither more nor less than that Dragon should get Stern's code. If he had the 'in' at Utting which he claimed to have this should be possible, only loyalty to Moscow Centre would prevent it. If he got the key to the code he would prove his loyalty to London Central beyond a doubt.

—*Talking to Strange Men,* Ruth Rendell

KEY POINTS

- Unauthorized intrusion into a computer system or network is one of the most serious threats to computer security.
- Intrusion detection systems have been developed to provide early warning of an intrusion so that defensive action can be taken to prevent or minimize damage.
- Intrusion detection involves detecting unusual patterns of activity or patterns of activity that are known to correlate with intrusions.
- One important element of intrusion prevention is password management, with the goal of preventing unauthorized users from having access to the passwords of others.

A significant security problem for networked systems is hostile, or at least unwanted, trespass by users or software. User trespass can take the form of unauthorized logon to a machine or, in the case of an authorized user, acquisition of privileges or performance of actions beyond those that have been authorized. Software trespass can take the form of a virus, worm, or Trojan horse.

All these attacks relate to network security because system entry can be achieved by means of a network. However, these attacks are not confined to network-based attacks. A user with access to a local terminal may attempt trespass without using an intermediate network. A virus or Trojan horse may be introduced into a system by means of a diskette. Only the worm is a uniquely network phenomenon. Thus, system trespass is an area in which the concerns of network security and computer security overlap.

Because the focus of this book is network security, we do not attempt a comprehensive analysis of either the attacks or the security countermeasures related to system trespass. Instead, in this Part we present a broad overview of these concerns.

This chapter covers with the subject of intruders. First, we examine the nature of the attack and then look at strategies intended for prevention and, failing that, detection. Next we examine the related topic of password management.

18.1 INTRUDERS

One of the two most publicized threats to security is the intruder (the other is viruses), generally referred to as a hacker or cracker. In an important early study of intrusion, Anderson [ANDE80] identified three classes of intruders:

- **Masquerader:** An individual who is not authorized to use the computer and who penetrates a system's access controls to exploit a legitimate user's account
- **Misfeasor:** A legitimate user who accesses data, programs, or resources for which such access is not authorized, or who is authorized for such access but misuses his or her privileges
- **Clandestine user:** An individual who seizes supervisory control of the system and uses this control to evade auditing and access controls or to suppress audit collection

The masquerader is likely to be an outsider; the misfeasor generally is an insider; and the clandestine user can be either an outsider or an insider.

Intruder attacks range from the benign to the serious. At the benign end of the scale, there are many people who simply wish to explore internets and see what is out there. At the serious end are individuals who are attempting to read privileged data, perform unauthorized modifications to data, or disrupt the system.

The intruder threat has been well publicized, particularly because of the famous "Wily Hacker" incident of 1986–1987, documented by Cliff Stoll [STOL88, 89]. In 1990 there was a nationwide crackdown on illicit computer hackers, with arrests, criminal charges, one dramatic show trial, several guilty pleas, and confiscation of massive amounts of data and computer equipment [STER92]. Many people believed that the problem had been brought under control.

In fact, the problem has not been brought under control. To cite one example, a group at Bell Labs [BELL92, BELL93] has reported persistent and frequent attacks on its computer complex via the Internet over an extended period and from a variety of sources. At the time of these reports, the Bell group was experiencing the following:

- Attempts to copy the password file (discussed later) at a rate exceeding once every other day
- Suspicious remote procedure call (RPC) requests at a rate exceeding once per week
- Attempts to connect to nonexistent "bait" machines at least every two weeks

Benign intruders might be tolerable, although they do consume resources and may slow performance for legitimate users. However, there is no way in advance to know whether an intruder will be benign or malign. Consequently, even for systems with no particularly sensitive resources, there is a motivation to control this problem.

An example that dramatically illustrates the threat occurred at Texas A&M University [SAFF93]. In August 1992, the computer center there was notified that one of its machines was being used to attack computers at another location via the Internet. By monitoring activity, the computer center personnel learned that there were several outside intruders involved, who were running password-cracking routines on various computers (the site consists of a total of 12,000 interconnected machines). The center disconnected affected machines, plugged known security holes, and resumed normal operation. A few days later, one of the local system managers detected that the intruder attack had resumed. It turned out that the attack was far more sophisticated than had been originally believed. Files were found containing hundreds of captured passwords, including some on major and supposedly secure servers. In addition, one local machine had been set up as a hacker bulletin board, which the hackers used to contact each other and to discuss techniques and progress.

An analysis of this attack revealed that there were actually two levels of hackers. The high level were sophisticated users with a thorough knowledge of the technology; the low level were the "foot soldiers" who merely used the supplied cracking programs with little understanding of how they worked. This teamwork combined the two most serious weapons in the intruder armory: sophisticated knowledge of how to intrude and a willingness to spend countless hours "turning doorknobs" to probe for weaknesses.

One of the results of the growing awareness of the intruder problem has been the establishment of a number of computer emergency response teams (CERTs). These cooperative ventures collect information about system vulnerabilities and disseminate it to systems managers. Unfortunately, hackers can also gain access to CERT reports. In the Texas A&M incident, later analysis showed that the hackers had developed programs to test the attacked machines for virtually every vulnerability that had been announced by CERT. If even one machine had failed to respond promptly to a CERT advisory, it was wide open to such attacks.

In addition to running password-cracking programs, the intruders attempted to modify login software to enable them to capture passwords of users logging on to systems. This made it possible for them to build up an impressive collection of compromised passwords, which was made available on the bulletin board set up on one of the victim's own machines.

In this section, we look at the techniques used for intrusion. Then we examine ways to detect intrusion. Finally, we look at password-based approaches to prevention.

Intrusion Techniques

The objective of the intruder is to gain access to a system or to increase the range of privileges accessible on a system. Generally, this requires the intruder to acquire information that should have been protected. In some cases, this information is in the form of a user password. With knowledge of some other user's password, an intruder can log in to a system and exercise all the privileges accorded to the legitimate user.

Typically, a system must maintain a file that associates a password with each authorized user. If such a file is stored with no protection, then it is an easy matter to gain access to it and learn passwords. The password file can be protected in one of two ways:

- **One-way function:** The system stores only the value of a function based on the user's password. When the user presents a password, the system transforms that password and compares it with the stored value. In practice, the system usually performs a one-way transformation (not reversible) in which the password is used to generate a key for the one-way function and in which a fixed-length output is produced.

- **Access control:** Access to the password file is limited to one or a very few accounts.

If one or both of these countermeasures are in place, some effort is needed for a potential intruder to learn passwords. On the basis of a survey of the literature and interviews with a number of password crackers, [ALVA90] reports the following techniques for learning passwords:

1. Try default passwords used with standard accounts that are shipped with the system. Many administrators do not bother to change these defaults.
2. Exhaustively try all short passwords (those of one to three characters).
3. Try words in the system's online dictionary or a list of likely passwords. Examples of the latter are readily available on hacker bulletin boards.
4. Collect information about users, such as their full names, the names of their spouse and children, pictures in their office, and books in their office that are related to hobbies.
5. Try users' phone numbers, Social Security numbers, and room numbers.
6. Try all legitimate license plate numbers for this state.
7. Use a Trojan horse (described in Section 18.2) to bypass restrictions on access.
8. Tap the line between a remote user and the host system.

The first six methods are various ways of guessing a password. If an intruder has to verify the guess by attempting to log in, it is a tedious and easily countered means of attack. For example, a system can simply reject any login after three password attempts, thus requiring the intruder to reconnect to the host to try again. Under these circumstances, it is not practical to try more than a handful of passwords. However, the intruder is unlikely to try such crude methods. For example, if an intruder can gain access with a low level of privileges to an encrypted password file, then the strategy would be to capture that file and then use the encryption mechanism of that particular system at leisure until a valid password that provided greater privileges was discovered.

Guessing attacks are feasible, and indeed highly effective, when a large number of guesses can be attempted automatically and each guess verified, without the guessing process being detectable. Later in this chapter, we have much to say about thwarting guessing attacks.

The seventh method of attack listed earlier, the Trojan horse, can be particularly difficult to counter. An example of a program that bypasses access controls was cited in [ALVA90]. A low-privilege user produced a game program and invited the system operator to use it in his or her spare time. The program did indeed play a game, but in the background it also contained code to copy the password file, which was unencrypted but access protected, into the user's file. Because the game was running under the operator's high-privilege mode, it was able to gain access to the password file.

The eighth attack listed, line tapping, is a matter of physical security. It can be countered with link encryption techniques, discussed in Section 7.1.

Other intrusion techniques do not require learning a password. Intruders can get access to a system by exploiting attacks such as buffer overflows on a program that runs with certain privileges. Privilege escalation can be done this way as well.

We turn now to a discussion of the two principal countermeasures: detection and prevention. Detection is concerned with learning of an attack, either before or after its success. Prevention is a challenging security goal and an uphill battle at all times. The difficulty stems from the fact that the defender must attempt to thwart all possible attacks, whereas the attacker is free to try to find the weakest link in the defense chain and attack at that point.

18.2 INTRUSION DETECTION

Inevitably, the best intrusion prevention system will fail. A system's second line of defense is intrusion detection, and this has been the focus of much research in recent years. This interest is motivated by a number of considerations, including the following:

1. If an intrusion is detected quickly enough, the intruder can be identified and ejected from the system before any damage is done or any data are compromised. Even if the detection is not sufficiently timely to preempt the intruder, the sooner that the intrusion is detected, the less the amount of damage and the more quickly that recovery can be achieved.
2. An effective intrusion detection system can serve as a deterrent, so acting to prevent intrusions.
3. Intrusion detection enables the collection of information about intrusion techniques that can be used to strengthen the intrusion prevention facility.

Intrusion detection is based on the assumption that the behavior of the intruder differs from that of a legitimate user in ways that can be quantified. Of course, we cannot expect that there will be a crisp, exact distinction between an attack by an intruder and the normal use of resources by an authorized user. Rather, we must expect that there will be some overlap.

Figure 18.1 suggests, in very abstract terms, the nature of the task confronting the designer of an intrusion detection system. Although the typical behavior of an intruder differs from the typical behavior of an authorized user, there is an overlap in these behaviors. Thus, a loose interpretation of intruder behavior, which will catch more intruders, will also lead to a number of "false positives," or authorized users identified as intruders. On the other hand, an attempt to limit false positives by a tight interpretation of intruder behavior will lead to an increase in false negatives, or intruders not identified as intruders. Thus, there is an element of compromise and art in the practice of intrusion detection.

In Anderson's study [ANDE80], it was postulated that one could, with reasonable confidence, distinguish between a masquerader and a legitimate user. Patterns of legitimate user behavior can be established by observing past history, and significant deviation from such patterns can be detected. Anderson suggests

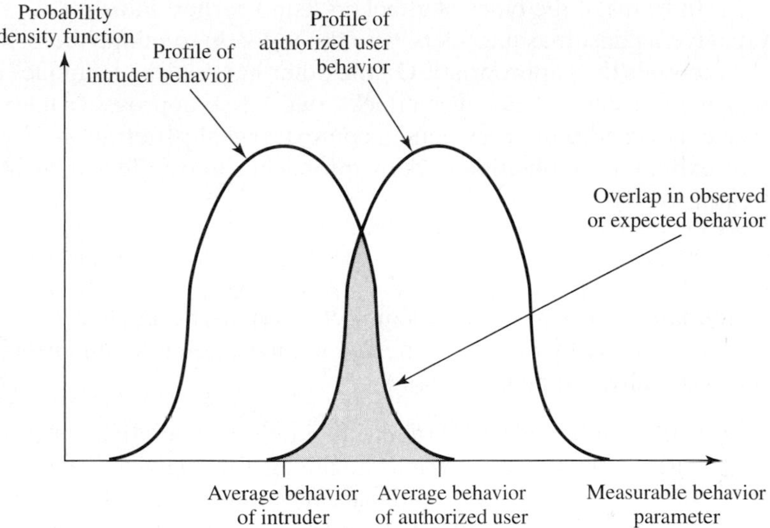

Figure 18.1 Profiles of Behavior of Intruders and Authorized Users

that the task of detecting a misfeasor (legitimate user performing in an unauthorized fashion) is more difficult, in that the distinction between abnormal and normal behavior may be small. Anderson concluded that such violations would be undetectable solely through the search for anomalous behavior. However, misfeasor behavior might nevertheless be detectable by intelligent definition of the class of conditions that suggest unauthorized use. Finally, the detection of the clandestine user was felt to be beyond the scope of purely automated techniques. These observations, which were made in 1980, remain true today.

[PORR92] identifies the following approaches to intrusion detection:

1. **Statistical anomaly detection:** Involves the collection of data relating to the behavior of legitimate users over a period of time. Then statistical tests are applied to observed behavior to determine with a high level of confidence whether that behavior is not legitimate user behavior.
   a. Threshold detection: This approach involves defining thresholds, independent of user, for the frequency of occurrence of various events.
   b. Profile based: A profile of the activity of each user is developed and used to detect changes in the behavior of individual accounts.
2. **Rule-based detection:** Involves an attempt to define a set of rules that can be used to decide that a given behavior is that of an intruder.
   a. Anomaly detection: Rules are developed to detect deviation from previous usage patterns.
   b. Penetration identification: An expert system approach that searches for suspicious behavior.

In a nutshell, statistical approaches attempt to define normal, or expected, behavior, whereas rule-based approaches attempt to define proper behavior.

In terms of the types of attackers listed earlier, statistical anomaly detection is effective against masqueraders, who are unlikely to mimic the behavior patterns of the accounts they appropriate. On the other hand, such techniques may be unable to deal with misfeasors. For such attacks, rule-based approaches may be able to recognize events and sequences that, in context, reveal penetration. In practice, a system may exhibit a combination of both approaches to be effective against a broad range of attacks.

Audit Records

A fundamental tool for intrusion detection is the audit record. Some record of ongoing activity by users must be maintained as input to an intrusion detection system. Basically, two plans are used:

- **Native audit records:** Virtually all multiuser operating systems include accounting software that collects information on user activity. The advantage of using this information is that no additional collection software is needed. The disadvantage is that the native audit records may not contain the needed information or may not contain it in a convenient form.
- **Detection-specific audit records:** A collection facility can be implemented that generates audit records containing only that information required by the intrusion detection system. One advantage of such an approach is that it could be made vendor independent and ported to a variety of systems. The disadvantage is the extra overhead involved in having, in effect, two accounting packages running on a machine.

A good example of detection-specific audit records is one developed by Dorothy Denning [DENN87]. Each audit record contains the following fields:

- **Subject:** Initiators of actions. A subject is typically a terminal user but might also be a process acting on behalf of users or groups of users. All activity arises through commands issued by subjects. Subjects may be grouped into different access classes, and these classes may overlap.
- **Action:** Operation performed by the subject on or with an object; for example, login, read, perform I/O, execute.
- **Object:** Receptors of actions. Examples include files, programs, messages, records, terminals, printers, and user- or program-created structures. When a subject is the recipient of an action, such as electronic mail, then that subject is considered an object. Objects may be grouped by type. Object granularity may vary by object type and by environment. For example, database actions may be audited for the database as a whole or at the record level.
- **Exception-Condition:** Denotes which, if any, exception condition is raised on return.
- **Resource-Usage:** A list of quantitative elements in which each element gives the amount used of some resource (e.g., number of lines printed or displayed, number of records read or written, processor time, I/O units used, session elapsed time).
- **Time-Stamp:** Unique time-and-date stamp identifying when the action took place.

Most user operations are made up of a number of elementary actions. For example, a file copy involves the execution of the user command, which includes doing access validation and setting up the copy, plus the read from one file, plus the write to another file. Consider the command

```
COPY GAME.EXE TO <Library>GAME.EXE
```

issued by Smith to copy an executable file GAME from the current directory to the <Library> directory. The following audit records may be generated:

Smith	execute	<Library>COPY.EXE	0	CPU = 00002	11058721678
Smith	read	<Smith>GAME.EXE	0	RECORDS = 0	11058721679
Smith	execute	<Library>COPY.EXE	write-viol	RECORDS = 0	11058721680

In this case, the copy is aborted because Smith does not have write permission to <Library>.

The decomposition of a user operation into elementary actions has three advantages:

1. Because objects are the protectable entities in a system, the use of elementary actions enables an audit of all behavior affecting an object. Thus, the system can detect attempted subversions of access controls (by noting an abnormality in the number of exception conditions returned) and can detect successful subversions by noting an abnormality in the set of objects accessible to the subject.
2. Single-object, single-action audit records simplify the model and the implementation.
3. Because of the simple, uniform structure of the detection-specific audit records, it may be relatively easy to obtain this information or at least part of it by a straightforward mapping from existing native audit records to the detection-specific audit records.

Statistical Anomaly Detection

As was mentioned, statistical anomaly detection techniques fall into two broad categories: threshold detection and profile-based systems. Threshold detection involves counting the number of occurrences of a specific event type over an interval of time. If the count surpasses what is considered a reasonable number that one might expect to occur, then intrusion is assumed.

Threshold analysis, by itself, is a crude and ineffective detector of even moderately sophisticated attacks. Both the threshold and the time interval must be determined. Because of the variability across users, such thresholds are likely to generate either a lot of false positives or a lot of false negatives. However, simple threshold detectors may be useful in conjunction with more sophisticated techniques.

Profile-based anomaly detection focuses on characterizing the past behavior of individual users or related groups of users and then detecting significant deviations. A profile may consist of a set of parameters, so that deviation on just a single parameter may not be sufficient in itself to signal an alert.

The foundation of this approach is an analysis of audit records. The audit records provide input to the intrusion detection function in two ways. First, the designer must decide on a number of quantitative metrics that can be used to measure user behavior. An analysis of audit records over a period of time can be used to determine the activity profile of the average user. Thus, the audit records serve to define typical behavior. Second, current audit records are the input used to detect intrusion. That is, the intrusion detection model analyzes incoming audit records to determine deviation from average behavior.

Examples of metrics that are useful for profile-based intrusion detection are the following:

- **Counter:** A nonnegative integer that may be incremented but not decremented until it is reset by management action. Typically, a count of certain event types is kept over a particular period of time. Examples include the number of logins by a single user during an hour, the number of times a given command is executed during a single user session, and the number of password failures during a minute.
- **Gauge:** A nonnegative integer that may be incremented or decremented. Typically, a gauge is used to measure the current value of some entity. Examples include the number of logical connections assigned to a user application and the number of outgoing messages queued for a user process.
- **Interval timer:** The length of time between two related events. An example is the length of time between successive logins to an account.
- **Resource utilization:** Quantity of resources consumed during a specified period. Examples include the number of pages printed during a user session and total time consumed by a program execution.

Given these general metrics, various tests can be performed to determine whether current activity fits within acceptable limits. [DENN87] lists the following approaches that may be taken:

- Mean and standard deviation
- Multivariate
- Markov process
- Time series
- Operational

The simplest statistical test is to measure the **mean and standard deviation** of a parameter over some historical period. This gives a reflection of the average behavior and its variability. The use of mean and standard deviation is applicable to a wide variety of counters, timers, and resource measures. But these measures, by themselves, are typically too crude for intrusion detection purposes.

A **multivariate** model is based on correlations between two or more variables. Intruder behavior may be characterized with greater confidence by considering such correlations (for example, processor time and resource usage, or login frequency and session elapsed time).

A **Markov process** model is used to establish transition probabilities among various states. As an example, this model might be used to look at transitions between certain commands.

A **time series** model focuses on time intervals, looking for sequences of events that happen too rapidly or too slowly. A variety of statistical tests can be applied to characterize abnormal timing.

Finally, an **operational model** is based on a judgment of what is considered abnormal, rather than an automated analysis of past audit records. Typically, fixed limits are defined and intrusion is suspected for an observation that is outside the limits. This type of approach works best where intruder behavior can be deduced from certain types of activities. For example, a large number of login attempts over a short period suggests an attempted intrusion.

As an example of the use of these various metrics and models, Table 18.1 shows various measures considered or tested for the Stanford Research Institute (SRI) intrusion detection system (IDES) [DENN87, JAVI91, LUNT88].

The main advantage of the use of statistical profiles is that a prior knowledge of security flaws is not required. The detector program learns what is "normal" behavior and then looks for deviations. The approach is not based on system-dependent characteristics and vulnerabilities. Thus, it should be readily portable among a variety of systems.

Rule-Based Intrusion Detection

Rule-based techniques detect intrusion by observing events in the system and applying a set of rules that lead to a decision regarding whether a given pattern of activity is or is not suspicious. In very general terms, we can characterize all approaches as focusing on either anomaly detection or penetration identification, although there is some overlap in these approaches.

Rule-based anomaly detection is similar in terms of its approach and strengths to statistical anomaly detection. With the rule-based approach, historical audit records are analyzed to identify usage patterns and to generate automatically rules that describe those patterns. Rules may represent past behavior patterns of users, programs, privileges, time slots, terminals, and so on. Current behavior is then observed, and each transaction is matched against the set of rules to determine if it conforms to any historically observed pattern of behavior.

As with statistical anomaly detection, rule-based anomaly detection does not require knowledge of security vulnerabilities within the system. Rather, the scheme is based on observing past behavior and, in effect, assuming that the future will be like the past. In order for this approach to be effective, a rather large database of rules will be needed. For example, a scheme described in [VACC89] contains anywhere from 10^4 to 10^6 rules.

Rule-based penetration identification takes a very different approach to intrusion detection, one based on expert system technology. The key feature of such systems is

Table 18.1 Measures That May Be Used for Intrusion Detection

Measure	Model	Type of Intrusion Detected
Login and Session Activity		
Login frequency by day and time	Mean and standard deviation	Intruders may be likely to log in during off-hours.
Frequency of login at different locations	Mean and standard deviation	Intruders may log in from a location that a particular user rarely or never uses.
Time since last login	Operational	Break-in on a "dead" account.
Elapsed time per session	Mean and standard deviation	Significant deviations might indicate masquerader.
Quantity of output to location	Mean and standard deviation	Excessive amounts of data transmitted to remote locations could signify leakage of sensitive data.
Session resource utilization	Mean and standard deviation	Unusual processor or I/O levels could signal an intruder.
Password failures at login	Operational	Attempted break-in by password guessing.
Failures to login from specified terminals	Operational	Attempted break-in.
Command or Program Execution Activity		
Execution frequency	Mean and standard deviation	May detect intruders, who are likely to use different commands, or a successful penetration by a legitimate user, who has gained access to privileged commands.
Program resource utilization	Mean and standard deviation	An abnormal value might suggest injection of a virus or Trojan horse, which performs side-effects that increase I/O or processor utilization.
Execution denials	Operational model	May detect penetration attempt by individual user who seeks higher privileges.
File Access Activity		
Read, write, create, delete frequency	Mean and standard deviation	Abnormalities for read and write access for individual users may signify masquerading or browsing.
Records read, written	Mean and standard deviation	Abnormality could signify an attempt to obtain sensitive data by inference and aggregation.
Failure count for read, write, create, delete	Operational	May detect users who persistently attempt to access unauthorized files.

the use of rules for identifying known penetrations or penetrations that would exploit known weaknesses. Rules can also be defined that identify suspicious behavior, even when the behavior is within the bounds of established patterns of usage. Typically, the rules used in these systems are specific to the machine and operating system. Also, such rules are generated by "experts" rather than by means of an automated analysis of audit records. The normal procedure is to interview system administrators and security analysts to collect a suite of known penetration scenarios and key events that threaten the security of the target system.[1] Thus, the strength of the approach depends on the skill of those involved in setting up the rules.

A simple example of the type of rules that can be used is found in NIDX, an early system that used heuristic rules that can be used to assign degrees of suspicion to activities [BAUE88]. Example heuristics are the following:

1. Users should not read files in other users' personal directories.
2. Users must not write other users' files.
3. Users who log in after hours often access the same files they used earlier.
4. Users do not generally open disk devices directly but rely on higher-level operating system utilities.
5. Users should not be logged in more than once to the same system.
6. Users do not make copies of system programs.

The penetration identification scheme used in IDES is representative of the strategy followed. Audit records are examined as they are generated, and they are matched against the rule base. If a match is found, then the user's *suspicion rating* is increased. If enough rules are matched, then the rating will pass a threshold that results in the reporting of an anomaly.

The IDES approach is based on an examination of audit records. A weakness of this plan is its lack of flexibility. For a given penetration scenario, there may be a number of alternative audit record sequences that could be produced, each varying from the others slightly or in subtle ways. It may be difficult to pin down all these variations in explicit rules. Another method is to develop a higher-level model independent of specific audit records. An example of this is a state transition model known as USTAT [ILGU93]. USTAT deals in general actions rather than the detailed specific actions recorded by the UNIX auditing mechanism. USTAT is implemented on a SunOS system that provides audit records on 239 events. Of these, only 28 are used by a preprocessor, which maps these onto 10 general actions (Table 18.2). Using just these actions and the parameters that are invoked with each action, a state transition diagram is developed that characterizes suspicious activity. Because a number of different auditable events map into a smaller number of actions, the rule-creation process is simpler. Furthermore, the state transition diagram model is easily modified to accommodate newly learned intrusion behaviors.

[1]Such interviews may even extend to reformed or unreformed crackers who will share their expertise for a fee [FREE93].

Table 18.2 USTAT Actions versus SunOS Event Types

USTAT Action	SunOS Event Type
Read	open_r, open_rc, open_rtc, open_rwc, open_rwtc, open_rt, open_rw, open_rwt
Write	truncate, ftruncate, creat, open_rtc, open_rwc, open_rwtc, open_rt, open_rw, open_rwt, open_w, open_wt, open_wc, open_wct
Create	mkdir, creat, open_rc, open_rtc, open_rwc, open_rwtc, open_wc, open_wtc, mknod
Delete	rmdir, unlink
Execute	exec, execve
Exit	exit
Modify_Owner	chown, fchown
Modify_Perm	chmod, fchmod
Rename	rename
Hardlink	link

The Base-Rate Fallacy

To be of practical use, an intrusion detection system should detect a substantial percentage of intrusions while keeping the false alarm rate at an acceptable level. If only a modest percentage of actual intrusions are detected, the system provides a false sense of security. On the other hand, if the system frequently triggers an alert when there is no intrusion (a false alarm), then either system managers will begin to ignore the alarms, or much time will be wasted analyzing the false alarms.

Unfortunately, because of the nature of the probabilities involved, it is very difficult to meet the standard of high rate of detections with a low rate of false alarms. In general, if the actual numbers of intrusions is low compared to the number of legitimate uses of a system, then the false alarm rate will be high unless the test is extremely discriminating. A study of existing intrusion detection systems, reported in [AXEL00], indicated that current systems have not overcome the problem of the base-rate fallacy. See Appendix 18A for a brief background on the mathematics of this problem.

Distributed Intrusion Detection

Until recently, work on intrusion detection systems focused on single-system standalone facilities. The typical organization, however, needs to defend a distributed collection of hosts supported by a LAN or internetwork. Although it is possible to mount a defense by using stand-alone intrusion detection systems on each host, a more effective defense can be achieved by coordination and cooperation among intrusion detection systems across the network.

Porras points out the following major issues in the design of a distributed intrusion detection system [PORR92]:

- A distributed intrusion detection system may need to deal with different audit record formats. In a heterogeneous environment, different systems will employ different native audit collection systems and, if using intrusion detection, may employ different formats for security-related audit records.

- One or more nodes in the network will serve as collection and analysis points for the data from the systems on the network. Thus, either raw audit data or summary data must be transmitted across the network. Therefore, there is a requirement to assure the integrity and confidentiality of these data. Integrity is required to prevent an intruder from masking his or her activities by altering the transmitted audit information. Confidentiality is required because the transmitted audit information could be valuable.
- Either a centralized or decentralized architecture can be used. With a centralized architecture, there is a single central point of collection and analysis of all audit data. This eases the task of correlating incoming reports but creates a potential bottleneck and single point of failure. With a decentralized architecture, there are more than one analysis centers, but these must coordinate their activities and exchange information.

A good example of a distributed intrusion detection system is one developed at the University of California at Davis [HEBE92, SNAP91]. Figure 18.2 shows the overall architecture, which consists of three main components:

- **Host agent module:** An audit collection module operating as a background process on a monitored system. Its purpose is to collect data on security-related events on the host and transmit these to the central manager.
- **LAN monitor agent module:** Operates in the same fashion as a host agent module except that it analyzes LAN traffic and reports the results to the central manager.
- **Central manager module:** Receives reports from LAN monitor and host agents and processes and correlates these reports to detect intrusion.

The scheme is designed to be independent of any operating system or system auditing implementation. Figure 18.3 [SNAP91] shows the general approach that is

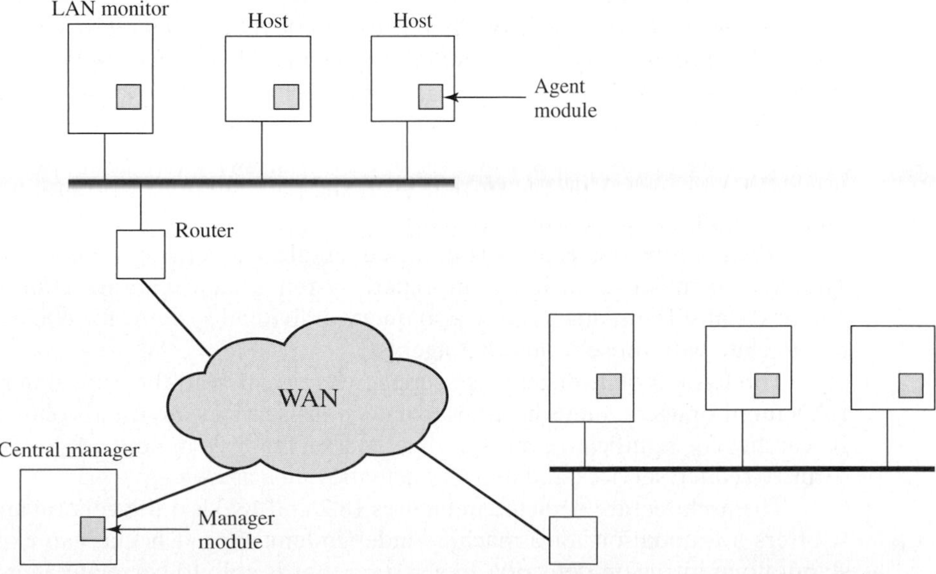

Figure 18.2 Architecture for Distributed Intrusion Detection

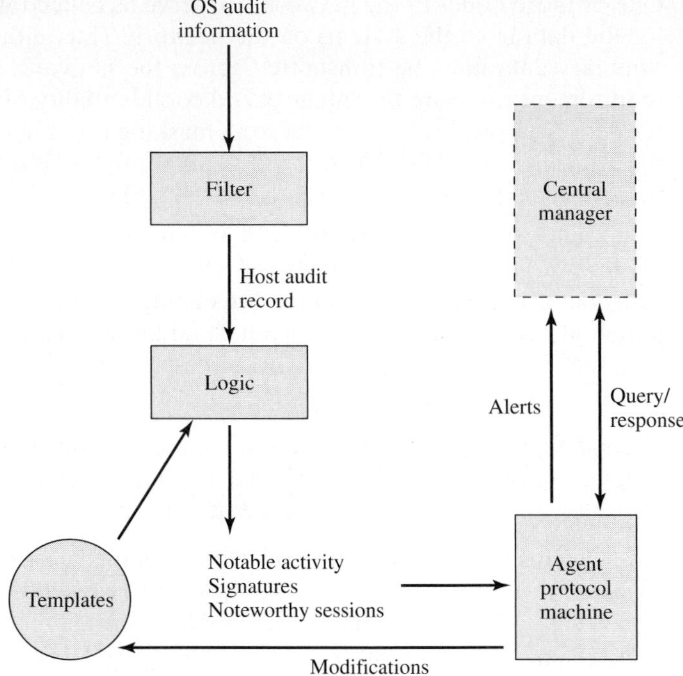

Figure 18.3 Agent Architecture

taken. The agent captures each audit record produced by the native audit collection system. A filter is applied that retains only those records that are of security interest. These records are then reformatted into a standardized format referred to as the host audit record (HAR). Next, a template-driven logic module analyzes the records for suspicious activity. At the lowest level, the agent scans for notable events that are of interest independent of any past events. Examples include failed file accesses, accessing system files, and changing a file's access control. At the next higher level, the agent looks for sequences of events, such as known attack patterns (signatures). Finally, the agent looks for anomalous behavior of an individual user based on a historical profile of that user, such as number of programs executed, number of files accessed, and the like.

When suspicious activity is detected, an alert is sent to the central manager. The central manager includes an expert system that can draw inferences from received data. The manager may also query individual systems for copies of HARs to correlate with those from other agents.

The LAN monitor agent also supplies information to the central manager. The LAN monitor agent audits host-host connections, services used, and volume of traffic. It searches for significant events, such as sudden changes in network load, the use of security-related services, and network activities such as *rlogin*.

The architecture depicted in Figures 18.2 and 18.3 is quite general and flexible. It offers a foundation for a machine-independent approach that can expand from stand-alone intrusion detection to a system that is able to correlate activity from a number of sites and networks to detect suspicious activity that would otherwise remain undetected.

Honeypots

A relatively recent innovation in intrusion detection technology is the honeypot. Honeypots are decoy systems that are designed to lure a potential attacker away from critical systems. Honeypots are designed to

- divert an attacker from accessing critical systems
- collect information about the attacker's activity
- encourage the attacker to stay on the system long enough for administrators to respond

These systems are filled with fabricated information designed to appear valuable but that a legitimate user of the system wouldn't access. Thus, any access to the honeypot is suspect. The system is instrumented with sensitive monitors and event loggers that detect these accesses and collect information about the attacker's activities. Because any attack against the honeypot is made to seem successful, administrators have time to mobilize and log and track the attacker without ever exposing productive systems.

Initial efforts involved a single honeypot computer with IP addresses designed to attract hackers. More recent research has focused on building entire honeypot networks that emulate an enterprise, possibly with actual or simulated traffic and data. Once hackers are within the network, administrators can observe their behavior in detail and figure out defenses.

Intrusion Detection Exchange Format

To facilitate the development of distributed intrusion detection systems that can function across a wide range of platforms and environments, standards are needed to support interoperability. Such standards are the focus of the IETF Intrusion Detection Working Group. The purpose of the working group is to define data formats and exchange procedures for sharing information of interest to intrusion detection and response systems and to management systems that may need to interact with them. The outputs of this working group include the following:

1. A requirements document, which describes the high-level functional requirements for communication between intrusion detection systems and requirements for communication between intrusion detection systems and with management systems, including the rationale for those requirements. Scenarios will be used to illustrate the requirements.
2. A common intrusion language specification, which describes data formats that satisfy the requirements.
3. A framework document, which identifies existing protocols best used for communication between intrusion detection systems, and describes how the devised data formats relate to them.

As of this writing, all of these documents are in an Internet-draft document stage.

18.3 PASSWORD MANAGEMENT

Password Protection

The front line of defense against intruders is the password system. Virtually all multiuser systems require that a user provide not only a name or identifier (ID) but also a password. The password serves to authenticate the ID of the individual logging on to the system. In turn, the ID provides security in the following ways:

- The ID determines whether the user is authorized to gain access to a system. In some systems, only those who already have an ID filed on the system are allowed to gain access.
- The ID determines the privileges accorded to the user. A few users may have supervisory or "superuser" status that enables them to read files and perform functions that are especially protected by the operating system. Some systems have guest or anonymous accounts, and users of these accounts have more limited privileges than others.
- The ID is used in what is referred to as discretionary access control. For example, by listing the IDs of the other users, a user may grant permission to them to read files owned by that user.

The Vulnerability of Passwords To understand the nature of the threat to password-based systems, let us consider a scheme that is widely used on UNIX, in which passwords are never stored in the clear. Rather, the following procedure is employed (Figure 18.4a). Each user selects a password of up to eight printable characters in length. This is converted into a 56-bit value (using 7-bit ASCII) that serves as the key input to an encryption routine. The encryption routine, known as crypt(3), is based on DES. The DES algorithm is modified using a 12-bit "salt" value. Typically, this value is related to the time at which the password is assigned to the user. The modified DES algorithm is exercised with a data input consisting of a 64-bit block of zeros. The output of the algorithm then serves as input for a second encryption. This process is repeated for a total of 25 encryptions. The resulting 64-bit output is then translated into an 11-character sequence. The hashed password is then stored, together with a plaintext copy of the salt, in the password file for the corresponding user ID. This method has been shown to be secure against a variety of cryptanalytic attacks [WAGN00].

The salt serves three purposes:

- It prevents duplicate passwords from being visible in the password file. Even if two users choose the same password, those passwords will be assigned at different times. Hence, the "extended" passwords of the two users will differ.
- It effectively increases the length of the password without requiring the user to remember two additional characters. Hence, the number of possible passwords is increased by a factor of 4096, increasing the difficulty of guessing a password.
- It prevents the use of a hardware implementation of DES, which would ease the difficulty of a brute-force guessing attack.

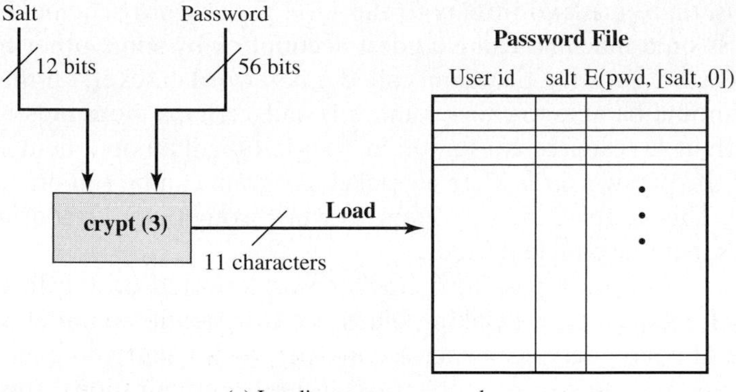

(a) Loading a new password

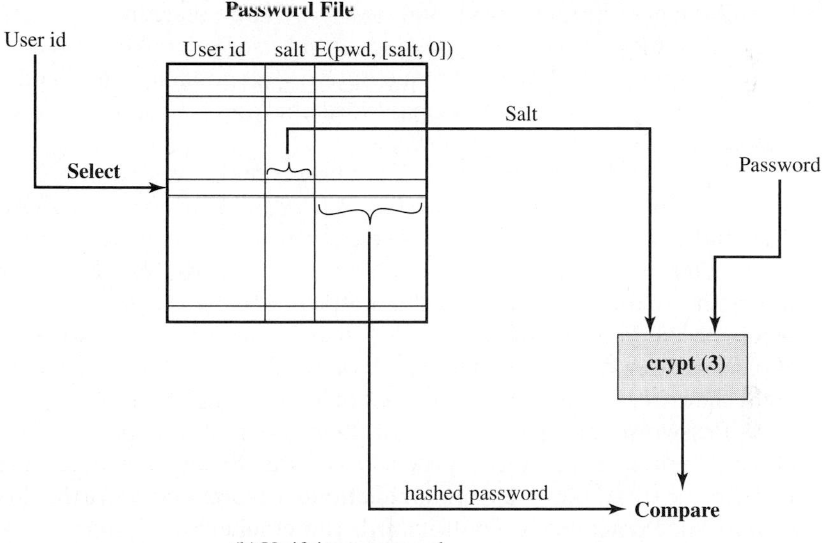

(b) Verifying a password

Figure 18.4 UNIX Password Scheme

When a user attempts to log on to a UNIX system, the user provides an ID and a password. The operating system uses the ID to index into the password file and retrieve the plaintext salt and the encrypted password. The salt and user-supplied password are used as input to the encryption routine. If the result matches the stored value, the password is accepted.

The encryption routine is designed to discourage guessing attacks. Software implementations of DES are slow compared to hardware versions, and the use of 25 iterations multiplies the time required by 25. However, since the original design of this algorithm, two changes have occurred. First, newer implementations of the algorithm itself have resulted in speedups. For example, the Internet worm described in Chapter 19 was able to do online password guessing of a few hundred passwords in a reasonably short time by using a more efficient encryption algorithm than the standard one stored on the UNIX systems that it attacked. Second, hardware performance continues to increase, so that any software algorithm executes more quickly.

Thus, there are two threats to the UNIX password scheme. First, a user can gain access on a machine using a guest account or by some other means and then run a password guessing program, called a password cracker, on that machine. The attacker should be able to check hundreds and perhaps thousands of possible passwords with little resource consumption. In addition, if an opponent is able to obtain a copy of the password file, then a cracker program can be run on another machine at leisure. This enables the opponent to run through many thousands of possible passwords in a reasonable period.

As an example, a password cracker was reported on the Internet in August 1993 [MADS93]. Using a Thinking Machines Corporation parallel computer, a performance of 1560 encryptions per second per vector unit was achieved. With four vector units per processing node (a standard configuration), this works out to 800,000 encryptions per second on a 128-node machine (which is a modest size) and 6.4 million encryptions per second on a 1024-node machine.

Even these stupendous guessing rates do not yet make it feasible for an attacker to use a dumb brute-force technique of trying all possible combinations of characters to discover a password. Instead, password crackers rely on the fact that some people choose easily guessable passwords.

Some users, when permitted to choose their own password, pick one that is absurdly short. The results of one study at Purdue University are shown in Table 18.3. The study observed password change choices on 54 machines, representing approximately 7000 user accounts. Almost 3% of the passwords were three characters or fewer in length. An attacker could begin the attack by exhaustively testing all possible passwords of length 3 or fewer. A simple remedy is for the system to reject any password choice of fewer than, say, six characters or even to require that all passwords be exactly eight characters in length. Most users would not complain about such a restriction.

Password length is only part of the problem. Many people, when permitted to choose their own password, pick a password that is guessable, such as their own name, their street name, a common dictionary word, and so forth. This makes the job of password cracking straightforward. The cracker simply has to test the password file against lists of likely passwords. Because many people use guessable passwords, such a strategy should succeed on virtually all systems.

Table 18.3 Observed Password Lengths [SPAF92a]

Length	Number	Fraction of Total
1	55	.004
2	87	.006
3	212	.02
4	449	.03
5	1260	.09
6	3035	.22
7	2917	.21
8	5772	.42
Total	13787	1.0

One demonstration of the effectiveness of guessing is reported in [KLEI90]. From a variety of sources, the author collected UNIX password files, containing nearly 14,000 encrypted passwords. The result, which the author rightly characterizes as frightening, is shown in Table 18.4. In all, nearly one-fourth of the passwords were guessed. The following strategy was used:

1. Try the user's name, initials, account name, and other relevant personal information. In all, 130 different permutations for each user were tried.
2. Try words from various dictionaries. The author compiled a dictionary of over 60,000 words, including the online dictionary on the system itself, and various other lists as shown.
3. Try various permutations on the words from step 2. This included making the first letter uppercase or a control character, making the entire word uppercase, reversing the word, changing the letter "o" to the digit "zero," and so on. These permutations added another 1 million words to the list.
4. Try various capitalization permutations on the words from step 2 that were not considered in step 3. This added almost 2 million additional words to the list.

Thus, the test involved in the neighborhood of 3 million words. Using the fastest Thinking Machines implementation listed earlier, the time to encrypt all these words for all possible salt values is under an hour. Keep in mind that such a thorough search could produce a success rate of about 25%, whereas even a single hit may be enough to gain a wide range of privileges on a system.

Access Control One way to thwart a password attack is to deny the opponent access to the password file. If the encrypted password portion of the file is accessible only by a privileged user, then the opponent cannot read it without already knowing the password of a privileged user. [SPAF92a] points out several flaws in this strategy:

- Many systems, including most UNIX systems, are susceptible to unanticipated break-ins. Once an attacker has gained access by some means, he or she may wish to obtain a collection of passwords in order to use different accounts for different logon sessions to decrease the risk of detection. Or a user with an account may desire another user's account to access privileged data or to sabotage the system.
- An accident of protection might render the password file readable, thus compromising all the accounts.
- Some of the users have accounts on other machines in other protection domains, and they use the same password. Thus, if the passwords could be read by anyone on one machine, a machine in another location might be compromised.

Thus, a more effective strategy would be to force users to select passwords that are difficult to guess.

Password Selection Strategies

The lesson from the two experiments just described (Tables 18.3 and 18.4) is that, left to their own devices, many users choose a password that is too short or too easy to guess. At the other extreme, if users are assigned passwords consisting of eight

Table 18.4 Passwords Cracked from a Sample Set of 13,797 Accounts [KLEI90]

Type of Password	Search Size	Number of Matches	Percentage of Passwords Matched	Cost/Benefit Ratio[a]
User/account name	130	368	2.7%	2.830
Character sequences	866	22	0.2%	0.025
Numbers	427	9	0.1%	0.021
Chinese	392	56	0.4%	0.143
Place names	628	82	0.6%	0.131
Common names	2239	548	4.0%	0.245
Female names	4280	161	1.2%	0.038
Male names	2866	140	1.0%	0.049
Uncommon names	4955	130	0.9%	0.026
Myths & legends	1246	66	0.5%	0.053
Shakespearean	473	11	0.1%	0.023
Sports terms	238	32	0.2%	0.134
Science fiction	691	59	0.4%	0.085
Movies and actors	99	12	0.1%	0.121
Cartoons	92	9	0.1%	0.098
Famous people	290	55	0.4%	0.190
Phrases and patterns	933	253	1.8%	0.271
Surnames	33	9	0.1%	0.273
Biology	58	1	0.0%	0.017
System dictionary	19683	1027	7.4%	0.052
Machine names	9018	132	1.0%	0.015
Mnemonics	14	2	0.0%	0.143
King James bible	7525	83	0.6%	0.011
Miscellaneous words	3212	54	0.4%	0.017
Yiddish words	56	0	0.0%	0.000
Asteroids	2407	19	0.1%	0.007
TOTAL	62727	3340	24.2%	0.053

[a] Computed as the number of matches divided by the search size. The more words that needed to be tested for a match, the lower the cost/benefit ratio.

randomly selected printable characters, password cracking is effectively impossible. But it would be almost as impossible for most users to remember their passwords. Fortunately, even if we limit the password universe to strings of characters that are reasonably memorable, the size of the universe is still too large to permit practical cracking. Our goal, then, is to eliminate guessable passwords while allowing the user to select a password that is memorable. Four basic techniques are in use:

- User education
- Computer-generated passwords

- Reactive password checking
- Proactive password checking

Users can be told the importance of using hard-to-guess passwords and can be provided with guidelines for selecting strong passwords. This **user education** strategy is unlikely to succeed at most installations, particularly where there is a large user population or a lot of turnover. Many users will simply ignore the guidelines. Others may not be good judges of what is a strong password. For example, many users (mistakenly) believe that reversing a word or capitalizing the last letter makes a password unguessable.

Computer-generated passwords also have problems. If the passwords are quite random in nature, users will not be able to remember them. Even if the password is pronounceable, the user may have difficulty remembering it and so be tempted to write it down. In general, computer-generated password schemes have a history of poor acceptance by users. FIPS PUB 181 defines one of the best designed automated password generators. The standard includes not only a description of the approach but also a complete listing of the C source code of the algorithm. The algorithm generates words by forming pronounceable syllables and concatenating them to form a word. A random number generator produces a random stream of characters used to construct the syllables and words.

A **reactive password checking** strategy is one in which the system periodically runs its own password cracker to find guessable passwords. The system cancels any passwords that are guessed and notifies the user. This tactic has a number of drawbacks. First, it is resource intensive if the job is done right. Because a determined opponent who is able to steal a password file can devote full CPU time to the task for hours or even days, an effective reactive password checker is at a distinct disadvantage. Furthermore, any existing passwords remain vulnerable until the reactive password checker finds them.

The most promising approach to improved password security is a **proactive password checker**. In this scheme, a user is allowed to select his or her own password. However, at the time of selection, the system checks to see if the password is allowable and, if not, rejects it. Such checkers are based on the philosophy that, with sufficient guidance from the system, users can select memorable passwords from a fairly large password space that are not likely to be guessed in a dictionary attack.

The trick with a proactive password checker is to strike a balance between user acceptability and strength. If the system rejects too many passwords, users will complain that it is too hard to select a password. If the system uses some simple algorithm to define what is acceptable, this provides guidance to password crackers to refine their guessing technique. In the remainder of this subsection, we look at possible approaches to proactive password checking.

The first approach is a simple system for rule enforcement. For example, the following rules could be enforced:

- All passwords must be at least eight characters long.
- In the first eight characters, the passwords must include at least one each of uppercase, lowercase, numeric digits, and punctuation marks.

These rules could be coupled with advice to the user. Although this approach is superior to simply educating users, it may not be sufficient to thwart password crackers. This scheme alerts crackers as to which passwords *not* to try but may still make it possible to do password cracking.

Another possible procedure is simply to compile a large dictionary of possible "bad" passwords. When a user selects a password, the system checks to make sure that it is not on the disapproved list. There are two problems with this approach:

- **Space:** The dictionary must be very large to be effective. For example, the dictionary used in the Purdue study [SPAF92a] occupies more than 30 megabytes of storage.
- **Time:** The time required to search a large dictionary may itself be large. In addition, to check for likely permutations of dictionary words, either those words most be included in the dictionary, making it truly huge, or each search must also involve considerable processing.

Two techniques for developing an effective and efficient proactive password checker that is based on rejecting words on a list show promise. One of these develops a Markov model for the generation of guessable passwords [DAVI93]. Figure 18.5 shows a simplified version of such a model. This model shows a language consisting of an alphabet of three characters. The state of the system at any time is the identity of the most recent letter. The value on the transition from one state to another represents the probability that one letter follows another. Thus, the probability that the next letter is b, given that the current letter is a, is 0.5.

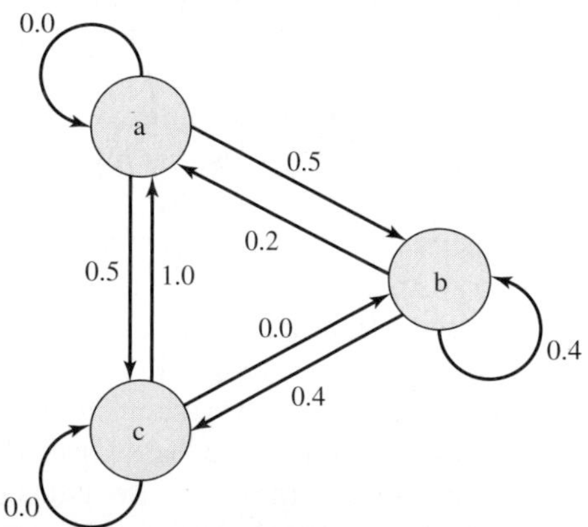

M = {3, {a, b, c} , T, 1 } where

$$T = \begin{bmatrix} 0.0 & 0.5 & 0.5 \\ 0.2 & 0.4 & 0.4 \\ 1.0 & 0.0 & 0.0 \end{bmatrix}$$

e.g., string probably from this language: abbcacaba

e.g., string probably not from this language: aacccbaaa

Figure 18.5 An Example Markov Model

In general, a Markov model is a quadruple $[m, A, \mathbf{T}, k]$, where m is the number of states in the model, A is the state space, $\mathbf{T}$ is the matrix of transition probabilities, and k is the order of the model. For a kth-order model, the probability of making a transition to a particular letter depends on the previous k letters that have been generated. Figure 18.5 shows a simple first-order model.

The authors report on the development and use of a second-order model. To begin, a dictionary of guessable passwords is constructed. Then the transition matrix is calculated as follows:

1. Determine the frequency matrix **f**, where $\mathbf{f}(i, j, k)$ is the number of occurrences of the trigram consisting of the ith, jth, and kth character. For example, the password *parsnips* yields the trigrams par, ars, rsn, sni, nip, and ips.
2. For each bigram ij, calculate $\mathbf{f}(i, j, \infty)$ as the total number of trigrams beginning with ij. For example, $\mathbf{f}(\mathrm{a}, \mathrm{b}, \infty)$ would be the total number of trigrams of the form aba, abb, abc, and so on.
3. Compute the entries of **T** as follows:

$$\mathbf{T}(i, j, k) = \frac{\mathbf{f}(i, j, k)}{\mathbf{f}(i, j, \infty)}$$

The result is a model that reflects the structure of the words in the dictionary. With this model, the question "Is this a bad password?" is transformed into the question "Was this string (password) generated by this Markov model?" For a given password, the transition probabilities of all its trigrams can be looked up. Some standard statistical tests can then be used to determine if the password is likely or unlikely for that model. Passwords that are likely to be generated by the model are rejected. The authors report good results for a second-order model. Their system catches virtually all the passwords in their dictionary and does not exclude so many potentially good passwords as to be user unfriendly.

A quite different approach has been reported by Spafford [SPAF92a, SPAF92b]. It is based on the use of a Bloom filter [BLOO70]. To begin, we explain the operation of the Bloom filter. A Bloom filter of order k consists of a set of k independent hash functions $H_1(x), H_2(x), \ldots, \mathrm{H}_k(x)$, where each function maps a password into a hash value in the range 0 to $N - 1$. That is,

$$H_i(\mathrm{X}_j) = y \qquad 1 \le i \le k; \qquad 1 \le j \le D; \qquad 0 \le y \le N - 1$$

where

X_j = jth word in password dictionary
D = number of words in password dictionary

The following procedure is then applied to the dictionary:

1. A hash table of N bits is defined, with all bits initially set to 0.
2. For each password, its k hash values are calculated, and the corresponding bits in the hash table are set to 1. Thus, if $H_i(\mathrm{X}_j) = 67$ for some (i, j), then the sixty-seventh bit of the hash table is set to 1; if the bit already has the value 1, it remains at 1.

When a new password is presented to the checker, its k hash values are calculated. If all the corresponding bits of the hash table are equal to 1, then the password is rejected. All passwords in the dictionary will be rejected. But there will also be some "false positives" (that is, passwords that are not in the dictionary but that produce a match in the hash table). To see this, consider a scheme with two hash functions. Suppose that the passwords *undertaker* and *hulkhogan* are in the dictionary, but *xG%#jj98* is not. Further suppose that

$$H_1(\text{undertaker}) = 25 \qquad H_1(\text{hulkhogan}) = 83 \qquad H_1(\text{xG\%\#jj98}) = 665$$
$$H_2(\text{undertaker}) = 998 \qquad H_2(\text{hulkhogan}) = 665 \qquad H_2(\text{xG\%\#jj98}) = 998$$

If the password xG%#jj98 is presented to the system, it will be rejected even though it is not in the dictionary. If there are too many such false positives, it will be difficult for users to select passwords. Therefore, we would like to design the hash scheme to minimize false positives. It can be shown that the probability of a false positive can be approximated by

$$P \approx (1 - e^{kD/N})^k = (1 - e^{k/R})^k$$

or, equivalently,

$$R \approx \frac{-k}{\ln(1 - P^{1/k})}$$

where

k = number of hash functions
N = number of bits in hash table
D = number of words in dictionary
R = N/D, ratio of hash table size (bits) to dictionary size (words)

Figure 18.6 plots P as a function of R for various values of k. Suppose we have a dictionary of 1 million words and we wish to have a 0.01 probability of rejecting a password not in the dictionary. If we choose six hash functions, the required ratio is $R = 9.6$. Therefore, we need a hash table of 9.6×10^6 bits or about 1.2 MBytes of storage. In contrast, storage of the entire dictionary would require on the order of 8 MBytes. Thus, we achieve a compression of almost a factor of 7. Furthermore, password checking involves the straightforward calculation of six hash functions and is independent of the size of the dictionary, whereas with the use of the full dictionary, there is substantial searching.[2]

[2]Both the Markov model and the Bloom filter involve the use of probabilistic techniques. In the case of the Markov model, there is a small probability that some passwords in the dictionary will not be caught and a small probability that some passwords not in the dictionary will be rejected. In the case of the Bloom filter, there is a small probability that some passwords not in the dictionary will be rejected. Again we see that taking a probabilistic approach simplifies the solution (e.g., see footnote 1 in Chapter 15).

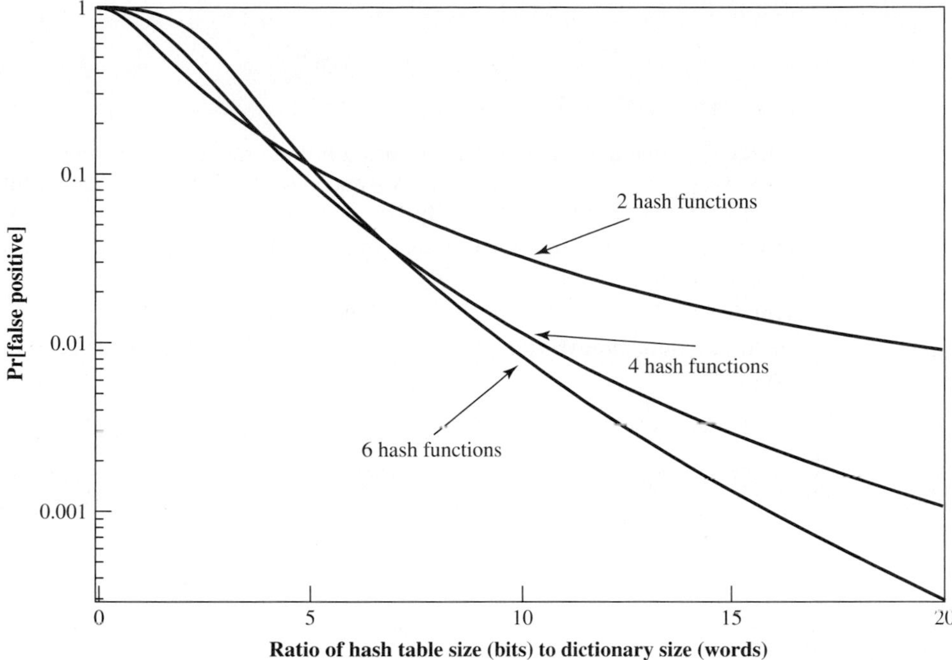

Figure 18.6 Performance of Bloom Filter

18.4 RECOMMENDED READING AND WEB SITES

Two thorough treatments of intrusion detection are [BACE00] and [PROC01]. A more concise but very worthwhile treatment is [BACE01]. Two short but useful survey articles on the subject are [KENT00] and [MCHU00]. [NING04] surveys recent advances in intrusion detection techniques. [HONE01] is the definitive account on honeypots and provides a detailed analysis of the tools and methods of hackers.

BACE00 Bace, R. *Intrusion Detection.* Indianapolis, IN: Macmillan Technical Publishing, 2000.

BACE01 Bace, R., and Mell, P. *Intrusion Detection Systems.* NIST Special Publication SP 800-31, November 2000.

HONE01 The Honeynet Project. *Know Your Enemy: Revealing the Security Tools, Tactics, and Motives of the Blackhat Community.* Reading, MA: Addison-Wesley, 2001.

KENT00 Kent, S. "On the Trail of Intrusions into Information Systems." *IEEE Spectrum*, December 2000.

MCHU00 McHugh, J.; Christie, A.; and Allen, J. "The Role of Intrusion Detection Systems." *IEEE Software*, September/October 2000.

NING04 Ning, P., et al. "Techniques and Tools for Analyzing Intrusion Alerts." *ACM Transactions on Information and System Security*, May 2004.

PROC01 Proctor, P., *The Practical Intrusion Detection Handbook.* Upper Saddle River, NJ: Prentice Hall, 2001.

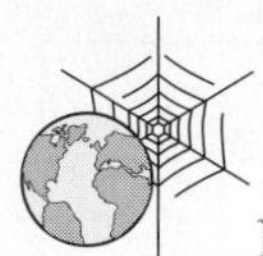

Recommended Web Sites:

- **CERT Coordination Center:** The organization that grew from the computer emergency response team formed by the Defense Advanced Research Projects Agency. Site provides good information on Internet security threats, vulnerabilities, and attack statistics.
- **Honeynet Project:** A research project studying the techniques of predatory hackers and developing honeypot products.
- **Honeypots:** A good collection of research papers and technical articles.
- **Intrusion Detection Working Group:** Includes all of the documents generated by this group.

18.5 KEY TERMS, REVIEW QUESTIONS, AND PROBLEMS

Key Terms

audit record Bayes' Theorem base-rate fallacy honeypot	intruder intrusion detection intrusion detection exchange format password	rule-based intrusion detection salt statistical anomaly detection

Review Questions

18.1 List and briefly define three classes of intruders.

18.2 What are two common techniques used to protect a password file?

18.3 What are three benefits that can be provided by an intrusion detection system?

18.4 What is the difference between statistical anomaly detection and rule-based intrusion detection?

18.5 What metrics are useful for profile-based intrusion detection?

18.6 What is the difference between rule-based anomaly detection and rule-based penetration identification?

18.7 What is a honeypot?

18.8 What is a salt in the context of UNIX password management?

18.9 List and briefly define four techniques used to avoid guessable passwords.

Problems

18.1 A taxicab was involved in a fatal hit-and-run accident at night. Two cab companies, the Green and the Blue, operate in the city. You are told that

- 85% of the cabs in the city are Green and 15% are Blue.
- A witness identified the cab as Blue.

The court tested the reliability of the witness under the same circumstances that existed on the night of the accident and concluded that the witness was correct in identifying the color of the cab 80% of the time. What is the probability that the cab involved in the incident was Blue rather than Green?

18.2 Assume that passwords are selected from four-character combinations of 26 alphabetic characters. Assume that an adversary is able to attempt passwords at a rate of one per second.

a. Assuming no feedback to the adversary until each attempt has been completed, what is the expected time to discover the correct password?

b. Assuming feedback to the adversary flagging an error as each incorrect character is entered, what is the expected time to discover the correct password?

18.3 Assume that source elements of length k is mapped in some uniform fashion into a target elements of length p. If each digit can take on one of r values, then the number of source elements is r^k and the number of target elements is the smaller number r^p. A particular source element x_i is mapped to a particular target element y_j.

a. What is the probability that the correct source element can be selected by an adversary on one try?

b. What is the probability that a different source element $x_k(x_i \neq x_k)$ that results in the same target element, y_j, could be produced by an adversary?

c. What is the probability that the correct target element can be produced by an adversary on one try?

18.4 A phonetic password generator picks two segments randomly for each six-letter password. The form of each segment is CVC (consonant, vowel, consonant), where V = <a, e, i, o, u> and C = $\overline{\text{V}}$.

a. What is the total password population?

b. What is the probability of an adversary guessing a password correctly?

18.5 Assume that passwords are limited to the use of the 95 printable ASCII characters and that all passwords are 10 characters in length. Assume a password cracker with an encryption rate of 6.4 million encryptions per second. How long will it take to test exhaustively all possible passwords on a UNIX system?

18.6 Because of the known risks of the UNIX password system, the SunOS-4.0 documentation recommends that the password file be removed and replaced with a publicly readable file called /etc/publickey. An entry in the file for user A consists of a user's identifier ID_A, the user's public key, PU_a, and the corresponding private key PR_a. This private key is encrypted using DES with a key derived from the user's login password P_a. When A logs in, the system decrypts E[Pa,PR_a] to obtain PR_a.

a. The system then verifies that P_a was correctly supplied. How?

b. How can an opponent attack this system?

18.7 The encryption scheme used for UNIX passwords is one way; it is not possible to reverse it. Therefore, would it be accurate to say that this is, in fact, a hash code rather than an encryption of the password?

18.8 It was stated that the inclusion of the salt in the UNIX password scheme increases the difficulty of guessing by a factor of 4096. But the salt is stored in plaintext in the same entry as the corresponding ciphertext password. Therefore, those two characters are known to the attacker and need not be guessed. Why is it asserted that the salt increases security?

18.9 Assuming that you have successfully answered the preceding problem and understand the significance of the salt, here is another question. Wouldn't it be possible to thwart completely all password crackers by dramatically increasing the salt size to, say, 24 or 48 bits?

18.10 Consider the Bloom filter discussed in Section 18.3. Define k = number of hash functions; N = number of bits in hash table; and D = number of words in dictionary.

a. Show that the expected number of bits in the hash table that are equal to zero is expressed as

$$\phi = \left(1 - \frac{k}{N}\right)^D$$

b. Show that the probability that an input word, not in the dictionary, will be falsely accepted as being in the dictionary is

$$P = (1 - \phi)^k$$

c. Show that the preceding expression can be approximated as

$$P \approx (1 - e^{-kD/N})^k$$

18.11 Design a file access system to allow certain users read and write access to a file, depending on authorization set up by the system. The instructions should be of the format

READ (F, User A): attempt by User A to read file F
WRITE (F, User A): attempt by User A to store a possibly modified copy of F

Each file has a *header record,* which contains authorization privileges; that is, a list of users who can read and write. The file is to be encrypted by a key that is not shared by the users but known only to the system.

APPENDIX 18A THE BASE-RATE FALLACY

We begin with a review of important results from probability theory, then demonstrate the base-rate fallacy.

Conditional Probability and Independence

We often want to know a probability that is conditional on some event. The effect of the condition is to remove some of the outcomes from the sample space. For example, what is the probability of getting a sum of 8 on the roll of two dice, if we know that the face of at least one die is an even number? We can reason as follows. Because one die is even and the sum is even, the second die must show an even number. Thus, there are three equally likely successful outcomes: (2, 6), (4, 4) and (6, 2), out of a total set of possibilities of [36 − (number of events with both faces odd)] = 36 − 3 × 3 = 27. The resulting probability is 3/27 = 1/9.

Formally, the **conditional probability** of an event A assuming the event B has occurred, denoted by $\Pr[A|B]$, is defined as the ratio

$$\Pr[A|B] = \frac{\Pr[AB]}{\Pr[B]}$$

where we assume $\Pr[B]$ is not zero.

In our example, $A = \{\text{sum of } 8\}$ and $B = \{\text{at least one die even}\}$. The quantity $\Pr[AB]$ encompasses all of those outcomes in which the sum is 8 and at least one die is even. As we have seen, there are three such outcomes. Thus, $\Pr[AB] =$

3/36 = 1/12. A moment's thought should convince you that Pr[B] = 3/4. We can now calculate

$$\Pr[A|B] = \frac{1/12}{3/4} = \frac{1}{9}$$

This agrees with our previous reasoning.

Two events A and B are called **independent** if $\Pr[AB] = \Pr[A]\Pr[B]$. It can easily be seen that if A and B are independent, $\Pr[A|B] = \Pr[A]$ and $\Pr[B|A] = \Pr[B]$.

Bayes' Theorem

One of the most important results from probability theory is known as Bayes' theorem. First we need to state the total probability formula. Given a set of mutually exclusive events $E_1, E_2, \ldots E_n$, such that the union of these events covers all possible outcomes, and given an arbitrary event A, then it can be shown that

$$\Pr[A] = \sum_{i=1}^{n} \Pr[A|E_i]\Pr[E_i] \tag{18.1}$$

Bayes' theorem may be stated as follows:

$$\Pr[E_i|A] = \frac{\Pr[A|E_i]P[E_i]}{\Pr[A]} = \frac{\Pr[A|E_i]P[E_i]}{\sum_{j=1}^{n} \Pr[A|E_j]\Pr[E_j]} \tag{18.2}$$

Figure 18.7a illustrates the concepts of total probability and Bayes' theorem.

Bayes' theorem is used to calculate "posterior odds," that is, the probability that something really is the case, given evidence in favor of it. For example, suppose we are transmitting a sequence of zeroes and ones over a noisy transmission line. Let S0 and S1 be the events a zero is sent at a given time and a one is sent, respectively, and R0 and R1 be the events that a zero is received and a one is

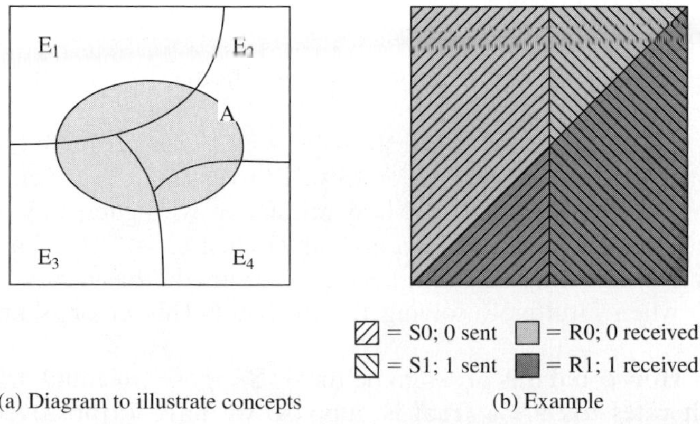

(a) Diagram to illustrate concepts (b) Example

Figure 18.7 Illustration of Total Probability and Bayes' Theorem

received. Suppose we know the probabilities of the source, namely Pr[S1] $= p$ and Pr[S0] $= 1 - p$. Now the line is observed to determine how frequently an error occurs when a one is sent and when a zero is sent, and the following probabilities are calculated: Pr[R0|S1] $= p_a$ and Pr[R1|S0] $= p_b$. If a zero is received, we can then calculate the conditional probability of an error, namely the conditional probability that a one was sent given that a zero was received, using Bayes' theorem:

$$\Pr[S1|R0] = \frac{\Pr[R0|S1]\Pr[S1]}{\Pr[R0|S1]\Pr[S1] + \Pr[R0|S0]\Pr[S0]} = \frac{p_a p}{p_a p + (1 - p_b)(1 - p)}$$

Figure 18.7b illustrates the preceding equation. In the figure, the sample space is represented by a unit square. Half of the square corresponds to S0 and half to S1, so Pr[S0] = Pr[S1] = 0.5. Similarly, half of the square corresponds to R0 and half to R1, so Pr[R0] = Pr[R1] = 0.5. Within the area representing S0, 1/4 of that area corresponds to R1, so Pr[R1/S0] = 0.25. Other conditional probabilities are similarly evident.

The Base-Rate Fallacy Demonstrated

Consider the following situation. A patient has a test for some disease that comes back positive (indicating he has the disease). You are told that

- The accuracy of the test is 87% (i.e., if a patient has the disease, 87% of the time, the test yields the correct result, and if the patient does not have the disease, 87% of the time, the test yields the correct result).
- The incidence of the disease in the population is 1%.

Given that the test is positive, how probable is it that the patient does not have the disease? That is, what is the probability that this is a false alarm? We need Bayes' theorem to get the correct answer:

$$\begin{aligned}\Pr[\text{well/positive}] &= \frac{\Pr[\text{positive/well}]\Pr[\text{well}]}{\Pr[\text{positive/disease}]\Pr[\text{disease}] + \Pr[\text{positive/well}]\Pr[\text{well}]} \\ &= \frac{(0.13)(0.99)}{(0.87)(0.01) + (0.13)(0.99)} = 0.937\end{aligned}$$

Thus, in the vast majority of cases, when a disease condition is detected, it is a false alarm.

This problem, used in a study [PIAT91], was presented to a number of people. Most subjects gave the answer 13%. The vast majority, including many physicians, gave a number below 50%. Many physicians who guessed wrong lamented, "If you are right, there is no point in making clinical tests!" The reason most people get it wrong is that they do not take into account the basic rate of incidence (the base rate) when intuitively solving the problem. This error is known as the *base-rate fallacy*.

How could this problem be fixed? Suppose we could drive both of the correct result rates to 99.9%. That is, suppose we have Pr[positive/disease] = 0.999 and Pr[negative/well] = 0.999. Plugging these numbers into the Equation (18.2), we get

Pr[well/positive] = 0.09. Thus, if we can accurately detect disease and accurately detect lack of disease at a level of 99.9%, then the rate of false alarms will be 9%. This is much better, but still not ideal. Moreover, again assume 99.9% accuracy, but now suppose that the incidence of the disease in the population is only 1/10000 = 0.0001. We then end up with a rate of false alarms of 91%. In actual situations, [AXEL00] found that the probabilities associated with intrusion detection systems were such that the false alarm rate was unsatisfactory.

CHAPTER 19

Malicious Software

What is the concept of defense: The parrying of a blow. What is its characteristic feature: Awaiting the blow.

—*On War,* Carl Von Clausewitz

KEY POINTS

- Malicious software is software that is intentionally included or inserted in a system for a harmful purpose.
- A virus is a piece of software that can "infect" other programs by modifying them; the modification includes a copy of the virus program, which can then go on to infect other programs.
- A worm is a program that can replicate itself and send copies from computer to computer across network connections. Upon arrival, the worm may be activated to replicate and propagate again. In addition to propagation, the worm usually performs some unwanted function.
- A denial of service (DoS) attack is an attempt to prevent legitimate users of a service from using that service.
- A distributed denial of service attack is launched from multiple coordinated sources.

This chapter examines malicious software (malware), especially viruses and worms.

19.1 VIRUSES AND RELATED THREATS

Perhaps the most sophisticated types of threats to computer systems are presented by programs that exploit vulnerabilities in computing systems. In this context, we are concerned with application programs as well as utility programs, such as editors and compilers.

We begin this section with an overview of the spectrum of such software threats. The remainder of the section is devoted to viruses and worms.

Malicious Programs

The terminology in this area presents problems because of a lack of universal agreement on all of the terms and because some of the categories overlap. Table 19.1, based principally on [SZOR05], is a useful guide.

Malicious software can be divided into two categories: those that need a host program, and those that are independent. The former are essentially fragments of programs that cannot exist independently of some actual application program, utility, or system program. Viruses, logic bombs, and backdoors are examples. The latter are self-contained programs that can be scheduled and run by the operating system. Worms and zombie programs are examples.

Table 19.1 Terminology of Malicious Programs

Name	Description
Virus	Attaches itself to a program and propagates copies of itself to other programs
Worm	Program that propagates copies of itself to other computers
Logic bomb	Triggers action when condition occurs
Trojan horse	Program that contains unexpected additional functionality
Backdoor (trapdoor)	Program modification that allows unauthorized access to functionality
Exploits	Code specific to a single vulnerability or set of vulnerabilities
Downloaders	Program that installs other items on a machine that is under attack. Usually, a downloader is sent in an e-mail.
Auto-rooter	Malicious hacker tools used to break into new machines remotely
Kit (virus generator)	Set of tools for generating new viruses automatically
Spammer programs	Used to send large volumes of unwanted e-mail
Flooders	Used to attack networked computer systems with a large volume of traffic to carry out a denial of service (DoS) attack
Keyloggers	Captures keystrokes on a compromised system
Rootkit	Set of hacker tools used after attacker has broken into a computer system and gained root-level access
Zombie	Program activated on an infected machine that is activated to launch attacks on other machines

We can also differentiate between those software threats that do not replicate and those that do. The former are programs or fragments of programs that are activated by a trigger. Examples are logic bombs, backdoors, and zombie programs. The latter consist of either a program fragment or an independent program that, when executed, may produce one or more copies of itself to be activated later on the same system or some other system. Viruses and worms are examples.

In the remainder of this subsection, we briefly survey some of the key categories of malicious software, with the exception of viruses and worms, which are covered in more detail later in this section.

Backdoor A backdoor, also known as a trapdoor, is a secret entry point into a program that allows someone that is aware of the backdoor to gain access without going through the usual security access procedures. Programmers have used backdoors legitimately for many years to debug and test programs. This usually is done when the programmer is developing an application that has an authentication procedure, or a long setup, requiring the user to enter many different values to run the application. To debug the program, the developer may wish to gain special privileges or to avoid all the necessary setup and authentication. The programmer may also want to ensure that there is a method of activating the program should something be wrong with the authentication procedure that is being built into the application. The backdoor is code that recognizes some special sequence of input or is triggered by being run from a certain user ID or by an unlikely sequence of events.

Backdoors become threats when unscrupulous programmers use them to gain unauthorized access. The backdoor was the basic idea for the vulnerability portrayed in the movie *War Games*. Another example is that during the development of Multics, penetration tests were conducted by an Air Force "tiger team" (simulating adversaries). One tactic employed was to send a bogus operating system update to a site running Multics. The update contained a Trojan horse (described later) that could be activated by a backdoor and that allowed the tiger team to gain access. The threat was so well implemented that the Multics developers could not find it, even after they were informed of its presence [ENGE80].

It is difficult to implement operating system controls for backdoors. Security measures must focus on the program development and software update activities.

Logic Bomb One of the oldest types of program threat, predating viruses and worms, is the logic bomb. The logic bomb is code embedded in some legitimate program that is set to "explode" when certain conditions are met. Examples of conditions that can be used as triggers for a logic bomb are the presence or absence of certain files, a particular day of the week or date, or a particular user running the application. Once triggered, a bomb may alter or delete data or entire files, cause a machine halt, or do some other damage. A striking example of how logic bombs can be employed was the case of Tim Lloyd, who was convicted of setting a logic bomb that cost his employer, Omega Engineering, more than $10 million, derailed its corporate growth strategy, and eventually led to the layoff of 80 workers [GAUD00]. Ultimately, Lloyd was sentenced to 41 months in prison and ordered to pay $2 million in restitution.

Trojan Horses A Trojan horse is a useful, or apparently useful, program or command procedure containing hidden code that, when invoked, performs some unwanted or harmful function.

Trojan horse programs can be used to accomplish functions indirectly that an unauthorized user could not accomplish directly. For example, to gain access to the files of another user on a shared system, a user could create a Trojan horse program that, when executed, changed the invoking user's file permissions so that the files are readable by any user. The author could then induce users to run the program by placing it in a common directory and naming it such that it appears to be a useful utility. An example is a program that ostensibly produces a listing of the user's files in a desirable format. After another user has run the program, the author can then access the information in the user's files. An example of a Trojan horse program that would be difficult to detect is a compiler that has been modified to insert additional code into certain programs as they are compiled, such as a system login program [THOM84]. The code creates a backdoor in the login program that permits the author to log on to the system using a special password. This Trojan horse can never be discovered by reading the source code of the login program.

Another common motivation for the Trojan horse is data destruction. The program appears to be performing a useful function (e.g., a calculator program), but it may also be quietly deleting the user's files. For example, a CBS executive was victimized by a Trojan horse that destroyed all information contained in his computer's memory [TIME90]. The Trojan horse was implanted in a graphics routine offered on an electronic bulletin board system.

Zombie A zombie is a program that secretly takes over another Internet-attached computer and then uses that computer to launch attacks that are difficult to trace to the zombie's creator. Zombies are used in denial-of-service attacks, typically against targeted Web sites. The zombie is planted on hundreds of computers belonging to unsuspecting third parties, and then used to overwhelm the target Web site by launching an overwhelming onslaught of Internet traffic. Section 19.3 discusses zombies in the context of denial of service attacks.

The Nature of Viruses

A virus is a piece of software that can "infect" other programs by modifying them; the modification includes a copy of the virus program, which can then go on to infect other programs.

Biological viruses are tiny scraps of genetic code—DNA or RNA—that can take over the machinery of a living cell and trick it into making thousands of flawless replicas of the original virus. Like its biological counterpart, a computer virus carries in its instructional code the recipe for making perfect copies of itself. The typical virus becomes embedded in a program on a computer. Then, whenever the infected computer comes into contact with an uninfected piece of software, a fresh copy of the virus passes into the new program. Thus, the infection can be spread from computer to computer by unsuspecting users who either swap disks or send programs to one another over a network. In a network environment, the ability to access applications and system services on other computers provides a perfect culture for the spread of a virus.

A virus can do anything that other programs do. The only difference is that it attaches itself to another program and executes secretly when the host program is run. Once a virus is executing, it can perform any function, such as erasing files and programs.

During its lifetime, a typical virus goes through the following four phases:

- **Dormant phase:** The virus is idle. The virus will eventually be activated by some event, such as a date, the presence of another program or file, or the capacity of the disk exceeding some limit. Not all viruses have this stage.
- **Propagation phase:** The virus places an identical copy of itself into other programs or into certain system areas on the disk. Each infected program will now contain a clone of the virus, which will itself enter a propagation phase.
- **Triggering phase:** The virus is activated to perform the function for which it was intended. As with the dormant phase, the triggering phase can be caused by a variety of system events, including a count of the number of times that this copy of the virus has made copies of itself.
- **Execution phase:** The function is performed. The function may be harmless, such as a message on the screen, or damaging, such as the destruction of programs and data files.

Most viruses carry out their work in a manner that is specific to a particular operating system and, in some cases, specific to a particular hardware platform. Thus, they are designed to take advantage of the details and weaknesses of particular systems.

```
program V :=

{goto main;
    1234567;

    subroutine infect-executable :=
        {loop:
        file := get-random-executable-file;
        if (first-line-of-file = 1234567)
            then goto loop
            else prepend V to file; }

    subroutine do-damage :=
        {whatever damage is to be done}

    subroutine trigger-pulled :=
        {return true if some condition holds}

main:   main-program :=
        {infect-executable;
        if trigger-pulled then do-damage;
        goto next;}

next:

}
```

Figure 19.1 A Simple Virus

Virus Structure A virus can be prepended or postpended to an executable program, or it can be embedded in some other fashion. The key to its operation is that the infected program, when invoked, will first execute the virus code and then execute the original code of the program.

A very general depiction of virus structure is shown in Figure 19.1 (based on [COHE94]. In this case, the virus code, V, is prepended to infected programs, and it is assumed that the entry point to the program, when invoked, is the first line of the program.

An infected program begins with the virus code and works as follows. The first line of code is a jump to the main virus program. The second line is a special marker that is used by the virus to determine whether or not a potential victim program has already been infected with this virus. When the program is invoked, control is immediately transferred to the main virus program. The virus program first seeks out uninfected executable files and infects them. Next, the virus may perform some action, usually detrimental to the system. This action could be performed every time the program is invoked, or it could be a logic bomb that triggers only under certain conditions. Finally, the virus transfers control to the original program. If the infection phase of the program is reasonably rapid, a user is unlikely to notice any difference between the execution of an infected and uninfected program.

A virus such as the one just described is easily detected because an infected version of a program is longer than the corresponding uninfected one. A way to thwart such a simple means of detecting a virus is to compress the executable file so that both the infected and uninfected versions are of identical length. Figure 19.2 [COHE94] shows in general terms the logic required. The key lines in this virus are

```
        program CV :=

{goto main;
        01234567;

        subroutine infect-executable :=
                {loop:
                        file := get-random-executable-file;
                if (first-line-of-file = 01234567) then goto loop;
           (1)  compress file;
           (2)  prepend CV to file;
           }

main:   main-program :=
                {if ask-permission then infect-executable;
           (3)  uncompress rest-of-file;
           (4)  run uncompressed file;}
           }
```

Figure 19.2 Logic for a Compression Virus

numbered, and Figure 19.3 [COHE94] illustrates the operation. We assume that program P_1 is infected with the virus CV. When this program is invoked, control passes to its virus, which performs the following steps:

1. For each uninfected file P_2 that is found, the virus first compresses that file to produce P'_2, which is shorter than the original program by the size of the virus.
2. A copy of the virus is prepended to the compressed program.
3. The compressed version of the original infected program, P'_1, is uncompressed.
4. The uncompressed original program is executed.

In this example, the virus does nothing other than propagate. As in the previous example, the virus may include a logic bomb.

Initial Infection Once a virus has gained entry to a system by infecting a single program, it is in a position to infect some or all other executable files on that system when

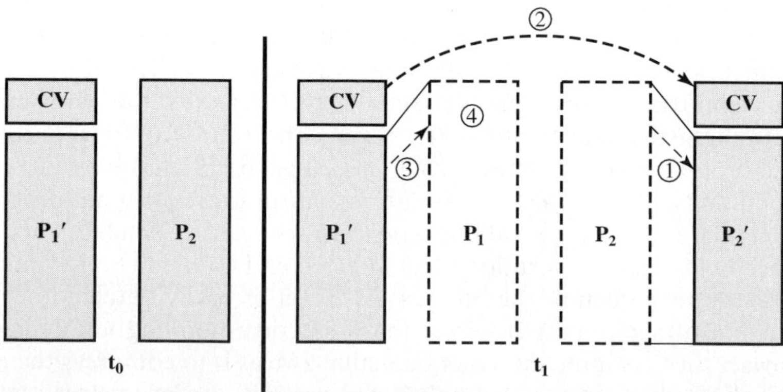

Figure 19.3 A Compression Virus

the infected program executes. Thus, viral infection can be completely prevented by preventing the virus from gaining entry in the first place. Unfortunately, prevention is extraordinarily difficult because a virus can be part of any program outside a system. Thus, unless one is content to take an absolutely bare piece of iron and write all one's own system and application programs, one is vulnerable.

Types of Viruses

There has been a continuous arms race between virus writers and writers of antivirus software since viruses first appeared. As effective countermeasures have been developed for existing types of viruses, new types have been developed. [STEP93] suggests the following categories as being among the most significant types of viruses:

- **Parasitic virus:** The traditional and still most common form of virus. A parasitic virus attaches itself to executable files and replicates, when the infected program is executed, by finding other executable files to infect.
- **Memory-resident virus:** Lodges in main memory as part of a resident system program. From that point on, the virus infects every program that executes.
- **Boot sector virus:** Infects a master boot record or boot record and spreads when a system is booted from the disk containing the virus.
- **Stealth virus:** A form of virus explicitly designed to hide itself from detection by antivirus software.
- **Polymorphic virus:** A virus that mutates with every infection, making detection by the "signature" of the virus impossible.
- **Metamorphic virus:** As with a polymorphic virus, a metamorphic virus mutates with every infection. The difference is that a metamorphic virus rewrites itself completely at each iteration, increasing the difficulty of detection. Metamorphic viruses my change their behavior as well as their appearance.

One example of a **stealth virus** was discussed earlier: a virus that uses compression so that the infected program is exactly the same length as an uninfected version. Far more sophisticated techniques are possible. For example, a virus can place intercept logic in disk I/O routines, so that when there is an attempt to read suspected portions of the disk using these routines, the virus will present back the original, uninfected program. Thus, *stealth* is not a term that applies to a virus as such but, rather, is a technique used by a virus to evade detection.

A **polymorphic virus** creates copies during replication that are functionally equivalent but have distinctly different bit patterns. As with a stealth virus, the purpose is to defeat programs that scan for viruses. In this case, the "signature" of the virus will vary with each copy. To achieve this variation, the virus may randomly insert superfluous instructions or interchange the order of independent instructions. A more effective approach is to use encryption. A portion of the virus, generally called a *mutation engine*, creates a random encryption key to encrypt the remainder of the virus. The key is stored with the virus, and the mutation engine itself is altered. When an infected program is invoked, the virus uses the stored random key to decrypt the virus. When the virus replicates, a different random key is selected.

Another weapon in the virus writers' armory is the virus-creation toolkit. Such a toolkit enables a relative novice to create quickly a number of different viruses. Although viruses created with toolkits tend to be less sophisticated than viruses designed from scratch, the sheer number of new viruses that can be generated creates a problem for antivirus schemes.

Macro Viruses

In the mid-1990s, macro viruses became by far the most prevalent type of virus. Macro viruses are particularly threatening for a number of reasons:

1. A macro virus is platform independent. Virtually all of the macro viruses infect Microsoft Word documents. Any hardware platform and operating system that supports Word can be infected.
2. Macro viruses infect documents, not executable portions of code. Most of the information introduced onto a computer system is in the form of a document rather than a program.
3. Macro viruses are easily spread. A very common method is by electronic mail.

Macro viruses take advantage of a feature found in Word and other office applications such as Microsoft Excel, namely the macro. In essence, a macro is an executable program embedded in a word processing document or other type of file. Typically, users employ macros to automate repetitive tasks and thereby save keystrokes. The macro language is usually some form of the Basic programming language. A user might define a sequence of keystrokes in a macro and set it up so that the macro is invoked when a function key or special short combination of keys is input.

Successive releases of Word provide increased protection against macro viruses. For example, Microsoft offers an optional Macro Virus Protection tool that detects suspicious Word files and alerts the customer to the potential risk of opening a file with macros. Various antivirus product vendors have also developed tools to detect and correct macro viruses. As in other types of viruses, the arms race continues in the field of macro viruses, but they no longer are the predominant virus threat.

E-mail Viruses

A more recent development in malicious software is the e-mail virus. The first rapidly spreading e-mail viruses, such as Melissa, made use of a Microsoft Word macro embedded in an attachment. If the recipient opens the e-mail attachment, the Word macro is activated. Then

1. The e-mail virus sends itself to everyone on the mailing list in the user's e-mail package.
2. The virus does local damage.

At the end of 1999, a more powerful version of the e-mail virus appeared. This newer version can be activated merely by opening an e-mail that contains the virus rather than opening an attachment. The virus uses the Visual Basic scripting language supported by the e-mail package.

Thus we see a new generation of malware that arrives via e-mail and uses e-mail software features to replicate itself across the Internet. The virus propagates itself as soon as activated (either by opening an e-mail attachment of by opening the e-mail) to all of the e-mail addresses known to the infected host. As a result, whereas viruses used to take months or years to propagate, they now do so in hours. This makes it very difficult for antivirus software to respond before much damage is done. Ultimately, a greater degree of security must be built into Internet utility and application software on PCs to counter the growing threat.

Worms

A worm is a program that can replicate itself and send copies from computer to computer across network connections. Upon arrival, the worm may be activated to replicate and propagate again. In addition to propagation, the worm usually performs some unwanted function. An e-mail virus has some of the characteristics of a worm, because it propagates itself from system to system. However, we can still classify it as a virus because it requires a human to move it forward. A worm actively seeks out more machines to infect and each machine that is infected serves as an automated launching pad for attacks on other machines.

Network worm programs use network connections to spread from system to system. Once active within a system, a network worm can behave as a computer virus or bacteria, or it could implant Trojan horse programs or perform any number of disruptive or destructive actions.

To replicate itself, a network worm uses some sort of network vehicle. Examples include the following:

- **Electronic mail facility:** A worm mails a copy of itself to other systems.
- **Remote execution capability:** A worm executes a copy of itself on another system.
- **Remote login capability:** A worm logs onto a remote system as a user and then uses commands to copy itself from one system to the other.

The new copy of the worm program is then run on the remote system where, in addition to any functions that it performs at that system, it continues to spread in the same fashion.

A network worm exhibits the same characteristics as a computer virus: a dormant phase, a propagation phase, a triggering phase, and an execution phase. The propagation phase generally performs the following functions:

1. Search for other systems to infect by examining host tables or similar repositories of remote system addresses.
2. Establish a connection with a remote system.
3. Copy itself to the remote system and cause the copy to be run.

The network worm may also attempt to determine whether a system has previously been infected before copying itself to the system. In a multiprogramming system, it may also disguise its presence by naming itself as a system process or using some other name that may not be noticed by a system operator.

As with viruses, network worms are difficult to counter.

The Morris Worm Until the current generation of worms, the best known was the worm released onto the Internet by Robert Morris in 1998. The Morris worm was designed to spread on UNIX systems and used a number of different techniques for propagation. When a copy began execution, its first task was to discover other hosts known to this host that would allow entry from this host. The worm performed this task by examining a variety of lists and tables, including system tables that declared which other machines were trusted by this host, users' mail forwarding files, tables by which users gave themselves permission for access to remote accounts, and from a program that reported the status of network connections. For each discovered host, the worm tried a number of methods for gaining access:

1. It attempted to log on to a remote host as a legitimate user. In this method, the worm first attempted to crack the local password file, and then used the discovered passwords and corresponding user IDs. The assumption was that many users would use the same password on different systems. To obtain the passwords, the worm ran a password-cracking program that tried
   (a) Each user's account name and simple permutations of it
   (b) A list of 432 built-in passwords that Morris thought to be likely candidates
   (c) All the words in the local system directory
2. It exploited a bug in the finger protocol, which reports the whereabouts of a remote user.
3. It exploited a trapdoor in the debug option of the remote process that receives and sends mail.

If any of these attacks succeeded, the worm achieved communication with the operating system command interpreter. It then sent this interpreter a short bootstrap program, issued a command to execute that program, and then logged off. The bootstrap program then called back the parent program and downloaded the remainder of the worm. The new worm was then executed.

Recent Worm Attacks The contemporary era of worm threats began with the release of the Code Red worm in July of 2001. Code Red exploits a security hole in the Microsoft Internet Information Server (IIS) to penetrate and spread. It also disables the system file checker in Windows. The worm probes random IP addresses to spread to other hosts. During a certain period of time, it only spreads. It then initiates a denial-of-service attack against a government Web site by flooding the site with packets from numerous hosts. The worm then suspends activities and reactivates periodically. In the second wave of attack, Code Red infected nearly 360,000 servers in 14 hours. In addition to the havoc it causes at the targeted server, Code Red can consume enormous amounts of Internet capacity, disrupting service.

Code Red II is a variant that targets Microsoft IISs. In addition, this newer worm installs a backdoor allowing a hacker to direct activities of victim computers.

In late 2001, a more versatile worm appeared, known as Nimda. Nimda spreads by multiple mechanisms:

- from client to client via e-mail
- from client to client via open network shares

- from Web server to client via browsing of compromised Web sites
- from client to Web server via active scanning for and exploitation of various Microsoft IIS 4.0 / 5.0 directory traversal vulnerabilities
- from client to Web server via scanning for the back doors left behind by the "Code Red II" worms

The worm modifies Web documents (e.g., .htm, .html, and .asp files) and certain executable files found on the systems it infects and creates numerous copies of itself under various filenames.

In early 2003, the SQL Slammer worm appeared. This worm exploited a buffer overflow vulnerability in Microsoft SQL server. The Slammer was extremely compact and spread rapidly, infecting 90% of vulnerable hosts within 10 minutes. Late 2003 saw the arrival of the Sobig.f worm, which exploited open proxy servers to turn infected machines into spam engines. At its peak, Sobig.f reportedly accounted for one in every 17 messages and produced more than one million copies of itself within the first 24 hours.

Mydoom is a mass-mailing e-mail worm that appeared in 2004. It followed a growing trend of installing a backdoor in infected computers, thereby enabling hackers to gain remote access to data such as passwords and credit card numbers. Mydoom replicated up to 1000 times per minute and reportedly flooded the Internet with 100 million infected messages in 36 hours.

State of Worm Technology

The state of the art in worm technology includes the following:

- **Multiplatform:** Newer worms are not limited to Windows machines but can attack a variety of platforms, especially the popular varieties of UNIX.
- **Multiexploit:** New worms penetrate systems in a variety of ways, using exploits against Web servers, browsers, e-mail, file sharing, and other network-based applications.
- **Ultrafast spreading:** One technique to accelerate the spread of a worm is to conduct a prior Internet scan to accumulate Internet addresses of vulnerable machines.
- **Polymorphic:** To evade detection, skip past filters, and foil real-time analysis, worms adopt the virus polymorphic technique. Each copy of the worm has new code generated on the fly using functionally equivalent instructions and encryption techniques.
- **Metamorphic:** In addition to changing their appearance, metamorphic worms have a repertoire of behavior patterns that are unleashed at different stages of propagation.
- **Transport vehicles:** Because worms can rapidly compromise a large number of systems, they are ideal for spreading other distributed attack tools, such as distributed denial of service zombies.
- **Zero-day exploit:** To achieve maximum surprise and distribution, a worm should exploit an unknown vulnerability that is only discovered by the general network community when the worm is launched.

19.2 VIRUS COUNTERMEASURES

Antivirus Approaches

The ideal solution to the threat of viruses is prevention: Do not allow a virus to get into the system in the first place. This goal is, in general, impossible to achieve, although prevention can reduce the number of successful viral attacks. The next best approach is to be able to do the following:

- **Detection:** Once the infection has occurred, determine that it has occurred and locate the virus.
- **Identification:** Once detection has been achieved, identify the specific virus that has infected a program.
- **Removal:** Once the specific virus has been identified, remove all traces of the virus from the infected program and restore it to its original state. Remove the virus from all infected systems so that the disease cannot spread further.

If detection succeeds but either identification or removal is not possible, then the alternative is to discard the infected program and reload a clean backup version.

Advances in virus and antivirus technology go hand in hand. Early viruses were relatively simple code fragments and could be identified and purged with relatively simple antivirus software packages. As the virus arms race has evolved, both viruses and, necessarily, antivirus software have grown more complex and sophisticated.

[STEP93] identifies four generations of antivirus software:

- First generation: simple scanners
- Second generation: heuristic scanners
- Third generation: activity traps
- Fourth generation: full-featured protection

A **first-generation** scanner requires a virus signature to identify a virus. The virus may contain "wildcards" but has essentially the same structure and bit pattern in all copies. Such signature-specific scanners are limited to the detection of known viruses. Another type of first-generation scanner maintains a record of the length of programs and looks for changes in length.

A **second-generation** scanner does not rely on a specific signature. Rather, the scanner uses heuristic rules to search for probable virus infection. One class of such scanners looks for fragments of code that are often associated with viruses. For example, a scanner may look for the beginning of an encryption loop used in a polymorphic virus and discover the encryption key. Once the key is discovered, the scanner can decrypt the virus to identify it, then remove the infection and return the program to service.

Another second-generation approach is integrity checking. A checksum can be appended to each program. If a virus infects the program without changing the checksum, then an integrity check will catch the change. To counter a virus that is sophisticated enough to change the checksum when it infects a program, an encrypted hash function can be used. The encryption key is stored separately from the program so that the virus cannot generate a new hash code and encrypt that. By using a hash function rather than a simpler checksum, the virus is prevented from adjusting the program to produce the same hash code as before.

Third-generation programs are memory-resident programs that identify a virus by its actions rather than its structure in an infected program. Such programs have the advantage that it is not necessary to develop signatures and heuristics for a wide array of viruses. Rather, it is necessary only to identify the small set of actions that indicate an infection is being attempted and then to intervene.

Fourth-generation products are packages consisting of a variety of antivirus techniques used in conjunction. These include scanning and activity trap components. In addition, such a package includes access control capability, which limits the ability of viruses to penetrate a system and then limits the ability of a virus to update files in order to pass on the infection.

The arms race continues. With fourth-generation packages, a more comprehensive defense strategy is employed, broadening the scope of defense to more general-purpose computer security measures.

Advanced Antivirus Techniques

More sophisticated antivirus approaches and products continue to appear. In this subsection, we highlight two of the most important.

Generic Decryption Generic decryption (GD) technology enables the antivirus program to easily detect even the most complex polymorphic viruses, while maintaining fast scanning speeds [NACH97]. Recall that when a file containing a polymorphic virus is executed, the virus must decrypt itself to activate. In order to detect such a structure, executable files are run through a GD scanner, which contains the following elements:

- **CPU emulator:** A software-based virtual computer. Instructions in an executable file are interpreted by the emulator rather than executed on the underlying processor. The emulator includes software versions of all registers and other processor hardware, so that the underlying processor is unaffected by programs interpreted on the emulator.
- **Virus signature scanner:** A module that scans the target code looking for known virus signatures.
- **Emulation control module:** Controls the execution of the target code.

At the start of each simulation, the emulator begins interpreting instructions in the target code, one at a time. Thus, if the code includes a decryption routine that decrypts and hence exposes the virus, that code is interpreted. In effect, the virus does the work for the antivirus program by exposing the virus. Periodically, the control module interrupts interpretation to scan the target code for virus signatures.

During interpretation, the target code can cause no damage to the actual personal computer environment, because it is being interpreted in a completely controlled environment.

The most difficult design issue with a GD scanner is to determine how long to run each interpretation. Typically, virus elements are activated soon after a program begins executing, but this need not be the case. The longer the scanner emulates a particular program, the more likely it is to catch any hidden viruses. However, the antivirus program can take up only a limited amount of time and resources before users complain.

Digital Immune System The digital immune system is a comprehensive approach to virus protection developed by IBM [KEPH97a, KEPH97b]. The motivation for this development has been the rising threat of Internet-based virus propagation. We first say a few words about this threat and then summarize IBM's approach.

Traditionally, the virus threat was characterized by the relatively slow spread of new viruses and new mutations. Antivirus software was typically updated on a monthly basis, and this has been sufficient to control the problem. Also traditionally, the Internet played a comparatively small role in the spread of viruses. But as [CHES97] points out, two major trends in Internet technology have had an increasing impact on the rate of virus propagation in recent years:

- **Integrated mail systems:** Systems such as Lotus Notes and Microsoft Outlook make it very simple to send anything to anyone and to work with objects that are received.
- **Mobile-program systems:** Capabilities such as Java and ActiveX allow programs to move on their own from one system to another.

In response to the threat posed by these Internet-based capabilities, IBM has developed a prototype digital immune system. This system expands on the use of program emulation discussed in the preceding subsection and provides a general-purpose emulation and virus-detection system. The objective of this system is to provide rapid response time so that viruses can be stamped out almost as soon as they are introduced. When a new virus enters an organization, the immune system automatically captures it, analyzes it, adds detection and shielding for it, removes it, and passes information about that virus to systems running IBM AntiVirus so that it can be detected before it is allowed to run elsewhere.

Figure 19.4 illustrates the typical steps in digital immune system operation:

1. A monitoring program on each PC uses a variety of heuristics based on system behavior, suspicious changes to programs, or family signature to infer that a virus may be present. The monitoring program forwards a copy of any program thought to be infected to an administrative machine within the organization.
2. The administrative machine encrypts the sample and sends it to a central virus analysis machine.
3. This machine creates an environment in which the infected program can be safely run for analysis. Techniques used for this purpose include emulation, or the creation of a protected environment within which the suspect program can be executed and monitored. The virus analysis machine then produces a prescription for identifying and removing the virus.
4. The resulting prescription is sent back to the administrative machine.
5. The administrative machine forwards the prescription to the infected client.
6. The prescription is also forwarded to other clients in the organization.
7. Subscribers around the world receive regular antivirus updates that protect them from the new virus.

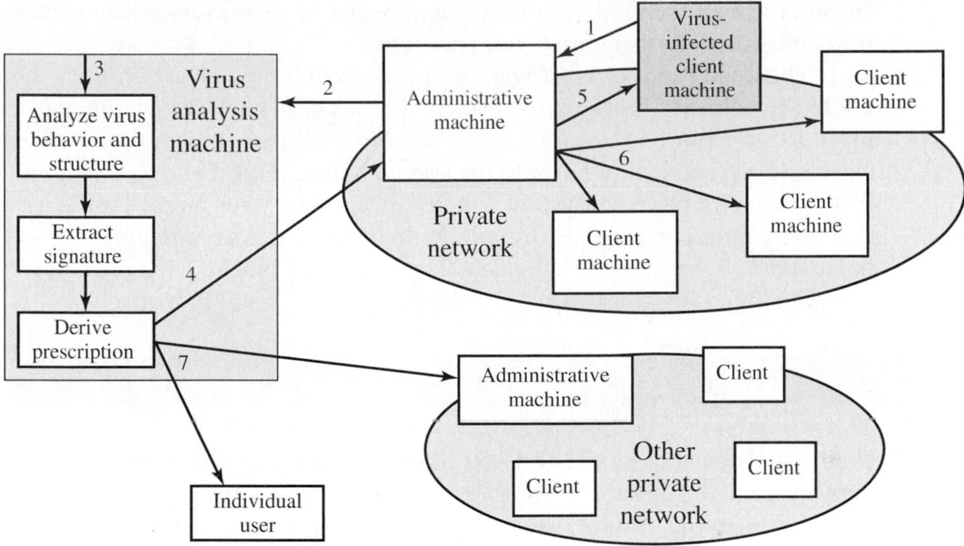

Figure 19.4 Digital Immune System

The success of the digital immune system depends on the ability of the virus analysis machine to detect new and innovative virus strains. By constantly analyzing and monitoring the viruses found in the wild, it should be possible to continually update the digital immune software to keep up with the threat.

Behavior-Blocking Software

Unlike heuristics or fingerprint-based scanners, behavior-blocking software integrates with the operating system of a host computer and monitors program behavior in real-time for malicious actions. The behavior blocking software then blocks potentially malicious actions before they have a chance to affect the system. Monitored behaviors can include the following:

- Attempts to open, view, delete, and/or modify files;
- Attempts to format disk drives and other unrecoverable disk operations;
- Modifications to the logic of executable files or macros;
- Modification of critical system settings, such as start-up settings;
- Scripting of e-mail and instant messaging clients to send executable content; and
- Initiation of network communications.

If the behavior blocker detects that a program is initiating would-be malicious behaviors as it runs, it can block these behaviors in real-time and/or terminate the offending software. This gives it a fundamental advantage over such established antivirus detection techniques as fingerprinting or heuristics. While there are literally trillions of different ways to obfuscate and rearrange the instructions of a virus or worm, many of which will evade detection by a fingerprint scanner or heuristic, eventually malicious code must make a well-defined request to the operating system. Given that the behavior blocker can intercept all such requests, it can identify and block malicious actions regardless of how obfuscated the program logic appears to be.

The ability to watch software as it runs in real time clearly confers a huge benefit to the behavior blocker; however, it also has drawbacks. Since the malicious code must actually run on the target machine before all its behaviors can be identified, it can cause a great deal of harm to the system before it has been detected and blocked by the behavior blocking system. For instance, a new virus might shuffle a number of seemingly unimportant files around the hard drive before infecting a single file and being blocked. Even though the actual infection was blocked, the user may be unable to locate their files, causing a loss to productivity or possibly worse.

19.3 DISTRIBUTED DENIAL OF SERVICE ATTACKS

Distributed denial of service (DDoS) attacks present a significant security threat to corporations, and the threat appears to be growing [VIJA02]. In one study, covering a three-week period in 2001, investigators observed more than 12,000 attacks against more than 5000 distinct targets, ranging from well-known ecommerce companies such as Amazon and Hotmail to small foreign ISPs and dial-up connections [MOOR01]. DDoS attacks make computer systems inaccessible by flooding servers, networks, or even end user systems with useless traffic so that legitimate users can no longer gain access to those resources. In a typical DDoS attack, a large number of compromised hosts are amassed to send useless packets. In recent years, the attack methods and tools have become more sophisticated, effective, and more difficult to trace to the real attackers, while defense technologies have been unable to withstand large-scale attacks [CHAN02].

A denial of service (DoS) attack is an attempt to prevent legitimate users of a service from using that service. When this attack comes from a single host or network node, then it is simply referred to as a DoS attack. A more serious threat is posed by a DDoS attack. In a DDoS attack, an attacker is able to recruit a number of hosts throughout the Internet to simultaneously or in a coordinated fashion launch an attack upon the target. This section is concerned with DDoS attacks. First, we look at the nature and types of attacks. Next, we examine means by which an attacker is able to recruit a network of hosts for attack launch. Finally, this section looks at countermeasures.

DDoS Attack Description

A DDoS attack attempts to consume the target's resources so that it cannot provide service. One way to classify DDoS attacks is in terms of the type of resource that is consumed. Broadly speaking, the resource consumed is either an internal host resource on the target system or data transmission capacity in the local network to which the target is attacked.

A simple example of an **internal resource attack** is the SYN flood attack. Figure 19.5a shows the steps involved:

1. The attacker takes control of multiple hosts over the Internet, instructing them to contact the target Web server.
2. The slave hosts begin sending TCP/IP SYN (synchronize/initialization) packets, with erroneous return IP address information, to the target.

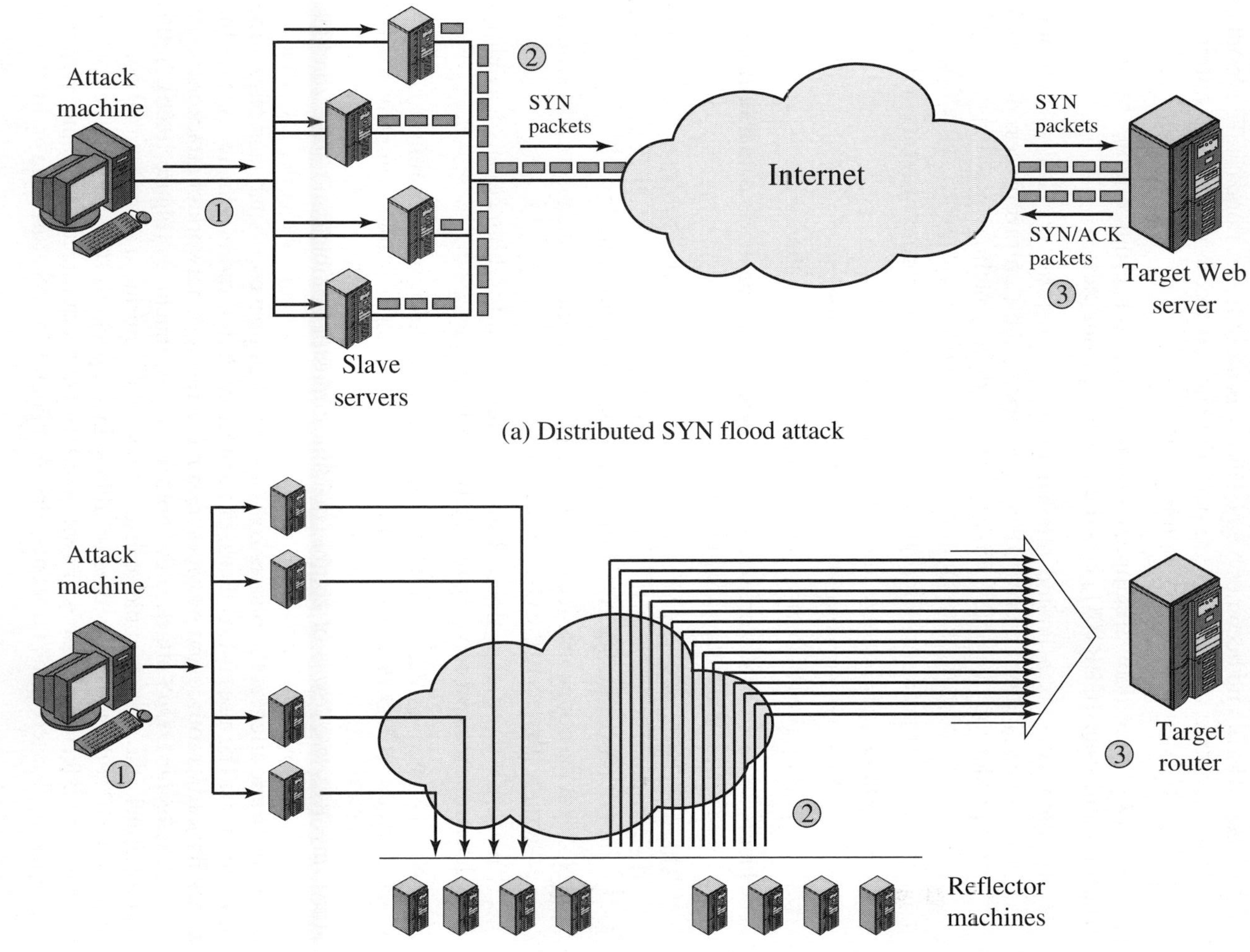

Figure 19.5 Examples of Simple DDoS Attacks

3. Each SYN packet is a request to open a TCP connection. For each such packet, the Web server responds with a SYN/ACK (synchronize/acknowledge) packet, trying to establish a TCP connection with a TCP entity at a spurious IP address. The Web server maintains a data structure for each SYN request waiting for a response back and becomes bogged down as more traffic floods in. The result is that legitimate connections are denied while the victim machine is waiting to complete bogus "half-open" connections.

The TCP state data structure is a popular internal resource target but by no means the only one. [CERT01] gives the following examples:

1. In many systems, a limited number of data structures are available to hold process information (process identifiers, process table entries, process slots, etc.). An intruder may be able to consume these data structures by writing a simple program or script that does nothing but repeatedly create copies of itself.
2. An intruder may also attempt to consume disk space in other ways, including
   - generating excessive numbers of mail messages
   - intentionally generating errors that must be logged
   - placing files in anonymous ftp areas or network-shared areas

Figure 19.5b illustrates an example of an **attack that consumes data transmission resources**. The following steps are involved:

1. The attacker takes control of multiple hosts over the Internet, instructing them to send ICMP ECHO packets[1] with the target's spoofed IP address to a group of hosts that act as reflectors, as described subsequently.
2. Nodes at the bounce site receive multiple spoofed requests and respond by sending echo reply packets to the target site.
3. The target's router is flooded with packets from the bounce site, leaving no data transmission capacity for legitimate traffic.

Another way to classify DDoS attacks is as either direct or reflector DDoS attacks. In a **direct DDoS** attack (Figure 19.6a), the attacker is able to implant zombie software on a number of sites distributed throughout the Internet. Often, the DDoS attack involves two levels of zombie machines: master zombies and slave zombies. The hosts of both machines have been infected with malicious code. The attacker coordinates and triggers the master zombies, which in turn coordinate and trigger the slave zombies. The use of two levels of zombies makes it more difficult to trace the attack back to its source and provides for a more resilient network of attackers.

A **reflector DDoS** attack adds another layer of machines (Figure 19.6b). In this type of attack, the slave zombies construct packets requiring a response that contain the target's IP address as the source IP address in the packet's IP header. These packets are sent to uninfected machines known as reflectors. The uninfected machines respond with packets directed at the target machine. A reflector DDoS attack can easily involve

[1]The Internet Control Message Protocol (ICMP) is an IP-level protocol for the exchange of control packets between a router and a host or between hosts. The ECHO packet requires the recipient to respond with an echo reply to check that communication is possible between entities.

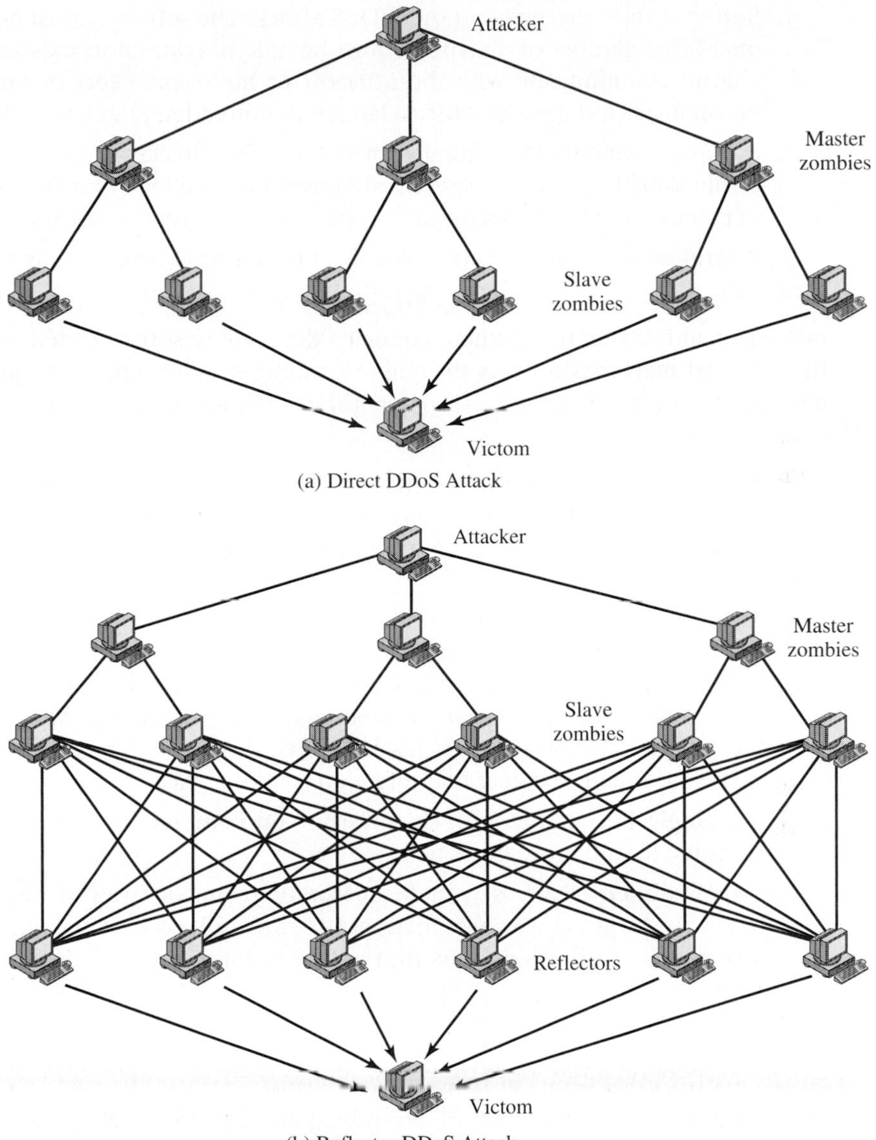

Figure 19.6 Types of Flooding-Based DDoS Attacks

more machines and more traffic than a direct DDoS attack and hence be more damaging. Further, tracing back the attack or filtering out the attack packets is more difficult because the attack comes from widely dispersed uninfected machines.

Constructing the Attack Network

The first step in a DDoS attack is for the attacker to infect a number of machines with zombie software that will ultimately be used to carry out the attack. The essential ingredients in this phase of the attack are the following:

1. Software that can carry out the DDoS attack. The software must be able to run on a large number of machines, must be able to conceal its existence, must be able to communicate with the attacker or have some sort of time-triggered mechanism, and must be able to launch the intended attack toward the target.
2. A vulnerability in a large number of systems. The attacker must become aware of a vulnerability that many system administrators and individual users have failed to patch and that enables the attacker to install the zombie software.
3. A strategy for locating vulnerable machines, a process known as scanning.

In the scanning process, the attacker first seeks out a number of vulnerable machines and infects them. Then, typically, the zombie software that is installed in the infected machines repeats the same scanning process, until a large distributed network of infected machines is created. [MIRK04] lists the following types of scanning strategies:

- **Random:** Each compromised host probes random addresses in the IP address space, using a different seed. This technique produces a high volume of Internet traffic, which may cause generalized disruption even before the actual attack is launched.
- **Hit-list:** The attacker first compiles a long list of potential vulnerable machines. This can be a slow process done over a long period to avoid detection that an attack is underway. Once the list is compiled, the attacker begins infecting machines on the list. Each infected machine is provided with a portion of list to scan. This strategy results in a very short scanning period, which may make it difficult to detect that infection is taking place.
- **Topological:** This method uses information contained on an infected victim machine to find more hosts to scan.
- **Local subnet:** If a host can be infected behind a firewall, that host then looks for targets in its own local network. The host uses the subnet address structure to find other hosts that would otherwise be protected by the firewall.

DDoS Countermeasures

In general, there are three lines of defense against DDoS attacks [CHAN02]:

- **Attack prevention and preemption (before the attack):** These mechanisms enable the victim to endure attack attempts without denying service to legitimate clients. Techniques include enforcing policies for resource consumption and providing backup resources available on demand. In addition, prevention mechanisms modify systems and protocols on the Internet to reduce the possibility of DDoS attacks.
- **Attack detection and filtering (during the attack):** These mechanisms attempt to detect the attack as it begins and respond immediately. This minimizes the impact of the attack on the target. Detection involves looking for suspicious patterns of behavior. Response involves filtering out packets likely to be part of the attack.

- **Attack source traceback and identification (during and after the attack):** This is an attempt to identify the source of the attack as a first step in preventing future attacks. However, this method typically does not yield results fast enough, if at all, to mitigate an ongoing attack.

The challenge in coping with DDoS attacks is the sheer number of ways in which they can operate. Thus DDoS countermeasures must evolve with the threat.

19.4 RECOMMENDED READING AND WEB SITES

For a thorough understanding of viruses, the book to read is [SZOR05]. Another excellent treatment is [HARL01]. Good overview articles on viruses and worms are [CASS01], [FORR97], [KEPH97], and [NACH97]. [MEIN01] provides a good treatment of the Code Red worm.

[PATR04] is a worthwhile survey of DDoS attacks. [MIRK04] is a thorough description of the variety of DDoS attacks and countermeasures. [CHAN02] is a good examination of DDoS defense strategies.

CASS01 Cass, S. "Anatomy of Malice." *IEEE Spectrum*, November 2001.

CHAN02 Chang, R. "Defending Against Flooding-Based Distributed Denial-of-Service Attacks: A Tutorial." *IEEE Communications Magazine*, October 2002.

FORR97 Forrest, S.; Hofmeyr, S.; and Somayaji, A. "Computer Immunology." *Communications of the ACM*, October 1997.

HARL01 Harley, D.; Slade, R.; and Gattiker, U. *Viruses Revealed*. New York: Osborne/McGraw-Hill, 2001.

KEPH97 Kephart, J.; Sorkin, G.; Chess, D.; and White, S. "Fighting Computer Viruses." *Scientific American*, November 1997.

MEIN01 Meinel, C. "Code Red for the Web." *Scientific American*, October 2001.

MIRK04 Mirkovic, J., and Relher, P. "A Taxonomy of DDoS Attack and DDoS Defense Mechanisms." *ACM SIGCOMM Computer Communications Review*, April 2004.

NACH97 Nachenberg, C. "Computer Virus-Antivirus Coevolution." *Communications of the ACM*, January 1997.

PATR04 Patrikakis, C.; Masikos, M.; and Zouraraki, O. "Distributed Denial of Service Attacks." *The Internet Protocol Journal*, December 2004.

SZOR05 Szor, P., *The Art of Computer Virus Research and Defense*. Reading, MA: Addison-Wesley, 2005.

Recommended Web Sites:

- **AntiVirus Online:** IBM's site on virus information
- **Vmyths:** Dedicated to exposing virus hoaxes and dispelling misconceptions about real viruses
- **DDoS Attacks/Tools:** Extensive list of links and documents

19.5 KEY TERMS, REVIEW QUESTIONS, AND PROBLEMS

Key Terms

auto-rooter backdoor digital immune system direct DDoS attack distributed denial of service (DDoS) downloaders e-mail virus exploits	flooder keylogger kit logic bomb macro virus malicious software (malware) polymorphic virus reflector DDoS attack	rootkit spammer program stealth virus trapdoor trojan horse virus worm zombie

Review Questions

19.1 What is the role of compression in the operation of a virus?

19.2 What is the role of encryption in the operation of a virus?

19.3 What are typical phases of operation of a virus or worm?

19.4 In general terms, how does a worm propagate?

19.5 What is a digital immune system?

19.6 How does behavior-blocking software work?

19.7 What is a DDoS?

Problems

19.1 There is a flaw in the virus program of Figure 19.1. What is it?

19.2 The question arises as to whether it is possible to develop a program that can analyze a piece of software to determine if it is a virus. Consider that we have a program D that is supposed to be able to do that. That is, for any program P, if we run D(P), the result returned is TRUE (P is a virus) or FALSE (P is not a virus). Now consider the following program:

```
Program CV :=
  { . . .
  main-program :=
         {if D(CV) then goto next:
                else infect-executable;
         }
next:
  }
```

In the preceding program, infect-executable is a module that scans memory for executable programs and replicates itself in those programs. Determine if D can correctly decide whether CV is a virus.

FIREWALLS

The function of a strong position is to make the forces holding it practically unassailable.

—*On War,* Carl Von Clausewitz

On the day that you take up your command, block the frontier passes, destroy the official tallies, and stop the passage of all emissaries.

—*The Art of War,* Sun Tzu

KEY POINTS

- A firewall forms a barrier through which the traffic going in each direction must pass. A firewall security policy dictates which traffic is authorized to pass in each direction.
- A firewall may be designed to operate as a filter at the level of IP packets, or may operate at a higher protocol layer.
- A trusted system is a computer and operating system that can be verified to implement a given security policy. Typically, the focus of a trusted system is access control. A policy is implemented that dictates what objects may be accessed by what subjects.
- The common criteria for information technology security is an international standards initiative to define a common set of security requirements and a systematic means of evaluating products against those requirements.

Firewalls can be an effective means of protecting a local system or network of systems from network-based security threats while at the same time affording access to the outside world via wide area networks and the Internet.

We begin this chapter with an overview of the functionality and design principles of firewalls. Next, we address the issue of the security of the firewall itself and, in particular, the concept of a trusted system, or secure operating system.

20.1 FIREWALL DESIGN PRINCIPLES

Information systems in corporations, government agencies, and other organizations have undergone a steady evolution:

- Centralized data processing system, with a central mainframe supporting a number of directly connected terminals
- Local area networks (LANs) interconnecting PCs and terminals to each other and the mainframe
- Premises network, consisting of a number of LANs, interconnecting PCs, servers, and perhaps a mainframe or two

- Enterprise-wide network, consisting of multiple, geographically distributed premises networks interconnected by a private wide area network (WAN)
- Internet connectivity, in which the various premises networks all hook into the Internet and may or may not also be connected by a private WAN

Internet connectivity is no longer optional for organizations. The information and services available are essential to the organization. Moreover, individual users within the organization want and need Internet access, and if this is not provided via their LAN, they will use dial-up capability from their PC to an Internet service provider (ISP). However, while Internet access provides benefits to the organization, it enables the outside world to reach and interact with local network assets. This creates a threat to the organization. While it is possible to equip each workstation and server on the premises network with strong security features, such as intrusion protection, this is not a practical approach. Consider a network with hundreds or even thousands of systems, running a mix of various versions of UNIX, plus Windows. When a security flaw is discovered, each potentially affected system must be upgraded to fix that flaw. The alternative, increasingly accepted, is the firewall. The firewall is inserted between the premises network and the Internet to establish a controlled link and to erect an outer security wall or perimeter. The aim of this perimeter is to protect the premises network from Internet-based attacks and to provide a single choke point where security and audit can be imposed. The firewall may be a single computer system or a set of two or more systems that cooperate to perform the firewall function.

In this section, we look first at the general characteristics of firewalls. Then we look at the types of firewalls currently in common use. Finally, we examine some of the most common firewall configurations.

Firewall Characteristics

[BELL94b] lists the following design goals for a firewall:

1. All traffic from inside to outside, and vice versa, must pass through the firewall. This is achieved by physically blocking all access to the local network except via the firewall. Various configurations are possible, as explained later in this section.
2. Only authorized traffic, as defined by the local security policy, will be allowed to pass. Various types of firewalls are used, which implement various types of security policies, as explained later in this section.
3. The firewall itself is immune to penetration. This implies that use of a trusted system with a secure operating system. This topic is discussed in Section 20.2.

[SMIT97] lists four general techniques that firewalls use to control access and enforce the site's security policy. Originally, firewalls focused primarily on service control, but they have since evolved to provide all four:

- **Service control:** Determines the types of Internet services that can be accessed, inbound or outbound. The firewall may filter traffic on the basis of IP address and TCP port number; may provide proxy software that receives and interprets each service request before passing it on; or may host the server software itself, such as a Web or mail service.

- **Direction control:** Determines the direction in which particular service requests may be initiated and allowed to flow through the firewall.
- **User control:** Controls access to a service according to which user is attempting to access it. This feature is typically applied to users inside the firewall perimeter (local users). It may also be applied to incoming traffic from external users; the latter requires some form of secure authentication technology, such as is provided in IPSec (Chapter 16).
- **Behavior control:** Controls how particular services are used. For example, the firewall may filter e-mail to eliminate spam, or it may enable external access to only a portion of the information on a local Web server.

Before proceeding to the details of firewall types and configurations, it is best to summarize what one can expect from a firewall. The following capabilities are within the scope of a firewall:

1. A firewall defines a single choke point that keeps unauthorized users out of the protected network, prohibits potentially vulnerable services from entering or leaving the network, and provides protection from various kinds of IP spoofing and routing attacks. The use of a single choke point simplifies security management because security capabilities are consolidated on a single system or set of systems.
2. A firewall provides a location for monitoring security-related events. Audits and alarms can be implemented on the firewall system.
3. A firewall is a convenient platform for several Internet functions that are not security related. These include a network address translator, which maps local addresses to Internet addresses, and a network management function that audits or logs Internet usage.
4. A firewall can serve as the platform for IPSec. Using the tunnel mode capability described in Chapter 16, the firewall can be used to implement virtual private networks.

Firewalls have their limitations, including the following:

1. The firewall cannot protect against attacks that bypass the firewall. Internal systems may have dial-out capability to connect to an ISP. An internal LAN may support a modem pool that provides dial-in capability for traveling employees and telecommuters.
2. The firewall does not protect against internal threats, such as a disgruntled employee or an employee who unwittingly cooperates with an external attacker.
3. The firewall cannot protect against the transfer of virus-infected programs or files. Because of the variety of operating systems and applications supported inside the perimeter, it would be impractical and perhaps impossible for the firewall to scan all incoming files, e-mail, and messages for viruses.

Types of Firewalls

Figure 20.1 illustrates the three common types of firewalls: packet filters, application-level gateways, and circuit-level gateways. We examine each of these in turn.

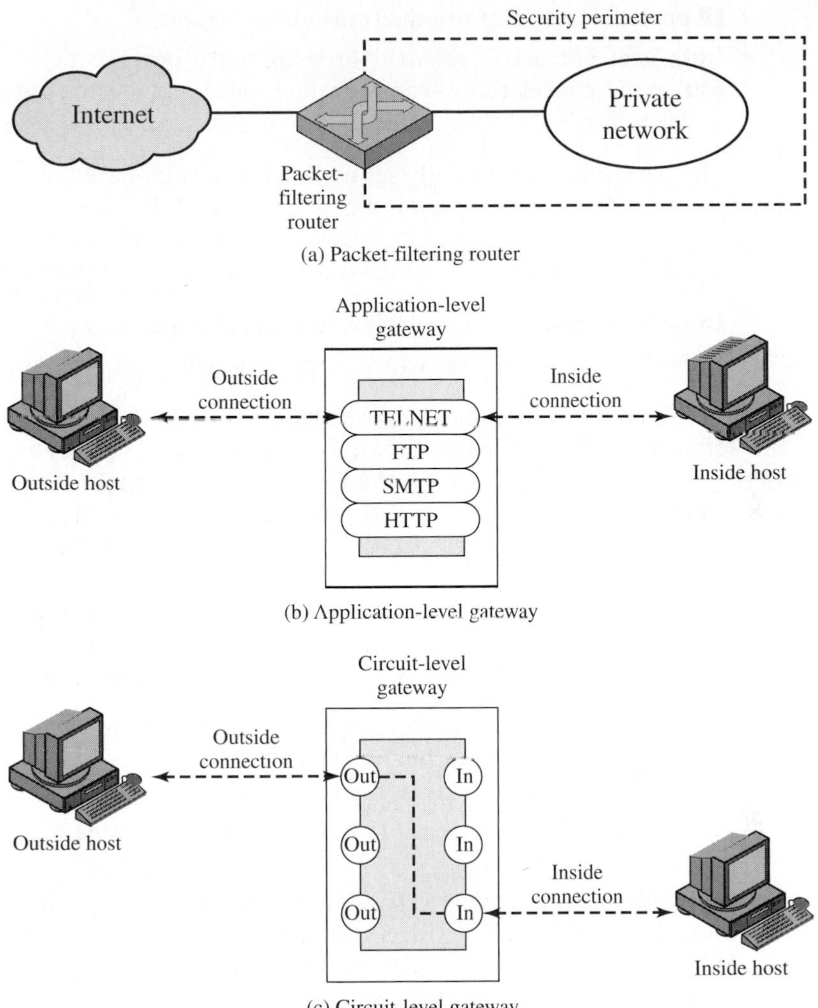

Figure 20.1 Firewall Types

Packet-Filtering Router A packet-filtering router applies a set of rules to each incoming and outgoing IP packet and then forwards or discards the packet. The router is typically configured to filter packets going in both directions (from and to the internal network). Filtering rules are based on information contained in a network packet:

- **Source IP address:** The IP address of the system that originated the IP packet (e.g., 192.178.1.1)
- **Destination IP address:** The IP address of the system the IP packet is trying to reach (e.g., 192.168.1.2)
- **Source and destination transport-level address:** The transport level (e.g., TCP or UDP) port number, which defines applications such as SNMP or TELNET

- **IP protocol field:** Defines the transport protocol
- **Interface:** For a router with three or more ports, which interface of the router the packet came from or which interface of the router the packet is destined for

The packet filter is typically set up as a list of rules based on matches to fields in the IP or TCP header. If there is a match to one of the rules, that rule is invoked to determine whether to forward or discard the packet. If there is no match to any rule, then a default action is taken. Two default policies are possible:

- **Default** = *discard*: That which is not expressly permitted is prohibited.
- **Default** = *forward*: That which is not expressly prohibited is permitted.

The default discard policy is more conservative. Initially, everything is blocked, and services must be added on a case-by-case basis. This policy is more visible to users, who are more likely to see the firewall as a hindrance. The default forward policy increases ease of use for end users but provides reduced security; the security administrator must, in essence, react to each new security threat as it becomes known.

Table 20.1, from [BELL94b], gives some examples of packet-filtering rule sets. In each set, the rules are applied top to bottom. The "*" in a field is a wildcard designator that matches everything. We assume that the default = discard policy is in force.

A. Inbound mail is allowed (port 25 is for SMTP incoming), but only to a gateway host. However, packets from a particular external host, SPIGOT, are blocked because that host has a history of sending massive files in e-mail messages.

B. This is an explicit statement of the default policy. All rule sets include this rule implicitly as the last rule.

C. This rule set is intended to specify that any inside host can send mail to the outside. A TCP packet with a destination port of 25 is routed to the SMTP server on the destination machine. The problem with this rule is that the use of port 25 for SMTP receipt is only a default; an outside machine could be configured to have some other application linked to port 25. As this rule is written, an attacker could gain access to internal machines by sending packets with a TCP source port number of 25.

D. This rule set achieves the intended result that was not achieved in C. The rules take advantage of a feature of TCP connections. Once a connection is set up, the ACK flag of a TCP segment is set to acknowledge segments sent from the other side. Thus, this rule set states that it allows IP packets where the source IP address is one of a list of designated internal hosts and the destination TCP port number is 25. It also allows incoming packets with a source port number of 25 that include the ACK flag in the TCP segment. Note that we explicitly designate source and destination systems to define these rules explicitly.

E. This rule set is one approach to handling FTP connections. With FTP, two TCP connections are used: a control connection to set up the file transfer and a data connection for the actual file transfer. The data connection uses a different port number that is dynamically assigned for the transfer. Most servers, and hence

Table 20.1 Packet-Filtering Examples

A

action	ourhost	port	theirhost	port	comment
block	*	*	SPIGOT	*	we don't trust these people
allow	OUR-GW	25	*	*	connection to our SMTP port

B

action	ourhost	port	theirhost	port	comment
block	*	*	*	*	default

C

action	ourhost	port	theirhost	port	comment
allow	*	*	*	25	connection to their SMTP port

D

action	src	port	dest	port	flags	comment
allow	{our hosts}	*	*	25		our packets to their SMTP port
allow	*	25	*	*	ACK	their replies

E

action	src	port	dest	port	flags	comment
allow	{our hosts}	*	*	*		our outgoing calls
allow	*	*	*	*	ACK	replies to our calls
allow	*	*	*	>1024		traffic to nonservers

most attack targets, live on low-numbered ports; most outgoing calls tend to use a higher-numbered port, typically above 1023. Thus, this rule set allows

—Packets that originate internally

—Reply packets to a connection initiated by an internal machine

—Packets destined for a high-numbered port on an internal machine

This scheme requires that the systems be configured so that only the appropriate port numbers are in use.

Rule set E points out the difficulty in dealing with applications at the packet-filtering level. Another way to deal with FTP and similar applications is an application-level gateway, described later in this section.

One advantage of a packet-filtering router is its simplicity. Also, packet filters typically are transparent to users and are very fast. [WACK02] lists the following weaknesses of packet filter firewalls:

- Because packet filter firewalls do not examine upper-layer data, they cannot prevent attacks that employ application-specific vulnerabilities or functions. For example, a packet filter firewall cannot block specific application commands; if a packet filter firewall allows a given application, all functions available within that application will be permitted.
- Because of the limited information available to the firewall, the logging functionality present in packet filter firewalls is limited. Packet filter logs normally contain the same information used to make access control decisions (source address, destination address, and traffic type).
- Most packet filter firewalls do not support advanced user authentication schemes. Once again, this limitation is mostly due to the lack of upper-layer functionality by the firewall.
- They are generally vulnerable to attacks and exploits that take advantage of problems within the TCP/IP specification and protocol stack, such as *network layer address spoofing*. Many packet filter firewalls cannot detect a network packet in which the OSI Layer 3 addressing information has been altered. Spoofing attacks are generally employed by intruders to bypass the security controls implemented in a firewall platform.
- Finally, due to the small number of variables used in access control decisions, packet filter firewalls are susceptible to security breaches caused by improper configurations. In other words, it is easy to accidentally configure a packet filter firewall to allow traffic types, sources, and destinations that should be denied based on an organization's information security policy.

Some of the attacks that can be made on packet-filtering routers and the appropriate countermeasures are the following:

- **IP address spoofing:** The intruder transmits packets from the outside with a source IP address field containing an address of an internal host. The attacker hopes that the use of a spoofed address will allow penetration of systems that employ simple source address security, in which packets from specific trusted internal hosts are accepted. The countermeasure is to discard packets with an inside source address if the packet arrives on an external interface.

- **Source routing attacks:** The source station specifies the route that a packet should take as it crosses the Internet, in the hopes that this will bypass security measures that do not analyze the source routing information. The countermeasure is to discard all packets that use this option.
- **Tiny fragment attacks:** The intruder uses the IP fragmentation option to create extremely small fragments and force the TCP header information into a separate packet fragment. This attack is designed to circumvent filtering rules that depend on TCP header information. Typically, a packet filter will make a filtering decision on the first fragment of a packet. All subsequent fragments of that packet are filtered out solely on the basis that they are part of the packet whose first fragment was rejected. The attacker hopes that the filtering router examines only the first fragment and that the remaining fragments are passed through. A tiny fragment attack can be defeated by enforcing a rule that the first fragment of a packet must contain a predefined minimum amount of the transport header. If the first fragment is rejected, the filter can remember the packet and discard all subsequent fragments.

Stateful Inspection Firewalls A traditional packet filter makes filtering decisions on an individual packet basis and does not take into consideration any higher layer context. To understand what is meant by context and why a traditional packet filter is limited with regard to context, a little background is needed. Most standardized applications that run on top of TCP follow a client/server model. For example, for the Simple Mail Transfer Protocol (SMTP), e-mail is transmitted from a client system to a server system. The client system generates new e-mail messages, typically from user input. The server system accepts incoming e-mail messages and places them in the appropriate user mailboxes. SMTP operates by setting up a TCP connection between client and server, in which the TCP server port number, which identifies the SMTP server application, is 25. The TCP port number for the SMTP client is a number between 1024 and 65535 that is generated by the SMTP client.

In general, when an application that uses TCP creates a session with a remote host, it creates a TCP connection in which the TCP port number for the remote (server) application is a number less than 1024 and the TCP port number for the local (client) application is a number between 1024 and 65535. The numbers less than 1024 are the "well-known" port numbers and are assigned permanently to particular applications (e.g., 25 for server SMTP). The numbers between 1024 and 65535 are generated dynamically and have temporary significance only for the lifetime of a TCP connection.

A simple packet-filtering firewall must permit inbound network traffic on all these high-numbered ports for TCP-based traffic to occur. This creates a vulnerability that can be exploited by unauthorized users.

A stateful inspection packet filter tightens up the rules for TCP traffic by creating a directory of outbound TCP connections, as shown in Table 20.2. There is an entry for each currently established connection. The packet filter will now allow incoming traffic to high-numbered ports only for those packets that fit the profile of one of the entries in this directory.

Application-Level Gateway An application-level gateway, also called a proxy server, acts as a relay of application-level traffic (Figure 20.1b). The user contacts

Table 20.2 Example Stateful Firewall Connection State Table [WACK02]

Source Address	Source Port	Destination Address	Destination Port	Connection State
192.168.1.100	1030	210.9.88.29	80	Established
192.168.1.102	1031	216.32.42.123	80	Established
192.168.1.101	1033	173.66.32.122	25	Established
192.168.1.106	1035	177.231.32.12	79	Established
223.43.21.231	1990	192.168.1.6	80	Established
219.22.123.32	2112	192.168.1.6	80	Established
210.99.212.18	3321	192.168.1.6	80	Established
24.102.32.23	1025	192.168.1.6	80	Established
223.212.212	1046	192.168.1.6	80	Established

the gateway using a TCP/IP application, such as Telnet or FTP, and the gateway asks the user for the name of the remote host to be accessed. When the user responds and provides a valid user ID and authentication information, the gateway contacts the application on the remote host and relays TCP segments containing the application data between the two endpoints. If the gateway does not implement the proxy code for a specific application, the service is not supported and cannot be forwarded across the firewall. Further, the gateway can be configured to support only specific features of an application that the network administrator considers acceptable while denying all other features.

Application-level gateways tend to be more secure than packet filters. Rather than trying to deal with the numerous possible combinations that are to be allowed and forbidden at the TCP and IP level, the application-level gateway need only scrutinize a few allowable applications. In addition, it is easy to log and audit all incoming traffic at the application level.

A prime disadvantage of this type of gateway is the additional processing overhead on each connection. In effect, there are two spliced connections between the end users, with the gateway at the splice point, and the gateway must examine and forward all traffic in both directions.

Circuit-Level Gateway A third type of firewall is the circuit-level gateway (Figure 20.1c). This can be a stand-alone system or it can be a specialized function performed by an application-level gateway for certain applications. A circuit-level gateway does not permit an end-to-end TCP connection; rather, the gateway sets up two TCP connections, one between itself and a TCP user on an inner host and one between itself and a TCP user on an outside host. Once the two connections are established, the gateway typically relays TCP segments from one connection to the other without examining the contents. The security function consists of determining which connections will be allowed.

A typical use of circuit-level gateways is a situation in which the system administrator trusts the internal users. The gateway can be configured to support application-level or proxy service on inbound connections and circuit-level functions for outbound connections. In this configuration, the gateway can incur the processing overhead of examining incoming application data for forbidden functions but does not incur that overhead on outgoing data.

An example of a circuit-level gateway implementation is the SOCKS package [KOBL92]; version 5 of SOCKS is defined in RFC 1928. The RFC defines SOCKS in the following fashion:

> The protocol described here is designed to provide a framework for client-server applications in both the TCP and UDP domains to conveniently and securely use the services of a network firewall. The protocol is conceptually a "shim-layer" between the application layer and the transport layer, and as such does not provide network-layer gateway services, such as forwarding of ICMP messages.

SOCKS consists of the following components:

- The SOCKS server, which runs on a UNIX-based firewall.
- The SOCKS client library, which runs on internal hosts protected by the firewall.
- SOCKS-ified versions of several standard client programs such as FTP and TELNET. The implementation of the SOCKS protocol typically involves the recompilation or relinking of TCP-based client applications to use the appropriate encapsulation routines in the SOCKS library.

When a TCP-based client wishes to establish a connection to an object that is reachable only via a firewall (such determination is left up to the implementation), it must open a TCP connection to the appropriate SOCKS port on the SOCKS server system. The SOCKS service is located on TCP port 1080. If the connection request succeeds, the client enters a negotiation for the authentication method to be used, authenticates with the chosen method, and then sends a relay request. The SOCKS server evaluates the request and either establishes the appropriate connection or denies it. UDP exchanges are handled in a similar fashion. In essence, a TCP connection is opened to authenticate a user to send and receive UDP segments, and the UDP segments are forwarded as long as the TCP connection is open.

Bastion Host A bastion host is a system identified by the firewall administrator as a critical strong point in the network's security. Typically, the bastion host serves as a platform for an application-level or circuit-level gateway. Common characteristics of a bastion host include the following:

- The bastion host hardware platform executes a secure version of its operating system, making it a trusted system.
- Only the services that the network administrator considers essential are installed on the bastion host. These include proxy applications such as Telnet, DNS, FTP, SMTP, and user authentication.
- The bastion host may require additional authentication before a user is allowed access to the proxy services. In addition, each proxy service may require its own authentication before granting user access.
- Each proxy is configured to support only a subset of the standard application's command set.

- Each proxy is configured to allow access only to specific host systems. This means that the limited command/feature set may be applied only to a subset of systems on the protected network.
- Each proxy maintains detailed audit information by logging all traffic, each connection, and the duration of each connection. The audit log is an essential tool for discovering and terminating intruder attacks.
- Each proxy module is a very small software package specifically designed for network security. Because of its relative simplicity, it is easier to check such modules for security flaws. For example, a typical UNIX mail application may contain over 20,000 lines of code, while a mail proxy may contain fewer than 1000.
- Each proxy is independent of other proxies on the bastion host. If there is a problem with the operation of any proxy, or if a future vulnerability is discovered, it can be uninstalled without affecting the operation of the other proxy applications. Also, if the user population requires support for a new service, the network administrator can easily install the required proxy on the bastion host.
- A proxy generally performs no disk access other than to read its initial configuration file. This makes it difficult for an intruder to install Trojan horse sniffers or other dangerous files on the bastion host.
- Each proxy runs as a nonprivileged user in a private and secured directory on the bastion host.

Firewall Configurations

In addition to the use of a simple configuration consisting of a single system, such as a single packet-filtering router or a single gateway (Figure 20.1), more complex configurations are possible and indeed more common. Figure 20.2 illustrates three common firewall configurations. We examine each of these in turn.

In the **screened host firewall, single-homed bastion** configuration (Figure 20.2a), the firewall consists of two systems: a packet-filtering router and a bastion host. Typically, the router is configured so that

1. For traffic from the Internet, only IP packets destined for the bastion host are allowed in.
2. For traffic from the internal network, only IP packets from the bastion host are allowed out.

The bastion host performs authentication and proxy functions. This configuration has greater security than simply a packet-filtering router or an application-level gateway alone, for two reasons. First, this configuration implements both packet-level and application-level filtering, allowing for considerable flexibility in defining security policy. Second, an intruder must generally penetrate two separate systems before the security of the internal network is compromised.

This configuration also affords flexibility in providing direct Internet access. For example, the internal network may include a public information server, such as a Web server, for which a high level of security is not required. In that case, the router can be configured to allow direct traffic between the information server and the Internet.

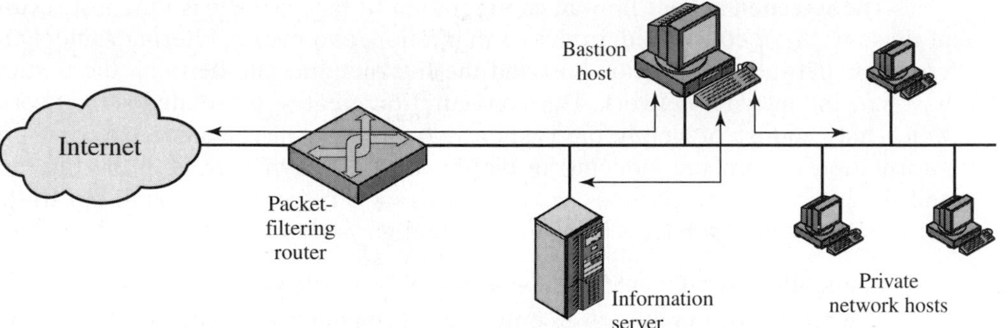

(a) Screened host firewall system (single-homed bastion host)

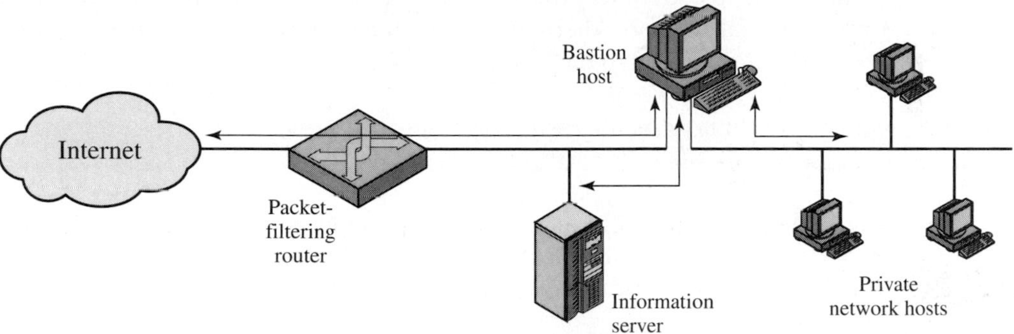

(b) Screened host firewall system (dual-homed bastion host)

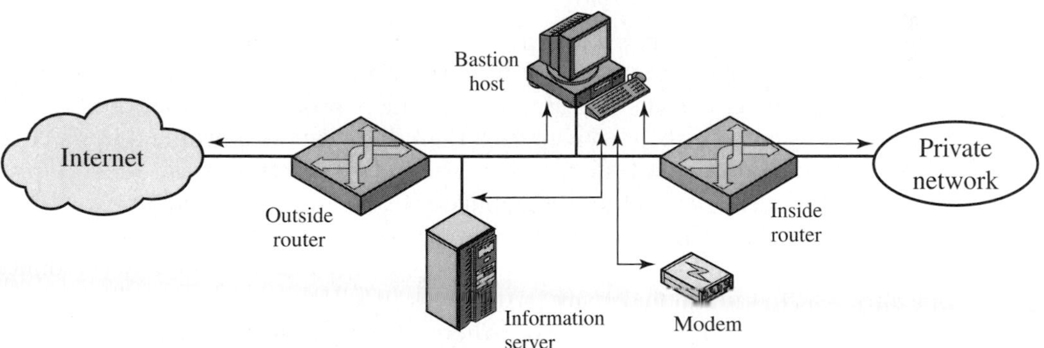

(c) Screened-subnet firewall system

Figure 20.2 Firewall Configurations

In the single-homed configuration just described, if the packet-filtering router is completely compromised, traffic could flow directly through the router between the Internet and other hosts on the private network. The **screened host firewall, dual-homed bastion** configuration physically prevents such a security breach (Figure 20.2b). The advantages of dual layers of security that were present in the previous configuration are present here as well. Again, an information server or other hosts can be allowed direct communication with the router if this is in accord with the security policy.

The **screened subnet firewall** configuration of Figure 20.2c is the most secure of those we have considered. In this configuration, two packet-filtering routers are used, one between the bastion host and the Internet and one between the bastion host and the internal network. This configuration creates an isolated subnetwork, which may consist of simply the bastion host but may also include one or more information servers and modems for dial-in capability. Typically, both the Internet and the internal network have access to hosts on the screened subnet, but traffic across the screened subnet is blocked. This configuration offers several advantages:

- There are now three levels of defense to thwart intruders.
- The outside router advertises only the existence of the screened subnet to the Internet; therefore, the internal network is invisible to the Internet.
- Similarly, the inside router advertises only the existence of the screened subnet to the internal network; therefore, the systems on the inside network cannot construct direct routes to the Internet.

20.2 TRUSTED SYSTEMS

One way to enhance the ability of a system to defend against intruders and malicious programs is to implement trusted system technology. This section provides a brief overview of this topic. We begin by looking at some basic concepts of data access control.

Data Access Control

Following successful logon, the user has been granted access to one or a set of hosts and applications. This is generally not sufficient for a system that includes sensitive data in its database. Through the user access control procedure, a user can be identified to the system. Associated with each user, there can be a profile that specifies permissible operations and file accesses. The operating system can then enforce rules based on the user profile. The database management system, however, must control access to specific records or even portions of records. For example, it may be permissible for anyone in administration to obtain a list of company personnel, but only selected individuals may have access to salary information. The issue is more than just one of level of detail. Whereas the operating system may grant a user permission to access a file or use an application, following which there are no further security checks, the database management system must make a decision on each individual access attempt. That decision will depend not only on the user's identity but also on the specific parts of the data being accessed and even on the information already divulged to the user.

A general model of access control as exercised by a file or database management system is that of an **access matrix** (Figure 20.3a). The basic elements of the model are as follows:

- **Subject:** An entity capable of accessing objects. Generally, the concept of subject equates with that of process. Any user or application actually gains access to an object by means of a process that represents that user or application.

	Program1	. . .	SegmentA	SegmentB
Process1	Read Execute		Read Write	
Process2				Read
⋮				

(a) Access matrix

Access control list for Program1: Process1 (Read, Execute)
Access control list for SegmentA: Process1 (Read, Write)
Access control list for SegmentB: Process2 (Read)

(b) Access control list

Capability list for Process1: Program1 (Read, Execute) SegmentA (Read, Write)
Capability list for Process2: Segment B (Read)

(c) Capability list

Figure 20.3 Access Control Structure

- **Object:** Anything to which access is controlled. Examples include files, portions of files, programs, and segments of memory.
- **Access right:** The way in which an object is accessed by a subject. Examples are read, write, and execute.

One axis of the matrix consists of identified subjects that may attempt data access. Typically, this list will consist of individual users or user groups, although access could be controlled for terminals, hosts, or applications instead of or in addition to users. The other axis lists the objects that may be accessed. At the greatest level of detail, objects may be individual data fields. More aggregate groupings, such as records, files, or even the entire database, may also be objects in the matrix. Each entry in the matrix indicates the access rights of that subject for that object.

In practice, an access matrix is usually sparse and is implemented by decomposition in one of two ways. The matrix may be decomposed by columns, yielding **access control lists** (Figure 20.3b). Thus, for each object, an access control list lists users and their permitted access rights. The access control list may contain a default, or public, entry. This allows users that are not explicitly listed as having special rights to have a default set of rights. Elements of the list may include individual users as well as groups of users.

Decomposition by rows yields **capability tickets** (Figure 20.3c). A capability ticket specifies authorized objects and operations for a user. Each user has a number of tickets and may be authorized to loan or give them to others. Because tickets may be dispersed around the system, they present a greater security problem than access control lists. In particular, the ticket must be unforgeable. One way to accomplish this is to have the operating system hold all tickets on behalf of users. These tickets would have to be held in a region of memory inaccessible to users.

The Concept of Trusted Systems

Much of what we have discussed so far has been concerned with protecting a given message or item from passive or active attacks by a given user. A somewhat different but widely applicable requirement is to protect data or resources on the basis of levels of security. This is commonly found in the military, where information is categorized as unclassified (U), confidential (C), secret (S), top secret (TS), or beyond. This concept is equally applicable in other areas, where information can be organized into gross categories and users can be granted clearances to access certain categories of data. For example, the highest level of security might be for strategic corporate planning documents and data, accessible by only corporate officers and their staff; next might come sensitive financial and personnel data, accessible only by administration personnel, corporate officers, and so on.

When multiple categories or levels of data are defined, the requirement is referred to as **multilevel security**. The general statement of the requirement for multilevel security is that a subject at a high level may not convey information to a subject at a lower or noncomparable level unless that flow accurately reflects the will of an authorized user. For implementation purposes, this requirement is in two parts and is simply stated. A multilevel secure system must enforce the following:

- **No read up:** A subject can only read an object of less or equal security level. This is referred to in the literature as the **Simple Security Property**.
- **No write down:** A subject can only write into an object of greater or equal security level. This is referred to in the literature as the ***-Property**[1] (pronounced *star property*).

These two rules, if properly enforced, provide multilevel security. For a data processing system, the approach that has been taken, and has been the object of much research and development, is based on the *reference monitor* concept. This approach is depicted in Figure 20.4. The reference monitor is a controlling element in the hardware and operating system of a computer that regulates the access of subjects to objects on the basis of security parameters of the subject and object. The reference monitor has access to a file, known as the *security kernel database*, that lists the access privileges (security clearance) of each subject and the protection attributes (classification level)

[1]The "*" does not stand for anything. No one could think of an appropriate name for the property during the writing of the first report on the model. The asterisk was a dummy character entered in the draft so that a text editor could rapidly find and replace all instances of its use once the property was named. No name was ever devised, and so the report was published with the "*" intact.

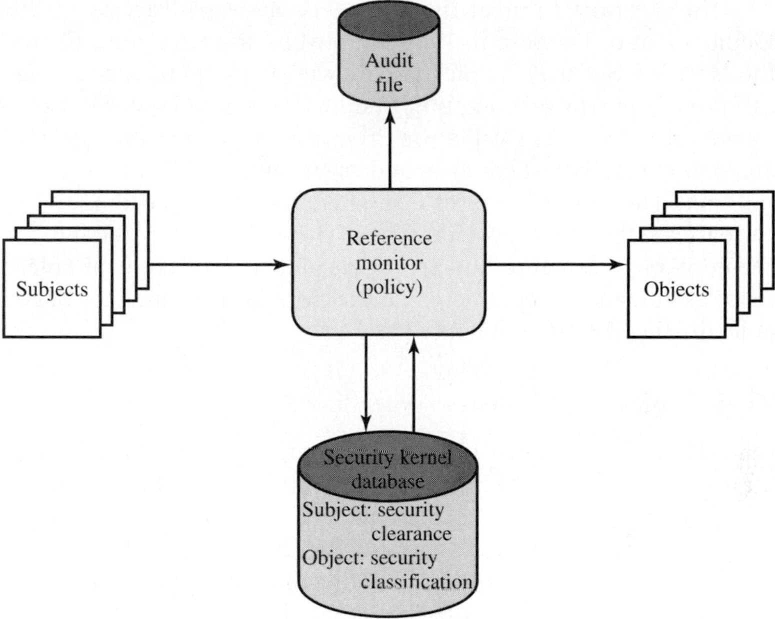

Figure 20.4 Reference Monitor Concept

of each object. The reference monitor enforces the security rules (no read up, no write down) and has the following properties:

- **Complete mediation:** The security rules are enforced on every access, not just, for example, when a file is opened.
- **Isolation:** The reference monitor and database are protected from unauthorized modification.
- **Verifiability:** The reference monitor's correctness must be provable. That is, it must be possible to demonstrate mathematically that the reference monitor enforces the security rules and provides complete mediation and isolation.

These are stiff requirements. The requirement for complete mediation means that every access to data within main memory and on disk and tape must be mediated. Pure software implementations impose too high a performance penalty to be practical; the solution must be at least partly in hardware. The requirement for isolation means that it must not be possible for an attacker, no matter how clever, to change the logic of the reference monitor or the contents of the security kernel database. Finally, the requirement for mathematical proof is formidable for something as complex as a general-purpose computer. A system that can provide such verification is referred to as a **trusted system**.

A final element illustrated in Figure 20.4 is an audit file. Important security events, such as detected security violations and authorized changes to the security kernel database, are stored in the audit file.

In an effort to meet its own needs and as a service to the public, the U.S. Department of Defense in 1981 established the Computer Security Center within the National Security Agency (NSA) with the goal of encouraging the widespread availability of trusted computer systems. This goal is realized through the center's Commercial Product Evaluation Program. In essence, the center attempts to evaluate commercially available products as meeting the security requirements just outlined. The center classifies evaluated products according to the range of security features that they provide. These evaluations are needed for Department of Defense procurements but are published and freely available. Hence, they can serve as guidance to commercial customers for the purchase of commercially available, off-the-shelf equipment.

Trojan Horse Defense

One way to secure against Trojan horse attacks is the use of a secure, trusted operating system. Figure 20.5 illustrates an example. In this case, a Trojan horse is used to get around the standard security mechanism used by most file management and operating systems: the access control list. In this example, a user named Bob interacts through a program with a data file containing the critically sensitive character string "CPE170KS." User Bob has created the file with read/write permission provided only to programs executing on his own behalf: that is, only processes that are owned by Bob may access the file.

The Trojan horse attack begins when a hostile user, named Alice, gains legitimate access to the system and installs both a Trojan horse program and a private file to be used in the attack as a "back pocket." Alice gives read/write permission to herself for this file and gives Bob write-only permission (Figure 20.5a). Alice now induces Bob to invoke the Trojan horse program, perhaps by advertising it as a useful utility. When the program detects that it is being executed by Bob, it reads the sensitive character string from Bob's file and copies it into Alice's back-pocket file (Figure 20.5b). Both the read and write operations satisfy the constraints imposed by access control lists. Alice then has only to access Bob's file at a later time to learn the value of the string.

Now consider the use of a secure operating system in this scenario (Figure 20.5c). Security levels are assigned to subjects at logon on the basis of criteria such as the terminal from which the computer is being accessed and the user involved, as identified by password/ID. In this example, there are two security levels, sensitive and public, ordered so that sensitive is higher than public. Processes owned by Bob and Bob's data file are assigned the security level sensitive. Alice's file and processes are restricted to public. If Bob invokes the Trojan horse program (Figure 20.5d), that program acquires Bob's security level. It is therefore able, under the simple security property, to observe the sensitive character string. When the program attempts to store the string in a public file (the back-pocket file), however, the *-Property is violated and the attempt is disallowed by the reference monitor. Thus, the attempt to write into the back-pocket file is denied even though the access control list permits it: The security policy takes precedence over the access control list mechanism.

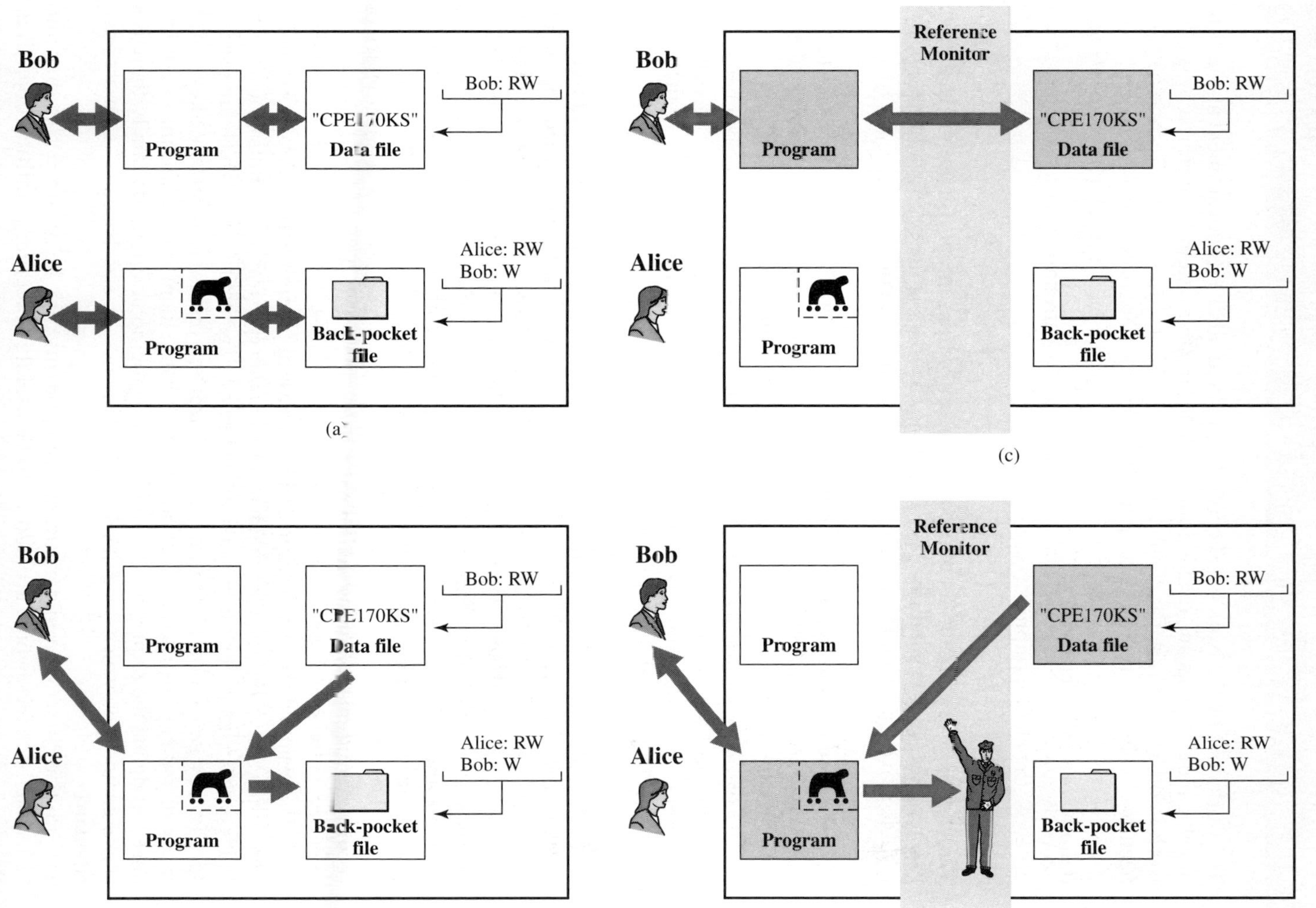

Figure 20.5 Trojan Horse and Secure Operating System

20.3 COMMON CRITERIA FOR INFORMATION TECHNOLOGY SECURITY EVALUATION

The work done by the National Security Agency and other U.S. government agencies to develop requirements and evaluation criteria for trusted systems is mirrored by similar work in other countries. The Common Criteria (CC) for Information Technology and Security Evaluation is an international initiative by standards bodies in a number of countries to develop international standards for specifying security requirements and defining evaluation criteria.

Requirements

The CC defines a common set of potential security requirements for use in evaluation. The term **target of evaluation** (TOE) refers to that part of the product or system that is subject to evaluation. The requirements fall in two categories:

- **Functional requirements:** Define desired security behavior. CC documents establish a set of security functional components that provide a standard way of expressing the security functional requirements for a TOE.
- **Assurance requirements:** The basis for gaining confidence that the claimed security measures are effective and implemented correctly. CC documents establish a set of assurance components that provide a standard way of expressing the assurance requirements for a TOE.

Both functional requirements and assurance requirements are organized into classes: A **class** is a collection of requirements that share a common focus or intent. Tables 20.3 and 20.4 briefly define the requirements classes for functional and assurance requirements. Each of these classes contains a number of families. The requirements within each **family** share security objectives, but differ in emphasis or rigor. For example, the audit class contains six families dealing with various aspects of auditing (e.g., audit data generation, audit analysis, and audit event storage). Each family, in turn, contains one or more components. A **component** describes a specific set of security requirements and is the smallest selectable set of security requirements for inclusion in the structures defined in the CC.

For example, the cryptographic support class of functional requirements includes two families: cryptographic key management and cryptographic operation. There are four components under the cryptographic key management family, which are used to specify: key generation algorithm and key size; key distribution method; key access method; and key destruction method. For each component, a standard may be referenced to define the requirement. Under the cryptographic operation family, there is a single component, which specifies an algorithm and key size based on a an assigned standard.

Sets of functional and assurance components may be grouped together into re-usable packages, which are known to be useful in meeting identified objectives. An example of such a package would be functional components required for Discretionary Access Controls.

Table 20.3 CC Security Functional Requirements

Class	Description
Audit	Involves recognizing, recording, storing and analyzing information related to security activities. Audit records are produced by these activities, and can be examined to determine their security relevance.
Cryptographic support	Used when the TOE implements cryptographic functions. These may be used, for example, to support communications, identification and authentication, or data separation.
Communications	Provides two families concerned with non-repudiation by the originator and by the recipient of data.
User data protection	Specifying requirements relating to the protection of user data within the TOE during import, export and storage, in addition to security attributes related to user data.
Identification and authentication	Ensure the unambiguous identification of authorized users and the correct association of security attributes with users and subjects.
Security management	Specifies the management of security attributes, data and functions.
Privacy	Provides a user with protection against discovery and misuse of his or her identity by other users.
Protection of the TOE security functions	Focused on protection of TSF (TOE security functions) data, rather than of user data. The class relates to the integrity and management of the TSF mechanisms and data.
Resource utilization	Supports the availability of required resources, such as processing capability and storage capacity. Includes requirements for fault tolerance, priority of service and resource allocation.
TOE access	Specifies functional requirements, in addition to those specified for identification and authentication, for controlling the establishment of a user's session. The requirements for TOE access govern such things as limiting the number and scope of user sessions, displaying the access history and the modification of access parameters.
Trusted path/channels	Concerned with trusted communications paths between the users and the TSF, and between TSFs.

Profiles and Targets

The CC also defines two kinds of documents that can be generated using the CC-defined requirements.

- **Protection profiles (PPs):** Define an implementation-independent set of security requirements and objectives for a category of products or systems that meet similar consumer needs for IT security. A PP is intended to be reusable and to define requirements that are known to be useful and effective in meeting the identified objectives. The PP concept has been developed to support the definition of functional standards, and as an aid to formulating procurement specifications. The PP reflects user security requirements
- **Security targets (STs):** Contain the IT security objectives and requirements of a specific identified TOE and defines the functional and assurance measures offered by that TOE to meet stated requirements. The ST may claim conformance to one or more PPs, and forms the basis for an evaluation. The ST is supplied by a vendor or developer.

Table 20.4 CC Security Assurance Requirements

Class	Description
Configuration management	Requires that the integrity of the TOE is adequately preserved. Specifically, configuration management provides confidence that the TOE and documentation used for evaluation are the ones prepared for distribution.
Delivery and operation	Concerned with the measures, procedures and standards for secure delivery, installation and operational use of the TOE, to ensure that the security protection offered by the TOE is not compromised during these events.
Development	Concerned with the refinement of the TSF from the specification defined in the ST to the implementation, and a mapping from the security requirements to the lowest level representation.
Guidance documents	Concerned with the secure operational use of the TOE, by the users and administrators.
Life cycle support	Concerned with the life-cycle of the TOE include lifecycle definition, tools and techniques, security of the development environment and the remediation of flaws found by TOE consumers.
Tests	Concerned with demonstrating that the TOE meets its functional requirements. The families address coverage and depth of developer testing, and requirements for independent testing.
Vulnerability assessment	Defines requirements directed at the identification of exploitable vulnerabilities, which could be introduced by construction, operation, misuse or incorrect configuration of the TOE. The families identified here are concerned with identifying vulnerabilities through covert channel analysis, analysis of the configuration of the TOE, examining the strength of mechanisms of the security functions, and identifying flaws introduced during development of the TOE. The second family covers the security categorization of TOE components. The third and fourth cover the analysis of changes for security impact, and the provision of evidence that procedures are being followed. This class provides building blocks for the establishment of assurance maintenance schemes.
Assurance maintenance	Provides requirements that are intended to be applied after a TOE has been certified against the CC. These requirements are aimed at assuring that the TOE will continue to meet its security target as changes are made to the TOE or its environment.

Figure 20.6 illustrates the relationship between requirements on the one hand and profiles and targets on the other. For a PP, a user can select a number of components to define the requirements for the desired product. The user may also refer to predefined packages that assemble a number of requirements commonly grouped together within a product requirements document. Similarly, a vendor or designer can select a number of components and packages to define an ST.

Figure 20.7 shows what is referred to in the CC documents as the security functional requirements paradigm. In essence, this illustration is based on the reference monitor concept but makes use of the terminology and design philosophy of the CC.

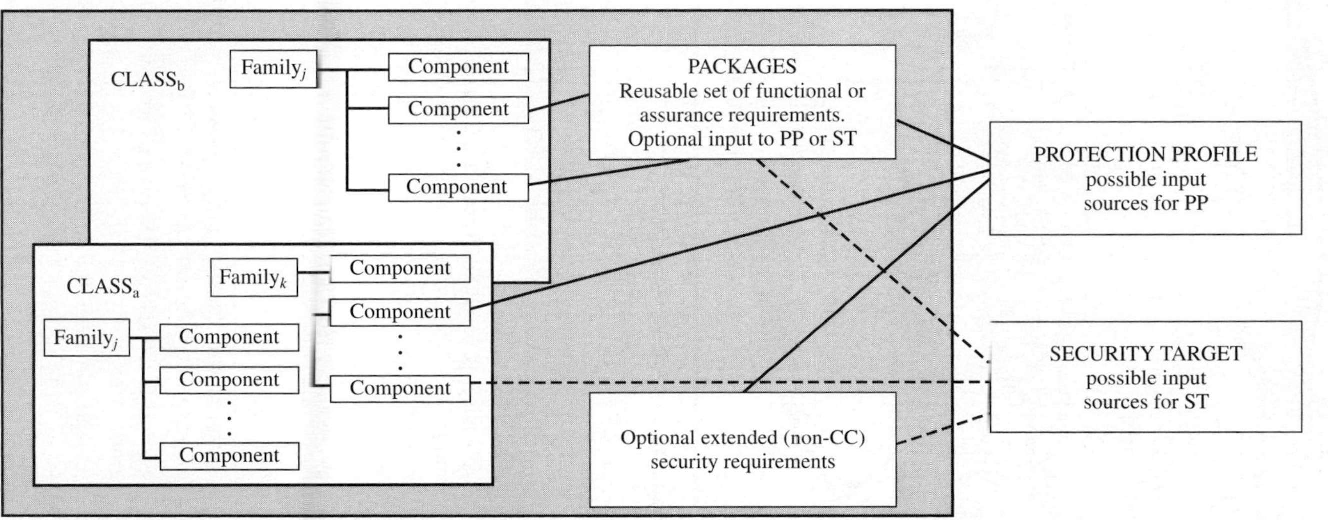

Figure 20.6 Organization and Construction of Common Criteria Requirements

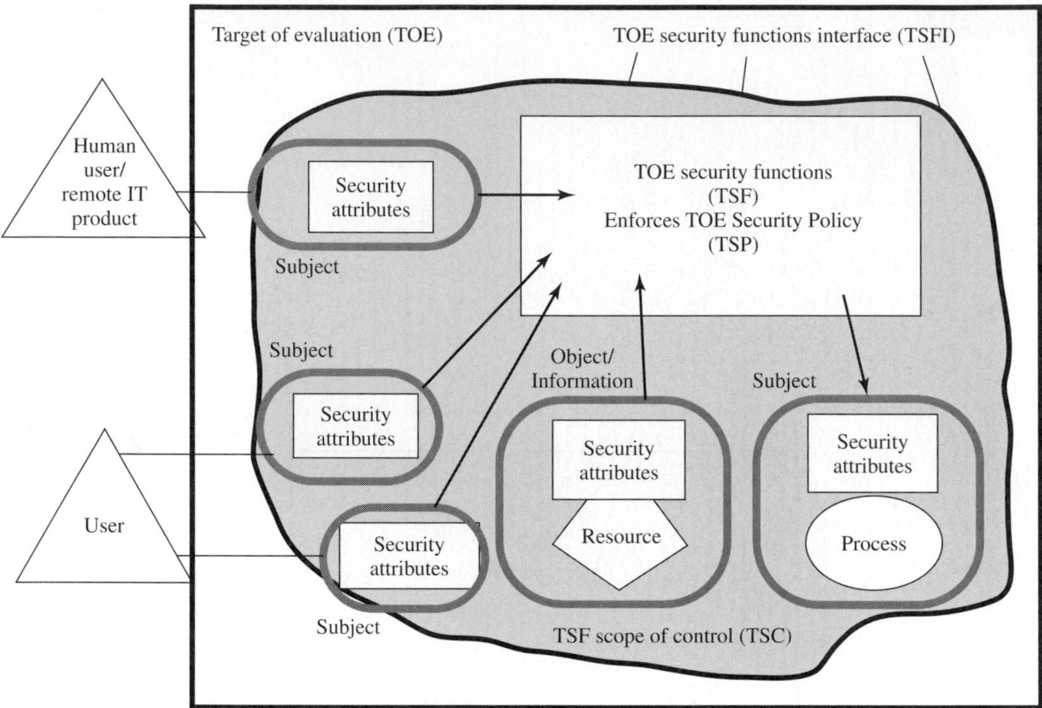

Figure 20.7 Security Functional Requirements Paradigm

20.4 RECOMMENDED READING AND WEB SITES

A classic treatment of firewalls is [CHAP00]. Another classic, recently updated, is [CHES03]. [LODI98], [OPPL97], and [BELL94b] are good overview articles on the subject. [WACK02] is an excellent overview of firewall technology and firewall policies. [AUDI04] and [WILS05] provide useful discussions of firewalls.

[GASS88] provides a comprehensive study of trusted computer systems. [PFLE03] and [GOLL99] also provide coverage. [FELT03] and [OPPL05] provide useful discussions of trusted computing.

AUDI04 Audin, G. "Next-Gen Firewalls: What to Expect." *Business Communications Review*, June 2004.

BELL94b Bellovin, S., and Cheswick, W. "Network Firewalls." *IEEE Communications Magazine*, September 1994.

CHAP00 Chapman, D., and Zwicky, E. *Building Internet Firewalls.* Sebastopol, CA: O'Reilly, 2000.

CHES03 Cheswick, W., and Bellovin, S. *Firewalls and Internet Security: Repelling the Wily Hacker*. Reading, MA: Addison-Wesley, 2003.

FELT03 Felten, E. "Understanding Trusted Computing: Will Its Benefits Outweigh Its Drawbacks?" *IEEE Security and Privacy*, May/June 2003.

GASS88 Gasser, M. *Building a Secure Computer System.* New York: Van Nostrand Reinhold, 1988.

GOLL99 Gollmann, D. *Computer Security.* New York: Wiley, 1999.

LODI98 Lodin, S., and Schuba, C. "Firewalls Fend Off Invasions from the Net." *IEEE Spectrum*, February 1998.

OPPL97 Oppliger, R. "Internet Security: Firewalls and Beyond." *Communications of the ACM*, May 1997.

OPPL05 Oppliger, R., and Rytz, R. "Does Trusted Computing Remedy Computer Security Problems?" *IEEE Security and Privacy*, March/April 2005.

PFLE03 Pfleeger, C. *Security in Computing.* Upper Saddle River, NJ: Prentice Hall, 1997.

WACK02 Wack, J.; Cutler, K.; and Pole, J. *Guidelines on Firewalls and Firewall Policy.* NIST Special Publication SP 800-41, January 2002.

WILS05 Wilson, J. "The Future of the Firewall." *Business Communications Review*, May 2005.

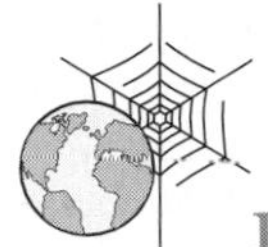

Recommended Web Sites:

- **Firewall.com:** Numerous links to firewall references and software resources.
- **Trusted Computing Group:** Vendor group involved in developing and promoting trusted computer standards. Site includes white papers, specifications, and vendor links.
- **Common Criteria Portal:** Official Web site of the common criteria project.

20.5 KEY TERMS, REVIEW QUESTIONS, AND PROBLEMS

Key Terms

access control list (ACL)	circuit-level gateway	packet-filtering router
access matrix	common criteria (CC)	reference monitor
access right	firewall	stateful inspection firewall
application-level gateway	multilevel security	subject
bastion host	object	trusted system
capability ticket		

Review Questions

20.1 List three design goals for a firewall.

20.2 List four techniques used by firewalls to control access and enforce a security policy.

20.3 What information is used by a typical packet-filtering router?

20.4 What are some weaknesses of a packet-filtering router?

20.5 What is the difference between a packet-filtering router and a stateful inspection firewall?

20.6 What is an application-level gateway?

20.7 What is a circuit-level gateway?

20.8 What are the differences among the three configurations of Figure 20.2?
20.9 In the context of access control, what is the difference between a subject and an object?
20.10 What is the difference between an access control list and a capability ticket?
20.11 What are the two rules that a reference monitor enforces?
20.12 What properties are required of a reference monitor?
20.13 What are the common criteria?

Problems

20.1 As was mentioned in Section 20.1, one approach to defeating the tiny fragment attack is to enforce a minimum length of the transport header that must be contained in the first fragment of an IP packet. If the first fragment is rejected, all subsequent fragments can be rejected. However, the nature of IP is such that fragments may arrive out of order. Thus, an intermediate fragment may pass through the filter before the initial fragment is rejected. How can this situation be handled?

20.2 In an IPv4 packet, the size of the payload in the first fragment, in octets, is equal to Total Length $-$ ($4 \times$ IHL). If this value is less than the required minimum (8 octets for TCP), then this fragment and the entire packet are rejected. Suggest an alternative method of achieving the same result using only the Fragment Offset field.

20.3 RFC 791, the IPv4 protocol specification, describes a reassembly algorithm that results in new fragments overwriting any overlapped portions of previously received fragments. Given such a reassembly implementation, an attacker could construct a series of packets in which the lowest (zero-offset) fragment would contain innocuous data (and thereby be passed by administrative packet filters), and in which some subsequent packet having a nonzero offset would overlap TCP header information (destination port, for instance) and cause it to be modified. The second packet would be passed through most filter implementations because it does not have a zero fragment offset. Suggest a method that could be used by a packet filter to counter this attack.

20.4 The necessity of the "no read up" rule for a multilevel secure system is fairly obvious. What is the importance of the "no write down" rule?

20.5 In Figure 20.5 one link of the Trojan horse copy-and-observe-later chain is broken. There are two other possible angles of attack by Drake: Drake logging on and attempting to read the string directly, and Drake assigning a security level of sensitive to the back-pocket file. Does the reference monitor prevent these attacks?

Appendix A

Standards and Standards-Setting Organizations

There are some dogs who wouldn't debase what are to them sacred forms. A very fine, very serious German Shepherd I worked with, for instance, grumbled noisily at other dogs when they didn't obey. When training him to retrieve, at one point I set the dumbbell on its end for the fun of it. He glared disapprovingly at the dumbbell and at me, then pushed it carefully back into its proper position before picking it up and returning with it, rather sullenly.

—***Adam's Task: Calling Animals by Name*, Vicki Hearne**

An important concept that recurs frequently in this book is standards. This appendix provides some background on the nature and relevance of standards and looks at the key organizations involved in developing standards for networking and communications.

A.1 THE IMPORTANCE OF STANDARDS

It has long been accepted in the telecommunications industry that standards are required to govern the physical, electrical, and procedural characteristics of communication equipment. In the past, this view has not been embraced by the computer industry. Whereas communication equipment vendors recognize that their equipment will generally interface to and communicate with other vendors' equipment, computer vendors have traditionally attempted to monopolize their customers. The proliferation of computers and distributed processing has made that an untenable position. Computers from different vendors must communicate with each other and, with the ongoing evolution of protocol standards, customers will no longer accept special-purpose protocol conversion software development. The result is that standards now permeate all the areas of technology discussed in this book.

There are a number of advantages and disadvantages to the standards-making process. The principal advantages of standards are as follows:

- A standard assures that there will be a large market for a particular piece of equipment or software. This encourages mass production and, in some cases, the use of large-scale-integration (LSI) or very-large-scale-integration (VLSI) techniques, resulting in lower costs.
- A standard allows products from multiple vendors to communicate, giving the purchaser more flexibility in equipment selection and use.

The principal disadvantages of standards are as follows:

- A standard tends to freeze the technology. By the time a standard is developed, subjected to review and compromise, and promulgated, more efficient techniques are possible.
- There are multiple standards for the same thing. This is not a disadvantage of standards per se, but of the current way things are done. Fortunately, in recent years the various standards-making organizations have begun to cooperate more closely. Nevertheless, there are still areas where multiple conflicting standards exist.

A.2 INTERNET STANDARDS AND THE INTERNET SOCIETY

Many of the protocols that make up the TCP/IP protocol suite have been standardized or are in the process of standardization. By universal agreement, an organization known as the Internet Society is responsible for the development and publication of these standards. The Internet Society is a professional membership organization that oversees a number of boards and task forces involved in Internet development and standardization.

This section provides a brief description of the way in which standards for the TCP/IP protocol suite are developed.

The Internet Organizations and RFC Publication

The Internet Society is the coordinating committee for Internet design, engineering, and management. Areas covered include the operation of the Internet itself and the standardization of protocols used by end systems on the Internet for interoperability. Three organizations under the Internet Society are responsible for the actual work of standards development and publication:

- **Internet Architecture Board (IAB):** Responsible for defining the overall architecture of the Internet, providing guidance and broad direction to the IETF
- **Internet Engineering Task Force (IETF):** The protocol engineering and development arm of the Internet
- **Internet Engineering Steering Group (IESG):** Responsible for technical management of IETF activities and the Internet standards process

Working groups chartered by the IETF carry out the actual development of new standards and protocols for the Internet. Membership in a working group is voluntary; any interested party may participate. During the development of a specification, a working group will make a draft version of the document available as an Internet Draft, which is placed in the IETF's "Internet Drafts" online directory. The document may remain as an Internet Draft for up to six months, and interested parties may review and comment on the draft. During that time, the IESG may approve publication of the draft as an RFC (Request for Comment). If the draft has not progressed to the status of an RFC during the six-month period, it is withdrawn from the directory. The working group may subsequently publish a revised version of the draft.

The IETF is responsible for publishing the RFCs, with approval of the IESG. The RFCs are the working notes of the Internet research and development community. A document in this series may be on essentially any topic related to computer communications and may be anything from a meeting report to the specification of a standard.

The work of the IETF is divided into eight areas, each with an area director and each composed of numerous working groups. Table A.1 shows the IETF areas and their focus.

The Standardization Process

The decision of which RFCs become Internet standards is made by the IESG, on the recommendation of the IETF. To become a standard, a specification must meet the following criteria:

Table A.1 IETF Areas

IETF Area	Theme	Example Working Groups
General	IETF processes and procedures	Policy Framework Process for Organization of Internet Standards
Applications	Internet applications	Web-related protocols (HTTP) EDI-Internet integration LDAP
Internet	Internet infrastructure	IPv6 PPP extensions
Operations and management	Standards and definitions for network operations	SNMPv3 Remote Network Monitoring
Routing	Protocols and management for routing information	Multicast routing OSPF QoS routing
Security	Security protocols and technologies	Kerberos IPSec X.509 S/MIME TLS
Transport	Transport layer protocols	Differentiated services IP telephony NFS RSVP
User services	Methods to improve the quality of information available to users of the Internet	Responsible Use of the Internet User services FYI documents

- Be stable and well understood
- Be technically competent
- Have multiple, independent, and interoperable implementations with substantial operational experience
- Enjoy significant public support
- Be recognizably useful in some or all parts of the Internet

The key difference between these criteria and those used for international standards from ITU is the emphasis here on operational experience.

The left-hand side of Figure A.1 shows the series of steps, called the *standards track*, that a specification goes through to become a standard; this process is defined in RFC 2026. The steps involve increasing amounts of scrutiny and testing. At each step, the IETF must make a recommendation for advancement of the protocol, and the IESG must ratify it. The process begins when the IESG approves the publication of an Internet Draft document as an RFC with the status of Proposed Standard.

The white boxes in the diagram represent temporary states, which should be occupied for the minimum practical time. However, a document must remain a Proposed Standard for at least six months and a Draft Standard for at least four months to allow time for review and comment. The gray boxes represent long-term states that may be occupied for years.

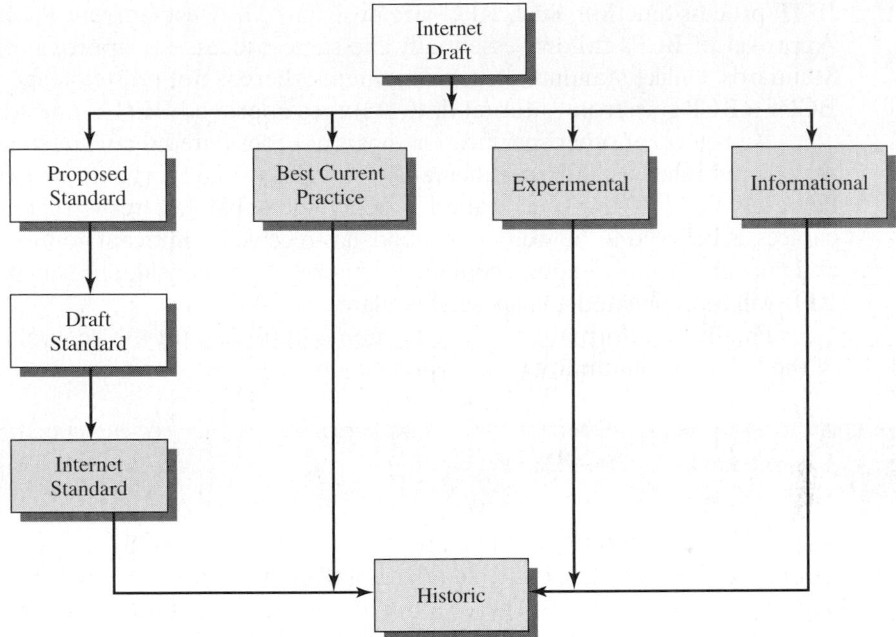

Figure A.1 Internet RFC Publication Process

For a specification to be advanced to Draft Standard status, there must be at least two independent and interoperable implementations from which adequate operational experience has been obtained.

After significant implementation and operational experience has been obtained, a specification may be elevated to Internet Standard. At this point, the Specification is assigned an STD number as well as an RFC number.

Finally, when a protocol becomes obsolete, it is assigned to the Historic state.

Internet Standards Categories

All Internet standards fall into one of two categories:

- **Technical specification (TS):** A TS defines a protocol, service, procedure, convention, or format. The bulk of the Internet standards are TSs.
- **Applicability statement (AS):** An AS specifies how, and under what circumstances, one or more TSs may be applied to support a particular Internet capability. An AS identifies one or more TSs that are relevant to the capability, and may specify values or ranges for particular parameters associated with a TS or functional subsets of a TS that are relevant for the capability.

Other RFC Types

There are numerous RFCs that are not destined to become Internet standards. Some RFCs standardize the results of community deliberations about statements of principle or conclusions about what is the best way to perform some operations or

IETF process function. Such RFCs are designated as Best Current Practice (BCP). Approval of BCPs follows essentially the same process for approval of Proposed Standards. Unlike standards-track documents, there is not a three-stage process for BCPs; a BCP goes from Internet draft status to approved BCP in one step.

A protocol or other specification that is not considered ready for standardization may be published as an Experimental RFC. After further work, the specification may be resubmitted. If the specification is generally stable, has resolved known design choices, is believed to be well understood, has received significant community review, and appears to enjoy enough community interest to be considered valuable, then the RFC will be designated a Proposed Standard.

Finally, an Informational Specification is published for the general information of the Internet community.

A.3 NATIONAL INSTITUTE OF STANDARDS AND TECHNOLOGY

The National Institute of Standards and Technology (NIST), part of the U.S. Commerce Department, issues standards and guidelines for use by U.S. government departments and agencies. These standards and guidelines are issued in the form of Federal Information Processing Standards (FIPS). NIST develops FIPS when there are compelling federal government requirements such as for security and interoperability and there are no acceptable industry standards or solutions.

- NIST announces the proposed FIPS in the *Federal Register* for public review and comment. At the same time that the proposed FIPS is announced in the *Federal Register*, it is also announced on NIST's Web site. The text and associated specifications, if applicable, of the proposed FIPS are posted on the NIST Web site.
- A 90-day period is provided for review and for submission of comments on the proposed FIPS to NIST. The date by which comments must be submitted to NIST is specified in the *Federal Register* and in the other announcements.
- Comments received in response to the *Federal Register* notice and to the other notices are reviewed by NIST to determine if modifications to the proposed FIPS are needed.
- A detailed justification document is prepared, analyzing the comments received and explaining whether modifications were made, or explaining why recommended changes were not made.
- NIST submits the recommended FIPS, the detailed justification document, and recommendations as to whether the standard should be compulsory and binding for Federal government use, to the Secretary of Commerce for approval.
- A notice announcing approval of the FIPS by the Secretary of Commerce is published in the *Federal Register*, and on NIST's Web site.

Although NIST standards are developed for U.S. government use, many of them are widely used in industry. AES and DES are prime examples.

APPENDIX B

PROJECTS FOR TEACHING CRYPTOGRAPHY AND NETWORK SECURITY

Analysis and observation, theory and experience must never disdain or exclude each other; on the contrary, they support each other.

—*On War*, Carl Von Clausewitz

Many instructors believe that research or implementation projects are crucial to the clear understanding of cryptography and network security. Without projects, it may be difficult for students to grasp some of the basic concepts and interactions among components. Projects reinforce the concepts introduced in the book, give the student a greater appreciation of how a cryptographic algorithm or protocol works, and can motivate students and give them confidence that they are capable of not only understanding but implementing the details of a security capability.

In this text, I have tried to present the concepts of cryptography and network security as clearly as possible and have provided numerous homework problems to reinforce those concepts. However, many instructors will wish to supplement this material with projects. This appendix provides some guidance in that regard and describes support material available in the instructor's supplement. The support material covers five types of projects:

- Research projects
- Programming projects
- Laboratory exercises
- Writing assignments
- Reading/report assignments

B.1 RESEARCH PROJECTS

An effective way of reinforcing basic concepts from the course and for teaching students research skills is to assign a research project. Such a project could involve a literature search as well as an Internet search of vendor products, research lab activities, and standardization efforts. Projects could be assigned to teams or, for smaller projects, to individuals. In any case, it is best to require some sort of project proposal early in the term, giving the instructor time to evaluate the proposal for appropriate topic and appropriate level of effort. Student handouts for research projects should include

- A format for the proposal
- A format for the final report
- A schedule with intermediate and final deadlines
- A list of possible project topics

The students can select one of the listed topics or devise their own comparable project. The instructor's supplement includes a suggested format for the proposal and final report as well as a list of fifteen possible research topics.

B.2 PROGRAMMING PROJECTS

The programming project is a useful pedagogical tool. There are several attractive features of stand-alone programming projects that are not part of an existing security facility:

1. The instructor can choose from a wide variety of cryptography and network security concepts to assign projects.
2. The projects can be programmed by the students on any available computer and in any appropriate language; they are platform and language independent.
3. The instructor need not download, install, and configure any particular infrastructure for stand-alone projects.

There is also flexibility in the size of projects. Larger projects give students more a sense of achievement, but students with less ability or fewer organizational skills can be left behind. Larger projects usually elicit more overall effort from the best students. Smaller projects can have a higher concepts-to-code ratio, and because more of them can be assigned, the opportunity exists to address a variety of different areas.

Again, as with research projects, the students should first submit a proposal. The student handout should include the same elements listed in Section A.1. The instructor's manual includes a set of twelve possible programming projects.

The following individuals have supplied the research and programming projects suggested in the instructor's manual: Henning Schulzrinne of Columbia University; Cetin Kaya Koc of Oregon State University; and David M. Balenson of Trusted Information Systems and George Washington University.

B.3 LABORATORY EXERCISES

Professor Sanjay Rao and Ruben Torres of Purdue University have prepared a set of laboratory exercises that are part of the instructor's supplement. These are implementation projects designed to be programmed on Linux but could be adapted for any Unix environment. These laboratory exercises provide realistic experience in implementing security functions and applications.

B.4 WRITING ASSIGNMENTS

Writing assignments can have a powerful multiplier effect in the learning process in a technical discipline such as cryptography and network security. Adherents of the Writing Across the Curriculum (WAC) movement (**http://wac.colostate.edu**) report substantial benefits of writing assignments in facilitating learning. Writing assignments lead to more detailed and complete thinking about a particular topic. In addition, writing assignments help to overcome the tendency of students to pursue a subject with a minimum of personal engagement, just learning facts and problem-solving techniques without obtaining a deep understanding of the subject matter.

The instructor's supplement contains a number of suggested writing assignments, organized by chapter. Instructors may ultimately find that this is the most important part of their approach to teaching the material. I would greatly appreciate any feedback on this area and any suggestions for additional writing assignments.

B.5 READING/REPORT ASSIGNMENTS

Another excellent way to reinforce concepts from the course and to give students research experience is to assign papers from the literature to be read and analyzed. The instructor's supplement includes a suggested list of papers, one or two per chapter, to be assigned. All of the papers are readily available either via the Internet or in any good college technical library. The instructor's supplement also includes a suggested assignment wording.

GLOSSARY

In studying the Imperium, Arrakis, and the whole culture which produced Maud'Dib, many unfamiliar terms occur. To increase understanding is a laudable goal, hence the definitions and explanations given below.

***—Dune,* Frank Herbert**

Some of the terms in this glossary are from the *Internet Security Glossary* [RFC 2828]. These are indicated in the glossary by an asterisk.

asymmetric encryption A form of cryptosystem in which encryption and decryption are performed using two different keys, one of which is referred to as the public key and one of which is referred to as the private key. Also known as public-key encryption.

authentication* The process of verifying an identity claimed by or for a system entity.

authenticator Additional information appended to a message to enable the receiver to verify that the message should be accepted as authentic. The authenticator may be functionally independent of the content of the message itself (e.g., a nonce or a source identifier) or it may be a function of the message contents (e.g., a hash value or a cryptographic checksum).

avalanche effect A characteristic of an encryption algorithm in which a small change in the plaintext or key gives rise to a large change in the ciphertext. For a hash code, the avalanche effect is a characteristic in which a small change in the message gives rise to a large change in the message digest.

bacteria Program that consumes system resources by replicating itself.

birthday attack This cryptanalytic attack attempts to find two values in the domain of a function that map to the same value in its range

block chaining A procedure used during symmetric block encryption that makes an output block dependent not only on the current plaintext input block and key, but also on earlier input and/or output. The effect of block chaining is that two instances of the same plaintext input block will produce different ciphertext blocks, making cryptanalysis more difficult.

block cipher A symmetric encryption algorithm in which a block of plaintext bits (typically 64 or 128) is transformed as a whole into a ciphertext block of the same length.

byte A sequence of eight bits. Also referred to as an *octet.*

cipher An algorithm for encryption and decryption. A cipher replaces a piece of information (an element in plaintext) with another object, with the intent to conceal meaning. Typically, the replacement rule is governed by a secret key.

ciphertext The output of an encryption algorithm; the encrypted form of a message or data.

code An unvarying rule for replacing a piece of information (e.g., letter, word, phrase) with another object, not necessarily of the same sort. Generally, there is no intent to conceal meaning. Examples include the ASCII character code (each character is represented by 7 bits) and frequency-shift keying (each binary value is represented by a particular frequency).

computationally secure Secure because the time and/or cost of defeating the security are too high to be feasible.

confusion A cryptographic technique that seeks to make the relationship between the statistics of the ciphertext and the value of the encryption key as complex as possible. This is achieved by the use of a complex scrambling algorithm that depends on the key and the input.

conventional encryption Symmetric encryption.

covert channel A communications channel that enables the transfer of information in a way unintended by the designers of the communications facility.

cryptanalysis The branch of cryptology dealing with the breaking of a cipher to recover information, or forging encrypted information that will be accepted as authentic.

cryptographic checksum An authenticator that is a cryptographic function of both the data to be authenticated and a secret key. Also referred to as a message authentication code (MAC).

cryptography The branch of cryptology dealing with the design of algorithms for encryption and decryption, intended to ensure the secrecy and/or authenticity of messages.

cryptology The study of secure communications, which encompasses both cryptography and cryptanalysis.

decryption The translation of encrypted text or data (called ciphertext) into original text or data (called plaintext). Also called deciphering.

differential cryptanalysis A technique in which chosen plaintexts with particular XOR difference patterns are encrypted. The difference patterns of the resulting ciphertext provide information that can be used to determine the encryption key.

diffusion A cryptographic technique that seeks to obscure the statistical structure of the plaintext by spreading out the influence of each individual plaintext digit over many ciphertext digits.

digital signature An authentication mechanism that enables the creator of a message to attach a code that acts as a signature. The signature is formed by taking the hash of the message and encrypting the message with the creator's private key. The signature guarantees the source and integrity of the message.

digram A two-letter sequence. In English and other languages, the relative frequency of various digrams in plaintext can be used in the cryptanalysis of some ciphers. Also called *digraph*.

discretionary access control* An access control service that enforces a security policy based on the identity of system entities and their authorizations to access system resources. (See: access control list, identity-based security policy, mandatory access control.) This service is termed "discretionary" because an entity might have access rights that permit the entity, by its own volition, to enable another entity to access some resource.

divisor One integer is said to be a devisor of another integer if there is no remainder on division.

encryption The conversion of plaintext or data into unintelligible form by means of a reversible translation, based on a translation table or algorithm. Also called enciphering.

firewall A dedicated computer that interfaces with computers outside a network and has special security precautions built into it in order to protect sensitive files on computers within the network. It is used to service outside network, especially Internet, connections and dial-in lines.

greatest common divisor The greatest common divisor of two integers, a and b, is the largest positive integer that divides both a and b. One integer is said to divide another integer if there is no remainder on division.

hash function A function that maps a variable-length data block or message into a fixed-length value called a hash code. The function is designed in such a way that, when protected, it provides an authenticator to the data or message. Also referred to as a message digest.

honeypot A decoy system designed to lure a potential attacker away from critical systems. A form of intrusion detection.

initialization vector A random block of data that is used to begin the encryption of multiple blocks of plaintext, when a block-chaining encryption technique is used. The IV serves to foil known-plaintext attacks.

intruder An individual who gains, or attempts to gain, unauthorized access to a computer system or to gain unauthorized privileges on that system.

intrusion detection system A set of automated tools designed to detect unauthorized access to a host system.

Kerberos The name given to Project Athena's code authentication service.

key distribution center A system that is authorized to transmit temporary session keys to principals. Each session key is transmitted in encrypted form, using a master key that the key distribution center shares with the target principal.

logic bomb Logic embedded in a computer program that checks for a certain set of conditions to be present on the system. When these conditions are met, it executes some function resulting in unauthorized actions.

mandatory access control A means of restricting access to objects based on fixed security attributes assigned to users and to files and other objects. The controls are mandatory in the sense that they cannot be modified by users or their programs.

man-in-the-middle attack A form of active wiretapping attack in which the attacker intercepts and selectively modifies communicated data in order to masquerade as one or more of the entities involved in a communication.

master key A long-lasting key that is used between a key distribution center and a principal for the purpose of encoding the transmission of session keys. Typically, the master keys are distributed by noncryptographic means. Also referred to as a key-encrypting key.

meet-in-the-middle attack This is a cryptanaltytic attack that attempts to find a value in each of the range and domain of the composition of two functions such that the forward mapping of one through the first function is the same as the inverse image of the other through the second function—quite literally meeting in the middle of the composed function.

message authentication A process used to verify the integrity of a message.

message authentication code (MAC) Cryptographic checksum.

message digest Hash function.

modular arithmetic A kind of integer arithmetic that reduces all numbers to one of a fixed set $[0 \ldots n - 1]$ for some number n. Any integer outside this range is reduced to one in this range by taking the remainder after division by n.

mode of operation A technique for enhancing the effect of a cryptographic algorithm or adapting the algorithm for an application, such as applying a block cipher to a sequence of data blocks or a data stream.

multilevel security A capability that enforces access control across multiple levels of classification of data.

multiple encryption Repeated use of an encryption function, with different keys, to produce a more complex mapping from plaintext to ciphertext.

nibble A sequence of four bits.

nonce An identifier or number that is used only once.

one-way function A function that is easily computed, but the calculation of its inverse is infeasible.

password* A secret data value, usually a character string, that is used as authentication information. A password is usually matched with a user identifier that is explicitly presented in the authentication process, but in some cases the identity may be implicit.

plaintext The input to an encryption function or the output of a decryption function.

primitive root If r and n are relatively prime integers with $n > 0$. and if $\phi(n)$ is the least positive exponent m such that $r^m \equiv 1 \bmod n$, then r is called a primitive root modulo n.

private key One of the two keys used in an asymmetric encryption system. For secure communication, the private key should only be known to its creator.

pseudorandom number generator A function that deterministically produces a sequence of numbers that are apparently statistically random.

public key One of the two keys used in an asymmetric encryption system. The public key is made public, to be used in conjunction with a corresponding private key.

public-key certificate Consists of a public key plus a User ID of the key owner, with the whole block signed by a trusted third party. Typically, the third party is a certificate authority (CA) that is trusted by the user community, such as a government agency or a financial institution.

public-key encryption Asymmetric encryption.

public-key infrastructure (PKI) The set of hardware, software, people, policies, and procedures needed to create, manage, store, distribute, and revoke digital certificates based on asymmetric cryptography.

relatively prime Two numbers are relatively prime if they have no prime factors in common; that is, their only common divisor is 1.

replay attacks An attack in which a service already authorized and completed is forged by another "duplicate request" in an attempt to repeat authorized commands.

residue When the integer a is divided by the integer n, the remainder r is referred to as the residue. Equivalently, $r = a \bmod n$.

residue class All the integers that have the same remainder when divided by n form a residue class (mod n). Thus, for a given remainder r, the residue class (mod n) to which it belongs consists of the integers $r, r \pm n, r \pm 2n, \ldots$.

RSA algorithm A public-key encryption algorithm based on exponentiation in modular arithmetic. It is the only algorithm generally accepted as practical and secure for public-key encryption.

secret key The key used in a symmetric encryption system. Both participants must share the same key, and this key must remain secret to protect the communication.

security attack* An assault on system security that derives from an intelligent threat; that is, an intelligent act that is a deliberate attempt (especially in the sense of a method or technique) to evade security services and violate the security policy of a system.

security mechanism A process (or a device incorporating such a process) that is designed to detect, prevent, or recover from a security attack.

security service A processing or communication service that enhances the security of the data processing systems and the information transfers of an organization. The services are intended to counter security attacks, and they make use of one or more security mechanisms to provide the service.

security threat* A potential for violation of security, which exists when there is a circumstance, capability, action, or event that could breach security and cause harm. That is, a threat is a possible danger that might exploit a vulnerability.

session key A temporary encryption key used between two principals.

steganography Methods of hiding the existence of a message or other data. This is different than cryptography, which hides the meaning of a message but does not hide the message itself.

stream cipher A symmetric encryption algorithm in which ciphertext output is produced bit-by-bit or byte-by-byte from a stream of plaintext input.

symmetric encryption A form of cryptosystem in which encryption and decryption are performed using the same key. Also known as conventional encryption.

trapdoor Secret undocumented entry point into a program, used to grant access without normal methods of access authentication.

trapdoor one-way function A function that is easily computed, and the calculation of its inverse is infeasible unless certain privileged information is known.

Trojan horse* A computer program that appears to have a useful function, but also has a hidden and potentially malicious function that evades security mechanisms, sometimes by exploiting legitimate authorizations of a system entity that invokes the program.

trusted system A computer and operating system that can be verified to implement a given security policy.

unconditionally secure Secure even against an opponent with unlimited time and unlimited computing resources.

virtual private network Consists of a set of computers that interconnect by means of a relatively unsecure network and that make use of encryption and special protocols to provide security.

virus Code embedded within a program that causes a copy of itself to be inserted in one or more other programs. In addition to propagation, the virus usually performs some unwanted function.

worm Program that can replicate itself and send copies from computer to computer across network connections. Upon arrival, the worm may be activated to replicate and propagate again. In addition to propagation, the worm usually performs some unwanted function.

zombie A program that secretly takes over another Internet-attached computer and then uses that computer to launch attacks that are difficult to trace to the zombie's creator.

REFERENCES

In matters of this kind everyone feels he is justified in writing and publishing the first thing that comes into his head when he picks up a pen, and thinks his own idea as axiomatic as the fact that two and two make four. If critics would go to the trouble of thinking about the subject for years on end and testing each conclusion against the actual history of war, as I have done, they would undoubtedly be more careful of what they wrote.

—*On War,* Carl von Clausewitz

ABBREVIATIONS

ACM Association for Computing Machinery
IEEE Institute of Electrical and Electronics Engineers
NIST National Institute of Standards and Technology

ADAM90 Adams, C., and Tavares, S. "Generating and Counting Binary Bent Sequences." *IEEE Transactions on Information Theory*, 1990.

ADAM94 Adams, C. "Simple and Effective Key Scheduling for Symmetric Ciphers." *Proceedings, Workshop in Selected Areas of Cryptography, SAC' 94.* 1994.

ADLE83 Adleman, L. "The Function Field Sieve." *Lecture Notes in Computer Science 877, Springer-Verlag*, 1983.

AGRA02 Agrawal, M.; Keyal, N.; and Saxena, N. "PRIMES is in P." *IIT Kanpur, Preprint*, August 2002. http://www.cse.iitk.ac.in/news/primality.pdf

AKL83 Akl, S. "Digital Signatures: A Tutorial Survey." *Computer*, February 1983.

ALVA90 Alvarc, A. "How Crackers Crack Passwords or What Passwords to Avoid." *Proceedings, UNIX Security Workshop II*, August 1990.

ANDE80 Anderson, J. *Computer Security Threat Monitoring and Surveillance.* Fort Washington, PA: James P. Anderson Co., April 1980.

AUDI04 Audin, G. "Next-Gen Firewalls: What to Expect." *Business Communications Review*, June 2004.

AXEL00 Axelsson, S. "The Base-Rate Fallacy and the Difficulty of Intrusion Detection." *ACM Transactions and Information and System Security*, August 2000.

BACE00 Bace, R. *Intrusion Detection.* Indianapolis, IN: Macmillan Technical Publishing, 2000.

BACE01 Bace, R., and Mell, P. *Intrusion Detection Systems.* NIST Special Publication SP 800-31, November 2000.

BARK91 Barker, W. *Introduction to the Analysis of the Data Encryption Standard (DES).* Laguna Hills, CA: Aegean Park Press, 1991.

BARR03 Barreto, P., and Rijmen, V. "The Whirlpool Hashing Function." *Submitted to NESSIE*, September 2000, revised May 2003.

BAUE88 Bauer, D., and Koblentz, M. "NIDX—An Expert System for Real-Time Network Intrusion Detection." *Proceedings, Computer Networking Symposium*, April 1988.

BELL90 Bellovin, S., and Merritt, M. "Limitations of the Kerberos Authentication System." *Computer Communications Review*, October 1990.

BELL92 Bellovin, S. "There Be Dragons." *Proceedings, UNIX Security Symposium III*, September 1992.

BELL93 Bellovin, S. "Packets Found on an Internet." *Computer Communications Review*, July 1993.

BELL94a Bellare, M, and Rogaway, P. "Optimal Asymmetric Encryption—How to Encrypt with RSA." *Proceedings, Eurocrypt '94*, 1994.

BELL94b Bellovin, S., and Cheswick, W. "Network Firewalls." *IEEE Communications Magazine*, September 1994.

BELL96a Bellare, M.; Canetti, R.; and Krawczyk, H. "Keying Hash Functions for Message Authentication." *Proceedings, CRYPTO '96*, August 1996; published by Springer-Verlag. An expanded version is available at http://www-cse.ucsd.edu/users/mihir

BELL96b Bellare, M.; Canetti, R.; and Krawczyk, H. "The HMAC Construction." *CryptoBytes*, Spring 1996.

BELL97 Bellare, M., and Rogaway, P. "Collision-Resistant Hashing: Towards Making UOWHF's Practical." *Proceedings, CRYPTO '97*, 1997; published by Springer-Verlag.

BELL00 Bellare, M.; Kilian, J.; and Rogaway, P. "The Security of the Cipher Block Chaining Message Authentication Code." *Journal of Computer and System Sciences*, December 2000.

BERL84 Berlekamp, E. *Algebraic Coding Theory.* Laguna Hills, CA: Aegean Park Press, 1984.

BETH91 Beth, T.; Frisch, M.; and Simmons, G. eds. *Public-Key Cryptography: State of the Art and Future Directions.* New York: Springer-Verlag, 1991.

BIHA93 Biham, E., and Shamir, A. *Differential Cryptanalysis of the Data Encryption Standard.* New York: Springer-Verlag, 1993.

BIHA00 Biham, E., and Shamir, A. "Power Analysis of the Key Scheduling of the AES Candidates" Proceedings, Second AES Candidate Conference, 24 October 2000. http://csrc.nist.gov/encryption/aes/round1/conf2/aes2conf.htm

BISH03 Bishop, M. *Computer Security: Art and Science.* Boston: Addison-Wesley, 2003.

BISH05 Bishop, M. *Introduction to Computer Security.* Boston: Addison-Wesley, 2005.

BLAC00 Black, J., and Rogaway, P.; and Shrimpton, T. " CBC MACs for Arbitrary-Length Messages: The Three-Key Constructions." *Advances in Cryptology—CRYPTO '00*, 2000.

BLAC02 Black, J., and Rogaway, P. "Black-Box Analysis of the Block-Cipher-Based Hash Function Constructions from PGV." *Advances in Cryptology—CRYPTO '02*, 2002.

BLAK99 Blake, I.; Seroussi, G.; and Smart, N. *Elliptic Curves in Cryptography.* Cambridge: Cambridge University Press, 1999.

BLOO70 Bloom, B. "Space/time Trade-Offs in Hash Coding with Allowable Errors." *Communications of the ACM,* July 1970.

BLUM86 Blum, L.; Blum, M.; and Shub, M. "A Simple Unpredictable Pseudo-Random Number Generator." *SIAM Journal on Computing*, No. 2, 1986.

BONE99 Boneh, D. "Twenty Years of Attacks on the RSA Cryptosystem." *Notices of the American Mathematical Society*, February 1999.

BONE02 Boneh, D., and Shacham, H. "Fast Variants of RSA." *CryptoBytes*, Winter/Spring 2002. http://www.rsasecurity.com/rsalabs

BORN03 Bornemann, F. "PRIMES is in P: A Breakthrough for Everyman." *Notices of the American Mathematical Society*, May 2003.

BRIG79 Bright, H., and Enison, R. "Quasi-Random Number Sequences from Long-Period TLP Generator with Remarks on Application to Cryptography." *Computing Surveys*, December 1979.

BRYA88 Bryant, W. *Designing an Authentication System: A Dialogue in Four Scenes.* Project Athena document, February 1988. Available at http://web.mit.edu/kerberos/www/dialogue.html

BURN97 Burn, R. *A Pathway to Number Theory.* Cambridge, England: Cambridge University Press, 1997.

CAMP92 Campbell, K., and Wiener, M. "Proof that DES Is Not a Group." *Proceedings, Crypto '92*, 1992; published by Springer-Verlag.

CASS01 Cass, S. "Anatomy of Malice." *IEEE Spectrum*, November 2001.

CERT01 CERT Coordination Center. "Denial of Service Attacks." June 2001. http://www.cert.org/tech_tips/denial_of_service.html

CHAN02 Chang, R. "Defending Against Flooding-Based Distributed Denial-of-Service Attacks: A Tutorial." *IEEE Communications Magazine*, October 2002.

CHAP00 Chapman, D., and Zwicky, E. *Building Internet Firewalls.* Sebastopol, CA: O'Reilly, 2000.

CHEN98 Cheng, P., et al. "A Security Architecture for the Internet Protocol." *IBM Systems Journal,* Number 1, 1998.

CHES97 Chess, D. "The Future of Viruses on the Internet." *Proceedings, Virus Bulletin International Conference*, October 1997.

CHES03 Cheswick, W., and Bellovin, S. *Firewalls and Internet Security: Repelling the Wily Hacker*. Reading, MA: Addison-Wesley, 2003.

COCK73 Cocks, C. *A Note on Non-Secret Encryption.* CESG Report, November 1973.

COHE94 Cohen, F. *A Short Course on Computer Viruses.* New York: Wiley, 1994.

COPP94 Coppersmith, D. "The Data Encryption Standard (DES) and Its Strength Against Attacks." *IBM Journal of Research and Development*, May 1994.

CORM01 Cormen, T.; Leiserson, C.; Rivest, R.; and Stein, C. *Introduction to Algorithms.* Cambridge, MA: MIT Press, 2001.

CRAN01 Crandall, R., and Pomerance, C. *Prime Numbers: A Computational Perspective.* New York: Springer-Verlag, 2001.

DAEM99 Daemen, J., and Rijmen, V. *AES Proposal: Rijndael, Version 2.* Submission to NIST, March 1999. http://csrc.nist.gov/encryption/aes

DAEM01 Daemen, J., and Rijmen, V. "Rijndael: The Advanced Encryption Standard." *Dr. Dobb's Journal*, March 2001.

DAEM02 Daemen, J., and Rijmen, V. *The Design of Rijndael: The Wide Trail Strategy Explained.* New York, Springer-Verlag, 2002.

DAMG89 Damgard, I. "A Design Principle for Hash Functions." *Proceedings, CRYPTO '89*, 1989; published by Springer-Verlag.

DAVI89 Davies, D., and Price, W. *Security for Computer Networks.* New York: Wiley, 1989.

DAVI93 Davies, C., and Ganesan, R. "BApasswd: A New Proactive Password Checker." *Proceedings, 16th National Computer Security Conference,* September 1993.

DAWS96 Dawson, E., and Nielsen, L. "Automated Cryptoanalysis of XOR Plaintext Strings." *Cryptologia*, April 1996.

DENN81 Denning, D. "Timestamps in Key Distribution Protocols." *Communications of the ACM*, August 1981.

DENN82 Denning, D. *Cryptography and Data Security.* Reading, MA: Addison-Wesley, 1982.

DENN83 Denning, D. "Protecting Public Keys and Signature Keys." *Computer*, February 1983.

DENN87 Denning, D. "An Intrusion-Detection Model." *IEEE Transactions on Software Engineering,* February 1987.

DESK92 Deskins, W. *Abstract Algebra.* New York: Dover, 1992.

DIFF76a Diffie, W., and Hellman, M. "New Directions in Cryptography." *Proceedings of the AFIPS National Computer Conference*, June 1976.

DIFF76b Diffie, W., and Hellman, M. "Multiuser Cryptographic Techniques." *IEEE Transactions on Information Theory*, November 1976.

DIFF77 Diffie, W., and Hellman, M. "Exhaustive Cryptanalysis of the NBS Data Encryption Standard." *Computer*, June 1977.

DIFF79 Diffie, W., and Hellman, M. "Privacy and Authentication: An Introduction to Cryptography." *Proceedings of the IEEE*, March 1979.

DIFF88 Diffie, W. "The First Ten Years of Public-Key Cryptography." *Proceedings of the IEEE*, May 1988. Reprinted in [SIMM92].

DOBB96 Dobbertin, H. "The Status of MD5 After a Recent Attack." *CryptoBytes*, Summer 1996.

DORA03 Doraswamy, N., and Harkins, D. *IPSec.* Upper Saddle River, NJ: Prentice Hall, 2003.

EFF98 Electronic Frontier Foundation. *Cracking DES: Secrets of Encryption Research, Wiretap Politics, and Chip Design.* Sebastopol, CA: O'Reilly, 1998

ELGA85 ElGamal, T. "A Public-Key Cryptosystem and a Signature Scheme Based on Discrete Logarithms." *IEEE Transactions on Information Theory*, July 1985.

ELLI70 Ellis, J. *The Possibility of Secure Non-Secret Digital Encryption.* CESG Report, January 1970.

ELLI99 Ellis, J. "The History of Non-Secret Encryption." *Cryptologia*, July 1999.

ENGE80 Enger, N., and Howerton, P. *Computer Security.* New York: Amacom, 1980.

ENGE99 Enge, A. *Elliptic Curves and Their Applications to Cryptography.* Norwell, MA: Kluwer Academic Publishers, 1999.

FEIS73 Feistel, H. "Cryptography and Computer Privacy." *Scientific American*, May 1973.

FEIS75 Feistel, H.; Notz, W.; and Smith, J. "Some Cryptographic Techniques for Machine-to-Machine Data Communications." *Proceedings of the IEEE*, November 1975.

FELT03 Felten, E. "Understanding Trusted Computing: Will Its Benefits Outweigh its Drawbacks?" *IEEE Security and Privacy*, May/June 2003.

FERN99 Fernandes, A. "Elliptic Curve Cryptography." *Dr. Dobb's Journal*, December 1999.

FLUH00 Fluhrer, S., and McGrew, D. "Statistical Analysis of the Alleged RC4 Key Stream Generator." *Proceedings, Fast Software Encryption 2000*, 2000.

FLUH01 Fluhrer, S.; Mantin, I.; and Shamir, A. "Weakness in the Key Scheduling Algorithm of RC4." *Proceedings, Workshop in Selected Areas of Cryptography,* 2001.

FORD95 Ford, W. "Advances in Public-Key Certificate Standards." *ACM SIGSAC Review*, July 1995.

FORR97 Forrest, S.; Hofmeyr, S.; and Somayaji, A. "Computer Immunology." *Communications of the ACM*, October 1997.

FRAN01 Frankel, S. *Demystifying the IPSec Puzzle.* Boston: Artech House, 2001.

FREE93 Freedman, D. "The Goods on Hacker Hoods." *Forbes ASAP*, 13 September 1993.

FUMY93 Fumy, S., and Landrock, P. "Principles of Key Management." *IEEE Journal on Selected Areas in Communications*, June 1993.

GARD72 Gardner, M. *Codes, Ciphers, and Secret Writing.* New York: Dover, 1972.

GARD77 Gardner, M. "A New Kind of Cipher That Would Take Millions of Years to Break." *Scientific American*, August 1977.

GARR01 Garrett, P. *Making, Breaking Codes: An Introduction to Cryptology.* Upper Saddle River, NJ: Prentice Hall, 2001.

GASS88 Gasser, M. *Building a Secure Computer System*. New York: Van Nostrand Reinhold, 1988.

GAUD00 Gaudin, S. "The Omega Files." *Network World*, June 26, 2000.

GILB03 Gilbert, H. and Handschuh, H. "Security Analysis of SHA-256 and Sisters." *Proceedings, CRYPTO '03*, 2003; published by Springer-Verlag.

GOLL99 Gollmann, D. *Computer Security.* New York: Wiley, 1999.

GONG92 Gong, L. "A Security Risk of Depending on Synchronized Clocks." *Operating Systems Review*, January 1992.

GONG93 Gong, L. "Variations on the Themes of Message Freshness and Replay." *Proceedings, IEEE Computer Security Foundations Workshop*, June 1993.

GRAH94 Graham, R.; Knuth, D.; and Patashnik, O. *Concrete Mathematics: A Foundation for Computer Science.* Reading, MA: Addison-Wesley, 1994.

GUTM02 Gutmann, P. "PKI: It's Not Dead, Just Resting." *Computer*, August 2002.

HAMM91 Hamming, R. *The Art of Probability for Scientists and Engineers.* Reading, MA: Addison-Wesley, 1991.

HANK04 Hankerson, D.; Menezes, A.; and Vanstone, S. *Guide to Elliptic Curve Cryptography.* New York: Springer, 2004.

HARL01 Harley, D.; Slade, R.; and Gattiker, U. *Viruses Revealed.* New York: Osborne/ McGraw-Hill, 2001.

HEBE92 Heberlein, L.; Mukherjee, B.; and Levitt, K. "Internetwork Security Monitor: An Intrusion-Detection System for Large-Scale Networks." *Proceedings, 15th National Computer Security Conference,* October 1992.

HELD96 Held, G. *Data and Image Compression: Tools and Techniques.* New York: Wiley, 1996.

HELL78 Hellman, M. "An Overview of Public Key Cryptography." *IEEE Communications Magazine*, November 1978.

HERS75 Herstein, I. *Topics in Algebra.* New York: Wiley, 1975.

HEVI99 Hevia, A., and Kiwi, M. "Strength of Two Data Encryption Standard Implementations Under Timing Attacks." *ACM Transactions on Information and System Security*, November 1999.

HEYS95 Heys, H., and Tavares, S. "Avalanche Characteristics of Substitution-Permutation Encryption Networks." *IEEE Transactions on Computers*, September 1995.

HONE01 The Honeynet Project. *Know Your Enemy: Revealing the Security Tools, Tactics, and Motives of the Blackhat Community.* Reading, MA: Addison-Wesley, 2001.

HORO71 Horowitz, E. "Modular Arithmetic and Finite Field Theory: A Tutorial." *Proceedings of the Second ACM Symposium and Symbolic and Algebraic Manipulation*, March 1971.

HUIT98 Huitema, C. *IPv6: The New Internet Protocol.* Upper Saddle River, NJ: Prentice Hall, 1998.

IANS90 I'Anson, C., and Mitchell, C. "Security Defects in CCITT Recommendation X.509—The Directory Authentication Framework." *Computer Communications Review*, April 1990.

ILGU93 Ilgun, K. "USTAT: A Real-Time Intrusion Detection System for UNIX." *Proceedings, 1993 IEEE Computer Society Symposium on Research in Security and Privacy*, May 1993.

IWAT03 Iwata, T., and Kurosawa, K. "OMAC: One-Key CBC MAC." *Proceedings, Fast Software Encryption*, FSE '03, 2003.

JAIN91 Jain, R. *The Art of Computer Systems Performance Analysis: Techniques for Experimental Design, Measurement, Simulation, and Modeling.* New York: Wiley, 1991.

JAKO98 Jakobsson, M.; Shriver, E.; Hillyer, B.; and Juels, A. "A practical secure physical random bit generator." *Proceedings of The Fifth ACM Conference on Computer and Communications Security*, November 1998.

JAVI91 Javitz, H., and Valdes, A. "The SRI IDES Statistical Anomaly Detector." *Proceedings, 1991 IEEE Computer Society Symposium on Research in Security and Privacy*, May 1991.

JONE82 Jones, R. "Some Techniques for Handling Encipherment Keys." *ICL Technical Journal*, November 1982.

JUEN85 Jueneman, R.; Matyas, S.; and Meyer, C. "Message Authentication." *IEEE Communications Magazine*, September 1988.

JUEN87 Jueneman, R. "Electronic Document Authentication." *IEEE Network Magazine*, April 1987.

JUN99 Jun, B., and Kocher, P. *The Intel Random Number Generator.* Intel White Paper, April 22, 1999.

JUNO04 Junod, P., and Vaudenay, S. "Perfect Diffusion Primitives for Block Ciphers: Building Efficient MDS Matrices." *Selected Areas in Cryptography 2004*, Waterloo, Canada, August 9–10, 2004.

JURI97 Jurisic, A., and Menezes, A. "Elliptic Curves and Cryptography." *Dr. Dobb's Journal*, April 1997.

KAHN96 Kahn, D. *The Codebreakers: The Story of Secret Writing.* New York: Scribner, 1996.

KALI95 Kaliski, B., and Robshaw, M. "The Secure Use of RSA." *CryptoBytes*, Autumn 1995.

KALI96a Kaliski, B., and Robshaw, M. "Multiple Encryption: Weighing Security and Performance." *Dr. $$$Dobb's Journal*, January 1996.

KALI96b Kaliski, B. "Timing Attacks on Cryptosystems." *RSA Laboratories Bulletin*, January 1996. http://www.rsasecurity.com/rsalabs

KATZ00 Katzenbeisser, S., ed. *Information Hiding Techniques for Steganography and Digital Watermarking.* Boston: Artech House, 2000.

KEHN92 Kehne, A.; Schonwalder, J.; and Langendorfer, H. "A Nonce-Based Protocol for Multiple Authentications" *Operating Systems Review*, October 1992.

KELS98 Kelsey, J.; Schneier, B.; and Hall, C. "Cryptanalytic Attacks on Pseudorandom Number Generators." *Proceedings, Fast Software Encryption*, 1998. http://www.schneier.com/paper-prngs.html

KENT00 Kent, S. "On the Trail of Intrusions into Information Systems." *IEEE Spectrum*, December 2000.

KEPH97a Kephart, J.; Sorkin, G.; Chess, D.; and White, S. "Fighting Computer Viruses." *Scientific American*, November 1997.

KEPH97b Kephart, J.; Sorkin, G.; Swimmer, B.; and White, S. "Blueprint for a Computer Immune System." *Proceedings, Virus Bulletin International Conference*, October 1997.

KITS04 Kitsos, P., and Koufopaviou, O. "Architecture and Hardware Implementation of the Whirlpool Hash Function." *IEEE Transactions on Consumer Electronics*, February 2004.

KLEI90 Klein, D. "Foiling the Cracker: A Survey of, and Improvements to, Password Security." *Proceedings, UNIX Security Workshop II*, August 1990.

KNUD98 Knudsen, L., et al. "Analysis Method for Alleged RC4." *Proceedings, ASIACRYPT '98*, 1998.

KNUT97 Knuth, D. *The Art of Computer Programming, Volume 1: Fundamental Algorithms.* Reading, MA: Addison-Wesley, 1997.

KNUT98 Knuth, D. *The Art of Computer Programming, Volume 2: Seminumerical Algorithms.* Reading, MA: Addison-Wesley, 1998.

KOBL92 Koblas, D., and Koblas, M. "SOCKS." *Proceedings, UNIX Security Symposium III*, September 1992.

KOBL94 Koblitz, N. *A Course in Number Theory and Cryptography.* New York: Springer-Verlag, 1994.

KOCH96 Kocher, P. "Timing Attacks on Implementations of Diffie-Hellman, RSA, DSS, and Other Systems." *Proceedings, Crypto '96*, August 1996.

KOCH98 Kocher, P.; Jaffe, J.; and Jun, B. Introduction to Differential Power Analysis and Related Attacks." http://www.cryptography.com/dpa/technical/index.html

KOHL89 Kohl, J. "The Use of Encryption in Kerberos for Network Authentication." *Proceedings, Crypto '89*, 1989; published by Springer-Verlag.

KOHL94 Kohl, J.; Neuman, B.; and Ts'o, T. "The Evolution of the Kerberos Authentication Service." in Brazier, F., and Johansen, D. *Distributed Open Systems.* Los Alamitos, CA: IEEE Computer Society Press, 1994. Available at http://web.mit.edu/kerberos/www/papers.html

KOHN78 Kohnfelder, L. *Towards a Practical Public-Key Cryptosystem.* Bachelor's Thesis, M.I.T., May 1978.

KONH81 Konheim, A. *Cryptography: A Primer.* New York: Wiley, 1981.

KORN96 Korner, T. *The Pleasures of Counting.* Cambridge, England: Cambridge University Press, 1996.

KUMA97 Kumar, I. *Cryptology.* Laguna Hills, CA: Aegean Park Press, 1997.

KUMA98 Kumanduri, R., and Romero, C. *Number Theory with Computer Applications.* Upper Saddle River, NJ: Prentice Hall, 1998.

LAM92a Lam, K., and Gollmann, D. "Freshness Assurance of Authentication Protocols" *Proceedings, ESORICS 92,* 1992; published by Springer-Verlag.

LAM92b Lam, K., and Beth, T. "Timely Authentication in Distributed Systems." *Proceedings, ESORICS 92,* 1992; published by Springer-Verlag.

LAND04 Landau, S. "Polynomials in the Nation's Service: Using Algebra to Design the Advanced Encryption Standard." American Mathematical Monthly, February 2004.

LE93 Le, A.; Matyas. S.; Johnson, D.; and Wilkins, J. "A Public Key Extension to the Common Cryptographic Architecture." *IBM Systems Journal*, No. 3, 1993.

LEHM51 Lehmer, D. "Mathematical Methods in Large-Scale Computing." *Proceedings, 2nd Symposium on Large-Scale Digital Calculating Machinery,* Cambridge: Harvard University Press, 1951.

LEUT94 Leutwyler, K. "Superhack." *Scientific American*, July 1994.

LEVE90 Leveque, W. *Elementary Theory of Numbers.* New York: Dover, 1990.

LEWA00 Lewand, R. *Cryptological Mathematics.* Washington, DC: Mathematical Association of America, 2000.

LEWI69 Lewis, P.; Goodman, A.; and Miller, J. "A Pseudo-Random Number Generator for the System/360." *IBM Systems Journal*, No. 2, 1969.

LIDL94 Lidl, R., and Niederreiter, H. *Introduction to Finite Fields and Their Applications.* Cambridge: Cambridge University Press, 1994.

LIPM00 Lipmaa, H.; Rogaway, P.; and Wagner, D. "CTR Mode Encryption." *NIST First Modes of Operation Workshop*, October 2000. http://csrc.nist.gov/encryption/ modes

LODI98 Lodin, S., and Schuba, C. "Firewalls Fend Off Invasions from the Net." *IEEE Spectrum*, February 1998.

LUNT88 Lunt, T., and Jagannathan, R. "A Prototype Real-Time Intrusion-Detection Expert System." *Proceedings, 1988 IEEE Computer Society Symposium on Research in Security and Privacy*, April 1988.

MADS93 Madsen, J. "World Record in Password Checking." *Usenet, comp.security.misc newsgroup,* August 18, 1993.

MANT01 Mantin, I., Shamir, A. "A Practical Attack on Broadcast RC4." *Proceedings, Fast Software Encryption*, 2001.

MARK97 Markham, T. "Internet Security Protocol." *Dr. Dobb's Journal*, June 1997.

MATS93 Matsui, M. "Linear Cryptanalysis Method for DES Cipher." *Proceedings, EUROCRYPT '93*, 1993; published by Springer-Verlag.

MATY91a Matyas, S. "Key Handling with Control Vectors." *IBM Systems Journal*, No.2, 1991.

MATY91b Matyas, S.; Le, A.; and Abraham, D. "A Key-Management Scheme Based on Control Vectors." *IBM Systems Journal*, No. 2, 1991.

MCHU00 McHugh, J.; Christie, A.; and Allen, J. "The Role of Intrusion Detection Systems." *IEEE Software*, September/October 2000.

MEIN01 Meinel, C. "Code Red for the Web." *Scientific American*, October 2001.

MENE97 Menezes, A.; van Oorschot, P.; and Vanstone, S. *Handbook of Applied Cryptography.* Boca Raton, FL: CRC Press, 1997.

MERK78 Merkle, R., and Hellman, M. "Hiding Information and Signatures in Trap Door Knapsacks." *IEEE Transactions on Information Theory*, September 1978.

MERK79 Merkle, R. *Secrecy, Authentication, and Public Key Systems.* Ph.D. Thesis, Stanford University, June 1979.

MERK81 Merkle, R., and Hellman, M. "On the Security of Multiple Encryption." *Communications of the ACM*, July 1981.

MERK89 Merkle, R. "One Way Hash Functions and DES." *Proceedings, CRYPTO '89*, 1989; published by Springer-Verlag.

MEYE82 Meyer, C., and Matyas, S. *Cryptography: A New Dimension in Computer Data Security.* New York: Wiley, 1982.

MEYE88 Meyer, C., and Schilling, M. "Secure Program Load with Modification Detection Code." *Proceedings, SECURICOM 88*, 1988.

MILL75 Miller, G. "Riemann's Hypothesis and Tests for Primality." *Proceedings of the Seventh Annual ACM Symposium on the Theory of Computing*, May 1975.

MILL88 Miller, S.; Neuman, B.; Schiller, J.; and Saltzer, J. "Kerberos Authentication and Authorization System." *Section E.2.1, Project Athena Technical Plan*, M.I.T. Project Athena, Cambridge, MA. October 27, 1988.

MIRK04 Mirkovic, J., and Relher, P. "A Taxonomy of DDoS Attack and DDoS Defense Mechanisms." *ACM SIGCOMM Computer Communications Review*, April 2004.

MIST96 Mister, S., and Adams, C. "Practical S-Box Design." *Proceedings, Workshop in Selected Areas of Cryptography, SAC' 96.* 1996.

MIST98 Mister, S., and Tavares, S. "Cryptanalysis of RC4-Like Ciphers." *Proceedings, Workshop in Selected Areas of Cryptography, SAC' 98.* 1998.

MITC90 Mitchell, C.; Walker, M.; and Rush, D. "CCITT/ISO Standards for Secure Message Handling." *IEEE Journal on Selected Areas in Communications*, May 1989.

MITC92 Mitchell, C.; Piper, F. ; and Wild, P. "Digital Signatures." In [SIMM92].

MIYA90 Miyaguchi, S.; Ohta, K.; and Iwata, M. "Confirmation that Some Hash Functions Are Not Collision Free." *Proceedings, EUROCRYPT '90*, 1990; published by Springer-Verlag.

MOOR01 Moore, M. " Inferring Internet Denial-of-Service Activity." *Proceedings of the 10th USENIX Security Symposium*, 2001.

MUFT89 Muftic, S. *Security Mechanisms for Computer Networks.* New York: Ellis Horwood, 1989.

MURP90 Murphy, S. "The Cryptanalysis of FEAL-4 with 20 Chosen Plaintexts." *Journal of Cryptology*, No. 3, 1990.

MUSA03 Musa, M.; Schaefer, E.; and Wedig, S. "A Simplified AES Algorithm and Its Linear and Differential Cryptanalyses." *Cryptologia*, April 2003.

MYER91 Myers, L. *Spycomm: Covert Communication Techniques of the Underground.* Boulder, CO: Paladin Press, 1991.

NACH97 Nachenberg, C. "Computer Virus-Antivirus Coevolution." *Communications of the ACM*, January 1997.

NECH92 Nechvatal, J. "Public Key Cryptography." In [SIMM92].

NECH00 Nechvatal, J., et al. *Report on the Development of the Advanced Encryption Standard.* National Institute of Standards and Technology. October 2, 2000.

NEED78 Needham, R., and Schroeder, M. "Using Encryption for Authentication in Large Networks of Computers." *Communications of the ACM*, December 1978.

NEUM90 Neumann, P. "Flawed Computer Chip Sold for Years." *RISKS-FORUM Digest*, Vol.10, No. 54, October 18, 1990.

NEUM93a Neuman, B., and Stubblebine, S. "A Note on the Use of Timestamps as Nonces." *Operating Systems Review*, April 1993.

NEUM93b Neuman, B. "Proxy-Based Authorization and Accounting for Distributed Systems." *Proceedings of the 13th International Conference on Distributed Computing Systems*, May 1993.

NICH96 Nichols, R. *Classical Cryptography Course.* Laguna Hills, CA: Aegean Park Press, 1996.

NING04 Ning, P., et al. "Techniques and Tools for Analyzing Intrusion Alerts." *ACM Transactions on Information and System Security*, May 2004.

NIST97 National Institute of Standards and Technology. "Request for Candidate Algorithm Nominations for the Advanced Encryption Standard." *Federal Register*, September 12, 1997.

ODLY95 Odlyzko, A. "The Future of Integer Factorization." *CryptoBytes*, Summer 1995.

OPPL97 Oppliger, R. "Internet Security: Firewalls and Beyond." *Communications of the ACM*, May 1997.

OPPL05 Oppliger, R., and Rytz, R. "Does Trusted Computing Remedy Computer Security Problems?" *IEEE Security and Privacy*, March/April 2005.

ORE67 Ore, O. *Invitation to Number Theory.* Washington, DC: The Mathematical Association of America, 1967,

ORE76 Ore, O. *Number Theory and Its History.* New York: Dover, 1976.

PARK88 Park, S., and Miller, K. "Random Number Generators: Good Ones are Hard to Find." *Communications of the ACM*, October 1988.

PATR04 Patrikakis, C.; Masikos, M.; and Zouraraki, O. "Distributed Denial of Service Attacks." *The Internet Protocol Journal*, December 2004.

PERL99 Perlman, R. "An Overview of PKI Trust Models." *IEEE Network*, November/ December 1999.

PFLE02 Pfleeger, C. *Security in Computing.* Upper Saddle River, NJ: Prentice Hall, 2002.

PFLE03 Pfleeger, C. *Security in Computing*. Upper Saddle River, NJ: Prentice Hall, 1997.

PIAT91 Piattelli-Palmarini, M. "Probability: Neither Rational nor Capricious." *Bostonia*, March 1991.

PIEP03 Pieprzyk, J.; Hardjono, T.; and Seberry, J. *Fundamentals of Computer Security.* New York: Springer-Verlag, 2003.

POHL81 Pohl, I., and Shaw, A. *The Nature of Computation: An Introduction to Computer Science.* Rockville, MD: Computer Science Press, 1981.

POIN02 Pointcheval, D. "How to Encrypt Properly with RSA." *CryptoBytes*, Winter/Spring 2002. http://www.rsasecurity.com/rsalabs

POPE79 Popek, G., and Kline, C. "Encryption and Secure Computer Networks." *ACM Computing Surveys*, December 1979.

PORR92 Porras, P. *STAT: A State Transition Analysis Tool for Intrusion Detection.* Master's Thesis, University of California at Santa Barbara, July 1992.

PREN93a Preneel, B.; Govaerta, R.; and Vandewalle, J. "Hash Functions Based on Block Ciphers: a Synthetic Approach." *Proceedings, Advances in Cryptology—CRYPTO '93*, 1993.

PREN93b Preneel, B. "Cryptographic Hash Functions." *Proceedings of the 3rd Symposium on State and Progress of Research in Cryptography*, 1993.

PREN96 Preneel, B., and Oorschot, P. "On the Security of Two MAC Algorithms." *Lecture Notes in Computer Science 1561; Lectures on Data Security*, 1999; published by Springer-Verlag.

PREN99 Preneel, B. "The State of Cryptographic Hash Functions." *Proceedings, EUROCRYPT '96*, 1996; published by Springer-Verlag.

PROC01 Proctor, P. *The Practical Intrusion Detection Handbook.* Upper Saddle River, NJ: Prentice Hall, 2001.

RABI78 Rabin, M. "Digitalized Signatures." In *Foundations of Secure Computation*, DeMillo, R.; Dobkin, D.; Jones, A.; and Lipton, R., eds. New York: Academic Press, 1978.

RABI80 Rabin, M. "Probabilistic Algorithms for Primality Testing." *Journal of Number Theory,* December 1980.

RAND55 Rand Corporation. *A Million Random Digits.* New York: The Free Press, 1955. http://www.rand.org/publications/classics/randomdigits

RESC01 Rescorla, E. *SSL and TLS: Designing and Building Secure Systems.* Reading, MA: Addison-Wesley, 2001.

RIBE96 Ribenboim, P. *The New Book of Prime Number Records.* New York: Springer-Verlag, 1996.

RIJM96 Rijmen, V.; Daemen, J.; Preneel, B.; Bosselares, A.; and Win, E. "The Cipher SHARK." *Fast Software Encryption, FSE '96*, 1996.

RITT91 Ritter, T. "The Efficient Generation of Cryptographic Confusion Sequences." *Cryptologia*, vol. 15 no. 2, 1991. http://www.ciphersbyritter.com/ARTS/CRNG2ART.HTM

RIVE78 Rivest, R.; Shamir, A.; and Adleman, L. "A Method for Obtaining Digital Signatures and Public Key Cryptosystems." *Communications of the ACM*, February 1978.

RIVE84 Rivest, R., and Shamir, A. "How to Expose an Eavesdropper." *Communications of the ACM*, April 1984.

ROBS95a Robshaw, M. *Stream Ciphers.* RSA Laboratories Technical Report TR-701, July 1995. http://www.rsasecurity.com/rsalabs

ROBS95b Robshaw, M. *Block Ciphers.* RSA Laboratories Technical Report TR-601, August 1995. http://www.rsasecurity.com/rsalabs

ROBS95c Robshaw, M. *MD2, MD4, MD5, SHA and Other Hash Functions.* RSA Laboratories Technical Report TR-101, July 1995. http://www.rsasecurity.com/ rsalabs

RODR02 Rodriguez, A., et al. *TCP/IP Tutorial and Technical Overview.* Upper Saddle River: NJ: Prentice Hall, 2002.

ROSE05 Rosen, K. *Elementary Number Theory and its Applications.* Reading, MA: Addison-Wesley, 2000.

ROSI99 Rosing, M. *Implementing Elliptic Curve Cryptography.* Greenwich, CT: Manning Publications, 1999.

RUBI97 Rubin, A. "An Experience Teaching a Graduate Course in Cryptography." *Cryptologia*, April 1997.

RUEP92 Rueppel, T. "Stream Ciphers." In [SIMM92].

SAFF93 Safford, D.; Schales, D.;, and Hess, D. "The TAMU Security Package: An Ongoing Response to Internet Intruders in an Academic Environment." *Proceedings, UNIX Security Symposium IV*, October 1993.

SAUE81 Sauer, C., and Chandy, K. *Computer Systems Performance Modeling.* Englewood Cliffs, NJ: Prentice Hall, 1981.

SCHA96 Schaefer, E. "A Simplified Data Encryption Standard Algorithm." *Cryptologia*, January 1996.

SCHN91 Schnorr, C. "Efficient Signatures for Smart Card." *Journal of Cryptology*, No. 3, 1991.

SCHN96 Schneier, B. *Applied Cryptography.* New York: Wiley, 1996.

SCHN00 Schneier, B. *Secrets and Lies: Digital Security in a Networked World.* New York: Wiley, 2000.

SHAM82 Shamir, A. "A Polynomial Time Algorithm for Breaking the Basic Merkle-Hellman Cryptosystem." *Proceedings, 23rd IEEE Symposium on the Foundations of Computer Science*, 1982.

SHAM03 Shamir, A., and Tromer, E. "On the Cost of Factoring RSA-1024." *CryptoBytes*, Summer 2003. http://www.rsasecurity.com/rsalabs

SHAN49 Shannon, C. "Communication Theory of Secrecy Systems." *Bell Systems Technical Journal*, No. 4, 1949.

SIMM92 Simmons, G., ed. *Contemporary Cryptology: The Science of Information Integrity.* Piscataway, NJ: IEEE Press, 1992.

SIMM93 Simmons, G. "Cryptology." *Encyclopaedia Britannica, Fifteenth Edition*, 1993.

SIMO95 Simovits, M. *The DES: An Extensive Documentation and Evaluation.* Laguna Hills, CA: Aegean Park Press, 1995.

SING99 Singh, S. *The Code Book: The Science of Secrecy from Ancient Egypt to Quantum Cryptography.* New York: Anchor Books, 1999.

SINK66 Sinkov, A. *Elementary Cryptanalysis: A Mathematical Approach.* Washington, DC: The Mathematical Association of America, 1966.

SMIT97 Smith, R. *Internet Cryptography.* Reading, MA: Addison-Wesley, 1997.

SNAP91 Snapp, S., et al. "A System for Distributed Intrusion Detection." *Proceedings, COMPCON Spring '91*, 1991.

SPAF92a Spafford, E. "Observing Reusable Password Choices." *Proceedings, UNIX Security Symposium III*, September 1992.

SPAF92b Spafford, E. "OPUS: Preventing Weak Password Choices." *Computers and Security*, No. 3, 1992.

STAL02 Stallings, W. "The Advanced Encryption Standard." *Cryptologia*, July 2002.

STAL04 Stallings, W. *Computer Networking with Internet Protocols and Technology.* Upper Saddle River, NJ: Prentice Hall, 2004.

STAL06 Stallings, W. "The Whirlpool Secure Hash Function." *Cryptologia*, January 2006.

STEI88 Steiner, J.; Neuman, C.; and Schiller, J. "Kerberos: An Authentication Service for Open Networked Systems." *Proceedings of the Winter 1988 USENIX Conference*, February 1988.

STEP93 Stephenson, P. "Preventive Medicine." *LAN Magazine*, November 1993.

STER92 Sterling, B. *The Hacker Crackdown: Law and Disorder on the Electronic Frontier.* New York: Bantam, 1992.

STIN02 Stinson, D. *Cryptography: Theory and Practice.* Boca Raton, FL: CRC Press, 2002.

STOL88 Stoll, C. "Stalking the Wily Hacker." *Communications of the ACM,* May 1988.

STOL89 Stoll, C. *The Cuckoo's Egg.* New York: Doubleday, 1989.

SZOR05 Szor, P. *The Art of Computer Virus Research and Defense.* Reading, MA: Addison-Wesley, 2005.

THOM84 Thompson, K. "Reflections on Trusting Trust (Deliberate Software Bugs)." *Communications of the ACM*, August 1984.

TIME90 Time, Inc. *Computer Security, Understanding Computers Series*. Alexandria, VA: Time-Life Books, 1990.

TIPP27 Tippett, L. *Random Sampling Numbers.* Cambridge, England: Cambridge University Press, 1927.

TSUD92 Tsudik, G. "Message Authentication with One-Way Hash Functions." *Proceedings, INFOCOM '92,* May 1992.

TUCH79 Tuchman, W. "Hellman Presents No Shortcut Solutions to DES." *IEEE Spectrum*, July 1979.

TUNG99 Tung, B. *Kerberos: A Network Authentication System.* Reading, MA: Addison-Wesley, 1999.

VACC89 Vaccaro, H., and Liepins, G. "Detection of Anomalous Computer Session Activity." *Proceedings of the IEEE Symposium on Research in Security and Privacy,* May 1989.

VANO90 van Oorschot, P., and Wiener, M. "A Known-Plaintext Attack on Two-Key Triple Encryption." *Proceedings, EUROCRYPT '90*, 1990; published by Springer-Verlag.

VANO94 van Oorschot, P., and Wiener, M. "Parallel Collision Search with Application to Hash Functions and Discrete Logarithms." *Proceedings, Second ACM Conference on Computer and Communications Security*, 1994.

VIJA02 Vijayan, J. "Denial-of-Service Attacks Still a Threat." *ComputerWorld*, April 8, 2002.

VOYD83 Voydock, V., and Kent., S. "Security Mechanisms in High-Level Network Protocols." *Computing Surveys*, June 1983.

WACK02 Wack, J.; Cutler, K.; and Pole, J. *Guidelines on Firewalls and Firewall Policy*. NIST Special Publication SP 800-41, January 2002.

WAGN00 Wagner, D., and Goldberg, I. "Proofs of Security for the UNIX Password Hashing Algorithm." *Proceedings, ASIACRYPT '00*, 2000.

WANG05 Wang, X.; Yin, Y.; and Yu, H. "Finding Collisions in the Full SHA-1. *Proceedings, Crypto '05*, 2005; published by Springer-Verlag.

WAYN96 Wayner, P. *Disappearing Cryptography.* Boston: AP Professional Books, 1996.

WEBS86 Webster, A., and Tavares, S. "On the Design of S-Boxes." *Proceedings, Crypto '85*, 1985; published by Springer-Verlag.

WIEN90 Wiener, M. "Cryptanalysis of Short RSA Secret Exponents." *IEEE Transactions on Information Theory,* vol. IT-36, 1990.

WILS05 Wilson, J. "The Future of the Firewall." *Business Communications Review*, May 2005.

WOO92a Woo, T., and Lam, S. "Authentication for Distributed Systems." *Computer*, January 1992.

WOO92b Woo, T., and Lam, S. " 'Authentication' Revisited." *Computer*, April 1992.

YUVA79 Yuval, G. "How to Swindle Rabin." *Cryptologia*, July 1979.

ZENG91 Zeng. K.; Yang, C.; Wei, D.; and Rao, T. "Pseudorandom Bit Generators in Stream-Cipher Cryptography." *Computer*, February 1991.

ZIV77 Ziv, J., and Lempel, A. "A Universal Algorithm for Sequential Data Compression." *IEEE Transactions on Information Theory,* May 1977.

Index

Acronyms

3DES	Triple Data Encryption Standard
AES	Advanced Encryption Standard
AH	Authentication Header
ANSI	American National Standards Institute
CBC	Cipher Block Chaining
CC	Common Criteria
CESG	Communications-Electronics Security Group
CFB	Cipher Feedback
CMAC	Cipher-Based Message Authentication Code
CRT	Chinese Remainder Theorem
DDoS	Distributed Denial of Service
DES	Data Encryption Standard
DoS	Denial of Service
DSA	Digital Signature Algorithm
DSS	Digital Signature Standard
ECB	Electronic Codebook
ESP	Encapsulating Security Payload
FIPS	Federal Information Processing Standard
IAB	Internet Architecture Board
IETF	Internet Engineering Task Force
IP	Internet Protocol
IPSec	IP Security
ISO	International Organization for Standardization
ITU	International Telecommunication Union
ITU-T	ITU Telecommunication Standardization Sector
IV	Initialization Vector
KDC	Key Distribution Center
LAN	Local Area Network
MAC	Message Authentication Code
MIC	Message Integrity Code
MIME	Multipurpose Internet Mail Extension
MD5	Message Digest, Version 5
MTU	Maximum Transmission Unit
NIST	National Institute of Standards and Technology
NSA	National Security Agency
OFB	Output Feedback
PCBC	Propagating Cipher Block Chaining
PGP	Pretty Good Privacy
PKI	Public Key Infrastructure
PRNG	Pseudorandom Number Generator
RFC	Request for Comments
RNG	Random Number Generator
RSA	Rivest-Shamir-Adelman
SET	Secure Electronic Transaction
SHA	Secure Hash Algorithm
SHS	Secure Hash Standard
S/MIME	Secure MIME
SNMP	Simple Network Management Protocol
SNMPv3	Simple Network Management Protocol Version 3
SSL	Secure Sockets Layer
TCP	Transmission Control Protocol
TLS	Transport Layer Security
UDP	User Datagram Protocol
WAN	Wide Area Network

Geraldo Khoe

101270449